Fodor's 96 Cruises and Ports of Call

"When it comes to information on regional history, what to see and do, and shopping, these guides are exhaustive."

—USAir Magazine

"Usable, sophisticated restaurant coverage, with an emphasis on good value."

—Andy Birsh, *Gourmet Magazine* columnist

"Valuable because of their comprehensiveness."

—Minneapolis Star-Tribune

"Fodor's always delivers high quality...thoughtfully presented...thorough."

—Houston Post

"An excellent choice for those who want everything under one cover."

—Washington Post

D0786082

Fodor's Travel Publications, Inc.
New York • Toronto • London • Sydney • Auckland

Fodor's Cruises and Ports of Call

Editor: M. T. Schwartzman
Contributors: Robert Blake, Claudette Covey, Janet Foley, Gail Gillen de Haas, Mary Ann Hemphill, Herb Hiller, Barbara Hults, Lori Lincoln, Marcy Pritchard, Melissa Rivers, Mary Ellen Schultz, Theodore W. Scull, Kate Sekules, Jordon Simon, Jonathan Siskin, Dinah A. Spritzer, Judith Wadson, Heidi Waldrop, Jane E. Zarem
Creative Director: Fabrizio La Rocca
Cartographer: David Lindroth
Technical Illustration: Christopher A. Wilson
Illustrator: Karl Tanner
Cover Photograph: Harvey Lloyd/The Stock Market
Cover Design: John Olenyik

Design: Vignelli Associates

Special Sales

Contents

Index *437*

Maps and Charts

At Sea with Cruises and Ports of Call 1996

A good cruise guide is like a trusted advisor. It's a place you can turn to for honest reviews of more than 100 ships. It tells you how to find a knowledgeable travel agent, recommends the best shore excursions, and gives you inside tips for enjoying your time in port. In the creation of Cruises and Ports of Call, we at Fodor's have gone to great lengths to provide you with the very best of all possible cruise companions, and, by extension, to make your cruise the best of all possible vacations.

About Our Writers

The information on these pages is courtesy of a whole roster of extraordinary writers.

Editor **M. T. Schwartzman** has cruised on every type of ship, in every level of luxury, to destinations the world over. While he calls Alaska his second home, for this edition he traveled to another Pacific destination—Hawaii—to personally review the $30 million refit of the 1950s-vintage *Independence*. By far, the biggest cruise story of the year was the controversial $45 million refit of the *Queen Elizabeth 2*, and back home in New York, our editor boarded the legendary liner to see what the commotion was all about.

But much of our book is about brand-new ships, and small-ship expert **Dinah Spritzer** traveled to Warren, Rhode Island, to visit Luther Blount, the founder of American Canadian Caribbean Line and, to many, the man who invented small-ship cruising. Dinah found Luther in his shipyard—where he builds his own vessels by hand—working on his latest creation, the *Niagara Prince*.

Talk about experienced cruisers—**Lori Lincoln** sailed on nine ships and visited two shipyards, and that was just in the preparation of this book. Lori cruised on big ships and small ships, luxury ships and party ships, on itineraries that ranged from Alaska to Egypt. Her shoreside adventures included mountain biking in Skagway and wandering through the open-air markets outside Istanbul. (A kilim rug now graces her New York apartment.)

Veteran Fodor's cruise reviewer **Heidi Waldrop** had ample opportunity to get her sea legs as well. She compared Dolphin Cruise Line with its upscale sister Majesty Cruise Line, but not before checking out Radisson Seven Seas' unique catamaran, the *Radisson Diamond*, and sampling the *Regent Star*'s unusual Panama Canal itinerary out of Montego Bay, which also called at Puerto Limon, Costa Rica.

Few people know adventure cruising better than **Ted Scull.** So we asked Ted to sail to Antarctica aboard the *Hanseatic*, the world's biggest and most luxurious expedition ship. The ship and the continent, he was happy to report, both lived up to their billing.

What's New

Big things are happening at Fodor's—and in cruising.

If this is not the first Fodor's guide you've purchased, you'll immediately notice our new look. More readable than ever? We think so—and we hope you do, too. One of the changes we hope you'll find most useful is the new *Ships at a Glance* chart for every cruise line. Now you can compare the key facilities of each line's ships at once.

Many readers have expressed an interest in how to find the best deals in cruising, so we've expanded our section on how to select a travel agent. In light of a recent bankruptcy of a Florida cruise-only agency, we list only agencies with a proven track record. But as we say in the section on choosing an agent, customer service is just as important as price, so we've added additional information on how each agency goes the extra mile for its passengers.

Even as we go to press, new ships are being launched, and even newer ships are being planned. The biggest ships in this book, weighing in at 70,000 tons, will soon be eclipsed by three 100,000-ton behemoths, two for Carnival Cruise Lines and one for Princess Cruises. On a somewhat sad note, the original Royal Viking Line passed into history this year. But RVL fans can still board their favorite ships: The *Queen* has become part of Royal Cruise Line, and the *Sun* is now the flagship of a new unit of Cunard Line, Cunard Royal Viking.

Health concerns aboard cruise ships have been making the headlines after an outbreak of Legionnaire's disease on Celebrity Cruises' *Horizon*. Two other unrelated incidents of gastrointestinal illness also made the news. At press time, the Centers for Disease Control, which already inspects cruise ships for food handling and other sanitary conditions, issued new guidelines for the operation of whirlpools aboard ships, which were suspected of contamination in the Legionnaire's outbreak.

Cruise lines have been on a spending spree in recent years, with no end in sight. At press time, more than 20 ships were on order through 1998. In addition to the 100,000-ton monsters mentioned above, of special note is a new 62,000-ton vessel for Holland America Line. Not only will it be the largest ship the line has ever built, but with a top speed of 25 knots, it will be one of the only ships specifically designed for around-the-world cruising. The unnamed vessel is scheduled for delivery in the fall of 1997.

How to Use This Book

Organization   For many first-time cruisers (and some experienced passengers as well) choosing a ship is a mind-boggling proposition. To help lay the groundwork for your choice, we begin this book with a new Cruise Primer. Within its pages you'll find definitions of all the different types of ships you're likely to encounter, a discussion of the cruise experiences you'll have aboard, advice on where to find the best deals—and how to choose a travel agent. You'll find out about the choices you have for dining and the cuisine and special diets available aboard most ships. You'll meet the people who will be your hosts at sea. And you'll learn everything you need to know for a satisfying and safe cruise vacation.

Cruise Ships and Lines Chapter 1 is the heart of this book. The discussion of each cruise line begins with the Fleet, which summarizes the vessels—are they big ships or small ships, new ships or old ships? Following the Fleet is the Cruise Experience, a detailed account of the onboard lifestyle each line cultivates. This section includes information on activities, dining, entertainment, service, and tipping. Finally, each ship has its own review, the Ship's Log, which describes the highlights of each vessel.

Ports of Call *Cruises and Ports of Call 1996* covers the major cruising regions of the Western Hemisphere. In Chapter 2, you'll find our choices for the best ashore in nearly 70 ports. We'll tell you how and where you'll come ashore and how to get around, where the best museums are and how to arrange for your favorite activities. All the most popular destinations are covered, whether your heading for Antarctica, Alaska, the Bahamas, Bermuda, the Caribbean, Northeastern United States and Canada, Panama Canal zone, or South America.

For each port, we've chosen the shore excursions that we think you'll like best. We've also created walking tours designed especially for cruise passengers on short port calls. Many cruise passengers like to play tennis or golf while in port, so we've identified those clubs, hotels, and courses that welcome cruise passengers. We've selected the best restaurants ashore as well.

The following credit-card abbreviations are used: **AE,** American Express; **D,** Discover; **DC,** Diners Club; **MC,** MasterCard; and **V,** Visa. Discover is not accepted outside the United States.

Itineraries After you've read all about the ships, and armchair-traveled to their different ports of call, you'll surely want to know which ships go where. So in Chapter 3, we've listed all the latest cruise itineraries for the late 1995 to mid-1996 cruise season.

Please Write to Us

Everyone who has worked on *Cruises and Ports of Call 1996* has taken enormous care to ensure the accuracy of the text. All prices and opening times we quote are based on information supplied to us at press time. However, the passage of time will always bring changes, so it's always a good idea to call ahead to confirm information in this guide when it matters—particularly if you have to travel far from your ship. The publisher cannot accept responsibility for any errors that may have occurred.

Was your ship as we described it? Was the food better? The service worse? The cabins smaller? Did our restaurant picks exceed your expectations? Did you find a museum we recommended a waste of time? Positive and negative, we love your feedback. So please send us a letter or postcard (we're at 201 East 50th Street, New York, NY 10022). If you have complaints, we'll look into them and revise our entries when the facts warrant it. We'll look forward to hearing from you. And in the mean time, have a wonderful cruise!

Cruise Primer

Choosing Your Cruise

The right ship is one that makes you comfortable. Every ship has its own personality, depending upon its size, when it was built, and for what purpose. Big ships are more stable and offer a huge variety of activities and facilities. Smaller ships feel intimate, like private clubs. Each type of ship satisfies a certain type of passenger, and for every big-ship fan there is somebody who would never set foot aboard one of these "floating resorts."

But when choosing your cruise, the type of ship isn't the only factor to consider. You also need to find out about the nature of the experience you will have—the lifestyle and activities available by day and after dark, the mealtime hours and dining-room dress codes, how roomy the ship is, and how good the service is apt to be. Equally important are your itinerary, the accommodations, and the cost of the cruise.

Types of Ships

Although all ocean liners are equipped with swimming pools, spas, nightclubs, theaters, and casinos, there are three distinct types: classic liners, cruise liners, and megaships. Many **classic liners**, ships constructed between 1950 and 1969 for transatlantic or other ocean crossings, are still sailing in the fleets of many cruise lines. Beginning in the 1960s, ship lines began to create vessels specifically for cruising. Some of these **cruise liners** were brand new; others were converted ferries or freighters. Vessels known as **megaships**, the biggest cruise ships ever built, first appeared in the late 1980s and, with their immense proportions and passenger capacities, immediately established a new standard of cruise-ship design.

Cruises are also available aboard a number of specialty ships: cruise yachts, expedition ships, motor-sailing ships, riverboats, and coastal cruisers.

Classic Liners With their long, sweeping hulls and stepped-back passenger decks, these vessels defined passenger-ship design for decades. Now serving cruise duty, they were originally configured to keep passengers happy during long ocean crossings. Typically, their cabins and closets are larger than those on vessels built for cruising. Deck space is sheltered, with fully or partially enclosed promenades that allow you to relax on deck even during foul weather. A few are still steam powered, without the vibrations sometimes associated with diesel power. Rich wood panels the walls, and fixtures may be the original brass. Smaller ships may feel cramped because of low ceilings in the lobby and corridors. But on the most opulent vessels, public spaces designed to inspire still do. There are balconies above the dining room where musicians can serenade diners; stained glass graces the cinemas and other public spaces; and grand staircases lead from one deck to another. Such traditional features have proved so enduring they have been incorporated in the plans for some of today's newest vessels.

Although classic ships typically carry between 600 and 1,000 passengers and weigh between 20,000 and 30,000 tons, a couple of them are among the largest passenger ships afloat.

Cruise Liners When ship builders stopped constructing vessels for transportation and started designing them for vacationing, the cruise liner entered the scene. On these ships, outdoor deck space is plentiful; stateroom space is not. Many have a wraparound outdoor promenade deck that allows you to stroll or jog the perimeter of the ship. Older cruise liners resemble the transatlantic ships from which they are descended: Decks are stacked one atop the other in steps, and the hull amid ships may appear to droop, so the bow and stern seem to curve upward. In the newest cruise liners, traditional meets trendy. You find atrium lobbies and expansive sun and sports decks, picture windows instead of portholes, and cabins that open onto private verandas. The smallest cruise liners carry 500 passengers and weigh in at 10,000 tons, while the largest accommodate 1,500 passengers, register 50,000 tons, and are stuffed with diversions—almost like megaships.

Megaships The centerpiece of most megaships is a three-, five-, or seven-story central atrium. However, these giant vessels are most easily recognized by their boxy profile: The hull and superstructure rise straight out of the water, as many as 14 stories tall, topped out by a huge sun or sports deck with a jogging track and swimming pool, which may be Olympic size. Some megaships, but not all, also have a wraparound promenade deck. Like the latest cruise liners, picture windows are standard equipment, and cabins in the top categories have private verandas. From their casinos and discos to their fitness centers, everything is proportionally bigger and more extravagant than on other ships. Between 1,500 and 2,500 passengers can be accommodated, and tonnage ranges from 60,000 to 70,000 or more.

Cruise Yachts At the opposite end of the spectrum from the megaship is the tiny cruise yacht. These intimate vessels carry from 100 to 300 passengers, weigh between 4,000 and 15,000 tons, and are like miniature ocean liners, with big-ship amenities such as fitness centers, casinos, lounges, and swimming pools. What sets these yachts apart from typical ocean liners is that passengers are treated like royalty. Cabins are all outside suites equipped with every creature comfort on the high seas from VCRs and stocked minibars to marble baths. Built into the stern of some of these vessels are retractable platforms, which are lowered for water sports when the ship is at anchor in calm waters.

Expedition Ships Vessels of this type are designed to reach into the most remote corners of the world. Shallow drafts allow them to navigate up rivers, close to coastlines, and into shallow coves. Hulls may be hardened for sailing in Antarctic ice. Motorized rubber landing craft known as Zodiacs, kept on board, make it possible for passengers to put ashore almost anywhere. However, because the emphasis during cruises aboard expedition ships tends to be on learning and exploring, the ships don't have casinos, showrooms, multiple bars and lounges, and other typical ocean-liner diversions. Instead, they have theaters for lectures, well-stocked libraries, and enrichment programs, led by experts, as entertainment. The smallest expedition ships carry fewer than 100 passengers and weigh just over 2,000 tons. The largest carries nearly 200 people and weighs 9,000 tons.

Motor-Sail Vessels A number of cruise vessels were designed as sailing ships. With their sails unfurled, they are an impressive sight. But since they must keep to a schedule, they cannot rely solely on wind power. So all are equipped with engines as well. Usually they employ both means of propulsion, a technique known as motor sailing, to put on a good show and make the next port on time. These vessels range from small windjammers carrying a handful of passengers to rather large clipper-style ships that approach the size of a small ocean liner and accommodate almost 400 passengers.

Riverboats Most riverboats sailing in today's cruise fleet are replicas of those that sailed the nation's rivers in the 19th century. The feeling is definitely Victorian: Parlors are furnished with Tiffany lamps and leather wing chairs, and rocking chairs line the outer decks. Smaller riverboats offer just a lounge or two and a dining room. Bigger ones may add a small health club, theater, and a few other amenities, while still retaining their traditional character. But even the largest riverboat, which carries more than 400 passengers, weighs only 3,000 tons.

Coastal Cruisers Closely related to the riverboat is its modern-day equivalent, the coastal cruiser. Designed more for exploring than entertaining, these yachtlike ships are able to sail to remote waterways and ports. Some have forward gangways for bow landings or carry a fleet of Zodiac landing craft. Unlike larger expedition ships, they do not have ice-hardened hulls. Weighing no more than 100 tons and carrying only about 100 passengers, coastal cruisers offer few on-board facilities and public spaces—perhaps just a dining room and a multipurpose lounge.

The Cruise Experience

Your cruise experience will be shaped by several factors, and to determine whether a particular ship's style will suit you, you need to do a bit of research. Is a full program of organized activities scheduled by day? What happens in the evening? Are there one or two seatings in the dining room? If there are more than one, you will not be allowed to arrive and exit as the spirit moves you but instead must show up promptly when service begins—and clear out within a specified time. What kind of entertainment is offered after dark? And how often do passengers dress up for dinner? Some cruises are fancier than others.

Equally important are the space ratio and the passenger-to-crew ratio. The latter indicates the number of passengers served by each crew member—the lower the ratio, the better the level of service. The space ratio, the gross tonnage of a ship divided by its passenger capacity, allows you to compare ships' roominess. The higher the ratio, the more spacious the vessel feels; it will feel quite large if the ratio is 40:1 or higher, cramped if the ratio is under 25:1.

Although no two cruises are quite the same, even aboard the same ship, the cruise experience tends to fall into three categories.

Formal Formal cruises embody the ceremony of cruising. Generally available on ocean liners and cruise yachts sailing for seven days or longer, formal cruises recall the days when traveling by ship was an event in itself. By day, shipboard lifestyle is generally unstructured, with few organized activities. Tea and bouillon may be served to the accompaniment of music from a classical trio in the afternoon. Ashore, passengers may be treated to a champagne beach party. Meals in the dining room are served in a single seating, and passengers are treated to the finest cuisine afloat. Jackets and ties for men are the rule for dinner, tuxedos are not uncommon, and the dress code is observed faithfully throughout the evening. Pianists, cabaret acts, and local entertainers provide nighttime diversion. Service is extremely attentive and personalized. Passenger-to-crew and space ratios are best. Because these cruises tend to attract destination-oriented passengers, shore excursions—such as private museum tours—sometimes are included in the fare, as are pre- or postcruise land packages and sometimes even tips.

Semiformal Semiformal cruises are a bit more relaxed than their formal counterparts. Meals are served in two seatings on ocean liners or one seating on specialty ships, menu choices are plentiful, and the cuisine is on a par with that available in better restaurants. Men tend to wear a jacket and tie to dinner most nights. Adding a distinct flair to the dining room is the common practice of staffing the restaurant with waiters of one nationality. Featured dishes may be prepared table side, and you often are able, with advance notice, to order a special diet, such as kosher, low salt, low cholesterol, sugar-free, or vegetarian (*see* Dining *in* On Board, *below*). There is a daily program of scheduled events, but there's time for more independent pursuits; passengers with similar interests are often encouraged to meet at appointed times for chess or checkers, deck games, and other friendly contests. Production-style shows are staged each evening, but the disco scene may not be too lively. Passenger-to-crew and space ratios assure good service and plenty of room for each passenger. Look for semiformal cruises aboard classic liners, cruise liners, megaships, and a few expedition ships on voyages of seven days or longer.

Casual Casual cruises are the most popular. Shipboard dress and lifestyle are informal. Meals in the dining room are served in two seatings on ocean liners and one seating on specialty ships; menus are usually not extensive, and the food is good but not extraordinary; your options may be limited if you have special dietetic requirements. Men dress in sport shirts and slacks for dinner most nights, in jackets and ties only two or three evenings of a typical seven-day sailing. Aboard casual ocean liners, activities are more diverse than on formal and semiformal ships, and there is almost always something going on, from bingo to beer-chugging contests. Las Vegas–style variety shows or Broadway revues headline the evening entertainment. Discos bop into the wee hours. Passenger-crew and space ratios are generally good, but service tends to be less personal. On specialty ships, activities on board will be limited as indicated in Types of Ships, *above.*

Look for casual cruises aboard classic liners, cruise liners, and megaships sailing three- to seven-day itineraries to fun-and-sun destinations; expedition ships; motor-sailing ships; riverboats; and coastal cruisers calling on more unusual ports.

Special-Interest Cruises

Aboard The cruise ships detailed in Chapter 1 carry primarily American
Foreign Ships passengers. But other vessels serve mostly British, German, or Italian passengers. Sailing aboard such ships can be a quite different experience than on their American-oriented counterparts. English may or may not be the first language spoken, and announcements are made in a number of different tongues. Cuisine and entertainment will be geared for European tastes. Ethnic dishes in the dining room and folkloric dancing in the showroom frequently reflect the origin of the ship's crew and passengers. There's often a single seating for meals, with passengers divided between two restaurants, and wine may be complimentary at dinner. The ships tend to be smaller and older than those marketed primarily to American passengers. But if the idea of cruising with people from other countries sounds appealing, you may find the experience extremely satisfying.

Booking a cruise on these ships is a bit different than reserving a cabin on a North American vessel. Most foreign vessels sail all over the world, so you must find out when the next U.S. port of call or Western Hemisphere itinerary is scheduled. Some of these lines maintain U.S. offices, others hire general sales agents (GSAs) who represent these ships and book their sailings. Several foreign lines and ships actively court U.S. passengers.

British **P&O** is the parent company of Los Angeles–based Princess Cruises. Three P&O ships, the 45,000-ton, 1,600-passenger *Canberra;* the 28,000-ton, 714-passenger *Sea Princess;* and the 67,000-ton, 2,000-passenger *Oriana*, occasionally board passengers in Fort Lauderdale or Los Angeles during their world cruises. Most passengers will be British, Australian, and American, in that order. P&O is represented in the United States by Golden Bear Travel (16 Digital Dr., Suite 100, Box 6115, Novato, CA 94948, tel. 415/382–8900 or 800/551–1000, fax 415/382–9086).

In addition to P&O, Golden Bear also acts as the GSA for the 6,700-ton, 160-passenger expedition ship *Bremen* (formerly SeaQuest's *Frontier Spirit*). During the North American winter, the ship sails to Antarctica and the Falkland Islands from South America. Other itineraries explore the east coast of South America, making forays into the Amazon and Orinoco rivers. Depending on the cruise, passengers will be a varied mix of Germans and North Americans, with a bilingual crew and meals served at one sitting.

Another foreign expedition ship marketed in the United States is the *Hanseatic* (*see* Radisson Seven Seas Cruises *in* Chapter 1), which at 9,000 tons is the largest expedition vessel afloat. The *Hanseatic* is attracting an increasing number of Americans on its cruises to Antarctica and Falkland Islands.

The Italian **Costa Cruise Lines** is reviewed in Chapter 1 for its ships that cater exclusively to the American market. Three of its other vessels—the 16,000-ton, 400-passenger *Daphne,* 16,500-ton, 800-passenger *EnricoCosta,* and 53,000-ton, 1,300-passenger *Costa-Classica*—attract a mainly European crowd. The *Daphne* sails on one of the longest and most interesting world cruises available, departing annually from Genoa, Italy, in December. The *EnricoCosta* sails out of Buenos Aires during the North American winter, catering to primarily Argentineans and Brazilians. The *CostaAllegra* sails year-round from Europe to the Caribbean. Itineraries emphasize finding secluded beaches rather than visiting popular port towns for sightseeing and shopping. Americans can book these ships through Costa's U.S. headquarters (tel. 800/462–6782).

For a cruise-yacht-type sailing aboard a foreign ship, consider the 15,000-ton, 500-passenger *Italian Prima.* This relatively new vessel was constructed from the hull up out of an existing ship, and now operates upscale cruises of the Caribbean for a European and American crowd. Contact Saga Holidays (tel. 617/262–2262). You can also take a windjammer cruise aboard a couple of foreign sailing ships (*see* Aboard Tall Ships, *below*).

Aboard Freighters For casual cruising, few ships are more relaxed than passenger freighters. Spending extended periods at sea with few port calls in between, these hybrid vessels attract a special breed of cruiser. Passengers tend to be older than the typical cruiser, and some ships have age limits, which range from 75 to 82. Passenger capacity is considerably smaller—most cargo liners carry up to 12 passengers, although the biggest accommodates 88. Because most of the space aboard ship is devoted to freight, passenger facilities are more limited than on ocean liners and usually consist of a dining room, small lounge, and exercise room. Outdoor deck space for passengers is provided at the stern, where there may be a small pool and whirlpool. Often, passengers share these facilities with the crew. Cabins are larger than on a typical cruise ship, but much more modestly decorated. There usually is no room service.

Unlike most cruise ships, which have precisely scheduled port calls, freighters stay in port as long as it takes to load or unload their cargo. This can be measured in hours or in days. Itineraries, too, are sometimes subject to change. Such journeys, which may last from four weeks to four months, depart the United States from East Coast, West Coast, and Gulf Coast ports. Some also travel the St. Lawrence River from ports on the Great Lakes and in Canada. Passengers may book passage one-way (and return by air) or stay aboard for the round-trip. Per diems average $100 a day. Two agencies specialize in booking freighter cruises and often act as the general sales agents for the biggest cargo liners.

Freighter World Cruises (180 S. Lake Ave., Suite 335, Pasadena, CA 91101, tel. 818/449–3106, fax 818/449–9573) publishes the "Freighter Space Advisory" every two weeks. This is the bible of freighter cruises, listing itineraries, cabin availability, and special fares. Brief descriptions detail the accommodations aboard the various ships.

TravLtips (Box 580188, Flushing, NY 11358, tel. 800/872–8584) publishes a bimonthly magazine with black-and-white photos and reports on freighter trips by passengers. The magazine also lists special offers.

Aboard Tall Ships Unfurling their sails for part of each day and night (and motor powered the rest of the time), windjammers differ only in size and amenities from the big motor-sailing cruise ships reviewed in Chapter 1, such as the *Star Clipper*, *Star Flyer*, or *Sea Cloud*. Most windjammers are restored tall ships, built as private yachts. Some are wooden hulled and others are constructed of steel; they may carry from 18 to more than 100 passengers. The facilities you find aboard vary with the vessel. Some windjammers have air-conditioning and lounges with TVs and VCRs. Cabins range in size from small to moderate. The simplest have upper and lower bunks, cold-water basins, and shared hand-pumped cool water showers; others may have double beds and tiny private showers and toilets. Food is hearty and simple. Beach picnics are features of the Caribbean experience, and lobster bakes are the highlight of New England cruises.

Ports tend to be off the beaten track—smaller ones that are rarely, if ever, visited by the large cruise ships. Most of the boats anchor off isolated shores for beachcombing and sunning; there's little organized sightseeing. Individual pursuits may include swimming, snorkeling, scuba diving, windsurfing, and dinghy sailing. Poking through villages and whale-watching are part of the New England experience.

Windjammer cruises appeal to nature lovers, photographers, sailors, and those who just want to get away from it all. As with the cruise-ship fleet, sailing styles vary—some are family oriented, others designed for adults only—so question the operator carefully. Major windjammer operators include the following:

The **Maine Windjammer Association** (Box 317P, Rockport, ME 04856, tel. 207/354–1090 or 800/624–6380, fax 207/354–0803) has 10 vessels based in Camden, Rockport, and Rockland.

Tall Ship Adventures (1839 S. Havana St., Aurora, CO 80012, tel. 303/755–7983 or 800/662–0090, fax 303/755–9007) offers three- to 14-day Caribbean cruises on the 39-passenger *Sir Francis Drake*.

Windjammer Barefoot Cruises (1759 Bay Rd., Box 190120, Miami Beach, FL 33119, tel. 305/672–6453 or 800/327–2601, fax 305/674–1219) has six tall ships plying the Caribbean plus a passenger freighter that acts as a supply ship (*see* Aboard Freighters, *above*).

Foreign tall ships that sail in the Caribbean during the winter include the **Lili Marleen** and **La Ponant.** The *Lili Marleen* was launched in 1995 and carries 50 passengers. Officers and crew are German. The *La Ponant* is a three-master built in 1991 and carries 64 passengers. Its cruises have a distinctly French flavor, from the cuisine to the itinerary, which calls mostly at French-speaking islands. Both ships can be booked through the Cruise Company of Greenwich (31 Brookside Dr., Greenwich, CT 06830, tel. 203/622–0203 or 800/825–0826).

Along America's Waterways A cruise need not be an ocean-going affair. Many major cruise lines, including Alaska Sightseeing/Cruise West, American Canadian Caribbean Line, Clipper Cruise Line, Delta Queen Steamboat Co., and Special Expeditions feature cruises that explore the rivers and protected waterways of the United States and Canada. Other options for exploring America by water include:

The **Alaska Marine Highway System** (Box 25535, Juneau, AK 99802, tel. 800/642–0066, fax 907/277–4829) has cabins aboard several ferries that serve the communities of Southeast and South-Central Alaska. Dining is cafeteria style with good American-style food.

Public rooms include an observation lounge, bar, and solarium. Many passengers are RV travelers transporting their vehicles (no roads connect the towns within the Inside Passage). Time spent in port is short—often just long enough to load and unload the ship. A weekly departure leaves from Bellingham, Washington, north of Seattle. Service to Alaska is also available from Prince Rupert, British Columbia, where the marine highway system connects with Canada's BC Ferries. Cabins on the Alaskan ferries book up as soon as they become available, but a number of tour operators sell packages that include accommodations. One of the oldest and largest is Knightly Tours (Box 16366, Seattle, WA 98116, tel. 206/938–8567 or 800/426–2123).

St. Lawrence Cruise Lines (253 Ontario St., Kingston, Ontario K7L 2Z4, Canada, tel. 613/549–8901 or 800/276–7868, fax 613/549–8410) operates the 64-passenger *Canadian Empress*, a replicated steamboat, on cruises along the St. Lawrence Seaway or the Ottawa River. Cabins are compact and all outside, the one public room serves as a restaurant, lounge, and bar. Sailings last four or five days; departures are scheduled from May to October. These very leisurely cruises attract mainly older Americans and Canadians who come aboard for relaxed sightseeing on the river and to explore Canadian history.

Theme Cruises   These increasingly popular sailings highlight a particular activity or topic. Onboard lectures and other events are coordinated with shoreside excursions. There are photography cruises, square-dancing cruises, sports cruises, financial-planning cruises, wine-tasting cruises, and more. The most popular destinations for theme cruises are Alaska and the Caribbean. To find out about theme cruises that might interest you, consult with the individual cruise lines or a travel agent. Such sailings usually are highlighted in the cruise line's brochure and past-passenger newsletters, or agency newsletters. The lines that offer the greatest variety of theme cruises are **American Hawaii Cruises, Cunard Line, Holland America Line, Norwegian Cruise Line, Premier Cruise Lines, Royal Caribbean Cruise Line, and Royal Cruise Line.**

How Long to Sail

After you choose the type of ship and cruise experience you prefer, you must decide on how long to sail: Do you want a two-day cruise to nowhere or a 100-day journey around the world? Two key factors to keep in mind are how much money you want to spend and how experienced are you at cruising—it probably wouldn't be a good idea to circumnavigate the globe your first time at sea.

Short cruises are ideal for first-time cruisers and families with children. In just two to five days you can get a quick taste of cruising without investing a lot of time or money—cruise lines set rates low to attract new passengers. You'll also have the chance to sail aboard some of the newest ships afloat, built exclusively for these runs. Short itineraries may include stops at one or two ports of call, or none at all. The most popular short cruises are three- and four-day sailings to the Bahamas or Key West and Cozumel out of Miami. From Los Angeles, three- and four-day cruises set sail for southern California and the Mexican Riviera.

After you have experienced a long weekend at sea, you may want to try a **weeklong cruise.** With seven days aboard ship, you get twice as much sailing time and a wider choice of destinations—as many as four to six ports, depending on whether you choose a loop or one-way itinerary (*see* Ship Itineraries, *below*). Since cruises are priced by a per-diem rate multiplied by the number of days aboard ship (*see* Cost, *below*), a weeklong cruise probably costs twice as much as a short cruise.

For some people, seven days is still too short—just when you learn your way around the ship, it's time to go home. On **10- or 11-day sailings,** you get more ports as well as more time at sea, but you won't pay as much as on **two-week sailings.** Many experienced cruisers feel it's just not worth the effort to board a ship for anything less than 14 days, so they opt for either a single 14-day itinerary or sign up for two seven-day trips back-to-back, combining sailings to eastern and western Caribbean ports of call, for example—and taking advantage of the discounts offered by some lines for consecutive sailings. Cruises that last longer than two weeks—**very long cruises**—require a lot of time and money and a love of cruising. If you have all these, then cruising can become more than a vacation—it can be a way of life.

Ship Itineraries

In choosing the best cruise for you, a ship's itinerary is another important factor. How long you sail will determine the variety and number of ports you visit, but so will the type of itinerary and where you sail from. Some cruises, known as **loop cruises,** start and end at the same point and usually explore ports close to one another; **one-way cruises** start at one port and end at another and range farther afield.

Most cruises to Bermuda, the Bahamas, the Mexican Riviera, and the Caribbean are loop cruises. On Caribbean itineraries, you often have a choice of departure points. Sailings out of San Juan, Puerto Rico, can visit up to six ports in seven days, while loop cruises out of Florida can reach up to four ports in the same time.

Cruises to Antarctica generally operate on one of two loop itineraries: most commonly from the tip of South America to the Antarctic Peninsula, but also from New Zealand or Australia to the Ross Sea. Because the latter itinerary covers much longer distances, you spend more time at sea and less on shore—though there is a stop at historic huts used by early Antarctic explorers.

The most common one-way itineraries are to Canada and New England or to South America. So-called "Caribazon" cruises combine a journey up or down the Amazon River with port calls in the Caribbean. Alaska sailings come as loop itineraries, generally only within the Inside Passage, and as one-way cruises, sailing across the Gulf of Alaska and giving you the chance to explore farther north on land before or after the cruise.

Many ships sailing the Caribbean or the Mexican Riviera in winter and spring move to Alaska or New England in summer and fall. Other ships spend part of the year in the Caribbean, part outside the Western Hemisphere. When a ship moves from one cruising area to another, it offers a **repositioning cruise,** which typically stops at less-visited ports and attracts fewer passengers. It often has a lower per diem than cruises to the most popular sailing destinations.

A handful of ships offer an annual one- to two-month **cruise around South America** or a three- to four-month **around-the-world cruise** that stops at dozens of fabulous ports. This continent-hopping itinerary typically costs from $20,000 per person for a small inside cabin to hundreds of thousands of dollars for a suite; partial segments, usually of 14 to 21 days, are also available.

Note: Cruise itineraries listed in Chapter 3 are for the late 1995–mid-1996 cruise season but are subject to change. Contact your travel agent or the cruise line directly for up-to-the-minute itineraries.

Cost

For one price, a cruise gives you all your meals, accommodations, and onboard entertainment. The only extras are tips, shore excursions, shopping, bar bills, and other incidentals. The axiom "the more you pay, the more you get" doesn't always hold true: While higher fares do prevail for better ships, which have more comfortable cabins, more attractive decor, and better service, the passenger in the least-expensive inside cabin eats the same food, sees the same shows, and shares the same amenities as one paying more than $1,000 per day for the top suite on any given ship. (A notable exception is aboard the *Queen Elizabeth 2*, where your dining-room assignment is based on your cabin category.)

A handy way to compare costs of different ships is to look at the per diem—the price of a cruise on a daily basis per passenger, based on double occupancy. (For instance, the per diem is $100 for a seven-day cruise that costs $700 per person when two people share the same cabin.)

For each ship reviewed in Chapter 1, average per diems are listed in three cabin categories: suites, outside cabins, and inside cabins (*see* Accommodations, *below*). Remember that these average per diems are meant for comparative purposes only—so you can see the relative costliness of one ship versus another. For actual cruise fares, which can vary wildly and are subject to widespread discounting, you'll need to contact your travel agent or cruise specialist. Of course, there will be additional expenses beyond your basic cruise fare. When you go to book a cruise, don't forget to consider these expenditures:

Pre- and post-cruise arrangements: If you plan to arrive a day or two early at the port of embarkation, or linger a few days for sightseeing after debarkation, estimate the cost of your hotel, meals, car rental, sightseeing, and other expenditures. Cruise lines sell packages for pre- and post-cruise stays that may or may not cost less than arrangements you make independently, so shop around.

Airfare: Be sure to check if the price of your cruise includes air transportation to and from the ship. If it does not, you can purchase your airline tickets and transfers from the cruise line. This is known as a fly-cruise package. Fly-cruise packages generally are convenient and reasonably priced. However, the cruise line chooses your airline and flight. Lines sometimes give passengers who make their own arrangements an air transportation credit of $200 or more, depending on the destination. By arranging your own airfare, you may get a lower fare and a more convenient routing. If you have frequent-flyer miles, you may be able to get a free ticket.

Pretrip incidentals: These may include trip or flight insurance, the cost of boarding your pets, airport or port parking, departure tax, visas, long-distance calls home, clothing, film or videotape, and other miscellaneous expenses.

Shore excursions and expenses: Costs for ship-organized shore excursions range from less than $20 for the cheapest city tour to almost $300 for the most expensive flightseeing packages. Review the descriptions of shore excursions in Chapter 2 to estimate how much you are likely to spend.

Amusement and gambling allowance: Video games, bingo, and gambling can set you back a bundle. If you plan to bet, budget for your losses—you'll almost certainly have them. You must be over 18 to gamble on a cruise ship.

Shopping: Include what you expect to spend for both inexpensive souvenirs and pricey duty-free purchases.

Onboard incidentals: Most cruise lines recommend that passengers tip their cabin steward, dining-room waiter, and assistant waiter a total of $8–$9 per person, per day. Tips for bartenders and others who have helped you will vary. Also figure in the bar tabs and the cost of wine with meals, laundry, beauty-parlor services, purchases in the gift shop, and other incidentals.

Accommodations

Cabins vary greatly depending upon the type of ship you choose. On every ship, though, there are different cabin categories priced according to their size, location, and amenities. Cruise brochures show the ship's layout deck by deck and the approximate location and shape of every cabin and suite. Use the deck plan to make sure the cabin you pick is not near public rooms, which may be noisy, or the ship's engines, which can vibrate at certain speeds, and make sure that you are near stairs or an elevator to avoid walking down long corridors every time you return to your cabin. Usually, the listing in the brochure of the ship's different cabin categories includes details on what kind of beds the cabin has, whether it has a window or a porthole, and what furnishings are provided. Brochures also usually show representative cabin layouts, but be aware that configurations within each category can differ. In Chapter 1, we have tried to indicate those outside cabins that may be partially obstructed by lifeboats or that overlook a public deck.

Cabin Size   Compared with land-based accommodations, many standard ship cabins seem tiny. The higher you go in the ship, the larger the quarters tend to be; outside cabins are generally bigger than inside ones (*see* Location, *below*).

Suites are the roomiest and best-equipped accommodations, but even aboard the same ship, they may differ in size, facilities, and price. Steward service may be more attentive to passengers staying in suites; top suites on some ships are even assigned private butlers. Most suites have a sitting area with a sofa and chairs; some have two bathrooms, occasionally with a whirlpool bath. The most expensive suites may be priced without regard to the number of passengers occupying them.

Location   On all ships, regardless of size or design, the bow (front) and stern (back) pitch up and down on the waves far more than the hull amidships (middle). Ships also experience a side to side motion known as roll. The closer your deck is to the true center of the ship—about halfway between the bottom of the hull and the highest deck and midway between the bow and the stern—the less you will feel the ship's movement. Some cruise lines charge more for cabins amidships; most charge more for the higher decks.

Outside cabins have portholes or windows (which cannot be opened); on the upper decks, the view from outside cabins may be partially obstructed by lifeboats or overlook a public deck. Because outside cabins are more desirable, newer ships are configured with mostly outside cabins or with outside cabins only. Increasingly, an outside cabin on an upper deck comes with a private veranda. Windows are mirrored in cabins that overlook an outdoor promenade so that passersby can't see in—at least by day; after dark, you need to draw your curtains.

Inside cabins on older vessels are often smaller and oddly shaped. On newer ships, the floor plans of inside cabins are virtually identical to those of outside cabins. Providing you don't feel claustrophobic without a window, inside cabins represent an excellent value.

Furnishings   All ocean liner and most specialty ship cabins are equipped with individually controlled air-conditioning, limited closet space, and a private bathroom—usually closet-size, with a toilet, small shower, and washbasin. More expensive cabins, especially on newer ships, may have a bathtub. Most cabins also have a small desk or dresser, a reading light, and, on many ships, a TV and sometimes even a VCR. Except on some older ocean liners and smaller specialty ships, all cabins also come with a phone.

Depending upon the ship and category, a cabin may have beds or berths. The most expensive cabins usually have king- or queen-size beds. Cabins priced in the mid-range often have doubles or twins. In cabins with twins, the beds may be positioned side-by-side or at right angles. On most newer ships, the twin beds in many cabins can be pushed together to form a double. If this is what you want, get written confirmation that your specific cabin number has this capability. Less expensive cabins and cabins on smaller or older ships, especially those that accommodate three or four people, may have upper and lower bunks, or berths; these are folded into the wall by day to provide more living space. Sofa beds replace upper berths on some newer ships.

Sharing Most cabins are designed to accommodate two people. When more than two share a cabin, such as when parents cruise with their children, the third and fourth passengers are usually offered a discount, thereby lowering the per-person price for the room for the entire group.

Sailing Alone Some ships, mostly older ones, have a few single cabins. But on most ships, passengers traveling on their own must pay a single supplement, which usually ranges from 125% to 200% of the double-occupancy per-person rate. On request, many cruise lines will match up two strangers of the same sex in a cabin at the standard per-person double-occupancy rate.

When to Go

Although the cruise industry is booming year-round, there are definite cruise seasons, and the most desirable times command the highest prices. Here are the most popular seasons:

- November–April in the Caribbean
- Mid-June–Labor Day in the Caribbean for families
- Late April–early October in Bermuda
- October–mid-May along the Mexican Riviera
- Early December–early March around South America
- Holidays, such as Christmas, Easter, and, in South America, Carnival time
- September–October, December–March, and May for the Panama Canal
- June–August and holidays in Hawaii
- Mid-May–late September in Alaska
- June–mid-October in Canada and the northeastern U.S. seacoast
- December–February for Antarctica

While the weather might be marginally cooler or drier during high season in the Caribbean and Mexican Riviera, there is no reason not to go to these areas during the low and shoulder seasons, when ships and ports are less crowded and fares are often lower. The one exception is to the Caribbean in the fall, when you risk an encounter with a tropical storm or hurricane. Alaska cruises run from late spring to early fall, but summer sailings are most in demand, and Antarctic cruises have a very short season because of extreme weather conditions.

Selecting a Cabin*

Penthouse Suite/Apartment

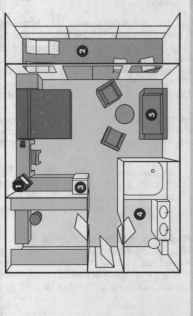

The largest accommodations on board, penthouse suites have sitting areas, queen size beds, vanity desks, and walk-in closets (with safes).

1. Although televisions are common, penthouse suites often have VCRs (and access to a video library) and stereos as well.

2. Private verandas, connected by sliding doors, are on some ships.

3. Most penthouse suites have refrigerators, often with stocked bars. Butler service is provided on some ships.

4. Twin sinks and Jacuzzi bathtubs (with shower) are typical.

5. The sofa can usually unfold into a bed for additional passengers.

Suite

Though much more expensive than regular cabins, suites are also larger, featuring double beds, sitting areas, televisions, and comparatively large closets.

1. Bathrooms are likely to have single sinks and bathtubs (with showers).

2. Refrigerators are often included, although alcoholic beverages may not be complimentary.

3. Suites, which tend to be on upper decks, usually have large picture windows.

4. The sofa can be converted into a bed.

Outside Cabin

Outside cabins usually have showers rather than bathtubs and seldom have refrigerators. Most cabins have phones, and many have televisions.

1 Twin beds are common, although many ships now offer a double bed. Upper berths for additional passengers fold into the wall.

2 Many cabins, especially those on lower decks, have portholes instead of picture windows. Cabins on newer ships, however, often have large windows.

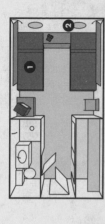

Inside Cabin

The least expensive accommodations, inside cabins have no portholes, tend to be tiny and oddly configured, have miniscule clothes closets, and bathrooms with showers only.

1 Almost all cabins have phones, but few have televisions.

2 Many inside cabins have upper and lower berths; the upper berth folds into the wall during the day, and the lower berth is made a couch.

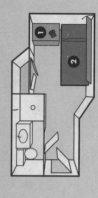

* Cruise lines offer a wide range of cabins, with a variety of names. This chart is intended as a general guide only.

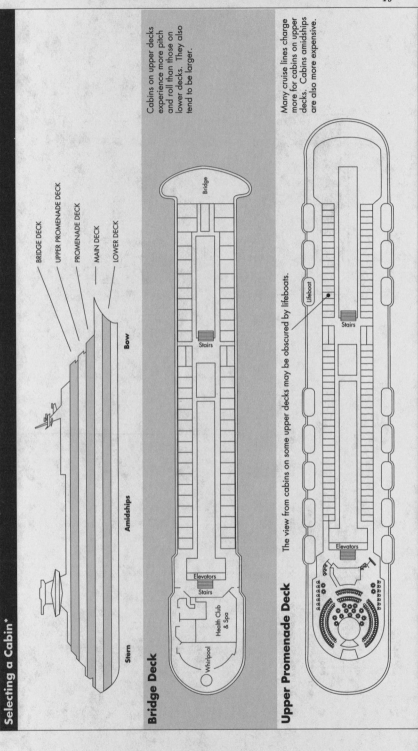

Selecting a Cabin*

BRIDGE DECK
UPPER PROMENADE DECK
PROMENADE DECK
MAIN DECK
LOWER DECK

Stern   Amidships   Bow

Bridge Deck

Bridge

Stairs

Elevators
Stairs

Whirlpool

Health Club
& Spa

Cabins on upper decks experience more pitch and roll than those on lower decks. They also tend to be larger.

Upper Promenade Deck

The view from cabins on some upper decks may be obscured by lifeboats.

Lifeboat

Stairs

Elevators

Many cruise lines charge more for cabins on upper decks. Cabins amidships are also more expensive.

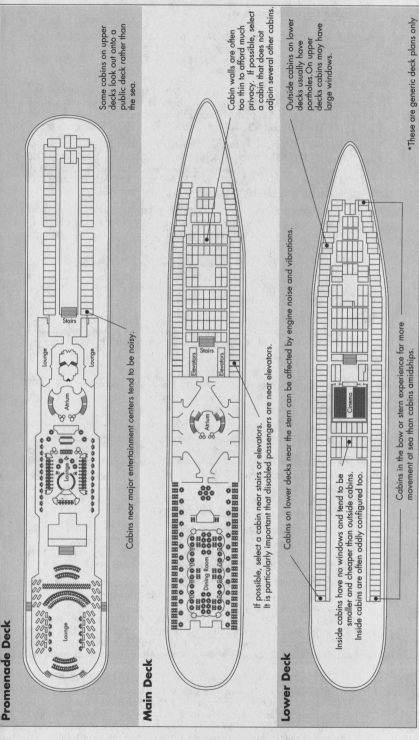

Promenade Deck

Some cabins on upper decks look out onto a public deck rather than the sea.

Cabins near major entertainment centers tend to be noisy.

Stairs
Lounge
Atrium
Lounge
Lounge
Lounge

Main Deck

Cabin walls are often too thin to afford much privacy. If possible, select a cabin that does not adjoin several other cabins.

Elevators
Stairs
Elevators
Atrium
Dining Room

If possible, select a cabin near stairs or elevators. It is particularly important that disabled passengers are near elevators.

Lower Deck

Outside cabins on lower decks usually have portholes. On upper decks cabins may have large windows.

Cabins on lower decks near the stern can be affected by engine noise and vibrations.

Cinema

Inside cabins have no windows and tend to be smaller and cheaper than outside cabins.
Inside cabins are often oddly configured too.

Cabins in the bow or stern experience far more movement at sea than cabins amidships.

*These are generic deck plans only

The Latest Information

Magazines   The quarterly ***Cruises & Tours*** profiles new ships and trends in cruising with roundup-style articles (Vacation Publications, 1502 Augusta Dr., Suite 415, Houston, TX 77057, tel. 713/974–6903; $15.80 per year).

The bimonthly ***Cruise Travel Magazine*** features a ship, cruise, and itinerary of the month, and publishes a cruise calendar every other issue (three times yearly) (World Publishing Co., Box 342, Mt. Morris, IL 61054, tel. 815/734–4151 or 800/877–5893; $9.97 per year).

Porthole, a bimonthly formerly known as *Cruise Digest Reports*, reviews two or three ships each issue, publishes the latest sanitation inspection scores, and takes a behind-the-scenes look at cruising (10 Fairway Dr., Suite 200, Deerfield Beach, FL 33441, tel. 305/746–5554, fax 305/427–0037; $35 per year).

Newsletters   ***The Millegram,*** published quarterly, relates cruise-industry news with short blurbs on new ships, shipbuilding contracts, and itinerary and ship-ownership changes (Bill Miller Cruises Everywhere, Box 1463, Secaucus, NJ 07096, tel. 201/348–9390; $15 per year).

The monthly ***Ocean & Cruise News*** reviews a different ship each month and reports on itinerary changes and discounted sailings (World Ocean & Cruise Liner Society, Box 92, Stamford, CT 06904, tel. and fax 203/329–2787; $28 per year).

Brochures   Cruise-line brochures usually contain the published price of each sailing. Use this when you comparison shop to tell how good a deal or discount an agent is offering. Deck plans are useful in selecting a cabin, and the fine print outlines the conditions of the cruise contract.

Videotapes   Videotapes—brochures on television—have become cruise lines' hottest sales tools. New ones are constantly being issued to highlight new itineraries and show off ships new and old.

A couple of independent companies produce cruise videos, too. You can choose from 150 cruise videos from **Vacations on Video** (7642 E. Gray Rd., Suite 103, Scottsdale, AZ 85260, tel. 602/483–1551, fax 602/483–0785; $7.95 per tape plus $3.75 shipping). Five ships are reviewed in each issue of the quarterly video magazine *Vacations Ashore & All the Ships at Sea* (173 Minuteman Causeway, Cocoa Beach, FL 32931, tel. 407/868–2131, fax 407/783–6122; $60 per year, $20 per issue, or $7 for a single ship review).

Other Sources   For practical information on cruising, contact **Cruise Lines International Association** (500 5th Ave., Suite 1407, New York, NY 10110; send self-addressed business-size envelope with 55¢ postage) for the free booklet, "Cruising—Answers to Your Questions."

For the most recent sanitation inspection scorecard, contact the Centers for Disease Control (CDC), which inspects all passenger ships sailing from American ports to foreign ports at least twice a year. (Ships that do not leave American waters, such as American Hawaii vessels, are not subject to the program. Instead, these ships are subject to state and U.S. Food and Drug Administration inspections.) Ships that score below 86 on a scale of 100 are still permitted to sail, as, according to the CDC, "a low score does not necessarily imply an imminent risk of an outbreak of gastrointestinal disease." These ships must make corrective repairs, however, and be reinspected within 30 to 60 days. The CDC rates cruise ships on the following: water, food preparation and handling, potential contamination of food, and general cleanliness, storage, and repair. For a free copy of the latest sanitation inspection report, write the Chief, Vessel Sanitation Program, National Center for Environmental Health (1015 North America Way, Room 107, Miami, FL 33132). You can also get a copy from the CDC's fax-back service at 404/332–4565. Request publication 510051.

Agencies that specialize in selling cruises can be good sources for the latest promotions and last-minute discounts. Some operate pre-recorded consumer hot lines while others publish free promotional magazines or newsletters (*see* Agencies to Contact *in* Booking Your Cruise, *below*).

Booking Your Cruise

Timing is important when booking your cruise. Since most cruise ships sail at or near capacity, especially during high seasons, you get the greatest choice and sometimes a discount if you make a reservation six months to a year in advance. If you book close to the sailing date, your choices may be more limited, but you may get an even better deal.

Getting the Best Cruise for Your Dollar

Like everything in retail, each cruise has a list price. However, the actual selling price can vary tremendously: These days, if you asked any 10 passengers on any given ship what they paid, they would give you 10 different answers. Discounts can range from 5% on a single fare to 50% on the second fare in a cabin. On really soft sailings, you may see newspaper ads offering fares that allow two passengers to sail for the price of one. The deepest discounts are in the Caribbean and Alaska.

Approach deep discounts with skepticism. Fewer than a dozen cabins may be offered at the discounted price, they may be inside cabins, and the fare may not include air transportation or transfers between the airport and the ship. Some may require that you leave almost immediately.

Deals and Discounts

Last-Minute Booking When cruise companies have cancellations or unsold cabins, they use cruise-only agencies and cruise specialists to recoup revenue. The closer the sailing date, the bigger the savings. Typically, you can save more than 25% for booking at the last minute, usually two weeks to a month ahead of departure. For the best discount, you have to be flexible, prepared to leave on as little as 24 hours' notice. You might end up spending your vacation at home—or you might luck into the travel bargain of a lifetime.

There's a down side. Cabin choice is limited, air transportation may not be included, and you may not get the meal seating you prefer. Also, think about why those cabins haven't been sold. Do you want to sail for less on the leftovers, or pay more to sail on a ship that is consistently full because it is consistently good?

Early Booking Discounts More and more cruise lines are offering discounts to customers who book early. Virtually every line sailing to Alaska runs some variation of an early booking discount program; similar incentives are becoming increasingly common for sailings to the Caribbean and other destinations. In addition to the discount, an early booking gives you a better choice of cabin and sailing date. Some lines guarantee that passengers who book early will receive any lower rate that the line subsequently posts on that particular cruise. Some lines offer an additional discount for paying the full fare in advance.

Using a Travel Agent

Most cruise lines do not sell directly to the public, so you must book through a travel agent. Don't just look for the lowest advertised price though; an agency should want your business not just now but in the future. Inquire about what extra services and added-values the agency gives to its passengers. This will tell you a lot about how serious the agency is about getting—and keeping—your business.

Cruise-Only Travel Agents "Cruise-only" travel agencies constitute one of the fastest-growing segments of the travel industry, and most major towns and cities have at least one. Their knowledgeable employees may have sailed on many ships. But that's only one of their strengths. Working together with specific cruise lines, cruise-only agencies obtain significant discounts by agreeing to sell large blocks of tickets. To make their quotas, they pass along savings to their clients. The discount you get depends on the agency, cruise line, season, current demand, and the popularity of the ship you have chosen. If the basic cost of your cruise does not include airfare, a cruise-only agency can sell you a fly-cruise package from the cruise line that includes round-trip air transportation and transfers. Similarly, cruise-only agencies can make your pre- or post-cruise vacation arrangements with a land package from the cruise line. .

Full-Service Travel Agents Unlike cruise-only agencies, which generally must sell you pre-packaged air and land arrangements, full-service travel agents can tailor your vacation to your specific needs and build a customized vacation if you want. But a full-service agent, who sells everything from theme-park vacations to motor-coach tours, may be less knowledgeable about the cruise lines and ships than his or her cruise-only counterpart. Some full-service agencies, however, specialize in cruising.

Choosing the Right Agency How do you find an honest, competent travel agent? Solicit recommendations from friends, family, and colleagues, especially those who have cruised before. Or look in the Yellow Pages for agents identified as members of CLIA (Cruise Lines International Association), NACOA (National Association of Cruise-Only Agencies), or ASTA (American Society of Travel Agents). Agents of the 20,000 CLIA affiliates nationwide have had extensive training, have cruised on several ships and inspected others, and have the background and resources to carefully match prospective passengers with the appropriate cruise line; agents who are CLIA Accredited Cruise Counsellors or Master Cruise Counsellors are most knowledgeable. Larger, well-established travel agencies—especially those that are cruise-only or are NACOA members—are more likely to employ experienced cruisers, but smaller agencies may give you more personal attention. Shop around, and book with the agency that gives you the best price *and* the best service.

One point is critical: To have a wonderful cruise, you need to pick the right ship. Bon vivants will find long cruises on certain formal ships boring; foodies and highbrows will be miserable on casual Caribbean cruises. A romantic getaway cannot be had in the company of families with howling children. Thus, an agent's first step should be to ask *you* questions about *your* lifestyle, vacation preferences, and expectations. If an agent places promotion of a specific ship or cruise line over consideration of your particular needs, move on.

Spotting Swindlers Always be on the lookout for a scam. Although reputable agencies far outnumber crooks, a handful of marketeers use deceptive and unethical tactics. The best way to avoid being fleeced is to deal with an agency that has been in business for at least five years. If you have any doubts about its credibility, consult your Better Business Bureau or consumer protection agency *before* you mail in any deposits. Or call the cruise line to verify the agent's reliability. Never allow yourself to be pressured into buying anything, and do not send money for a voucher that may be redeemed for a cruise at some later, unspecified date. Be wary of bait-and-switch tactics: If you're told that an advertised bargain cruise is sold out, do not be persuaded to book a more expensive substitute. Also, if you're told that your cruise reservation was canceled because of overbooking and that you must pay extra for a confirmed rescheduled sailing, demand a full refund. Finally, if ever you fail to receive a voucher or ticket on the promised date, place an inquiry immediately.

Agencies to Contact
The agencies listed below specialize in booking cruises, have been in business at least five years, and emphasize customer service as well as price. Publications such as *Cruise Travel Magazine* and *Cruises & Tours* (*see* The Latest Information *in* Choosing Your Cruise, *above*) also list agencies.

Cruise Only
Cruise Fairs of America (2029 Century Park E, Suite 950, Los Angeles, CA 90067, tel. 310/556–2925 or 800/456–4386, fax 310/556–2254), established in 1987, has a fax-back service for information on the latest deals. The agency also publishes a twice-yearly newsletter with tips on cruising.

Cruise Headquarters (4225 Executive Sq. #1600, La Jolla, CA 92037, tel. 619/453–1201 or 800/424–6111, fax 619/453–0653), established in 1988, specializes in creating personalized shoreside arrangements.

Cruise Line, Inc. (4770 Biscayne Blvd., Penthouse 1, Miami, FL 33137, tel. 305/576–0036 or 800/777–0707, fax 305/576–0073), established in 1983, publishes *World of Cruising* magazine and a number of brochures, including a "Guide to First Time Cruising," and a "Guide to Shipboard Wedding Packages."

Cruise Pro (2527 E. Thousand Oaks Blvd., Thousand Oaks, CA 91362, tel. 805/371–9884 or 800/222–7447; in CA, 800/258–7447; fax 805/371–9084), established in 1983, has special discounts for members of its Voyager's Club ($15 to join).

Cruise Quarters of America (1241 E. Dyer Rd., Suite 110, Santa Ana, CA 92705, tel. 714/754–0280 or 800/648–2444, fax 714/850–1974), established in 1986, is a division of Associated Travel International, one of the country's largest travel companies, and has a VIP club (tel. 800/517–5391) for upscale cruise planning.

Crui$e Value (c/o Golden Bear Travel, 16 Digital Dr., Suite 100, Box 6115, Novato, CA 94948, tel. 415/382–8900 or 800/551–1000 outside CA, fax 415/382–9086) is the cruise-only division of a full-service travel company that also acts as general sales agent for a number of foreign cruise ships. The agency's "Mariner Club" runs hosted cruises for passengers who would like to travel as part of a group.

CruiseMasters (3415 Sepulveda Blvd., Suite 645, Los Angeles, CA 90034, tel. 310/397–7175 or 800/242–9000, fax 310/397–3568), established in 1987, gives each passenger a personalized, bound guide to their ship's ports of call. The agency's Family Cruise Club serves parents cruising with their children. A World Cruise Desk is dedicated to booking very long cruises.

Cruises of Distinction (93 Dorsa Ave., Livingston, NJ 07039, tel. 201/716–0088 or 800/634–3445, fax 201/716–9893), established in 1984, publishes a free 80-page cruise catalog four times a year. For a fee ($39), you can receive notification of unadvertised specials by mail or fax.

Don Ton Cruise Tours (3151 Airway Ave., E–1, Costa Mesa, CA 92626, tel. 714/545–3737 or 800/432–3491, fax 714/545–5275), established in 1972, features a variety of special-interest clubs, including a short-notice club, singles club, family cruise club, and adventure cruise club. Call for a complete list.

Kelly Cruises (1315 W. 22nd St., Suite 105, Oak Brook, IL 60521, tel. 708/990–1111 or 800/837–7447, fax 708/990–1147), established in 1986, publishes a quarterly newsletter highlighting new ships and special rates. Passengers can put their name on a free mailing list for last-minute deals.

Vacations at Sea (4919 Canal St., New Orleans, LA 70119, tel. 504/482–1572 or 800/749–4950, fax 504/486–8360), established in 1983, puts together its own pre- and post-cruise land packages and hosted tours.

Full Service   **Ambassador Tours** (120 Montgomery St., Suite 400, San Francisco, CA 94104, tel. 415/981–5678 or 800/989–9000, fax 415/982–3490), established in 1955, does 80% of its business in cruises.
Time to Travel (582 Market St., San Francisco, CA 94104, tel. 415/421–3333 or 800/524–3300, fax 415/421–4857), established in 1935, does 90% of its business in cruises.
Trips 'n Travels, (1024 Kane Concourse, Bay Harbor, FL 33154, tel. 305/864–2222 or 800/331–2745, fax 305/861–8809) does 80% of its business in cruises. The agency's concierge service arranges theater tickets and so forth in ports of call.
White Travel Service (127 Park Rd., West Hartford, CT 06119, tel. 203/233–2648 or 800/547–4790, prerecorded cruise hot line 203/236–6176, fax 203/236–6177), founded in 1972, does most of its business in cruises.

Payment

Handing money over to your travel agent constitutes a contract, so before you pay your deposit, review the cruise brochure to find out the provisions of the cruise contract. What is the payment schedule and cancellation policy? Will there be any additional charges before you can board your ship, such as transfers, port fees, or local taxes? If your air connection requires you to spend an evening in a hotel near the port before or after the cruise, is there an extra cost?

If possible, pay your deposit and balance with a credit card. This gives you some recourse if you need to cancel, and you can ask the credit-card company to intercede on your behalf in case of problems.

Deposit   Most cruises must be reserved with a refundable deposit of $200–$500 per person, depending upon how expensive the cruise is; the balance is due 45–60 days before you sail. If the cruise is less than 45 days away, however, you may have to pay the entire amount immediately.

Cancellation   Your entire deposit or payment may be refunded if you cancel your reservation between 45 and 60 days before departure; the grace period varies from line to line. If you cancel later than that, you will forfeit some or all of your deposit (*see* Waivers and Insurance, *below*). An average cancellation charge is $100 one month before sailing, $100 plus 50% of the ticket price between 15 and 30 days prior to departure, and $100 plus 75% of the ticket price between 14 days and 24 hours ahead of time. If you simply fail to show up when the ship sails, you will lose the entire amount. Many travel agents also assess a small cancellation fee. Check their policy.

Waivers and   Cruise lines sell two types of policies that protect you in the event of
Insurance   cancellation or trip interruption. **Waivers** provide a full refund if you cancel your trip for any reason, usually up to 72 hours before sailing; the cost to cover a seven-day cruise is about $65. **Insurance** protects against cancellation for specified reasons plus trip delay, interruption, medical expenses, emergency evacuation, and lost, stolen, or damaged luggage; the cost to cover a seven-day cruise is about $99. Neither of these cruise-line programs protects you against cruise-line default (*see* Insurance, *below*).

Before You Go

Tickets, Vouchers, and Other Travel Documents

After you make the final payment to your travel agent, the cruise line will issue your cruise tickets and vouchers for airport–ship transfers. Depending on the airline, and whether you have purchased a fly-cruise package, you may receive your plane tickets or charter flight vouchers at the same time; you may also receive vouchers for any shore excursions, although most cruise lines issue these aboard ship. Should your travel documents not arrive when promised, contact your travel agent or call the cruise line directly. If you book late, tickets may be delivered directly to the ship.

Once aboard, you may be asked to turn over your passport for group immigration clearance (*see* Passports and Visas, *below;* Embarkation *in* Arriving and Departing, *below*) or to turn over your return plane ticket so the ship's staff may reconfirm your flight home. Otherwise, keep travel documents in a safe place, such as the safe in your cabin or at the purser's office.

Passports and Visas

U.S. Citizens American citizens boarding ships in the United States usually need neither a passport nor visas to call at ports in the Caribbean. However, carrying a passport is always a good idea. If you are boarding a ship outside the United States, such as in San Juan, Puerto Rico, you'll need the appropriate entry requirements for that country (*see* Chapter 2 for specific rules).

Many ships that ply Central and South American ports have the local immigration officials inspect and stamp all the passengers' passports at the same time, so the boarding card issued to each passenger is the only document you'll need to get on or off the ship. But there are some countries, especially in South America, from which you must obtain a visa stamp in advance. Your travel agent should inform you if you need a visa and should even help you obtain it, through a visa service by mail or directly from the consulate or embassy. (There may be a charge of up to $25 for this service, added to the visa charge of about $5.)

Passport You can pick up new and renewal application forms at any of the 13
Renewal U.S. Passport Agency offices and at some post offices and courthouses. Although passports are usually mailed within four weeks of your application's receipt, allow five weeks or more from April through summer. Call the Department of State Office of Passport Services' information line (tel. 202/647–0518) for fees, documentation requirements, and other details.

If your passport is lost or stolen abroad, report the loss immediately to the nearest embassy or consulate and to the local police. If you can provide the consular officer with the information contained in the passport, he or she will usually be able to issue you a new passport promptly. For this reason, keep a photocopy of the data page of your passport separate from your money and traveler's checks. Also leave a photocopy with a relative or friend at home.

Non-U.S. If you plan to cruise from an American gateway, such as Miami or
Citizens Los Angeles, and return to the United States at the end of the trip, you may need a passport from your own country, along with a B-2 visa, which allows multiple entries into the United States.

Canadians An identity card will be sufficient for entry and reentry into the United States. Passport application forms are available at 28 regional passport offices as well as post offices and travel agencies. Whether for a first or a subsequent passport, you must apply in person.

Children under 16 may be included on a parent's passport but must have their own to travel alone. Passports are valid for five years and are usually mailed within two to three weeks of an application's receipt. For fees, documentation requirements, and other information in English or French, call the passport office (tel. 819/994–3500 or 800/567–6868).

U.K. Citizens British citizens need a valid passport to enter the United States. However, if you will be boarding your ship within 90 days, you probably won't need a visa. You will need to fill out the Visa Waiver Form 1-94W, supplied by the airline. Applications for new and renewal passports are available from main post offices as well as at six passport offices, located in Belfast, Glasgow, Liverpool, London, Newport, and Peterborough. You may apply in person at all passport offices, or by mail to all except the London office. Children under 16 may travel on an accompanying parent's passport. All passports are valid for 10 years. Allow a month for processing.

Vaccinations and Inoculations

Unless you plan to cruise to exotic or out-of-the-way destinations, you probably will not need any shots. However, if you are middle-age or overweight or have high blood pressure, diabetes, or other chronic health problems, your doctor may wish to prescribe certain inoculations (such as a flu shot) not normally recommended.

If you intend to visit some of the more remote Central or South American jungles, you may have to take antimalaria pills; depending on the prescription, you begin taking them a few days to three weeks in advance of your trip to build immunity. Hepatitis, once rare, now crops up periodically throughout the Americas; check with your doctor about whether or not to have a gamma-globulin shot. Cruise ships regularly avoid regions that have typhoid, typhus, and cholera. If it's been years or decades since you received a polio vaccination, and you're headed for South America, it's advisable to take a booster dose. It's also a good idea to have a tetanus shot if you haven't had one within the past five years or so. Visit your doctor for shots three or four weeks before your trip since some vaccinations must be given in a series.

Certain rarely given inoculations, such as that for yellow fever (necessary if you are going into the Amazon), are administered, at a nominal cost, only by U.S. Health Department clinics. Your physician or the local hospital can give you the address and hours of the nearest facility. After getting such a shot, you will be given an International Certificate of Vaccination to carry with your passport.

For up-to-date health advisories on the ports to which you will be sailing, contact the Centers for Disease Control's International Travelers Hotline (tel. 404/639–2572). This automated system provides vaccination requirements and recommendations by geographic area.

Cruising with Children

Children are much more common aboard cruise ships. According to CLIA, 25% of cruise passengers are now families traveling together. To serve this growing market, a new family-oriented cruise-only agency, Family Cruise Club, has been launched by Los Angeles-based CruiseMasters (*see* Agencies to Contact *in* Booking Your Cruise, *above*).

Discounted fares range from free passage on off-peak sailings to $400 per child during high season. Some cruise lines, such as American Hawaii Cruises, Celebrity Cruises, Norwegian Cruise Line, Fantasy Cruises, and Seawind Cruise Line, allow children under two to sail without charge. Airfares and shore excursions also are frequently discounted. For single parents sailing with their children, Premier Cruise Lines offers a reduced single supplement of 25% (normally the charge is 100%).

Activities and Supervision Lines that frequently sail with children aboard may have costumed staff to entertain younger passengers. Premier Cruise Lines has Looney Tunes favorites, such as Bugs Bunny and Daffy Duck, running around its ships; Norwegian Cruise Line has Universal Studios characters, including Woody Woodpecker and Rocky and Bullwinkle; and aboard Dolphin Cruise Line or Majesty Cruise Line you can sail with the Flintstones or Jetsons. At least during summer vacation and holiday periods, many other lines now have supervised play areas for children and teenagers. Programs include arts and crafts, computer instruction, games and quizzes, kids' movies, swimming-pool parties, scavenger hunts, ship tours, magic shows, snorkeling lessons, kite flying, cooking classes, and teaching sessions on the history of the ports to be visited. Find out in advance whether there are special programs for your child's age group, how many hours of supervised activities are scheduled each day, whether meals are included, and what the counselor-to-child ratio is. Royal Caribbean Cruise Line and Celebrity Cruises have programs for children in three separate age groups; Carnival Cruise Lines' Camp Carnival is divided into four age groups.

Some ships provide day care and baby-sitting for younger children at no extra charge, while others charge a nominal hourly rate. On many ships, baby-sitting is by private arrangement (at a negotiated price). If you plan to bring an infant or toddler, be sure to request a crib, high chair, or booster seat in advance and bring plenty of diapers and formula.

Ships with two dinner seatings routinely assign passengers with children to the earlier seating; some lines will not permit children to eat in the dining room on their own. If your kids are picky eaters, check ahead to see if special children's menus are offered. (*See* Chapter 1 for specific information on each cruise line's policies and programs regarding children.)

Publications Several excellent sources on family travel exist. But above all, call the line and determine exactly what children's programs will be available during your sailing, and talk it over with your travel agent.

The most comprehensive guide on family sailing is *Cruising with Children*, which contains the nitty-gritty details—from pricing to kids' programs to crib availability—on 30 cruise lines. It is available from **Travel With Your Children** (TWYCH, 45 W. 18th St., 7th Floor Tower, New York, NY 10011, tel. 212/206–0688; $20 plus $3 postage). TWYCH's newsletter *Family Travel Times*, issued 10 times a year (annual subscription $55), features a column on cruising. The Family Cruise Club publishes a newsletter for young cruisers and a brochure for adults called *Is It Your First Time? The Parent's Guide to Cruising*.

Hints for Passengers with Disabilities

The official position of the International Council of Cruise Lines, which represents cruise lines in Washington, is that the Americans with Disabilities Act does not apply to cruise ships. The council argues that most cruise ships, as foreign-flag vessels, are not subject to domestic U.S. laws and cites engineering concerns as well. Seaworthiness and accessibility, the council argues, are not always compatible. Disclaimers on every cruise brochure allow ships to refuse passage to anyone whose disability might endanger others. Most ships require that you travel with an able-bodied companion if you use a wheelchair or have mobility problems.

If you have a mobility problem, even though you do not use a wheel-chair, tell your travel agent. Each cruise line sets its own policies; choose the line that is most accommodating. Also be careful to select a ship that is easy to get around. Ships vary even within the fleet of the same line. (*See* Chapter 1 for specific recommendations on which ships are suitable for passengers with mobility problems.) Follow up by making sure that the cruise line is fully informed of your disabili-ties and any special needs. Get written confirmation of any promises that have been made to you about a special cabin or transfers to and from the airport. The line may request a letter from your doctor stating that you need neither a wheelchair nor a companion, or that you will not require special medical attention on board.

If you have any type of chronic health problem that may require medical attention, notify the ship's doctor soon after you board so he or she will be prepared to treat you appropriately, if necessary.

Passengers in Wheelchairs The latest cruise ships have been built with accessibility in mind, and many older ships have been modified to accommodate passen-gers in wheelchairs. The key areas to be concerned about are access to public rooms, outer decks, and, of course, cabins. If you need a specially equipped cabin, book as far in advance as possible and ask specific questions of your travel agent or a cruise line representa-tive. Specifically, ask how your cabin is configured and equipped. Is the entrance level or ramped? Are all doorways at least 30 inches wide (wider if your wheelchair is not standard size)? Are pathways to beds, closets, and bathrooms at least 36 inches wide and unob-structed? In the bathroom, is there 42 inches of clear space in front of the toilet and are there grab bars behind and on one side of it and in the bathtub or shower? Ask whether there is a three-prong outlet in the cabin, and whether the bathroom has a hand-held shower-head, a bath bench, or roll-in shower or shower stall with fold-down seat, if you need them. For specific information about individual ships, *see* Accessibility *in* Chapter 1.

The best cruise ship for passengers who use wheelchairs is one that ties up right at the dock at every port, at which time a ramp or even an elevator is always made available. Unfortunately, it's hard to as-certain this in advance, for a ship may tie up at the dock at a particu-lar port on one voyage and, on the next, anchor in the harbor and have passengers transported to shore via tender. Ask your travel agent to find out which ships are scheduled to dock on which cruises. If a tender is used, some ships will have crew members carry the wheelchair and passenger from the ship to the tender. Unfortunate-ly, other ships point-blank refuse to take wheelchairs on tenders, especially if the water is choppy. At some ports, ships always tender because docking facilities are unavailable. For more information about where and whether ships dock or tender, *see* Coming Ashore for each port *in* Chapter 2.

Passengers with Vision Impairments Some ships allow guide dogs to accompany passengers with vision impairments; however, if your cruise is scheduled to visit foreign ports (as most do), you may not be able to take a guide dog ashore, depending on the country. To avoid potential quarantine upon re-turning to the United States, guide dogs should have their shots up-dated within seven days of sailing, and owners should carry the dog's valid health and rabies certificates.

Hawaii is especially strict about importing animals. No dog, not even guide dogs, may step ashore without being quarantined for 120 days unless it arrives from an area recognized by the state as rabies-free. Guide dogs may remain aboard visiting ships during port calls for up to 48 hours. That period begins upon docking at the first Ha-waiian port and includes all time spent in Hawaiian waters.

Pregnant Women Considering advanced pregnancy a disability, cruise lines may re-fuse passage to pregnant women. "Advanced" usually refers to the third trimester. If you are pregnant, check on the cruise line's policy before you book passage.

Organizations Several organizations provide travel information for people with disabilities, usually for a membership fee, and some publish newsletters and bulletins. Among them are the **Information Center for Individuals with Disabilities** (Fort Point Pl., 27–43 Wormwood St., Boston, MA 02210, tel. 617/727–5540 or 800/462–5015 in MA between 11 and 4, or leave message; TTY 617/345–9743); **Mobility International USA** (Box 10767, Eugene, OR 97440, tel. and TTY 503/343–1284, fax 503/343–6812), the U.S. branch of an international organization based in Belgium (*see below*) that has affiliates in 30 countries; **MossRehab Hospital Travel Information Service** (tel. 215/456–9603, TTY 215/456–9602); the **Travel Industry and Disabled Exchange** (TIDE, 5435 Donna Ave., Tarzana, CA 91356, tel. 818/344–3640, fax 818/344–0078); and **Travelin' Talk** (Box 3534, Clarksville, TN 37043, tel. 615/552–6670, fax 615/552–1182).

In the United Kingdom Important information sources include the **Royal Association for Disability and Rehabilitation** (RADAR, 12 City Forum, 250 City Rd., London EC1V 8AF, tel. 0171/250–3222), which publishes travel information for people with disabilities in Britain, and **Mobility International** (Rue de Manchester 25 B1070 Brussels, Belgium, tel. 00–322–410–6297), an international clearinghouse of travel information for people with disabilities.

Travel Agencies and Tour Operators **Accessible Journeys** (35 W. Sellers Ave., Ridley Park, PA 19078, tel. 610/521–0339 or 800/846–4537, fax 610/521–6959) arranges escorted trips for travelers with disabilities and provides licensed caregivers to accompany those who require aid. **Flying Wheels Travel** (143 W. Bridge St., Box 382, Owatonna, MN 55060, tel. 507/451–5005 or 800/535–6790) is a travel agency specializing in domestic and worldwide cruises for people with mobility problems.

Publications *Wheels and Waves: A Cruise-Ferry Guide for the Physically Handicapped* ($13.95, tel. 800/637–2256 or 800/247–6553) describes more than 200 ships, including 100 with accessible cabins. It is a publication of Wheels Aweigh (17105 San Carlos Blvd., Ft. Myers, FL 33931).

Several free publications are available from the U.S. Consumer Information Center (Box 100, Pueblo, CO 81009, tel. 719/948–3334): "New Horizons for the Air Traveler with a Disability" (include Dept. 355A in the address), a U.S. Department of Transportation booklet, describes changes resulting from the 1986 Air Carrier Access Act and from the 1990 Americans with Disabilities Act. "Fly Smart" (Dept. 575B), a pocket-size brochure, details flight safety tips. "Access Travel: Airports" (Dept. 575A), describes facilities and services for people with disabilities at more than 500 airports worldwide.

Travelin' Talk Directory (*see* Organizations, *above*) was published in 1993. This 500-page resource book ($35 check or money order with a money-back guarantee) is packed with information for travelers with disabilities. Twin Peaks Press (Box 129, Vancouver, WA 98666, tel. 206/694–2462 or 800/637–2256) publishes the *Directory of Travel Agencies for the Disabled* ($19.95), which lists more than 370 agencies worldwide, and *Wheelchair Vagabond* ($14.95), a collection of personal travel tips. Add $2 per book for shipping.

Hints for Older Passengers

For older travelers, cruise vacations strike an excellent balance: They offer a tremendous variety of activities and destinations in one convenient package. You can do as much or as little as you want, meet new people, see new places, enjoy shows and bingo, learn to play bridge, or take up needlepoint—all within a safe, familiar environment. Cruises are *not* a good idea for those who are bedridden, have a serious medical condition that is likely to flare up on board, or are prone to periods of confusion or severe memory loss.

No particular rules apply to senior citizens on cruises, but certain freighter cruises do have an age limit (*see* Special-Interest Cruises, *above*). Those who want a leisurely, relaxed pace will probably be happiest on ships that attract a higher percentage of older passengers: luxury ocean liners, cruise yachts, and expedition ships on voyages of longer than seven days. Passengers who are less than spry should look for a ship where the public rooms are clustered on one deck and select a cabin near an elevator or stairway amidships. Do not book a cabin with upper and lower berths.

Only a couple of cruise lines, notably Royal Caribbean, Premier, and Fantasy, have reduced rates for senior citizens, but senior citizens may be able to take advantage of local discounts ashore. When in port, showing proof of age often results in reduced admissions, half fares on public transportation, and special dining rates.

Several cruise lines employ "gentleman hosts," who act as dancing and bridge partners for single ladies traveling alone. Among these lines are the Delta Queen Steamboat Company, Regency Cruises, Royal Cruise Line, and Sun Line Cruises.

Organizations The **American Association of Retired Persons** (AARP, 601 E St. NW, Washington, DC 20049, tel. 202/434–2277) provides independent travelers who are members of the AARP (open to those age 50 or older; $8 per person or couple annually) with the Purchase Privilege Program, which books cruises through AARP Travel Experience from American Express (400 Pinnacle Way, Suite 450, Norcross, GA 30071, tel. 800/927–0111 or 800/745–4567).

Two other organizations offer discounts on cruises, along with such nontravel perks as magazines and newsletters: the **National Council of Senior Citizens** (1331 F St. NW, Washington, DC 20004, tel. 202/347–8800; membership $12 annually) and **Mature Outlook** (6001 N. Clark St., Chicago, IL 60660, tel. 312/465–6466 or 800/336–6330; $9.95 annually).

Tour Operators **Saga International Holidays** (222 Berkeley St., Boston, MA 02116, tel. 617/262–2262 or 800/343–0273) caters to those over age 60 who like to travel in groups. **SeniorTours** (508 Irvington Rd., Drexel Hill, PA 19026, tel. 215/626–1977 or 800/227–1100) arranges Caribbean cruises.

Publications *The 50+ Traveler's Guidebook: Where to Go, Where to Stay, What to Do*, by Anita Williams and Merrimac Dillon (St. Martin's Press, 175 5th Ave., New York, NY 10010; $12.95), is available in bookstores and offers many useful tips. "The Mature Traveler" (Box 50820, Reno, NV 89513, tel. 702/786–7419; $29.95), a monthly newsletter, lists discounts on cruises.

Hints for Gay and Lesbian Passengers

Organizations The **International Gay Travel Association** (Box 4974, Key West, FL 33041, tel. 305/292–0217, 800/999–7925, or 800/448–8550), which has 700 members, will provide you with names of travel agents and cruise lines that specialize in gay travel.

Tour Operators and Travel Agencies Some of the largest agencies serving gay travelers include: **Advance Travel** (10700 N.W. Freeway, #160, Houston, TX 77092, tel. 713/682–2002 or 800/695–0880), **Islanders/Kennedy Travel** (183 W. 10th St., New York, NY 10014, tel. 212/242–3222 or 800/988–1181), **Now Voyager** (4406 18th St., San Francisco, CA 94114, tel. 415/626–1169 or 800/255–6951), and **Yellowbrick Road** (1500 W. Balmoral Ave., Chicago, IL 60640, tel. 312/561–1800 or 800/642–2488). Tour operators that book cruises for gay passengers include: **R.S.V.P. Travel**

Productions (tel. 800/328–7787) operates many gay cruises while **Olivia** (tel. 800/631–6277) provides the same service for lesbian travelers.

Publications The premier international travel magazine for gays and lesbians is *Our World* (1104 N. Nova Rd., Suite 251, Daytona Beach, FL 32117, tel. 904/441–5367; $35 for 10 issues). **"Out & About"** (tel. 203/789–8518 or 800/929–2268; $49 for 10 issues, full refund if you aren't satisfied) is a monthly newsletter that reports on cruise lines that are gay-friendly.

What to Pack

You will naturally pack differently for the tropics than for an Alaskan cruise, but even if you're heading for warmer climates, bring along a sweater in case of cool evening ocean breezes or overactive air-conditioning. In both Alaska and the Caribbean, a rain slicker may come in handy. (To find out what to pack for cruises to Antarctica, *see* Chapter 2.) Make sure you bring at least one pair of comfortable walking shoes for exploring port towns. Shorts or slacks are convenient for shore excursions, but remember that in Latin America women are expected to dress modestly and men to wear slacks. In Chapter 1, we indicate how many formal evenings are typical on each ship—usually two per seven-day cruise. Men should pack a dark suit, a tuxedo, or a white dinner jacket. Women should pack one long gown or cocktail dress for every two or three formal evenings on board. Most ships have semiformal evenings, when men should wear a jacket and tie. On a few ships, men should wear a jacket and tie every evening (*see* The Cruise Experience *in* Choosing Your Cruise, *above*). A few lines have no dress codes or guidelines.

Generally speaking, plan on one outfit for every two days of cruising, especially if your wardrobe contains many interchangeable pieces. Ships often have convenient laundry facilities as well (*see* Shipboard Services *in* On Board, *below*). And don't overload your luggage with extra toiletries and sundry items; they are easily available in port and in the ship's gift shop (though usually at a premium price). Soaps, and sometimes shampoos and body lotion, are often placed in your cabin compliments of the cruise line.

Bring an extra pair of eyeglasses or contact lenses in your carry-on luggage. If you have a health problem that requires a prescription drug, pack enough to last the duration of the trip or have your doctor write a prescription using the drug's generic name, because brand names vary from country to country. Always carry prescription drugs in their original packaging to avoid problems with customs officials. Don't pack them in luggage that you plan to check in case your bags go astray. Pack a list of the offices that supply refunds for lost or stolen traveler's checks.

Electricity Most cruise ships use U.S.-type 110V, 60-cycle electricity and grounded plugs, but others employ 220V, 50-cycle current and are fitted with European- or English-type outlets. In that case, to use U.S.-purchased electric appliances on board, you'll need an adapter plug. Unless the appliance is dual-voltage and made for travel, you'll also need a converter. (*See* Chapter 1 for details on each ship's voltage.) For a copy of the free brochure "Foreign Electricity is No Deep Dark Secret," send a stamped, self-addressed envelope to adapter-converter manufacturer Franzus Company (Customer Service, Dept. B50, Murtha Industrial Park, Box 142, Beacon Falls, CT 06403, tel. 203/723–6664).

Luggage

Allowances Cruise passengers can bring aboard as much luggage as they like
On Board Ship and are restricted only by the amount of closet space in their cabin.

If you are flying to your point of embarkation, be aware of the airline's luggage policies. Because luggage is often tossed about and stacked as it is moved between ship and airport, bring suitcases that can take abuse.

In Flight Free airline baggage allowances depend on the airline, the route, and the class of your ticket; ask in advance. In general, on domestic flights and on international flights between the United States and foreign destinations, you are entitled to check two bags—neither exceeding 62 inches (length + width + height), or weighing more than 70 pounds. A third piece may be brought aboard; its total dimensions are generally limited to less than 45 inches, so it will fit easily under the seat in front of you or in the overhead compartment. In the United States, the Federal Aviation Administration gives airlines broad latitude to limit carry-on allowances and tailor them to different aircraft and operational conditions. Charges for excess, oversize, or overweight pieces vary.

If you are flying between two foreign destinations, note that baggage allowances may be determined not by piece but by weight— generally 88 pounds of luggage in first class, 66 pounds in business class, and 44 pounds in economy. If your flight between two cities abroad *connects* with your transatlantic or transpacific flight, the piece method still applies.

Safeguarding Your Luggage When your cruise documents arrive, they will often include luggage tags bearing the name of your ship. Place one on each piece of luggage before leaving home: These tags will identify your luggage to cruise line officials if there is an automatic luggage pull service at the airport on arrival. Also tag your bags inside and out with your name, address, and phone number. (If you use your home address, cover it so that potential thieves can't see it.) Put a copy of your itinerary inside each bag, so you can easily be tracked, and itemize your bags' contents and their worth in case they go astray.

When you check in for your pre- or post-cruise flight, make sure that the tag attached by baggage handlers bears the correct three-letter code for your destination. If your bags do not arrive with you, or if you detect damage, immediately file a written report with the airline before you leave the airport.

Insurance

Travel insurance can protect your investment, replace your luggage and its contents, or provide for medical coverage should you fall ill during your trip. Most travel agencies and many insurance agents sell specialized health-and-accident, flight, trip-cancellation, and luggage insurance as well as comprehensive policies with some or all of these features. Before you make any purchase, review your existing health and home-owner policies to find out whether they cover expenses incurred while traveling.

Baggage Insurance In the event of loss, damage, or theft on domestic flights, airline liability is $2,000 per passenger, excluding the valuable items such as jewelry and cameras that are listed in your ticket's fine print. On international flights, airlines' liability is $20 per kilogram for checked baggage (roughly about $640 per 70-pound bag) and $400 per passenger for unchecked baggage. Excess-valuation insurance can be bought directly from the airline at check-in for about $10 per $1,000 worth of coverage. However, you cannot buy it at any price for the rather extensive list of excluded items shown on your airline ticket.

Flight Insurance Often bought as a last-minute impulse at the airport, flight insurance pays a lump sum when a plane crashes either to a beneficiary if the insured dies or sometimes to a surviving passenger who loses eyesight or a limb. Like most impulse buys, flight insurance is expensive and basically unnecessary. It supplements the airlines' coverage described in the limits-of-liability paragraphs on your ticket. Charging an airline ticket to a major credit card often automatically entitles you to coverage, which may also extend to travel by bus, train, and ship.

Health-and-Accident Insurance Specific policy provisions of supplemental health-and-accident insurance for travelers include reimbursement for $1,000 to $150,000 worth of medical and/or dental expenses caused by an accident or illness during a trip. The personal-accident or death-and-dismemberment provision pays a lump sum to your beneficiaries if you die or to you if you lose a limb or your eyesight; the lump sum awarded can range from $15,000 to $500,000. The medical-assistance provision may reimburse you for the cost of referrals, evacuation, or repatriation and other services, or it may automatically enroll you as a member of a particular medical-assistance company that will provide those services.

Trip Insurance **Trip-cancellation-and-interruption insurance** protects you in the event you are unable to undertake or finish your trip, especially if your cruise arrangements do not allow changes or cancellations. The amount of coverage you purchase should equal the cost of your trip should you, a traveling companion, or a family member fall ill, forcing you to stay home, plus the nondiscounted one-way airline ticket you would need to buy if you had to return home early. Read the fine print carefully, especially sections defining "family member" and "preexisting medical conditions." Be aware that trip-cancellation-and-interruption insurance does not protect you in the event that your travel agency or tour operator defaults. To protect yourself against an agency or supplier's failure to deliver, you must purchase **bankruptcy or default insurance.** Another way to protect yourself is to buy a cruise packaged by one of the 33 members of the United States Tour Operators Association (USTOA, 211 E. 51st St., Suite 12B, New York, NY 10022, tel. 212/750–7371), which requires members to maintain $1 million each in an account to reimburse clients in case of default. Even better, pay for travel arrangements with a major credit card, so you can refuse to pay the bill if services have not been rendered—and let the card company fight your battles.

Companies to Contact Travel insurance covering baggage, health, and trip cancellation or interruption is available from **Access America, Inc.** (Box 90315, Richmond, VA 23230, tel. 804/285–3300 or 800/284–8300), **Carefree Travel Insurance** (Box 310, 120 Mineola Blvd., Mineola, NY 11501, tel. 516/294–0220 or 800/323–3149), **Near Travel Services** (Box 1339, Calumet City, IL 60409, tel. 708/868–6700 or 800/654–6700), **Tele-Trip** (Mutual of Omaha Plaza, Box 31716, Omaha, NE 68131, tel. 800/228–9792), **Travel Insured International** (Box 280568, East Hartford, CT 06128, tel. 203/528–7663 or 800/243–3174), **Travel Guard International** (1145 Clark St., Stevens Point, WI 54481, tel. 715/345–0505 or 800/826–1300), and **Wallach & Company** (107 W. Federal St., Box 480, Middleburg, VA 22117, tel. 703/687–3166 or 800/237–6615).

U.K. Residents Most tour operators, travel agents, and insurance agents sell policies covering accident, medical expenses, personal liability, trip cancellation, and loss or theft of personal property. You can also buy an annual travel-insurance policy valid for every trip (usually of less than 90 days) you make during the year in which it's purchased. Make sure you will be covered if you have a preexisting medical condition or are pregnant. The Association of British Insurers, a trade association representing 450 insurance companies, advises extra medical coverage for visitors to the United States.

For advice by phone or a free booklet, "Holiday Insurance," that sets out what to expect from a holiday-insurance policy and gives price guidelines, contact the association (51 Gresham St., London EC2V 7HQ, tel. 0171/600–3333; 30 Gordon St., Glasgow G1 3PU, tel. 0141/226–3905; Scottish Provident Bldg., Donegall Sq. W, Belfast BT1 6JE, tel. 01232/249176; call for other locations).

Planning for Expenses

Some ships will not cash personal checks or take certain credit cards. Consult your cruise documents to determine which forms of payment are accepted aboard ship. The purser's office usually cashes traveler's checks, and on some ships, you can even open an account there and get cash when you need it; it will be added to your bill along with onboard purchases, and you pay at the end of the cruise. Cashiers at onboard casinos also cash traveler's checks and dispense cash advances on your credit card, even to those who don't intend to gamble.

Foreign Currency U.S. dollars, traveler's checks, and credit cards are accepted in almost every port frequented by cruise ships. Many local businesses and vendors actually prefer receiving U.S. dollars. But there are always times when foreign currency will come in handy—for museum and theater admissions, public buses, telephones, vending machines, and small tips. When you change money, change only as much as you need (since it can be difficult to reconvert it to U.S. dollars), and do it at a bank or money-exchange booth, where you will probably get better rates than at hotels, restaurants, shops, or the ship's purser's office. If you do change too much, look for the box that several cruise lines keep somewhere near the purser's office or reception desk, where passengers' leftover local bills and coins go to local charities or UNICEF.

Traveler's Checks The most widely recognized are **American Express, Citicorp, Thomas Cook,** and **Visa,** which are sold by major commercial banks. Both American Express and Thomas Cook issue checks that can be countersigned and used by you or your traveling companion. Typically, the issuing company or the bank at which you make your purchase charges 1% to 3% of the checks' face value as a fee. Some foreign banks charge as much as 20% of the face value as the fee for cashing traveler's checks in a foreign currency. Buy a few checks in small denominations to cash toward the end of your trip, so you won't be left with excess foreign currency. Record the numbers of checks as you spend them, and keep this list separate from the checks.

Cash Machines While there are many itineraries that never get near a port with automated-teller machines, ATMs are proliferating and can be found in most major tourist areas as well as aboard some ships; many are tied to international networks such as **Cirrus** and **Plus.** You can use your bank card at ATMs to withdraw money from an account and get cash advances on a credit-card account if your card has been programmed with a personal identification number, or PIN. Check in advance on limits on withdrawals and cash advances within specified periods. Ask whether your bank-card or credit-card PIN will need to be reprogrammed for use in the area you'll be visiting. Four digits are commonly used overseas. Note that Discover is accepted only in the United States. On cash advances you are charged interest from the day you receive the money from ATMs as well as from tellers. Within the United States, transaction fees for ATM withdrawals outside your home turf may be higher than for withdrawals at home. Abroad, although transaction fees for withdrawals may be higher than fees for withdrawals at home, Cirrus and Plus exchange rates are excellent, because they are based on wholesale rates only offered by major banks.

For specific Cirrus locations, call 800/424–7787. For U.S. Plus locations, call 800/843–7587 and press the area code and first three digits of the number you're calling from (or of the calling area where you want an ATM); for foreign Plus locations, consult the Plus directory at your local bank. Before traveling internationally, plan ahead: Obtain ATM locations and the names of affiliated cash-machine networks before departure.

Photography

Bring with you all the film, tapes, and batteries that you need. Such items are more expensive abroad or in the ship's commissary, and often the particular brand or size you want is not available. Never pack your film in your luggage and try to avoid X-ray machines by asking for hand inspection. Such a request is always granted at U.S. airports; it's up to the inspector abroad. Don't depend on a lead-lined bag to protect film in checked luggage—the airline or cruise line may increase the radiation to see what's inside. Call the Kodak Information Center (tel. 800/242-2424) for details.

Many long-distance shots cannot be captured with a normal lens, so bring a telephoto if possible. An 81-series amber-warming filter will remove excess blues that predominate at sea level and will protect your lens against sand and salt spray. Polarizing filters enhance bright skies and seas.

If you intend to charge video-camera batteries aboard ship, make certain that the ship supplies 110V–120V current, or that you use the proper converter (*see* Electricity, *above*). Don't attempt to attach your camcorder to the television in your cabin in order to play back tapes—many ships' televisions use European broadcast standards, making them incompatible with U.S.-purchased video equipment.

Further Reading

If you want to learn about the modern sailing era, read *Great Cruise Ships and Ocean Liners from 1954 to 1986*, by William H. Miller, Jr. Miller has assembled a marvelous collection of rare black-and-white photographs of many of history's greatest superliners, accompanied by a wealth of history and anecdotes that make wonderful shipboard reading.

Peter Freuchen's *Book of the Seven Seas* is an ambitious novel incorporating all that's best from the mythology, history, and exploration of the world's oceans. John Maxtone-Graham's three books, *The Only Way to Cross, Liners to the Sun,* and *Crossing & Cruising,* chronicle the growth of shipping from a mode of travel to a mode of pleasure. David McCullough's *The Path Between the Seas* is a fascinating account of the construction of the Panama Canal, from its ill-fated French origins to the battle against yellow fever and the creation of the country of Panama.

Arriving and Departing

Most cruises to the Caribbean, the Bahamas, and the eastern coasts of Mexico and South America leave from one of Florida's three main ports: **Miami, Fort Lauderdale,** and **Port Canaveral.** Less frequently, they originate in **Galveston,** in **New Orleans,** or from a Caribbean island such as **Puerto Rico** or **Aruba.** Cruises to the Mexican Riviera often leave from **Los Angeles,** and typical Alaskan trips originate in **Vancouver** or **San Francisco** (a few positioning cruises begin or end in Los Angeles as well). Most cruises to Bermuda originate in **New York.** You'll have to fly to **Honolulu** for most Hawaiian cruises and to **South America, Australia,** or **New Zealand** for cruises to Antarctica.

If you have purchased a fly-cruise package, you will be met by a cruise-company representative when your plane lands at the port city and then shuttled directly to the ship in buses or minivans. Some cruise lines arrange to transport your luggage between airport and ship—you don't have to hassle with baggage claim at the start of your cruise or with baggage check-in at the end. If you decide not to buy the fly-cruise package but still plan to fly, ask your travel agent if you can use the ship's transfer bus anyway; if you do, you may be required to purchase a round-trip transfer voucher ($5–$20). Otherwise, you will have to take a taxi to the ship.

If you live close to the port of embarkation, bus transportation may be available. If you are part of a group that has booked a cruise together, this transportation may be part of your package. Another option for those who live close to their point of departure is to drive to the ship. The major U.S. cruise ports all have parking facilities.

East Coast Ports

Fort Lauderdale Also known as Port Everglades, Florida's Fort Lauderdale cruise port is the second largest in the world after Miami's—and is aiming to become the largest. The port is right in the middle of downtown Fort Lauderdale, but it's so spread out that you need a car or taxi to get around.

Long-Term Parking A 2,500-space parking garage and street-level parking are quite close to the terminals; free shuttles are available to those lots that are farther away. The cost is $7 per day.

From the Airport Fort Lauderdale–Hollywood International Airport is about 5–10 minutes away from the docks. The ride in a metered taxi costs about $10.

Miami The Port of Miami is on Dodge Island, across from the downtown area via a five-lane bridge. Just before the bridge on the mainland is the large and attractive Bayside Marketplace, whose waterfront ambience, two stories of shops and restaurants, and street entertainers provide a pleasant alternative to the cruise terminals if you arrive before boarding begins. Free shuttle buses are available to Bayside from the cruise terminals.

Long-Term Parking Street-level lots are right in front of the cruise terminals. Just leave your luggage with a porter, tip him, and park. The cost is $8 per day.

From the Airport Miami International Airport is about 20–30 minutes away from the docks. The flat rate for a taxi to the Port of Miami is $14 for up to five people. Limousines are available for $5.50 per person.

New York City Though still less than charming, New York's Hudson River docks, on Manhattan's west-side waterfront, have been cleaned up considerably in recent years. If you're early and don't want to spend the wait exploring your own ship, walk over to neighboring Pier 86's *Intrepid* Sea-Air-Space Museum, where you can view a battleship, an aircraft carrier (with a variety of planes), and a submarine.

Long-Term Parking Outdoor long-term parking is available on the fenced-in top level of the pier for $15.50 per day.

From the Airport La Guardia, Newark, and John F. Kennedy airports are not too far from Manhattan, but with traffic it can take an hour and a half to get to the docks in a taxi. Pier porters expect a tip, even if they carry your bags only a few feet.

Taxis are metered, so your actual cost will depend upon how much time you spend in traffic. On a good day expect the following: From **JFK,** a cab ride takes about one hour and costs about $45. From **La Guardia,** figure at least 40 minutes and a $35 fare. From **Newark International Airport,** a cab ride might take 45 minutes and cost about $50; however, the meters click away in traffic, so always budget up to double the expected fare for your taxi ride. Passengers pay for all bridge and tunnel tolls. Tip 15%.

Port Near the Kennedy Space Center and Cocoa Beach, Florida's Port
Canaveral Canaveral is used primarily by ships that combine their sailings
with a pre- or post-cruise package at an Orlando theme park. The
terminals are not yet as efficient at processing passengers as those
at Miami and Fort Lauderdale, and a sense of confusion prevails during the busiest check-in periods.

Long-Term An outdoor long-term parking lot is located directly outside the ter-
Parking minal and costs $6 per day.

From the The Orlando airport is 45 minutes away from the docks. Taxi rates
Airport are very expensive, so try taking the $20-per-person **Cocoa Beach
Shuttle** (tel. 800/633–0427) bus instead, but call first to make a reser-
vation.

West Coast Ports

Los Angeles The World Cruise Center in San Pedro has consolidated the old Port
of Los Angeles cruise facilities into one modern center. Porters expect to be tipped.

A shuttle bus (25¢) runs from the World Cruise Center to Ports O'
Call Village, a shopping center with a rustic seaside motif about a
half mile away; downtown San Pedro; and the Cabrillo Marine Museum. Turn left out of the center for a quarter-mile stroll to the L.A.
Maritime Museum.

Long-Term Outdoor long-term parking is a five-minute walk from the terminals;
Parking a free shuttle bus also serves the lots. Parking is $6.60 per day.

From the Most passengers arriving by air use Los Angeles International Air-
Airport port (LAX), about 20 miles from the cruise-ship docks; the trip can
take from 20 minutes to 1½ hours, depending on traffic. Long Beach
Airport is only about 12 miles away, but rather small. John Wayne/
Orange County Airport is from 45 minutes to an hour away.

Taxis are metered, and the ride from LAX will cost at least $40. Sev-
eral shuttle services run vans between LAX and the cruise port for
about $21 per person or about $50 for up to four people; they are
boarded curbside at the airport.

San Francisco The entire dock area of San Francisco is a tourist neighborhood of
entertainment, shops, and restaurants called the Embarcadero.
There's plenty to see and do within easy walking distance of the
cruise-ship terminals. With your back to the cruise pier, turn right
to get to Fisherman's Wharf, Ghirardelli Square, and the Maritime
Museum. If you don't want to walk, Bus 32 travels along the Embarcadero. You can also pick up a ferry to Alcatraz at Pier 41.

Long-Term A five-story public garage is located one block from the cruise termi-
Parking nal at Pier 35. Parking is $8 per day.

From the San Francisco International Airport, one of the busiest in the coun-
Airport try, is about 14 miles from the cruise pier. The trip from the airport
to the cruise pier costs a flat rate of $24 and takes 25–30 minutes,
depending upon traffic. Less expensive (about $8–$10 per person)
shuttle buses can be picked up curbside at the airport, but they take
longer. Make sure the shuttle will drop you off at the cruise pier.

Vancouver Many travelers consider British Columbia's Vancouver one of the
most beautiful cities in the world, so it is only appropriate that its
pier is also one of the most convenient and attractive. Right on the
downtown waterfront, the Canada Place terminal is instantly recognizable by its rooftop of dramatic sails. Inside are shops and restaurants. Porters are courteous and taxis plentiful.

If you are early, consider visiting historic Gastown just a couple of
blocks away (to the left if you have your back to the water).

Long-Term Parking   Parking at **Citipark** (tel. 604/684–2251) at Canada Place costs C$14 per day. However, you must arrive from two to four hours prior to departure time, and advance reservations are strongly recommended. Cheaper rates (less than $10 a day) are available at hotels near the terminal, but you will need to take a cab between your car and the ship.

From the Airport   Vancouver International Airport is approximately 11 miles away from Canada Place, but the road weaves through residential neighborhoods instead of highways. A taxi from the airport costs about $25 and takes about 25 minutes.

Cruise-line bus transfers from the Vancouver and Seattle airports are the most convenient, providing baggage handling and, for those with flights into Seattle, customs clearance. If for some reason you cannot connect with one of these buses, Airport Express provides fast, frequent bus service between the Vancouver airport and the pier for about $14 one way, $28 round-trip. From Seattle, Quick Shuttle makes the four- to five-hour bus trip (in season) for about $22 one way, $40 round-trip; disembark at the Sandman Inn, about eight blocks from the port. From there, take a cab to the pier.

Embarkation

Check-In   On arrival at the dock, you must check in before boarding your ship. (A handful of smaller cruise ships handle check-in at the airport.) An officer will collect or stamp your ticket, inspect or even retain your passport or other official identification, ask you to fill out a tourist card, check that you have the correct visas, and collect any unpaid port or departure tax. Seating assignments for the dining room are often handed out at this time, too. You may also register your credit card to open a shipboard account, although that may be done later at the purser's office (*see* Shipboard Accounts *in* On Board, *below*).

After this you may be required to go through a security check and to pass your hand baggage through an X-ray inspection. These are the same machines in use at airports, so ask to have your photographic film inspected visually.

Although it takes only five or 10 minutes per family to check in, lines are often long, so aim for off-peak hours. The worst time tends to be immediately after the ship begins boarding; the later it is, the less crowded. For example, if boarding begins at 2 PM and continues until 4:30, try to arrive after 3:30.

Boarding the Ship   Before you walk up the gangway, the ship's photographer will probably take your picture; there's no charge unless you buy the picture (usually $6). On board, stewards may serve welcome drinks in souvenir glasses—for which you're usually charged between $3 and $5 cash.

You will either be escorted to your cabin by a steward or, on a smaller ship, given your key by a ship's officer and directed to your cabin. Some elevators are unavailable to passengers during boarding, since they are used to transport luggage. You may arrive to find your luggage outside your stateroom or just inside the door; if it doesn't arrive within a half hour before sailing, contact the purser. If you are among the unlucky few whose luggage doesn't make it to the ship in time, the purser will trace it and arrange to have it flown to the next port.

Visitors' Passes   Some cruise ships permit passengers to invite guests on board prior to sailing, although most cruise lines prohibit all but paying passengers for reasons of security and insurance liability. Cruise companies that allow visitors usually require that you obtain passes several weeks in advance; call the lines for policies and procedures.

Most ships do not allow visitors while the ship is docked in a port of call. If you meet a friend on shore, you won't be able to invite him or her back to your stateroom.

Disembarkation

The last night of your cruise is full of business. On most ships you must place everything except your hand luggage outside your cabin door, ready to be picked up by midnight. Color-coded tags, distributed to your cabin in a debarkation packet, should be placed on your luggage before the crew collects it. Your designated color will later determine when you leave the ship and help you retrieve your luggage on the pier.

Your shipboard bill is left in your room during the last day; to pay the bill (if you haven't already put it on your credit card) or to settle any questions, you must stand in line at the purser's office. Tips to the cabin steward and dining staff are distributed on the last night.

The next morning, in-room breakfast service is usually not available because stewards are too busy. Most passengers clear out of their cabins as soon as possible, gather their hand luggage, and stake out a chair in one of the public lounges to await the ship's clearance through customs. Be patient—it takes a long time to unload and sort thousands of pieces of luggage. Passengers are disembarked by groups according to the color-coded tags placed on luggage the night before; those with the earliest flights get off first. If you have a tight connection, notify the purser before the last day, and he or she may be able to arrange faster preclearing and debarkation for you.

Customs and Duties

On Departure   If you plan to take more than $10,000 in cash, traveler's checks, or other negotiable instruments (such as bearer bonds or money orders) in or out of the United States, you must file Customs Form 4790 before you leave. U.S. residents bringing any foreign-made equipment from home, such as cameras, are wise to carry the original receipts with them or to register the items with U.S. Customs before leaving home (Form 4457). Otherwise, you may end up paying duty on your return.

Returning   To ease customs clearance at the end of your cruise, keep a detailed
Home   record of your purchases, save all receipts, and pack your overseas purchases on top of all your other belongings, in case the customs officer wishes to inspect them.

U.S. Customs   Before your ship lands, each individual or family must fill out a customs declaration, regardless of whether anything was purchased abroad. If you have fewer than $1,400 worth of goods, you will not need to itemize purchases. Be prepared to pay whatever duties are owed directly to the customs inspector, with cash or check.

U.S. Customs now preclears a number of ships sailing in and out of Miami and other ports—it's done on the ship before you disembark. In other ports you must collect your luggage from the dock, then stand in line to pass through the inspection point. This can take up to an hour.

Allowances. You may bring home $400 worth of foreign goods duty-free if you've been out of the country for at least 48 hours and haven't already used the $400 exemption, or any part of it, in the past 30 days. Note that these are the *general* rules, applicable to most countries; if you're returning from a cruise that called in the U.S. Virgin Islands, the duty-free allowance is higher—$1,200.

Alcohol and Tobacco. Travelers 21 or older may bring back 1 liter of alcohol duty-free, provided the beverage laws of the state through which they reenter the United States allow it. In the case of the U.S. Virgin Islands, 5 liters are allowed. In addition, 100 non-Cuban cigars and 200 cigarettes are allowed, regardless of your age. From the U.S. Virgin Islands, 1,000 cigarettes are allowed, but only 200 of them may have been acquired elsewhere. Antiques and works of art more than 100 years old are duty-free.

Gifts. Duty-free, travelers may mail packages valued at up to $200 to themselves, up to $100 to others with a limit of one parcel per addressee per day (including alcohol or tobacco products or perfume valued at up to $5); mark the package "For Personal Use" or "Unsolicited Gift" and write the nature of the gift and its retail value on the outside.

For More Information. For a copy of "Know Before You Go," a free brochure detailing what you may and may not bring back to the United States, rates of duty, and other pointers, contact the U.S. **Customs Service** (Box 7407, Washington, DC 20044, tel. 202/927–6724).

Canadian Customs **Allowances.** Once per calendar year, when you've been out of Canada for at least seven days, you may bring in C$300 worth of goods duty-free. If you've been away less than seven days but more than 48 hours, the duty-free exemption drops to C$100 but can be claimed any number of times (as can a C$20 duty-free exemption for absences of 24 hours or more). You cannot combine the yearly and 48-hour exemptions, use the $300 exemption only partially (to save the balance for a later trip), or pool exemptions with family members. Goods claimed under the C$300 exemption may follow you by mail; those claimed under the lesser exemptions must accompany you.

Alcohol and Tobacco. Alcohol and tobacco products may be included in the yearly and 48-hour exemptions but not in the 24-hour exemption. If you meet the age requirements of the province through which you reenter Canada, you may bring in, duty-free, 1.14 liters (40 imperial ounces) of wine or liquor *or* two dozen 12-ounce cans or bottles of beer or ale. If you are 16 or older, you may bring in, duty-free, 200 cigarettes, 50 cigars or cigarillos, and 400 tobacco sticks or 400 grams of manufactured tobacco. Alcohol and tobacco must accompany you on your return.

Gifts. An unlimited number of gifts valued up to C$60 each may be mailed to Canada duty-free. These do not count as part of your exemption. Label the package "Unsolicited Gift—Value under $60." Alcohol and tobacco are excluded.

For More Information. For more information, including details of duties on items that exceed your duty-free limit, ask the Revenue Canada Customs and Excise and Taxation Department (2265 St. Laurent Blvd. S, Ottawa, Ontario, K1G 4K3, tel. 613/993–0534) for a copy of the free brochure "I Declare/Je Déclare."

U.K. Customs **Allowances.** When returning from cruises that called at countries outside the European Union, you may import duty-free 200 cigarettes, 100 cigarillos, 50 cigars or 250 grams of tobacco; 1 liter of spirits or 2 liters of fortified or sparkling wine; 2 liters of still table wine; 60 milliliters of perfume; 250 milliliters of toilet water; plus £136 worth of other goods, including gifts and souvenirs.

For More Information. For further information or a copy of "A Guide for Travellers," which details standard customs procedures as well as what you may bring into the United Kingdom from abroad, contact HM Customs and Excise (Dorset House, Stamford St., London SE1 9NG, tel. 0171/202–4227).

U.S. Customs for Foreigners If you hold a foreign passport and will be returning home within hours of docking, you may be exempt from all U.S. Customs duties. Everything you bring into the United States must leave with you when you return home. When you reach your own country, you will have to pay appropriate duties there.

On Board

Checking Out Your Cabin

The first thing to do upon arriving at your cabin or suite is to make sure that everything is in order. If there are two twin beds instead of the double bed you wanted, or other serious problems, ask to be moved *before* the ship departs. Unless the ship is full, you can usually persuade the chief housekeeper or hotel manager to allow you to change cabins. It is customary to tip the stewards who assist you in moving to another cabin.

Since your cabin is your home away from home for a few days or weeks, everything should be to your satisfaction. Take a good look around: Is the cabin clean and orderly? Do the toilet, shower, and faucets work? Check the telephone and television. Again, major problems should be addressed immediately. Minor concerns, such as not enough bath towels or pillows, can wait until the frenzy of embarkation has subsided.

Your dining time and seating-assignment card may be in your cabin; now is the time to check it and immediately request any changes.

Shipboard Accounts

Virtually all cruise ships operate as cashless societies. Passengers charge onboard purchases and settle their accounts at the end of the cruise with a credit card, traveler's checks, or cash. You can sign for wine at dinner, drinks at the bar, shore excursions, gifts in the shop—virtually any expense you may incur aboard ship. On some lines, an imprint from a major credit card is necessary to open an account. Otherwise, a cash deposit may be required and a positive balance maintained to keep the shipboard account open. Either way, you will want to open a line of credit soon after settling into your cabin if an account was not opened for you at embarkation. This easily can be arranged by visiting the purser's office, located in the central atrium or main lobby.

The Crew

Cruise ships carry a full complement of crew (the people who actually sail the ship) and staff (the employees who feed, serve, and entertain you while you are on board). It's highly unlikely that you will see or meet the great majority of the ship's employees, since most work behind the scenes in the engine room, galleys, and other areas that are off-limits to passengers. Here are some with whom you will come in contact:

Officers **Captains** have many years of experience at sea and are officially certified and licensed as master mariners by their governments. On cruise ships, the captain is responsible not only for sailing the ship and ensuring its safety, but also for setting the tenor of the cruise. Most are charming, sophisticated diplomats who act as troubleshooters for almost any onboard problem. The **staff captain,** who is second-in-command to the captain, also holds master mariner papers and is fully qualified to take over should the captain become incapacitated. Usually, the staff captain oversees day-to-day operations of the crew in matters of navigation and seamanship. Smaller ships may not carry a staff captain, in which case the second-in-command is the **first mate.**

Cruise and Hotel Staff The **chief purser** is the ship's accountant, responsible for a number of services, such as check cashing, money changing, account payments, safe-deposit boxes, customs, and daily schedules. The shipboard **hotel manager,** who serves much the same function as a land-based hotel manager, supervises all housekeeping and dining-room staff. The hotel manager is the final authority on any problems you may have with your cabin, the food, or any other aspect of the ship. Small and medium-size ships that do not have a hotel manager split these responsibilities between the staff captain and the chief purser.

The **cruise director**—usually dressed in a brightly colored blazer rather than a uniform—is probably the most visible person on the ship. Besides planning, scheduling, and directing all shipboard social activities, the cruise director acts as an ombudsman and troubleshooter. The **entertainment director** oversees entertainment activities, from lounge music to guest lecturers. The **shore excursion director** sells tour tickets, gives an informative talk on each port before docking, and arranges almost everything on land—including tour buses, guides, and admissions to attractions. On smaller ships, the cruise director may take on the duties of one or both of the latter positions.

The **chief steward** oversees the dining room, the galley, the Lido, and the pantry, and supervises all waiters, busboys, and maître d's. Talk to the chief steward first if you have any complaints about the food or the service; if you don't get satisfaction, see the hotel manager. On some ships, the title of chief steward is used for the officer in charge of the room stewards, in which case the duties described above are often assumed by the maître d' or dining-room manager. Talk to the maître d' if you have any dietary preferences, wish to change tables, or want a picnic lunch packed for a trek ashore.

The **room steward/stewardess** or **cabin steward/stewardess** cleans and tidies your cabin throughout the voyage and also usually delivers any food or drink ordered through room service. Depending upon the ship, your steward may be visible enough that you become quite friendly, or you may seldom see him or her until the last evening, when tips traditionally are distributed. If there are any maintenance problems with your cabin or if you have special requests, such as extra pillows, first talk to your steward. If necessary, your next recourse is the **chief housekeeper,** who supervises the small army of stewards and cleaning and laundry personnel.

Tipping

For better or worse, tipping is an integral part of the cruise experience. Most companies pay their cruise staff nominal wages and expect tips to make up the difference. Most cruise lines have recommended tipping guidelines (*see* Chapter 1), and on many ships "voluntary" tipping for beverage service has been replaced with a mandatory 15% service charge, which is added to every bar bill. On the other hand, the most expensive luxury lines include tipping in the cruise fare and prohibit crew members from accepting any additional gratuities. On most small adventure ships, a collection box is placed in the dining room or lounge on the last full day of the cruise, and passengers are encouraged to contribute anonymously.

Dining

Restaurants The chief meals of the day are served in the main dining room, which on most ships can accommodate only half the passengers at once. So meals are usually served in two sittings—early (or main) and late (or second) seatings—usually from 1½ to 2½ hours apart. Early seating for dinner is generally between 6 and 6:30, late seating between 8 and 8:30.

Most cruise ships have a cafeteria-style restaurant, usually located near the swimming pool, where you can eat lunch and breakfast (dinner is usually served only in the dining room). Many ships provide self-serve coffee or tea in their cafeteria around the clock, as well as buffets at midnight.

A handful of ships also have alternative restaurants for ethnic cuisines, such as Italian, Chinese, or Japanese food. Other ships have pizzerias, ice-cream parlors, and caviar or cappuccino bars; there may be an extra charge at these facilities.

Meals Ocean liners serve food nearly around the clock. There may be up to four breakfast options: early morning coffee and pastries on deck, breakfast in bed via room service, buffet-style breakfast in the cafeteria, and breakfast in the dining room. There may also be two or three choices for lunch, mid-afternoon hors d'oeuvres, and midnight buffets. You can eat whatever is on the menu, in any quantity, at as many of these meals as you wish. Room service is traditionally, but not always, free (*see* Shipboard Services, *below*).

Seatings When it comes to your dining-table assignment, you should have options on four important points: early or late seating; smoking or no-smoking section; a table for two, four, six, or eight; and special dietary needs. When you receive your cruise documents, you will usually receive a card asking for your dining preferences. Fill this out and return it to the cruise line, but remember that you will not get your seating assignment until you board the ship. Check it out immediately, and if your request was not met, see the maître d'—usually there is a time and place set up for changes in dining assignments.

On some ships, seating times are strictly observed. Ten to 15 minutes after the scheduled mealtime, the dining-room doors are closed. On other ships, passengers may enter the dining room at their leisure, but they must be out by the end of the seating. When a ship has just one seating, passengers may enter any time while the kitchen is open and are never rushed.

Seating assignments on some ships apply only for dinner. Several have open seating for breakfast or lunch, which means you may sit anywhere at any time. Smaller or more luxurious ships offer open seating for all meals.

Changing Tables Dining is a focal point of the cruise experience, and your companions at meals may become your best friends on the cruise. However, if you don't enjoy the company at your table the maître d' can usually move you to another one if the dining room isn't completely full—a tip helps. He will probably be reluctant to comply with your request after the first full day at sea, however, because the waiters, busboys, and wine steward who have been serving you up to that point won't receive their tips at the end of the cruise. Be persistent if you are truly unhappy.

Cuisine Most ships sailing in the Western Hemisphere serve food geared to the American palate, but there are also theme dinners featuring the cuisine of a particular country. Some European ships, especially smaller vessels, may offer a particular cuisine throughout the cruise—Scandinavian, German, Italian, or Greek, perhaps—depending on the ship's or the crew's nationality. Aboard all cruise ships, the quality of the cooking is generally good, but even a skilled chef is hard-put to serve 500 or more extraordinary dinners per hour. On the other hand, the presentation is often spectacular, especially at gala midnight buffets.

There is a direct relationship between the cost of a cruise and the quality of its cuisine. The food is very sophisticated on some (mostly expensive) lines, among them Crystal Cruises, Cunard Line, and Seabourn Cruise Line. In the more moderate price range, Celebrity

Cruises has gained renown for the culinary stylings of French chef Michel Roux, who acts as a consultant to the line.

Special Diets With notification well in advance, many ships can provide a kosher, low-salt, low-cholesterol, sugar-free, vegetarian, or other special menu. However, there's always a chance that the wrong dish will somehow be handed to you. Especially when it comes to soups and desserts, it's a good idea to ask about the ingredients.

Large ships usually offer an alternative "light" or "spa" menu based upon American Heart Association guidelines, using less fat, leaner cuts of meat, low-cholesterol or low-sodium preparations, smaller portions, salads, fresh-fruit desserts, and healthy garnishes. Some smaller ships may not be able to accommodate special dietary needs. Vegetarians generally have no trouble finding appropriate selections on ship menus.

Wine Wine at meals costs extra on most ships; the prices are usually comparable to those in shoreside restaurants and are charged to your shipboard account. On some ships, however—most notably Italian, French, and Greek vessels—meals are accompanied by table wine (*see* Aboard Foreign Ships *in* Choosing Your Cruise, *above*). A handful of luxury vessels include both wine and liquor.

The Captain's Table It is both a privilege and a marvelous experience to be invited to dine one evening at the captain's table. Although some seats are given to celebrities, repeat passengers, and passengers in the most expensive suites, other invitations are given at random to ordinary passengers. Any passenger can request an invitation from the chief steward or the hotel manager, although there is no guarantee you will be accommodated. The captain's guests always wear a suit and tie or a dress, even if the dress code for that evening is casual. On many ships, passengers may also be invited to dine at the other officers' special tables, or officers may visit a different passenger table each evening.

Bars

Ship's bars, whether adjacent to the pool or attached to one of the lounges, tend to be the social centers of a ship. Except on a handful of luxury-class ships where everything is included in the ticket price, bars operate on a pay-as-it's-poured basis. Rather than demand cash after every round, however, most ships allow passengers to charge drinks to their accounts. Prices are comparable to what you'd pay at home.

In international waters there are, technically, no laws against teenage drinking, but almost all ships require passengers to be over 18 or 21. Many cruise ships have chapters of Alcoholics Anonymous (aka "Friends of Bill W") or will organize meetings on request. Look for meeting times and places in the daily program slipped under your cabin door each night.

Entertainment

Lounges and Nightclubs On ocean liners, the main entertainment lounge, which may also be called a theater or showroom, schedules nightly musical revues, magic acts, comedians, and variety shows. Generally, the larger the ship, the bigger and more elaborate the productions. Newer ships—and some older ones as well—sometimes feature multitier seating balconies. During the rest of the day the room is used for group activities, such as shore-excursion talks or bingo games.

Many larger ships have a second showroom, used for bingo or trivia contests while the main show is under way elsewhere. Entertainers and ballroom dancing may go on here late into the night. Elsewhere you may find a disco, nightclub, or cabaret, usually built around a bar and dance floor. Music is provided by a piano player, disc jockey, or small performing ensembles such as country-and-western duos or jazz combos.

On smaller ships the entertainment options are more limited, sometimes consisting of no more than a piano around which passengers gather. There may be a main lounge where scaled-down revues are staged.

Library Most cruise ships have a library with anywhere from 500 to 1,500 volumes, including everything from the latest best-sellers to reference works. Many shipboard libraries also stock videotapes.

Movie Theaters All but the smallest vessels have a movie theater. The films are frequently one or two months past their first release but not yet available on videotape or cable TV. Films rated "R" are edited to minimize sex and violence. On a weeklong voyage, a dozen different films may be screened, each one repeated at various times during the day. Theaters are also used for lectures, religious services, and private meetings.

With a few exceptions, ocean liners equip their cabins with closed-circuit TVs; these show movies (continuously on some newer ships), shipboard lectures, and regular programs (thanks to satellite reception). Ships with VCRs in the cabins usually provide a selection of movies on cassette at no charge (a deposit is usually required).

Casinos Once a ship is 12 miles off American shores, it is in international waters and gambling is permitted. (Some "cruises to nowhere," in fact, are little more than sailing casinos.) All ocean liners, as well as many cruise yachts and motor-sailing ships, have casinos. On larger vessels, they usually have poker, baccarat, blackjack, roulette, craps, and slot machines. House stakes are much more modest than those at Las Vegas or Atlantic City. On most ships the maximum bet is $200; some ships allow $500. Payouts on the slot machines (some of which take as little as a nickel) are generally much lower, too. Credit is never extended, but many casinos have handy credit-card machines that dispense cash for a hefty fee. Exceptions are the Caesars Palace at Sea casinos aboard the *Crystal Harmony* and *Crystal Symphony*, which are regulated by the Nevada Gaming Commission, offer the same gambling limits as in Las Vegas, and, by prior arrangement, will extend credit.

Children are officially barred from the casinos, but it's common to see them playing the slots rather than the adjacent video machines. Most ships offer free individual instruction and even gambling classes in the off-hours. Casinos are usually open from early morning to late night, although you may find only unattended slot machines before evening. In adherence to local laws, casinos are always closed while in port.

Game Rooms Most ships have a game or card room with card tables and board games. These rooms are for serious players and are often the site of friendly round-robin competitions and tournaments. Most ships furnish everything for free (cards, chips, games, and so forth), but a few charge $1 or more for each deck of cards. Be aware that professional cardsharps and hustlers have been fleecing ship passengers almost as long as there have been ships.

There are small video arcades in most medium and large ships. A few also have a room with personal computers equipped with games and popular business programs such as WordPerfect and Lotus 1-2-3, all available at no charge.

Bingo and Other Games The daily high-stakes bingo games are even more popular than the casinos. You can play for as little as a dollar a card. Most ships have a snowball bingo game with a jackpot that grows throughout the cruise into hundreds or even thousands of dollars.

Another popular cruise pastime are the so-called "horse races": Fictional horses are auctioned off to "owners." Individual passengers can buy a horse or form "syndicates." Bids usually begin at around $25 and can top $1,000 per horse. Races are then "run" according to dice throws or computer-generated random numbers. The audience bets on their favorites.

Sports and Fitness

Swimming Pools
All but the smallest ships have at least one pool, some of them elaborate affairs with water slides or retractable roofs; hot tubs and whirlpools are quite common. Pools may be filled with fresh water or salt water; some ships have one of each. While in port or during rough weather, the pools are usually emptied or covered with canvas. Many are too narrow or short to allow swimmers more than a few strokes in any direction; none have diving boards, and not all are heated. Often there are no lifeguards. Wading pools are sometimes provided for small children.

Sun Deck
The top deck is usually called the Sun Deck or Sports Deck. On some ships this is where you'll find the pool or whirlpool; on others it is dedicated to volleyball, table tennis, shuffleboard, and other such sports. A number of ships have paddle-tennis courts, and a few have golf driving ranges. (Skeet shooting is usually offered at the stern of a lower deck.) Often, at twilight or after the sun goes down, the Sun Deck is used for dancing, barbecues, limbo contests, or other social activities.

Exercise and Fitness Rooms
Most newer ships and some older ones have well-equipped fitness centers, many with massage, sauna, and whirlpools. An upper-deck fitness center often has an airy and sunny view of the sea; an inside, lower-deck health club is often dark and small unless it is equipped with an indoor pool or beauty salon. Many ships have full-service exercise rooms with bodybuilding equipment, stationary bicycles, rowing machines, treadmills, aerobics classes, and personal fitness instruction. Some ships even have structured cruise-length physical fitness programs, which may include lectures on weight loss or nutrition. These often are tied in with a spa menu in the dining room. Beauty salons adjacent to the health club may offer spa treatments such as facials and mud wraps. The more extensive programs are often sold on a daily or weekly basis.

Promenade Deck
Many vessels designate certain decks for fitness walks and may post the number of laps per mile. Fitness instructors may lead daily walks around the Promenade Deck. A number of ships discourage jogging and running on the decks or ask that no one take fitness walks before 8 AM or after 10 PM, so as not to disturb passengers in cabins. With the advent of the megaship (*see* Types of Ships, *above*), walking and jogging has in many cases moved up top to tracks on the Sun or Sports deck.

Shipboard Services

Room Service
A small number of ships have no room service at all, except when the ship's doctor orders it for an ailing passenger. Many offer only breakfast (Continental on some, full on others), while others provide no more than a limited menu at certain hours of the day. Most, however, have certain selections that you can order at any time. Some luxury ships have unlimited round-the-clock room service. There may or may not be a charge for room service (other than for drinks). Check before you order.

Minibars
An increasing number of ships equip their more expensive cabins with small refrigerators or minibars stocked with snacks, soft drinks, and liquors, which may or may not be free.

Laundry and Dry Cleaning	All but the smallest ships and shortest cruises offer laundry services—full-service, self-service, or both. Use of machines is generally free, although some ships charge for detergent, use of the machines, or both. Valet laundry service includes cabin pickup and delivery and usually takes 24 hours. Most ships also offer dry-cleaning services.
Hairdressers	Even the smallest ships have a hairdresser on staff. Larger ships have complete beauty parlors, and some have barbershops. Book hairdressers well in advance, especially before such popular events as the farewell dinner.
Film Processing	Many cruise ships have color-film processing and printing equipment to develop film overnight. It's expensive but convenient.
Photographer	The staff photographer, a near-universal fixture on cruise ships, records every memorable, photogenic moment. The thousands of photos snapped over the course of a cruise are displayed publicly in special cases every morning and are offered for sale, usually for $6 for a 5″ × 7″ color print or $12 for a 8″ × 10″. If you want a special photo or a portrait, the photographer is usually happy to oblige. Many passengers choose to have a formal portrait taken before the captain's farewell dinner—the dressiest evening of the cruise. The ship's photographer usually anticipates this demand by setting up a portable studio near the dining-room entrance.
Religious Services	Most ships provide nondenominational religious services on Sundays and religious holidays, and a number offer daily Catholic masses and Friday-evening Jewish services. The kind of service held depends upon the clergy the cruise line invites on board. Usually religious services are held in the library, the theater, or one of the private lounges, although a few ships have actual chapels.
Communications *Shipboard*	Most cabins have loudspeakers and telephones. Generally, the loudspeakers cannot be switched off because they are needed to broadcast important notices. Telephones are used to call fellow passengers, order room service, summon a doctor, leave a wake-up call, or speak with any of the ship's officers or departments.
Ship to Shore	Satellite facilities make it possible to call anywhere in the world from most ships. Most are also equipped with telex and fax machines, and some provide credit-card phones. It may take as long as a half hour to make a connection, but unless a storm is raging outside, conversation is clear and easy. On older ships, voice calls must be put through on short-wave wireless or via the one phone in the radio room. Newer ships are generally equipped with direct-dial phones in every cabin for calls to shore. Be warned: The cost of sending any message, regardless of the method, can be quite expensive— up to $15 a minute. If possible, wait until you go ashore to call home.

Health

Medical Care	All but the tiniest ships carry at least one doctor, and larger ones have fully equipped infirmaries, staffed with doctors and nurses, most of whom have emergency-room experience and who are prepared to handle medical emergencies. Doctors have office hours and make cabin calls if you are bedridden. Fees for office visits are usually nominal—$20–$40 for a consultation, including any medicine you may need—but not always: The charge can run into the hundreds of dollars for broken bones or emergency surgery, for which you must pay cash, by check, or with a credit card; you may then apply for reimbursement from your insurance company when you get home. In addition, most ships carry small quantities of the most frequently dispensed prescription drugs, from insulin to hypertension pills.
	If you become seriously ill or injured and happen to be near a modern major city, you may be taken to a medical facility shoreside. But if

you're farther afield, you may have to be airlifted off the ship by helicopter and flown either to the nearest American territory or to an airport where you can be taken by charter jet to the United States. If you have any reason to feel that you could have a medical emergency, ask your travel agent about buying trip or health insurance (*see* Insurance *in* Before You Go, *above*).

Seasickness Modern cruise ships, unlike their earlier transatlantic predecessors, are relatively motion-free vessels with computer-controlled stabilizers, and they usually sail in comparatively calm waters. If you have a history of seasickness, though, it's best to get treatment *before* you begin to feel ill. The easiest, most painless method is to ask your doctor or the ship's doctor to prescribe a Transderm patch, good for about 72 hours, which tapes behind your ear; the medicine, contained in a semipermeable membrane, is automatically absorbed through the skin into your bloodstream. Side effects can be strong and may include blurred vision and a dulled sense of taste. Two other antimotion drugs are Bonine and Dramamine, both sold over the counter (in fact, many cruise ships hand out free packets of Dramamine at the purser's office or in the dining room); their one undesirable side effect is drowsiness. Some swear by wristbands (with an embedded plastic button) that employ acupressure to ward off seasickness; they're sold through travel-supply catalogues, at some travel agencies, and in some ships' shops. If you do feel seasick, don't talk about it; stay away from anybody complaining about seasickness, and go out on deck. Breathe in the fresh air. Look at the horizon rather than the waves. Get involved in fun activities. This is one problem that, when ignored, will often go away. Typically, seasickness does not last longer than three to 10 hours. In an emergency, ships' doctors can administer a shot that quickly relieves all symptoms of seasickness.

Potable Water Water and food on board any ship listed in this book is as safe as at any stateside restaurant. Canada, Bermuda, Puerto Rico, the Virgin Islands, and a handful of other well-developed countries and islands are quite safe in terms of sanitation, but at many other ports, precautions are in order. Local water may taste good, but it can contain bacteria to which locals are immune but visitors are susceptible. Diarrhea and intestinal disorders can result.

In such situations, drink only bottled water that is clearly more than tap water put into a container. Because the glass you use may have been washed in suspect water, drink beer or soda straight from the can or bottle. In tropical climates, stay away from fruits or raw vegetables that you don't peel yourself.

Swimming Water While swimming in the sea or salt water doesn't present any health hazard (unless the area is polluted, as in Acapulco), swimming in rivers, freshwater lakes, and streams in undeveloped countries may expose you to harmful microorganisms or aquatic parasites. So, unless you are on a ship-sponsored shore excursion or have been specifically told by the cruise director that the local creeks and lakes are safe, stick with the ocean or chlorinated swimming pools.

Lifeboats

By international law all ships must be equipped with lifeboats, and according to Coast Guard regulations and the SOLAS (Safety of Life at Sea) convention, every cruise ship must conduct at least one lifeboat drill, mandatory for all passengers, early in the voyage. Every passenger must correctly don a life preserver, which is usually found in the cabin under the bed or in the closet. On the back of the cabin door or nearby on the wall will be an instruction chart and possibly a map indicating how to get to your lifeboat mustering station. At the signal for abandoning ship—six long blasts of the ship's horn, followed by six short blasts—every passenger must proceed to a mustering station. All ships follow this drill with at least one full-fledged crew practice (usually while most passengers are ashore at one of the ports of call), and some ships have additional emergency drills during the cruise.

Make certain that the ship's purser knows if you or your spouse has some physical infirmity that may hamper a speedy exit from your cabin. In case of a real emergency, the purser can quickly dispatch a crew member to assist you. If you are traveling with children, be sure child-size life jackets are placed in your cabin.

World Time Zones

Numbers below vertical bands relate each zone to Greenwich Mean Time (0 hrs.).
Local times frequently differ from these general indications,
as indicated by light-face numbers on map.

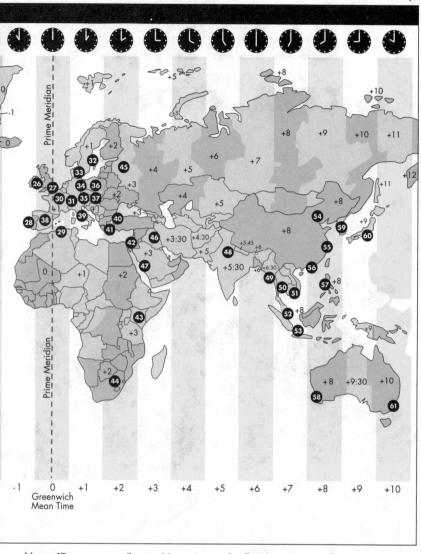

1 Cruise Lines and Ships

Abercrombie & Kent

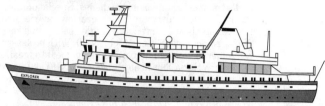

The Fleet   MS *Explorer*

The *Explorer* has a long and illustrious history. In previous incarnations, it was the *Lindblad Explorer* and later the *Society Explorer*. When built in 1969, it incorporated many design features that set the standard for later expedition ships: It was the first to feature an ice-hardened hull, a relatively shallow draft, a small profile for entering otherwise inaccessible coves and harbors, and a fleet of Zodiacs. The *Explorer* was the first ship to offer adventure cruises to Antarctica, and has sailed longer and farther than any other expedition ship.

Ship at a Glance

	Dining Rooms	Bars	Casino	Fitness Center	Pools	Average Per Diem
Explorer	1	1	○	●	1	$460

Cruise Experience   Abercrombie & Kent (A&K)—better known for its luxury safaris and land tours to exotic locales—entered the cruise scene in 1992 when it purchased the *Explorer*. One of the industry's foremost advocates of environmentally sensitive travel, or ecotourism, A&K appeals to well-educated, sophisticated travelers looking to expand their horizons. Its cruises underline this commitment to ecology by emphasizing an environmentally friendly philosophy during lectures, shore excursions, and Zodiac explorations. Lecturers and staff are familiar with ecological issues and urge passengers to avoid damaging the environment and not to disturb, harass, or interfere with the wildlife. Passengers tend to be couples 55–60 and above. Many are repeaters, and some may be aboard for their 10th time or more. There are few younger couples or single passengers.

Activities   There is no daily program of organized events because most activity takes place off the ship. Once at anchor, the *Explorer* launches its fleet of Zodiacs, which can make landfall nearly anywhere as conditions allow. Naturalists lead these waterborne excursions, which frequently encounter penguins, seals, sea lions, humpback whales, and a host of other marine creatures and seabirds. There's no charge to participate, but passengers should be in reasonably good physical condition and have a sense of adventure: The unpredictable Antarctic climate sometimes means rough seas, and land outings can require long periods of hiking on icy, rugged terrain.

Landings are frequent, and many passengers try to be on every excursion. Those who choose to stay aboard can pass the time with a book from the ship's library or a visit to the captain on the bridge, which is always open to passengers.

Chart Symbols. Ships at a Glance. ●: *Fully equipped;* ◑: *Partially equipped;* ○: *Not equipped.* Cabins and Rates. **D:** *Double bed;* **K:** *King-size bed;* **Q:** *Queen-size bed;* **T:** *Twin bed;* **U/L:** *Upper and lower berths;* ●: *All cabins have this facility;* ○: *No cabins have this facility;* ◑: *Some cabins have this facility*

Dining Food is of the hearty, Northern European variety—not bad, not gourmet. You'll find heavy meat dishes, standard buffet breakfasts, and a smattering of American dishes. Special dietary needs are not easily handled, although there are low-calorie selections on the menus. Meals are served at a single seating in a rather diminutive dining room; dinner is at roughly 7:30. With no assigned seating arrangements, you can hop around from meal to meal, mingling with fellow travelers. This is no glamour cruise: The two semiformal evenings are frequently attended by casually dressed passengers who have wisely junked fancier duds to economize on packing space. There is no smoking in the dining room.

Other food service includes lunch and breakfast buffets, which are sometimes presented deckside, weather permitting. Coffee and tea are available all day. Room service, too, is always available, but since there are no in-cabin phones, you must either find a steward or arrange delivery in advance.

Entertainment Except for enrichment talks and occasional screenings of documentary films or videos in the lecture hall, entertainment is a matter of making your own fun. There is a good selection of fiction and nonfiction books in the ship's library, along with magazines and board games. Before dinner every night, passengers are invited to meet with the naturalists for an informal recap of the day's events and to preview the next day's agenda. After dinner, passengers may gather around the piano for an impromptu sing-along. After-dinner drinks are served here and members of the crew and staff often mingle with passengers in this informal setting.

Service and Tipping Instead of deferential white-glove service, you'll find naturalists and lecturers eating with and moving about among the passengers—like members of the family. A service charge is included in the cruise fare, and tips are not accepted.

Destinations The ship that originally launched cruising to the "White Continent" spends November through April sailing there from southern Chile. The rest of the year is spent outside the Western Hemisphere. (For detailed itineraries, *see* Chapter 3.)

For More Information Abercrombie & Kent (1520 Kensington Rd., Oak Brook, IL 60521, tel. 708/954–2944 or 800/323–7308).

MS Explorer

Specifications *Type of ship:* Expedition
Cruise experience: Casual
Size: 2,398 tons
Number of cabins: 51
Outside cabins: 100%
Year built: 1969

Passengers: 96
Crew: 67 (European, American, and Filipino)
Officers: German
Passenger/crew ratio: 1.4 to 1

Ship's Log Compared with the newest generation of expedition ships, such as the *Bremen* or *Hanseatic*, the *Explorer* is a bit small and spartan. The design is strictly practical, with narrow decks, exposed pipes, and cramped quarters. The *Explorer*'s compact size, however, enables all passengers to disembark onto Zodiacs in 15 minutes, allowing for several landings per day and additional time for shore excursions. Despite the *Explorer*'s age and size, the ship, with its red hull, continues to be a beacon to adventure cruisers, some of whom would never dream of sailing to Antarctica on any other ship.

Cabins and Rates	Beds	Phone	TV	Sitting Area	Fridge	Tub	Average Per Diem*
Suite	T	○	○	●	●	○	$662–$682

| Outside | T | ○ | ○ | ○ | ○ | ○ | $419–$502 |

Rates are for Antarctica. Airfare and port taxes are extra.

Cabins are tiny; each has a wooden desk with a view through a porthole or picture window. In the daytime, beds are converted into side-by-side sofas. Closet space is extremely limited; all accommodations have hair dryers. Cabins on the Boat Deck look onto the public promenade.

Outlet voltage: 220 AC.

Single supplement: 140%–170% of double-occupancy rate.

Discounts: A third passenger in a cabin pays half the double-occupancy rate; no cabins accommodate four passengers. Passengers who book early can save $500 per person, and there is a 20% discount for booking back-to-back Antarctica cruises.

Sports and Fitness   **Health club:** Reclining bike, ski machines, free weights, sauna.

Recreation: Small pool (not filled on Antarctica cruises).

Facilities   **Public rooms:** Lounge, lecture hall; access to navigation bridge.

Shops: Small gift shop, beauty salon.

Health care: Doctor on call.

Child care: None.

Services: Laundry service.

Accessibility   Because there is no elevator aboard, this ship is not recommended for wheelchair users.

Alaska Sightseeing/Cruise West

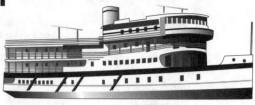

The Fleet   MV *Spirit of Alaska*
MV *Spirit of Columbia*
MV *Spirit of Discovery*
MV *Spirit of '98*

Alaska Sightseeing's philosophy is that smaller is better: Each vessel measures less than 200 feet in length, weighs less than 100 tons, and carries no more than 101 passengers. Because they have shallow drafts, these small ships can hug the shoreline and explore narrow inlets, fjords, and rivers that bigger cruise ships must bypass. The *Spirit of Alaska* and *Spirit of Columbia* have bow ramps that allow passengers to go ashore where docking or dropping anchor would otherwise be impossible.

Ships at a Glance

	Dining Rooms	Bars	Casino	Fitness Center	Pools	Average Per Diem
Spirit of Alaska	1	1	○	◐	0	$406
Spirit of Columbia	1	1	○	◐	1	$351
Spirit of Discovery	1	1	○	◐	0	$412
Spirit of '98	1	1	○	◐	0	$420

Cruise Experience   Alaska Sightseeing lets nature take center stage. Passengers are encouraged to spend their time out on deck, scanning the shore for wildlife. The captain may linger awhile when a foraging bear is sighted or a pod of whales is encountered. Guests may visit the wheelhouse anytime during daylight hours. Itineraries call for less time in port, and more time for shipboard touring, than is typical of cruises aboard large ocean liners. Passengers who sail this way are well-traveled nature lovers. Because there are so few people aboard, individual interests can be indulged, and sailing schedules are flexible enough to allow for extra time to watch a calving glacier or photograph eagles. Upon request, crew members will awaken guests to view the northern lights.

Activities   There are no showgirls, no midnight buffets, and no aerobics classes. Talks given by park naturalists or the cruise director are the only organized activities aboard ship. In addition to wildlife watching, popular pastimes include shuffleboard, checkers, cards, and comparing notes on the day's events.

Dining   Food is plentiful and tasty; cuisine is classic American. Local catches and produce are often on the menu, as are home-baked breads and

Chart Symbols. Ships at a Glance. **●:** *Fully equipped;* **◑:** *Partially equipped;* ○: *Not equipped.* Cabins and Rates. **D:** *Double bed;* **K:** *King-size bed;* **Q:** *Queen-size bed;* **T:** *Twin bed;* **U/L:** *Upper and lower berths;* **●:** *All cabins have this facility;* ○: *No cabins have this facility;* **◑:** *Some cabins have this facility*

desserts. Meals are served in a single, open seating (dinner at 7 or 7:30). Passengers may choose from two entrées each evening. Like the rest of the Alaska Sightseeing cruise experience, dining is very informal, and food presentation is less important than the view outside. Leave all your dress clothes at home: No one dons anything resembling high fashion, even for the Captain's Dinner. Special dietary requests should be made at time of booking.

An early-riser Continental breakfast in the lounge is followed each morning by full breakfast in the dining room, where lunch also is served. Fresh fruit, coffee, tea, and other beverages are available throughout the day. Snacks are usually served around 4 and hors d'oeuvres at 6. There is no room service, except by special arrangement and in the Owner's Suite on the *Spirit of '98*.

Entertainment Most Alaska Sightseeing passengers would rather rise early than revel late into the night. Mingling in the lounge and discussing the day's wildlife sightseeing are the highlights of most evenings. On Crew night, you'll learn why the ship's engineer is called a "mule." There's also movie night, a karaoke night, and a casino night, when the stakes are Alaska Sightseeing sweatshirts.

Service and The all-American crew is enthusiastic and informative. Even with *Tipping* myriad ship duties, these young hosts find time to form close friendships with their guests. Recommended tipping is $5–$10 per person, per diem. Passengers place their tips in an envelope on the last evening of the cruise and leave them, anonymously, in the lounge.

Destinations Among the few American-flagged vessels sailing the Inside Passage, these are the only ships that home port in Seattle during the Alaska season. Spring and fall itineraries take in northern California's Napa Valley, Oregon's Columbia and Snake rivers or the stretch of the Inside Passage that borders British Columbia. (For detailed itineraries, *see* Chapter 3.)

For More Alaska Sightseeing/Cruise West (4th & Battery Bldg., Suite 700, **Information** Seattle, WA 98121, tel. 800/426–7702).

MV Spirit of Alaska

Specifications *Type of ship:* Coastal cruiser   *Passengers:* 82
Cruise experience: Casual   *Crew:* 20 (American)
Size: 97 tons   *Officers:* American
Number of cabins: 39   *Passenger/crew ratio:* 4 to 1
Outside cabins: 100%   *Year built:* 1980

Ship's Log Alaska Sightseeing's original overnight vessel is still its coziest. You are never by yourself in the lounge, and meals in the homey dining room resemble a family affair soon after the cruise has begun. Sleek and small, the *Spirit of Alaska* feels like a real yacht. A bow ramp adds to the sense of adventure, allowing passengers to put ashore at tiny islands and beaches where few other cruise travelers ever visit.

Cabins and Rates

	Beds	Phone	TV	Sitting Area	Fridge	Tub	Average Per Diem*
Suite	Q	○	○	●	○	○	$506
Outside	D	○	○	○	○	○	$406
Inside	D	○	○	○	○	○	$306

Rates are for Alaska. Airfare and port taxes are extra.

The *Spirit of Alaska* offers the widest variety of accommodations of any Alaska Sightseeing vessel, from top-deck suites with two picture windows to claustrophobic lower-deck cabins with a porthole. Most cabins are very small. Toilets and showers are a combined unit.

Outlet voltage: 110 AC.

Single supplement: 175% of double-occupancy rate.

Discounts: Four cabins (two category AA, two category A) are available as triples at reduced per diems. Early booking discounts are $50 and $100 per person, additional $50 discount for early final payment.

Fitness   **Health club:** StairMaster, exercise bike, rowing machine.

Recreation: Unobstructed circuit for jogging.

Facilities   **Public rooms:** Lounge, bar; access to navigation bridge.

Accessibility   Four main deck cabins, the aft dining room, and the forward lounge are located on a single level. There is no elevator.

MV Spirit of Columbia

Specifications   *Type of ship:* Coastal cruiser   *Passengers:* 70
Cruise experience: Casual   *Crew:* 18 (American)
Size: 98 tons   *Officers:* American
Number of cabins: 33   *Passenger/crew ratio:* 3.9 to 1
Outside cabins: 50%   *Year built:* 1979

Ship's Log   The latest addition to the AS/CW fleet was American Canadian Cruise Line's *New Shoreham II* before Alaska Sightseeing bought it in early 1994. The ship was renamed the *Spirit of Columbia* to reflect its positioning out of Portland on Columbia and Snake river cruises spring through fall. Although cut from the same mold as Alaska Sightseeing's *Spirit of Alaska*, it has one notable feature: a unique bow ramp design that allows passengers to walk directly from the forward lounge onto shore. The *Spirit of Columbia*'s interior design was inspired by the national park lodges of the American West; colors are drawn from a muted palette of rust, evergreen, and sand.

Cabins and Rates	Beds	Phone	TV	Sitting Area	Fridge	Tub	Average Per Diem*
Suite	Q or T	○	●	●	●	◐	$456
Outside	Q or T	○	◐	○	◐	○	$351
Inside	T	○	○	○	○	○	$256

*Rates are for the Columbia and Snake rivers. Airfare and port taxes are extra.

After purchasing the *Spirit of Columbia*, Alaska Sightseeing built a new bridge deck with six suites. The Owner's Suite stretches the width of the vessel; located just under the bridge, its row of foward-facing windows give a captain's-eye view of the ship's progress. All suites have a TV/VCR, minirefrigerator, and an armchair and a desk. Deluxe cabins have a side table and chair. All cabins have modest-size closets and drawers between or under the beds. A watercolor print, depicting Pacific Northwest scenery, hangs in each cabin. Color schemes are similar to the shades found in the public rooms. Patterns were based on Native American designs from the desert Southwest.

Outlet voltage: 110 AC.

Single supplement: 175% of double-occupancy rate.

Discounts: $50 and $100 per person for booking early, additional $50 discount for early final payment.

Sports and Fitness	**Health club:** StairMaster, exercise bike, rowing machine.
	Recreation: Stern swimming platform, unobstructed circuit (12 laps = 1 mile) for jogging.
Facilities	**Public rooms:** Lounge; access to navigation bridge.
Accessibility	Four main-deck cabins, the aft dining room, and forward lounge, are located on a single level. There is no elevator.

MV Spirit of Discovery

Specifications

Type of ship: Coastal cruiser   *Passengers:* 84
Cruise experience: Casual   *Crew:* 21 (American)
Size: 94 tons   *Officers:* American
Number of cabins: 43   *Passenger/crew ratio:* 4 to 1
Outside cabins: 100%   *Year built:* 1976

Ship's Log Floor-to-ceiling windows in the main lounge provide stunning views of glaciers, wildlife, and other passing scenery for passengers aboard this snazzy yacht. Blue-suede chairs, a wraparound bench sofa at the bow, and a mirrored ceiling make the chrome-filled lounge look extra-swank. From here, passengers have direct access to a large outdoor viewing deck, one of two aboard. This is especially convenient for those who don't want to trudge upstairs every time a whale is spotted. Another advantage of the *Discovery* is its small workout room. In good weather, the equipment is moved to an outside deck under a protective canopy.

Cabins and Rates

	Beds	Phone	TV	Sitting Area	Fridge	Tub	Average Per Diem*
Outside	T	○	○	○	○	○	$412

Rates are for Alaska. Airfare and port taxes are extra.

Although the cabins are small, their picture windows are larger than on any other Alaska Sightseeing ship, and they are decorated with photographs of Alaska wildlife. All cabins have individual climate control and a vanity with a desk and chair. Deluxe cabins have refrigerators and minibars, plus TVs and VCRs. Two cabins are reserved for single travelers. The bathrooms' tight toilet/shower/sink configuration is the ship's most unappealing quality.

Outlet voltage: 110 AC.

Single supplement: 175% of double-occupancy rate.

Discounts: $50 and $100 per person for booking early, additional $50 discount for early final payment.

Fitness	**Health club:** StairMaster, exercise bike, rowing machine.
Facilities	**Public rooms:** Bar/lounge; access to navigation bridge.
	Shops: Small gift shop.
Accessibility	This ship is not recommended for wheelchair users.

MV Spirit of '98

Specifications

Type of ship: Coastal cruiser   *Passengers:* 101
Cruise experience: Casual   *Crew:* 23 (American)
Size: 96 tons   *Officers:* American
Number of cabins: 49   *Passenger/crew ratio:* 4.4 to 1
Outside cabins: 100%   *Year built:* 1984

Ship's Log With its rounded stern and wheelhouse, old-fashioned smokestack, and Victorian decor, the *Spirit of '98* evokes the feel of a turn-of-the-century steamship even though it was built in 1984. As the largest

Alaska Sightseeing ship, it also is the most elegant. Inside and out, mahogany adorns this ship, including the sculptured sideboard in its main lounge, where massive floral curtains conjure up the days of the cancan and the player piano is in constant demand. Overstuffed chairs upholstered in crushed velvet complete the Gold Rush–era motif. For private moments, there are plenty of nooks and crannies aboard ship, along with the cozy Soapy's Parlor at the stern, with a small bar and a few tables and chairs.

Cabins and Rates		Beds	Phone	TV	Sitting Area	Fridge	Tub	Average Per Diem*
Suite		K	○	●	●	●	●	$635
Outside		Q or T	○	○	●	○	○	$420

Rates are for Alaska. Airfare and port taxes are extra.

The small but comfortable cabins are appointed with mahogany headboards and Audubon prints. Each has a picture window that may be opened. All cabins have individual climate control, separate showers and toilet in the bathrooms, and excellent light for bedtime reading. Most have both closet and drawer space for storage. In addition, Deluxe and Category 1 cabins have a sitting area, and the single Owner's Suite comes with a living room; game/meeting room; separate bedroom; TV; VCR; fully stocked, complimentary wet bar; and oversize bathroom.

Outlet voltage: 110 AC.

Single supplement: 175% of double-occupancy rate.

Discounts: Two category 1 cabins can be booked as triples at reduced per diems. Early booking discounts are $50 and $100 per person, additional $50 discount for early final payment.

Sports and Fitness **Health club:** StairMaster, exercise bike, rowing machine.

Recreation: Unobstructed circuit (12 laps = 1 mile) for jogging.

Facilities **Public rooms:** Bar/lounge; access to navigation bridge.

Accessibility Two cabins are accessible to wheelchair users. All public decks and rooms are accessible by elevator.

American Canadian Caribbean Line

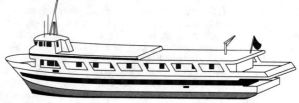

Caribbean Prince

The Fleet *Caribbean Prince*
Mayan Prince
Niagara Prince

ACCL's vessels are the personal creations of the line's owner, Luther H. Blount, who builds them in his Rhode Island shipyard. Their efficient layout and durability are the result of Blount's 45 years of shipbuilding experience—he has designed and constructed ferries, sightseeing boats, and small ships now operated by other cruise lines, such as Alaska Sightseeing/Cruise West. For ACCL, he has created a fleet of small yachtlike ships that are custom designed for cruising inland waterways and coastlines, with retractable pilothouses, shallow drafts, bow ramps, and rear swimming platforms.

Ships at a Glance

	Dining Rooms	Bars	Casino	Fitness Center	Pools	Average Per Diem
Caribbean Prince	1	0	○	○	1	$185
Mayan Prince	1	0	○	○	1	$182
Niagara Prince	1	0	○	○	1	$188

Cruise Experience ACCL's passengers prefer a casual, relaxed, and intimate shipboard environment to the glamour and luxury of pricier cruise lines. But rock-bottom rates mean that ACCL offers few traditional services and facilities—sheets and towels are changed every *other* day, and it's even suggested that you pack your own beach towel. These no-frills cruises are an excellent value, nevertheless. Everything is included in the base price except tips and shore excursions. No alcohol is sold on board, although you are free to bring your own. At several ports, the crew can arrange to have liquor delivered directly to the ship. Mixers and other nonalcoholic drinks are available free from the bar at all hours.

New England charm and personal service make passengers feel like they're sailing on the family yacht. In a sense, they are, and Blount and his family personally send off every cruise that departs from the line's base in Warren, Rhode Island. Once underway, passengers find themselves on easy terms with one another as well as with the crew. The line is similar in its informal ambience and limited amenities to Alaska Sightseeing, but the latter's cabins and public spaces are decidedly more elegant. ACCL cruisers tend to be educated and older (63 on average), and children under 14 are not permitted. On some Caribbean cruises you can board a day early and use the

Chart Symbols. Ships at a Glance. ●: *Fully equipped;* ◐: *Partially equipped;* ○: *Not equipped.* Cabins and Rates. **D:** *Double bed;* **K:** *King-size bed;* **Q:** *Queen-size bed;* **T:** *Twin bed;* **U/L:** *Upper and lower berths;* ●: *All cabins have this facility;* ○: *No cabins have this facility;* ◐: *Some cabins have this facility*

ship as a floating hotel for $50 per passenger, $100 per couple. In keeping with Blount's down-home hospitality, passengers embarking in Warren may park their cars in the shipyard free of charge while cruising.

Activities Life aboard ship is laid-back, with almost no organized activities. Onboard diversions include bingo, bridge, chess, golf putting, and backgammon. In the Caribbean, the focus is on beachcombing and water sports. Two Sailfish, snorkeling equipment, and a 21-seat glass-bottom boat are available free to passengers; you can swim or sail from the stern platform. Fishing from ship or beach is encouraged; bring your own tackle. Shore excursions tend to be informative and extremely worthwhile; if the local tour guides don't meet ACCL standards, the ship supplies a guide. The average price for shore excursions is only $12; the most expensive (in Belize) costs $25.

Dining Hearty, homemade fare, such as sandwiches on fresh-baked bread and classic pastas, are interspersed with such gourmet treats as chilled gazpacho and crab-stuffed pastry. Generally speaking though, cuisine is basic American, and many offerings use fresh seafood and produce picked up in ports along the way. Breakfast is buffet, lunch is family style, and an open-seating dinner is served at 6. There is only one choice of dinner entrée; the chef will prepare a special dish for passengers who want another option, but special diets, including low fat, kosher, sugar-free, and low salt, must be requested at least two weeks before departure. Passengers can help themselves any time to tea, coffee, lemonade, and snacks, such as fruit and homemade cookies. There are no formal nights and no room service.

Entertainment Local musicians frequently come aboard during port calls, and there's an electric piano for those who want to make their own music. Every evening, movies are shown on a VCR in the main lounge. Otherwise most passengers pass the time playing cards or reading.

Service and Tipping Service is quite casual. Tips are given via anonymous envelopes that you place in a basket in the lounge (tip $9 per diem per passenger); the total is pooled among the crew.

Destinations Itineraries are as idiosyncratic as the line itself and take in offbeat islands in New England, the Caribbean, Central America, and the Bahamas; jungle rivers in Venezuela and Belize; the Panama Canal; the coastline of the Atlantic and the Gulf of Mexico; the Mississippi River and the Great Lakes; and, in autumn, the Erie Canal and St. Lawrence Seaway. (For detailed itineraries, *see* Chapter 3.)

For More Information American Canadian Caribbean Line (Box 368, Warren, RI 02885, tel. 401/247–0955 or 800/556–7450).

Caribbean Prince

Specifications | | |
| --- | --- |
| *Type of ship:* Coastal cruiser | *Passengers:* 78 |
| *Cruise experience:* Casual | *Crew:* 17 (American) |
| *Size:* 89.5 tons | *Officers:* American |
| *Number of cabins:* 39 | *Passenger/crew ratio:* 4.6 to 1 |
| *Outside cabins:* 84% | *Year built:* 1983 |

Ship's Log The *Caribbean Prince*, one of the smallest cruise ships afloat, looks like a cross between an oversize yacht and a little ferry. It is Blount's most austere creation. The vessel's interior is made mostly of fiberglass and aluminum; a few Caribbean prints are the only hints of decor aboard. There are only two public rooms. The dining room, furnished with mahogany cabinets, tables for six, and pink- and blue-flowered curtains, doubles by day as a recreation room and lobby. On the same deck forward is a small lounge, where the bartender dispenses nonalcoholic drinks or will mix whatever concoctions you wish from liquor you bring aboard. Though the ship is tiny, there is ample room on deck for lounge chairs and a barbecue.

Cabins and Rates		Beds	Phone	TV	Sitting Area	Fridge	Tub	Average Per Diem*
	Outside	T or D	○	○	○	○	○	$185
	Inside	T	○	○	○	○	○	$136

Airfare and port taxes are extra.

It doesn't get more no-frills than this—metal lockers, pale beige walls, and beds covered not with spreads but with blue velour blankets. The more expensive cabins have chairs, full-length closets, and mahogany trim. Take only the essentials on board; there is very little storage space. Reading lights and vanity mirrors are in every cabin, but you'll have to go outside your cabin to see yourself in a full-length mirror, which are found in the corridors. All cabins have picture windows except cabins 20–22, which are inside and have one extra-wide bed (42 inches). Sun Deck cabins have partially obstructed views. Cabin keys are issued only upon request.

Outlet voltage: 110 AC.

Single supplement: 175% of double-occupancy rate (cabins 20–22 only). The supplement is waived for passengers who agree to share with another single traveler even if one is not found by the time of sailing.

Discounts: 15% per passenger when three passengers share a cabin. You get a 10% discount when booking consecutive cruises.

Sports and Fitness **Recreation:** Early-morning exercises, fishing, snorkeling, sailing, unobstructed circuit on Sun Deck (11 laps = 1 mile) for jogging, swimming platform.

Facilities **Public rooms:** Lounge.

Accessibility There are no facilities specifically equipped for wheelchair users. All public rooms are on one deck, though, along with a number of passenger cabins.

Mayan Prince

Specifications *Type of ship:* Coastal cruiser   *Passengers:* 92
Cruise experience: Casual   *Crew:* 17 (American)
Size: 92 tons   *Officers:* American
Number of cabins: 46   *Passenger/crew ratio:* 5 to 1
Outside cabins: 87%   *Year built:* 1992

Ship's Log The *Mayan Prince* was inspired by passenger feedback, collected with questionnaires on the *Caribbean Prince*. Well designed and modern in both layout and convenience, the *Mayan Prince* has individual cabin temperature controls and 20% more deck space than its predecessor. Slightly bigger than the *Caribbean Prince*, it also carries 14 more passengers. There is still a noticeable lack of artwork, except for the few Mayan prints that dot the public areas, Mayan-inspired designs on the curtains, and a small display of Mayan artifact replicas. There is little use of decorative wood; instead, most of the ship's interior is made of painted aluminum and other metal.

As on the *Caribbean Prince*, there are two public rooms. The dining room seats passengers in groups of six or eight. The galley faces the dining area, so passengers can chat easily with the chef. After dinner, travelers can walk directly into the forward lounge and relax on a blue vinyl wraparound couch or in armchairs upholstered in a bright rainbow tweed, watch a movie on one of the two televisions, or select a paperback from the bookshelves. During the day, passengers gather here to disembark by a ramp when the ship makes bow landings.

Cabins and Rates		Beds	Phone	TV	Sitting Area	Fridge	Tub	Average Per Diem*
	Outside	T or D	○	○	◑	○	○	$182
	Inside	T or D	○	○	○	○	○	$138

Airfare and port taxes are extra.

Like the *Caribbean Prince*, the *Mayan Prince*'s cabins are tiny and spartan, appointed in beige and blue and equipped with a reading light and vanity mirror; you must leave your cabin to see yourself in a full-length mirror. Floral curtains have the same Mayan pattern as those in the public rooms. Bathrooms have a state-of-the-art silent commode—not the roaring vacuum-type systems found on other ships. Cabins with numbers in the 50s and 60s have full-length wooden closets; others have small metal lockers. In contrast to the *Caribbean Prince*, all cabins have drawers, but you should still pack lightly just the same. Top-level cabins open directly onto an outdoor deck. All cabins have picture windows except cabins 20–22, which are inside and have one extra-wide bed (42 inches). Cabin keys are issued only upon request.

Outlet voltage: 110 AC.

Single supplement: 175% of double-occupancy rate (cabins 20–22 only). The supplement is waived for passengers who agree to share with another single traveler even if one is not found by the time of sailing.

Discounts: 15% per passenger when three passengers share a cabin. You get a 10% discount when booking consecutive cruises.

Sports and Fitness **Recreation:** Informal workouts, fishing, snorkeling, unobstructed circuit on Sun Deck for jogging, swimming platform.

Facilities **Public rooms:** Lounge.

Accessibility There are no facilities specifically equipped for wheelchair users. All public areas are on one deck, though, along with a number of passenger cabins.

Niagara Prince

Specifications *Type of ship:* Coastal cruiser   *Passengers:* 84
Cruise experience: Casual   *Crew:* 17 (American)
Size: 99 tons   *Officers:* American
Number of cabins: 42   *Passenger/crew ratio:* 5 to 1
Outside cabins: 95%   *Year built:* 1994

Ship's Log The newest ACCL ship is also the line's largest and spiffiest. Slightly sleeker than its sisters, the *Niagara* was built for both canal and ocean cruising. Rather than the retractable wheelhouses found on the other two ships, it employs a unique ballasting system that submerges the vessel 10 inches so it can pass under the bridges of the Erie Canal. The *Niagara* has the widest swimming platform of any ACCL vessel, and is one of the only cruise ships that can launch or pick up a tender without stopping.

Although dining room and lounge are laid out almost identically to those aboard the line's other ships, they are located on a higher deck for easier access to the outside. Wide wraparound windows give better viewing, too. Both rooms are appointed in the standard ACCL furnishings—round tables in the dining room, wraparound couch and overstuffed armchairs in the lounge—but the upholstery and carpeting, with mauve and teal accents, are brighter and more sumptuous than on the *Caribbean* or *Mayan Prince*. Similarly, Caribbean watercolors and pastel prints brighten up the public rooms and corridors.

	Beds	Phone	TV	Sitting Area	Fridge	Tub	Average Per Diem*
Outside	T or D	○	○	◑	○	○	$188
Inside	T or D	○	○	○	○	○	$109

Cabins and Rates (row label)

*Airfare and port taxes are extra.

Cabins remain small but storage space has been improved with roomier metal lockers and drawers. The *Niagara* is Blount's first attempt at interior decorating—tweed teal carpeting and vibrant green and mauve trim are considerable improvements from the stark staterooms of his previous ships. Prints and treasure maps depicting ports visited by ACCL add a nice finishing touch. In another plus, most staterooms have a chair and table. Along with quiet commodes, cabins have individual climate controls. Cabins with numbers in the 50s, 60s, and 70s have sliding picture windows. A few cabins have portholes. Beds in most cabins can be converted to doubles upon request. There are two inside cabins. Cabin keys are issued only upon request.

Outlet voltage: 110 AC.

Single supplement: 175% of double-occupancy rate (cabins 20–22 only). The supplement is waived for passengers who agree to share with another single traveler even if one is not found by the time of sailing.

Discounts: 15% per passenger when three passengers share a cabin. You get a 10% discount when booking consecutive cruises.

Sports and Fitness **Recreation:** Informal workouts, fishing, snorkeling, unobstructed circuit on Sun Deck for jogging, swimming platform.

Facilities **Public rooms:** Lounge.

Accessibility There is a stair lift for each deck and all public areas are accessible to wheelchair users. Two cabins are accessible to wheelchair users as well.

American Hawaii Cruises

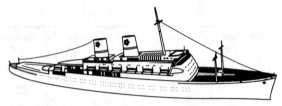

The Fleet SS *Constitution*
SS *Independence*

Built in 1951, these were the first modern liners to sail between New York and the Mediterranean; it was the *Constitution* that brought Grace Kelly and her wedding party to Monaco for her marriage to Prince Rainier in 1956. Other famous passengers have included Ernest Hemingway and California governor Ronald Reagan. By the early 1990s, though, the glory of these ships was faded, and American Hawaii committed $60 million to reverse their deterioration. Topping the list of improvements was redecoration of the public rooms and cabins. Making it easier for passengers to get around the ships, which were built for three-class travel, was a top priority, too. At press time, work on the *Independence* had been completed (*see* Ship's Log, *below*), while the *Constitution* was scheduled to go into dry dock for similar refurbishments in mid- to late 1995.

Ships at a Glance

	Dining Rooms	Bars	Casino	Fitness Center	Pools	Average Per Diem
Constitution	2/1	3	○	◐	2	$256
Independence						

Cruise Experience This is really two cruise experiences in one. Fans of classic liners built for transatlantic travel will appreciate the finer points of these ships' design. Particularly noteworthy are the enclosed promenades, whose huge brass and glass doors open to the sea, letting in cool ocean breezes when the ship is docked or at anchor. Other "they don't make them like that anymore" qualities include heavy wooden doors with brass-rimmed portholes, which lead between inside and outside decks. Original cabin furnishings include light fixtures, medicine cabinets, bureaus, and pullman-style folding beds.

For many other passengers, the attraction of these ships is the chance to see Hawaii's major islands at an affordable price. In all, the ships visit five ports on four islands in seven days, without the need to change hotels and to make intra-island plane connections. Because the ships sail solely within Hawaii, the emphasis of the cruise, both aboard ship and ashore, is on the islands. The daily program of activities includes a full slate of Hawaii crafts classes, storytelling, and other island traditions. You can learn to make jewelry from sea shells or to play the ukulele. Whale watching, too, is a big event, and local environmental representatives come aboard ship to lecture and point out the huge creatures. The line's shore excursion booklet lists more than 50 choices, ranging from bus tours to rainforest hikes. Whether you're aboard for the ship or for the islands,

Chart Symbols. Ships at a Glance. ●: *Fully equipped;* ◐: *Partially equipped;* ○: *Not equipped.* Cabins and Rates. **D:** *Double bed;* **K:** *King-size bed;* **Q:** *Queen-size bed;* **T:** *Twin bed;* **U/L:** *Upper and lower berths;* ●: *All cabins have this facility;* ○: *No cabins have this facility;* ◐: *Some cabins have this facility*

make no mistake—this is not a luxury cruise. It is, however, a very good value. In fact, you'll find a number of nice touches aboard, such as complimentary bon-voyage mai-tais, free soft drinks, and no-charge laundry machines. Dramamine, aspirin, and acetaminophen are always available for free at the purser's office. For all these, there's often a charge on some higher priced lines. Another appealing quality is the ships' casual atmosphere, which emphasizes comfort and relaxation over pomp and circumstance.

This combination of convenience and value attracts passengers in all age ranges. Aboard one of these liners you'll find everyone except younger couples. A typical mix includes families with younger children, middle-age couples, and older passengers celebrating their 50th wedding anniversary.

Activities Shoreside activities are emphasized, and there are more than 50 excursions to choose from, including flightseeing by helicopter over an active volcano, bicycling down the slopes of a dormant volcano, or visiting Hawaii Volcanoes National Park—you should be detecting a theme here. Also big are whale watching, snorkeling, and kayaking.

Passengers who stay aboard by day will find plenty to do, from the usual cruise activities to ukulele, hula, lei making, palm weaving, and Hawaiian-language lessons. There are also such typical cruise diversions as line-dancing classes and, of course, bingo. Movies are screened daily in the ship's cinema-style theater. Be sure to see *An Affair to Remember*—the shipboard shots were filmed aboard the *Constitution*.

Dining American cuisine—steaks, seafood, and lamb—dominates the daily menus, and although food is well prepared, dishes tend to be bland. An effort is made whenever possible to use local ingredients. The Kona coffee and Hawaiian pineapple are particularly noteworthy. Traditional Hawaiian "plate lunches" top the menu in the dining room at the midday meal, and fresh local fish is always a selection at dinner. A Pu'uwai (Healthy Heart) program is available for low-fat, low-cholesterol entrées. The extensive wine list offers Californian, French, and German vintages.

On the *Independence*, passengers are assigned to one of two dining rooms at random. The *Constitution* has a single dining room. On both ships, the dining rooms are below decks, and although they lack panoramic windows, they are bright and colorful. There are two open seatings for dinner (6 and 8), breakfast and lunch are open seating. There is one semiformal/formal evening each cruise; otherwise all dress is casual. On the first evening, dinner is a grand buffet. Passengers don Hawaiian fashions for the Polynesian dinner.

Breakfast and lunch are also served in a midship buffet. These are just as good as meals in the dining room, and taking your lunch or breakfast here has the added benefit of allowing you to sit outside on deck or in an enclosed promenade. Service also can be slow in the dining room for breakfast and lunch.

Other food service includes Continental breakfast of coffee, pastries, and fruit in one of the bars; afternoon hors d'oeuvres in the lounges; and complimentary brown-bag lunches for those going ashore for the day. A midnight buffet rounds out the day's food service. Coffee, soft drinks, and juices are available 24 hours, as is room service.

Entertainment Passengers looking for a throbbing disco or casino will not find it here. (Because they never leave American waters, there is no gambling aboard either vessel.) Instead, you'll find pajama parties, 1950s sock hops, and karaoke nights, as well as traditional cruise-ship musical reviews in the main showroom and a piano player who takes requests in another lounge. There's also an orchestra for big-band dancing. All the entertainers, from the singers to the orchestra members, are accomplished musicians.

Service and Tipping The American crew is this line's great strength. Each member of the hotel staff—cabin stewards, waiters, waitresses, and bartenders—wears a badge identifying his or her name and home state, making for instant and easy conversation. Recommended tips per passenger, per diem are: dining-room waiter, $3.50; assistant waiter, $1.75; cabin steward, $3.50. A 15% gratuity is automatically added to bar and wine service.

Destinations Like the name says, American Hawaii sails only in the Aloha state. (For detailed itineraries, *see* Chapter 3.)

For More Information American Hawaii Cruises (2 North Riverside Plaza, Chicago, IL 60606, tel. 312/466–6000 or 800/765–7000).

SS Constitution and SS Independence

Specifications *Type of ship:* Classic liner *Passengers:* 796/828
Cruise experience: Casual *Crew:* 315 (American)
Size: 30,090 tons *Officers:* American
Number of cabins: 398/414 *Passenger/crew ratio:* 2.5 to 1
Outside cabins: 44%/43% *Year built:* 1951

Ship's Log Age has its virtues, such as spacious cabins and enclosed, teak-lined promenades. A $30 million refit of the *Independence* in late 1994 created several new public rooms. The main lounge, often referred to as the ship's "living room," is a study in polished teak and rattan, with French doors that open onto the enclosed promenades. The adjoining bar is just as stylish, highlighted by an old-fashioned jukebox and Tiffany-style lamps. Not everything has been rejuvenated, though. There is still a fair amount of rot and rust on the outside decks—about what you'd expect on a ship that's been at sea for four decades. But there is another reason for the decay: You rarely see anybody painting and scraping as they should be. On the other hand, the improvements made during dry dock were expertly executed. Most impressive is a grand, outdoor staircase, which links the two pool decks and promenade deck for easy access. The *Constitution* was scheduled to undergo similar renovations at press time.

Cabins and Rates	Beds	Phone	TV	Sitting Area	Fridge	Tub	Average Per Diem*
Suite	K, Q, or T	●	●	●	●	●	$314
Outside	K, Q, D, T, or U/L	●	○	◑	●	◑	$256
Inside	D, T, or U/L	●	○	◑	●	◑	$242

Rates are for Hawaii. Airfare and port taxes are extra.

Cabins come in 50 different configurations priced in 13 categories. Spaciousness can differ significantly even within the same category, so if roominess is most important to you, ask for a cabin configured to hold third and fourth passengers. If a double or queen-size bed is most important, emphasize that when booking.

Forty cabins, including six solarium suites on the Bridge Deck, were added to the *Independence* during the recent refit, and similar expansion is planned for the *Constitution*. The new suites are roomy and feature high ceilings and skylights, but they lack the traditional charm of these ships' original accommodations, which incorporate such classic hallmarks as in-the-round tiled showers and built-in half-moon sinks in the bathrooms. Decor in all cabins uses a kaleidoscope of colorful Hawaiian motifs. Patterns evoke a range of island imagery, from local flora to aloha shirts. Each cabin also has been given its own Hawaiian name.

Outlet voltage: 110 AC.

Single supplement: 200% of double-occupancy rate for suites, 160% for most other categories. Some inside cabins are available as singles for a $100 surcharge over the double-occupancy per diem.

Discounts: A third or fourth passenger in a cabin pays $695 (cruise only) for a seven-day cruise. Children under 18 traveling with two full-fare adults in select cabin categories sail for $195 year-round.

Sports and Fitness
Health club: Exercise equipment including Lifecycles and StairMasters, saunas, massage (extra charge).

Recreation: Aerobics and stretch-and-tone classes, two freshwater pools, unobstructed circuit on wraparound promenade (7 laps = 1 mile) for jogging.

Facilities
Public rooms: Three bars, main lounge, showroom, study, conference room, cinema.

Shops: Shopping arcade, beauty parlor/barber, photo gallery.

Health care: Doctor and nurse on call.

Child care: Supervised activities for children ages 5–16 during summer and holidays, youth recreation center, baby-sitting arranged privately with staff members.

Services: Self-service laundry, dry cleaning arranged off-ship, photo lab on *Independence.*

Accessibility
Although these ships do not have designated cabins for wheelchair users, the line makes an effort to assign passengers with mobility problems to larger cabins off a main hallway on the Main Deck or on the decks above. Elevators are accessible to passengers using folding wheelchairs. Passengers with mobility problems must be accompanied by an able-bodied individual.

Carnival Cruise Lines

Jubilee

The Fleet MS *Celebration*
MS *Ecstasy*
MS *Fantasy*
MS *Fascination*
TSS *Festivale*
MS *Holiday*
MS *Imagination*
MS *Inspiration*
MS *Jubilee*
MS *Sensation*
MS *Tropicale*

Carnival ships are like floating theme parks, and all the line's vessels share this fun-house aura to some degree. A real automobile, bus, or trolley car may be parked in one of the bars just as part of the decor. The effect is most exaggerated on the newer, bigger ships, but even the older, smaller ones have their share of whimsy. No Carnival vessel carries less than 1,000 passengers, and the line continues to build ever-bigger megaships. Its latest project, scheduled to be launched in 1996, will be a 100,000-ton behemoth carrying more than 3,000 passengers.

Ships at a Glance

	Dining Rooms	Bars	Casino	Fitness Center	Pools	Average Per Diem
Celebration/Jubilee	2	7	●	●	2	$205
Ecstasy/Fantasy Fascination/Imagination Inspiration/Sensation	2	9	●	●	2	$208
Festivale	1	5	●	●	2	$208
Holiday	2	7	●	●	2	$211
Tropicale	1	6	●	●	2	$206

Cruise Experience Due to its success, Carnival is the standard by which all lower-priced cruise lines are measured. Advertising hype aside, not even its critics can deny that the line delivers what it promises: Activities and entertainment are nonstop, food is plentiful, and cabins are spacious and comfortable. Though there's nothing exotic about it, and it has none of the gentility or grace of some other lines, brash and sometimes crass Carnival does throw a great party.

Passengers are young, or at least young at heart. More singles cruise on Carnival than on any other line, although the average passenger's age is 42 and you'll still find many cruisers older than 55.

Chart Symbols. Ships at a Glance. ●: *Fully equipped;* ◑: *Partially equipped;* ○: *Not equipped.* Cabins and Rates. **D:** *Double bed;* **K:** *King-size bed;* **Q:** *Queen-size bed;* **T:** *Twin bed;* **U/L:** *Upper and lower berths;* ●: *All cabins have this facility;* ○: *No cabins have this facility;* ◑: *Some cabins have this facility*

Many families are attracted to Carnival as well. To cater to this diverse clientele, the line has sought to upgrade its image in recent years without straying from its "Fun Ship" formula. The decor on its latest ships is slightly more subdued if no less fanciful, passengers under 18 must be accompanied by an adult 21 or older (although older ships still attract a spring-break crowd), and drinks and other shipboard purchases may now be charged to a shipboard account. If you're looking for a good tan, island hopping, and a variety of nighttime entertainment, Carnival delivers the goods at a reasonable price.

Activities Carnival vessels offer every activity that a cruise ship can, including beer-drinking contests, greased-pole pillow fights, bingo, masquerade parties, pool games, water-balloon tosses, and trivia contests. No one can do it all, but many passengers try. Activity is centered around movement—from room to room and deck to deck. There are no lounges for curling up with a good book, except for the small libraries.

Dining The line has worked hard in recent years to shed its image as the McDonald's of the cruise industry, and though in the past the selections gravitated toward middle-of-the-road Italian-American fare, such as pastas, pizzas, surf-and-turf combinations, chops, and roasts, the current menus have become healthier and more diverse. Seafood and poultry are served in light sauces, and specialties may include fajitas or blackened swordfish. Vegetarian dishes are available on all lunch and dinner menus, too. All ships have quiche-and-salad bars. Children's lunch and dinner menus offer favorites like ravioli, hamburgers, and fish-and-chips. Meals are nothing less than feasts, with oversize but attractively arranged portions, noisy conversation, overly friendly waiters, and strolling musicians. French night, Spanish night, and other theme dinners feature special dishes and costumed waiters. The food quality is average, but the quantity and hoopla associated with its presentation make it seem better than it is.

The dining room has two seatings per meal (dinner at 6 and 8). Tables are assigned, though you may ask to be placed at a table of your peers, or with families traveling with children. Two formal evenings are held on cruises of four days or longer, one on three-day cruises. Requests for special diets should be made at the time of booking. Kosher food is not available. There is no smoking in the dining room.

Breakfast and lunch buffets are served on the Lido Deck, as are midmorning snacks and afternoon tea. Coffee is on 24 hours a day; specialty coffees are available (at extra cost) on the newer ships. Every night there's a midnight buffet; some ships even offer a still-later buffet for those who party into the wee hours. All ships feature 24-hour room service from a limited menu.

Entertainment The action begins just after sunrise and continues well into the night. Disco music begins throbbing by mid-afternoon on deck and around the pool. At any given time you can choose from an abundance of contests, parties, classes, games, bar and lounge entertainers, and bands. In-cabin movies are limited to one film run several times a day. Carnival wants its passengers out and about its ships.

Carnival's performers are among the most diverse group at sea. There are musicians, magicians, dancers, comedians, jugglers, and other specialty acts. On the larger ships it's not unusual to have a country-and-western duo, a full-size dance band, a rock-and-roll group, a '40s swing band, a song stylist, a cocktail pianist, *and* a classical-music quartet, all performing simultaneously—in addition to the action in the disco and the teenage dance club. Even the smaller Carnival ships have more entertainment options than most cruise lines' largest. Carnival's casinos are the largest afloat, and heavy emphasis is placed on gambling. Main lounge shows can be high-tech extravaganzas. On the newest ships, Carnival has taken these productions light years ahead of what used to be standard revues with laser lighting, superior sound systems, and state-of-the-art stages.

Year-round children's programs include "Coketail" parties, kite-flying contests, arts and crafts, bridge tours, and bingo. Baby-sitting is available in the playroom for a nominal charge. The newer ships have teen clubs with video games and music.

Service and Tipping
In the past, the pressure to tip on Carnival ships has been considerable. Here, too, the line is working to bring a little more grace to its cruises. Still, the more generous passengers usually get the best service. Tip the room steward and the waiter $3 each per passenger per diem, the busboy $1.50. Bellboys, deck stewards, and room-service waiters expect to be tipped at the time of service; 15% is customary. Tip the maître d' and the head waiter at your own discretion and whenever you request a special service, such as a change in your table assignment. A 15% service charge is automatically added to all bar bills.

Destinations
True to its festive reputation, Carnival's ships call on sun-and-fun ports throughout the Caribbean, Bahamas, and Mexican Riviera, with one ship spending the summer in Alaska. Land/sea packages combine a stay at Walt Disney World with a cruise. Itineraries run from three to 11 days. (For detailed itineraries, *see* Chapter 3.)

For More Information
Carnival Cruise Lines (Carnival Pl., 3655 N.W. 87th Ave., Miami, FL 33178, tel. 305/599–2600).

MS Celebration and MS Jubilee

Specifications
Type of ship: Cruise liner
Cruise experience: Casual
Size: 47,262 tons
Number of cabins: 743
Outside cabins: 61%

Passengers: 1,486
Crew: 670 (international)
Officers: Italian
Passenger/crew ratio: 2.2 to 1
Year built: 1987/1986

Ship's Log
Showy, brassy art; brightly colored walls; neon lights; spectacularly lighted ceilings and floors—when it comes to design and decor, there is nothing subtle about these vessels. Just about every decorative material imaginable—wrought iron, stained glass, wood paneling, padded leather, Plexiglas—has been used to startling effect. Scattered throughout the two ships are a trolley car, a Wizard of Oz–theme disco, a '20s Speakeasy Café, and other imaginative touches. The result is overwhelming and is guaranteed to keep your adrenaline flowing from the moment you get up until you collapse into bed. Both ships have an arcade of lounges and bars, each with its own motif, several dance floors, and a number of small nooks. The large bars are awfully rowdy. The main entertainment lounges are spacious steel-and-marble extravaganzas, as flashy and tacky as anything aglow in Las Vegas. Discos on both ships have a futuristic, sci-fi look.

Cabins and Rates

	Beds	Phone	TV	Sitting Area	Fridge	Tub	Average Per Diem*
Suite	T or K	●	●	●	●	●	$290
Outside	T, K, or U/L	●	●	○	●	○	$208
Inside	T, K, or U/L	●	●	○	●	○	$197

*Rates are for seven-day cruises. Airfare and port taxes are extra.

Cabins are of similar size, shape, and appearance, decorated in bright colors and wood tones. The Veranda Suite, however, has a whirlpool and a private balcony. Closed-circuit TV plays films all day and most of the night.

Outlet voltage: 110 AC.

Single supplement: 150%–200% of double-occupancy rate. Carnival can match up to four same-sex adults in a cabin for $650 each on seven-day cruises.

Discounts: A third or fourth passenger in a cabin pays $60 per diem (cruise only). You get a discount of up to $1,000 for booking early, and up to $250 for arranging your own airfare.

Sports and Fitness	**Health club:** Gym with exercise equipment; men's and women's spas with whirlpools, saunas, facial- and body-treatment center.

Recreation: Aerobics classes, shuffleboard, table tennis, trapshooting, two pools, children's wading pool, unobstructed circuit for jogging.

Facilities	**Public rooms:** Seven bars, six entertainment lounges, casino, disco, library, card room, video-game room.

Shops: Gift shops, beauty salon/barber.

Health care: Doctor and nurse on call.

Child care: Playroom, youth programs in four age groups run by counselors, baby-sitting arranged privately with youth counselor.

Services: Full- and self-service laundry, photographer.

Accessibility	Fourteen cabins on each ship are accessible to wheelchair users.

MS Ecstasy, MS Fantasy, MS Fascination, MS Imagination, MS Inspiration, and MS Sensation

Specifications

Type of ship: Megaship
Cruise experience: Casual
Size: 70,367 tons
Number of cabins: 1,020/1,022 (Fantasy)
Outside cabins: 60.7%

Passengers: 2,040/2,044 (Fantasy)
Crew: 920 (international)
Officers: Italian
Passenger/crew ratio: 2.2 to 1
Years built: 1990–1996

Ship's Log

These six $225 million ships, the newest in the Carnival fleet, appeal to the kind of crowd that loves Atlantic City and Las Vegas. They are identical in all but decor, though all share the marble, brass, mirrors, and electric lights that heighten Carnival's now-notorious hyperactivity. In addition to Olympic-size pools, the ships also have unique banked and padded jogging tracks with a special surface; their casinos and fitness centers are among the largest afloat. Each is built around a central, seven-story atrium.

Big, bright, bold, and brassy, the *Fantasy* lives up to its name, resembling a series of fantastic Hollywood sets rather than a cruise ship. Fifteen miles of bright neon tubing snake through the ship. The public rooms are lavishly decorated in elaborate motifs; the Cats Lounge, for example, was inspired by the famous musical, and Cleopatra's Bar re-creates the interior of an Egyptian tomb.

The *Ecstasy* and *Sensation* are less futuristic and more elegant. The *Ecstasy*'s cityscape motif links the public areas: City Lights Boulevard evokes an urban street scene, the Rolls Royce Café is built around an antique Rolls, the Metropolis Bar is home to a skyscraper-like neon sculpture, and the entrance to the Chinatown lounge is guarded by twin lion-head Foo dog sculptures reminiscent of ancient China. The *Sensation* takes a more subtle approach. Public rooms indulge the senses with lush greenery and carved wood in the Oak Room or a copy of the sculpture *David* in the Michelangelo Lounge.

A portal of arched hands invites passengers to enter the Touch of Class piano bar, where, once inside, passengers sit in the palms of still more hands.

The *Fascination* takes the movie-set theme quite literally: Public rooms evoke a Hollywood motif, and likenesses of tinsel-town legends populate its salons and lounges. Life-size figures portray Marilyn Monroe, James Dean, Bette Davis, Gary Cooper, John Wayne, and Humphrey Bogart—just to name a few.

The *Imagination* and *Inspiration* were scheduled to be launched in late 1995 and mid-1996 respectively. At press time, no details were available on their interior decor.

Cabins and Rates		Beds	Phone	TV	Sitting Area	Fridge	Tub	Average Per Diem*
	Suite	T, K, or Q	●	●	●	●	◑	$243–$290
	Outside	T or K	●	●	●	●	○	$180–$208
	Inside	T, K, or U/L	●	●	○	○	○	$171–$197

Lower rates are for three-day cruises; higher rates are for seven-day cruises. Airfare and port taxes are extra.

Cabins are decorated in bright colors and wood tones. Each is quite spacious, with closed-circuit TV and private safes. Veranda Suites and Demi Suites have private balconies, wet bars, and VCRs. Veranda Suites have tubs with whirlpool jets. Some outside cabins on the Veranda Deck have partially obstructed views.

Outlet voltage: 110 AC.

Single supplement: 150%–200% of double-occupancy rate. Carnival can match up to four same-sex adults in a cabin for $275 (three-day cruises) or $395 (four-day cruises) each.

Discounts: A third or fourth passenger in a cabin pays $60 per diem (cruise only) for a seven-day cruise and about $66 per diem (cruise only) for three- and four-day cruises. You get a discount of up to $400 for early booking and up to $250 for arranging your own airfare on three- and four-day cruises.

Sports and Fitness

Health club: Gym, aerobics room, massage room, women's and men's locker rooms with steam rooms and saunas, fitness machines, two whirlpools, facial and body treatments.

Recreation: Aerobics classes, shuffleboard, table tennis, trapshooting, two outdoor pools (one with slide), children's wading pool, four outdoor whirlpools, banked jogging track (11 laps = 1 mile) for jogging.

Facilities

Public rooms: Nine bars and lounges, casino, disco, card room, library.

Shops: Boutiques, drugstore, beauty salon/barber.

Health care: Doctor and nurse on call.

Child care: Playroom, teen center (with video games), youth programs in four age groups run by counselors, baby-sitting arranged privately with youth counselor.

Services: Full- and self-service laundry, photographer.

Accessibility

Twenty cabins, all on the Empress Deck of each ship, are accessible to wheelchair users.

TSS Festivale

Specifications *Type of ship:* Classic liner *Passengers:* 1,146
Cruise experience: Casual *Crew:* 580 (international)
Size: 38,175 tons *Officers:* Italian
Number of cabins: 580 *Passenger/crew ratio:* 2 to 1
Outside cabins: 53% *Year built:* 1961

Ship's Log Carnival purchased this vessel, built in 1961 as the *Transvaal Castle*, in 1978 and refurbished it in 1986. Although the ship now has been infused with Carnival's signature whimsy, its age and original design are still apparent. Many of the cabins are roomy, but original fixtures are often chipped, cracked, or corroded.

This ship does not offer the glitz and glitter some Carnival passengers desire, but its classic lines, winged bridge, and single smokestack make it one of the best-looking ships in the fleet. The public areas, too, retain much of the original wood paneling and have polished brass railings and doors. The decor is conservative by Carnival standards, with muted colors, classic etched glass, and a fabulous art deco steel stairway. The Tradewinds and Copa Cabana lounges are reminiscent of 1930s film sets. The Gaslight Café looks like a mishmash of every B movie ever made, mixing teak paneling with a mirrored ceiling, petite pink tables, and overstuffed purple chairs.

Cabins and Rates

	Beds	Phone	TV	Sitting Area	Fridge	Tub	Average Per Diem*
Suite	T	○	○	●	○	◑	$290
Outside	Q, T, or U/L	○	○	○	○	●	$208
Inside	Q, T or U/L	○	○	○	○	○	$197

*Rates are for seven-day cruises. Airfare and port taxes are extra.

Recalling the ship's heyday as an ocean liner, some suites have wooden headboards, full-length mirrors, and separate sitting rooms. Demi Suite V55 does not have a bathtub. Some outside cabins on the Veranda Deck have partially obstructed views.

Outlet voltage: 110 AC.

Single supplement: 150%–200% of double-occupancy rate. Carnival can match up to four same-sex adults in a cabin for $650 each.

Discounts: A third or fourth passenger in a cabin pays $57 per diem (cruise only) for seven-day cruises and about $75 (cruise only) for 10- and 11-day cruises. You get a discount of up to $1,000 for booking early and up to $250 for arranging your own airfare.

Sports and Fitness **Health club:** Exercise equipment, sauna, massage room, facial- and body-treatment center.

Recreation: Aerobics classes, shuffleboard, table tennis, trapshooting, two pools, wading pool, unobstructed circuit (7½ laps = 1 mile) for jogging.

Facilities **Public rooms:** Five bars, four entertainment lounges, casino, disco, cinema, library, video-game room.

Shops: Boutique, gift shop, liquor/sundries shop, beauty salon/barber.

Health care: Doctor and nurse on call.

Child care: Playroom, play deck, youth programs in three age groups with counselors, baby-sitting arranged privately with youth counselor.

Services: Laundry service, photographer.

Accessibility There are no cabins specifically equipped for wheelchair users.

MS Holiday

Specifications

Type of ship: Cruise liner	*Passengers:* 1,452
Cruise experience: Casual	*Crew:* 660 (international)
Size: 46,052 tons	*Officers:* Italian
Number of cabins: 726	*Passenger/crew ratio:* 2.2 to 1
Outside cabins: 62%	*Year built:* 1985

Ship's Log One of the first generation of "superliners" built for Carnival, the *Holiday* was the forerunner of the line's megaships. On the outside, it ushered in the age of boxy hulls and superstructures that rise straight out of the water. Inside, it took Carnival's palatial, theme-park atmosphere to new extremes. A bar called the Bus Stop has red-top luncheonette stools, traffic signs, and an actual red-and-white bus from the 1930s. Another bar, Carnegie's, has the luxurious look of a private club, with overstuffed leather chairs and sofas, and glass-door library shelves. Rick's American Café is straight from *Casablanca*. The *Holiday* ushered in Carnival's first extra-wide, enclosed walkway that runs along the port side of the Promenade Deck. The teak passageway called Broadway connects the casino and all the bars and lounges on the deck. The main entertainment lounge, the Americana, is a six-level, curved room that accommodates more than 900 passengers. The Gaming Club Casino has more than 100 slot machines and 250 seats.

Cabins and Rates

	Beds	Phone	TV	Sitting Area	Fridge	Tub	Average Per Diem*
Suite	T/K	●	●	●	●	●	$243–$277
Outside	T, K, or U/L	●	●	○	○	○	$180–$197
Inside	T or K	●	●	○	○	○	$171–$184

Lower rates are for three-day cruises; higher rates are for four-day cruises. Airfare and port taxes are extra.

The slightly larger-than-average cabins are appointed in bright colors and wood tones. The Veranda Suites have a sitting room, private balcony, and whirlpool. All cabins have wall safes.

Outlet voltage: 110 AC.

Single supplement: 150%–200% of double-occupancy rate. Carnival can match up to four same-sex adults in a cabin for $650 each.

Discounts: A third or fourth passenger in a cabin pays $60 per diem (cruise only) for a seven-day cruise and about $66 per diem (cruise only) for three- and four-day cruises. You get a discount of up to $1,000 for booking early and up to $250 for arranging your own airfare.

Sports and Fitness **Health club:** Exercise equipment, spas with whirlpools, sauna, massage room, facial- and body-treatment center.

Recreation: Aerobics, shuffleboard, table tennis, trapshooting, two outdoor pools, wading pool, unobstructed circuit for jogging.

Facilities	**Public rooms:** Seven bars, four entertainment lounges, casino, disco, library, video-game room.
	Shops: Boutique, gift shop, beauty salon/barber.
	Health care: Doctor and nurse on call.
	Child care: Playroom, youth programs in four age groups run by counselors, baby-sitting arranged privately with youth counselor.
	Services: Full- and self-service laundry, photographer.
Accessibility	Fifteen cabins are accessible to wheelchair users.

MS Tropicale

Specifications

Type of ship: Cruise liner	*Passengers:* 1,022
Cruise experience: Casual	*Crew:* 550 (international)
Size: 36,674 tons	*Officers:* Italian
Number of cabins: 511	*Passenger/crew ratio:* 1.9 to 1
Outside cabins: 63%	*Year built:* 1981

Ship's Log The *Tropicale* has been a very influential ship for its resortlike qualities. Responding to passenger suggestions, Carnival created a vessel ideal for cruising, with plenty of open space; a good choice of bars, lounges, and play areas; and a spectacular swimming pool. From the outside, the *Tropicale* is recognizable by its clean lines; sloping superstructure; oversize portholes; and the raked, double-winged funnel near the stern. The interior is ultramodern and spans the entire spectrum of colors. The Exta-Z Disco's dance floor, for instance, is alive with red and yellow lights, the elaborate ceiling with blue, green, and red neon lights. Indirect lighting sets a more appetizing mood in the Riviera Restaurant, which, with its rattan furniture, resembles a tropical grand hotel.

Cabins and Rates

	Beds	Phone	TV	Sitting Area	Fridge	Tub	Average Per Diem*
Suite	T/K	●	●	●	●	●	$290
Outside	T, K, or U/L	●	●	○	○	○	$208
Inside	T, K, or U/L	●	●	○	○	○	$197

*Rates are for seven-day cruises. Airfare and port taxes are extra.

Cabins are of similar size and appearance, comfortable and larger than average; the majority have twin beds that can be made into a king. Decor is a mix of bright colors and wood tones. Veranda Suites have private balconies. Most outside cabins have large square windows rather than portholes.

Outlet voltage: 110 AC.

Single supplement: 150%–200% of double-occupancy rate. Carnival can match up to four same-sex adults in a cabin for $650 each.

Discounts: A third or fourth passenger in a cabin pays $57 per diem (cruise only). You get a discount of up to $1,000 for booking early and up to $250 for arranging your own airfare.

Sports and Fitness **Health club:** Exercise equipment, men's and women's saunas and massage rooms, facial- and body-treatment center.

Recreation: Aerobics classes, shuffleboard, table tennis, trapshooting, two pools, wading pool, small, unobstructed circuit for jogging.

Facilities **Public rooms:** Six bars and lounges, casino, disco, card room, library, video-game room.

Shops: Gift shops, beauty salon/barber.

Health care: Doctor and nurse on call.

Child care: Playroom, youth programs in three age groups run by counselors, baby-sitting arranged privately with youth counselor.

Services: Full- and self-service laundry, photographer.

Accessibility Eleven cabins are accessible to wheelchair users.

Celebrity Cruises

The Fleet
MV *Century*
MV *Galaxy*
MV *Horizon*
SS *Meridian*
MV *Zenith*

Celebrity operates one of cruising's newest fleets. With the exception of the classic *Meridian* (the former *Galileo*), all its ships have been built since the line's inception in 1990. The older *Meridian*, a vintage transatlantic liner that was renamed and redesigned during a $55 million renovation in 1990, has a cozy feel because all its public rooms are together on one deck. The newer vessels are more spacious and elegant. They feel more like Caribbean all-inclusive resorts than ships. The line's new Century-class vessels, a series of three 70,000-ton megaships, represent the very latest trends in cruise-ship design.

Ships at a Glance

	Dining Rooms	Bars	Casino	Fitness Center	Pools	Average Per Diem
Century/Galaxy	1	11	●	●	2	$331
Horizon/Zenith	1	9/7	●	●	2	$317
Meridian	1	7	●	●	1	$292

Cruise Experience
Celebrity Cruises provides a more upscale—and expensive—alternative to its sister line, Fantasy Cruises, including roomier accommodations, slightly more personalized service, and more amenities. On any of its ships, you will experience an outstanding cruise—the cuisine is certainly the best in this price category. Celebrity attracts everyone from older couples to honeymooners for its Bermuda and repositioning cruises. Passengers are decidedly older, averaging in their mid-fifties, on the 10- and 11-day Caribbean sailings. Aboard the *Meridian* and the *Zenith*, the summertime children's programs are the best on board any upscale cruise line.

Activities
Though not party ships, Celebrity packs plenty of fun. Activities include pool and card games, shuffleboard, snorkeling instruction, "horse racing," skeet shooting, and golf putting. Passengers are not pressured to participate, and many choose to read or relax on their own in a lounge chair.

Dining
Celebrity has risen nicely above typical cruise cuisine by hiring chef Michel Roux, proprietor of two of Britain's finest restaurants, as a consultant. Roux's experience in creating and cooking for large numbers of discriminating diners has been put to wonderful use. Food is truly outstanding; both familiar and exotic dishes have been

Chart Symbols. Ships at a Glance. ●: *Fully equipped;* ◖: *Partially equipped;* ○: *Not equipped.* Cabins and Rates. **D:** *Double bed;* **K:** *King-size bed;* **Q:** *Queen-size bed;* **T:** *Twin bed;* **U/L:** *Upper and lower berths;* ●: *All cabins have this facility;* ○: *No cabins have this facility;* ◖: *Some cabins have this facility*

customized to appeal to the mellow palate of American cruisers. To keep things fresh, the menu rotates constantly. At least one "lean and light" entrée is offered at every meal. A complete vegetarian menu is available for lunch and dinner. Dinner is at two assigned seatings (6:15 and 8:30). Two formal evenings are held each cruise. Special diets, such as kosher or salt-free, can be catered to when booked in advance or with the maître d' on the day of sailing.

Outside the dining room, options include an enormous café on the Marina Deck, which is open for breakfast, lunch, and afternoon tea. Limited room service is available 24 hours.

Entertainment   Celebrity's ships present lavish, if predictable, variety shows, enlivened by the occasional surprise guest (e.g., performers from a Russian circus). Smaller lounges offer low-key jazz and big-band music. Karaoke parties are popular, and the discos rock until 3 AM.

Service and   Service is friendly and first class—rapid and accurate in the dining
Tipping   room, but sometimes slower and uneven in the bars. Waiters, stewards, and bartenders are enthusiastic, take pride in their work, and try to please—though not all have full command of English. Tip your room steward and your waiter $3 each per passenger per diem, the busboy $1.50. Celebrity also recommends tipping the chief housekeeper $5 per passenger per cruise and the maître d' $7.50 per passenger per cruise. Bar stewards should be tipped 15% of the bill at the time of service.

Destinations   Celebrity offers Bermuda cruises out of New York during the summer. During winter it operates 10- and 11-day Caribbean cruises out of San Juan that visit up to eight ports. Year-round sailings from Fort Lauderdale cruise the Caribbean for seven days. (For detailed itineraries, *see* Chapter 3.)

For More   Celebrity Cruises (5200 Blue Lagoon Dr., Miami, FL 33126, tel.
Information 800/437–3111).

MV Century and MV Galaxy

Specifications   *Type of ship:* Megaship   *Passengers:* 1,750
                     Cruise experience: Semi-   *Crew:* 853 (international)
                     formal   *Officers:* Greek
                     Size: 70,000 tons   *Passenger/crew ratio:* 2.1 to 1
                     Number of cabins: 875   *Year built:* 1995
                     Outside cabins: 64%

Ship's Log   The *Century* is designed to appeal to both present-day and 21st-century cruisers. It has public rooms to satisfy virtually every taste: There's the cozy Michael's Club, a British-style pub appointed in wood paneling and overstuffed leather chairs, and the high-tech Images video bar—as colorful as it sounds. Unlike its predecessors in the Celebrity fleet, the *Century* has a glass-domed, three-story atrium at its center. Another departure from the design of its fleetmates is a single-level dining room whose ceilings rise two stories high and a two-deck theater with a stage large enough for full-scale musical productions.

The *Galaxy*, second in the series, will be even more extravagant. There will be two atrium lobbies—one three stories and the other four—plus a multilevel observation lounge in a "futuristic setting." At press time, the *Galaxy* was scheduled to enter service in fall 1996.

Cabins and Rates	Beds	Phone	TV	Sitting Area	Fridge	Tub	Average Per Diem*
Suite	D	●	●	●	○	●	$442–$556

| Outside | D or T/K | ● | ● | ● | ○ | ○ | $285–$378 |
| Inside | D or T/K | ● | ● | ○ | ○ | ○ | $239–$278 |

Rates include airfare. Port taxes are extra.

While the size of the cabins aboard the *Century* remains much the same as aboard the *Horizon* and *Zenith*, a number of amenities, such as televisions and minibars, have been added to all categories. Each deck has been given its own color theme, and every cabin is decorated in corresponding colors. Bathtubs in the Royal and Penthouse suites have whirlpool jets and verandas.

Outlet voltage: 110/220 AC.

Single supplement: 150%–200% of double-occupancy rate.

Discounts: A third or fourth passenger in a cabin pays $135 per diem. Children 2–12 traveling with two full-paying adults pay $120 per diem. Children under two travel free. You get a discount for booking early.

Sports and Fitness

Health club: Aerobics, stationary bikes, weight machines, free weights, treadmills, rowing machines, saunas, massage rooms, steam rooms, spa treatments.

Recreation: Electronic golf simulator, shuffleboard, table tennis, trapshooting, swimming, volleyball, basketball, darts, snorkeling, exercise classes, jogging track, two pools.

Facilities

Public rooms: Eleven bars, four entertainment lounges, casino, cinema, card room, library, video-game room, conference center.

Shops: Atrium boutiques.

Health care: Doctor on call.

Child care: Playroom; baby-sitting arranged with crew member.

Services: Photographer, full- and self-service laundry, beauty shop/barber.

Accessibility

Eight cabins are accessible to wheelchair users. Passengers with mobility problems must provide their own small, collapsible wheelchairs and travel with an able-bodied companion.

MV Horizon and MV Zenith

Specifications

Type of ship: Cruise liner
Cruise experience: Semi-formal
Size: 46,811/47,255 tons
Number of cabins: 677/687
Outside cabins: 79%/84%

Passengers: 1,354/1,374
Crew: 642/657 (international)
Officers: Greek
Passenger/crew ratio: 2.1 to 1
Year built: 1990/1992

Ship's Log

With a navy band of paint encircling their otherwise white hulls, these ships cut a sharp profile at sea. The interiors are indisputably gracious, airy, and comfortable. The design makes the most of natural light through strategically placed oversize windows. The nine passenger decks sport several bars, entertainment lounges, and ample deck space. Wide corridors, broad staircases, seven elevators, and well-placed signs make it easy to get around. Decor is contemporary and attractive, the artwork pleasant rather than memorable. The Zenith has a slightly different layout from its sister ship: There are two fewer bars—though others have been enlarged—more suites, a larger health club, more deck space, and a meeting room.

Cabins and Rates		Beds	Phone	TV	Sitting Area	Fridge	Tub	Average Per Diem*
	Suite	D	●	●	●	○	●	$327–$542
	Outside	D or T/K	●	●	●	○	○	$285–$349
	Inside	D or T/K	●	●	○	○	○	$239–$278

Rates include airfare. Port taxes are extra.

The cabins are modern and quite roomy. Furnishings include a nightstand, a desk, and a small glass-top coffee table. Closets are reasonably large, as are bathrooms. Bedtime readers will find the lone lamp on the nightstand insufficient, especially in rooms with double beds. Every cabin is equipped with a television showing CNN and other broadcasts. The suites are enormous. They have large sitting areas, tubs with whirlpool jets, 24-hour room service, and a private butler. The view from many outside cabins on the Bermuda Deck is partially obstructed by lifeboats.

Outlet voltage: 110/220 AC.

Single supplement: 150%–200% of double-occupancy rate.

Discounts: A third or fourth passenger in a cabin pays $135 per diem. Children 2–12 traveling with two full-paying adults pay $77 (Bermuda) or $120 (Caribbean) per diem. Children under two travel free. You get a discount for booking early.

Sports and Fitness

Health club: Bright, sunny upper-deck spa with sauna, massage, weight machines, stationary bicycles, rowing machine, stair climber, treadmill, separate mirrored aerobics area, massage, facial/body treatments.

Recreation: Exercise classes, putting green, shuffleboard, snorkeling, trapshooting, Ping-Pong, two pools, three whirlpools, unobstructed circuit (5 laps = 1 mile) for jogging.

Facilities

Public rooms: Nine bars and lounges (*Horizon*) or seven bars and lounges (*Zenith*), showroom, casino, disco, card room, library/reading room, video-game room.

Shops: Gift shop, boutique, perfume shop, cigarette/liquor store, photo shop.

Health care: Doctor and nurse on call.

Child care: Playroom, teen room on Sun Deck, youth programs in three age groups supervised by counselors in summer (*Zenith*), baby-sitting arranged with crew member.

Services: Photographer, laundry service, beauty shop/barber.

Accessibility

Four cabins with 39½-inch doorways are accessible to wheelchair users. Specially equipped public elevators are 35½ inches wide, but certain public areas may not be wide enough for wheelchairs. Passengers with mobility problems must provide their own small, collapsible wheelchairs and travel with an able-bodied companion.

SS Meridian

Specifications

Type of ship: Classic liner
Cruise experience: Semiformal
Size: 30,440 tons
Number of cabins: 553
Outside cabins: 53%

Passengers: 1,106
Crew: 580 (international)
Officers: Greek
Passenger/crew ratio: 1.9 to 1
Year built: 1967

Ship's Log The *Meridian* radiates a relaxed, personable charm—it's like staying in someone's home. The dining-room food is even better than on its fleetmates, although the same cannot be said about the lunch and breakfast buffets. Two crowds seem to prefer this ship: Families take advantage of the children's program, which is broken down into three age groups. Older passengers appreciate the ship's lineage, its traditional design, and intimate public areas—most of which are on the same deck, allowing easy access. But there are drawbacks that discourage singles and young couples: The health club is neither as large nor as bright as aboard the newer ships, and the Marina Cafe doubles as a dreary disco at night.

Cabins and Rates

	Beds	Phone	TV	Sitting Area	Fridge	Tub	Average Per Diem*
Suite	T	●	●	●	○	●	$377–$404
Outside	T or D	●	○	◐	○	○	$254–$331
Inside	T, D, or U/L	●	○	○	○	○	$180–$231

Rates include airfare. Port taxes are extra.

Cabins are similar in size and amenities to those aboard the *Horizon* and *Zenith*; however, they are decorated in a somewhat jarring scheme of orange, red, and purple sunset hues. Bathtubs in the Presidential, Starlight, and Deluxe suites have whirlpool jets. Outside cabins on the Horizon Deck have floor-to-ceiling windows. Many outside cabins on the Atlantic Deck have obstructed or partially obstructed views.

Outlet voltage: 110/220 AC.

Single supplement: 150%–200% of double-occupancy rate.

Discounts: A third or fourth passenger in a cabin pays $113 (Caribbean) per diem. Children 2–12 sharing a cabin with two full-paying adults pay $59–$99 per diem. Children under two travel free. Special single-parent rates are sometimes available. You get a discount for booking early.

Sports and Fitness **Health club:** Stationary bikes, weight machines, treadmills, rowing machines, sauna, massage, facial/body treatment.

Recreation: Exercise classes, putting green, golf driving, shuffleboard, snorkeling, trapshooting, Ping-Pong, pool, children's pool, three outdoor whirlpools, unobstructed circuit on Captain's Deck (8 laps = 1 mile).

Facilities **Public rooms:** Seven bars, four entertainment lounges (including main showroom), casino, disco, cinema, card room/library, video-game room, chapel/synagogue.

Shops: Boutique, perfumery, drugstore, photo shop, beauty salon/barber.

Health care: Doctor on call.

Child care: Playroom with large windows, patio, and wading pool; youth programs in three age groups with counselors in summer; baby-sitting arranged privately with crew members.

Services: Photographer, laundry service, beauty shop/barber.

Accessibility Two cabins are accessible to wheelchair users. Celebrity requires that passengers using wheelchairs travel with an able-bodied adult who will take full responsibility in case of emergency.

Clipper Cruise Line

Yorktown Clipper

The Fleet MV *Nantucket Clipper*
MV *Yorktown Clipper*

The yachtlike *Nantucket Clipper* and *Yorktown Clipper* are small, stylish coastal cruisers with a casual, country-club feel. With their shallow drafts and Zodiac landing craft, they are well suited to exploring remote and otherwise inaccessible waters.

Ships at a Glance	Dining Rooms	Bars	Casino	Fitness Center	Pools	Average Per Diem
Nantucket Clipper *Yorktown Clipper*	1	1	○	○	0	$330

Cruise Experience Clipper Cruise Line offers two distinct styles of cruising: Clipper Classic and Clipper Adventure. Classic-series cruises focus on destinations with cultural and historical appeal, while adventure cruises sail to regions renowned for their scenic beauty and wildlife-viewing opportunities. On adventure cruises, Zodiacs ferry passengers to remote beaches, pristine forests, small villages, and wildlife refuges; a team of naturalists and lecturers conduct seminars aboard ship and unusual walking tours on shore. Classic cruises dock at marinas or at town piers, eliminating the need for tenders or taxis.

Compared with other small ship lines, Clipper's Caribbean and East Coast experience is more sophisticated and service-oriented than life aboard an American Canadian Caribbean Line vessel. In Alaska, Clipper combines the creature comforts of Alaska Sightseeing with the educational emphasis of Special Expeditions. Passengers are older (typically in their mid-sixties), wealthier, and better-educated than the average cruise passenger.

Activities Clipper is noted for its cultural bent, and on each cruise a naturalist, historian, or other expert leads lectures and field trips. Apart from these occasional talks and excursions, organized activities are few. Board games and card games are popular, but reading and socializing are the main onboard activities. In the Caribbean, snorkeling off the side of the ship is popular.

Dining Clipper's American cuisine is quite good. Selections are limited, however, and portions rather small. As with any cruise though, you can always order more. Dinner (at 7:30) is served at one open seating. There are two "dressy" evenings per cruise, but formal attire is not necessary. Special dietary requests should be made in writing three weeks before departure; no kosher meals are available. Other food service includes a Continental breakfast served in the Observation Lounge and fresh chocolate-chip cookies available in the after-

---

Chart Symbols. Ships at a Glance. **●:** *Fully equipped;* **◑:** *Partially equipped;* ○: *Not equipped.* Cabins and Rates. **D:** *Double bed;* **K:** *King-size bed;* **Q:** *Queen-size bed;* **T:** *Twin bed;* **U/L:** *Upper and lower berths;* **●:** *All cabins have this facility;* ○: *No cabins have this facility;* **◑:** *Some cabins have this facility*

noon. Coffee and tea can be had at any time, but there is no room service.

Entertainment There are no discos, casinos, or musical revues aboard Clipper's ships. Though local entertainers sometimes perform on board and movies may be shown, evenings are low-key; socializing in the lounge over drinks is about as rowdy as this crowd usually gets. Many passengers venture ashore to enjoy the nightlife or take evening strolls.

Service and Tipping Though small, the American staff is young, energetic, and capable, working nicely together to provide good service without lobbying for tips. On the last evening passengers are asked to leave tips in an envelope on the purser's desk (tip $8 per passenger per diem); these are pooled and distributed.

Destinations The Clipper Classic series is available to the eastern U.S. seaboard, New England and Canada, the Great Lakes, and northern California. Clipper Adventure cruises sail to Alaska, the Pacific Northwest, Mexico, Central America, western South America, and Antarctica. (For detailed itineraries, *see* Chapter 3.)

For More Information Clipper Cruise Line (7711 Bonhomme Ave., St. Louis, MO 63105, tel. 800/325–0010).

MV Nantucket Clipper and MV Yorktown Clipper

Specifications
Type of ship: Coastal cruiser *Passengers:* 102/138
Cruise experience: Casual *Crew:* 32/40 (American)
Size: 95 tons/97 tons *Officers:* American
Number of cabins: 51/69 *Passenger/crew ratio:* 3.2 to
Outside cabins: 100% 1/3.5 to 1
Year built: 1984/1988

Ship's Log The *Clipper*s look more like boxy yachts than cruise ships. Their signature design is dominated by a large bridge and large picture windows that ensure bright interior public spaces. There are only a few public rooms, and deck space is limited. The glass-walled Observation Lounge is small enough to foster conversation that can be heard anywhere in the room, so it's usually quite friendly. The ships' coziness can engender camaraderie or claustrophobia, but generally passengers are made to feel like invited guests. A knowledgeable crew offers advice as to what and what not to see in port. And day or night, you're usually welcome to stop by the bridge for a cup of coffee with the captain and crew.

Cabins and Rates

	Beds	Phone	TV	Sitting Area	Fridge	Tub	Average Per Diem*
Outside	T	O	O	O	O	O	$330

*Airfare and port taxes are extra.

The all-outside cabins are small. How the designers stuffed two beds, a dresser, a desk, a bathroom, and a closet into such a tiny space is a great mystery. Nicely finished in pastel fabrics and accented with blond woods and prints on the walls, they make a comfortable home at sea. Most cabins have a picture-window view, a few have portholes. Category Two cabins open onto the public promenade.

Outlet voltage: 110 AC.

Single supplement: 150% of double-occupancy rate.

Discounts: A third passenger in a cabin pays $600–$2,100 per cruise, depending upon the itinerary.

Sports and Fitness **Recreation:** Snorkeling equipment and instruction, unobstructed circuit for jogging; no organized deck sports or facilities.

Facilities **Public rooms:** Small lounge serves as living room, bar, card room, and entertainment center; there are TVs in the dining room and lounge.

Shops: Souvenir items available.

Health care: None.

Accessibility There are no facilities specifically equipped for wheelchair users.

Club Med

The Fleet *Club Med 1*

The huge *Club Med 1* is like a small ocean liner with sails. Built by the French shipyard that produced the graceful *Windstar* ships, the *Club Med 1* is a distinctive, sleek, white vessel that combines ancient sail power with cutting-edge technology. It is also one of the largest passenger sailing ships afloat.

Ship at a Glance

	Dining Rooms	Bars	Casino	Fitness Center	Pools	Average Per Diem
Club Med 1	2	5	●	●	2	$300

Cruise Experience
Club Med, known for fun-in-the-sun villages, has taken its activity-packed vacations and sent them to sea. There's always something to do, and the ship's team of cruise directors (known as G.O.s or *gentils organisateurs*) makes sure that everybody has a good time. There's no pressure to join in, though, and a laid-back atmosphere prevails.

A Club Med cruise is international—on the *Club Med 1*'s Caribbean sailings, only 20% to 30% of the passengers may be American. The majority come from Europe, particularly from France. Shipboard announcements are made in English, French, and German, and all the G.O.s speak English. Because a Club Med cruise costs more than its land-based vacations, passengers tend to be more affluent. Most are couples in their mid-thirties to sixties, who have never been to a Club Med village before.

Activities
On a typical day in the Caribbean, the *Club Med 1* drops anchor in a protected bay. For those who want to go ashore, there's tender service. For those who stay aboard, the most popular activities are water sports, such as sailing, snorkeling, and scuba diving (for certified divers only). Every day, weather permitting, a large platform is lowered from the stern, creating a diving and sunning deck at water level. The G.O.s are always on hand to provide instruction on using the ship's water-sports equipment, as well as to lead traditional cruise diversions, such as bridge lessons. Calisthenics and aerobics are conducted on deck and in the pool.

Dining
Just like in France, dinner is a big event, and lasts longer than many Americans may be accustomed to. Cuisine is mainly French and Continental, with low-calorie, nonfat, and vegetarian dishes available upon request. Dinner is served from 7:30 to 9:30 in two restaurants—the main dining room, where seating is open, and an indoor-outdoor café, where reservations are required. Twice a week, passengers dress for dinner, but neither jackets nor ties are required for men on any evening; Women dress "casually elegant," nothing

---

Chart Symbols. Ships at a Glance. ●: *Fully equipped;* ◐: *Partially equipped;* ○: *Not equipped.* Cabins and Rates. **D:** *Double bed;* **K:** *King-size bed;* **Q:** *Queen-size bed;* **T:** *Twin bed;* **U/L:** *Upper and lower berths;* ●: *All cabins have this facility;* ○: *No cabins have this facility;* ◐: *Some cabins have this facility*

more fancy than a basic black dress or a smart pantsuit. Beer and Club Med's private-label wines are complimentary at lunch and dinner; other wines may be ordered at an additional charge.

Breakfast and lunch are served in the indoor-outdoor café; lunch is also served in the main dining room. Except for the complimentary Continental breakfast served in the cabin, there is a charge for 24-hour room service. A limited in-cabin menu ranges from $3 cheese sandwiches to $25 caviar platters.

Entertainment A piano bar, a disco, and a cabaret lounge with performances by G.O.s and local bands constitute the entertainment. Don't look for the Las Vegas–style shows you see on some ships. A favorite on every cruise is "Carnival Night," when passengers masquerade in elaborate costumes and stage makeup provided by the crew.

Service and Tipping The G.O.s are neither servile nor condescending. The friendly and informal staff seem genuinely enthused and eager to help passengers. No tips are accepted.

Destinations Thanks to its shallow draft, *Club Med 1* can sail into small Caribbean harbors in such places as Les Saintes, Mayreau, Carriacou, and Tintamarre. In summer, the ship sails the Mediterranean. (For detailed itineraries, *see* Chapter 3.)

For More Information Club Med (40 W. 57th St., New York, NY 10019, tel. 800/258–2633 or 800/453–7447).

Club Med 1

Specifications *Type of ship:* Motor-sail *Passengers:* 376
Cruise experience: Casual *Crew:* 200 (international)
Size: 14,000 tons *Officers:* French
Number of cabins: 188 *Passenger/crew ratio:* 1.8 to 1
Outside cabins: 100% *Year built:* 1989

Ship's Log There's no mistaking the *Club Med 1* when all seven white sails are unfurled. It is a vessel of beauty and grace, reminiscent of the great clipper ships of old. Its main power source is the wind, augmented by nonpolluting electric diesel engines, all controlled by a state-of-the-art computer. A draft of only 15 feet allows the ship to sail safely into small, off-the-beaten-path harbors.

Eschewing the chrome, neon, and plastic decor of today's glitzy megaships, Club Med wisely opted instead for a yachtlike ambience achieved through rich teak and mahogany decks and paneling. The public rooms are furnished in an art deco style, with muted blue and beige fabrics, and are wrapped in large windows that make you feel very much at one with the sea.

Cabins and Rates

	Beds	Phone	TV	Sitting Area	Fridge	Tub	Average Per Diem*
Suite	T/K	●	●	●	●	○	$440
Outside	T/K	●	●	●	●	○	$300

Rates are for the Caribbean. Airfare and port taxes are extra.

Cabins are all outside, not huge but roomy, and appointed in a modern yet nautical style, with mahogany furnishings, twin brass-trimmed portholes, and stark white walls. Each is equipped with local and closed-circuit TV, a telephone, a radio, an honor bar, two minisafes, a hair dryer, and terry robes.

Outlet voltage: 110/220 AC.

Single supplement: 130% of double-occupancy rates.

Discounts: A third passenger in a cabin pays 80% of Bali Deck double-occupancy rates.

Sports and Fitness

Health club: Spacious top-deck fitness center with sea-view windows and modern weight-training machines, stationary bikes, rowing machines, and treadmill; massage, tanning, sauna, facials, manicures, and hairstyling.

Recreation: Aerobics and other exercise classes, Windsurfers, Sunfish sailboats, scuba equipment (for certified divers), waterskiing off swimming platform, two pools, two Zodiac dive boats, unobstructed circuit for jogging.

Facilities

Public rooms: Five bars, disco, casino, theater.

Shops: Gift shop, beauty salon.

Health care: Doctor and nurse on call.

Child care: Children under 10 not allowed; G.O.s supervise daytime activities for teenagers.

Services: Bank, laundry service, pressing service.

Accessibility There are no facilities specifically equipped for wheelchair users.

Commodore Cruise Line

The Fleet SS *Enchanted Isle*
SS *Enchanted Seas*

Built in 1957, these vessels were originally named the *Brasil* and *Argentina* and designed for all–first class passenger service between New York and South America. Over the years, the ships were rechristened with many names, and saw service with Holland America Line and later Bermuda Star Line as the *Bermuda Star* and *Queen of Bermuda*. Unfortunately, these ships have not aged gracefully. Signs of their many years at sea include corroded brass, thick layers of paint, and scarred and pitted wood. On the other hand, if you look closely, you can still see touches of these ship's original art deco design.

Ships at a Glance		Dining Rooms	Bars	Casino	Fitness Center	Pools	Average Per Diem
Enchanted Isle		1	6	●	◐	1	$140–
Enchanted Seas							$155

Cruise Experience A casual onboard atmosphere, low prices, and the chance to sail on a classic-style liner are this line's chief attractions. Commodore is most popular among couples in their forties to sixties, who enjoy spending quiet time sunning and relaxing on deck. Families with children will appreciate being able to fit three, four, or five passengers in many of the staterooms at greatly reduced rates. In all, the line makes up for what it lacks in elegance and amenities with value and passenger satisfaction, which is why many consider the line one of cruising's best buys.

Activities Daily events run the gamut of typical ocean-liner activities, but at a pace somewhat less frenetic than on other sun-and-fun cruises. Choices include bingo, scavenger hunts, wine-and-cheese tastings, food-carving demonstrations, and poolside games.

Dining Commodore's strictly American fare is what one would expect from an economy cruise line: adequate, correctly prepared, but far from memorable. Dinner is served at two assigned seatings (6 and 8:30); there is a single, open-seating breakfast. There are two formal evenings. Low-fat, no-sugar, low-salt, vegetarian, and low-calorie diets are available, but kosher meals are not. There is no smoking in the dining room. Buffet breakfasts and lunches are served daily in the Lido or Bistro, as are ice cream, cakes, and cookies at teatime, but you are better off taking your meals in the dining room. There is no room service.

Chart Symbols. Ships at a Glance. ●: *Fully equipped;* ◐: *Partially equipped;* ○: *Not equipped.* Cabins and Rates. **D:** *Double bed;* **K:** *King-size bed;* **Q:** *Queen-size bed;* **T:** *Twin bed;* **U/L:** *Upper and lower berths;* ●: *All cabins have this facility;* ○: *No cabins have this facility;* ◐: *Some cabins have this facility*

Entertainment This is Commodore's strong suit. The push toward a highly charged, good-time attitude is reflected primarily in the revitalized entertainment. Shows may take a destination as a theme, and the general shipboard atmosphere reflects the ports, too: Embarkation staff, waiters, and bartenders wear colorful uniforms—Mexican sombreros, Caribbean tropical wear, or perhaps Dixieland jazz tuxedos, depending upon the ship's itinerary. A disco and piano bar continue the party well into the wee hours.

Service and Tipping Tip the room steward and waiter $3 each per passenger per diem, and the busboy $2. A 15% service charge is automatically added to beverage purchases.

Destinations The *Enchanted Isle* sails from Barbados on deep Caribbean cruises. The *Enchanted Seas*'s home port is New Orleans for sailings to the western Caribbean. (For detailed itineraries, *see* Chapter 3.)

For More Information Commodore Cruise Lines (800 Douglas Rd., Coral Gables, FL 33134, tel. 305/529–3000).

SS Enchanted Isle and SS Enchanted Seas

Specifications *Type of ship:* Classic liner
Cruise experience: Casual
Size: 23,395 tons/23,500 tons
Number of cabins: 367/369
Outside cabins: 77%/79%
Year built: 1957

Passengers: 731/726
Crew: 350/330 (international)
Officers: European and Scandinavian
Passenger/crew ratio: 2.1 to 1/2.2 to 1

Ship's Log These are a very handsome ships from the outside but less thoughtfully designed inside. Public rooms are fairly small and irregularly shaped. The lack of bright, open spaces can make it feel cramped at times, and some of the facilities—the gym, for example—look like afterthoughts. The minuses are balanced, however, by the fact that the passenger capacity is relatively low and cabins are quite large.

Cabins and Rates

	Beds	Phone	TV	Sitting Area	Fridge	Tub	Average Per Diem*
Suite	D or T	●	●	●	○	●	$200
Outside	D or T	●	●	◐	○	◐	$140–$155
Inside	D or T	●	●	◐	○	○	$110–$130

*Rates are for the Caribbean. Airfare and port taxes are extra.

Cabins are large, with plentiful closet space. The top three categories have additional amenities such as sitting areas, desks, and real bathtubs. Recent redecorations aboard both ships have helped spruce things up, but the age of these ships is still apparent in cracked bathroom tiles and worn bathroom fixtures. The view from outside cabins on the Navigation Deck (*Isle*) or Sun Deck (*Seas*) is partially obstructed, except cabins 222–224 on both ships. Outside cabins on the Boat Deck (both ships) look onto a public promenade.

Outlet voltage: 110 AC.

Single supplement: 150%–200% of double-occupancy rate. Commodore will match two same-sex adults in a cabin at the double-occupancy rate.

Discounts: A third or fourth passenger in a cabin pays $106 per diem (*Isle*) or $56 per diem (*Seas*). A child under 17 sharing with two adults pays $42 per diem (*Seas*). You get a $250 discount for arranging your own airfare and a discount for booking early.

Sports and Fitness

Health club: Small inside exercise room, sauna.

Recreation: Aerobics, golf driving, table tennis, shuffleboard, skeet shooting, pool.

Facilities

Public rooms: Six bars, four entertainment lounges (five on *Seas*), casino, disco, cinema, card/writing room (*Seas*), library, video-game room.

Shops: Duty-free boutique, gift ship, beauty salon/barber.

Health care: Doctor on call.

Child care: Playroom, baby-sitting, youth programs run by counselors during holidays and in summer.

Services: Full- and self-service laundry, photographer, film processing.

Accessibility Elevators are accessible to wheelchair users, and public doorways with ledges are fitted with ramps. However, cabin bathrooms have a step, and there is no elevator service to the lowest passenger deck on each ship.

Costa Cruise Lines

The Fleet
MV *CostaAllegra*
MV *CostaClassica*
MV *CostaRomantica*

Costa Classica

In the 1990s, Costa has completely reinvented itself. Its North America fleet consists of three distinguished ships, the *Allegra*, *Classica*, and *Romantica*, which combine European traditions with modern technology. Aboard these liners, you'll find elaborate architectural flourishes, inspired by the line's Italian heritage. Design details, such as intricate mosaic bordering, hand-painted murals, and marble fountains, bring the Old World into the New. These gleaming vessels have completely replaced the line's older ships, which now carry primarily European passengers (*see* Aboard Foreign Ships *in* Cruise Primer).

Ships at a Glance

	Dining Rooms	Bars	Casino	Fitness Center	Pools	Average Per Diem
Allegra	1	4	●	●	1	$250
CostaClassica *CostaRomantica*	1	2	●	●	2	$285

Cruise Experience
Costa is known for an exuberant, indulgent experience it calls "cruising Italian style." The result is like having a festival in a stately European hotel. The ships themselves are elegant and sleek, but the mood on board is distinctly jovial—as exhibited by the singing waiters who prepare specialty dishes at your table and the toga party on the last night of the cruise. Overall, the *Allegra* has a more informal attitude, design, and decor, but all three ships operate as cash-free societies (passengers use a Costa "credit card" to pay for shore excursions and onboard expenses), just one of the many refinements found aboard this very European line.

Activities
Costa offers the usual bag of merriments—bingo, skeet shooting, and myriad get-togethers—along with more unusual offerings: lectures on wine, astrology, and Italian history, for instance. In keeping with the Italian flair for romance, Costa's captains invite married couples to renew their vows in a special ceremony—after which they'll happily sell you champagne. An onboard snorkeling school gives lessons during Caribbean sailings. The ships' spas are more elaborate than most.

Dining
With the introduction of its new ships, Costa has revamped its gastronomic experience, keeping old favorites and introducing some delightful alternatives. In the main dining room you'll find the usual lavish fare, with rich pasta dishes as well as beef and fresh fish. Veg-

---

Chart Symbols. Ships at a Glance. ●: *Fully equipped;* **◑:** *Partially equipped;* ○: *Not equipped.* Cabins and Rates. **D:** *Double bed;* **K:** *King-size bed;* **Q:** *Queen-size bed;* **T:** *Twin bed;* **U/L:** *Upper and lower berths;* **●:** *All cabins have this facility;* ○: *No cabins have this facility;* **◑:** *Some cabins have this facility*

etarian dishes also appear on the lunch and dinner menus. Dining-room meals are served at two assigned seatings (dinner at 6:15 and 8:30). Breakfast and lunch are sometimes open when in port. Two formal nights are scheduled on each seven-day cruise. Low-calorie spa meals are available, but special dietary requests, as well as arrangements for birthday and anniversary celebrations, should be made in writing at least four weeks in advance.

Snacks between meals can be found at the poolside gelati stand and at a Viennese-style patisserie and a café serving individual gourmet pizzas. At least three times per cruise, chefs set up a pasta buffet poolside—cooking several different dishes on the spot. On the Lido Deck, you can help yourself to early-morning coffee with juice and pastries, a full buffet breakfast and lunch, and afternoon snacks. The eating day concludes with a midnight buffet. Each cruise has one pizza/focaccia poolside party, an outdoor barbecue, and a buffet/galley tour. Room service is available around the clock but is limited to sandwiches and Continental breakfast. (Passengers who book suites are entitled to order in-room dinners from the dining-room menu, complete with linens and china.)

Entertainment The festive atmosphere aboard ship includes theme nights: Most popular are the Italian *Festa* and the Roman Bacchanal, for which passengers fashion togas out of bedsheets. Otherwise, entertainment is fairly typical, from cabaret shows to dancing to sing-alongs in the piano bar.

Service and Tipping With the new ships has come an equally improved level of service and attention to detail. A 24-hour Concierge Desk handles special requests, and the crew tends to its passengers with traditional European deference. Tip the room steward and waiter $3 each per passenger per diem, the head waiter $1, the busboy $1.50.

Destinations Costa ships sail throughout the Caribbean in winter, returning to their home waters each summer for a variety of European and Mediterranean cruises. (For detailed itineraries, *see* Chapter 3.)

For More Information Costa Cruise Lines (World Trade Center, 80 S.W. 8th St., Miami, FL 33130, tel. 800/462–6782).

MV CostaAllegra

Specifications

Type of ship: Cruise liner	*Passengers:* 800
Cruise experience: Semi-formal	*Crew:* 400 (international)
	Officers: Italian
Size: 30,000 tons	*Passenger/crew ratio:* 2 to 1
Number of cabins: 405	*Year built:* 1992
Outside cabins: 60%	

Ship's Log Less streamlined and modernist than its fleetmates, the *Allegra* has an unpretentious atmosphere that attracts a similar crowd. The ship is comfortable and easy to get around, with all the public rooms on one deck, including a staircase descending into the main dining room. The designers made wonderful use of sunlight and sea in the public areas: A stunning plant-filled atrium caps the health club, and the boxy aft of the ship allows high windows in the dining room, with a splendid view of the ocean. Public areas have the feel of being underwater because of a series of skylit, water-filled compartments overhead and large portholes peering into the main swimming pool above.

Cabins and Rates

	Beds	Phone	TV	Sitting Area	Fridge	Tub	Average Per Diem*
Suite	Q, T	●	●	●	●	●	$365
Outside	Q, T	●	●	○	○	○	$250

| Inside | U/L | ● | ● | ○ | ○ | ○ | $165 |

Rates include airfare. Port taxes are extra.

Inside and outside cabins are equally spacious, all decorated with Italian furnishings accented in burnished wood and woven fabrics. Some cabins have twins that convert to a queen and all have built-in hair dryers and safes. The Grand Suite, on the bow, has large windows on two sides but no balcony. Like the Grand Suite, standard suites have whirlpool bathtubs and walk-in closets, but they have private balconies. Suites receive flowers, fruit, and pastry and candy baskets replenished daily.

Outlet voltage: 110/220 AC.

Single supplement: 200% of double-occupancy rate for suites, 150% for other cabins.

Discounts: A third or fourth passenger in a cabin pays $70 per diem. You get a discount for arranging your own airfare.

Sports and Fitness **Health club:** Stair climbers, Lifecycles, treadmills, free weights, aerobic and stretch classes, massage and facial-treatment center.

Recreation: Pool, three Jacuzzis, jogging track.

Facilities **Public rooms:** Four bars, two entertainment lounges, casino, disco, card room, library, meeting room, chapel.

Shops: Boutique, perfume and jewelry shop, photo shop, beauty salon/barber.

Health care: Doctor on call.

Child care: Supervised children's center, baby-sitting.

Services: Laundry service, photographer.

Accessibility Elevators and public lavatories are accessible to wheelchair users, as are eight cabins.

MV CostaClassica and MV CostaRomantica

Specifications *Type of ship:* Cruise liner *Passengers:* 1,300
Cruise experience: Semi- *Crew:* 650 (international)
formal *Officers:* Italian
Size: 53,000 tons/54,000 tons *Passenger/crew ratio:* 2 to 1
Number of cabins: 654 *Year built:* 1991/1993
Outside cabins: 67%

Ship's Log At $325 million each, the *CostaClassica* and *CostaRomantica* are among the world's most expensively built cruise ships per passenger. They have the regal bearing of a fine European hotel—with plenty of cool Italian marble and handmade ceramic tile—but a sassy, charged Italian spirit. Despite their size, an intimate, yachtlike ambience can be found aboard both ships. The second pool, for instance, is an often uncrowded place to be alone with a good book. On the *Romantica*, the wicker cabanas forward on the top deck are ideal for a private moment with a sunset.

On both ships, dining is a grand affair amidst Italian marble floors, Louis XIV–style chairs, and murals. Fare is Northern Italian, plus classic crowd-pleasers such as lobster and beef Wellington. Two theme dinners highlight foods of the Renaissance and Roman eras. By contrast, early breakfasts and buffet lunches are served in a contemporary-style Italian café with hand-painted tiles and marble tables. You can also eat light at the salad bar or build your own sandwich at Leonardo's deli. Rounding out the classical suggestions of these ships are the main showrooms, where typical Las Vegas–style revues are staged in a faithful reproduction of a Renaissance theater with tiered seating for excellent views all around.

Only differences in interior design distinguish these otherwise identical sister ships. The *Classica* sports a decidedly modern, minimalist edge—some consider it too severe. The *Romantica* is softer, with more use of wood and pastel colors. In the *Romantica*'s main dining room, a noise-absorbing ceiling mutes the din reflected off the Italian marble floors. The design of the lunch buffet on the *Romantica* provides for a smoother flow of traffic.

Cabins and Rates		Beds	Phone	TV	Sitting Area	Fridge	Tub	Average Per Diem*
	Suite	Q	●	●	●	●	●	$390–$427
	Outside	Q or T	●	●	●	○	○	$285
	Inside	T or U/L	●	●	●	○	○	$232

*Rates include airfare. Higher suite rates are for the Classica. *Port taxes are extra.*

Cherry-wood furniture, designer fabrics, watercolor prints of European cities on the walls, and roomy bathrooms highlight the large cabins. Light sleepers may grumble, however, about the thin walls. Current movies are shown continuously on cabin TVs. Some twins convert to a queen. Staterooms that accommodate three passengers offer upper and lower berths. Suites sleep up to four, using a twin sofa bed and a twin Murphy bed along with the queen-size bed; in addition to a sitting area, the suites have a graceful, wood-rimmed balcony large enough to accommodate two chaise longues with room to spare. On the *Romantica*, some suites also come with floor-to-ceiling windows.

Outlet voltage: 110/220 AC.

Single supplement: 200% of double-occupancy rate, 150% for other cabins.

Discounts: A third or fourth passenger in a cabin pays $70 per diem on Caribbean sailings (cruise only). You get a discount for arranging your own airfare.

Sports and Fitness **Health club:** Aerobics studio; exercise room with free weights, Lifecycles, treadmills, stair climbers, circuit weight-training system; whirlpool spas, roman bath, steam and sauna rooms; massage and facial-treatment center; juice bar.

Recreation: Two pools, jogging track.

Facilities **Public rooms:** Two bars, two entertainment lounges, casino, disco, card room, library, conference center/chapel.

Shops: Boutique, perfume shop, jewelry/gift shop, photo shop, sports-clothing shop, gourmet deli, beauty salon/barber.

Health care: Doctor on call.

Child care: Playroom, supervised youth activity center, baby-sitting.

Services: Laundry service, photographer.

Accessibility Elevators and public lavatories are accessible to wheelchair users, as are six cabins.

Crystal Cruises

The Fleet *Crystal Harmony*
Crystal Symphony

Counted among the world's most luxurious ocean liners, the Crystal fleet stands out due to its modern design and amenities. Unlike other luxury ships, such as the *Cunard Royal Viking Sun*, Crystal's ships are more like upscale land resorts. Crystal's dining rooms seat only half the ships' complement at one time—a major departure from tradition on ships in this price category.

Ships at a Glance	Dining Rooms	Bars	Casino	Fitness Center	Pools	Average Per Diem
Crystal Harmony	3*	7	●	●	2	$455
Crystal Symphony	3*	6	●	●	2	$455

*includes two alternative restaurants

Cruise Experience A cruise aboard Japanese-owned Crystal Cruises is for affluent passengers who are accustomed to the best. Life aboard the *Crystal Harmony* or *Crystal Symphony* is not as intimate or unstructured as on Cunard Line's *Sea Goddess*, nor quite as formal or sedentary as aboard Cunard's *Sagafjord*. The *Harmony* and *Symphony* are designed for those who love physical activity and fine food and are willing to pay a premium for them.

Crystal combines the best of Japanese technical know-how with a European flair for service and attention. Engines, radar, and navigational equipment are state-of-the-art. Business services for the high-powered executive include audiovisual, translation, and satellite telecommunications equipment, as well as fax machines, computers, and secretarial services. And the spacious fitness centers are arguably the seagoing world's most advanced. White-glove service, stellar cuisine, air-conditioned tenders with toilets, and a contemporary interior complete the effect of total luxury and comfort.

Activities To the typical litany of ocean-liner diversions, Crystal adds high-tech sports facilities, such as a computerized electronic golf course and driving range; high-powered intellectual and cultural debates and destination-oriented lectures by scholars, political figures, and diplomats; a busy fitness center and spa, with lots of pampering; and the first Caesars-Palace-at-Sea casinos.

Dining The Japanese aesthetic is evident in Crystal's lavish, distinctive food presentations. Although, unlike other lines in this price category, Crystal seats passengers for dinner in two seatings (6:30 and 8:30), on any particular night passengers may also choose to dine at

---

Chart Symbols. Ships at a Glance. ●: *Fully equipped;* ◑: *Partially equipped;* ○: *Not equipped.* Cabins and Rates. **D:** *Double bed;* **K:** *King-size bed;* **Q:** *Queen-size bed;* **T:** *Twin bed;* **U/L:** *Upper and lower berths;* ●: *All cabins have this facility;* ○: *No cabins have this facility;* ◑: *Some cabins have this facility*

no extra charge in a Japanese restaurant on the *Harmony* or in a Chinese restaurant aboard the *Symphony*. A third choice, the Prego Italian restaurant, is found on both ships. To complement dinner, each ship has an extensive wine cellar. Two formal evenings are scheduled each week, but men wear a jacket and tie to dinner virtually every night.

The canopy-covered indoor-outdoor Lido Cafe serves breakfast, mid-morning bouillon, and lunch. The swim-up bar in the Neptune Pool (on the *Harmony* only) and grill serves hot dogs, hamburgers, sandwiches, and pizza. The Bistro sells specialty coffees and wine and serves international cheeses. Room service is available 24 hours a day. Passengers can order from the full dining-room menu at lunch and dinner, sandwiches and pizza at other times.

Entertainment There are pre- and post-dinner cabarets, Broadway-quality shows in the main lounge, a piano bar, before- and after-dinner dancing, a harpist, a trio (sometimes classical), a sing-along piano bar, and the casino. Local entertainers are sometimes brought on board to entertain during the ships' frequent parties.

Service and Tipping Crystal's staff members are well trained, highly motivated, and thoroughly professional. Tip the steward and the waiter $3 each per passenger per diem, the busboy $2. In the alternative restaurants, tip $5 per passenger per meal.

Destinations Crystal brings its refined level of cruising to the Caribbean, Panama Canal, Mexico, Alaska, and South America in the Western Hemisphere. (For detailed itineraries, *see* Chapter 3.)

For More Information Crystal Cruises (2121 Ave. of the Stars, Los Angeles, CA 90067, tel. 800/446–6620).

Crystal Harmony and Crystal Symphony

Specifications *Type of ship:* Cruise liner   *Passengers:* 960
Cruise experience: Formal   *Crew:* 545/530 (European)
Size: 49,400 tons/50,000 tons   *Officers:* Norwegian and
Number of cabins: 480   Japanese
Outside cabins: 96%/100%   *Passenger/crew ratio:* 1.7 to
Year built: 1990/1995   1/1.8 to 1

Ship's Log The *Crystal Harmony*, exceptionally sleek and sophisticated, contradicts the conventional wisdom that all new state-of-the-art ships must look like high-rise, barge-bound hotels. Technologically advanced and superbly equipped, it is tastefully decorated as well. Harmonious colors, lots of plants and neoclassical sculptures, and a light-and-airy design give a sense of both luxury and simplicity. At the center is a multilevel atrium, Crystal Plaza—a study in glass stairways and railings, brass fixtures, and dazzling white walls. The Vista Lounge is a beautiful wedding-white room with oversize observation windows. A portion of the Lido Deck is covered by a retractable canopy. With one of the highest space ratios afloat, there's never a feeling of claustrophobia, in either the public rooms or the hallways.

The *Crystal Symphony* is the biggest ship to be built with all outside cabins since the *Royal Princess* (*see* Princess Cruises). Inside, it differs from its sibling in a lighter color scheme for the decor and several larger public rooms. Repeat Crystal passengers will find that their favorite rooms, such as the Palm Lounge and Lido Cafe, have been expanded. The *Symphony*'s two-story atrium and casino are twice the size of the same spaces aboard the *Harmony*. The *Symphony*'s Lido also has separate lines for healthy and hearty fare.

Cabins and Rates		Beds	Phone	TV	Sitting Area	Fridge	Tub	Average Per Diem*
Suite	T/K	●	●	●	●		●	$683
Outside (with veranda)	T/Q	●	●	●	●		●	$455
Outside (without veranda)	T/Q	●	●	●	●		●	$416

Rates are for the Panama Canal. Airfare and port taxes are extra.

Thanks to the skillful use of paneling and mirrors, the large staterooms appear even larger. Each is beautifully decorated, and equipped with 14-channel TVs (including CNN and ESPN), VCRs, hair dryers, and robes. Penthouses have verandas and Jacuzzis (butler service is available); certain standard cabins have verandas as well. Some cabins on the Horizon and Promenade decks have obstructed views (Crystal's brochures clearly identify rooms with limited views). Cabins on the Promenade Deck look out onto a public walkway.

Outlet voltage: 110/220 AC.

Single supplement: 110%–170% of double-occupancy rate.

Discounts: A third passenger in a cabin pays the minimum per-person fare for that cruise. Children under 12 with two full-paying adults pay half the minimum per-person fare. You get up to $300 discount for arranging your own airfare. Repeat passengers get a 5% discount.

Sports and Fitness

Health club: Spa with state-of-the-art equipment (stationary bikes, rowing machines, stair climbers, treadmills), free weights, saunas, steam rooms, massage, exercise classes, weight-reduction regimens, body and facial care, makeup services.

Recreation: Aerobics, jazz-dance, exercise classes, paddle tennis, shuffleboard, skeet shooting, Ping-Pong, basketball, two pools (one for laps), two whirlpools, unobstructed circuit for jogging.

Facilities

Public rooms: Seven bars (*Harmony*), six bars (*Symphony*), six entertainment lounges, casino, disco, cinema, card room, library (books and videotapes), video-game room, smoking room.

Shops: Shopping arcade of boutiques, beauty salon/barber.

Health care: Doctors and nurses on call.

Child care: Youth programs with counselors during holidays or whenever a large number of children are on board, baby-sitting arranged privately with crew members.

Services: Concierge service, full- and self-service laundry, dry cleaning, photographer, video-camera rentals, film processing, secretarial and photocopy services, translation equipment for meetings.

Accessibility Two penthouses and two standard cabins are accessible to wheelchair users. Passengers must provide their own small, traveling wheelchairs. All public areas are accessible.

Cunard Line Limited

QE 2

The Fleet MV *Cunard Countess*
SS *Cunard Crown Dynasty*
MS *Cunard Royal Viking Sun*
RMS *Queen Elizabeth 2*
MS *Sagafjord*
MV *Sea Goddess I*
MS *Vistafjord*

Her Majesty's fleet is as diverse as the former empire. Continuing the tradition of transatlantic passage is the classic *Queen Elizabeth 2*, a giant liner built to weather the storms of the North Atlantic. Tradition on a more intimate scale can be found aboard the elegant *Sagafjord*, *Vistafjord*, and *Royal Viking Sun*. Smaller still are the tiny *Sea Goddess* yacht. The *Countess* delivers tradition, too, but without the pomp and circumstance. Giving Cunard a contemporary choice is the snazzy *Crown Dynasty*, the most modern of the line's vessels.

Ships at a Glance

	Dining Rooms	Bars	Casino	Fitness Center	Pools	Average Per Diem
Countess	1	4	●	●	1	$160
Crown Dynasty	1	4	●	●	1	$338
QE 2	5	6	●	●	4	$437
Royal Viking Sun	2*	5	●	●	2	$615
Sagafjord *Vistafjord*	1/2*	4	●	●	2	$545/ $442
Sea Goddess	1	3	●	●	1	$642

**includes alternative restaurant*

Cruise Experience Cunard's three divisions, Queen Elizabeth 2, Cunard Crown, and Cunard Royal Viking, each represent a distinct style of cruising, distinguished by shipboard atmosphere, level of service, and pricing. Specific details on activities, dining, entertainment, and service are covered under each Ship's Log. In general, though, the qualities that define each brand are as follows:

Cunard Crown This three-ship division, comprised of the *Cunard Crown Dynasty*, the *Cunard Countess*, and *Cunard Princess* (which sails in Europe year-round and is not reviewed in this chapter), brings the Cunard brand of cruising to a broader audience than the line's other ships. With low to moderate prices, the Cunard Crown ships attract the youngest crowd of Cunard's vessels.

Chart Symbols. Ships at a Glance. **●:** *Fully equipped;* **◑:** *Partially equipped;* ○: *Not equipped.* Cabins and Rates. **D:** *Double bed;* **K:** *King-size bed;* **Q:** *Queen-size bed;* **T:** *Twin bed;* **U/L:** *Upper and lower berths;* **●:** *All cabins have this facility;* ○: *No cabins have this facility;* **◑:** *Some cabins have this facility*

Cunard Royal Viking Cunard's newest division is named for its latest acquisition, the *Royal Viking Sun*. In this group are the line's finest vessels. Fans of the now disbanded Royal Viking Line will find the name, and many of the traditions, carried on aboard RVL's former flagship. Many of these passengers will also appreciate the understated elegance of the *Sagafjord* and *Vistafjord*. The yachtlike *Sea Goddess* offers cruises affordable to only a very few; passengers on this ship enjoy the highest standards of luxury and service available.

Queen Elizabeth 2 As perhaps the most famous ship in cruising, the *QE2* has the name recognition and loyal following to establish it as its own brand in the Cunard family. The grande dame of the seas is the only cruise ship to still offer passage in different classes. But other than eating and sleeping, all passengers enjoy the same facilities and amenities. Transatlantic sailings attract ship aficionados who are as interested in the ship's history and legacy as they are in its fine dining. Many are repeat passengers, who share stories about their many previous crossings.

Destinations The sun never sets on the Cunard fleet; in the Western Hemisphere, the line sails to every major destination from Alaska to Argentina.

For More Information Cunard Line Limited (555 5th Ave., New York, NY 10017, tel. 800/528–6273 for Cunard Crown or Queen Elizabeth 2 and 800/458–9000 for Cunard Royal Viking).

MV Cunard Countess

Specifications *Type of ship:* Cruise liner
Cruise experience: Casual
Size: 17,593 tons
Number of cabins: 398
Outside cabins: 66%

Passengers: 796
Crew: 350 (mainly British)
Officers: British
Passenger/crew ratio: 2.3 to 1
Year built: 1976

Ship's Log The *Cunard Countess* is an affordable ship that caters to a relaxed, informal, and mostly European crowd. The vessel's Caribbean itinerary, which calls at six different ports in seven days, is especially good for first-time cruisers looking for something a little more sophisticated than a Carnival cruise. But since these are among the least expensive cruises available, don't mistake the Cunard name for an automatic stamp of luxury. The ship is compact, cabins are small, but public rooms are spacious; the Showtime Lounge, for example, features a 40-square-foot, black marble dance floor. The Starlight Lounge, a card and entertainment room, is one of the ship's highlights; furnished in art nouveau style, it commands a magnificent view of sea. Public areas and cabins were refurbished in the fall of 1992—furniture was reupholstered and new navy-and-gold carpeting was installed.

Activities In addition to typical ocean-liner activities, the ship has a 24-hour health club. Exercise options continue ashore in the form of hikes, sports programs, and competitive runs—the *Countess* is known for its extensive shore excursion program.

Dining Food is above average, and the service is usually excellent. The dining room has two assigned seatings per meal (dinner at 6:30 and 8:30) and a midnight buffet. There are two formal evenings per week. A special fitness diet is available, though special dietary requests should be made two weeks before sailing. The Lido serves early morning coffee and pastries, light breakfast, mid-morning bouillon, and light lunch. Help-yourself coffee and tea are available all day, and afternoon tea is served. Room service may be ordered 24 hours a day from a limited menu.

Entertainment Variety shows in the main lounge are the main event of evening entertainment, and there's an indoor-outdoor nightclub and a piano bar. You can ballroom dance, disco dance, or on certain evenings, dress up for the Masquerade Ball. The *Countess*'s music theme cruises are especially popular, so be sure to book well in advance if you're interested.

Service and Tipping Service is excellent. Tip the room steward and the waiter $3 each per passenger per diem, the busboy $1.50; the wine steward gets 15% of the wine bill.

Cabins and Rates

	Beds	Phone	TV	Sitting Area	Fridge	Tub	Average Per Diem*
Suite	T	●	●	●	●	●	$223
Outside	T	●	○	○	○	○	$160
Inside	T or U/L	●	○	○	○	○	$135

Rates are for the Caribbean. Airfare and port taxes are extra.

Cabins are small but convert into sitting rooms during the day. Recent renovations include thicker mattresses, beds set in an L-shape arrangement, and more luggage space. Cabinetwork consists of colorfully laminated desks and dressers.

Outlet voltage: 110 AC.

Single supplement: 150% of double-occupancy rate; if a confirmed reservation is made at least 30 days prior to sailing, the single supplement may be waived. Cunard will match two same-sex adults in a cabin for the double-occupancy rate.

Discounts: A third or fourth passenger in a cabin pays $127–$142 per diem. You get a discount for arranging your own airfare.

Sports and Fitness **Health club:** 24-hour gym with free weights, computerized weight machines, rowing machines, stationary bikes, ballet barre, sauna, massage; aerobics, stretch, yoga, and other exercise classes.

Recreation: Basketball, golf driving, paddle tennis, table tennis, shuffleboard, pool, two outdoor whirlpools.

Facilities **Public rooms:** Four bars, three entertainment lounges, casino, disco, cinema, card room, library/writing room.

Shops: Small arcade of boutiques and gift shops, beauty salon/barber.

Health care: Doctor on call.

Child care: Wading pool, baby-sitting, youth programs run by counselors during holidays or in summer.

Services: Laundry service, photographer.

Accessibility Not all public areas are accessible to wheelchair users, and wheelchairs are not permitted on tenders. Passengers must provide their own small, portable wheelchair.

SS Crown Dynasty

Specifications *Type of ship:* Cruise liner   *Passengers:* 800
Cruise experience: Semi-   *Crew:* 320 (Filipino)
formal   *Officers:* Northern European
Size: 20,000 tons   *Passenger/crew ratio:* 2.5 to 1
Number of cabins: 400   *Years built:* 1993
Outside cabins: 69.5%

Ship's Log Cunard advertises the *Dynasty* in the same brochures as the *Countess*. The newer Crown vessel is impressive in its shipboard appointments. Clever use of glass yields an especially spacious result. Other design touches are at once elegant and dramatic: A skylight and three window walls brighten the Bon Vivant dining room, where tiered seating allows unobstructed sea views. In the Crown Plaza atrium, a five-story wall of glass offers a spectacular view as well, and a grand staircase and a glass elevator complete the space.

The one flaw in this otherwise finely conceived vessel has been passenger complaints about the service. Otherwise, everything about the *Crown Dynasty* is first-rate. Single passengers in particular should consider sailing on one of these ships because there is no single surcharge.

Activities The *Crown Dynasty* offers "low density, low impact" activities, such as bingo, pool games, "horse racing," wine tasting, "whodunit" evenings, and crafts classes. The "Seafit" health-and-fitness program combines aerobics, water exercises, walking tours of ports, and low-calorie, low-cholesterol, low-sodium cuisine.

Dining The American and Continental cuisine is rich and varied, and there are always light and healthy offerings, and desserts are good but not excessively rich. The dining room's innovative, tiered design affords unobstructed sea views from nearly every table. Dinner is served at two assigned seatings (6 and 8:15); breakfast and lunch have open seating. Two formal nights are scheduled on each weeklong cruise. Special dietary requests must be made in writing at least two weeks before sailing.

The Palm Court Café, a bright indoor-outdoor facility, serves breakfast, lunch, snacks, and outdoor grill selections. Afternoon tea and midnight buffets are offered. Room service is available 24 hours a day but is limited to sandwiches and Continental breakfast.

Entertainment Entertainment is not dazzling, but this seems to suit passengers just fine. Broadway-style shows, cabarets, and dancing take place in the Scheherezade Lounge, which has large windows that are great for sea viewing by day. Jazz combos and dance music are featured in the aft lounge, Reflections, while music videos and disco pounds out until the wee hours of the morning in the Chameleon Club. Those who would rather stay in their cabins at night can enjoy in-room movies.

Service and Tipping Service on the *Crown Dynasty* is erratic: Sometimes it is very good, other times less so. Tip the steward and the waiter $2.50 each per passenger per diem, the busboy $1.50. A 15% service charge is added to bar bills.

Cabins and Rates

	Beds	Phone	TV	Sitting Area	Fridge	Tub	Average Per Diem*
Suites	D	●	●	●	●	○	$435
Outside	T/D	●	●	◑	◑	○	$338
Inside	T/D	●	●	○	○	○	$236

Rates are for the Panama Canal. Port taxes are extra.

Light woods, brass accents, and pastel colors combine to create very pleasant and airy cabins. Standard staterooms are furnished with two lower beds that convert to a double, remote-control TVs (including CNN), ample storage, and a safe. Each Deluxe Suite has a double bed, a sitting area, an extra closet, and a refrigerator. Ten suites have private balconies.

Outlet voltage: 110 AC.

Single supplement: No surcharge, subject to confirmation 30 days prior to sailing; earlier confirmation at 150% of double-occupancy rate.

Discounts: A third passenger in a cabin pays $64 per diem, as does a child under 15 sailing with a single parent. You get a discount for arranging your own airfare.

Sports and Fitness

Health club: Nautilus equipment, aerobics, juice bar, sauna, steam room, massage, facials.

Recreation: Unobstructed circuit for jogging.

Facilities

Public rooms: Four lounges, casino, disco, cinema, library, meeting room.

Shops: Boutiques, beauty salon with manicures and pedicures.

Child care: Teen/youth center.

Accessibility

Four cabins (two inside, two outside) and the elevators are accessible to wheelchair users. The line recommends that passengers with mobility problems travel with an able-bodied companion.

MS Cunard Royal Viking Sun

Specifications

Type of ship: Cruise liner
Cruise experience: Formal
Size: 38,000 tons
Number of cabins: 384
Outside cabins: 94.8%

Passengers: 756
Crew: 460 (European)
Officers: Norwegian
Passenger/crew ratio: 1.6 to 1
Year built: 1988

Ship's Log

At press time, the former flagship of Royal Viking Line was in transition. When built in 1988, no expense was spared in outfitting the *Sun*, but since that time the ship's former owners had let the vessel slip into a tired appearance, with faded upholstery and paint-chipped furniture. To reverse the wear, Cunard spent $11 million in May 1995 to refurbish the *Sun*'s public rooms. New carpeting was installed and furnishings received new coverings. In addition, a new alternative restaurant was tentatively scheduled to open in October 1995.

As with all of the former Royal Viking Line ships, the *Sun* was built for long-distance cruising. Its interior is spacious and designed for maximum comfort. A feeling of light and space is created by the use of floor-to-ceiling windows and two glass-walled elevators. The vessel also has its share of small lounges. Best is the Oak Room, an old-world retreat of leather chairs, nautical paintings, and a simulated fireplace. Unfortunately, these attractive rooms are little-used, creating a dead space in the middle of the ship. At the bow is the Stella Polaris Room, an observation lounge with 180° views.

The *Sun* has a very loyal following. Its passenger repeat rate is 66%, so many passengers know the ship, the staff, and often fellow passengers, well. The clientele tends to be older (fifties to mid-seventies), experienced, and sophisticated, with enough time and money to take long voyages. Foreign travelers make up about 20% of Royal Viking's clientele and are assisted by an international staff. Life on board tends toward the formal, and neat attire is required at all times.

Activities

Fun on the *Sun* runs the gamut of ocean-liner diversions, from the typical—trivia quizzes, board- and card-game tournaments, dance lessons, arts-and-crafts classes, and fashion shows—to the more genteel—wine-tastings, napkin-folding demonstrations, bridge instruction, and a needlepoint club. Gentlemen hosts sail aboard the *Sun* to act as social partners for single women traveling alone. Four times each year, well-known chefs board the ship to offer cooking demonstrations and mingle with passengers. On all cruises there's a Goren bridge program and a staff golf pro, who conducts clinics. On world cruises, the *Sun* pulls out all the stops, scheduling special lectures and entertainment, gifts and parties.

Passengers concerned with keeping their minds and bodies in shape can sign up for as many as seven daily classes from the ship's Golden Door Spa at Sea program, conducted by staff from the famous spa in California, and enrich themselves by attending the World Affairs Program lecture series. Talks cover a diverse range of topics and are designed to give passengers greater insight into the ship's ports of call. You may learn, for example, that Samuel Cunard founded Cunard Line in Halifax, Nova Scotia (see Chapter 2, Ports of Call).

Dining The *Royal Viking Sun*'s cuisine has long been touted as some of cruising's best, and that's not an idle boast. Chefs from highly acclaimed restaurants frequently sail on board to prepare meals for passengers. Healthful menu selections at each meal are tied in with the ship's Golden Door Spa at Sea program.

All meals in the dining room are served in a single, assigned seating. Dinner is served from 7:30 to 9:00. On a Royal Viking ship, virtually every night is a formal night, and passengers are expected to dress smartly even on informal evenings. The dress code is in effect from 6 PM onward, enforced by the passengers themselves, who revel in showing off their finest.

Befitting such elaborate ceremony, much care and attention is devoted to food preparation, and passengers never see the same menu twice. Caviar may be ordered at any dinner, even when it isn't on the menu, and just about any special order can be prepared with 24 hours' notice. However, special dietary requests (such as for diabetics or vegetarians) should be made in writing at least four weeks before sailing.

More casual dining is also available. The Garden Café serves early morning coffee and an extensive buffet lunch. On occasional evenings when dinner is served, the Garden Café serves as the ship's alternative restaurant. The outdoor Pool Bar serves hamburgers, hot dogs, and sandwiches during the day. Other food service on the *Sun* includes mid-morning bouillon, afternoon snacks, elegant afternoon teas, evening sandwiches, and a midnight buffet. On Norwegian Day, passengers feast on a midday Norwegian Grand Buffet and enjoy Norwegian folk entertainment in the evening. Room service is always available, from a full menu at mealtimes and limited service at other times.

Entertainment Shipboard performances on the *Sun*, which cater to an older audience, have improved under Cunard. Hollywood celebrities and big-name entertainers are occasional headliners. In addition to the main showroom productions, there are occasional cabarets or game shows. Classical-music recitals and performances by solo harpists and pianists are common. Two movies are shown daily, and the library is stocked with 700 videotapes for cabin VCRs.

Service and Tipping Royal Viking has set the standard of service for every other luxury cruise line, and the *Sun*'s passenger-to-crew ratio is just about the best among cruise ships. Concierges handle special requests, whether you want to make a restaurant reservation ashore or hire a baby-sitter. Gratuities for cabin stewards and waiters are included in the cruise fare. Maître d's, butlers, and night stewards may be tipped for unusual service, but they never solicit a gratuity. A 15% service charge is automatically added to bar and wine purchases.

Cabins and Rates	Beds	Phone	TV	Sitting Area	Fridge	Tub	Average Per Diem*
Suite	T/K	●	●	●	●	●	$889
Outside	T/K	●	●	●	●	◑	$564

Inside	T	●	●	○	●	◐	$413

*Rates are for a 15-day world-cruise segment and include airfare. Port taxes are extra.

Cabins are oversize, beautifully furnished, and equipped with all the amenities, including walk-in closets, bathrobes, lockable drawers, TVs (including CNN), and VCRs. Penthouses, deluxe bedrooms, and 40% of the outside cabins have verandas. The remarkable Owner's Suite features a large veranda and two bathrooms, one with a whirlpool in a glassed-in alcove looking out at the ocean. Penthouses and the Owner's Suite also come with butler service. Cabins on the Promenade Deck look onto a public area.

Outlet voltage: 110/220 AC.

Single supplement: 125%–200% of double-occupancy rate.

Discounts: A third passenger in a cabin pays the minimum fare. A child under 12 sharing a cabin with two adults pays half the minimum. Various discounts are offered for repeaters, first-time cruisers, and early booking. You get a discount for arranging your own airfare.

Sports and Fitness **Health club:** Golden Door Spa at Sea with fitness classes, exercise equipment, free weights, aerobics floor, saunas, and massage.

Recreation: Aerobics and other exercise classes, badminton, croquet, golf driving, putting course, computerized golf simulator, table tennis, shuffleboard, quoits, trapshooting, two pools (one with swim-up bar), whirlpool, unobstructed circuit (4 laps = 1 mile) for jogging.

Facilities **Public rooms:** Five bars, four entertainment lounges, casino, disco, cinema, card room, library (books and videotapes), photo gallery.

Shops: Gift shops, beauty salon (with facials and massages).

Health care: Doctor and two nurses on call.

Child care: Children's programs only during Christmas cruises, baby-sitting arranged through concierge.

Services: Concierge, laundry service, dry cleaning and pressing, two launderettes, ironing room, photographer, film processing.

Accessibility Four staterooms have L-shaped bed configurations for greater wheelchair maneuverability and are specially equipped. Wheelchair users must travel with an able-bodied companion and provide their own 22-inch wheelchair.

RMS Queen Elizabeth 2

Specifications *Type of ship:* Classic liner
Cruise experience: Semi-formal/Formal
Size: 67,139 tons
Number of cabins: 900
Outside cabins: 70%
Year built: 1969

Passengers: 1,850
Crew: 1,000 (international)
Officers: British
Passenger/crew ratio: 1.8 to 1 (varies according to cabin category)

Ship's Log The *Queen Elizabeth 2* is the last of its kind: Put into service in 1969 as a transatlantic liner, the *QE2* is the only cruise ship that still makes regularly scheduled crossings of the Atlantic between New York and England and the only one that assigns passengers to dine according to their cabin class in one of five restaurants.

The ship has undergone numerous refits, including one that transformed it into a military carrier during the Falklands War. Most recently, Cunard spent $45 million to upgrade many of the cabins and create several new public rooms. Among the most noteworthy are the Golden Lion, styled after a traditional English pub and a new Lido, which, with its generous use of blond woods, floor-to-ceiling glass, and brass finishings, brings a contemporary touch to this very traditional ship. Celebrating that tradition is a new "Heritage Trail" exhibit, which showcases Cunard memorabilia and artifacts. New works of art were also commissioned, depicting Cunard ships throughout the ages. All told, the renovation consumed 8,000 gallons of paint, 40,000 square yards of carpeting were laid, and 2,000 new lighting fixtures were installed.

Despite this major investment, the *Queen Elizabeth 2* continues to show its age. Many of the problems evident before the last refurbishment were still apparent after the ship came out of dry dock. Dented and corroded ceiling panels, cracked banisters repaired with plastic packing tape, and bathroom grouting stained with mold were among the details left unimproved.

Yet, for a traditional crossing of the Atlantic, this remains the purist's choice and therein, perhaps, lies the ship's continuing appeal: It's the sole survivor of a bygone era.

Activities Without diverging from the traditional fare of bingo, "horse racing," and similar get-togethers, the *QE2* also serves up a sophisticated agenda of daily activities. These include numerous lectures and seminars, classical-music concerts, fashion shows, computer courses, and an extensive fitness program. Art-history buffs will appreciate the "Heritage Trail" displays found throughout the ship. The ship's library is one of the most impressive at sea.

Dining In terms of dining, the *QE2* is a four-class ship, and passengers are assigned to one of five dining rooms according to their cabin category. The best is the Queen's Grill, a celebrated gourmet restaurant featuring tableside cooking and roast carving, where you can order virtually anything, even if it's not on the menu. Below this room are the Princess Grill and Britannia Grill, top-notch restaurants where you can also order off the menu. The Caronia is the ship's first-class restaurant, and is also single seating. (Past passengers should note that this restaurant is now located where the Mauretania used to be, to the displeasure of some long-time cruisers.) The Mauretania room is a grand, spacious restaurant for all other passengers, and serves dinner in two seatings (6:30 and 8:30). Two or three formal evenings are held each week in all the restaurants, though dinners in the Queen's Grill, Britannia Grill, and Princess Grill are rarely casual.

On transatlantic crossings, a special supervised early dinner for children allows parents to dine on their own. Spa meals are available, but other dietary requests should be made at least three weeks ahead. The ship's wine cellar stocks more than 20,000 bottles.

Early morning coffee and pastries, a buffet breakfast and lunch, and hamburgers and hot dogs are served in the new Lido. Health-conscious passengers may opt for the breakfast (and sometimes lunch) spa buffets. Other food service includes mid-morning bouillon, a traditional high tea, and a midnight buffet; 24-hour room service from a limited menu is available.

Entertainment Foremost among the *QE2*'s new public rooms are its rebuilt public lounges. The main showroom, the Grand Lounge, has been outfitted with a new stage, dance floor, carpeting, and upgraded sound-and-light system. The former Midships Bar has been reincarnated as the Chart Room Bar; its centerpiece is the piano from the *Queen Mary*, and the truly nostalgic can listen to cocktail music before dinner here and reminisce. In these rooms and others, the "City at Sea" comes alive at night with variety shows, cabaret, classical-music concerts, disco parties, and more. A highlight of *QE2* entertainment is a series of talks given by such celebrities as Jeremy Irons, Meryl

Streep, Jason Robards, Art Buchwald, and Barbara Walters. Dance and talent contests and costume parties are also held. The liner has its own 20-station TV network. A daily newspaper is published on board.

Service and Tipping
Service in the grill- and first-class staterooms and restaurants is impeccable because that's where the most—and the best—staff members work. The service at all levels of the ship, however, is above average. Unfortunately, Cunard suffers from occasional labor problems, and there have been a few incidents of work slowdowns or stoppages. Also, some passengers find the British attitude a bit stuffy and unspontaneous. In the Mauretania Restaurant, tip the cabin steward and waiter $3 each per passenger per diem; in the Columbia Restaurant, $4; in the Queen's and Princess grills, $5. A 10% service charge is added to bar bills.

Cabins and Rates

	Beds	Phone	TV	Sitting Area	Fridge	Tub	Average Per Diem*
Grill Class	Q or T/D	●	●	●	●	●	$895–$1,223
Caronia Class	Q or T	●	●	◐	◐	◐	$615
Mauretania Class	T or U/L	●	●	○	○	○	$370

Rates are for transatlantic crossings. Airfare and port taxes are extra.

During the most recent refit, it seems that the lower category cabins got the most attention. Lower-deck accommodations revealed brand-new bathrooms upon inspection, but some upper-category cabins had old facilities that needed a good cleaning. Before booking, check carefully that your particular cabin number has been renovated, and get it in writing.

Suites accommodate up to four passengers, at no extra charge per passenger, making them more economical for a family of four than two luxury cabins. Penthouse Suites, with verandas and whirlpools, are the largest, most luxurious accommodations afloat; first-class cabins (all with VCRs) also are spacious. Luxury cabins, except No. 8184, have private verandas. Lifeboats partially obstruct the view from some cabins on the Sports Deck, and Boat Deck cabins look onto a public promenade.

Outlet voltage: 110 AC.

Single supplement: 175%–200% of double-occupancy rate; several single cabins are available at $179–$726 per diem.

Discounts: A third or fourth passenger in a cabin pays half the minimum fare in the cabin's restaurant grade. Various discounts exist for combining consecutive itineraries, booking and paying early on the World Cruise, and arranging your own airfare.

Sports and Fitness
Health club: Thalassotherapy pool, inhalation room, French hydrotherapy bath treatment, computerized nutritional and lifestyle evaluation, aerobics and exercise classes, weight machines, Lifecycles, rowers, StairMasters, treadmills, sauna, whirlpools, hydrocalisthenics, massage.

Recreation: Putting green, golf driving range, paddle tennis, table tennis, shuffleboard, tetherball, trapshooting, volleyball, two outdoor and two indoor pools, four whirlpools, sports area with separate clubhouses for adults and teens.

Facilities
Public rooms: Six bars, five entertainment lounges, casino, disco, cinema, card room, library/reading room, video-game room, execu-

tive boardroom, Epson computer center, chapel/synagogue, art gallery.

Shops: Arcade with men's formal rental shop, Harrods, designer boutiques (Burberry, Pringle, Wedgwood), florist, beauty center, barbershop.

Health care: Extensive hospital with full staff of doctors and nurses.

Child care: A nursery is staffed by two British nannies, who watch over children age two to eight. Counselors supervise children eight to 12. At breakfast and lunch, children can eat by themselves in the Lido or Pavilion cafés.

Services: Laundry service, dry cleaning, valet service, ironing room, photographer, film processing.

Accessibility   Ramps were installed in public corridors during the most recent refit, but many public rooms still have a step or two up or down. Four cabins have been refitted to accommodate wheelchair users.

MS Sagafjord and MS Vistafjord

Specifications   *Type of ship:* Cruise liner   *Passengers:* 589/736
Cruise experience: Formal   *Crew:* 352/379 (mainly
Size: 24,474/24,492 tons   Scandinavian)
Number of cabins: 321/387   *Officers:* Norwegian
Outside cabins: 90%/81%   *Passenger/crew ratio:* 1.7 to
Year built: 1965/1973   1/1.9 to 1

Ship's Log   The *Sagafjord* and *Vistafjord* add a Scandinavian touch to Cunard's British demeanor. Both are superb vessels, renowned for their European-style service and international environment. Their passengers tend to be older (late fifties and up) and more demanding than those on the *Countess* and prefer a slower pace to the hustle and bustle of the *QE2*. They also are a loyal bunch: It's easy to find passengers aboard for their fifth time or more. Both ships recently underwent $15 million refurbishments that further enhanced these already fine ships.

Though built eight years apart, the *Vistafjord* is the sister ship of the *Sagafjord*. The *Vistafjord* is slightly longer and larger; cabins are the same size, but the additional 66 staterooms mean more passengers share the same amount of public space. Among its newest creature comforts, built during the last renovation, are 11 Penthouse Suites, and a new Italian restaurant, the 40-seat Tivoli, which introduced alternative dining to the ship.

The *Sagafjord*, with its lower space and passenger–crew ratios, has captured numerous cruise-industry awards, and it deserves every accolade: From the white-glove service to the legendary cuisine, it has few peers. The new dining room, in particular, is perhaps the most elegant at sea: Passengers make their entrance from a grand staircase into a room of unusually high ceilings graced by three crystal chandeliers. Another noteworthy space is the piano bar. It's reached by a circular staircase, much like on a submarine. Two seating levels are cantilevered overlooking the outdoor decks aft, enclosed by an atrium-style wall of glass.

In all other respects there is almost no difference between the two ships. Both the dining rooms and the Grand Ballrooms can accommodate all passengers at once. Throughout the ship, indirect lighting helps to highlight the original artwork and the delicate carvings. Additional light, softened by the use of rich wood paneling and potted plants, emanates through large picture windows. The stern's elegant tiering of polished woods and white paint resembles a grand staircase.

Activities Shipboard diversions reflect the sophisticated tastes of the ships' clientele—among them, dance classes, bridge tours, video golf lessons, and card and board games. Both ships showcase leading personalities from stage and screen, as well as literary and political figures, in their onboard lecture programs.

Dining Menus may be similar to those of other cruise lines, but the food preparation and service are outstanding. Meals are served in a single seating, with a large number of one- and two-person tables. Dinner is served between 7 and 9. Every evening is at least semiformal. Both ships feature an extensive wine collection. All menus offer a healthy alternative, as well as a dessert suitable for diabetics. Special dietary requests should be made one month in advance, but culinary cravings are accommodated with no fuss.

On the Lido Deck, early morning juice and coffee, breakfast and lunch buffets, mid-morning bouillon, and afternoon tea are served. Breakfast in the Lido includes hot entrées cooked to order. The lunch buffet offers great variety, from caviar and smoked salmon at the salad bar to grilled hot dogs and hamburgers. Room service is available at any time.

Entertainment Entertainment is more low-key—with less variety but more sophistication—than aboard most ships. In addition to Broadway-style revues, you're likely to find a jazz band, a concert pianist, or an operatic performer featured. On any given night, passengers might listen to a light musical revue, dance to two different orchestras, or enjoy cabaret in the charming nightclubs. Popular special events include costume balls and theme parties.

Service and Tipping The staff are highly professional and dignified without being stuffy and are clearly interested in the convenience of the passengers. Tip the room steward $4 per passenger per diem, the waiter $5. A 15% gratuity is recommended for the wine steward.

Cabins and Rates

	Beds	Phone	TV	Sitting Area	Fridge	Tub	Average Per Diem*
Suite	Q or T/D	●	●	●	●	●	$1,123/ $894
Outside	Q or T	●	○	●	○	◑	$545/ $442
Inside	T	●	○	●	○	◑	$377/ $320

Rates include airfare. Higher rates are for Alaska (Sagafjord). Lower rates are for the Caribbean (Vistafjord). Port taxes are extra.

Scandinavian furnishings and generous use of polished wood and brass sets a nautical tone in the spacious cabins. Closets and extra cabinets are plentiful. Bathtubs are full-size. Terry-cloth robes and fresh fruit, delivered daily, are among the first-class amenities enjoyed in all cabin categories. Other luxury touches include card-key safes, refrigerators, hair dryers, and VCRs. Some staterooms have verandas and even separate sitting rooms; most have large picture windows. Lifeboats partially obstruct the view from some outside cabins on the Sun and Officer's decks. Cabins on the Promenade Deck look out onto a public area, and some are actually between decks—with the floor of the upper-level Officer's Deck cutting across the window. Cabins with televisions include CNN broadcasts.

Outlet voltage: 110 AC.

Single supplement: 175% of double-occupancy rate; some single rooms are available.

Discounts: A third or fourth passenger in a cabin pays $183–$277 per diem. You get a discount for arranging your own airfare.

Sports and Fitness

Health club: Excellent below-decks facility, with stationary bikes, rowing machines, free weights, hydrocalisthenics, sauna, massage.

Recreation: Aerobics and other exercise classes, golf driving, shuffleboard, table tennis, trapshooting, whirlpools, indoor pool, outdoor pool, unobstructed circuit (7 laps = 1 mile) for jogging.

Facilities

Public rooms: Four bars, three entertainment lounges, small casino, cinema, card room, library.

Shops: Gift shop, beauty salon, barbershop.

Health care: Doctor on call.

Child care: Baby-sitting can be arranged.

Services: Full- and self-service laundry, dry cleaning, photographer, film processing.

Accessibility

Small travel wheelchairs are needed to fit in cabin doorways and rest rooms. If advised in advance, the housekeeper will place a ramp over the ledge at the entrance to cabin bathrooms. However, bathrooms are often too small for wheelchair maneuvering. Elevators are accessible. Passengers with mobility problems are assisted ashore on tenders when seas are calm.

Sea Goddess I

Specifications

Type of ship: Cruise yacht
Cruise experience: Formal
Size: 4,250 tons
Number of cabins: 58
Outside cabins: 100%
Year built: 1984

Passengers: 116
Crew: 89 (American and European)
Officers: Norwegian
Passenger/crew ratio: 1.3 to 1

Ship's Log

Sea Goddess I was designed to raise the level of cruise luxury (and prices) to new heights, and largely, it has succeeded. Life aboard ship is unstructured, elegant, and unforgettable. Once you've paid the exorbitant fare, there are no more out-of-pocket expenses. Cruise fares really do include everything imaginable, from drinks to caviar any time of day or night. Inside and out, the *Sea Goddess I* looks like a royal yacht—from its dramatic profile and upswept twin funnels to the marble dance floor in the Main Salon and fine Oriental rugs in the lobby. A shallow draft allows it to anchor in out-of-the-way coves and unfrequented ports, where the stern's water-sports platform can be lowered for snorkeling, sailing, windsurfing, and swimming (weather permitting). Though small, this intimate, romantic ship offers ample room for 59 couples to enjoy what, in many ways, still sets the standard for luxurious vacations afloat.

Activities

No structured shipboard activities are offered; passengers set their own pace. Special-interest cruises include lectures and seminars; epicurean cruises, for example, feature guest chefs and talks by California vintners. A Golden Door Spa fitness trainer offers exercise classes and designs personal programs. At port, the accommodating staff can arrange entry to exclusive onshore clubs for tennis, golf, gambling, and dancing. The *Sea Goddess's* beach parties are renowned for endless quantities of champagne and caviar.

Dining

In the tradition of the finest restaurants, the kitchen caters to special requests, preparing dishes individually as they are ordered. The quality of the food is excellent but, given the limited kitchen space, not as good as that in the *QE2*'s Queen's Grill. Fine wines and after-dinner drinks are served, and Beluga caviar is dispensed as freely as the champagne. Meals are served in a single, open seating (dinner from 8 to 10). Two formal evenings are held each week, but passengers tend to dress elegantly every night. The Outdoor Café serves coffee, breakfast, and lunch, but full service is available any time. Room service will provide anything day or night, including full-course meals—all served on china and linen.

Entertainment Entertainment is understated, featuring perhaps a pianist or a dance trio in the piano bar, or local entertainment from the day's port of call. Since there is no showroom aboard, no production-style shows are staged. Many passengers visit the casinos or nightclubs in town while in port.

Service and Tipping With one of the best passenger-to-crew ratios, the ship offers attentive and personal service. The aim is to make you feel that all your needs, wishes, and perhaps even fantasies will be fulfilled. An elegant black-tie midnight dinner for two on the deck? No problem. Chilled champagne and caviar brought ashore to you while you sunbathe in a quiet, white-sand cove? You have but to ask. No tipping is allowed.

Cabins and Rates		Beds	Phone	TV	Sitting Area	Fridge	Tub	Average Per Diem*
	Suite	Q or T	●	●	●	●	●	$642

Rates are for the Caribbean and include airfare. Port taxes are extra.

Cabins on the *Sea Goddess I* set the standard for modern seafaring comfort. Oversize picture windows overlooking the sea top the list of amenities in the all-outside, all-suite accommodations. Each has an electronic safe, a stereo, a remote-control color TV (including CNN) and VCR, and a minibar. The refrigerator can be stocked with any food from the kitchen or any liquor, wine, or beverage you'd like, at no charge; a personal-preference form is mailed to every passenger before sailing, so the crew can stock the cabin and the kitchen accordingly. A few suites have removable adjoining walls for those who want even more space and a second bathroom; the cost is about 150% of the single-cabin rate. Cabins on Deck Five look onto the Promenade. Cabin 315 is a larger suite that doesn't cost more.

Outlet voltage: 110 AC.

Single supplement: 150%–175% of double-occupancy rate.

Discounts: You get a 50% discount for booking consecutive cruises, and a discount for arranging your own airfare.

Sports and Fitness **Health club:** Gym, sauna, massage, showers. Golden Door Spa personnel will develop individualized fitness programs.

Recreation: Skeet shooting, water sports (windsurfing, snorkeling, sailing, waterskiing off the stern swimming platform), pool, unobstructed circuit for jogging.

Facilities **Public rooms:** Three bars, two entertainment lounges, casino, library (books and videotapes).

Shops: Gift shop, beauty salon/barber.

Health care: Doctor on call.

Child care: Baby-sitting can be arranged privately.

Services: Laundry service, dry cleaning.

Accessibility Cabin doorways and rest rooms are not large enough for wheelchairs. Wheelchairs may not be taken on launches at ports where the ship must anchor offshore, preventing wheelchair users from going ashore.

Delta Queen Steamboat Company

The Fleet *American Queen*
Delta Queen
Mississippi Queen

Evocative of the great floating palaces about which Mark Twain lovingly wrote, these boats (they're *not* ships) are the only remaining overnight paddle-wheel riverboats in the country. Nostalgia is the name of the game: They ply the Mississippi River System at a leisurely 6–7 mph. The tiny, wooden *Delta Queen* is like a homey bed-and-breakfast. The *American Queen* and *Mississippi Queen* are steamboating's answer to megaships. The largest paddle wheelers ever built, they dwarf the size of the *Delta Queen*.

Ships at a Glance

	Dining Rooms	Bars	Casino	Fitness Center	Pools	Average Per Diem
American Queen	1	4	○	●	1	$397
Delta Queen	1	3	○	◐	0	$397
Mississippi Queen	1	3	○	●	0	$397

Cruise Experience Delta Queen preserves "Life on the Mississippi" with 19th-century charm, plus 20th-century air-conditioning and other newfangled doodads. These floating wedding cakes are outfitted in Victorian-style gingerbread trim, Tiffany-type stained glass, polished brass, crystal chandeliers, plush carpeting, and warm wood paneling. Public areas have cushy leather wing chairs and handsomely upholstered Chesterfield sofas. On deck, you can watch the country go by from oversize wooden rocking chairs, old-fashioned porch swings, and white-iron patio furniture—and you can do so while munching freshly made popcorn or a hot dog. Most passengers are well-heeled retirees, many of whom return time and again—the Paddlewheel Steamboatin' Society of America hosts a Champagne and Punch Reception for repeat passengers. For single women passengers sailing alone, senior gentlemen act as hosts and social partners.

A Riverlorian (the steamboat company's term for river historian) gives lively talks about the river, explains how to find mile markers and read the river charts, answers questions, lends books, and provides free binoculars. The captain's lecture is a not-to-be-missed event. Passengers can try their hands at playing the calliopes. There's little pressure to participate in anything; you can do as little or as much as you like. The size of the boats governs the scope of the onboard activities and entertainment; these are covered individual-

Chart Symbols. Ships at a Glance. ●: *Fully equipped;* ◐: *Partially equipped;* ○: *Not equipped.* Cabins and Rates. **D:** *Double bed;* **K:** *King-size bed;* **Q:** *Queen-size bed;* **T:** *Twin bed;* **U/L:** *Upper and lower berths;* ●: *All cabins have this facility;* ○: *No cabins have this facility;* ◐: *Some cabins have this facility*

ly under Ship's Log. Although Louisiana allows riverboat gambling, there are no casinos aboard.

Theme cruises are often scheduled. Topics may include the Kentucky Derby, the Civil War, baseball, and fall foliage. Two special events should be noted: One is the annual Great Steamboat Race, an 11-night cruise from New Orleans to St. Louis that steams toward the finish line on the Fourth of July. It replicates a famous 19th-century race between the *Natchez* and the *Robert E. Lee*. This is a wildly popular cruise: Crews challenge each other to tests of speed and maneuverability, pitting the *DQ* against the *MQ*, and passengers gussy up for the annual Floozy Contest. With their flags flying and calliopes whistling away, the boats race at a dizzying 12 mph or so, while landlubbers line the shore and cheer them on. At Christmas, the Bonfire cruises are also enormously popular. Replicating an age-old Cajun custom (the bonfires light the way for Papa Noel), a huge bonfire is lit along the levee, and there is a spectacular fireworks display. Shores and boat decks are lined with folks shouting Christmas greetings back and forth—and Papa Noel does pay a visit.

Dining If bigger is better, then it shows most in Delta Queen's food: The food on the *MQ* is superior to that aboard the *DQ*, and the presentation on the *MQ* is more spectacular than on the *DQ* as well. Dinner on the *MQ* is a bit dressier than on the *DQ*, but formal wear is never required. The *MQ*'s 200-seat dining room is on the Observation Deck and offers better views; the only good river view in the low-lying *DQ* dining room is from a window seat. At press time, the *American Queen* was still under construction, so no evaluation of its food was possible, but passengers should expect an experience comparable to the dining found aboard the *Mississippi Queen*.

Aboard all three boats, five meals are served daily. Dinner is scheduled in two seatings (6 and 8 on the MQ and AQ, 5:30 and 7 on the DQ). Menus are more Continental than South Louisianian, and the renditions of regional dishes are on the mild side. Every meal includes at least one "Heart Smart" selection. "Theme" meals include an old-fashioned family-style picnic, with waiters in jeans passing around huge platters of fried chicken, barbecue ribs, corn bread, corn on the cob, potato salad, and such. Passengers with special dietary needs should notify the company a month in advance. The only room service is for Continental breakfast.

Destinations and Ports of Call Because the Delta Queen Steamboat Company's ports are not covered in Chapter 2, we've tried to give you a general idea of how time is spent ashore on a typical riverboat cruise. (For detailed itineraries, *see* Chapter 3.)

The boats never paddle for more than two days without putting into port, where they are usually docked for at least a half day. Shore excursions visit plantation homes, historic towns and Civil War battlefields, sleepy villages, and major metropolises. Tours are either by bus or on foot, and, since there are scores of ports, there is a wide range available.

The excursions to Houmas House plantation ($6.50 adults, $4 children) and Nottoway Plantation ($9 adults, $3.50 children), both west of New Orleans, involve a stroll at your leisure across the levee and the lawn; tickets can be purchased on board or at the house. The Battlefield and Siege Tour ($20 adults, $15.50 children) is a three-hour bus tour of Mississippi's vast Vicksburg National Military Park. In Iowa, gambling is the name of the game on a $10, 3½-hour cruise on the *Silver Eagle*, a four-deck riverboat with slot and poker machines and 26 gaming tables. The most expensive excursion is the Cajun Tour in Baton Rouge, a 3½-hour bus tour to French Settlement ($35 per person).

In some ports the steamboat company provides a free shuttle into town. This is fine if you want to poke around on your own; however, the shore excursions are narrated and take you to plantation homes that you can't always reach on foot. In other ports, you can simply amble down the gangplank and walk to the sights.

Service and Tipping The staff and crew are extraordinarily friendly and helpful, not at all intrusive. Dining-room service is superb. The night before debarkation, instructions and envelopes for tips are left in each stateroom. Tip waiters, waitresses, and cabin attendants $3.50 per person per night; busboys $2.25 per person per night; maître d's $5 per couple per cruise; porters $1.50 per bag. An automatic 15% is added to wine and bar purchases.

For More Information Delta Queen Steamboat Co. (30 Robin St. Wharf, New Orleans, LA 70130, tel. 504/586–0631 or 800/543–1949).

American Queen

Specifications
Type of boat: Riverboat *Passengers:* 436
Cruise experience: Casual *Crew:* 165 (American)
Size: 4,700 tons *Officers:* American
Number of cabins: 222 *Passenger/crew ratio:* 2.6 to 1
Outside cabins: 75% *Year built:* 1995

Ship's Log The largest steamboat ever built for the Mississippi River system, the *American Queen* is based on the great paddle wheelers of the past. The *AQ*'s designers studied such famous river giants as the *J.M. White*, the *Robert E. Lee*, and the *New Orleans*. At the *AQ*'s stern, a huge, red paddle wheel is not just for show—its 60 tons churn the muddy Mississippi, propelling the boat forward. Two immense, black, fluted smokestacks signify the presence of authentic steam engines, salvaged from a 1930s river dredge. The retractable pilothouse was modeled after the one on the turn-of-the-century *Charles Rebstock*, another famous riverboat; on its roof stands a 6-foot-high, rooster-shaped weather vane. Inside, the nostalgia continues. At the stern, a sweeping grand staircase is based on the one once found aboard the *J.M. White*. Bookcases in the Gentlemen's Cardroom and Ladies' Parlor are stocked with firsthand accounts of exploration, how-to books, and novels from a century ago. More Victoriana can be found in the Mark Twain Gallery, a long, narrow room overlooking the dining salon. Scattered throughout the boat's various public rooms are more than 200 pieces of artwork, most in their original frames from the 1860s to 1890s.

Activities On the *AQ*, you can be as active or as relaxed as you want. On the leisurely side, you can do nothing more strenuous than write a letter in the card room or ladies' parlor, or sip a mint julep in the observation lounge. You can learn to read navigational charts and maps in the chart room, with help from the Riverlorian, or watch the world go by from a swing in the glass-enclosed Porch of America, where there's a soda fountain and a player piano. More active types can join their fellow passengers at bingo, bridge, and board games, plus dance lessons and sing-alongs.

Entertainment The evening's entertainment begins at dinner, when passengers are serenaded by a band playing antique musical instruments. The Grand Saloon is the main showroom for floor shows by night and lectures by day, and is the venue for dancing to a big band, cabarets, and vaudeville shows. The Saloon's design is especially noteworthy: It was conceived as a miniature opera house, like the ones commonly found in small river towns during the 1880s. In the Calliope Bar, entertainment on a smaller scale includes storytelling, movies, and recitals—all evocative of the Victorian era.

Cabins and Rates

	Beds	Phone	TV	Sitting Area	Fridge	Tub	Average Per Diem*
Suite	Q or T	●	○	●	○	●	$497
Outside	T	●	○	●	○	◐	$397
Inside	T	●	○	○	○	○	$227

*Rates are for a seven-night river cruise. Airfare and port taxes are extra.

Cabins continue the Victorian theme with reproduction wallpaper, floral carpeting, artwork, lighting fixtures, and period furnishings—some have authentic antique bureaus. Outside accommodations have bay windows for panoramic views of the river, private verandas, or direct access to an outdoor promenade through windowed French doors. Top-category suites are furnished with antique queen-size beds. Complimentary champagne, fresh fruit, and cheese are provided to passengers in suites and upper-category outside staterooms. Twenty-seven cabins have private verandas, while six cabins have partially obstructed views due to exterior staircases, which are shown clearly on the brochure deck plans.

Outlet voltage: 110 AC.

Single supplement: 150%–175% of double-occupancy rate.

Discounts: A third passenger in a cabin pays $100 per diem. One child 16 or younger cruises free in some staterooms, when sharing a cabin with two full-fare adults. You get a discount for booking early.

Sports and Fitness

Health club: StairMaster, stationary bikes, treadmills.

Recreation: Small swimming pool.

Facilities

Public rooms: Four bars, showroom/lecture hall, theater, card room, ladies' parlor, observation deck.

Shops: Victorian gift shop, beauty/barber shop.

Health care: None.

Child care: Passengers may make private baby-sitting arrangements with a staff or crew member.

Accessibility

Nine cabins are accessible to wheelchair users. Elevators and wide hallways are accessible; however, passengers with mobility problems are advised to travel with a companion who can assist them.

Delta Queen

Specifications

Type of boat: Riverboat	*Passengers:* 174
Cruise experience: Casual	*Crew:* 75 (American)
Size: 3,360 tons	*Officers:* American
Number of cabins: 87	*Passenger/crew ratio:* 2.3 to 1
Outside cabins: 100%	*Year built:* 1926

Ship's Log

If the *Delta Queen* were a song she'd be "Up the Lazy River." This grande dame of America's most famous river first sailed the waters of the Sacramento River and served her country during World War II as a U.S. Navy ferry on San Francisco Bay. She began cruising the Mississippi River system after World War II. In the late '60s, due to federal legislation banning boats with wooden superstructures, she seemed doomed for demolition, but the hue and cry raised by preservationists and nostalgia buffs resulted in a congressional exemption, under which she still sails. The tiny four-decker is a designated National Historic Landmark and is listed on the National Register of Historic Places. Because the boat is made of wood, smoking is restricted to designated areas and forbidden in the cabins.

Activities A person can while away a fair amount of time just sitting on deck in a rocking chair or swing. The *DQ* is really not for type-A personalities. Bingo and bridge, quilting and hat making, trivia and kite-flying contests are about as hectic as things get. Tours are conducted of the pilothouse, and passengers are encouraged to visit the engine room and have a cup of coffee with the crew, who will cheerfully show you how the engines and the 44-ton paddle operate.

Entertainment The boat is so small the dining room has to do extra duty as a lecture and concert hall, a movie theater, and a nightclub. As a result, there is a great deal of moving about of chairs and tables between meals and during various functions. The nightly floor shows range from outstanding classical ragtime concerts to corny country hoedowns. Jokes and music are geared toward the older crowd. After the show, the orchestra plays music for dancing, while up in the Texas Lounge a pianist/vocalist entertains with standards and show tunes, mostly from the '40s and '50s, as she does during the cocktail hour. Sing-alongs are also popular, and the Texas Lounge features a great Dixieland band.

Cabins and Rates

	Beds	Phone	TV	Sitting Area	Fridge	Tub	Average Per Diem*
Suite	Q or T	○	○	●	○	●	$497
Outside	Q	○	○	●	○	○	$397
Inside	Q	○	○	●	○	○	$227

Rates are for a seven-night river cruise. Airfare and port taxes are extra.

One of the standard jokes aboard the *DQ* is, "You didn't realize that the brochure picture of your cabin was actual size, did you?" They *are* quite tiny (baths are minuscule), but all cabins are outside. A slight disadvantage here is that in order to have any privacy it's necessary to keep your shades or shutters closed: There is a lot of activity on the wraparound decks. Accommodations on the Cabin Deck have inside entrances, while those on the Sun and Texas decks have outside entrances. The most charming aspect of these small accommodations is their original wood paneling. All also come with complimentary soap, shampoo, and body lotion, wall-to-wall carpeting, and limited closet and storage space. Suites 307 and 308 are up front, on either side of the pilothouse. Superior staterooms 117, 118, 121, and 122 on the Cabin Deck, and staterooms 207, 208, 227, 228, and 230 on the Texas Deck, have partially obstructed river views. Complimentary champagne, fresh fruit, and cheese are provided to passengers in suites and superior staterooms.

Outlet voltage: 110 AC.

Single supplement: 150%–175% of double-occupancy rate.

Discounts: No cabins accommodate third or fourth passengers. There is a discount for booking early.

Sports and Fitness **Health club:** Stationary bike, rowing machine.

Recreation: Unobstructed circuits for jogging.

Facilities **Public rooms:** Three lounges.

Shops: Gift shop.

Health care: None.

Child care: Passengers may make private baby-sitting arrangements with a crew member.

Accessibility The *Delta Queen* has no facilities for wheelchair users. However, passengers with mobility problems can travel aboard the boat provided they can traverse stairways.

Mississippi Queen

Specifications *Type of boat:* Riverboat   *Passengers:* 420
Cruise experience: Casual   *Crew:* 165 (American)
Size: 3,364 tons   *Officers:* American
Number of cabins: 207   *Passenger/crew ratio:* 2.6 to 1
Outside cabins: 64%   *Year built:* 1976

Ship's Log The seven-deck *Mississippi Queen* combines the traditions of steamboating with resort-style facilities. She was built in 1976 at a cost of $27 million and refurbished in 1989. There is infinitely more space, in public areas, on decks, and in the cabins, than aboard the *DQ*. Her huge calliope is the world's largest. Some passengers debark without ever having completely gotten their bearings.

Activities In addition to bingo, bridge, masquerades, lectures, and contests, the *MQ* offers a gym with exercise machines, classes, a sauna, and whirlpool; shuffleboard; full-service beauty shop (perms, cuts, facials, manicures); a first-run movie theater (*Showboat* is frequently screened); a library; and a conference center with audiovisual equipment.

Entertainment As on the *AQ*, evening entertainment centers on floor shows in the Grand Saloon. There are cabarets with Dixieland bands, ragtime and rinky-dink piano sessions, banjo players, and singers and dancers; the *MQ*'s renditions of the Andrews Sisters, Sophie Tucker, and Al Jolson; Mardi Gras bashes; Broadway-style show revues; and barbershop quartets. The ship employs two "dance hosts," who dance with single female passengers. The bars and lounges are large and lively—the Paddlewheel Lounge is a glitzy, two-tier affair on the Observation and Texas decks.

Cabins and Rates

	Beds	Phone	TV	Sitting Area	Fridge	Tub	Average Per Diem*
Suite	Q or T	●	○	●	○	●	$497
Outside	T	●	○	●	○	●	$397
Inside	T	●	○	●	○	●	$227

*Rates are for a seven-night river cruise. Airfare and port taxes are extra.

While none of the staterooms is huge, and some are quite small, they're great places to settle in and contemplate the river in peace and quiet. Utilitarian furnishings evoke little in the way of character, and the wood paneling found aboard the *DQ* is absent. But closet and storage space, while not vast, is more generous than on the *DQ*. Of the outside cabins, 94 have private verandas. Inside cabins, however, are not for the claustrophobic. The four Victorian-style suites are another story entirely. Two are adjacent to the pilothouse, with windows facing forward and to the side for a captain's-eye view of the river; two are adjacent to the paddle wheel, with its lulling, sleep-inducing sounds. Staterooms 131, 132, 141, 220, 221, 327, and 328 have partially obstructed river views. Suites, and some outside and inside staterooms, can accommodate more than two passengers. Complimentary champagne, fresh fruit, and cheese are provided passengers in suites and superior staterooms.

Outlet voltage: 110 AC.

Single supplement: 150%–175% of double-occupancy rate.

Discounts: A third passenger in a cabin pays $100 per diem. One child 16 or younger cruises free in some staterooms, when sharing a cabin with two full-fare adults. You get a discount for booking early.

Sports and Fitness
Health club: Stationary bike, treadmill, exercise classes, stair climber.

Recreation: Shuffleboard, sauna, whirlpool spa.

Facilities
Public rooms: Three bars, two lounges, showroom, lecture hall, theater/conference center, library, game room, activity center.

Shops: Gift shop, beauty/barbershop.

Health care: None.

Child care: Passengers may make private baby-sitting arrangements with a staff or crew member.

Accessibility
There is one cabin accessible to wheelchair users. Elevators and wide hallways are accessible; however, passengers with mobility problems are advised to travel with a companion who can assist them.

Dolphin Cruise Line

Dolphin IV

The Fleet SS *Dolphin IV*
SS *OceanBreeze*
SS *SeaBreeze*

Under the Dolphin banner sail a collection of steam-powered older ships. All are 35–40 years old and have been refitted since Dolphin was founded in 1984.

Ships at a Glance

	Dining Rooms	Bars	Casino	Fitness Center	Pools	Average Per Diem
Dolphin IV	1	4	●	○	1	$191
OceanBreeze	1	3	●	●	1	$235
SeaBreeze	1	5	●	◑	1	$192

Cruise Experience While there never has been anything fancy about a Dolphin cruise, passengers get their money's worth, and perhaps a bit more. Despite its fleet of older vessels, the line has established a reputation for caring about its passengers. Value is the word most often associated with Dolphin—which keeps a loyal following coming back again and again. Unlike some lower-price cruise lines, Dolphin offers a comprehensive shipboard account system: Passengers sign for all purchases and settle their accounts at the end of the cruise.

Activities For adults, Dolphin includes all the typical ocean-liner diversions, such as bingo, pool games, dance classes, and trivia contests. As the official cruise line of Hanna-Barbera, Dolphin's children's program features youth counselors dressed as Yogi Bear, Fred Flintstone, and other cartoon characters, who frolic with kids and lead such daily events as scavenger hunts, teen parties, and talent shows. The tiny island that the *Dolphin IV* visits for its private beach parties is one of the most picturesque.

Dining Menus are extensive and innovative, and food quality is well above average. Children's menus reflect the Hanna-Barbera theme with such specialties as the "Astro Dog" or "Zoinks Sundae." Waiters hustle and go out of their way to please; what's more, they're genuinely friendly, not just tip-hungry. There are two assigned seatings per meal. A pianist entertains at dinner (6 and 8). Formal nights are scheduled twice on every weeklong cruise and once on every three- or four-day sailing. Make special dietary requests in writing seven days before sailing.

Buffet breakfast and lunch in the open-air cafés are excellent, by any standard. Other food service includes 24-hour self-serve coffee and

Chart Symbols. Ships at a Glance. ●: *Fully equipped;* ◑: *Partially equipped;* ○: *Not equipped.* Cabins and Rates. D: *Double bed;* K: *King-size bed;* Q: *Queen-size bed;* T: *Twin bed;* U/L: *Upper and lower berths;* ●: *All cabins have this facility;* ○: *No cabins have this facility;* ◑: *Some cabins have this facility*

tea, afternoon cookies and cake, a midnight buffet, and 24-hour room service from a limited menu.

Entertainment Shows in the main lounge feature the usual variety of singers, comedians, and jugglers. An orchestra performs nightly for dancing.

Service and Tipping Staff members are energetic, thorough, and unusually personable. Tip the room steward $3.50 per passenger per diem, the waiter $3, the busboy $1.50. The maître d' should get $4 per passenger per cruise, the wine steward or bartender 15% of your final tab.

Destinations Except for the *OceanBreeze*, which makes Aruba its home port for southern Caribbean and Panama Canal sailings, all Dolphin ships sail from Miami to the Bahamas and the Caribbean. (For detailed itineraries, *see* Chapter 3.)

For More Information Dolphin Cruise Line (901 South America Way, Miami, FL 33132, tel. 800/992-4299).

SS Dolphin IV

Specifications

Type of ship: Cruise liner	*Passengers:* 588
Cruise experience: Casual	*Crew:* 285 (international)
Size: 13,007 tons	*Officers:* Greek
Number of cabins: 294	*Passenger/crew ratio:* 2.1 to 1
Outside cabins: 70.4%	*Year built:* 1956

Ship's Log The *Dolphin IV* was the freighter *Ithaca* before Dolphin bought it more than a decade ago; it was last renovated in 1991. A masterful conversion enlarged the ship's superstructure and gave the stern a terrace. The ship's design yields more usable space than most other small ships, although it carries a comparatively high number of passengers. The interior combines classic wood paneling and brass trim with bright, upbeat colors and large windows. The Barbizon Restaurant is narrow, with a low ceiling, but mirrors along the walls help create a sense of space and light. The Lido is remarkably well organized, with service divided between a cold buffet and a barbecue; passengers seldom must stand in line. Indeed, for comfort, convenience, and variety, the *Dolphin IV*'s Lido is one of the best. The disco, however, is small and claustrophobic, located deep in the belly of the ship and accessible only via a flight of steep steps.

Cabins and Rates

	Beds	Phone	TV	Sitting Area	Fridge	Tub	Average Per Diem*
Suite	D	●	○	●	○	○	$225
Outside	D, T, or U/L	●	○	○	○	○	$191
Inside	D, T, or U/L	●	○	○	○	○	$145

Airfare and port taxes are extra.

Cabins are small but perfectly adequate for short cruises. Desks and dressers are laminated in white and other colors. Views from some outside cabins on the Boat Deck are partially obstructed.

Outlet voltage: 110/220 AC.

Single supplement: 150% of double-occupancy rate.

Discounts: A third or fourth passenger in a cabin pays $30–$50 per diem. You get a discount of up to $200 per passenger for booking 90 days in advance.

Sports and Fitness **Recreation:** Aerobics, table tennis, shuffleboard, skeet shooting, pool, unobstructed circuit for jogging.

Facilities **Public rooms:** Four bars, two entertainment lounges, casino, disco, card room, small library/movie room, video-game room.

Shops: Gift shop, beauty salon/barber.

Health care: Doctor on call.

Child care: Playroom, baby-sitting, youth programs with counselors year-round.

Services: Photographer.

Accessibility Cabins on the Atlantis Deck, the Boat Deck, or the forward Barbizon Deck are recommended for wheelchair users. Lower decks and several public areas are not accessible, but public lavatories are accessible to passengers using standard-size wheelchairs. Passengers with mobility problems must be accompanied by a an able-bodied companion.

SS OceanBreeze

Specifications *Type of ship:* Classic liner   *Passengers:* 776
Cruise experience: Casual   *Crew:* 310 (international)
Size: 21,667 tons   *Officers:* Greek
Number of cabins: 384   *Passenger/crew ratio:* 2.5 to 1
Outside cabins: 61.3%   *Year built:* 1955

Ship's Log The *OceanBreeze* is Dolphin's most elegant ship, although it's still far more casual than a Princess or even a Royal Caribbean vessel. Fans of the now-defunct Admiral Cruise Lines may remember the *OceanBreeze* in its former life as the *Azure Seas*. After joining the line in 1992, it underwent extensive renovations. Though still no luxury ship, Dolphin has brightened the decor, remodeled cabins, and added a children's room. Probably the ship's most stunning feature is the huge two-level casino on the Boat and Promenade decks, where you can chance it on 123 slot machines or try your luck in every other kind of gambling endeavor imaginable. The atmosphere is decidedly festive and upbeat. Passengers are welcomed aboard with an introductory show and verbal tour of the ship in the Rendezvous Lounge. The evening entertainment is lively and professional; rollicking theme nights include country-and-western and rock-and-roll parties.

Cabins and Rates

	Beds	Phone	TV	Sitting Area	Fridge	Tub	Average Per Diem*
Suite	D	●	●	●	●	●	$292
Outside	D	●	○	○	○	○	$235
Inside	D	●	○	○	○	○	$170

*Airfare and port taxes are extra.

Because this is an older vessel, cabins are fairly large. The new decor is a tasteful array of muted blues, pinks, and greens. All cabins have a double or two lower beds, plenty of closet and dresser space, and carpeting, and are minimally equipped with climate control and a radio. The plush Owner's Suite is a two-bedroom pad with all the usual amenities plus a minibar. Outside cabins on the Atlantis Deck look out onto a public promenade.

Outlet voltage: 110/220 AC.

Single supplement: 150% of double-occupancy rate.

Discounts: A third or fourth passenger in a cabin pays $70 per diem. You get a discount of up to $900 per cabin for early booking.

Sports and Fitness	**Health club:** Exercise equipment, whirlpool, sauna. **Recreation:** Table tennis, heated pool.
Facilities	**Public rooms:** Three bars and lounges, casino, disco, cinema, card room/library, video-game room, meeting room. **Shops:** Gift shop, beauty salon/barber. **Health care:** Doctor on call. **Child care:** Playroom, baby-sitting, youth programs with counselors year-round. **Services:** Laundry service, dry cleaning, photographer, film processing.
Accessibility	Passengers with mobility problems must be accompanied by an able-bodied adult companion.

SS SeaBreeze

Specifications	*Type of ship:* Classic liner *Cruise experience:* Casual *Size:* 21,010 tons *Number of cabins:* 421 *Outside cabins:* 62.5%	*Passengers:* 840 *Crew:* 400 (international) *Officers:* Greek *Passenger/crew ratio:* 2.1 to 1 *Year built:* 1958

Ship's Log The *SeaBreeze* was completely refurbished when it joined the Dolphin fleet in 1989, having previously seen service as Premier's *Royale* and Costa's *Frederico 'C*. The exterior is not beautiful, with twin cargo booms on the fo'c'sle, a bulky superstructure, and a large, squarish stack amidships. But the *SeaBreeze* does offer plenty of deck space, easily accommodating the small swimming pool and three honeycomb-shape whirlpools—maybe the most popular attractions on board. The interior is appointed in shades of blue, lavender, and peach, and the ship retains many of its original brass fixtures.

Cabins and Rates

	Beds	Phone	TV	Sitting Area	Fridge	Tub	Average Per Diem*
Suite	Q or T	●	○	●	○	●	$229
Outside	D, T, or U/L	●	○	○	○	◐	$192
Inside	D, T, or U/L	●	○	○	○	○	$136

*Airfare and port taxes are extra.

Cabins are small and simply furnished in a melange of blues, greens, and yellows. Mirrors are employed generously. Furniture is minimal. Only suites have desks; standard cabins have pull-out writing tables. Outside cabins on the Daphne Deck look onto a public promenade, and the view from most outside cabins on La Bohème Deck is obstructed by lifeboats.

Outlet voltage: 110/220 AC.

Single supplement: 150% of double-occupancy rate.

Discounts: A third or fourth passenger in a cabin pays $70 per diem. You get a discount of up to $700 per cabin for early booking.

Sports and Fitness	**Health club:** Exercise equipment, two whirlpools, massage. **Recreation:** Aerobics, basketball, golf driving, table tennis, scuba and snorkeling lessons, shuffleboard, skeet shooting, pool, unobstructed circuit for jogging.

Facilities **Public rooms:** Five bars, four entertainment lounges, casino, disco, cinema, video-game room.

Shops: Gift shop, beauty salon/barber.

Health care: Doctor on call.

Child care: Playroom, baby-sitting, youth programs with counselors year-round.

Services: Laundry service, dry cleaning, photographer, film processing.

Accessibility Public areas are accessible to wheelchair users, although bathroom and cabin entrances have doorsills. Cabin bathroom doorways are 20 inches wide. Passengers with mobility problems must travel with an able-bodied adult companion.

Fantasy Cruises

The Fleet SS *Britanis*

This is the oldest ship in the Americas, dating from 1932. Rather than polish and glitz, it has a distinct personality—a quality that is often missing on some of the large, cookie-cutter cruise ships being built today. As of press time, the *Britanis* was under long-term charter to the U.S. military. It was, however, expected to resume cruising under the Fantasy banner at the conclusion of that agreement.

Ship at a Glance

	Dining Rooms	Bars	Casino	Fitness Center	Pools	Average Per Diem
Britanis	1	5	●	◑	2	$180

Cruise Experience Fantasy makes no claim to be a luxury line; it is, rather, the budget version of its upscale sister, Celebrity Cruises. Lively, organized activities and plentiful shore excursions characterize Fantasy cruises, which are among the least expensive available. Not surprisingly, the low prices and many discounts—available to senior citizens, honeymooners, and even groups of friends—attract people on a budget. A large share of passengers are young couples (average age: mid-forties). Many travel with children—kids under 12 sail free on some cruises. Unfortunately, it's difficult to forget about money once you're aboard. Fantasy is a cash-and-carry cruise line: Only bar drinks can be signed for—everything else must be paid for in cash.

Activities Shipboard life centers on organized group games, including such mainstays as trivia and dance contests, the shipboard version of the Honeymoon Game, and poolside fun. The atmosphere is convivial and decidedly informal, with passengers often finding themselves caught up in a bridge game with the sociable Greek officers. Impromptu Greek dance classes are not uncommon.

Dining Food is among the best aboard any budget line and even compares favorably with a number of more expensive lines. Cuisine, tailored to the American palate, features such standbys as lobster, steak, and cream soups, prepared with a traditional European influence. Continental specialties appear at each meal, and rich desserts round out the menus. Meals are served at two assigned seatings (dinner at 6:30 and 8:30). Two formal evenings are held each week, but men seldom don anything fancier than a sport jacket and tie—this is not a tuxedo crowd. Special dietary requests should be made in writing at least two weeks before sailing. Early morning tea or coffee, breakfast, and lunch buffets are served on the Lido, although the fare is a poor second choice to the dining room. Other food service includes

---

Chart Symbols. Ships at a Glance. ●: *Fully equipped;* ◑: *Partially equipped;* ○: *Not equipped.* Cabins and Rates. **D:** *Double bed;* **K:** *King-size bed;* **Q:** *Queen-size bed;* **T:** *Twin bed;* **U/L:** *Upper and lower berths;* ●: *All cabins have this facility;* ○: *No cabins have this facility;* ◑: *Some cabins have this facility*

mid-morning bouillon, afternoon tea, and a midnight buffet. Room service from a limited menu is available 24 hours.

Entertainment Fantasy's entertainment follows the typical ocean liner formula in presenting run-of-the-mill acts and entertainers. There are no celebrities or big-name acts, and there's a distinct lack of flair overall. Nevertheless, the variety shows, passenger talent contests, and masquerade contests are all infused with the same bonhomie that enlivens the daytime activities.

Service and Tipping Fantasy Cruises employs a large number of crew members, partially because its older vessel requires more hands and partially to ensure that passengers receive plenty of attention and service. Tip the room steward and the waiter $2.50 each per passenger per diem, the busboy $1.20, and the maître d' and chief steward $1 each. Tip the wine steward 15%. A 15% service charge is added to any purchase for which you sign at the bar.

Destinations The *Britanis* makes a circumnavigation of South America each fall and sails to the western Caribbean the rest of the year. It is expected to resume these itineraries when it returns to cruise service.

For More Information Fantasy Cruises (5200 Blue Lagoon Dr., Miami, FL 33126, tel. 800/423–2100).

SS Britanis

Specifications

Type of ship: Classic liner	*Passengers:* 926
Cruise experience: Casual	*Crew:* 532 (international)
Size: 26,000 tons	*Officers:* Greek
Number of cabins: 463	*Passenger/crew ratio:* 1.7 to 1
Outside cabins: 38.6%	*Year built:* 1932

Ship's Log Built in the '30s as a transpacific liner and used as a troop carrier during World War II, the *Britanis* is the oldest cruise ship still sailing in the Western Hemisphere. It is also one of only a handful of American-built ships still in service (*see* American Hawaii Cruises, *above*). After many changes in name and decor, the ship still retains the look and feel of an old ocean liner. It is, for example, one of the few passenger ships still sailing that has twin smokestacks, one slightly forward and the other slightly astern. Many original fixtures, such as teak decks and brass fittings, remain, although not all in pristine condition. Much of the interior is art deco.

Cabins and Rates

	Beds	Phone	TV	Sitting Area	Fridge	Tub	Average Per Diem*
Suite	D or T	●	○	○	○	○	$260
Outside	D or T	●	○	○	○	○	$180
Inside	T	●	○	○	○	○	$100

Airfare and port taxes are extra.

The *Britanis* has one of the highest percentages of inside, windowless cabins of any cruise ship. As is typical of cabins on converted ocean liners, there is more closet space but fewer amenities—such as radios, TVs, and minibars—than on newer ships.

Outlet voltage: 110 AC.

Single supplement: 150%–200% of double-occupancy rate.

Discounts: Passengers 65 or older receive a 50% discount when traveling with another full-paying passenger. Children under two sail free; children 2–12 traveling with a full-paying adult receive a discount. A third or fourth passenger in a cabin pays about $65–$95 per diem.

Sports and Fitness

Health club: Small gym with stationary bikes and fitness machines, sauna.

Recreation: Aerobics and other exercise classes, golf putting, table tennis, shuffleboard, skeet shooting, pool, partially obstructed circuits (9 laps = 1 mile; 6 laps around the Boat Deck = 1 mile) for jogging.

Facilities

Public rooms: Five bars, three entertainment lounges, casino, disco, cinema, card room/library, game room, TV lounge, smoking room, no-smoking lounge.

Shops: Gift shops, beauty salon/barber.

Health care: Doctor on call.

Child care: Youth programs with counselors during holidays and in summer, baby-sitting arranged privately with crew member.

Services: Laundry service, photographer, film processing.

Accessibility There are no facilities specifically equipped for wheelchair users.

Holland America Line

Rotterdam

The Fleet MS *Maasdam*
MS *Nieuw Amsterdam*
MS *Noordam*
SS *Rotterdam*
MS *Ryndam*
MS *Statendam*
MS *Veendam*
MS *Westerdam*

When you sail aboard a Holland America vessel, you know you're on a ship. Nautical antiques and memorabilia, from historic artifacts to nostalgic soap boxes, reflect the line's 100-year-plus seafaring heritage. All the line's vessels were originally built for Holland America except the *Westerdam*, which was purchased as the *Homeric* from Home Lines, stretched, and rechristened. Four new sister ships, the *Statendam*, *Maasdam*, *Ryndam*, and *Veendam* are the biggest and most spacious the line has ever built.

Ships at a Glance

	Dining Rooms	Bars	Casino	Fitness Center	Pools	Average Per Diem
Maasdam/Ryndam Statendam/Veendam	1	7	●	●	2	$320
Nieuw Amsterdam Noordam	1	8	●	●	2	$285
Rotterdam	1	7	●	●	2	$353
Westerdam	1	7	●	●	2	$285

Cruise Experience Founded in 1873, Holland America is one of the oldest names in cruising. Steeped in the traditions of the transatlantic crossing, its cruises are conservative affairs renowned for their grace and gentility. No money changes hands (you sign for everything), and loudspeaker announcements are kept to a minimum. A noteworthy feature is the Passport to Fitness program, combining fitness activities and spa cuisine. Participation in shore excursions and special activities is emphasized, but passengers are otherwise left to their own devices.

Holland America passengers tend to be better educated, older, and less active than those traveling on sister line Carnival's ships, but younger and less affluent than those on a cruise line like Cunard Royal Viking. Passenger satisfaction is high, as is the percentage of repeat passengers. Holland America is known throughout the industry for its almost fanatical devotion to safety and sanitation. All ships exceed every international safety standard, and kitchens and

Chart Symbols. Ships at a Glance. ●: *Fully equipped;* ◑: *Partially equipped;* ○: *Not equipped.* Cabins and Rates. **D:** *Double bed;* **K:** *King-size bed;* **Q:** *Queen-size bed;* **T:** *Twin bed;* **U/L:** *Upper and lower berths;* ●: *All cabins have this facility;* ○: *No cabins have this facility;* ◑: *Some cabins have this facility*

dining rooms are exceptionally clean. Like only a few other lines, it maintains its own school (in Indonesia) to train staff members, rather than hiring them out of a union hall.

If you're looking for a refined and relaxing cruise, you'll never go wrong taking one of Holland America's ships or shore excursions. If, however, you like dawn-to-midnight entertainment, nonstop partying, or lots of young families on board, you should probably choose another cruise line.

Activities Holland America offers the full complement of organized group activities, such as poolside games, dance classes, trivia contests, and bingo, as well as the more offbeat karaoke machines, which allow passengers to sing along with orchestrated recordings. Nevertheless, relaxing in a deck chair and letting the world take care of itself while the ship's staff takes care of you is the prime attraction of a Holland America cruise.

Dining Food is good by cruise-ship standards, served on Rosenthal china. The emphasis is on American cuisine, with an occasional Dutch or Indonesian dish for variety. Dinner menus often include fish fresh from the market in that day's port of call, and every menu includes a spa selection. Special dinner menus are available for children. Breakfast and lunch are open seating; dinner is served at two assigned seatings (6:15 and 8:15). There are two formal evenings each week, three during a 10-day cruise. Special diets are catered to if requests are made one month in advance.

The menus for Holland America's breakfast and lunch buffets, served in the Lido, often outdo its dining-room selections. Once during each cruise there's an Indonesian lunch and an outdoor barbecue dinner. Every day there's a deck lunch of barbecued hot dogs and hamburgers, pasta, stir-fries, or make-your-own tacos. The Lido also features a self-serve ice-cream/frozen-yogurt parlor. Other food service includes mid-morning bouillon or iced tea, traditional afternoon tea served in an inside lounge, and hot hors d'oeuvres served during the cocktail hour. Passengers can help themselves to tea and coffee at any time; 24-hour room service is available from a limited menu.

Entertainment Apart from a disco, the entertainment is slanted toward an older audience. Main lounge shows, offered twice nightly, feature big-band sounds, comedy, magic and dance acts, and revues. You'll also find dance orchestras, a piano bar, string trios, and dance quartets. The Filipino members of the crew put on a show once during each cruise and there also is a passenger talent show one evening. Cabin TVs, standard on all ships except the *Rotterdam*, have superb closed-circuit service, including CNN broadcasts. Rare appearances are made by big-name performers and guest lecturers.

Service and Tipping In the 1970s Holland America adopted a "no tips required" policy. Staff members perform their duties with great pride and professionalism. In turn, passengers don't feel the pressure or the discomfort of having crew members solicit tips. As it happens, about 80% of Holland passengers give tips comparable to those recommended on other lines—but entirely at their own discretion. Perhaps that's because the crew seems to take a genuine, personal interest in passengers, learning not only their names but habits and personal preferences.

As Holland America absorbs its new ships, service has been spotty at times. Passengers may experience some momentary lapses, but they will also find the finer moments that Holland America has become known for—bartenders who make personalized bookmarks for guests and roll napkins into flowers for the ladies, for example.

Destinations In the Western Hemisphere, Holland America offers six different Caribbean itineraries, two Alaska itineraries, Panama Canal transits, and sailings to Hawaii. (For detailed itineraries, *see* Chapter 3.)

For More Information Holland America Line (300 Elliott Ave. W, Seattle, WA 98119, tel. 800/426–0327).

MS Maasdam, MS Ryndam, MS Statendam, and MS Veendam

Specifications

Type of ship: Cruise liner
Cruise experience: Semi-formal
Size: 55,451 tons
Number of Cabins: 633
Outside cabins: 77%

Passengers: 1,266
Crew: 571 (Indonesian and Filipino)
Officers: Dutch
Passenger/crew ratio: 2.2 to 1
Years built: 1993–1996

Ship's Log These ships can best be described as classic-revival, combining the old and new in one neat package. From the outside, they look bigger than their 55,000 tons, thanks to their megaship profile. Inside, they dramatically express Holland America's past in a two-tier dining room, replete with dual grand staircases framing an orchestra balcony—the latter first introduced on the *Nieuw Amsterdam* of 1938.

Although these four ships are structurally identical, Holland America has given each its own distinct personality. Layout and decor of the public rooms differ from ship to ship; it is here that parent company Carnival's influence shows. For the first time, public rooms have whimsical themes. The Crow's Nest on the *Statendam* draws its inspiration from *Composition with Red, Blue and Yellow* by Dutch abstract painter Piet Mondrian. The same room on the *Maasdam* evokes Alaska's northern lights; the theme on the *Ryndam* is the glaciers of Alaska. (At press time, details on the *Veendam*'s public rooms were unavailable.)

The *Statendam* and *Ryndam* are more typical of Holland America than the *Maasdam*. In a central, three-story atrium, a fountain of bronze mermaids or fish, respectively, state the ships' connection to the sea. On the *Maasdam*, this space is occupied by a modern, green glass sculpture of no nautical significance. Similarly, a wall of televisions on the *Maasdam* displays computer-generated video art.

A big improvement on these ships over some previous Holland America cruise liners is the tiered showroom, where terraced seating creates good lines of sight all around. Aboard the *Maasdam*, notice the depictions of Henry Hudson's ship, the *Half Moon*, on the showroom light fixtures—a fitting reminder of Holland America's maritime heritage.

Cabins and Rates

	Beds	Phone	TV	Sitting Area	Fridge	Tub	Average Per Diem*
Suite	T/Q	●	●	●	○	●	$370
Outside	T/Q	●	●	●	○	●	$320
Inside	T/Q	●	●	●	○	●	$270

*Rates are for the Caribbean. Airfare and port taxes are extra.

Every standard cabin comes with a small sitting area with a sofa; outside cabins have tubs in the bath, inside cabins just showers. All have wall-mounted hair dryers. Closet space is excellent, but drawer space is limited. Color schemes are in muted blues, peaches, and grays, with plenty of wood paneling. A fruit basket is refilled each day, and every passenger gets a canvas tote bag. Penthouse Suites are huge and all deluxe staterooms and suites have verandas, whirl-pool tubs, VCRs, and minibars.

Outlet voltage: 110 AC.

Single supplement: 200% of double-occupancy rates in suites and deluxe staterooms, 150% elsewhere.

Discounts: A third or fourth passenger pays about $130–$150 per diem. You get discounts for booking early and for arranging your own airfare.

Sports and Fitness

Health club: Hydro-fitness exercise equipment, Lifecycles, Life-steps, treadmills, massage, aerobics studio, saunas, steam rooms.

Recreation: Fitness programs and classes, shuffleboard, skeet shooting, two whirlpools, two pools (one with retractable glass roof), practice tennis courts (*Maasdam* and *Ryndam*), unobstructed circuit on wraparound promenade (4 laps = 1 mile) for jogging, cushioned jogging track (14.5 laps = 1 mile; *Statendam* only).

Facilities

Public rooms: Seven bars, five lounges, showroom, casino, disco, cinema, card and puzzle room, video-game room, meeting rooms.

Shops: Several boutiques and gift shops, beauty salon/barber.

Health care: Doctors and nurses on board.

Child care: Youth programs with counselors offered when demand warrants it; baby-sitting arranged privately with crew members.

Services: Full- and self-service laundry, dry cleaning, photographer, film processing.

Accessibility Six cabins are specially equipped for wheelchair users. Corridors are wide, elevators and public lavatories are accessible.

MS Nieuw Amsterdam and MS Noordam

Specifications

Type of ship: Cruise liner
Cruise experience: Semi-formal
Size: 33,930 tons
Number of cabins: 607
Outside cabins: 68%

Passengers: 1,214
Crew: 542 (Indonesian and Filipino)
Officers: Dutch
Passenger/crew ratio: 2.2 to 1
Year built: 1983/1984

Ship's Log The N-ships, as they are sometimes called, evoke the days of Dutch exploration, from early New York to India. Dutch nautical antiques, scattered liberally throughout, give the vessels a sense of identity and history. Passengers will be struck by how conveniently laid out and comfortable the liners are. Although these ships are not particularly large, their designers managed to capture a sense of space with extra-wide teak promenades, oversize public rooms, and wide corridors. It's hard to pick a favorite room from among the many bars and lounges; however, with their polished hardwood floors and twin balconies, the Admiral's Lounge on the *Noordam* and the Stuyvesant Lounge on the *Nieuw Amsterdam* are always popular.

Cabins and Rates

	Beds	Phone	TV	Sitting Area	Fridge	Tub	Average Per Diem*
Suite	K	●	●	●	●	●	$316
Outside	Q or T	●	●	○	○	◑	$285
Inside	Q or T	●	●	○	○	○	$260

Rates are for the Caribbean. Airfare and port taxes are extra.

Cabins are spotless, comfortable, and relatively large. The Art Deco–inspired Northern European furnishings are among the most handsome to be found aboard any cruise ship. A fruit basket is refilled each day, and every passenger gets a canvas tote bag. Views from most cabins on the Boat and Navigation decks (including the Staterooms Deluxe) are partially obstructed.

Outlet voltage: 110/220 AC.

Single supplement: 200% of double-occupancy rate in Staterooms Deluxe, 150% elsewhere. Holland America can arrange for two same-sex adults to share a cabin at the double-occupancy rate.

Discounts: A third or fourth passenger in a cabin pays $60–$108 (Caribbean) or $79–$100 (Alaska) per diem. You get discounts for booking early and for arranging your own airfare.

Sports and Fitness   **Health club:** Jogging and rowing machines, stationary bicycles, barbells, isometric pulleys, massage, dual saunas, loofah scrubs, Kerstin facials, health-care program.

Recreation: Exercise classes, golf putting, paddle and deck tennis, shuffleboard, trapshooting, two pools, whirlpool, unobstructed circuit (5 laps = 1 mile) for jogging.

Facilities   **Public rooms:** Eight bars, three entertainment lounges, casino, disco, cinema, card room, library, video-game room, computer room.

Shops: Boutiques, gift shop, beauty salon/barber.

Health care: Doctor on call.

Child care: Youth programs with counselors offered when demand warrants it, baby-sitting arranged privately with crew member.

Services: Full- and self-service laundry, dry cleaning, photographer, film processing.

Accessibility   Elevators and four staterooms on each ship are accessible to wheelchair users. They are Category-B cabins, which are Deluxe Outside Double rooms on the Navigation Deck.

SS Rotterdam

Specifications   *Type of ship:* Classic liner
Cruise experience: Semi-formal
Size: 38,645 tons
Number of cabins: 575
Outside cabins: 53%

Passengers: 1,075
Crew: 603 (Indonesian and Filipino)
Officers: Dutch
Passenger/crew ratio: 1.8 to 1
Year built: 1959

Ship's Log   The *Rotterdam*, the flagship of the line, carries the name of four previous Holland America ships, including the line's very first vessel. The current *Rotterdam* was launched in 1959 as a transatlantic liner, rebuilt in 1969 for cruising, and last refurbished in 1989. At that time the ship was given a brighter look, including new carpets and upholstery throughout and new tile for the pool. However, the beautiful wood floors, decks, and paneling have been retained, as were the shopping arcade and one of the largest double-decker movie theaters afloat. Although significantly larger than the N-ships, the *Rotterdam* carries fewer passengers. On the upper promenade deck is the impressive Ritz Carlton ballroom, with two levels connected by a curved grand staircase. The ceiling lighting in the ballroom is dazzling.

Cabins and Rates	Beds	Phone	TV	Sitting Area	Fridge	Tub	Average Per Diem*
Suite	Q	●	○	●	●	●	$474
Outside	D or T	●	○	◐	○	◐	$353
Inside	D or T	●	○	○	○	◐	$255

*Rates are for Alaska. Airfare and port taxes are extra.

The Rotterdam is Holland America's only ship that does not have televisions in each cabin. A fruit basket is refilled each day, and every passenger gets a canvas tote bag. Views from most cabins on the Sun and Boat decks are partially obstructed. Passengers on B Deck use the upper decks to go from one end of the ship to the other because the dining room blocks passage.

Outlet voltage: 110 AC.

Single supplement: 200% of double-occupancy rate for Staterooms Deluxe, 150% elsewhere. There are several single cabins at $246–$332 per diem (inside) and $332–$418 per diem (outside). Holland America can arrange for two same-sex adults to share a cabin at the double-occupancy rate.

Discounts: A third or fourth passenger in a cabin pays $60–$100 per diem. You get discounts for booking early and for arranging your own airfare.

Sports and Fitness

Health club: Stationary bicycles, weight machine, exercise board, indoor pool, sauna, massage.

Recreation: Exercise classes, golf driving, paddle and deck tennis, shuffleboard, trapshooting, indoor pool, outdoor pool, partially enclosed circuit for jogging.

Facilities

Public rooms: Seven bars, five entertainment lounges, casino, disco, cinema, card room, library/writing room, smoking lounge, video-game room, computer center.

Shops: Boutique, drugstore, newsstand, gift shop, beauty salon/barber.

Health care: Doctor on call.

Child care: Youth programs with counselors during holidays and in summer, baby-sitting arranged privately with crew member.

Services: Full- and self-service laundry, dry cleaning, photographer, film processing.

Accessibility

Although some entranceways have doorsills, ramps have been placed over the key ones to improve access for wheelchair users. All public rooms, except the dining room, are located on a single deck. All public areas are accessible. No cabins are specifically equipped for passengers with mobility problems.

MS Westerdam

Specifications

Type of ship: Cruise liner
Cruise experience: Semi-formal
Size: 53,872 tons
Number of cabins: 747
Outside cabins: 66%

Passengers: 1,494
Crew: 620 (Indonesian and Filipino)
Officers: Dutch
Passenger/crew ratio: 2.4 to 1
Year built: 1986

Ship's Log

Holland America purchased Home Line's two ships in 1988 just to obtain this one, then called the *Homeric*. An additional $84 million investment made the rechristened *Westerdam* into a bigger version of the *Nieuw Amsterdam* and *Noordam*. On the outside, the ship has the angular, muscular look common to ships this big that retain a stepped-back deck design. Inside, it is unusually comfortable and spacious, largely because it was lengthened by 130 feet during its refurbishment. Into this new space were put a host of bars, cafés, shops, and lounges, as well as a photo-processing studio. The dining room is noteworthy because, unlike on many ships where the restaurant occupies a strategic perch with expansive views, on the *Westerdam* it is located far below decks. Nevertheless, passengers will find an eating venue that is a rich and elegant melange of wood veneers, polished brass and crystal chandeliers.

Cabins and Rates	Beds	Phone	TV	Sitting Area	Fridge	Tub	Average Per Diem*
Suite	T	●	●	●	○	●	$325
Outside	Q, T, or D	●	●	◐	○	◐	$285
Inside	T	●	●	○	○	○	$262

Rates are for the Caribbean. Airfare and port taxes are extra.

Cabins are large, with plenty of storage space; all but the least expensive feature a sitting area with a convertible couch. The use of blond wood and ivory tones adds to the overall sense of airiness. A fruit basket is refilled each day, and every passenger gets a canvas tote bag.

Outlet voltage: 110 AC.

Single supplement: 200% of double-occupancy rate for suites or staterooms deluxe, 150% elsewhere. Holland America will arrange for two same-sex adults to share a cabin at the double-occupancy rate.

Discounts: A third or fourth passenger in a cabin pays $70–$90 (Caribbean) or $79–$100 (Alaska) per diem. You get discounts for booking early and for arranging your own airfare.

Sports and Fitness

Health club: Hydro-fitness exercise equipment, dual saunas, massage, loofah scrubs, facials, health-care program.

Recreation: Exercise classes, golf putting, paddle and deck tennis, shuffleboard, skeet shooting (Caribbean), basketball, two pools (one with retractable glass roof), three whirlpools, unobstructed circuit (4 laps = 1 mile) for jogging.

Facilities

Public rooms: Seven bars, two entertainment lounges, casino, disco, cinema, card room, library, video-game room, meeting room.

Shops: Boutiques, drugstore, beauty salon/barber.

Health care: Doctor on call.

Child care: Youth programs with counselors when demand warrants it.

Services: Full- and self-service laundry, dry cleaning, photographer, film processing.

Accessibility Elevators and four cabins are accessible to wheelchair users.

Majesty Cruise Line

The Fleet MV *Royal Majesty*

The sole ship in the fleet of Majesty Cruise Line was built specifically to sail on three- and four-day cruises, and is one of the few upscale
cruise liners sailing these short itineraries. Thoroughly modern in
its appointments, the *Royal Majesty* was designed to attract passengers who might otherwise sail aboard Holland America or Celebrity. To that end, it combines the best qualities of both these lines,
and the result is a contemporary vessel with burnished woods and
polished brass bathed in warm, natural light.

Ship at a Glance

	Dining Rooms	Bars	Casino	Fitness Center	Pools	Average Per Diem
Royal Majesty	1	3	●	●	1	$239

Cruise Experience The *Royal Majesty* delivers a level of sophistication rarely found on
three- and four-day cruises. The ship excels in its onboard appoint-
ments, activities, and innovative entertainment, but falls somewhat
short of the competition when it comes to dining. Passengers looking
for action amid their refinement will like the ship's Regal Bodies fitness program of aerobics and weight lifting and the Club Nautica
program of snorkeling and diving. There's also a full-service spa for
more relaxed rejuvenation.

Activities Majesty mixes standard cruise activities—pool games, trivia contests, bingo, dance classes—with a daily program of more off-beat
options, such as early morning Tai Chi classes and wine tasting seminars. The Club Nautica water-sports program takes passengers off
the ship in each port for snorkeling and dive safaris, led by an ex-
pert-in-residence. You can't earn certification, but you can get your
flippers wet during scuba classes for beginners, too. Activities for
younger passengers include scavenger hunts and talent shows, led
by youth counselors dressed as Yogi Bear and Fred Flintstone. Majesty, along with sister line Dolphin, is the official cruise line of
Hanna-Barbera, which is good for families cruising together but can
seem somewhat incongruous in the elegantly appointed dining
room.

Dining Dining aboard Majesty is probably this ship's most disappointing effort. The cuisine is about equal to the food served on Majesty's sister
line, Dolphin, and while that's quite good for a lower-priced line, its
not what you'd expect from a ship in this class. Menus lack imagination, from the presentation to the flavoring, but they are extensive,
with choices to suit every taste. Dinner always includes five entrées
plus a vegetarian and "light" selection. Service is sophisticated,
though, and there's piano music to dine by. Kids get their own

---

Chart Symbols. Ships at a Glance. ●: *Fully equipped;* ◑:
Partially equipped; ○: *Not equipped.* Cabins and Rates. **D:**
Double bed; **K:** *King-size bed;* **Q:** *Queen-size bed;* **T:** *Twin bed;*
U/L: *Upper and lower berths;* ●: *All cabins have this facility;*
○: *No cabins have this facility;* ◑: *Some cabins have this
facility*

menus, featuring fun foods such as "Yummy Yogi Pizza" and "Bam-Bam's Chilly-Willy Hot Dog." Formal nights are scheduled twice on every weeklong sailing and once on every three- and four-day cruise. Make special dietary requests in writing seven days before sailing.

A better choice than the dining room for lunch or breakfast are the buffets—the spreads are impressive and the food quite tasty. Other food service includes pizza and ice cream twice a day; afternoon tea with sandwiches, cookies, and cake; and a midnight buffet. Coffee and tea are available 24 hours a day, as is room service from a limited menu.

Entertainment   As with its daily schedule of activities, the *Royal Majesty*'s nightly program of entertainment features typical cruise-ship song-and-dance productions, plus some novel alternatives: one-act plays, classical guitar recitals, and an elaborate medieval-style festival. There's also masquerade parties and karaoke nights.

Service and   Tip the room steward $3.50 per passenger per diem, the waiter $3,
Tipping   the busboy $1.50. The maître d' should get $5 per passenger per cruise, the wine steward or bartender 15% of your final tab.

Destinations   During fall, winter, and spring, the *Royal Majesty* sails from Miami on three- and four-day cruises to the Bahamas or Mexico's Yucatan. In summer, it repositions to Boston for cruises to Bermuda. (For detailed itineraries, *see* Chapter 3.)

For More   Majesty Cruise Lines (901 South America Way, Miami, FL 33132,
Information   tel. 800/645–8111).

MV Royal Majesty

Specifications   *Type of ship:* Cruise liner   *Passengers:* 1,056
Cruise experience: Semi-   *Crew:* 500 (international)
formal   *Officers:* Greek
Size: 32,400 tons   *Passenger/crew ratio:* 2.1 to 1
Number of cabins: 528   *Year built:* 1992
Outside cabins: 65%

Ship's Log   The "royal" theme reigns throughout the ship, from the Queen of Hearts Card Room to the House of Lords Executive Conference Room to the Royal Fireworks Lounge. Excellent use of light and space creates bright, inviting public areas from which passengers can enjoy fine sea views. The Royal Observatory Panorama Bar is a favorite perch from which to watch the ship pull into and out of ports of call. The Cafe Royale is where you'll want to be for breakfast and lunch; its perch just above the bridge makes for panoramic views forward. At the other end of the ship, the Piazza San Marco serves pizza and ice cream twice a day amid sweeping views aft.

Cabins and Rates	Beds	Phone	TV	Sitting Area	Fridge	Tub	Average Per Diem*
Suite	D	●	●	●	●	○	$343
Outside	D	●	●	○	○	○	$239
Inside	T/D	●	●	○	○	○	$156

Rates are for three-night Bahamas cruises. Airfare and port taxes are extra.

Like the rest of the ship, cabin decor is tasteful and classy. Color schemes are understated earth tones complemented with wood furnishings and moldings. Each stateroom comes with robes, color TV (including CNN), five channels of music, direct-dial ship-to-shore telephones, hair dryers, security safes, and ironing boards. Suites and some outside cabins have a minibar, a queen-size bed, and an enormous ocean-view picture window. Views from many cabins on Queen's Deck are obstructed by lifeboats; cabins on Princess Deck look out onto a public promenade.

Outlet voltage: 110 AC.

Single supplement: 150% of double-occupancy rate.

Discounts: A third or fourth passenger in a cabin pays $127–$150 per diem. You get a discount of up to $100 for arranging your own airfare and a discount of $50 per passenger if you book 100 days in advance.

Sports and Fitness

Health club: Fitness center with LifeCircuit, weights, stair climber, stationary bikes, rowing machines, and treadmills; aerobics studio with exercise and dance classes; spa with body and facial treatments.

Recreation: Pool, two whirlpools, jogging track.

Facilities

Public rooms: Three bars, showroom, casino, disco, card room, library, meeting rooms, board room.

Shops: Gift shop, beauty salon.

Child care: Playroom, splash pool, baby-sitting, youth program with counselors year-round.

Services: Photographer.

Accessibility

The ship is fully accessible to wheelchair users, including four elevators, rest rooms on various decks, and four specially equipped staterooms.

Norwegian Cruise Line

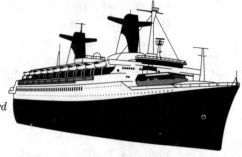

The Fleet
MS *Dreamward*
MS *Leeward*
SS *Norway*
MS *Seaward*
MS *Windward*

NCL has a hodgepodge of big ships and small ships, old ships and new ships. The *Norway*, formerly the *France*, was built in 1962 and is still the longest cruise ship afloat. NCL's newest ships, the *Dreamward* and *Windward*, are state-of-the-art vessels with mostly outside cabins (some with private balconies), picture windows, multiple restaurants, and tiered public rooms.

Ships at a Glance

	Dining Rooms	Bars	Casino	Fitness Center	Pools	Average Per Diem
Dreamward *Windward*	4*	8	●	●	2	$300
Leeward	3*	5	●	●	1	$250
Norway	3*	5	●	●	2	$270
Seaward	3*	8	●	●	2	$255

*includes alternative Italian restaurant

Cruise Experience
NCL was the originator of the modern formula for cruising: Its ships offer a full schedule of activities and entertainment, generous portions of American-style food, and a wide range of popular ports. NCL tries to be everything to everyone, so its passengers tend to span generations, economic brackets, and lifestyles. The newer ships, however, attract a younger, partying crowd, while the *Norway* and *Seaward* appeal to an older, more affluent group.

In years past, the line's onboard experience lacked the polish found aboard its competitors. Recently, that has begun to change. Refinements include traditional afternoon high tea served by white-gloved waiters to the accompaniment of classical music, an out-of-this-world Chocoholic Bar, and specialty coffees served in the main dining rooms. Around the pools, passengers will notice more attendants at the ready with towels and spritzers upon request.

Activities
NCL doesn't skimp here. It's not unusual to see 30 different classes, contests, games, demonstrations, lectures, and performances scheduled for a single day. The line keeps in step with America's changing lifestyles: Fitness programs have been beefed up considerably and children's programs have been instituted. New adventure-oriented excursions appeal to sporting types. In the

Chart Symbols. Ships at a Glance. **●:** *Fully equipped;* **◐:** *Partially equipped;* ○: *Not equipped.* Cabins and Rates. **D:** *Double bed;* **K:** *King-size bed;* **Q:** *Queen-size bed;* **T:** *Twin bed;* **U/L:** *Upper and lower berths;* **●:** *All cabins have this facility;* ○: *No cabins have this facility;* **◐:** *Some cabins have this facility*

Caribbean, a limited number of passengers can sign up for snorkeling or scuba-diving tours, and in Alaska, they can go mountain biking, sea kayaking, or glacier hiking.

An extensive schedule of theme cruises enliven the usual offerings of bingo, trivia contests, dance classes, wine tastings, and vegetable-carving demonstrations. Most popular is the sports series aboard the *Norway* and *Dreamward*, when famous football, basketball, hockey, and baseball players—just to name a few—meet and play with passengers. Other theme cruises frequently highlight music, from country music to jazz to '50s and '60s pop (all on the *Norway*). Most upper Caribbean itineraries include an all-day beach party on NCL's own Bahamian island, Great Stirrup Cay, with snorkeling, beach games, and a barbecue.

Dining The food is plentiful but average; standards are highest on the *Norway*. Cuisine is a combination of American and Continental, usually with at least one Norwegian fish appetizer or entrée at lunch or dinner. (Caviar is served at an extra charge.) "Light entrée" options are available, but special dietary requests should be made one month prior to sailing. There are two assigned seatings for dinner (6 and 8:30); breakfast and lunch are open seating when ships are in port. Two formal evenings are held each week.

The *Leeward*, *Norway*, and *Seaward* each have two dining rooms to which passengers are assigned according to the location of their cabin; on the *Dreamward* and *Windward*, passengers are assigned to one of three dining rooms at random.

On all the ships, a small alternative restaurant, called Le Bistro, serves Italian cuisine à la carte at no additional cost. Passengers are served on a first-come, first-served basis (no reservations accepted). Because only a small number of passengers are served at one time, the food tends to be better prepared than in the main dining rooms.

Lidos on all NCL ships serve a buffet breakfast and lunch (the *Seaward*'s Lido also serves dinner). There's also an ice-cream parlor aboard each vessel except the *Leeward*. Midnight buffets are served every evening. Room service is available 24 hours a day from a limited menu.

Entertainment Everything one would expect from a cruise is available in full measure on NCL ships, including Las Vegas–style variety shows, dance orchestras, piano bars, and discos. The *Norway*, *Seaward*, *Dreamward*, and *Windward* go so far as to feature scaled-down Broadway shows and revues, although the productions don't approach the elaborate, high-tech shows aboard Carnival's newest ships. The *Norway*'s music cruises have headlined such celebrities as Ricky Skaggs, the Bellamy Brothers, Tanya Tucker, the Tommy Dorsey Orchestra, Mary Wilson, and Paul Revere and the Raiders. In-cabin TVs on all ships show CNN broadcasts and movies all day.

Service and Tipping The general level of service on NCL ships is very good, but *Norway* passengers usually get treated a little better. Tip the room steward and the waiter each $3 per passenger per diem, the busboy $1.50. A 15% service charge is added to the bar tab, and a tip of 50¢ or $1 is expected each time room service is ordered.

Destinations NCL's itineraries are as varied as its fleet, sailing to well-traveled and off-the-beaten-path ports in the Caribbean, plus the Bahamas, Bermuda, Southern California, the Mexican Riviera, and Alaska. (For detailed itineraries, *see* Chapter 3.)

For More Information Norwegian Cruise Line (95 Merrick Way, Coral Gables, FL 33134, tel. 800/327–7030).

MS Dreamward and MS Windward

Specifications

Type of ship: Cruise liner	*Passengers:* 1,242/1,246
Cruise experience: Casual	*Crew:* 483 (international)
Size: 41,000 tons	*Officers:* Norwegian
Number of cabins: 623	*Passenger/crew ratio:* 2.6 to 1
Outside cabins: 85%	*Year built:* 1992/1993

Ship's Log Like most sister ships, these identical twins differ only in decor. Public rooms even have the same names, making it a breeze to get around on one if you have already sailed on the other. Terraced decks give panoramic views forward and aft, and walls of glass line the length of the ship. Multilevel public rooms include the Terrace dining room, the Stardust show lounge, and the two-deck-high Casino Royale, where the action includes roulette, craps, blackjack, and slot machines. Instead of one, big dining room, four smaller restaurants create a more intimate ambience. Even the biggest, the Terrace, seats only 282 on several levels and has windows on three sides. Matching these two ships' variety of eateries is a variety of special menus, theme meals, and children's menus. Dinner has two assigned seatings, but breakfast and lunch are open, so you can try the other restaurants or opt for hamburgers and hot dogs at the casual Sports Bar & Grill.

Showroom productions are the usual festive affairs, including the full-length Broadway-style shows that NCL is famous for. A proscenium stage makes these productions NCL's most elaborate yet, although the line's productions lag behind Carnival's, whose newest ships feature even more high-tech stage equipment, and, consequently more elaborate shows. After the show, the lounge metamorphoses into a late-night disco. The Sports Bar & Grill transmits live ESPN and NFL broadcasts on multiple screens. There's plenty of space for relaxing on the five-tier Sun Deck, and the especially broad Promenade Deck is good for walking and jogging.

Cabins and Rates

	Beds	Phone	TV	Sitting Area	Fridge	Tub	Average Per Diem*
Suite	T/Q	●	●	●	●	◐	$330–$360
Outside	T/Q	●	●	●	○	○	$270–$320
Inside	T/Q	●	●	○	○	○	$220–$265

*Airfare and port taxes are extra.

The *Dreamward* and *Windward* have an unusually high percentage of outside cabins, most with picture windows. Standard cabins, with their Caribbean villa look and feel, are among the prettiest at sea. The suites have floor-to-ceiling windows; some have private balconies and special amenities that include daily fruit baskets, champagne, trays of hors d'oeuvres, and concierge service. Adjoining suites are available on the Norway, International, and Star decks. Outside cabins have couches that convert into beds. Deluxe suites can accommodate up to four people and adjoining U-shape suites work well for families of up to six. Some cabins on the Norway Deck have obstructed views.

Outlet voltage: 110 AC.

Single supplement: 150%–200% of double-occupancy rate.

Discounts: A third or fourth passenger in a cabin (including children) pays $99–$114 per diem. You get as much as a $250 discount for arranging your own airfare and discounts for booking early.

Sports and Fitness	**Health club:** Lifecycles, Lifesteps, exercise equipment, Jacuzzis, a variety of massage treatments.

Recreation: Basketball court, exercise course, two pools, golf range, unobstructed cushioned circuit for jogging.

Facilities **Public rooms:** Eight bars, entertainment lounge/theater, observation lounge/nightclub, casino, library, video-game room, conference center.

Shops: Gift shops and boutiques, beauty salon/barber.

Health care: Doctor on call.

Child care: Playroom; organized youth programs with counselors in three age groups year-round, four age groups during holidays and in summer; guaranteed baby-sitting.

Accessibility All decks and activities are accessible to wheelchair users, except the Sky Deck and public lavatories. Travel with an able-bodied companion is required. Six specially equipped cabins are accessible to wheelchair users, 28 for passengers with hearing impairments.

MS Leeward

Specifications *Type of ship:* Cruise liner *Passengers:* 950
Cruise experience: Casual *Crew:* 400 (international)
Size: 25,000 tons *Officers:* Norwegian
Number of cabins: 475 *Passenger/crew ratio:* 2.4 to 1
Outside cabins: 67% *Year built:* 1992

Ship's Log The sleek *Leeward* joined Norwegian Cruise Line in 1995, after seeing service as a cruise-ferry on the Baltic Sea as the *Viking Saga*. Already sleek and attractive inside and out, the vessel underwent a $60 million refit before being rechristened the *Leeward*. As with the *Dreamward* and *Windward*, this ship incorporates expansive windows overlooking the sea. A sports bar and grill, a NCL first on the *Dreamward* and *Windward*, has been put aboard the *Leeward* as well. Passengers are assigned to one of two main dining rooms for dinner, and they can always choose to eat in the 80-seat alternative restaurant, Le Bistro.

Cabins and Rates	Beds	Phone	TV	Sitting Area	Fridge	Tub	Average Per Diem*
Suite	D or T	●	●	●	●	○	$285–$315
Outside	D & U or T/D	●	●	○	○	○	$255–$270
Inside	D & U	●	●	○	○	○	$180–$190

*Airfare and port taxes are extra.

Cabins are decorated in hues of dusty rose and gray. All have televisions; none, not even the suites, have tubs. Two owner's suites have private balconies and Jacuzzis; eight penthouses have balconies and a separate bedroom and living room.

Outlet voltage: 110 AC.

Single supplement: 150%–200% of double-occupancy rate.

Discounts: A third or fourth passenger in a cabin pays $99 per diem. You get up to $250 off for arranging your own airfare and discounts for booking early.

Sports and Fitness

Health club: Exercise equipment, full-service spa.

Recreation: Aerobics and other exercise classes, table tennis, skeet shooting, snorkeling lessons and excursions, pool, Jacuzzis, unobstructed circuit for jogging.

Facilities

Public rooms: Five bars and lounges, casino, disco, library, meeting rooms.

Shops: Duty-free shops and gift boutique, barber/beauty salon.

Health care: Doctor on call.

Child care: Playroom; youth programs with counselors in three age groups year-round, four age groups during holidays and in summer; guaranteed baby-sitting.

Services: Laundry service, photographer, film processing.

Accessibility

Six cabins and five elevators are accessible to wheelchair users. All decks and public rooms are accessible, except for the beauty salon. No public rest rooms are accessible.

SS Norway

Specifications

Type of ship: Classic liner	*Passengers:* 2,032
Cruise experience: Semi-formal	*Crew:* 900 (international)
	Officers: Norwegian
Size: 76,049 tons	*Passenger/crew ratio:* 2.3 to 1
Number of cabins: 1,016	*Year built:* 1962
Outside cabins: 56.9%	

Ship's Log

Deep within the huge hull of the *Norway* beats a Gallic heart. The ship began life in 1962 as the *France*, built with French government subsidies to be the biggest, most beautiful transatlantic liner afloat—a symbol for a country impressed with its own style and stature. Unfortunately, travelers weren't impressed that it took the *France* six days to cross the Atlantic when a jet could fly the distance in seven hours. The ship was sold to Norwegian Cruise Line in 1979 and extensively refitted for vacation cruises.

One of the best-looking ocean liners ever built, the *Norway* has an incredible amount of deck space, as well as a cavernous interior. The enclosed International Deck is so large and wide that its tree-edged walkways, lined with sidewalk cafés, bars, shops, and boutiques, resemble an upscale shopping mall. The port walkway is named Fifth Avenue, and the starboard side, Champs-Elysées.

The *Norway* has undergone two major refurbishments in the past several years. The first added almost 3,000 tons to its gross tonnage, making it the largest ship afloat—although it will soon lose that title. Among the additions were two new decks, a 6,000-square-foot spa (spa packages include calorie-controlled lunches), a new restaurant, and 124 luxury staterooms (54 with private balconies). The second and most recent restored the ship to its former art deco glory. Much of the original *France* is still visible in the wood decks, slate floors, magnificent artwork, sweeping staircases, and sparkling chandeliers. The Windward and Leeward dining rooms are as large as hotel banquet halls. It's easy to get lost among the plethora of bars and lounges; many passengers never see all the public rooms.

Cabins and Rates

	Beds	Phone	TV	Sitting Area	Fridge	Tub	Average Per Diem*
Suite	K, Q, or T	●	●	●	●	●	$365
Outside	D, T, or U/L	●	●	○	◐	◐	$270

Inside	D, T, or U/L	●	●	○	○	◑	$215

Airfare and port taxes are extra.

Most suites and cabins are larger than those of comparably priced ships. Standard cabins have portholes, upper categories have picture windows. Suites offer concierge service. Each Owner's Suite has a private wraparound balcony, a living room, a master bedroom and second bedroom, a dressing room, a bathroom, and a whirlpool. Some Grand Deluxe Suites have a separate living room and a second bedroom, a whirlpool, and a powder room. Most Penthouse Suites have private balconies. Olympic Deck cabins look onto the jogging track. Most cabins on the Fjord and Olympic decks have obstructed or partially obstructed views.

Outlet voltage: 110 AC.

Single supplement: 150%–200% of double-occupancy rate. A few inside single cabins are available at $207–$271 per diem.

Discounts: A third or fourth passenger in a cabin pays $99 per diem. You get up to $250 off for arranging your own airfare and discounts for booking early.

Sports and Fitness

Health club: Fitness center with 16 treatment rooms (for massage, reflexology, herbal treatment, hydrotherapy, thermal body wraps, and more), two saunas, two steam rooms, body-jet showers, Cybex Eagle strength-training equipment, Lifecycles and Lifesteps, whirlpool, indoor pool for water exercise. The spa's beauty salon (separate from the ship's main salon) offers facials and other beauty treatments.

Recreation: Aerobics and other exercise classes, basketball, deck Olympics, golf driving and putting, paddleball, table tennis, shuffleboard, skeet shooting, snorkeling classes and excursions, volleyball, two outdoor pools, unobstructed cushioned circuit for jogging.

Facilities

Public rooms: Five bars and lounges, cabaret, casino, disco, theater, library, video-game room, two meeting rooms.

Shops: Arcade of gift shops and boutiques, beauty salon/barber.

Health care: Doctor on call.

Child care: Playroom; youth programs with counselors in three age groups year-round, four age groups during holidays and in summer; guaranteed baby-sitting.

Services: Concierge service in suites, laundry service, drycleaning, photographer, film processing.

Accessibility

The *Norway* has nine cabins accessible to wheelchair users. All public areas except the Sun Deck pool are accessible. The ship's size forces it to anchor offshore at most ports; boarding the tenders can pose a difficulty for passengers with mobility problems, who must travel with an able-bodied companion and provide their own small, collapsible wheelchairs.

MS Seaward

Specifications

Type of ship: Cruise liner	*Passengers:* 1,504
Cruise experience: Casual	*Crew:* 630 (international)
Size: 42,000 tons	*Officers:* Norwegian
Number of cabins: 752	*Passenger/crew ratio:* 2.4 to 1
Outside cabins: 67.7%	*Year built:* 1988

Ship's Log

Compared with other ships built in the late 1980s, the *Seaward* is surprisingly spartan. A spacious pool deck is well equipped with back-to-back swimming pools and twin Jacuzzis, but there's more all-weather carpeting than teak decking. The Crystal Court, a two-story lobby, is also disappointingly modest for a ship of such recent vintage.

On the positive side, the *Seaward*'s two large dining rooms are gracious and welcoming, their many tables set with white linens and formal stemware. The newest addition to the ship, the Le Bistro Italian restaurant, is a more casual alternative for dinner. The bars and lounges are inviting and plushly appointed, and there are two showrooms—one for small-scale shows by bands and comedians and another for full-scale musical productions. (Be sure to get to the Cabaret Lounge early; its single-level construction makes viewing difficult for those at the back and sides of the room.)

	Beds	Phone	TV	Sitting Area	Fridge	Tub	Average Per Diem*
Suite	T/D	●	●	●	●	●	$350
Outside	T/D	●	●	○	○	○	$255
Inside	T/D or U/L	●	●	○	○	○	$220

Cabins and Rates

*Airfare and port taxes are extra.

Standard cabins are appointed in white and colored cabinetwork with brass and wood-tone accents. Rounded picture windows in outside cabins look like elongated portholes. Some cabins on the Norway and Star decks have obstructed or partially obstructed views.

Outlet voltage: 110 AC.

Single supplement: 150%–200% of double-occupancy rate. A few inside single cabins are available at $207–$271 per diem.

Discounts: A third or fourth passenger in a cabin pays $99 per diem. You get up to $250 off for arranging your own airfare and discounts for booking early.

Sports and Fitness

Health club: Exercise equipment, massage, sauna.

Recreation: Aerobics and other exercise classes, basketball, golf driving, table tennis, shuffleboard, skeet shooting, snorkeling lessons and excursions, volleyball, two pools, two Jacuzzis, unobstructed cushioned circuit (4 laps = 1 mile) for jogging.

Facilities

Public rooms: Eight bars and lounges, casino, disco, cabaret, card room/library.

Shops: Several stores, beauty salon/barber.

Health care: Doctor on call.

Child care: Playroom; youth programs with counselors in three age groups year-round, four age groups during holidays and in summer; guaranteed baby-sitting.

Services: Laundry service, dry cleaning, photographer, film processing.

Accessibility

The *Seaward* has excellent facilities for wheelchair users. Four cabins are specially equipped, and no area of the ship is inaccessible to passengers with mobility problems, who must travel with an able-bodied companion and provide their own small, collapsible wheelchairs.

Premier Cruise Lines

The Fleet   *Star/Ship Atlantic*
Star/Ship Oceanic   **Starship Oceanic**

These two ships, known collectively as The Big Red Boat, are instantly recognizable by their cherry-color hulls. Premier has acquired its fleet from a venerable name of cruising past: The *Atlantic* and *Oceanic* both sailed under the same names for now-defunct Home Lines. The ships were refitted to suit the family cruise market. A recreation center for children ages two and older has its own wading pool and sundeck, teenagers have their own recreation room, and many cabins can accommodate three, four, or even five passengers.

Ships at a Glance

	Dining Rooms	Bars	Casino	Fitness Center	Pools	Average Per Diem
Atlantic	1	5	●	●	3	$259
Oceanic	1	6	●	●	2	$259

Cruise Experience   Premier invented family cruising in 1984 and still runs one of the best child-care and youth programs on the high seas. (There's even a special price structure for single parents.) Formerly the official cruise line of Walt Disney World, the line now carries Looney Tunes characters, such as Bugs Bunny and Daffy Duck, on every sailing. If you don't like children, don't sail with Premier—but you don't have to have a family to enjoy these lively, unpretentious cruises. Increasingly, they are popular with honeymooners who want to combine a cruise with a visit to Florida. For senior citizens, the line offers a 10%–15% discount.

Premier is the only line to operate three- and four-day cruises exclusively. These may be bought cruise-only, or combined with a land package to Orlando-area theme parks for five- or seven-day vacations. Choices include Walt Disney World, Universal Studios, Sea World, Kennedy Space Center's Spaceport USA, and the Major League Baseball Players' Alumni Fantasy Camp.

Activities   For adults, Premier offers traditional cruise activities—"horse racing," bingo, pool games, trivia contests, bridge tournaments—as well as extensive fitness programs and facilities. Young children and teenagers have their own activities centers, video-game room, and counselor-supervised programs.

Dining   Food is good basic fare. The waiters are exceptionally good with children, but don't look for elegance or snappy service, especially with the high number of children served. The menu, decor, and waiters' costumes change nightly to reflect a theme—French, Italian, Ca-

---

Chart Symbols. Ships at a Glance. **●**: *Fully equipped;* **◖**: *Partially equipped;* ○: *Not equipped.* Cabins and Rates. **D**: *Double bed;* **K**: *King-size bed;* **Q**: *Queen-size bed;* **T**: *Twin bed;* **U/L**: *Upper and lower berths;* **●**: *All cabins have this facility;* ○: *No cabins have this facility;* **◖**: *Some cabins have this facility*

ribbean, American. A children's menu is available, with such favorites as hamburgers, hot dogs, and macaroni and cheese. Meals are served at two assigned seatings (6 and 8:15 for dinner). If you are traveling with small children, it's smart to sign up for the first seating. If you wish a more sedate environment, you would be wise to select the late seating. There is one semiformal evening on each cruise. Special dietary requests should be made in writing at least four weeks prior to sailing.

Early morning coffee is served on the Pool Deck, as are extensive breakfast and lunch buffets. Other food service includes a make-your-own sundae bar, afternoon tea, midnight buffet, and a late-night omelet bar. Room service is available 24 hours from a limited menu.

Entertainment Looney Tunes characters roam the decks to play with children (and adults, who seem to get into the act when no one is looking). You can even arrange for your child to be tucked into bed at night by his or her favorite character, or to have breakfast with the Looney Tunes. Otherwise, entertainment is traditional, featuring variety shows, magicians, films, and theme parties. After the sun goes down, Premier presents Las Vegas–style revues, cabaret acts, piano playing, and other adult forms of entertainment. (The comedy, however, is strictly PG-13, instead of the R-rated material most ships offer late-night passengers.) Premier also features large casinos with row upon row of slot machines. In-cabin TVs show CNN broadcasts.

Service and Tipping Generally, the crew is superb at handling children and all their wants. They're patient, always smiling, and ready to give a helping hand. Tip the room steward and the waiter each $3 per passenger per diem, the busboy $1.50, both slightly more for the four-night cruise. Tip the headwaiter $2 per passenger per cruise for a three-night cruise, $3 for a four-night cruise. When you sign for bar and wine bills, a 15% service charge is automatically added.

Destinations The *Atlantic* and *Oceanic* sail on three- and four-day cruises to the Bahamas. (For detailed itineraries, *see* Chapter 3.)

For More Information Premier Cruise Lines (Box 517, Cape Canaveral, FL 32920, tel. 800/473–3262).

Star/Ship Atlantic

Specifications

Type of ship: Cruise liner	*Passengers:* 1,550
Cruise experience: Casual	*Crew:* 500 (international)
Size: 36,500 tons	*Officers:* Greek
Number of cabins: 549	*Passenger/crew ratio:* 3.1 to 1
Outside cabins: 73%	*Year built:* 1982

Ship's Log The *Atlantic* is a generic-looking cruise ship that previously sailed as the *Atlantic* for Home Lines. During a major refurbishment in 1989, the public rooms and casino were enlarged, extra cabins were added, and more facilities for children were installed. Like its fleetmate the *Oceanic*, it features a retractable, transparent roof over the Riviera Pool. Most daytime activities are centered on the Promenade Deck, which has an ice-cream parlor, a well-equipped sports-and-fitness center, and two pools with adjacent sun areas.

Youngsters age two or older can enjoy Pluto's Playhouse in the Children's Recreation Center (the largest of any ship sailing the Bahamas), as well as a shallow children's pool. For older children, the Space Station Teen Center has a jukebox and a dance floor, and the Star Fighter Arcade is packed with state-of-the-art video games.

Cabins and Rates	Beds	Phone	TV	Sitting Area	Fridge	Tub	Average Per Diem*
Suite	Q or T	●	●	●	○	●	$293
Outside	Q, T, or U/L	●	●	●	○	●	$259
Inside	D, T, or U/L	●	●	○	○	◐	$233

Airfare and port taxes are extra.

Cabins are simply furnished, but many can accommodate three, four, or five passengers.

Outlet voltage: 110 AC.

Single supplement: 200% of double-occupancy rate. Single parents traveling with children under 17 pay 125% on cabin categories 3–8.

Discounts: A third, fourth, or fifth passenger in a cabin pays $449–$569 (cruise only) and $529–$749 (cruise/hotel), depending upon sailing season. You can save up to $400 for booking early and $200 for arranging your own airfare. Senior citizens receive a 10% discount on peak sailings, 15% on shoulder-season sailings, and 20% on off-peak sailings on cabin categories 3–8.

Sports and Fitness **Health club:** Lifecycles, Universal weights, minitrampolines, sit-up boards, massage.

Recreation: Aerobics and other exercise classes, table tennis, snorkeling lessons, shuffleboard, skeet shooting, volleyball, whirlpools, three pools, wading pool, jogging track.

Facilities **Public rooms:** Five bars, three entertainment lounges, casino, disco, cinema, video-game room.

Shops: Three gift shops, beauty salon/barber.

Health care: Doctor on call.

Child care: Children's recreation center (age two and up), with wading pool, sundeck, supervised programs aboard ship and ashore; teen programs and playroom; baby-sitting for children ages two to 12.

Services: Laundry service, photographer.

Accessibility Accessibility aboard ship for wheelchair users is limited. Passengers with mobility problems may have difficulty boarding the tenders that ferry passengers to Port Lucaya and Salt Cay.

Star/Ship Oceanic

Specifications *Type of ship:* Classic liner *Passengers:* 1,609
Cruise experience: Casual *Crew:* 530 (international)
Size: 40,000 tons *Officers:* Greek
Number of cabins: 590 *Passenger/crew ratio:* 3 to 1
Outside cabins: 44% *Year built:* 1965

Ship's Log In the tradition of having prominent ladies christen ships, Minnie Mouse was the celebrity wielding the champagne bottle when the *Oceanic* was inaugurated as a Premier ship in 1986. The exterior is stunning, with the classic lines of a transatlantic liner. The ship boasts two pools that can be covered by a retractable, transparent dome in the event of rain. The Seven Continents Restaurant is huge and well lighted, with wide aisles and ample space between the tables, but it tends to become noisy. The casino is one of the largest on any cruise ship; children under 18 are forbidden to play the slot machines, but a video arcade is nearby.

Cabins and Rates

	Beds	Phone	TV	Sitting Area	Fridge	Tub	Average Per Diem*
Suite	Q, D, or T	●	●	●	○	●	$293
Outside	D, T, or U/L	●	●	◐	○	●	$259
Inside	D, T, or U/L	●	●	○	○	◐	$233

Airfare and port taxes are extra.

Cabins are simply furnished; many accommodate three, four, or five passengers.

Outlet voltage: 110 AC.

Single supplement: 200% of double-occupancy rate. Single parents traveling with children under 17 pay 125% on cabin categories 3–8.

Discounts: A third, fourth, or fifth passenger in a cabin pays $449–$569 (cruise only) and $529–$749 (cruise/hotel) depending upon sailing season. You can save up to $400 for booking early and $200 for arranging your own airfare. Senior citizens receive a 10% discount on peak sailings, 15% on shoulder-season sailings, and 20% on off-peak sailings on cabin categories 3–8.

Sports and Fitness

Health club: Lifecycles, Universal weight equipment, minitrampolines, sit-up boards, massage.

Recreation: Aerobics and other exercise classes, basketball, table tennis, pool volleyball, snorkeling lessons, shuffleboard, skeet shooting, tennis practice, volleyball, two adjacent swimming pools, wading pool, three whirlpools, jogging track.

Facilities

Public rooms: Six bars, four entertainment lounges, casino, disco, cinema, reading room, video-game room.

Shops: Two gift shops, beauty salon/barber.

Health care: Doctor on call.

Child care: Children's recreation center (age two and up), with wading pool, sundeck, supervised programs aboard ship and ashore; teen programs and playroom; 24-hour baby-sitting for children ages two to 12.

Services: Laundry service, photographer.

Accessibility

Accessibility aboard ship for wheelchair users is limited. Passengers with mobility problems may have difficulty boarding the tenders that ferry passengers to Port Lucaya and Salt Cay.

Princess Cruises

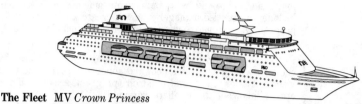

Star Princess

The Fleet
MV *Crown Princess*
MV *Golden Princess*
MV *Island Princess*
MV *Pacific Princess*
MV *Regal Princess*
MV *Royal Princess*
TSS *Sky Princess*
MV *Star Princess*

Princess proves that big can be classy aboard its increasingly huge, upscale megaships. The largest ships in the Princess fleet weigh in at 70,000 tons but carry only 1,590 passengers, a small complement for a ship this size. And Princess is looking at an even bigger future: In late 1995 it expected delivery of the mammoth 77,000-ton *Sun Princess*, to be followed by its sister, the new *Dawn Princess*. In 1997, the *Grand Princess*, a 100,000-ton giant too big to fit through the Panama Canal, will arrive, and will vie with Carnival's 100,000-tonner for the title of largest cruise ship ever built.

Ships at a Glance

	Dining Rooms	Bars	Casino	Fitness Center	Pools	Average Per Diem
Crown Princess Regal Princess	1	9	●	●	2	$300
Golden Princess	1	7	●	●	2	$350
Island Princess Pacific Princess	1	6	●	●	2	$350
Royal Princess	1	7	●	●	3	$400
Sky Princess	1	7	●	●	2	$300
Star Princess	1	7	●	●	3	$300

Cruise Experience
Most of us remember Princess ships from the cheerful TV series the *Love Boat*. In the real world, Princess Cruises is the refined North American arm of British shipping giant P&0. In 1988 Princess acquired Sitmar, an upscale Italian line, which infused the parent company with a refreshing hint of Italian exuberance.

Passengers tend to be older, experienced travelers who expect superior service and won't accept less. Even on the line's biggest ships, they are treated like guests at a fine hotel while they enjoy all the services and activities of a shoreside, all-inclusive resort. (On Caribbean sailings, passengers can even earn scuba certification). Shipboard purchases can be signed for and accounts settled at the end of the cruise.

Chart Symbols. Ships at a Glance. ●: *Fully equipped;* ◐: *Partially equipped;* ○: *Not equipped.* Cabins and Rates. **D:** *Double bed;* **K:** *King-size bed;* **Q:** *Queen-size bed;* **T:** *Twin bed;* **U/L:** *Upper and lower berths;* ●: *All cabins have this facility;* ○: *No cabins have this facility;* ◐: *Some cabins have this facility*

Activities Many Princess passengers are content to take it easy, although there's plenty to keep them busy if they prefer. All the expected ocean-liner activities are offered—dance lessons, bingo, "horse racing," and bridge and backgammon tournaments. Fitness facilities include an exercise manager who can create a customized fitness program. An extensive water-sports program includes scuba-diving classes held in the pools.

On the *Golden Princess, Sky Princess,* and *Star Princess,* youth centers, with a children's pool and sundeck, provide daily supervised activities year-round; children's programs are available on the other ships when the numbers warrant it.

Dining The mostly Italian dining-room staff supervise meals with élan and pride. Each night at dinner the headwaiter prepares a fresh pasta dish tableside. Continental cuisine is presented with flair and fanfare—the baked Alaska, in particular, is reason for a grand parade—but sometimes it is a bit disappointing to the palate. Alternative low-fat, low-cholesterol, and low-sodium selections are offered at every meal. Caviar, or just about anything else, may be ordered even when it is not on the menu. Meals are served at two assigned seatings (dinner at 6:15 and 8:15); breakfast and lunch may be open seating when the ship is in port. Two formal evenings are held on seven-day cruises, three on nine- to 16-day cruises. Special dietary requests are well handled, but they should be made in writing three weeks before sailing. There is no smoking in the dining room.

The Lido serves breakfast and lunch buffets but the food is usually better in the dining room. Other food service includes mid-morning bouillon, afternoon tea, and a midnight buffet; 24-hour room service is limited to sandwiches and beverages except during dinner, when a full menu is served. The *Crown, Regal, Sky,* and *Star* have free pizza parlors open throughout the afternoon and evening. On the *Crown, Regal, Royal,* and *Star,* a patisserie serves complimentary desserts and specialty coffees for an extra charge.

Entertainment Princess emphasizes entertainment suitable for the entire family, with a little more flair and flash than its chief rivals. Evening diversions include musical revues, variety shows, cabarets, a piano bar, a dance orchestra and combo, and a disco. Local musicians sometimes come aboard and perform. In-cabin TVs show movies, CNN, and ESPN.

Service and Tipping Princess places heavy emphasis on keeping passengers happy and satisfied. Generally, the service is excellent and unobtrusive, though passengers occasionally complain of stuffiness among British crew members. The Italian dining-room staff is a great deal of fun, however, and the room service is exceptional. Tip the room steward and waiter $3 each per passenger per diem, the waiter's assistant $1.75. The maître d' and the headwaiter may be tipped at the passenger's discretion for a job well done. A 15% gratuity is automatically added to bar and wine charges.

Destinations The Princess fleet is like a small navy, sailing to virtually every Western Hemisphere cruise destination. Itineraries cover Alaska, the Caribbean, Hawaii, the Mexican Riviera, New England and Canada, South America, and the Panama Canal. (For detailed itineraries, *see* Chapter 3.)

For More Information Princess Cruises (10100 Santa Monica Blvd., Los Angeles, CA 90067, tel. 310/553–1770).

MV Crown Princess and MV Regal Princess

Specifications *Type of ship:* Megaship
Cruise experience: Semi-
formal
Size: 70,000 tons
Number of cabins: 795
Outside cabins: 80%

Passengers: 1,590
Crew: 696 (international)
Officers: Italian
Passenger/crew ratio: 2.2 to 1
Year built: 1990/1991

Ship's Log Supposedly modeled on the curves of a dolphin, these sister ships look more like oversize, seafaring versions of the Japanese bullet train. The unusual exteriors are a blend of the traditional (note the single, upright funnel) and the avant-garde. The company's biggest and best-equipped ships to date, the *Crown* and the *Regal* each feature a dramatic, domed observation lounge/casino/entertainment area, a million-dollar art collection, and a three-story atrium foyer. The ships are almost as large as Royal Caribbean Cruise Line's 74,000-ton megaship, *Majesty of the Seas*, but they hold about 1,200 fewer passengers (counting upper and lower berths). The ships also have a high percentage of outside cabins, many of which have private verandas. These comfortable ships manage to avoid overwhelming passengers with their sheer size by creating a soft, warm interior, appointed with cozy couches and armchairs; art deco furnishings; light-wood panels; polished metals; and muted coral, blue, and aqua tones.

Cabins and Rates

	Beds	Phone	TV	Sitting Area	Fridge	Tub	Average Per Diem*
Suite	T/Q	●	●	●	●	●	$350
Outside	T/Q or U/L	●	●	●	●	○	$300
Inside	T/Q	●	●	●	●	○	$250

Rates include airfare, except in Alaska. Port taxes are extra.

Cabins are pleasantly appointed in contemporary wood and upholstered furnishings with framed prints on the walls. Each has a walk-in closet, a refrigerator, a separate dressing area, and a safe. Terry robes and fresh-fruit baskets are also found in each stateroom. Outside cabins have large picture windows. Most outside cabins on the Aloha and Baja decks (including all suites and minisuites) have private verandas. The view from the F-category outside cabins on Dolphin Deck is obstructed.

Outlet voltage: 110 AC.

Single supplement: 200% of double-occupancy rate for deluxe category suite and minisuites, 150%–160% for other cabins.

Discounts: A third or fourth passenger in a cabin pays $86–$116 per diem. You get a discount for early booking and for arranging your own airfare.

Sports and Fitness

Health club: Sizable below-decks facility with aerobics room, steam room, sauna, weight machines, stationary bikes, other exercise equipment, massage, beauty parlor.

Recreation: Exercise classes, golf driving, Ping-Pong, scuba and snorkeling lessons (scuba certification available), shuffleboard, skeet shooting, two pools (one with a waterfall, the other with a swim-up bar), two whirlpools, unobstructed jogging track (6 laps = 1 mile).

Facilities	**Public rooms:** Nine bars, five entertainment lounges, domed observation lounge, casino, disco, cinema/conference center, card room, library.

Shops: Two-level arcade of boutiques, gift shops, drugstore, hairdresser.

Health care: Two doctors and two nurses on call.

Child care: Children's program with youth counselor when 15 or more children on board.

Services: Laundry service, dry cleaning, photographer, film processing.

Accessibility   Ten cabins are accessible to wheelchair users.

MV Golden Princess

Specifications	*Type of ship:* Cruise liner *Cruise experience:* Semi-formal *Size:* 28,000 tons *Number of cabins:* 415 *Outside cabins:* 85%	*Passengers:* 830 *Crew:* 410 (European) *Officers:* British, Italian, Finnish *Passenger/crew ratio:* 2 to 1 *Year built:* 1973

Ship's Log   The *Golden* sailed formerly with Royal Viking Line as the *Royal Viking Sky*; it was later operated by NCL as the *Sunward* and for a short while in Europe by Birka Lines as the *Birka Queen*. Built as one of Royal Viking Line's original ships, it was designed to that line's exacting standards and exudes a classic grace.

Princess has kept the *Golden* in pristine condition. A recent refurbishment spruced up the ship with new carpet, drapes, and furnishings. No structural renovation is planned, though, because the ship is leased, leaving the single-level showroom as a poor venue for viewing the splashy production shows. On the other hand, excellent views of the sea can be had outdoors from the terraced decks aft, where two pools and a Jacuzzi are found, or inside from the Observatory Lounge, a perch high above the bow with wraparound views from high-back leather chairs.

Cabins and Rates		Beds	Phone	TV	Sitting Area	Fridge	Tub	Average Per Diem*
	Suite	D/T	●	●	●	●	●	$400
	Outside	D/T	●	●	◑	◑	◑	$350
	Inside	D/T	●	●	○	○	○	$300

*Airfare included, except in Alaska. Port taxes are extra.

Suites have verandas; suite 8 has a partially obstructed view. Minisuites and outside deluxe staterooms have large picture windows. Outside deluxe staterooms 24, 26–33, and 35 are larger accommodations priced the same as other cabins in this category. European-size double beds are slightly smaller than standard American size. Terry robes and fresh-fruit baskets are in each stateroom.

Outlet voltage: 110 AC.

Single supplement: 200% of double-occupancy rate for suites, 150%–160% for other cabins.

Discounts: A third or fourth passenger in a cabin pays about $87–$141 per diem. You get a discount of up to $250 for arranging your own airfare. You get an additional discount for booking early.

Sports and Fitness **Health club:** Lifecycles, Lifesteps, rowing machines, free weights, sauna.

Recreation: Shuffleboard, golf driving, Ping-Pong, basketball, paddle tennis, one whirlpool, two pools, unobstructed circuit (5 laps = 1 mile) for jogging.

Facilities **Public rooms:** Seven bars and lounges, showroom, casino, disco, library, two small conference rooms.

Shops: Several boutiques and gift shops, photo gallery and shop, beauty salon/barber.

Health care: Doctor and two nurses on call.

Child care: Youth center and programs with counselors offered year-round.

Services: Full- and self-service laundry, dry cleaning, photographer, film processing.

Accessibility Ramps have been installed throughout the ship and most of the elevators are accessible to wheelchair users; however, some areas remain inaccessible.

MV Island Princess and MV Pacific Princess

Specifications *Type of ship:* Cruise liner
Cruise experience: Semi-formal
Size: 20,000 tons
Cabins: 305
Outside cabins: 77.5%

Passengers: 640
Crew: 350 (international)
Officers: British
Passenger/crew ratio: 1.8 to 1
Year built: 1972/1971

Ship's Log Though the *Island Princess* and *Pacific Princess* are the smallest vessels in the Love Boat fleet, they are spacious and attractive. Both also carry large crews, which results in superior service—from the fresh flowers everywhere to the white-gloved stewards who are always close by.

Most outdoor activities take place around the cloverleaf-shape swimming pool, protected by a retractable canopy called the Sun Dome. The interiors are modern and impressive—particularly the two-story lobby, with its spectacular staircase, floor-to-ceiling mirrors, and glass paneling. The dining rooms are well lighted and roomy, with plenty of tables for two.

In an effort to remain popular in the competitive cruise market, both ships completed multimillion refurbishments recently—the *Pacific Princess* in September 1992, the *Island Princess* in October 1994. The ships now have completely new interiors, including electrically controlled sliding glass doors leading to the pool deck, a new Veranda buffet, new colors and patterns, and a new collection of contemporary art. The jogging track has been resurfaced for better traction.

Cabins and Rates

	Beds	Phone	TV	Sitting Area	Fridge	Tub	Average Per Diem*
Suite	D/T	●	●	●	●	●	$400
Outside	T	●	●	◐	◐	○	$350
Inside	T	●	●	◐	◐	○	$300

Airfare included. Port taxes are extra.

Some cabins on the Promenade Deck look onto a public area. Terry robes and fresh-fruit baskets are found in each stateroom.

Outlet voltage: 110 AC.

Single supplement: 200% of double-occupancy rate for deluxe category suites and minisuites, 150%–160% for other cabins.

Discounts: A third or fourth passenger in a cabin pays $132–$169 per diem (*Pacific Princess*) or $285–$350 per diem (*Island Princess*). You get a discount for early booking on most itineraries, and for arranging your own airfare.

Sports and Fitness

Health club: Lifecycles, rowing machines, weights, weight machines, saunas, massage.

Recreation: Aerobics and other exercise classes, golf driving, table tennis, shuffleboard, skeet shooting, two pools, unobstructed circuit (18 laps = 1 mile) for jogging.

Facilities

Public rooms: Six bars, four entertainment lounges, casino, disco, cinema, card room, library/writing room.

Shops: Gift shop, beauty salon/barber.

Health care: Doctor and two nurses on call.

Child care: Daytime youth programs with counselors when more than 15 children on board.

Services: Laundry service, dry cleaning, photographer.

Accessibility

Public lavatories and four cabins on each ship are equipped with wide toilet stalls and hand bars to accommodate passengers with mobility problems. All four elevators are accessible.

MV Royal Princess

Specifications

Type of ship: Cruise liner
Cruise experience: Semi-formal
Size: 45,000 tons
Cabins: 600
Outside cabins: 100%

Passengers: 1,200
Crew: 520 (international)
Officers: British
Passenger/crew ratio: 2.4 to 1
Year built: 1984

Ship's Log

Among big ships, the *Royal Princess* is one of only two that offers all outside staterooms (the other is the *Crystal Symphony*). Add to this 2 acres of open deck space forward, aft, and amidship, including a wraparound promenade, and you see why this is one of the most acclaimed cruise liners ever built—and the flagship of the Princess fleet.

The Horizon Lounge and Bar offers a breathtaking, 360° view of the sea from its position atop the ship. Lovely as it is, the lounge is rarely crowded. Most other public rooms are clustered on the Riviera Deck. The two main showrooms—the circular International Lounge and the plush and frilly cabaret-style Riviera Club—boast excellent acoustics. The Continental dining room has a bright, airy feel thanks to its pastel color scheme, a touch of art deco brass, and walls of windows to let in the sunlight.

Cabins and Rates

	Beds	Phone	TV	Sitting Area	Fridge	Tub	Average Per Diem*
Suite	Q	●	●	●	●	●	$400
Outside	T/Q	●	●	◐	●	●	$350

Airfare included. Port taxes are extra.

Cabins are all outside, and all standard staterooms are the same size. Each is finished in a different wood by category: oak veneers in the penthouses, teak in the suites, mahogany in the minisuites, and teak again in the standard cabins. Penthouses, suites, minisuites, and Aloha Deck outside cabins have private verandas. Even the smallest cabins are well equipped, with details and amenities not found in standard accommodations aboard many other ships, such as double sinks, shower/bathtubs, refrigerators, and large windows. Higher-priced cabins have wall safes, and penthouses have whirlpools. Terry robes and fresh-fruit baskets are found in each stateroom. Categories H, HH, I, J, JJ, and K are outside cabins with partially or entirely obstructed views.

Outlet voltage: 110 AC.

Single supplement: 200% of double-occupancy rate for suites or outside cabins with verandas, 150%–160% for other cabins.

Discounts: A third or fourth passenger in a cabin pays $132–$150 per diem. You get a discount for early booking and for arranging your own airfare.

Sports and Fitness

Health club: Five high-tech stationary bikes, rowing machines, whirlpool; adjacent beauty center with two saunas, two massage rooms, spa treatments.

Recreation: Aerobics and other exercise classes, golf driving, table tennis, pool sports, shuffleboard, skeet shooting, three pools (one for laps, a circular one surrounded by dipping pools, and another wading pool, all on Lido Deck), Jacuzzi, unobstructed circuit (3.5 laps = 1 mile) for jogging.

Facilities

Public rooms: Seven bars, four entertainment lounges, casino, disco, cinema, card room, library, video-game room.

Shops: Gift shop, beauty salon/barber.

Health care: Two doctors and two nurses on call.

Child care: Daytime youth programs with counselors when more than 15 children on board.

Services: Full- and self-service laundry, dry cleaning, photographer, film processing.

Accessibility

Four cabins and all public areas, except the self-service laundry room, are accessible to wheelchair users. Several public lavatories are grab bar–equipped. Raised thresholds leading to outside decks are especially high, but ramps are located at selected entrances.

TSS Sky Princess

Specifications

Type of ship: Cruise liner	*Passengers:* 1,200
Cruise experience: Semi-formal	*Crew:* 535 (international)
	Officers: British
Size: 46,000 tons	*Passenger/crew ratio:* 2.2 to 1
Number of cabins: 600	*Year built:* 1984
Outside cabins: 64%	

Ship's Log

Formerly Sitmar's *Fairsky*, the *Sky Princess* underwent a major refurbishment in 1992. A huge showroom—with a tiered floor, a large stage, and new light and sound systems—was installed. In addition to redecorating the entire ship, Princess expanded the shopping area. Three swimming pools are on deck, plus plenty of space for sunning.

Cabins and Rates

	Beds	Phone	TV	Sitting Area	Fridge	Tub	Average Per Diem*
Suite	T/D	●	●	●	●	◗	$350
Outside	T	●	●	○	○	○	$300
Inside	T	●	●	○	○	○	$250

Airfare included, except in Alaska. Port taxes are extra.

Suites have verandas. Many cabins have two upper berths to accommodate third and fourth passengers. Terry robes and fresh-fruit baskets are found in each stateroom.

Outlet voltage: 110 AC.

Single supplement: 200% of double-occupancy rate for suites and minisuites, 150%–160% for other cabins.

Discounts: A third or fourth passenger in a cabin pays $122–$131. You get a discount for early booking and for arranging your own airfare.

Sports and Fitness

Health club: Nautilus machines; sit-up board, three Lifecycles, two stationary bikes, ballet barre, sauna, massage room, large whirlpool.

Recreation: Aerobics and other exercise classes, paddle and table tennis, pool games, shuffleboard, skeet shooting, volleyball, three pools (one for children), scuba certification, jogging track (15 laps = 1 mile).

Facilities

Public rooms: Seven bars, five entertainment lounges, casino, disco, card room, library, video-game room.

Shops: Four boutiques/gift shops, beauty salon/barber.

Health care: Doctor and two nurses on call.

Child care: Youth center (open 9 AM–midnight) with separate rooms for teens and younger children (older than six months), games, video games, wide-screen TV, children's pool, sundeck, programs supervised by counselors year-round.

Services: Full- and self-service laundry, dry cleaning, photographer, film processing.

Accessibility Six cabins and all six elevators are accessible to wheelchair users.

MV Star Princess

Specifications

Type of ship: Megaship
Cruise experience: Semiformal
Size: 63,500 tons
Number of cabins: 736
Outside cabins: 77.6%

Passengers: 1,494
Crew: 600 (international)
Officers: Italian
Passenger/crew ratio: 2.5 to 1
Year built: 1989

Ship's Log The *Star Princess*, the first new ship to be built after Sitmar and Princess merged, is striking for its size alone: It has 12 public decks. Princess resisted the temptation to cram in as many cabins and staterooms as possible, and as a result, the ship is extremely spacious. Its centerpiece is the Plaza, a dramatic three-deck-high atrium topped by a dome. Perhaps the most engaging public room is the Windows on the World Lounge, with its 360° view of the sea. A million-dollar collection of contemporary art is placed throughout the ship, both in the public rooms and in individual cabins. Daytime activities revolve around the Pool Deck, where two swimming pools and four whirlpools are connected by a walkway and waterfalls, and passengers can swim to the splash bar.

Cabins and Rates

	Beds	Phone	TV	Sitting Area	Fridge	Tub	Average Per Diem*
Suite	T/Q	●	●	●	●	●	$350
Outside	T/Q	●	●	○	●	○	$300
Inside	T/Q	●	●	○	●	○	$250

Airfare included, except in Alaska. Port taxes are extra.

Standard cabins are spacious, with twin beds that convert to queen-size, a built-in safe, minifridges, and remote-control color TVs. Terry robes and fresh-fruit baskets are also found in each stateroom. The suites have separate sitting areas, marble baths, and king-size beds. Outside cabins have large picture windows; the suites and minisuites have verandas with sliding glass doors. Some outside cabins have obstructed views. Most cabins have upper berths to accommodate a third or fourth passenger.

Outlet voltage: 110 AC.

Single supplement: 200% of double-occupancy rate for suites and minisuites, 150%–160% for other cabins.

Discounts: A third or fourth passenger in a cabin pays $109–$134 per diem. You get a discount for early booking and for arranging your own airfare.

Sports and Fitness

Health club: Nautilus equipment, aerobics area, sauna, steam room, massage, beauty treatments.

Recreation: Exercise classes, shuffleboard, skeet shooting, volleyball, three pools, four whirlpools, scuba certification, jogging track (5 laps = 1 mile).

Facilities

Public rooms: Seven bars, seven lounges, casino, disco, cinema, card room, library.

Shops: Four boutiques/gift shops, beauty salon/barber.

Health care: Two doctors and two nurses on call.

Child care: Youth center (open 9 AM–midnight) for children ages two to 17, with games, video games, wide-screen TV, children's pool and sundeck, programs supervised by counselors year-round.

Services: Full- and self-service laundry, dry cleaning, photographer, film processing.

Accessibility

Ten cabins and all nine elevators are accessible to wheelchair users.

Radisson Seven Seas Cruises

The Fleet MS *Hanseatic*
SSC *Radisson Diamond*

At first glance, these two ships would seem to have nothing in common, but a closer look reveals many similarities. Each is the biggest of its kind: The *Radisson Diamond* is the largest twin-hull ship ever built for cruising, while the *Hanseatic* claims the title of biggest expedition ship afloat. Both were built by the same Finnish shipyard, and have space and passenger-to-crew ratios as good as any ship afloat. In late 1994, Radisson joined forces with Seven Seas Cruise Line, and now represents the luxury, yachtlike *Song of Flower* (which sails year-round outside the regions covered by this book) and the expedition ship *Hanseatic* to North American passengers.

Ships at a Glance

	Dining Rooms	Bars	Casino	Fitness Center	Pools	Average Per Diem
Hanseatic	1	1	○	●	1	$750
Radisson Diamond	2	4	●	●	1	$600

Cruise Experience The *Diamond* and the *Hanseatic*, built to cruise the Caribbean and Antarctica, respectively, deliver vastly different cruise experiences. For that reason, details on dining, activities, entertainment, and service are covered individually under each Ship's Log.

For More Information Radisson Seven Seas Cruises (600 Corporate Dr., Suite 410, Fort Lauderdale, FL 33334, tel. 800/333–3333).

MS Hanseatic

Type of ship: Expedition
Cruise experience: Casual
Size: 9,000 tons
Number of cabins: 94
Outside cabins: 100%
Year built: 1993

Passengers: 188
Crew: 125 (European and Filipino)
Officers: German
Passenger/crew ratio: 1.5 to 1

Ship's Log The *Hanseatic* is the world's newest, biggest, and most luxurious expedition ship. It carries all the standard expedition features—a hardened hull for plowing through Antarctic ice and 14 Zodiac landing craft for exploring otherwise inaccessible shores—in a level of comfort unusual for an adventure ship. There's a small fitness center and spa, for instance, with a whirlpool, swimming pool, sauna, and massage therapy. The ship's passenger-to-crew ratio rivals the standards of the cruise world's most expensive ships. Due to its relatively large size, the *Hanseatic* is equipped with a more varied

Chart Symbols. Ships at a Glance. **●:** *Fully equipped;* **◑:** *Partially equipped;* ○: *Not equipped.* Cabins and Rates. **D:** *Double bed;* **K:** *King-size bed;* **Q:** *Queen-size bed;* **T:** *Twin bed;* **U/L:** *Upper and lower berths;* **●:** *All cabins have this facility;* ○: *No cabins have this facility;* **◑:** *Some cabins have this facility*

selection of public rooms than most expedition ships. There's a cruise ship–style lounge for evening entertainment; a full-size lecture hall, which doubles as a cinema; and a top-deck observation lounge with 180° views of the sea. You can always visit the captain on the navigation bridge in between the enrichment lectures and Zodiac excursions that are the hallmark of the expedition experience.

The *Hanseatic*'s very high standards of comfort, especially as compared with the earlier generation of expedition ships, attract people who might not otherwise take such a cruise. It also means that the hard-core adventure traveler with special interests will be sharing the experience with more mainstream, general-interest passengers. Increasingly, these passengers are Americans, especially on Antarctica cruises, but at other times the passenger list may be mostly German, as the ship is marketed extensively in Europe as well.

Activities Zodiac explorations are the primary daytime event aboard the *Hanseatic*. In preparation for these shoreside explorations, a team of experts, such as naturalists, marine biologists, geologists, or anthropologists, brief passengers in the Darwin Lounge, a state-of-the-art facility with video and sound systems. The experts then accompany passengers ashore. Hitting the beach in a Zodiac usually means a wet landing, but the *Hanseatic* also carries two cruise ship–style enclosed tenders.

Dining Menus are distinctly European, with an emphasis on central European cooking rather the Continental cuisine more familiar to American cruise-ship passengers. This means excellent cream soups, very good salads, a game dish every night, and rich desserts—Americans may find the diet somewhat heavy-handed. A "light" menu is always available at dinnertime, though. The food is expertly presented, but portions are generally small by American standards.

The main restaurant is a spacious room, surrounded on three sides by windows. Meals are served in a single, open seating (dinner from 7 to 9:30). Breakfasts and lunches are hot and cold buffets or from a menu, while dinners are served from a menu only. The captain hosts a table several times during the cruise. A jacket and tie is standard attire for the welcome and farewell dinners, but otherwise, dress is "smart casual."

A second restaurant, the informal café, also serves light breakfast and lunch. Menus are the standard buffets of salads, hot dogs, hamburgers, hot pastas, and soups, but the main dining room is so attractive that meals here become an afterthought. There are outside tables, though, for warm-weather alfresco dining.

Entertainment Cabaret shows, orchestras, and dancing are nighttime staples in the Explorer Lounge. Throughout the day, documentary and feature films are shown in the Darwin Hall, as well as over closed-circuit television in the cabins. A four-piece band plays at afternoon tea, and for before and after dinner dancing. A resident pianist also performs pre- and post-dinner music in the Observation Lounge, and may also hold a classical-music evening.

Service and Tipping Service is excellent and the standard of English spoken by the crew is very high. The cabin staff is female and the dining-room staff is male and female—all young, energetic Germans or northern Europeans. Tips are included in the *Hanseatic*'s cruise fares, but gratuities are allowed for special service. Still, additional tipping is not expected and is never solicited.

Destinations In the Western Hemisphere, the *Hanseatic* sails to Antarctica and the Canadian Arctic, plus both coasts of North and South America. You're not likely to find a more comfortable ship going to these remote destinations. (For detailed itineraries, *see* Chapter 3.)

Cabins and Rates		Beds	Phone	TV	Sitting Area	Fridge	Tub	Average Per Diem*
Suite	D	●	●	●	●	●		$1,100
Outside	D or T	●	●	●	●	●		$750

Rates are for Antarctica. Airfare included.

Standard cabins are unusually spacious for an expedition ship. All are outside with ocean views, and come with a sitting area, marble bathroom, color television/VCR and refrigerator stocked with complimentary nonalcoholic drinks. Private butler service is available for suites and some upper-category double staterooms.

Outlet voltage: 220 AC.

Single supplement: 50% for all categories except A staterooms and suites, where two full fares are required.

Discounts: You can save $500 per person for booking early or for booking back-to-back cruises.

Sports and Fitness **Health club:** Top-deck facility with exercise equipment, free weights, sauna, massage, and glass-enclosed whirlpool.

Recreation: Swimming pool.

Facilities **Public rooms:** Main lounge with dance floor and bar, observation lounge with bar, library (books and videos), cinema.

Shops: Boutique, beauty salon.

Health care: Doctor and nurse on call.

Child care: Baby-sitting arranged privately with crew member.

Services: Laundry service, dry cleaning, photographer, film processing.

Accessibility Two cabins are accessible to wheelchair users, as are all elevators and decks except Cinema Deck. Many voyages require Zodiac landings at all or most ports, which may make it difficult for passengers with mobility impairments to go ashore.

SSC Radisson Diamond

Type of ship: Cruise liner
Cruise experience: Semi-formal
Size: 20,000 tons
Number of cabins: 177
Outside cabins: 100%

Passengers: 354
Crew: 192 (international)
Officers: Finnish
Passenger/crew ratio: 1.8 to 1
Year built: 1992

Ship's Log As wide as an ocean liner but only as long as a yacht, the *Diamond* is the only cruise ship ever to receive a *Popular Mechanics* design and engineering award. The futuristic catamaran resembles a spider perched over the sea. While the twin-hull design actually does make the ship more stable and reduce the chance of getting seasick, the difference in motion takes some getting used to. During a storm there is none of the normal pitch and roll, but stabilizers cause a very slight side-to-side jerking motion—which only becomes an issue if you are wearing high heels and trying to keep your balance. The *Diamond* was specifically built to stage meetings and conventions at sea, so in addition to being one of the most stable cruise ships afloat, it is also especially spacious.

A cruise aboard *Diamond* is pure class all the way, catering to the passenger who has seen many ships and has specific demands of a cruise ship. Impeccable service and attention to detail, combined with some of the most extensive business facilities afloat, give the *Diamond* the feel of a seagoing Radisson hotel, the company that handles all the ship's hotel operations. Whether traveling on this ship for business or pleasure, the *Diamond* and Radisson ensure that every passenger is treated like a guest at a fine luxury resort.

Activities In keeping with the ship's relaxed mood, there are few organized events on board. People gather at their leisure around such activities as dancing lessons, card games, backgammon, and shuffleboard. The *Diamond* also has an extensive book and videotape library. At least once a cruise (weather permitting), water activities are held off the large marina platform, which is built into the stern of the ship and lowers into the water. Passengers can swim in a small netted pool, ride on a Jet Ski, or snorkel.

A number of theme cruises are scheduled each year; the most popular are culinary and literary. The ship's lecture series headlines speakers on a wide range of topics from banking to Broadway musicals. Ashore, the *Diamond* offers some interesting alternatives to the usual shore excursions: In St. Maarten you can race on an "America's Cup" 12-meter sailboat.

Dining Dining aboard the *Diamond* reflects its elegant and exclusive demeanor. International cuisine is served in the Grand Dining Room—one of the prettiest dining rooms afloat—in one open seating, so you dine when and with whomever you want (dinner is served 7:30–10). There's one formal night per cruise, with elegant casual attire the norm other evenings—a little more relaxed than on other ships in this price category.

A second dinner option is the intimate gourmet Italian restaurant, also with one seating at 8. Six wonderful courses are served from a fixed menu in a festive atmosphere. Reservations should be made as soon as you board, because the restaurant is very popular.

Breakfast and lunch buffets are served in the Grill (at night this is the Italian restaurant). Early-riser coffee is served daily beginning at 6:30 AM, and afternoon tea is served with rich pastries in the Windows Lounge or the Grill. Room service is available 24 hours a day from an extensive menu; in-room dinners are served complete with linen napery, crystal, china, and flowers.

Entertainment Evening entertainment is generally mellow and consists of cabaret-style shows, a pianist, a small musical combo, and comedians. Partyers can stay as late as they like in the disco and the casino.

Service and Tipping Cabin service is expertly provided by female Austrian, Swiss, and Scandinavian cabin stewardesses; the dining-room staff is mostly female as well. The *Radisson Diamond* has a no-tipping policy.

Destinations The *Diamond* gives passengers a choice of wintertime Caribbean itineraries lasting 3, 4, 7, or 10 days, as well as Panama Canal transits. Summer and fall are spent cruising the Mediterranean. (For detailed itineraries, *see* Chapter 3.)

Cabins and Rates

	Beds	Phone	TV	Sitting Area	Fridge	Tub	Average Per Diem*
Suite	Q or T	●	●	●	●	●	$600

Airfare and port taxes are extra.

Cabins are all outside on three upper decks; most have a private balcony, others have a large bay window. None have obstructed views. Soothing mauve, sky-blue, or sea-green fabrics are accented by birch wood, and each cabin has a stocked minibar and refrigerator. Bathrooms are spacious, with marble vanities, tubs, and hair dryers. In-cabin TVs show CNN and feature films.

Outlet voltage: 110 AC.

Single supplement: 125% of double-occupancy rate.

Discounts: Up to 50% off the second week of a cruise when selected itineraries are combined for a sailing of 14 days or longer.

Sports and Fitness
Health club: Aerobics studio, weight room, Lifecycles, Lifesteps, Liferowers, Jacuzzi, and body-toning spa with massage and herbal-wrap treatments.

Recreation: Golf driving range with nets, putting green, minigolf; shuffleboard; water sports, including snorkeling, windsurfing, jet skiing, and swimming; jogging track.

Facilities
Public rooms: Four bars, entertainment lounge/disco, casino, library, conference center and boardroom.

Shops: Boutique, drugstore, beauty salon/barber.

Health care: Doctor and nurse on call.

Child care: None.

Services: Laundry service, photographer, film-developing service, business center with software library, fax, publishing facilities, personal computer hookups.

Accessibility
Elevators, public lavatories, and two cabins are accessible to wheelchair users.

Regency Cruises

The Fleet *Regent Isle*
Regent Rainbow
Regent Sea
Regent Spirit
Regent Star
Regent Sun

Regency operates the biggest collection of former transatlantic ocean liners afloat. For cruise buffs, sailing on ships that crossed the oceans can be a great thrill. All these charming, mature ships are comfortable and friendly rather than modern and glitzy. Many have enclosed promenades; other classic features include stained glass, orchestra balconies in the dining rooms, and full-screen cinemas.

Ships at a Glance

	Dining Rooms	Bars	Casino	Fitness Center	Pools	Average Per Diem
Regent Isle	2	5	●	●	3	$157
Regent Rainbow	1	6	●	●	1	$242
Regent Sea	1	3	●	●	1	$186
Regent Spirit	1	5	●	●	1	$199
Regent Star	1	4	●	●	2	$295
Regent Sun	1	5	●	●	2	$253

Cruise Experience Regency has carved a niche for itself by offering affordable cruises to unusual destinations. Passengers tend to be experienced cruisers who want to see more than the typical Caribbean loop but can't afford pricier lines or first-timers looking for an inexpensive vacation. Alaska cruises draw mostly families and younger folks.

Besides its interesting itineraries, Regency delivers a level of onboard refinement not often found on a lower-priced cruise. As on the more expensive lines, passengers sign for all onboard purchases, settling their accounts when they debark. European-style service and outstanding Continental cuisine are among the other features usually associated with higher-priced cruise lines. Gentlemen hosts, who act as dancing and bridge partners for single female passengers, are on board during sailings of seven days or longer. A resident naturalist and a geologist accompany each Alaska sailing. Nevertheless, these are not luxury cruises, and passengers should not expect the elegance of the *Queen Elizabeth 2*, the *Rotterdam*, or even the *Norway*.

Chart Symbols. Ships at a Glance. **●:** *Fully equipped;* **◑:** *Partially equipped;* ○: *Not equipped.* Cabins and Rates. **D:** *Double bed;* **K:** *King-size bed;* **Q:** *Queen-size bed;* **T:** *Twin bed;* **U/L:** *Upper and lower berths;* **●:** *All cabins have this facility;* ○: *No cabins have this facility;* **◑:** *Some cabins have this facility*

In addition to Regency's low published rates, substantial discounts are given for advance bookings, back-to-back or repeat cruises, or trips during the shoulder season. Special deals like second-honeymoon packages, which include a number of romantic perks, are a nice touch.

Activities Regency offers bingo, crafts classes, dance lessons, duplicate bridge, wine tasting, pool games, scavenger hunts, trivia quizzes, and other typical activities. On the *Regent Spirit* and *Regent Sun*, onboard snorkeling and scuba instruction is offered in the Caribbean.

Dining Cuisine is interesting and compares more favorably to a fine restaurant than a typical cruise line. Portions are hearty. "Lean and Light" entrées are excellent. Breakfast and lunch are often open seating. Dinner is served in two assigned seatings (6 and 8:15). There are two formal evenings on each seven-night cruise. Write one month ahead for special diet requests or kosher selections.

The Lido café serves good breakfast and lunch buffets, and an outdoor grill offers hot dogs, hamburgers, and chicken for lunch. Other food offerings are mid-morning bouillon, afternoon tea, hot and cold hors d'oeuvres before dinner, and a gracious midnight buffet; snack hours are long and fill the gaps between meals. Room service is prompt, accurate, and available 24 hours from a limited menu.

Entertainment You'll see nightly variety shows or movies, and dance to disco or a big-band orchestra. At some ports, local folkloric performers come aboard. Other lively and not-so-lively participatory games and activities include "horse racing," passenger talent shows, Liar's Club, and the well-attended "Mr. and Mrs." newlyweds game. A singles party is held early in the cruise. Overall, the entertainment is wholesome (no off-color jokes or Las Vegas–style dancers) and appropriate for children. About five recent films are shown weekly in the ships' theaters.

Service and Tipping With relatively low passenger-to-crew ratios, service is superior to similarly priced lines. Because Regency respects its employees, treats them well, and even provides entertainment for them, there is a low personnel turnover. This fosters dignified, competent service that is even overconscientious at times. The line is one of the few with all female cabin stewards. Most of the staff is recruited from Europe, and although language lessons are given on board, new employees sometimes have an initial problem with English. Tip the cabin stewardess and the dining-room waiter $3 each per passenger per diem, the busboy $1.50.

Destinations Regency is known for its innovative itineraries throughout the Western Hemisphere. The line is one of the few that uses Montego Bay, Jamaica, and Cozumel, Mexico, as home ports. (For detailed itineraries, *see* Chapter 3.)

For More Information Regency Cruises (260 Madison Ave., New York, NY 10016, tel. 212/972–4499).

Regent Isle

Specifications *Type of ship:* Classic liner   *Passengers:* 925
Cruise experience: Casual   *Crew:* 450 (European)
Size: 25,000 tons   *Officers:* Italian
Number of cabins: 464   *Passenger/crew ratio:* 2 to 1
Outside cabins: 51.2%   *Year built:* 1957

Ship's Log A former Sitmar and then Princess ship, the *Regent Isle* joined the Regency fleet in late 1995. Built in 1957 as an ocean liner and refurbished in 1993, the ship retains much of its original look, with teakwood decks, glass-paneled library bookshelves, muted pastel interiors, and wood paneling. As is often the case on converted ocean liners, however, public space is relatively limited.

Cabins and Rates	Beds	Phone	TV	Sitting Area	Fridge	Tub	Average Per Diem*
Suite	D	●	●	●	●	●	$205
Outside	T or U/L	●	○	○	○	○	$157
Inside	T or U/L	●	○	○	○	○	$125

Rates are for the Caribbean. Airfare and port taxes are extra.

Because the ship was built as a liner, cabins are larger than average and include such features as oversize closets, full-length mirrors, and wood trim. Outside views from cabins on the Aloha Deck are obstructed by lifeboats; cabins on the Baja Deck look onto a public promenade. All cabins, except suites and cabins in the lowest categories, have two upper berths.

Outlet voltage: 110 AC.

Single supplement: 140%–200% of double-occupancy rate. Regency will match same-sex single passengers; if no roommate is found, the single supplement is waived.

Discounts: A third or fourth passenger in a cabin pays $44.50–$49.50 per diem for a two-day cruise or $71–$85 per diem for a five-day cruise. A child sharing a cabin with two adults pays $24.50–$29.50 per diem for a two-day cruise or $51–$65 per diem for a five-day cruise.

Sports and Fitness	**Health club:** Exercise equipment including stationary bikes, rowing and Universal machines, treadmill, and free weights; men's and women's saunas; massage.

Recreation: Aerobics and other exercise classes, shuffleboard, three pools, partially obstructed circuit for jogging.

Facilities	**Public rooms:** Five bars, seven lounges, casino, disco, cinema, card room, library.

Shops: Boutiques, beauty salon/barber.

Health care: Doctor and nurse on call.

Child care: Youth programs with counselors on two- and five-day Caribbean cruises, baby-sitting arranged privately with staff member.

Services: Laundry service, photographer, film processing.

Accessibility	Ramps have been installed throughout the ship and most of the elevators are accessible to wheelchair users; however, some areas remain inaccessible.

Regent Rainbow

Specifications	*Type of ship:* Classic liner	*Passengers:* 960
	Cruise experience: Casual	*Crew:* 420 (mostly European)
	Size: 25,000 tons	*Officers:* Greek
	Number of cabins: 484	*Passenger/crew ratio:* 2.3 to 1
	Outside cabins: 68%	*Year built:* 1957

Ship's Log	Regency put $75 million into restoring the former *Santa Rosa*, and they've done a commendable job. In the Chanterelle dining room, classic touches include an orchestra balcony and a stained-glass ceil-

ing; it's an appropriate venue for the excellent cuisine, prepared by expertly trained French chefs. After dinner, most passengers head up to the Bridge Deck for dancing to an orchestra in the Starlight Lounge or bopping the night away in the Sky Room disco. A casino provides all the usual tables, from blackjack to Caribbean stud poker. A well-appointed fitness center has saunas and a massage room.

Cabins and Rates		Beds	Phone	TV	Sitting Area	Fridge	Tub	Average Per Diem*
	Suites	D	●	●	●	●	○	$350
	Outside	D, T	●	●	◐	◐	◐	$242
	Inside	D, T	●	●	○	○	○	$205

*Rates are for the Panama Canal. Airfare and port taxes are extra.

Cabins are spacious. Many have large picture windows. All have color TV (including CNN), telephone, radio, and climate control.

Outlet voltage: 110 AC.

Single supplement: 140%–200% of double-occupancy rate. Regency will match same-sex single passengers; if no roommate is found, the single supplement is waived.

Discounts: A third or fourth passenger in a cabin pays about $70 per diem.

Sports and Fitness

Health club: Exercise equipment including step machine, treadmill, Nautilus, and free weights; sauna; massage.

Recreation: Aerobics and other exercise classes, golf driving range, shuffleboard, Ping-Pong, one pool, two whirlpools, jogging track.

Facilities

Public rooms: Six bars, six lounges, casino, disco, card room, library.

Shops: Boutiques, beauty salon/barber.

Health care: Infirmary, doctor on call.

Child care: Youth programs with counselors on Alaska cruises and during major holidays, baby-sitting arranged privately with staff member.

Services: Laundry service, photographer.

Accessibility Four cabins are accessible to wheelchair users.

Regent Sea

Specifications

Type of ship: Classic liner
Cruise experience: Casual
Size: 22,000 tons
Number of cabins: 361
Outside cabins: 96%
Year built: 1957

Passengers: 729
Crew: 365 (European/international)
Officers: Greek
Passenger/crew ratio: 2 to 1

Ship's Log The *Gripsholm*, a legendary Swedish-American luxury liner, fell on hard times and underwent several incarnations before Regency purchased the ship and transformed it into the *Regent Sea*. The vessel retains its classic lines and much of its original handsome woods and brass fixtures. It's also one of the few remaining cruise ships with twin smokestacks and a wraparound, glass-enclosed promenade. The latter allows you to enjoy Alaska's spectacular scenery without having to brave its sometimes soggy climate.

The public rooms (except the dining room, theater, and gymnasium) are on one deck, which makes it easy to get your bearings. But, as on many older ships, the dining room cuts the Main Deck in half, forcing passengers to go up a deck, across, and then down again to get past the dining room when it's closed. Although the *Sea* is well maintained and appointed, don't look for opulence. The decor is a blend of traditional and modern, with a fairly successful marriage of old wood and highly polished mirrors and brass.

Cabins and Rates		Beds	Phone	TV	Sitting Area	Fridge	Tub	Average Per Diem*
	Suites	T or D	●	○	●	◐	●	$249
	Outside	T or U/L	●	○	◐	○	◐	$186
	Inside	T or D	●	○	○	○	○	$153

*Rates are for world cruise. Airfare and port taxes are extra.

Cabins come in many different configurations, and are quite large compared with those on some newer ships. Storage space is unusually abundant. Some categories have three or four closets, some with built-in shoe racks, and alcoves where steamer trunks once were stored. Most cabins are outside, but lifeboats obstruct the view of some on the Sun Deck, where all suites and cabins look onto a public promenade (privacy is afforded in these cases with one-way-mirror windows). It takes a few detours to reach the forward cabins on the Bolero and Allegro decks (the bottom two decks), accessible only by the forward stairways.

Outlet voltage: 110 AC.

Single supplement: 130%–200% of double-occupancy rate. Regency will match same-sex single passengers; if no roommate is found, the single supplement is waived.

Discounts: A third or fourth passenger in a cabin pays $90–$119 per diem. A child under 18 in a cabin with two adults pays $75–$104 per diem.

Sports and Fitness

Health club: Exercise equipment including stationary bikes, rowing and Universal machines, treadmill, and free weights; whirlpools; men's and women's saunas; massage.

Recreation: Aerobics and other exercise classes, golf driving range, shuffleboard, Ping-Pong, pool, unobstructed indoor-outdoor circuit for jogging.

Facilities

Public rooms: Three bars, nine lounges, casino, disco, cinema, library.

Shops: Boutiques, beauty salon/barber.

Health care: Doctor on call.

Child care: Youth programs with counselors on Alaska cruises and during major holidays, baby-sitting arranged privately with staff member.

Services: Laundry service, photographer.

Accessibility Two cabins are accessible to wheelchair users. All elevators and public rooms are reached from a level deck.

Regent Spirit

Specifications *Type of ship:* Classic liner   *Passengers:* 400
Cruise experience: Casual   *Crew:* 200 (mostly European)

Size: 12,500 tons
Number of cabins: 211
Outside cabins: 100%

Officers: Greek
Passenger/crew ratio: 2 to 1
Year built: 1962

Ship's Log Every cabin is an outside one on Regency's smallest ship. The almost yachtlike *Spirit* is tiny for an ocean liner but shares a number of classic elements with its larger fleetmates, from the long, sweeping lines of the hull to the stained-glass ceiling in the Monte Carlo Court. The Lido Cafe adds a contemporary touch: A glass-enclosed wall looks out onto the pool and potted plants (or passengers) soak up the sunlight that streams through. It's a nice, bright spot for buffet lunch or a cup of coffee any time.

Cabins and Rates

	Beds	Phone	TV	Sitting Area	Fridge	Tub	Average Per Diem*
Suites	D	●	●	●	●	○	$313
Outside	D, T	●	●	○	○	◐	$199

*Rates are for Central America. Airfare and port taxes are extra.

Cabins are all outside but relatively small compared with those aboard Regency's other ships. All are appointed in a clean, contemporary decor of upholstered chairs, mirrors, and white surfaces. Many have picture windows, and a very high proportion have real bathtubs. All have color TV, telephone, radio, and climate control.

Outlet voltage: 220 AC.

Single supplement: 140%–200% of double-occupancy rate. Regency will match same-sex single passengers; if no roommate is found, the single supplement is waived.

Discounts: A third or fourth passenger in a cabin pays $67–$75 per diem. A child under 18 in a cabin with two adults pays $63–$70 per diem.

Sports and Fitness **Health club:** Exercise equipment including stationary bikes, rowing and Universal machines, treadmill, and free weights; sauna; massage.

Recreation: Aerobics and other exercise classes, golf driving range, pool, onboard scuba and snorkeling instruction, jogging track.

Facilities **Public rooms:** Five bars, six lounges, casino, disco, cinema, card room, library.

Shops: Boutiques, beauty salon/barber.

Health care: Doctor on call.

Child care: Youth programs with counselors during major holidays, baby-sitting arranged privately with staff member.

Services: Laundry service, photographer.

Accessibility Four cabins are accessible to wheelchair users.

Regent Star

Specifications *Type of ship:* Classic liner
Cruise experience: Casual
Size: 24,500 tons
Number of cabins: 474
Outside cabins: 61.3%
Year built: 1957

Passengers: 950
Crew: 450 (European/international)
Officers: Greek
Passenger/crew ratio: 2 to 1

Ship's Log The *Star*—formerly the *Statendam*—is a handsome vessel that has delighted cruisers for decades. Although its capacity of 950 passengers is a lot for a ship this size, its public rooms, including the main dining room, are spacious, and the two-to-one ratio of passengers to crew assures personal attention. The *Star*'s interior is streamlined and contemporary, and most of the public rooms, including the Cordon Bleu dining room, feature large windows. With a classic-style glass enclosed promenade deck, the ship is especially well suited for its summer sailings in Alaska.

Cabins and Rates

	Beds	Phone	TV	Sitting Area	Fridge	Tub	Average Per Diem*
Outside	D, T, or U/L	●	○	◐	○	◑	$295
Inside	D, T, or U/L	●	○	○	○	◑	$212

Rates are for Alaska. Airfare and port taxes are extra.

Unusual built-in amenities evoke the *Star*'s days as a transatlantic liner. In several categories, a private foyer off the main hallway serves two cabins. Cubbyholes in the wall next to each berth can keep a water glass or book for bedtime reading. Brass guards on vanities secure toiletries, and hideaway writing tables pull out from the dressers. Some baths feature real tubs and medicine cabinets. Views from cabins on the Bridge Deck are obstructed by lifeboats. On the Upper Promenade Deck cabins look onto a public promenade; one-way-mirror windows afford privacy.

Outlet voltage: 110 AC.

Single supplement: 130%–200% of double-occupancy rate. Regency will match same-sex single passengers; if no roommate is found, the single supplement is waived.

Discounts: A third or fourth passenger in a cabin pays $90–$118 per diem. A child under 18 in a cabin with two adults pays $75–$104 per diem. Cabin S18 is a sitting room that can be booked for an extra $985 (with no additional passengers) or $1,065 (for each additional passenger) with cabin S16 or S17 to form a large suite.

Sports and Fitness **Health club:** Lower-deck gym with exercise equipment, including stationary bikes, rowing and Universal machines, treadmill, and free weights; indoor pool; sauna; massage.

Recreation: Aerobics and other exercise classes, Ping-Pong, shuffleboard, trapshooting, outdoor pool, two whirlpools, golf driving range, basketball hoop, unobstructed circuit for jogging.

Facilities **Public rooms:** Four bars, four entertainment lounges, casino, disco, card room.

Shops: Boutiques, beauty salon/barber.

Health care: Doctor on call.

Child care: Youth programs with counselors on Alaska cruises and during major holidays, baby-sitting arranged privately with staff member.

Services: Laundry service, photographer.

Accessibility Two cabins are accessible to wheelchair users. All elevators and public rooms are reached from a level deck. The Sports Deck is inaccessible.

Regent Sun

Specifications	
Type of ship: Classic liner	*Passengers:* 836
Cruise experience: Casual	*Crew:* 410 (European/
Size: 25,500 tons	international)
Number of cabins: 419	*Officers:* Greek
Outside cabins: 81.9%	*Passenger/crew ratio:* 2 to 1
Year built: 1964	

Ship's Log The *Regent Sun*—formerly Royal Cruise Line's *Royal Odyssey* and still retaining original Israeli art from its days as the *Shalom*—became Regency Cruises' flagship in 1988. Though it is a relatively seasoned ship, Regency keeps its appearance pristine. Among its noteworthy attributes are the library, which looks out onto an enclosed promenade similar to the one aboard the *Regent Sea*. The cinema is notable for its back-lit stained-glass panels. It also has direct access to the enclosed promenade.

Low ceilings can make corridors and the lobby feel cramped, but numerous public rooms provide varied retreats. The Yacht Club is a small lounge suitable for a quiet drink, and the Panorama Lounge is rarely crowded. For more active socializing, the Monte Carlo Court is busy when a band is playing or when the predinner hors d'oeuvres are served, and the Lido Cafe is rather light and airy with wicker furnishings. The Casino Royale is small compared with casinos aboard some megaships but nicely proportioned for a ship this size; its glass enclosure effectively prevents underage children from playing the slot machines. The Regency Lounge, which is the main showroom, offers good visibility, padded seats, and easy access. The Cordon Rouge Dining Room is small, pretty, and well laid out, offering a range of seating options.

Cabins and Rates	Beds	Phone	TV	Sitting Area	Fridge	Tub	Average Per Diem*
Suite	K or T	●	○	●	○	◑	$330
Outside	T	●	○	◑	○	◑	$253
Inside	T	●	○	○	○	○	$199

*Rates are for Northeastern United States and Canada.
Airfare and port taxes are extra.*

Cabins and closets are average size and modestly but tastefully furnished. Decor uses bright colors and blond woods. The look is modular, a reflection of the tastes popular at the time the ship was built. Cabins and corridors are color coordinated—each deck in a different scheme—so passengers can easily find their cabin. Lifeboats obstruct the view from many cabins on Riviera Deck. Some cabins on Promenade Deck look onto a public walkway; one-way-mirror windows provide privacy. Inside cabins are unusually large.

Outlet voltage: 110 AC.

Single supplement: 130%–200% of double-occupancy rate. Regency will match same-sex single passengers; if no roommate is found, the single supplement is waived.

Discounts: A third or fourth passenger in a cabin pays $80–$106 per diem. A child under 18 in a cabin with two adults pays $42–$89 per diem.

Sports and Fitness **Health club:** Below-deck gym with exercise equipment including stationary bikes, rowing and Universal machines, free weights; indoor swimming pool; men's and women's saunas; massage.

Recreation: Aerobics and other exercise classes, deck tennis, miniature golf and driving cage, Ping-Pong, shuffleboard, outdoor pool, onboard scuba and snorkeling instruction.

Facilities　**Public rooms:** Five bars, four entertainment lounges, casino, disco, cinema, card room, library, video-game room.

Shops: Boutique, beauty salon/barber.

Health care: Doctor on call.

Child care: Youth programs with counselors on New England/Canada summer cruises and during major holidays, baby-sitting arranged privately with staff member.

Services: Laundry service, photographer.

Accessibility　Two cabins have wider doors and bathrooms for wheelchair users. Public rooms are reached from a level deck. The Bridge Deck, where the deck-tennis court and golf driving cage are located, is inaccessible. There is a single step to get into the gym.

Renaissance Cruises

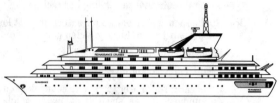

The Fleet *Renaissance IV*

Renaissance's cruising yacht is a relatively tiny vessel, similar in size to Cunard's *Sea Goddess*. But unlike other vessels in this class, it lacks the sumptuous surroundings—and the hefty price tag—of such competitors in the luxury-small-ship category as Seabourn Cruise Line or Silversea Cruises. Renaissance built eight of these ships, but only one sails within the Western Hemisphere.

Ship at a Glance

	Dining Rooms	Bars	Casino	Fitness Center	Pools	Average Per Diem
Renaissance IV	1	1	◐	◐	1	$225

Cruise Experience Though outwardly similar to Cunard's *Sea Goddess*, the lifestyle aboard this Renaissance yacht places less emphasis on elegance. Although men dress for dinner most nights, it's not quite the tuxedo crowd found aboard the line's pricier competitors. Culture, not couture, accounts for Renaissance's appeal. Ports are chosen for the sake of adventure and education, and the itineraries are among the most unusual you'll find. The ships sail mostly at night, allowing for maximum time during daylight for exploring the islands.

Passengers are typically intellectual, culturally minded individuals. They are experienced cruisers, in their late fifties or early sixties, who want to learn about the world as they travel in supreme comfort that is still priced less than other luxury yachts. Like other cultural cruises, Renaissance provides passengers with pre-trip reading lists. A number of special-interest tour operators, such as the Smithsonian Institution, charter other Renaissance vessels for educational tours.

Activities Don't look for pool games, trivia contests, or other traditional cruise pastimes. Renaissance passengers prefer more introspective activities, such as enjoying a reading selection from the ship's library or viewing a first-run video on their in-suite VCR. However, Renaissance does have a small casino and extensive water-sports equipment, such as Sunfish, waverunners, and snorkeling gear.

Dining The cuisine is international, with a focus on nouvelle light dishes with fresh ingredients. Meals in the restaurant are at a single open seating (dinner at 7:30). Men are expected to wear a jacket and tie to dinner. The extensive wine cellar is moderately priced. There is no smoking in the dining room. Early morning coffee, breakfast, and lunch are available on deck, weather permitting. A late-night snack is served; 24-hour room service from a limited menu is available. A questionnaire is mailed to passengers before their trip so that the

Chart Symbols. Ships at a Glance. ●: *Fully equipped;* ◐: *Partially equipped;* ○: *Not equipped.* Cabins and Rates. **D:** *Double bed;* **K:** *King-size bed;* **Q:** *Queen-size bed;* **T:** *Twin bed;* **U/L:** *Upper and lower berths;* ●: *All cabins have this facility;* ○: *No cabins have this facility;* ◐: *Some cabins have this facility*

cabin refrigerator may be stocked with their favorite beverages and snacks. (There is a charge for whatever is consumed.)

Entertainment Since most passengers go ashore during the day, the ship's limited entertainment is confined to the evening hours, when a small two- or three-piece band performs in the main lounge. There's also a piano bar. Local entertainers are sometimes brought on board to perform. The library is well stocked with best-sellers, old favorites, reference works, and recently released videos.

Service and Tipping Service is elegant, unobtrusive, and omnipresent, though a bit short of flawless. Tip the stewardess $3 per passenger per diem, the dining-room staff $5 (dining-room tips are pooled). A 15% gratuity is automatically added to the bar bill. All tips may be charged to your shipboard account, if you'd rather not use cash.

Destinations In the Western Hemisphere, Renaissance sails to large and small islands throughout the Caribbean. (For detailed itineraries, *see* Chapter 3.)

For More Information Renaissance Cruises (1800 Eller Dr., Suite 300, Box 350307, Fort Lauderdale, FL 33335-0307, tel. 800/525–2450).

Renaissance IV

Specifications *Type of ship:* Cruise yacht
Cruise experience: Semi-formal
Size: 4,500 tons
Number of cabins: 50
Outside cabins: 100%

Passengers: 104
Crew: 67 (European)
Officers: Italian
Passenger/crew ratio: 1.6 to 1
Year built: 1991

Ship's Log The Renaissance ship isn't graced with long, lean lines, but makes up for its outwardly awkward appearance with an impressive interior. Subtle earth tones dominate, and many of the walls are paneled in rich, dark woods accented by polished brass. Throughout the ship extensive and effective use is made of mirrors, polished teak, marble, and tasteful modern art. The atmosphere is refined and warm, and (because the ship is small) friendly—like a private club.

Cabins and Rates	Beds	Phone	TV	Sitting Area	Fridge	Tub	Average Per Diem*
Suite	T/Q	●	●	●	●	○	$225

Rates are for the Caribbean. Airfare and port taxes are extra.

Every cabin on the *Renaissance IV* is an outside suite, but they come in six different categories. All are large compared with those on other small upscale cruise ships, and mirror tiling makes them seem even larger. Bathrooms have teak floors and marble paneling and are equipped with hair dryers; none have bathtubs, however—an unusual omission for this type of ship. Beds can be configured as either twins or queen size. Rooms have VCRs and a lockable drawer. Most cabins on the Erikson, Marco Polo, and Columbus decks look onto public promenades. Top category Renaissance Suites have oversize, walk-in closets and private verandas that look out to sea with no obstructions.

Outlet voltage: 110 AC.

Single supplement: $995 over the double-occupancy rate.

Discounts: A third or fourth passenger in a cabin pays $995 per cruise.

Sports and Fitness **Health club:** Massage, sauna.

Recreation: Zodiacs, sailfish, snorkeling, pool, whirlpool, unobstructed circuits for jogging.

Facilities **Public rooms:** Piano bar, lounge, small casino, library.

Shops: Gift shop, hairdresser.

Health care: Doctor on call.

Child care: None.

Services: Laundry service.

Accessibility There are ledges at the entrance to cabin bathrooms and at the doors that lead from the outer decks to the inside of the ship. There is no official policy regarding wheelchair users, but Renaissance advises that these cruises may be too strenuous for passengers with mobility problems.

Royal Caribbean Cruise Line

Sovereign of the Seas

The Fleet
MS *Legend of the Seas*
MS *Majesty of the Seas*
MS *Monarch of the Seas*
MS *Nordic Empress*
MS *Song of America*
MS *Song of Norway*
MS *Sovereign of the Seas*
MS *Splendour of the Seas*
MS *Sun Viking*
MS *Viking Serenade*

For sheer size and capacity, Royal Caribbean established the standard for big ships when it introduced the *Sovereign of the Seas* in 1988. Later sister ships, the *Majesty* and *Monarch*, were even bigger. The line's latest new-builds are slightly scaled-down, yet still giants at 70,000 tons. The first, *Legend of the Seas*, debuted in spring 1995. A sister, the *Splendour of the Seas*, is scheduled to follow in spring 1996. Four more megaships are on order for delivery through 1998. Cantilevered from the top of the funnel is the hallmark of every RCCL ship: the glass-enclosed Viking Crown Lounge, with its bird's-eye view. Another trademark is the musical-comedy theme found in all the public rooms. Despite the immense size of some of these vessels, cabins are comfortable but neither luxurious nor spacious.

Ships at a Glance

	Dining Rooms	Bars	Casino	Fitness Center	Pools	Average Per Diem
Legend of the Seas *Splendour of the Seas*	1	5	●	●	2	$321
Majesty of the Seas *Monarch of the Seas* *Sovereign of the Seas*	2	10	●	●	2	$299–$314
Nordic Empress	1	6	●	●	1	$309
Song of Norway	1	5	●	●	1	$308
Song of America	1	6	●	●	2	$292
Sun Viking	1	6	●	●	1	$277
Viking Serenade	2	6	●	●	1	$296

Cruise Experience
RCCL is one of the best-run and most-popular cruise lines. While the fleet comprises ships of almost every size, the company's philosophy remains consistent: Offer every imaginable activity in a resortlike atmosphere between port calls at a variety of destina-

Chart Symbols. Ships at a Glance. ●: *Fully equipped;* ◐: *Partially equipped;* ○: *Not equipped.* Cabins and Rates. **D:** *Double bed;* **K:** *King-size bed;* **Q:** *Queen-size bed;* **T:** *Twin bed;* **U/L:** *Upper and lower berths;* ●: *All cabins have this facility;* ○: *No cabins have this facility;* ◐: *Some cabins have this facility*

tions. RCCL draws customers from every age group and economic bracket, all lured by the prospect of a cruise experience that is above average but certainly not upscale.

Activities Life on board is similar to that of the party ships run by Carnival, but slightly more sophisticated and conservative. Among the many activities offered are cash bingo (plus free poolside bingo for prizes), board and card games, arts and crafts, pool games, dance classes, golf driving and putting, and "horse racing." Following current fitness trends, the ships also feature numerous exercise activities and well-equipped gyms. Most Caribbean cruises have daylong beach parties in a cove at CocoCay, a private Bahamian island. The line's "Golf Ahoy" program includes greens time at private courses in Florida, the Caribbean, Bermuda, the Bahamas, and Baja Mexico.

Dining Food is above-average Continental fare, served at two assigned seatings per meal (dinner at 6:15 and 8:30). Two formal evenings are held on each seven-day cruise, one on three- and four-day cruises. The line's Sovereign sisters have two dining rooms—the closest you get to intimate aboard these huge vessels. Health-conscious eaters or those just watching their diet can order menu selections that conform to American Heart Association guidelines, but RCCL is not equipped to handle special dietary requests, other than providing vegetarian and children's dishes at all meals.

The Lido-style indoor-outdoor café serves early morning coffee, a buffet breakfast, and lunch. Other food service includes afternoon tea (with a make-your-own sundae bar), a midnight buffet, and late-night sandwich service in the lounges. Room service is available 24 hours from a limited menu. In-cabin multicourse dinners can be ordered from a selection of dishes off the evening's dining-room menu.

Entertainment This is one of RCCL's strong suits. The company follows the established formula for cruise-ship entertainment, but with a dash of pizzazz and professionalism that most other lines often lack. Nightly variety shows, late-night comedy and solo cabaret acts, steel-drum combos, passenger talent shows, and theme parties are staged on each cruise.

Service and Tipping The crew is generally enthusiastic and personable, although service can be slow—not surprising given the number of passengers that must be served on the larger ships. Unfortunately, crew members display little subtlety in soliciting tips. Tip the room steward and the waiter each $3 per passenger per diem, the busboy $1.50; the headwaiter gets $2.50 per passenger per cruise (for excellent service only). Tips for bar staff should be given at the time of service.

Destinations Royal Caribbean still calls its namesake home, but the line also sails to Alaska, Bermuda, Mexico, Hawaii, and the Panama Canal in the Western Hemisphere. (For detailed itineraries, *see* Chapter 3.)

For More Information Royal Caribbean Cruise Line (1050 Caribbean Way, Miami, FL 33132, tel. 305/539–6000).

MS Legend of the Seas and MS Splendour of the Seas

Specifications *Type of ship:* Megaship   *Passengers:* 1,804
Cruise experience: Casual   *Crew:* 732 (international)
Size: 70,000 tons   *Officers:* Norwegian
Number of cabins: 902   *Passenger/crew ratio:* 2.4 to 1
Outside cabins: 65%   *Year built:* 1995

Ship's Log RCCL's second generation of megaships blend many hallmarks of the RCCL design and add some new twists as well. For the first time, RCCL's signature seven-deck atrium lobby and Royal Crown observation lounge are combined in one 14-story unit. Other innovations include the cruise world's first miniature golf courses, landscaped to imitate real links with greens, sand traps, and water hazards. The Solarium, an indoor-outdoor public space set around the pool, uses a new design that increases the amount of glass in the retractable roof and minimizes the need for steel supports. The Solarium's Roman-inspired decor uses lightweight plastics and plaster to simulate a setting of marble and stone. Each ship also has a star-gazing platform on the highest forward deck.

The dining rooms aboard the *Legend* and *Splendour* are two-level extravaganzas, flanked on either side by 20-foot walls of glass. In the center, a revolving platform supports a grand piano. A grand staircase connects the upper and lower dining levels. Main show-rooms span two decks as well, but rather than a balconied design, there is a single, sloping, amphitheater-style floor. At the stage, a real orchestra pit can be raised and lowered. Unlike many other showrooms, passengers sit in real theater seats rather than in groupings of lounge chairs and couches.

Cabins and Rates	Beds	Phone	TV	Sitting Area	Fridge	Tub	Average Per Diem*
Suite	T/Q	●	●	●	●	●	$460
Outside	T/Q	●	●	●	○	○	$321
Inside	T/Q	●	●	●	○	○	$299

Airfare included. Port taxes are extra.

The *Legend* and *Splendour* have larger cabins than RCCL's earlier megaships and more with balconies (231 compared with 60). All cabins have a sitting area—even inside cabins—and are appointed in pretty pastels with brass accents and wood moldings. Bathrooms lack hair dryers, an odd omission on a ship otherwise so well equipped. The Royal Suite, largest on the ship, has a bedroom, dining room, and living room with a baby grand piano. Other suites have separate sleeping and living quarters, too, but no piano. Standard equipment does include refrigerators, bars, and real bathtubs.

Outlet voltage: 110/220 AC.

Single supplement: 150% of double-occupancy rate; however, less expensive singles can be had if you're willing to wait for your cabin assignment until embarkation time.

Discounts: A third or fourth passenger in a cabin pays about $100 per diem. Senior-citizen discounts are offered on specific sailings. You get a discount for arranging your own airfare and for booking early on standard inside and outside cabins only.

Sports and Fitness

Health club: Rowing machines, treadmills, stationary bikes, massage, men's and women's saunas, outdoor whirlpools.

Recreation: Aerobics and fitness program, miniature golf, table tennis, shuffleboard, skeet shooting, snorkeling lessons, two pools, jogging track.

Facilities

Public rooms: Five bars, four entertainment lounges, casino, disco, theater, card room, library, video-game room.

Shops: Five boutiques and gift shops, beauty salon/barber.

Health care: Two doctors and four nurses on call.

Child care: Teen center, children's playroom, year-round supervised youth programs in three age groups, baby-sitting privately arranged with crew member, cribs available but must be requested at time of booking. Two family cabins with a parent's bedroom, children's bedroom, two bathrooms, living area, and private balcony.

Services: Laundry service, dry cleaning, photographer, film processing.

Accessibility These ships are well suited for wheelchair users, with accessible elevators, wide corridors, and specially equipped public lavatories. Seventeen cabins are designed for passengers with mobility problems. The tenders that ferry passengers ashore are easy to board. If seas are rough, crew members will carry passengers and their wheelchairs on board.

MS Majesty of the Seas, MS Monarch of the Seas, and MS Sovereign of the Seas

Specifications *Type of ship:* Megaship
Cruise experience: Casual
Size: 73,941/73,941/73,192 tons
Number of cabins: 1,177/1,177/1,138
Outside cabins: 63%

Passengers: 2,354/2,354/2,278
Crew: 822/822/808 (international)
Officers: Norwegian
Passenger/crew ratio: 2.8 to 1
Year built: 1992/1991/1988

Ship's Log *Majesty of the Seas* and *Monarch of the Seas*, identical sister ships, are two of the largest vessels built specifically for cruising. The slightly smaller *Sovereign of the Seas* was the prototype for the fleet and has only a few design differences: The layout of some public rooms is different, and the larger ships have just one theater, 39 more cabins, and teen nightclubs. All three ships incorporate an incredible range of facilities and amenities.

Each ship is as tall as the Statue of Liberty and three football fields long. The Viking Crown Lounge is 14 stories above sea level, higher than any lounge on any other line's ship. Given such enormous dimensions, these ships are often described in superlatives. Their immense size, however, also means that you can spend seven days on board and never feel that you're really at sea. Lines, too, can be long, and the service, while efficient, sometimes lacks a personal touch. Nevertheless, these are excellent ships for first-time passengers because they have everything a cruise was ever meant to have.

The heart of each ship is a dramatic five-story atrium accented with brass railings and curving stairways as well as signature glass elevators. An arcade with 10 shops sells everything from fur coats to jewelry. During mealtimes and in the afternoon, passengers are serenaded with music. The dining room serves a different international menu each evening; waiters dress accordingly, and musicians stroll among the tables playing music to match the cuisine.

Cabins and Rates	Beds	Phone	TV	Sitting Area	Fridge	Tub	Average Per Diem*
Suite	T/Q	●	●	●	◐	●	$347–$368
Outside	T/Q	●	●	◐	○	◐	$299–$314
Inside	T/Q	●	●	○	○	○	$264–$278

Airfare included. Port taxes are extra.

Standard cabins on the *Majesty* and *Monarch* are appointed in nautical blues, on the *Sovereign* in shades of pink. Cabins on the Promenade Deck look onto a public area. Concierge service is provided for passengers in suites. Many cabins have one or two upper berths in addition to beds. In-cabin TVs show CNN broadcasts.

Outlet voltage: 110/220 AC.

Single supplement: 150% of double-occupancy rate; however, less expensive singles can be had if you're willing to wait for your cabin assignment until embarkation time.

Discounts: A third or fourth passenger in a cabin pays about $100 per diem. Senior-citizen discounts are offered on specific sailings. You get a discount for arranging your own airfare and for booking early on standard inside and outside cabins only.

Sports and Fitness

Health club: Rowing machines, treadmills, stationary bikes, massage, men's and women's saunas, outdoor whirlpool.

Recreation: Aerobics and fitness program, basketball, table tennis, shuffleboard, skeet shooting, snorkeling lessons, two pools, unobstructed circuits for jogging.

Facilities

Public rooms: Ten bars, seven entertainment lounges, casino, disco, two cinemas (*Sovereign*) or one cinema (*Majesty* and *Monarch*), card room, library, video-game room, teen centers (*Majesty, Monarch*).

Shops: Ten boutiques and gift shops, beauty salon/barber.

Health care: Two doctors and four nurses on call.

Child care: Playroom, year-round supervised youth programs in three age groups, baby-sitting privately arranged with crew member, cribs available but must be requested at time of booking. *Monarch* and *Majesty* each have a family cabin (No. 1549) with a parent's bedroom, children's bedroom, two bathrooms, living area, and private balcony.

Services: Laundry service, dry cleaning, photographer, film processing.

Accessibility

These ships are well suited for wheelchair users, with 18 accessible elevators, wide corridors, and specially equipped public lavatories. Four cabins on the *Majesty* and *Monarch*, two inside and two outside, are designed for passengers with mobility problems. The *Sovereign* doesn't have the specially equipped cabins, but has 10 cabins with extra-wide doors. The tenders ferrying passengers to the CocoCay beach party are easy to board; if seas are rough, crew members will carry passengers and their wheelchairs on board. CocoCay is all sand, however, which makes moving about in a wheelchair difficult.

MS Nordic Empress

Specifications

Type of ship: Cruise liner	*Passengers:* 1,600
Cruise experience: Casual	*Crew:* 671 (international)
Size: 48,563 tons	*Officers:* International
Number of cabins: 800	*Passenger/crew ratio:* 2.3 to 1
Outside cabins: 60%	*Year built:* 1990

Ship's Log

The *Nordic Empress*—a distinctive-looking ship with huge rear bay windows—was specifically designed for the three- and four-day cruise market. Much thought was put into making it easy for passengers to learn their way about the ship on such a short voyage. The result was such innovative answers as a single main corridor running down only one side of each deck.

The interior, filled with large and festive public rooms, is a glittering combination of art deco and futuristic designs. At the center of the ship is an incredible nine-story atrium that dazzles with light, glass, chrome, and even cascading waterfalls. Vying for attention is cruising's only triple-level casino and a spacious double-decker dining room with a sensational view of the sea. The commodious showroom and the disco also rise two decks. Because of the stern windows, the *Empress*'s Windjammer Café is forward rather than aft, where most Lidos are traditionally situated. The unusually configured and decorated Sun Deck is more like a private club, with its sail-like canopies, gazebos, and fountains.

<table>
<tr><td>**Cabins and Rates**</td><td></td><td>Beds</td><td>Phone</td><td>TV</td><td>Sitting Area</td><td>Fridge</td><td>Tub</td><td>Average Per Diem*</td></tr>
<tr><td></td><td>Suite</td><td>Q</td><td>●</td><td>●</td><td>●</td><td>●</td><td>●</td><td>$358</td></tr>
<tr><td></td><td>Outside</td><td>T/Q</td><td>●</td><td>●</td><td>○</td><td>○</td><td>◐</td><td>$309</td></tr>
<tr><td></td><td>Inside</td><td>T/Q</td><td>●</td><td>●</td><td>○</td><td>○</td><td>○</td><td>$275</td></tr>
</table>

Airfare included. Port taxes are extra.

Cabins are average in size but have spacious closets. Interiors are in Scandinavian blond woods and white trim with light pastels and contemporary furnishings. Bathrooms are bright, compact, and intelligently laid out. In-cabin TVs show CNN broadcasts. Some cabins are not insulated well against noise. Views from some cabins on the Mariner Deck are obstructed by lifeboats. Suites have private verandas.

Outlet voltage: 110/220 AC.

Single supplement: 150% of double-occupancy rate; however, less expensive singles can be had if you're willing to wait for your cabin assignment until embarkation time.

Discounts: A third or fourth passenger in a cabin pays about $65 per diem. Senior-citizen discounts are offered on specific sailings. You get a discount for arranging your own airfare and for booking early on standard inside and outside cabins only.

Sports and Fitness **Health club:** Gym with aerobics area, rowing machine, stationary bicycles, free weights, sauna, steam room, and massage.

Recreation: Aerobics and other exercise classes, skeet shooting, table tennis, shuffleboard, pool, children's pool, four whirlpools, unobstructed circuit (5 laps = 1 mile) for jogging.

Facilities **Public rooms:** Six bars, three entertainment lounges, casino, disco, video-game room, conference center.

Shops: Gift shop, beauty salon/barber.

Health care: Doctor and two nurses on call.

Child care: Kid/Teen Center playroom on Sun Deck has supervised programs in three age groups year-round; baby-sitting arranged privately with crew member, cribs available but must be requested at time of booking.

Services: Laundry service, photographer.

Accessibility The *Nordic Empress* is well suited for wheelchair users, although official company policy requires that an able-bodied traveling companion accompany wheelchair users. Four cabins are accessible, with wide doors, level floors, and oversize bathrooms with rails. Most elevators accommodate standard-size wheelchairs.

MS Song of America

Specifications *Type of ship:* Cruise liner   *Passengers:* 1,402
Cruise experience: Casual   *Crew:* 535 (international)
Size: 37,584 tons   *Officers:* Norwegian
Number of cabins: 701   *Passenger/crew ratio:* 2.6 to 1
Outside cabins: 57%   *Year built:* 1982

Ship's Log The *Song of America* is unusually handsome. Despite its size, it looks more like a yacht than a cruise ship, though its width gives it space and stability that a yacht could never manage. Plentiful chrome, mirrors, and overhead lights give the ship a flashier look than other RCCL vessels, but the overall effect is clean, crisp, and airy. A refurbishment finished in 1994 ensured that the *Song of America* kept its youthful appearance.

Cabins and Rates

	Beds	Phone	TV	Sitting Area	Fridge	Tub	Average Per Diem*
Suite	T or D	●	●	●	●	●	$393
Outside	T or D	●	●	○	○	○	$292
Inside	T or T/D	●	●	○	○	○	$256

*Airfare included. Port taxes are extra.

Standard outside cabins are done in nautical blue; inside cabins are a bright orange. In-cabin TVs show CNN broadcasts. Suites on the Promenade Deck look onto a public area.

Outlet voltage: 110/220 AC.

Single supplement: 150% of double-occupancy rate; however, less expensive singles are available if you are willing to wait for your cabin assignment until embarkation time.

Discounts: A third or fourth passenger in a cabin pays $107 per diem. Senior-citizen discounts are offered on specific sailings. You get a discount for arranging your own airfare and for booking early on standard inside and outside cabins only.

Sports and Fitness

Health club: Rowing machines, treadmills, stationary bikes, massage, men's and women's saunas.

Recreation: Aerobics, table tennis, ring toss, snorkeling lessons, shuffleboard, skeet shooting, two pools, unobstructed circuits for jogging.

Facilities

Public rooms: Six bars, four entertainment lounges, casino, disco, cinema, card room.

Shops: Gift shop, drugstore, beauty salon/barber.

Health care: Doctor on call.

Child care: Youth programs with counselors in three age groups during holidays and in summer, baby-sitting arranged privately with crew member, cribs available but must be requested at time of booking.

Services: Laundry service, dry cleaning, photographer, film processing.

Accessibility

Accessibility aboard this ship is limited. Doorways have lips, and public bathrooms are not specially equipped. Passengers with mobility problems must bring a portable wheelchair and be escorted by an able-bodied companion. Tenders are easy to board; if seas are rough, crew members will carry passengers and their wheelchairs.

MS Song of Norway

Specifications

Type of ship: Cruise liner
Cruise experience: Casual
Size: 23,000 tons
Number of cabins: 502
Outside cabins: 65.2%

Passengers: 1,004
Crew: 423 (international)
Officers: Norwegian
Passenger/crew ratio: 2.4 to 1
Year built: 1970

Ship's Log

This is a historic if unheralded ship. The *Song of Norway* was the first ship of fledgling Royal Caribbean Cruise Line when it was launched in 1970. Eight years later, it became one of the first cruise ships to be split and stretched. In what later became a common procedure, the ship was cut in two, fitted with a new midsection, and then reassembled. The lengthening increased passenger capacity by 300 and added new deck space and public rooms. As a result, the *Song of Norway* has a superb Sun Deck with an unusually large pool for swimming laps. The lobby, while not the soaring atriums of later RCCL ships, is handsomely accented in wood paneling and marble.

Cabins and Rates		Beds	Phone	TV	Sitting Area	Fridge	Tub	Average Per Diem*
Suite		D or T/D	●	●	●	●	●	$371
Outside		D/U, T/D, or T	●	○	○	○	○	$308
Inside		D/L, D/U, or T	●	○	○	○	○	$270

Airfare included. Port taxes are extra.

Decorative touches in standard cabins include brass-accented wall sconces. Cabins on the Promenade Deck look onto a public area.

Outlet voltage: 110 AC.

Single supplement: 150% of double-occupancy rate; however, less expensive singles are available if you are willing to wait for your cabin assignment until embarkation time.

Discounts: A third or fourth passenger in a cabin pays $87–$150 per diem. Senior-citizen discounts are offered on specific sailings. You get a discount for arranging your own airfare, and for booking early on standard inside and outside cabins only.

Sports and Fitness

Health club: Stationary bikes, rowing machines, treadmills, separate men's and women's saunas and massage rooms.

Recreation: Aerobics, basketball, dancercise, table tennis, shuffleboard, skeet shooting, yoga, snorkeling lessons, pool, unobstructed circuit for jogging.

Facilities

Public rooms: Five bars, three entertainment lounges, casino, disco.

Shops: Gift shop, beauty salon/barber.

Child care: Youth programs with counselors in three age groups during holidays or in summer, baby-sitting arranged privately with crew member, cribs available but must be requested at time of booking.

Health care: Doctor on call.

Services: Laundry service, dry cleaning, photographer, film processing.

Accessibility

Accessibility aboard these ships is limited. The Viking Crown Lounge is inaccessible to wheelchair users. Doorways throughout the ship have lips, and public bathrooms are not specially equipped. Passengers with mobility problems must bring their own traveling wheelchair, and they must be escorted by an able-bodied companion.

MS Sun Viking

Specifications *Type of ship:* Cruise liner   *Passengers:* 714
Cruise experience: Casual   *Crew:* 341 (international)
Size: 18,556 tons   *Officers:* Norwegian
Number of cabins: 357   *Passenger/crew ratio:* 2.1 to 1
Outside cabins: 68.9%   *Year built:* 1972

Ship's Log   The *Sun Viking* is RCCL's smallest ship. Unlike the *Song of Norway*, the line's other vintage 1970s ship, it has never been lengthened—meaning fewer public rooms, less space to play in, and small cabins. Nevertheless, passengers are lured back to it time and again because they feel more in touch with the sea here than on the larger vessels. Certainly, passengers and crew get to know one another better. Don't expect to find a busy, partying atmosphere on this ship. One important feature is the swimming pool, which has a shallow area around the perimeter for wading.

Cabins and Rates

	Beds	Phone	TV	Sitting Area	Fridge	Tub	Average Per Diem*
Suite	D or T	●	○	●	●	●	$340
Outside	D/U or T	●	○	○	◑	○	$277
Inside	D/L or T	●	○	○	○	○	$245

*Airfare included. Port taxes are extra.

Cabins are significantly smaller than on comparable ships. Decorative touches include brass-accented wall sconces. Suites and cabins on the Promenade Deck look onto a public area.

Outlet voltage: 110 AC.

Single supplement: 150% of double-occupancy rate; however, less expensive singles are available if you're willing to wait for your cabin assignment until embarkation.

Discounts: A third or fourth passenger in a cabin pays $107 per diem. Senior-citizen discounts are offered on specific sailings. You get a discount for arranging your own airfare, and for booking early on standard inside and outside cabins only.

Sports and Fitness   **Health club:** Exercise equipment, men's and women's saunas.

Recreation: Aerobics and other exercise classes, basketball, table tennis, ring toss, shuffleboard, skeet shooting, pool, unobstructed circuits for jogging.

Facilities   **Public rooms:** Six bars, three entertainment lounges, small casino (slot machines), disco.

Shops: Boutique, gift shop, beauty salon/barber.

Health care: Doctor on call.

Child care: Youth programs run by counselors in three age groups during holidays and in summer, baby-sitting arranged privately with crew member, cribs available but must be requested at time of booking.

Services: Laundry service, dry cleaning, photographer, film processing.

Accessibility   Accessibility aboard this ship is limited. Doorways have lips, and public bathrooms are not specially equipped. The Viking Crown Lounge is inaccessible to wheelchair users. A portable wheelchair and an able-bodied traveling companion are required.

MS Viking Serenade

Specifications

Type of ship: Cruise liner
Cruise experience: Casual
Size: 40,132 tons
Number of cabins: 756
Outside cabins: 63%

Passengers: 1,512
Crew: 612 (international)
Officers: International
Passenger/crew ratio: 2.4 to 1
Year built: 1982, rebuilt 1991

Ship's Log Formerly Admiral Cruises' *Stardancer*, the *Viking Serenade* was originally designed as the world's only cruise ship/car ferry, which explains why it looks more like a barge than a cruise ship. However, RCCL spent $75 million to convert the car deck into cabins, add a three-story atrium, renovate the existing cabins and public rooms, and add the company's signature observation deck, the glass-enclosed Viking Crown Lounge. Other features are a much-enlarged casino, a shopping arcade, a teen disco, and a state-of-the-art fitness center. Designs and furnishings are bright and contemporary. Brass, glass, mirrors, and stainless steel are used extensively.

Cabins and Rates

	Beds	Phone	TV	Sitting Area	Fridge	Tub	Average Per Diem*
Suite	Q	●	●	●	●	●	$354
Outside	T	●	●	◐	◐	◐	$296
Inside	T	●	●	○	○	○	$236

Airfare included. Port taxes are extra.

Standard outside cabins are pretty, with frilly window treatments; standard inside cabins feature murals in the window's place. In-cabin TVs show CNN broadcasts. The larger outside staterooms on Club Deck have partially obstructed views.

Outlet voltage: 110/220 AC.

Single supplement: 150% of double-occupancy rate; however, less expensive singles are available if you are willing to wait for your cabin assignment until embarkation time.

Discounts: A third or fourth passenger in a cabin pays $65 per diem. Senior-citizen discounts are offered on specific sailings. You get a discount for arranging your own airfare and for booking early on standard inside and outside cabins only.

Sports and Fitness **Health club:** Top-deck spa with rowing machines, stationary bikes, free weights, sauna.

Recreation: Aerobics and other exercise classes, Ping-Pong, shuffleboard, trapshooting, pool with retractable dome, unobstructed circuit (8 laps = 1 mile) for jogging.

Facilities **Public rooms:** Six bars, four entertainment lounges, casino, disco, card room/library.

Shops: Gift shop, beauty salon/barber.

Health care: Doctor on call.

Child care: Playroom; teen club with soda bar, video games, and dance floor; children's programs with counselors in three age groups year-round, cribs available but must be requested at time of booking.

Services: Laundry service, dry cleaning, photographer.

Accessibility Four cabins and all public areas are accessible to wheelchair users.

Royal Cruise Line

Crown Odyssey

The Fleet MS *Crown Odyssey*
MS *Queen Odyssey*
MS *Royal Odyssey*
MS *Star Odyssey*

Royal Cruise Line's vessels are spacious, gracious ships built for long-distance cruising. The *Royal Odyssey* and *Star Odyssey* have classic lines reminiscent of the great transatlantic liners. The newer *Crown Odyssey* and yachtlike *Queen Odyssey* tend more toward modern cruise sensibilities than the classic style, but are equally as comfortable and refined.

Ships at a Glance

	Dining Rooms	Bars	Casino	Fitness Center	Pools	Average Per Diem
Crown Odyssey	1	6	●	●	3	$278
Queen Odyssey	1	4	●	●	1	$481
Royal Odyssey *Star Odyssey*	1	4	●	●	1	$300

Cruise Experience Although it's a maritime tradition to christen ships with aristocratic names, few shipping companies live up to the superlatives that such appellations imply. Royal Cruise Line is an exception, however, for its reputation is as good as its name. The royal treatment—luxurious cabins and amenities and, above all, superb service by the predominantly Greek staff—is in store for all passengers who board its ships. It's no surprise that, on average, 40%–50% of guests—and as many as 85% on certain cruises—are repeat passengers. New itineraries, in particular, draw plenty of repeaters eager to sail again with Royal. Theme sailings, such as "Big Band" cruises, are also popular. (Royal has one of cruising's most extensive theme programs.) Greek Night epitomizes the Royal Cruise Line experience. On this evening, the crew shares its pride in its Greek heritage. The flavors of Greece top the menu at dinner; afterwards, the cruise staff joins in an exuberant show of Greek folk dances and songs. Passengers tend to be in their fifties or older, successful, and well traveled. Children are rarely taken on Royal cruises, and only during school vacations. In many respects, Royal Cruise Line appeals to the same type of passenger who would like Holland America. Both lines emphasize an Old World civility and the tradition of travel by ship.

In addition to excellent service, Royal is known for its wide-ranging itineraries, well-organized shore excursions, fine cuisine, and professional entertainment. Sensitivity to the needs of its passengers and willingness to go the extra mile mark Royal's programs and ac-

---

Chart Symbols. Ships at a Glance. ●: *Fully equipped;* ◑: *Partially equipped;* ○: *Not equipped.* Cabins and Rates. **D:** *Double bed;* **K:** *King-size bed;* **Q:** *Queen-size bed;* **T:** *Twin bed;* **U/L:** *Upper and lower berths;* ●: *All cabins have this facility;* ○: *No cabins have this facility;* ◑: *Some cabins have this facility*

tivities. For instance, representatives of the cruise line meet passengers at major U.S. gateways and fly with travelers to their point of embarkation. Once aboard ship, they act as an adjunct to the cruise staff. For single female passengers sailing alone, senior gentlemen act as hosts and social partners. These men are carefully screened; they are forbidden to play favorites or become romantically involved.

Activities A variety of cruise activities are offered, including aerobics, dance, and language classes; card and board games; trivia contests; and visits to the navigation bridge. The New Beginnings program offers lectures on fitness, nutrition, and self-improvement. Other lectures cover subjects ranging from the ports visited to estate planning and investments. Unlike some other lines, Royal's port talks are much more than promotional announcements on where to find the best shopping. Speakers share their insights into the ports visited, enriching passengers' shoreside experience. Shore excursions are outstanding; at least 70% of passengers partake in one or more tours.

Dining The primarily Continental cuisine is good but not always great. What the chefs prepare best, not surprisingly, is Greek dishes. The dining-room stewards are superb: After the first meal, they know each passenger's preferences and serve meals accordingly. If you take skim milk in your coffee, it will be delivered automatically. No one would ever categorize the Greek waiters as stiff and formal; they have big personalities and excellent senses of humor.

Meals on the *Crown Odyssey* are served in two assigned seatings for lunch and dinner (6:30 and 8:30); breakfast is open. On the *Queen Odyssey*, *Royal Odyssey*, and *Star Odyssey*, all meals are served in a single seating (dinner from 7 to 9:30; open seating on the *Queen*, tables assigned on the *Royal* and *Star*). On all four ships, two formal evenings are held during each cruise; other evenings are semiformal.

Every menu carries a low-calorie, low-cholesterol selection approved by the American Heart Association; a booklet in each cabin explains the ship's AHA dining program, offers tips on battling appetite, and provides a photo of each dish along with a nutritional breakdown. Entrées that meet AHA guidelines include skewered scallops with asparagus spears, chicken Salinas (with cold artichoke hearts and lemon), and broiled marinated salmon with apricots. Other dietary requests should be made in writing five weeks before sailing.

Early morning coffee, breakfast, and lunch buffets are served on deck and in one of the lounges. Other service includes mid-morning bouillon, afternoon tea, and a late-night buffet. Room service is available around the clock, though selection is dictated by kitchen hours.

Entertainment The entertainment aboard Royal's ships caters to the tastes of a mostly older clientele. Some acts bring down the house, but others aren't quite ready for Broadway. In addition to a nightly variety show and first-run movies, there are cabarets, piano and harp duos, and dancing (ballroom or disco). Big-name entertainers are sometimes on board, as are literary or film celebrities. A passenger talent night and a costume party are held once every cruise. A singles cocktail party and a repeaters party (for passengers who have sailed with Royal before) are other regular features.

Service and Royal prides itself on a highly professional staff noted for their *Tipping* warm, personal style. The dining-room staff, in particular, love to spoil the passengers. Most of the crew have been working together on Royal ships since the company was formed in 1971. A majority of the waiters and stewards were trained in first-class European hotels, and the level of service reflects this. Tips are pooled and distributed among the crew. Tip $9–$10 per passenger per diem on the *Crown, Royal,* and *Star*; $12 per passenger per diem on the *Queen.*

Destinations The *Crown Odyssey*'s destinations in the Western Hemisphere include Hawaii, the Mexican Riviera, and Panama Canal; the *Royal Odyssey* sails to Alaska, the eastern U.S. seaboard and Canada, and the Panama Canal; the *Star Odyssey* visits the Panama Canal; and the *Queen Odyssey* explores the Caribbean. (For detailed itineraries, *see* Chapter 3.)

For More Information Royal Cruise Line (1 Maritime Plaza, San Francisco, CA 94111, tel. 415/956–7200).

MS Crown Odyssey

Specifications *Type of ship:* Cruise liner
Cruise experience: Semiformal
Size: 34,250 tons
Number of cabins: 526
Outside cabins: 78%

Passengers: 1,052
Crew: 470 (Greek)
Officers: Greek
Passenger/crew ratio: 2.2 to 1
Year built: 1988

Ship's Log The *Crown Odyssey* is showier than the more traditional *Royal* and *Star:* If the latter could be likened to antique lamps, then the former is more like a big crystal chandelier. The *Crown*'s art deco interior is a mosaic of textures and materials, including marble, wood, glass, stainless steel, and brass. Passengers have 10 decks to wander. At the mirrored entrance to Theo's Bar is the centerpiece of the ship: a modern sculpture of a peacock in a glass cage. (Fiber optics in the peacock's fantail change color constantly.) Equally spectacular is the Top of the Crown Lounge, with its 360° view of the sea and the ship's interior through floor-to-ceiling windows.

Much emphasis is placed on physical fitness. The Health Center, styled after a Roman bath, has tile walls with inlaid mosaics and Italian white rattan furniture. Its offerings include low-impact programs for older passengers, a health bar, indoor whirlpools, and even an indoor pool. Dining in the Seven Continents restaurant is an experience difficult to top. Royal Doulton china, European linen, and silver set the tone for meals that are superbly prepared and deftly served.

Cabins and Rates

	Beds	Phone	TV	Sitting Area	Fridge	Tub	Average Per Diem*
Suite	T/D	●	●	●	●	●	$585
Outside	T	●	●	○	○	◑	$278
Inside	T/D	●	●	○	○	◑	$174

Rates are for Hawaii. Airfare and port taxes are extra.

Suites are spacious and comfortable. Wood paneling and trim are used extensively, and suites also have fully mirrored closets and phones for worldwide communications. The 16 Penthouse Deck suites are decorated in themes suggested by their names (Taj Mahal, Bel Air, Shangri-la) and have private balconies, marble bathrooms, walk-in closets, whirlpool baths, and butler service. Some superior deluxe apartments can be combined with an adjoining cabin to provide 1,000 square feet of space. Superior deluxe suites and junior suites on the Riviera Deck have bay windows with panoramic views. Views from most cabins on the Lido Deck are partially or fully obstructed by lifeboats.

Outlet voltage: 110/220 AC.

Single supplement: 160%–200% of double-occupancy rate; some cabins available at an additional $75 per diem on selected sailings.

Discounts: A third or fourth passenger in a cabin pays 60% of the double-occupancy rate. You get a discount of 10%–50% for early booking. Repeat passengers and those who book their own flights are eligible for additional discounts.

Sports and Fitness

Health club: Eight-station Universal gym with full-time fitness instructor, four Lifecycles, treadmill, rower, free weights, ballet barre, indoor pool, two whirlpools, massage, health bar, men's and women's saunas, full-service beauty center (herbal wraps, facials, and more).

Recreation: Table tennis, shuffleboard, exercise classes (some geared toward older passengers), outdoor pool, children's pool, two outdoor whirlpools, unobstructed circuits for jogging.

Facilities

Public rooms: Six bars, five entertainment lounges, casino, disco, cinema, card room, library.

Shops: Two boutiques, sundries shop, beauty salon/barber.

Health care: Doctor on call.

Child care: Organized youth programs with counselors during selected holidays only.

Services: Laundry service, pressing, dry cleaning, 24-hour information desk, photographer, film processing.

Accessibility

Four cabins are equipped with sit-down showers, grip bars around the shower and toilet areas, and tilting mirrors.

MS Queen Odyssey

Specifications

Type of ship: Cruise yacht
Cruise experience: Formal
Size: 10,000 tons
Number of cabins: 106
Outside cabins: 100%

Passengers: 212
Crew: 145 (international)
Officers: Greek
Passenger/crew ratio: 1.6 to 1
Year built: 1992

Ship's Log

The *Queen Odyssey* joined Royal Cruise Line in January 1995. Originally designed as the third Seabourn sister, but commissioned as the *Royal Viking Queen*, the vessel brings a new dimension to the Royal experience. As the *Royal Viking Queen*, the ship was known for its superior service, dining, and attention to detail, and Royal Cruise Line has kept its crew intact. The captain and officers, however, are now Greek as on other Royal Cruise Line ships. By virtue of its smaller size, the *Queen* offers passengers greater intimacy than its larger fleetmates. In fact there are opportunities aboard the *Queen* not available on Royal's larger ships: A fold-out marina at the stern lowers in calm waters (weather permitting) for swimming, waterskiing, boating, and other water sports. A Zodiac is carried aboard for making landfall in truly remote (and otherwise inaccessible) spots. Another specially designed craft accompanies the ship on Amazon itineraries, enabling passengers to explore the river's smaller tributaries. Dining and service are a notch above Royal's bigger ships, and with low introductory pricing the *Queen* is attracting a younger crowd.

Cabins and Rates

	Beds	Phone	TV	Sitting Area	Fridge	Tub	Average Per Diem*
Suite	Q or T	●	●	●	●	●	$481

Rates are for the Caribbean. Port taxes are extra.

All the *Queen*'s staterooms are outside suites with a living area, bedroom area, and large picture windows looking out to sea. The spacious living space is matched only by the spacious storage space: Walk-in closets come in every cabin. The Owner's Suite is highlighted by a white marble bathroom. In the larger suites, French doors separate the living room and bedroom. Standard suites are finished in wood moldings and cabinetwork, complemented by blue fabrics. Each is outfitted with a TV (including CNN), VCR, and refrigerator; minibars are stocked with complimentary snacks and beverages.

Outlet voltage: 110/220 AC.

Single supplement: 125%–200% of double-occupancy rate.

Discounts: A third passenger in a cabin pays the minimum fare. A child under 12 sharing a cabin with two adults pays half the minimum. Various discounts are offered for repeaters, first-time cruisers, and early booking. You get a discount of $300–$800 for arranging your own airfare.

Sports and Fitness

Health club: Exercise equipment including Liferowers, Lifecycles, step machine, treadmill, free weights, aerobics floor, saunas, massage.

Recreation: Retractable platform for water sports, wind-sheltered pool, three whirlpools, unobstructed circuit for jogging.

Facilities

Public rooms: Four bars, two entertainment lounges, casino, library, boardroom.

Shops: Boutique, beauty salon.

Health care: Doctor and nurse on call.

Child care: None.

Services: Concierge, full- and self-service laundry, dry cleaning, photographer, film processing, satellite communications, fax capabilities.

Accessibility

Four staterooms are accessible to wheelchair users. Passengers with mobility problems must travel with an able-bodied companion and provide their own 22-inch wheelchair.

MS Royal Odyssey and MS Star Odyssey

Specifications

Type of ship: Cruise liner
Cruise experience: Semi-formal
Size: 28,000 tons
Number of cabins: 399/404
Outside cabins: 87%/88%

Passengers: 750
Crew: 410 (Greek)
Officers: Greek
Passenger/crew ratio: 1.8 to 1
Year built: 1973/1972

Ship's Log

These nearly identical sister ships were originally intended for globe-trotting itineraries, and they provide passengers with plenty of room during extended periods at sea. Staterooms are oversize, public areas are spacious, and the dining rooms can seat the ship's full complement at once.

The *Royal Odyssey* is fresh from a $20 million refurbishment that has lightened up the look of the ship. Bleached woods and an abundance of halogen lighting have replaced the subdued ambience that some passengers may remember from the ship's days as the *Royal Viking Sea*. The center of shipboard life is the Odyssey Lounge, where passengers can sink into comfortably appointed sofas and swivel chairs. The Panorama Lounge, a perch atop the ship even higher than the bridge, is an excellent observation point for wraparound views of Panama Canal transits or whale watching. Other shipboard spots of note include the three outdoor whirlpools on

Penthouse Deck; Yanni's Hearth, which serves freshly baked cinnamon buns poolside each morning and cookies in the afternoon; and the Odyssey Bar, where sunbathers can take a buffet breakfast and lunch without ever having to going inside.

The *Star Odyssey* came to Royal Cruise Line from Norwegian Cruise Line, where it sailed as the *Westward*. Before that, it was the *Royal Viking Star*. A multimillion-dollar refurbishment reduced the ship's passenger capacity from 860 to 750, and restored the ship's original one-seating dining room. The *Star* features the same public rooms and passenger facilities as the *Royal*, although some are located on a different deck, while others are appointed with a different decor or laid out in a different configuration. The Horizon Fitness center, saunas, and gymnasium, for example, are located at the very top deck on the *Star*; on the *Royal* this facility is found two decks down. There are two whirlpools on Penthouse Deck rather than three. A Panorama Lounge is found on the *Star* in the same place as on the *Royal*, but its layout differs. And the main Odyssey Show Lounge on the *Star* has a sloping floor; on the *Royal* it is tiered.

	Beds	Phone	TV	Sitting Area	Fridge	Tub	Average Per Diem*
Suite	T or D	●	●	●	●	●	$757
Outside	T or D	●	●	◐	○	○	$300
Inside	T	●	●	○	○	○	$168

Cabins and Rates

Rates are for Northeastern United States and Canada. Airfare and port taxes are extra.

The roomy accommodations on both these ships were thoroughly redone before they joined the Royal fleet. Tastefully appointed standard cabins come in pastel shades that vary by deck. Color schemes come in various combinations of pastel blues, greens, and ivory. Penthouse apartments are individually decorated. Each of the nine penthouses also has a private veranda. Every cabin comes with two lockable drawers, three-channel radio, telephone for worldwide calls, individually controlled thermostat, full-length mirrors, wall-mounted hair dryers and closed-circuit color television. Recent video releases are shown daily, as are movie classics relevant to the itinerary. Some cabins also have refrigerators.

Outlet voltage: 110/220 AC.

Single supplement: 160%–200% of double-occupancy rate; $75 per diem on selected sailings. There are 49 inside and outside cabins for single occupancy on the *Royal* and 33 on the *Star*.

Discounts: A third or fourth passenger in a cabin pays 60% of the double-occupancy rate. You get a discount of 10%–50% for early booking. Repeat passengers and those who book their own flights are eligible for additional discounts.

Sports and Fitness

Health club: Weights, treadmills, rowers, Lifecycles, aerobics, full-time fitness director, juice bar, sauna, beauty enter with herbal wraps and facials.

Recreation: Golf driving range, paddle-tennis court, table tennis, shuffleboard, pool, whirlpools (three on *Royal*, two on *Star*), unobstructed circuit (6 laps = 1 mile) for jogging.

Facilities

Public rooms: Four bars, four entertainment lounges, casino, disco, cinema, card room, library, writing room, reading rooms.

Shops: Gift shop, beauty salon, barber shop, photo shop/gallery.

Health care: Doctor and two nurses on call.

Child care: Organized youth programs with counselors during selected holidays only.

Services: Laundry service, pressing, dry cleaning, 24-hour information desk, photographer, film processing.

Accessibility Two cabins on the *Royal,* but none on the *Star* are outfitted for wheelchair users; there is a step up to cabin bathrooms. Most public rooms are accessible, and portable ramps are available. Passengers with mobility problems must travel with a companion and provide a 22-inch portable wheelchair.

Seabourn Cruise Line

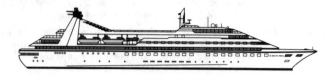

The Fleet *Seabourn Pride*
Seabourn Spirit

The streamlined Seabourn ships always attract attention when they pull into port. Like all cruise yachts, every cabin is an outside suite. A platform at the stern lowers for water sports, but it is used sparingly and only in the calmest waters.

Ships at a Glance		Dining Rooms	Bars	Casino	Fitness Center	Pools	Average Per Diem
Seabourn Pride		1	3	●	●	1	$875–$995
Seabourn Spirit							

Cruise Experience Of the millions of people who go on cruises, only a few can afford the type of voyage offered by Seabourn. Inspired by the luxury cruises of Cunard's *Sea Goddess*, Seabourn vessels deliver the same exceptional service, but a greater choice of activities. Certainly, no expense was spared in the construction and decoration of the *Seabourn Pride* and *Seabourn Spirit*. From the crystal glassware in the staterooms to the huge expanse of marble in the circular atrium, Seabourn represents the pinnacle of cruising elegance. These ships are among the most spacious ships afloat, too, and notably so in the all-suite accommodations, which are the highlight of the ship.

Passengers pay an extremely high price for such luxury. As a result, the majority are middle-age or older. While this is reflected in the generally low-key activities and entertainment, there is plenty in the way of water sports to keep even passengers in their thirties busy.

Activities Seabourn lets passengers enjoy the ship's facilities at their own pace, and there are few organized activities. There's a small casino, a library with a good selection of books and videos, and a card room. Water sports are popular on cruises to warm-weather destinations. Anchored in the calm waters of a cove or bay, the ship can lower its stern to create a platform with a central swimming area protected by wire netting; from this platform passengers can swim, sail, water-ski, or ride banana boats—weather permitting. For more sedate explorations, the ship also carries paddleboats and a glass-bottom boat.

The few scheduled events include a diverse enrichment series of lectures. Well-known personalities talk about everything from cruising to cuisine. Speakers include renowned chefs, editors of major travel and lifestyle publications, and celebrities. The line's "Signature Series" excursions include invitations to private golf clubs of championship caliber and behind-the-scenes tours of shoreside attractions.

Chart Symbols. Ships at a Glance. **●:** *Fully equipped;* **◐:** *Partially equipped;* ○: *Not equipped.* Cabins and Rates. **D:** *Double bed;* **K:** *King-size bed;* **Q:** *Queen-size bed;* **T:** *Twin bed;* **U/L:** *Upper and lower berths;* **●:** *All cabins have this facility;* ○: *No cabins have this facility;* **◐:** *Some cabins have this facility*

Dining The outstanding cuisine has a French accent and is strongly nouvelle-influenced in presentation and portions. Meals are prepared to order, and passengers are free to ask for dishes not on the menu. The fine food is complemented by a superb wine list. The dining room is formal and large, with tables spaced so far apart they would make a New York restaurateur swoon. Tables are unassigned, and passengers may dine at any time during meal hours (dinner is from 7:30 to 10). Typically, passengers line up fellow tablemates in the afternoon, perhaps meeting before dinner for drinks at the bar—it can be a bit like arranging a new dinner party every day. Two formal evenings are held each week, but gentlemen are expected to wear a jacket and tie virtually every night. The formality of the dining room, which works so successfully for dinner, seems stuffy at breakfast and lunch.

For more informal meals, the Veranda Café is a delightful spot. With its rattan furniture and tightly packed tables, it is the ship's cheeriest room. Located on the same deck as the pool, the café serves opulent buffet breakfasts and lunches, as well as a few items cooked to order, like eggs, hot dogs, hamburgers, and fresh pastas. The Veranda Café is also the venue for theme dinners. Served one or two nights per cruise, these informal events are very popular; a table must be reserved in advance.

Room service is superb and available 24 hours. At least once during your cruise, be sure to have dinner in your cabin; it's a romantic affair with personal service and beautifully prepared cuisine served course by course. Breakfast in the cabin is also presented with grace and panache.

Entertainment In the small show lounge, solo artists give nightly performances, and there's a cabaret-style show twice a week. Nightly dancing and piano music round out the low-key evening entertainment.

Service and The passenger-to-crew ratio is among the lowest of any ship. No tipping is allowed, yet the European service crew is professional, personable, and eager to accommodate virtually any personal request.

Destinations In the Western Hemisphere, Seabourn sails to the northeastern United States and Canada, the Caribbean, South America, the West Coast, Mexican Riviera, and Alaska. (For detailed itineraries, *see* Chapter 3.)

For More Seabourn Cruise Line (55 Francisco St., San Francisco, CA 94133, **Information** tel. 415/391–7444 or 800/929–9595).

Seabourn Pride and Seabourn Spirit

Specifications | | |
|---|---|
| *Type of ship:* Cruise yacht | *Passengers:* 204 |
| *Cruise experience:* Formal | *Crew:* 140 (international) |
| *Size:* 10,000 tons | *Officers:* Norwegian |
| *Number of cabins:* 106 | *Passenger/crew ratio:* 1.5 to 1 |
| *Outside cabins:* 100% | *Year built:* 1988/1989 |

Ship's Log Aesthetically, the Seabourn ships may be the most striking small ships afloat. With their sleek lines and twin funnels that resemble airfoils, they are streamlined and futuristic. Generous use of glass, brass, and marble inside is subtle and sophisticated, a sensation heightened by the ship's spaciousness. The refined color schemes of peach, blue, and soft beige add to the light and airy feel aboard ship. From morning until sunset, passengers take a break from sunbathing around the Sky Bar—a simple outdoor gathering spot that is the premier daytime attraction.

The other most popular spot is the Club/Casino, with its piano bar and the sloping picture windows that form the stern wall. Spotlights, potted plants, and glass partitions make this an attractive room for preprandial cocktails and after-dinner dancing. The darker

Magellan Lounge on the deck below has none of the Club/Casino's charm, but its gently tiered floor makes it ideal for musical revues and lectures. Two decks up is the magnificent Constellation Lounge; from its position above the bridge it has a commanding view of the sea through a semicircle of large picture windows.

Cabins and Rates	Beds	Phone	TV	Sitting Area	Fridge	Tub	Average Per Diem*
Suite	Q or T	●	●	●	●	●	$875–$995

Lower rates are for the Caribbean. Higher rates are for Alaska. Airfare included. Port taxes are extra.

Five-foot-high picture windows, a sitting area, stocked bar and refrigerator, TV (including CNN) and VCR, large marble bath with twin sinks and tub/shower, and walk-in closets are among the creature comforts of every suite. Here, as in the rest of the ship, glass, blond woods, and mirrors are used to great effect. Refrigerators/bars are stocked with a large selection of liquors, beer, and soft drinks; there's a charge for liquor refills. Unlimited soft drinks are complimentary here, as throughout the ship. All cabins have coffee tables that convert to dining tables, and safes. The Owner's Suites at the front of the ship have curved bow windows that make you feel as though you're on your own yacht, but midship Owner's Suites are larger.

Outlet voltage: 110/220 AC.

Single supplement: 110%–$150% of double-occupancy rate; 200% for Owner's and Regal suites.

Discounts: A third passenger in a suite pays 50% the double-occupancy rate. You get a $300–$900 discount for arranging your own airfare. Passengers who pay in full 12 months in advance receive a 10% discount; those who pay six to 11 months in advance receive 5% off the fare. Certain cruises may be combined for a savings of up to 50% on one of the cruises. A "frequent cruiser" program offers early booking discounts to passengers who sail 45–120 days in a 36-month period.

Sports and Fitness

Health club: Aerobics rooms, exercise equipment (including Nautilus), weight-training classes, massage, steam room, sauna, health and beauty treatments (herbal wraps, facials, dietary counseling, personalized fitness programs).

Recreation: Aerobics and other exercise classes, shuffleboard, skeet shooting, small pool, three whirlpools, sailing, windsurfing, waterskiing, snorkeling, unobstructed circuit for jogging.

Facilities

Public rooms: Three bars, two lounges, casino, card room, library (books and videos), business center.

Shops: Clothing boutique, gift shop, beauty salon/barber.

Health care: Doctor on call.

Child care: Baby-sitting arranged with purser's office.

Services: Full- and self-service laundry, dry cleaning, overnight shoe-shine service, photographer, film processing.

Accessibility

Three Seabourn Suites (type A) are laid out for easier access by wheelchair users. All elevators and public areas are accessible, and public lavatories are specially equipped. Passengers with mobility problems are required to travel with an able-bodied adult. In small ports to which passengers must be ferried by tender, wheelchair users may have trouble getting ashore.

Seawind Cruise Line

The Fleet TSS *Seawind Crown*

The Portuguese *Seawind Crown* was built in 1961 as the *Infante Dom Enrique* and became the sole ship of Seawind Cruise Line 30 years later. A handsome ship with classic lines, polished brass, and rich wood, it also has plenty of deck space and nicely apportioned public rooms. A $2 million renovation in late 1994 added 50 cabins and increased passenger capacity to 728. Still, the *Seawind Crown* remains a spacious ship for its size.

Ship at a Glance

	Dining Rooms	Bars	Casino	Fitness Center	Pools	Average Per Diem
Seawind Crown	1	5	●	●	2	$275

Cruise Experience Relatively low prices, including free airfare from 43 U.S. gateways, early booking discounts of up to $450 per person, and a reputation for solid service have made this one-ship line popular among cost-conscious cruisers. Originally built for Scandinavian and German passengers, the ship still attracts an international mix of Europeans, South Americans, and North Americans. Couples who want to renew their marriage vows can arrange for the captain to officiate in the ship's chapel, followed by a cocktail reception in honor of the "newlyweds."

Activities Though English is the ship's first language, activities are conducted in English, Spanish, Portuguese, and German to accommodate the large number of European and South American passengers. The daily program is typical: bingo, singles get-togethers, and deck games.

Dining The food is good but unspectacular, with European, Portuguese, and Greek influences, and a few ethnic dishes, such as lamb kebabs or Greek salad, are offered from time to time. Lunch and dinner are presented at two assigned seatings (dinner at 6:30 and 8:30) in the nicely appointed Vasco da Gama Dining Room. Two formal evenings are scheduled during each weeklong cruise. Other options include morning buffets, snacks, and elaborate midnight buffets. Unfortunately, there is no open-air or poolside meal service; buffets are served in the below-decks dining room. Other than Continental breakfast, there is very limited room service.

Entertainment This small ship offers an ambitious but fair caliber troupe of entertainers, including four regular dancers, a handful of guest singers, and typically a visiting magician or comedian. Latin and Caribbean music are performed throughout the day on various decks and in various lounges.

Chart Symbols. Ships at a Glance. **●**: *Fully equipped;* **◖**: *Partially equipped;* ○: *Not equipped.* Cabins and Rates. **D**: *Double bed;* **K**: *King-size bed;* **Q**: *Queen-size bed;* **T**: *Twin bed;* **U/L**: *Upper and lower berths;* **●**: *All cabins have this facility;* ○: *No cabins have this facility;* **◖**: *Some cabins have this facility*

Service and
Tipping

Seawind's staff is gracious, due in part to the intimate onboard ambience—you'll probably get to know several staff members fairly well on a seven-day cruise. Tip your waiter $3 per diem per passenger, the busboy $1.50, the cabin steward $3; the headwaiter gets $5 per week per passenger. A 15% service charge is automatically added to the bar bill.

Destinations

From its home port in Aruba, the *Seawind Crown* sails two different itineraries throughout the southern Caribbean. A land-sea program includes three to seven nights at the La Cabana resort in Aruba. (For detailed itineraries, *see* Chapter 3.)

For More
Information

Seawind Cruise Line (1750 Coral Way, Miami, FL 33145, tel. 305/854-7800).

TSS Seawind Crown

Specifications

Type of ship: Classic liner
Cruise experience: Semi-formal
Size: 24,000 tons
Number of cabins: 362
Outside cabins: 68%

Passengers: 728
Crew: 320 (European)
Officers: Greek and Portuguese
Passenger/crew ratio: 2.1 to 1
Year built: 1961

Ship's Log

This ship's most outstanding feature is its proportions: More than 43,000 square feet of deck space and suites that measure 500 square feet—more than double what you find on many ships. Among the ship's offerings are an array of bars and lounges, an extensive shopping gallery, a well-equipped exercise room, and two swimming pools. An asset for southern Caribbean enthusiasts is that the *Crown* spends several more hours in Curaçao and Grenada than do most ships.

Cabins and
Rates

	Beds	Phone	TV	Sitting Area	Fridge	Tub	Average Per Diem*
Suite	D	●	●	●	●	○	$375
Outside	D, T, or U/L	●	●	○	●	◑	$275
Inside	D, T, or U/L	●	●	○	●	○	$250

*Rates are for the Caribbean and include airfare.

Cabins are large but oddly configured, appointed in pastel hues, and outfitted with a telephone, minifridge, and closed-circuit TV. Bathrooms are spacious but equipped with European-style handheld shower nozzles. Many cabins overlook a public promenade.

Outlet voltage: 220 AC.

Single supplement: 150%–200% of double-occupancy rate for all categories except the smallest inside cabins (category M), for which single passengers pay no extra charge.

Discounts: A third or fourth passenger in a cabin pays $895 per seven-week cruise. You get a discount of up to $200 for arranging your own airfare, and a $450 discount for booking 60 days in advance. Children under age two pay $100 per week.

Sports and
Fitness

Health club: Rowing machines, treadmill, sauna, massage.

Recreation: Volleyball, two pools, unobstructed circuits for jogging.

Facilities

Public rooms: Five bars and lounges, showroom, casino, disco, cinema, card room, library, chapel.

Shops: Boutiques gallery, beauty salon/barber.

Health care: A doctor and a nurse are on call.

Child care: Playroom, daily chaperoned children's activities.

Services: Photo service, photo shop.

Accessibility There are four elevators and two cabins accessible to wheelchair users. Passengers who use wheelchairs must state this at the time of booking and must travel with an able-bodied adult.

Silversea Cruises

The Fleet MV *Silver Cloud*
MV *Silver Wind*

Silversea aims to narrow the gap between ocean-liner and small-ship cruising, with such features as a full-size showroom, a domed dining room, several bars, and shops that are larger than those found aboard Seabourn and Sea Goddess. At more than 16,000 tons, the *Silver Cloud* and *Silver Wind* are designed to be more stable than their competitors in the open sea, yet they are still agile enough to navigate relatively shallow waters or narrow channels.

Ships at a Glance

	Dining Rooms	Bars	Casino	Fitness Center	Pools	Average Per Diem
Silver Cloud Silver Wind	1	3	●	●	1	$640

Cruise Experience Larger ships mean more facilities and room for passengers. For example, the Silversea ships have larger swimming pools and more deck space than other cruise yachts. The all-inclusive packaging is the most comprehensive at sea, including selected shore excursions and all beverages aboard ship, alcoholic and otherwise. (A few special vintages are extra.) Each booking comes with a complimentary pre-cruise hotel room for passengers who arrive early and free travel insurance. But, depending on the itinerary, Silversea may still cost hundreds of dollars a day less than its competitors.

Activities Silversea emphasizes water sports for the active passenger. Choices include waterskiing, wave running, windsurfing, snorkeling, and swimming. Aboard ship, passengers can join the morning aerobics classes, work out in small exercise rooms, swim in the teak-lined pool, or jog on the promenade deck. For the less athletically inclined, there are card and board games, celebrity speakers, foreign-language classes, chess and bridge competitions, and a large library stocked with books, videotapes, and compact discs. Two IBM-compatible computers with CD-ROM drives are also found in the library.

Dining Continental, American, and regional specialties tied to the itinerary top Silversea's wide-ranging menus. Panoramic windows line the domed dining room, which accommodates all passengers in a single, open seating (dinner is from 7:30 to 9:30). Meals are served in a setting of candlelight and fresh flowers, French crystal and Italian china. Two formal nights are scheduled each week, but passengers are expected to primp for dinner every evening. Most special dietary requests should be submitted well in advance.

Chart Symbols. Ships at a Glance. ●: *Fully equipped;* ◑: *Partially equipped;* ○: *Not equipped.* Cabins and Rates. **D:** *Double bed;* **K:** *King-size bed;* **Q:** *Queen-size bed;* **T:** *Twin bed;* **U/L:** *Upper and lower berths;* ●: *All cabins have this facility;* ○: *No cabins have this facility;* ◑: *Some cabins have this facility*

Another room with a view for dining is the Terrace Cafe, which overlooks an open deck. Although the specialties of the house are pastas and gelati, almost any dish from the dining room may be ordered. Seating is mostly indoor, with a few outdoor tables. Theme dinners are served here three or four times a week. Room service is available 24 hours from an unlimited menu.

Entertainment Production-style shows are staged nightly in the Venetian Lounge showroom, featuring resident performers as well as local talent. Films and lectures are presented here as well. Another bar presents live music for dancing; a small casino adjoins the upper level. Passengers may also view films in-cabin on closed-circuit broadcasts or from the library's selection of videotapes.

Service and Tipping Silversea's staff has been recruited from some of the finest lines in cruising, such as Crystal and Seabourn. Tipping is included in the cruise fare, and no additional gratuities are accepted.

Destinations Silversea counts the eastern U.S. seaboard and Canada, the Caribbean, South America, and the Panama Canal among its worldwide sailings. (For detailed itineraries, *see* Chapter 3.)

For More Information Silversea Cruises (110 E. Broward Blvd., Fort Lauderdale, FL 33301, tel. 305/522–4477 or 800/722–6655).

Silver Cloud and Silver Wind

Specifications *Type of ship:* Cruise yacht   *Passengers:* 296
Cruise experience: Formal   *Crew:* 196
Size: 16,800 tons   *Officers:* Italian
Number of cabins: 148   *Passenger/crew ratio:* 1.5 to 1
Outside cabins: 100%   *Year built:* 1994

Ship's Log The *Silver Cloud* and *Silver Wind* have taken the cruise yacht category to new extremes of size and spaciousness. The additional space their tonnage allows has been put to use in the public rooms, particularly in the two-tier showroom, where a movable stage makes full-scale productions possible. Unlike the *Sea Goddess* and Seabourn ships, there is no retractable marina at the stern for water sports; the Silversea ships use one of the tender platforms instead. They do, however, have larger pools and more open deck space.

The decor aboard the Silversea ships is subtle yet distinctive and meant to evoke the great steamships of the past. Brass sconces, wood paneling, and brass-ringed portholes in the dining room deliver the desired effect. Throughout the ship, there is an obvious attention to detail. Note, for instance, the inlaid designs in the dining room's hardwood floor.

Cabins and Rates	Beds	Phone	TV	Sitting Area	Fridge	Tub	Average Per Diem*
Suite	Q, T	●	●	●	●	●	$640

Rates are for the Amazon and include airfare and port taxes.

As with every luxury cruise yacht, every warmly appointed cabin is an outside suite. Large picture windows, walk-in closets, marble bathrooms with robes, slippers, and a wall-mounted hair dryer are among the many amenities, along with a writing table stocked with personalized stationary, a basket of fresh fruit replenished daily, and flowers and champagne upon arrival. Other standard equipment includes remote-controlled television with closed-circuit and satellite broadcasts (including CNN), a VCR, refrigerator (stocked with complimentary beverages), and wall safe. Except for Vista

Suites, all accommodations open onto a teak veranda with floor-to-ceiling sliding glass doors.

Outlet voltage: 110/220 AC.

Single supplement: A limited number of suites are available for single occupancy on each cruise. Single passengers pay 125% of the double-occupancy rate for Vista or Veranda suites, 200% for Grand, Owner, or Silver suites.

Discounts: A third or fourth passenger in the Vista pays 50% of the double-occupancy rate. A third through sixth passenger in the Veranda, Silver, or Grand Suite pays 50% of the Veranda double-occupancy rate. Passengers who combine two or more consecutive sailings can save up to $3,000. Passengers who pay six months in advance receive a 15% discount; those who make deposits four months in advance receive 10% off.

Sports and Fitness

Health club: Fitness center with exercise equipment, spa treatments, sauna, and massage rooms.

Recreation: Pool, two whirlpools, water sports, unobstructed circuit for jogging.

Facilities

Public rooms: Three bars, observation area, showroom, casino, library/computer center, card/conference room.

Shops: Boutique, beauty salon/barber, photo shop.

Health care: Doctor and nurse on call.

Child care: None.

Services: Laundry service, dry cleaning, photographer, film processing, fax.

Accessibility Two cabins are accessible to wheelchair users on the *Silver Wind*.

Society Expeditions

The Fleet MS *World Discoverer*

The *World Discoverer* conforms to exacting standards for adventure cruises, including a hardened hull to plow through ice-choked channels and a fleet of Zodiac landing craft, which allow passengers to make landfall virtually anywhere. Equipped to explore, this ship makes good use of its capabilities, and has on a number of occasions made a name for itself in the annals of cruising. In 1985 it made the first Northwest Passage crossing by a passenger ship, and later made headlines again with an unscheduled excursion across the Bering Strait during an Alaskan cruise. The U.S. government fined the line for this historic bold stroke; these days, a crossing to the Russian Far East is part of its regular itineraries.

Ship at a Glance	Dining Rooms	Bars	Casino	Fitness Center	Pools	Average Per Diem
World Discoverer	1	3	○	◑	●	$475

Cruise Experience Ranging far and wide throughout the Western Hemisphere, the *World Discoverer* draws well-traveled cruisers, largely retired professionals. About 80% come from the United States and the remaining 20% from countries in Europe. Many have sailed aboard the *World Discoverer* before. A spirit of camaraderie usually develops between everyone on board, as passengers mingle with each other and the ship's officers and crew. Central to this shared experience are the Zodiac excursions off the ship. Together, small bands of passengers search for wildlife and explore little-visited shorelines from Antarctica to the Arctic.

Activities These are active cruises. Two or three excursions daily may include shoreside walks or hikes over rough terrain. Away teams are led by naturalists, anthropologists, historians, and botanists, who also lecture aboard ship to enrich passengers' appreciation for the creatures they see and the places they visit. Those who stay aboard will also find an assortment of pastimes, whether it be checking out a good book from the library or working out in the modest gym.

Dining Food is basic, no-frills fare, served in a single, open seating in the Marco Polo dining room. Portions for all meals are hearty, from the American-style breakfasts to the Continental cuisine served at dinner. Considering the remote regions visited and the inability to frequently stock the ship, the produce is surprisingly fresh at all times.

Entertainment Enrichment talks conducted by the staff scientists are a daily event in the Lecture Hall, which also doubles as the ship's theater for the

---

Chart Symbols. Ships at a Glance. **●**: *Fully equipped;* **◑**: *Partially equipped;* ○: *Not equipped.* Cabins and Rates. **D**: *Double bed;* **K**: *King-size bed;* **Q**: *Queen-size bed;* **T**: *Twin bed;* **U/L**: *Upper and lower berths;* **●**: *All cabins have this facility;* ○: *No cabins have this facility;* **◑**: *Some cabins have this facility*

occasional film or video screening. For those who just want to watch the passing scenery, there are 180° panoramic views through the windows of the observation lounge.

Service and Tipping The amiable European and Filipino dining-room staff and cabin attendants perform their duties quickly and efficiently. Recommended tipping is $8–$9 per person per day.

Destinations From Alaska to Antarctica, the *World Discoverer* sails some of the most interesting itineraries to be found anywhere. Of special note are its Bering Sea and Arctic Ocean cruises. (For detailed itineraries, *see* Chapter 3.)

For More Information Society Expeditions (2001 Western Ave., Suite 300, Seattle, WA 98121, tel. 800/548–8669).

MS World Discoverer

Specifications *Type of ship:* Expedition *Passengers:* 138
Cruise experience: Casual *Crew:* 75 (international)
Size: 3,153 tons *Officers:* German
Number of cabins: 71 *Passenger/crew ratio:* 1.8 to 1
Outside cabins: 100% *Year built:* 1974

Ship's Log With its blue hull, white funnel, and picture windows lining the ship, the *World Discoverer* strikes a dramatic pose wherever it drops anchor. Although not the largest or most luxurious expedition ship afloat, it delivers adventure in a warm and comfortable environment, with a touch of cruise-ship amenities. Onboard facilities include an observation lounge, cocktail lounge, library, lecture hall, a small fitness center with a sauna, and a swimming pool—the ship even carries water-sports equipment.

Cabins and Rates

	Beds	Phone	TV	Sitting Area	Fridge	Tub	Average Per Diem*
Suite	T	●	○	●	○	●	$680
Outside	T or U/L	●	○	○	○	○	$475

Rates are for Alaska. Airfare and port taxes are extra.

A European minimalism is softened by pastel colors in the small, spartan, all-outside cabins. Stainless-steel accents and molded contours lend a modern edge to the decor. The otherwise simple appointments are more than adequate for the typical adventure passenger, who tends to be active and use the cabin for little besides sleep. There are three suites aboard, as well as five single cabins. All accommodations are outside, and come with individual climate control, ample storage space, and hair dryers in the bathrooms. Cabins 100–103 and 110–113 have picture windows.

Outlet voltage: 220 AC.

Single supplement: 150% of double-occupancy rates; however, five single outside cabins are available at $423–$562 per cruise.

Discounts: A third or fourth passenger in a cabin pays $1,750–$3,450 per cruise, depending upon the itinerary.

Sports and Fitness **Health club:** Tiny gym, sauna, solarium, massage (sometimes).

Recreation: Pool, equipment for diving, fishing, snorkeling, waterskiing, windsurfing.

Facilities **Public rooms:** Three bars, two lounges, observation lounge, cinema/lecture hall, library/card room; navigation bridge open to passengers.

Shops: Gift shop, beauty salon/barber.

Health care: Doctor on call.

Accessibility There are no facilities specifically equipped for wheelchair users.

Special Expeditions

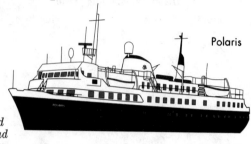

Polaris

The Fleet MS *Polaris*
MV *Sea Bird*
SY *Sea Cloud*
MV *Sea Lion*

Like other small-ship lines, Special Expeditions operates a collection of shallow-draft vessels designed to explore nature and visit remote ports. The yachtlike *Sea Bird* and *Sea Lion* are tiny, and even the *Polaris* is among the smallest of expedition ships. While all carry Zodiacs for wet landings almost anywhere, none of these vessels—not even the *Polaris*—has an ice-hardened hull. Very different from these three ships is the *Sea Cloud*, an authentic tall ship.

Ships at a Glance

	Dining Rooms	Bars	Casino	Fitness Center	Pools	Average Per Diem
Polaris	1	1	○	○	○	$550
Sea Bird/Sea Lion	1	1	○	○	○	$400
Sea Cloud	1	1	○	○	○	$700

Cruise Experience
Special Expeditions cruises attract a slightly younger, less affluent, more easygoing crowd than other adventure lines. Unlike guest experts on some ships who are treated either as employees or celebrities, specialists on Special Expeditions cruises eat and socialize with passengers. You'll feel less like a paying spectator and more like part of a grand adventure. Because all shore excursions, snorkeling, entrance fees, and lectures are included in the fare, few financial surprises await you.

Special Expeditions' primary vessels, the *Sea Bird* and *Sea Lion*, are neither as plushly appointed as Clipper's similar ships nor as roomy as Alaska Sightseeing's larger vessels. Where Special Expeditions excels is in its staff, especially the lecturers. In fact, Special Expeditions sails with more top experts aboard than any other small-ship line.

Activities
These are fairly regimented cruises. From the early morning broadcasts over the intercom system and set mealtimes to the daily schedule of lectures and shore excursions, the day is mapped out in fliers placed in your cabin at night. In tropical waters more emphasis is placed upon individual leisure activities, like snorkeling and sailing. Shipboard activities consist mainly of numerous lectures given by the staff of naturalists and historians on the wildlife and culture of the ports of call.

Chart Symbols. Ships at a Glance. ●: *Fully equipped;* ◐: *Partially equipped;* ○: *Not equipped.* Cabins and Rates. **D:** *Double bed;* **K:** *King-size bed;* **Q:** *Queen-size bed;* **T:** *Twin bed;* **U/L:** *Upper and lower berths;* ●: *All cabins have this facility;* ○: *No cabins have this facility;* ◐: *Some cabins have this facility*

Dining   Hearty meals draw on fresh ingredients available in ports along the way and are influenced by North American and European cooking traditions. The diet, more homey than gourmet, is somewhat heavy (especially if you help yourself to seconds), but with all the adventure activity you will quickly burn off the calories. Meals are served in a single, open seating (dinner from about 7 to 8:30). Passengers are expected to dress smartly on two designated evenings. Passengers can help themselves to coffee and cookies at any time. Special dietary requests are not easily handled. Room service is available only if you are ill.

Entertainment   Although there is no organized entertainment, the captain will occasionally invite local performers to dinner and have them play or sing in the lounge afterward. Otherwise, passengers play cards or board games at night or read. Most passengers hit the sack early to rest up for the next day's adventures.

Service and   Besides the sheer adventure of a Special Expeditions cruise, it is the
Tipping   warmth, competence, and intelligence of the crew that passengers remember. Crew members are very special; they engender trust, respect, and friendship. Tips are given anonymously by placing cash (or not-so-anonymous personal checks) in an envelope at the purser's office, where they're then pooled and divided among the crew. Tip $8 per passenger per diem.

Destinations   In the Western Hemisphere, the line's special expeditions extend from Alaska to the Amazon. (For detailed itineraries, *see* Chapter 3.)

For More   Special Expeditions (720 5th Ave., New York, NY 10019, tel. 212/
Information   265–7740 or 800/762–0003).

MS Polaris

Specifications   *Type of ship:* Expedition   *Passengers:* 80
Cruise experience: Casual   *Crew:* 44 (Filipino and
Size: 2,214 tons   Swedish)
Number of cabins: 41   *Officers:* Swedish
Outside cabins: 100%   *Passenger/crew ratio:* 1.8 to 1
Year built: 1960

Ship's Log   The *Polaris* began its life as a Scandinavian ferry and was later converted for expedition service. It lacks a wealth of amenities, but is well suited for adventure cruises. The main public room is more like an oversize living room than a cruise-ship lounge. Before dinner, passengers gather here to recap the day's events and hear informal talks by the naturalists. After dinner, videos are shown. Serving as the ship's library is an even smaller room at the stern—well stocked with reference books, best-sellers, and atlases. The dining room commands a magnificent view of the sea. For views below the waterline, the vessel is stocked with snorkeling equipment and carries a glass-bottom boat.

Cabins and Rates	Beds	Phone	TV	Sitting Area	Fridge	Tub	Average Per Diem*
Outside	T	○	○	◑	○	○	$550

Airfare and port taxes are extra.

Cabins are tiny, narrow, and poorly lighted, but they all have sea views. Stylistically speaking, the furnishings are purely practical.

Outlet voltage: 220 AC (bathrooms 110 AC).

Single supplement: 150% of double-occupancy rate in categories 1 and 2.

Discounts: A third or fourth passenger in a cabin pays half the double-occupancy rate.

Facilities **Public rooms:** Lounge/bar, library; navigation bridge open to passengers.

Shops: Small gift shop, beauty salon/barber.

Health care: Doctor on call.

Services: Laundry service.

Accessibility This ship is not recommended for passengers with mobility problems.

MV Sea Bird and MV Sea Lion

Specifications *Type of ship:* Coastal cruiser   *Passengers:* 70
Cruise experience: Casual   *Crew:* 21 (American)
Size: 99.7 tons   *Officers:* American
Number of cabins: 37   *Passenger/crew ratio:* 3.3 to 1
Outside cabins: 100%   *Year built:* 1982/1981

Ship's Log The lilliputian *Sea Lion* and *Sea Bird* look like hybrids of ferries and riverboats. While technically oceangoing vessels, they mostly sail on rivers and protected waterways. Their shallow drafts allow them to enter waters that would ground larger ships, even the *Polaris*. Homey and very friendly, the *Sea Lion* and the *Sea Bird* carry almost the same number of passengers as the *Polaris*, despite their smaller size. The ships' storage capacity, the size of the crews, and the number of public areas have been cut back as a result. Lectures, films, and other entertainment are held in the single lounge/bar, which also holds the ship's small reference library. These ships are not for claustrophobics, or for those who easily become seasick. They rock noticeably in rough waters. Packets of Dramamine are available from the purser's office.

Cabins and Rates	Beds	Phone	TV	Sitting Area	Fridge	Tub	Average Per Diem*
Suite	T/D	○	○	●	○	○	$460
Outside	T/D	○	○	○	○	○	$400

Airfare and port taxes are extra.

The cabins are among the smallest afloat, so form follows function to maximize space and minimize waste.

Outlet voltage: 110 AC.

Single supplement: 150% of double-occupancy rate in the smallest cabins only.

Discounts: No cabins are available for third or fourth passengers.

Facilities **Public rooms:** Lounge/bar, library; navigation bridge open to passengers.

Shops: Gift shop.

Health care: Doctor on board only on Baja California cruises; otherwise, the ship, never far from land, will dock in a U.S. or Canadian port if care is required.

Services: Laundry service.

Accessibility These ships are not recommended for passengers with mobility problems.

SY Sea Cloud

Specifications	*Type of ship:* Motor-sail *Passengers:* 60

Specifications

Type of ship: Motor-sail
Cruise experience: Casual
Size: 2,323 tons
Number of cabins: 32
Outside cabins: 100%

Passengers: 60
Crew: 65 (German)
Officers: German
Passenger/crew ratio: .92 to 1
Year built: 1932

Ship's Log

The four-masted *Sea Cloud*, perhaps the most beautiful barque afloat, is a vision of maritime grace and elegance. When it was built, as the *Hussar V*, for the heiress Marjorie Merriweather Post and financier E. F. Hutton, it was the world's largest privately owned yacht. It's led a colorful life since then: as a naval weather station during World War II, as the yacht of Dominican dictator Molina Trujillo, and as carrier of numerous Hollywood stars and even the Duke and Duchess of Windsor. Eventually, a dispute over ownership left the ship rotting and derelict until a group of German investors refurbished and relaunched it in 1978.

Every attempt has been made to keep the *Sea Cloud* true to its origins, an artifact of a grander, more glamorous era. Every inch of this classic sailing yacht is finely polished and crafted. It's truly a sight to watch crew members scamper up the 20-story masts to unfurl the ship's 29 billowing sails (which cover 34,000 square feet). Auxiliary engines are fired up when necessary, but cruising under sail is much quieter, smoother, and more romantic.

Many of the original wood panels, desks, antiques, and other furnishings have been meticulously restored. Life on board is informal, laid-back, and unhurried, with few organized activities. Despite the air of privilege, no formal nights are scheduled. The *Sea Cloud* allows you to feel the waves under you, to list side to side with the winds, to experience the energy of the sea. Bring plenty of Dramamine.

Cabins and Rates

	Beds	Phone	TV	Sitting Area	Fridge	Tub	Average Per Diem*
Suite	K	○	○	●	○	●	$1,000
Outside	D/T	○	○	◑	○	◑	$700

*Airfare and port taxes are extra.

Cabins and suites are individually decorated and laid out. Most prized are the Owner's Suites, with original chandeliers and non-working fireplaces. Suites and deluxe staterooms have safes. Closet space is generous, and newer cabins have windows rather than portholes. Views from some Upper Deck cabins are partially obstructed by lifeboats. Cabins on the Promenade Deck look out onto public areas.

Outlet voltage: 220 AC.

Single supplement: 150% of double-occupancy rate; some single cabins are available.

Discounts: No cabins are available for third or fourth passengers.

Sports

Recreation: Snorkeling, unobstructed circuit for jogging.

Facilities

Public rooms: Lounge/bar, library; navigation bridge open to passengers.

Shops: Gift shop.

Health care: Doctor on call.

Services: Laundry service.

Accessibility

This ship is not recommended for passengers with mobility problems.

Star Clippers

The Fleet *Star Clipper*
Star Flyer

Taller, faster, and bigger than the original clippers, these sister ships re-create the 19th century vessels that supplied the California Gold Rush. First-time sailors and seasoned yachtsmen alike will appreciate Star Clippers' attention to sailing's finer details. The ships rely chiefly on sail power, with a single engine used only in flat calms and to maneuver in tight harbors. Some concessions have been made to modern technology: The ships are equipped with anti-rolling systems that keep them upright at high speeds and prevent rocking while at anchor.

Ships at a Glance

	Dining Rooms	Bars	Casino	Fitness Center	Pools	Average Per Diem
Star Clipper *Star Flyer*	1	2	○	○	2	$185

Cruise Experience Old-fashioned sailing is the key to Star Clippers' appeal. Guests can pitch the sails, help steer the ship, and learn about navigational techniques from the captain. Most, however, opt to take in the nautical ambience as they lounge on the upper deck. While Star Clippers' sailing philosophy is similar to a windjammer cruise (*see* Special-Interest Cruises *in* Cruise Primer), the vessels' facilities were designed with a more upscale passenger in mind: They have greater public space and larger cabins with hair dryers, televisions, and telephones, plus two swimming pools aboard. As cruise ships, their amenities fall somewhere in between Special Expedition's authentic *Sea Cloud* and the high-tech, computer-controlled vessels of Club Med and Windstar, but at a more affordable price. However, the differences are more than a matter of creature comforts: The Star Clippers are true sailing vessels, albeit with motors, while Club Med and Windstar vessels are ocean liners with masts and sails.

Star Clippers' crowd is an international one: About half the 170 passengers are European (French, German, and Swedish). Nearly all are couples, ranging from honeymooners to well-traveled retirees. The ships' officers mix socially with passengers and eat with passengers during dinner.

Activities Passengers do their own thing. The only organized activities are daily aerobics classes, talks on ports of call, knot-tying lessons, and afternoon captain's tales. Scrabble, checkers, and other board games are played in the library. Snorkeling, windsurfing, waterskiing, and sailing are available whenever the ship is at anchor; the ship carries its own banana boat and four Zodiacs, two for daily diving excursions

---

Chart Symbols. Ships at a Glance. ●: *Fully equipped;* ◑: *Partially equipped;* ○: *Not equipped.* Cabins and Rates. **D:** *Double bed;* **K:** *King-size bed;* **Q:** *Queen-size bed;* **T:** *Twin bed;* **U/L:** *Upper and lower berths;* ●: *All cabins have this facility;* ○: *No cabins have this facility;* ◑: *Some cabins have this facility*

and two for waterskiing. Night dives are particularly popular. Divers must be certified, but pool instruction is given to beginners who are interested.

Dining   Star Clippers has hired a new executive chef and created new menus in an effort to improve what had been a weakness. The wine list is excellent. Passengers are charged for all nonalcoholic drinks except during breakfast, dinner, and some lunches. Tables and booths seat eight to 10, so dining tends to be a family-style event. Dinner is served at an open seating from 7:30 to 10. Formal attire is never required in the dining room; collared shirts for men is about as dressy as it gets. Special dietary requests, with the exception of vegetarian meals, are not easily accommodated.

Other food service includes Continental breakfast in the piano bar and a buffet breakfast, with omelets cooked to order, served in the dining room. Lunchtime beach barbecues are a favorite among passengers. Lunch buffets are also served on deck or in the dining room, followed by hors d'oeuvres in the afternoon. Midnight sandwiches conclude the eating day in the piano bar. There is no room service.

Entertainment   The piano bar, with its friendly piano player/singer, is the main gathering spot for low-key evening diversion. Passengers often request songs and join the show, especially on crew-passenger talent night. Local musical groups board the ship at happy hours for short but colorful performances. Two disco nights are held each cruise on a semi-enclosed upper deck. Traditional crab races, as practiced by the sailors of yesteryear, are another evening highlight. Several movies play throughout the night on in-cabin televisions.

Service and Tipping   Cabin service is excellent; dining-room service is a bit harried. The international crew works well together and is generally helpful, if not overly attentive. Tip the room steward $3 per diem and dining-room staff $5 per diem.

Destinations   Stopping at ports rarely visited by larger ships, the *Star Flyer* and *Star Clipper* cruise the Caribbean from home ports in St. Maarten and Barbados. When the two vessels meet at sea, a race at full sail often ensues. (For detailed itineraries, *see* Chapter 3.)

For More Information   Star Clippers (4101 Salzedo Ave., Coral Gables, FL 33146, tel. 800/442–0551).

Star Clipper and Star Flyer

Specifications
Type of ship: Motor-sail   *Passengers:* 170
Cruise experience: Casual   *Crew:* 72 (international)
Size: 3,025 tons   *Officers:* International
Number of cabins: 85   *Passenger/crew ratio:* 2.3 to 1
Outside cabins: 83%   *Year built:* 1991/1992

Ship's Log   These long, slender white ships have sharp pointed bows to cut quickly through the water, narrowly curved steel hulls, teak decks and trim, and four tapered steel masts rigged with 16 sails. Two small, saltwater swimming pools are surrounded by sunning areas on the aft and sundecks. The pool on the latter has a glass bottom, so patrons of the piano bar can view swimmers from below. Deck-chair mats can be used as floats in the pool or in the ocean. Most social activity takes place on the Tropical Deck, either outside at the bar or inside the chrome-finished piano bar. Here, passengers gather to chat and relax on leather, semicircular booths. Navy blue and beige lend a nautical air to the room. A winding grand stairway leads from the bar to the dining room, appointed in the same blue/beige decor, teak and marble trim, and handsome nautical art.

Cabins and Rates	Beds	Phone	TV	Sitting Area	Fridge	Tub	Average Per Diem*
Outside	T	●	●	●	○	○	$185
Inside	T	●	●	●	○	○	$170

Rates are for Caribbean. Airfare and port taxes are extra.

Accommodations are somewhat small but closets are roomy. Each cabin has a vanity and a tiny corner sitting area with a built-in seat and an upholstered stool. Outside cabins have portholes; only a very few have picture windows. Showers and sink faucets are the push type and require constant pressing to maintain water flow. Ten cabins have an additional berth that folds out of the wall for a third passenger. A hardcover illustrated history of Star Clippers is placed in each cabin prior to embarkation.

Outlet voltage: 110/220 AC.

Single supplement: 150% of double-occupancy rate.

Discounts: A third passenger in a cabin pays $395. You get a discount of up to $500 per person for booking more than a year in advance and a 10% discount for booking 120 days in advance on selected sailings. Passengers combining two consecutive seven-day cruises save $300.

Sports and Fitness **Recreation:** Four fitness instructors, water-sports equipment, scuba gear for certified divers.

Facilities **Public rooms:** Two bars, one lounge, library.

Shops: Gift shop.

Health care: Nurse on call.

Child care: There are no organized children's programs or provisions for young children, but older children are welcome.

Accessibility These ships are not recommended for passengers with mobility problems.

Sun Line Cruises

The Fleet   TSS *Stella Solaris*

This former French passenger liner once sailed as the *Camboge* on long ocean voyages between France, Indochina, and the Far East. It was completely rebuilt in 1973 as a cruise liner, so that only the graceful hull and quiet steam engines remain from the original ship. Today it sails with a Greek flavor instilled by its officers, crew, and owners, who operate Sun Line as a true family business.

Ship at a Glance

	Dining Rooms	Bars	Casino	Fitness Center	Pools	Average Per Diem
Stella Solaris	1	4	◐	◐	1	$300

Cruise Experience   Sun Line specializes in long cruises offering unusual itineraries normally available only on much more expensive ships. Though Amazon cruises have been attracting the younger set recently, most passengers are older than on other ships, most likely because of the time and money required for extended cruises. Passengers enjoy a number of genteel touches while en route to their exotic destinations. Two gentlemen travel with the ship so single ladies will have partners for dancing, dining, bridge games, and other social activities. Catholic Mass is celebrated every morning, the Jewish Sabbath every Friday evening, and a Protestant service every Sunday. Passengers can leave their shoes for the steward to polish and return by morning. Nearly half of those who sail on Sun Line are repeat passengers.

Activities   Expert lecturers from North American universities and prominent research societies conduct a shipboard enrichment program, with talks covering local ports, history, art, stargazing, wildlife, and other subjects. Of particular note are talks by Captain Loren McIntyre, credited with discovering the source of the Amazon, who helped Sun Line pioneer Amazon cruising in 1983. Traditional activities, such as bingo, card and board games, and trivia contests, as well as classes in bridge, arts and crafts, and ballroom and Greek dancing are also scheduled.

Dining   The cuisine is essentially Continental, with Greek specialties featured at lunch and a different ice-cream sundae each day. Low-sodium, low-cholesterol, and low-fat selections are available at every meal. The wine list is eclectic, ranging from very modest Italian and Greek vintages to expensive Bordeaux. Dinner is served at two assigned seatings (6:30 and 8:30). Two formal evenings are held on seven-day cruises, three or four on cruises longer than 12 days. Men should wear a jacket and tie for all "informal" dinners, and women a cocktail dress or pantsuit. On "casual" nights, sportswear is suffi-

---

Chart Symbols. Ships at a Glance. ●: *Fully equipped;* ◐: *Partially equipped;* ○: *Not equipped.* Cabins and Rates. **D:** *Double bed;* **K:** *King-size bed;* **Q:** *Queen-size bed;* **T:** *Twin bed;* **U/L:** *Upper and lower berths;* ●: *All cabins have this facility;* ○: *No cabins have this facility;* ◐: *Some cabins have this facility*

cient. Special dietary requests should be made in writing two weeks before sailing. The Lido café serves early morning coffee and pastries, a buffet breakfast, mid-morning bouillon, and a buffet lunch. Afternoon tea is served in the Solaris lounge. Self-serve coffee and iced tea are available at all times. Room service is available 24 hours from a limited menu.

Entertainment In addition to nightly variety shows, Sun Line offers piano music, cabarets, dance bands, late-night disco, and passenger talent shows. Local performers are often brought on board to perform. Greek Night is an exuberant celebration of Sun Line's heritage that includes dancing, ethnic food, bouzouki music, singing, more dancing, and plenty of toasts with ouzo or wine. Movie lovers have a choice of an afternoon or an evening screening in a 275-seat cinema. After the evening show, the orchestra gets a good crowd in the lounge for ballroom dancing until midnight, after which night owls flock to the disco.

Service and Sun Line is proud of the way it treats the crew. Some crew members
Tipping have been with the company for more than 30 years; others inherited their positions from their fathers. As a result, the service is personable and efficient. Tips are pooled among the crew according to the rules of the Greek Stewards' Union; tip $8 or $9 per passenger per diem. Passengers are asked not to tip individual crew members except the beautician, barber, and masseuse.

Destinations In winter, the *Solaris* sails Amazon, Caribbean, and Panama Canal itineraries. In summer, the ship sails outside the Western Hemisphere. (For detailed itineraries, *see* Chapter 3.)

For More Sun Line Cruises (1 Rockefeller Plaza, Suite 315, New York, NY
Information 10020, tel. 800/872–6400 or 800/368–3888 in Canada).

TSS Stella Solaris

Specifications | *Type of ship:* Cruise liner | *Passengers:* 620 |
|---|---|
| *Cruise experience:* Semi-formal | *Crew:* 310 (Greek and Filipino) |
| *Size:* 18,000 tons | *Officers:* Greek |
| *Number of cabins:* 329 | *Passenger/crew ratio:* 2 to 1 |
| *Outside cabins:* 76% | *Year built:* 1953; rebuilt 1973 |

Ship's Log An attractive ship with curving lines, teak decks, and hardwood railings, the *Solaris* is a homey ship with a friendly atmosphere. Spacious and with relatively few passengers aboard, it's designed for easy mixing. The centrally located foyer serves as a village green of sorts, where several times a day, everyone pauses or passes through on their way to the restaurant, one of the lounges, a favorite bar, or other rendezvous point. The boat deck, the prime outdoor gathering area, attracts sizeable numbers of early morning walkers (not many joggers on this ship) doing their constitutional rounds. As the day wears on, many take to the sheltered deck chairs that line both sides of the wide promenade.

Cabins and Rates

	Beds	Phone	TV	Sitting Area	Fridge	Tub	Average Per Diem*
Suite	D or T	●	●	●	○	●	$375
Outside	T	●	●	○	○	◐	$300
Inside	T	●	●	○	○	○	$250

Rates are for the Amazon. Airfare and port taxes are extra.

Cabins come in either green, salmon, or gold, and most are well apportioned; storage space is especially generous. Many can be connected as adjoining staterooms. Each is equipped with a lockable drawer for valuables. Suites on the Boat Deck (category 1) look out onto a public promenade through one-way glass, and have a large walk-in closet and a sitting area with coffee table, sofa, and chairs. Superior inside and standard outside cabins have upper berths for third and fourth passengers. A third passenger may also be accommodated in a sofa bed in the deluxe suites.

Outlet voltage: 110/220 AC.

Single supplement: 150%–200% of double-occupancy rate. Same-sex singles can be matched in a cabin; each pays the double-occupancy rate.

Discounts: A third or fourth passenger in a cabin pays the minimum fare for the cruise. You get a discount for arranging your own airfare, and a 10%–35% discount for early booking. Special incentives are offered to repeat passengers on selected dates. Two passengers sail for the price of one on round-trip Amazon cruises and spring and fall transatlantic crossings. Children 2–11 sharing a cabin with two adults pay 50% of the minimum fare for the cruise. Children under two pay $35 per diem.

Sports and Fitness

Health club: Fitness equipment, sauna, massage.

Recreation: Aerobics, table tennis, shuffleboard, pool, unobstructed circuit (7 laps = 1 mile) for jogging.

Facilities

Public rooms: Four bars, three entertainment lounges, casino, disco, cinema, card room, library/writing room.

Shops: Gift shop, beauty salon/barber.

Health care: Doctor and two nurses on call.

Child care: Playroom, youth programs with counselors when demand warrants it, baby-sitting arranged privately with crew member.

Services: Laundry service, pressing service, photographer, film processing, shoe shines.

Accessibility

All public areas except the disco are accessible to wheelchair users. No cabin is specially equipped, and cabin and bathroom entrances have raised thresholds. Bathroom entries are 21½ inches wide. Any passenger who uses a wheelchair must be accompanied by an able-bodied companion.

Windstar Cruises

The Fleet *Wind Spirit*
Wind Star

In creating Windstar's vessels, the designers crossed a 19th-century sailing ship with an ultramodern yacht. They took the latest in hull technology and put four masts on top, then added computers to control the six sails. At the touch of a button, 22,000 feet of canvas unfurl in two minutes—a spectacular sight to see. The sails are usually enough to power the ship, but in calm winds, diesel engines are employed to help with propulsion. Inspired as much by today's luxury cruise liners as yesterday's clippers, Windstar celebrates the new as well as the old.

Ships at a
Glance

	Dining Rooms	Bars	Casino	Fitness Center	Pools	Average Per Diem
Wind Spirit *Wind Star*	1	2	◑	◑	1	$456

Cruise Experience Few modern vessels capture the feeling of being at sea the way a Windstar ship does. But while the ship's design may be reminiscent of sailing vessels of yore, the amenities and shipboard service are among the best at sea. Life on board is unabashedly sybaritic, attracting a sophisticated crowd happy to sacrifice bingo and masquerade parties for the attractions of remote islands and water sports. Surprisingly, the daily rates are little more than those charged on the large, upscale ocean liners.

Activities Shipboard life is unregimented and unstructured. No group activities are held; passengers pursue their own interests. Chief among these is water sports. In calm waters, the ship lowers a platform built into the stern, creating a water-level deck for swimming and sunning. Snorkels, masks, and fins are distributed to passengers, free of charge, at the beginning of the week and are theirs to use for the duration of the cruise. Other water sports include waterskiing, kayaking, windsurfing, sailing, and even fishing. Banana-boat rides are always popular (the banana boat is a large, yellow inflatable that sits up to five people as it's pulled at a rapid rate of speed by another boat). There is a small casino on board, but gambling is not a priority for most Windstar passengers.

Dining Windstar's food is among the best served by any cruise line. Dinner is open seating, and passengers can wander in any time between 7:30 and 9:30. Elaborate formal wear is not considered appropriate; men generally do not wear a tie or jacket to dinner. Special dietary requests should be made four weeks before sailing. Breakfast and lunch are served in the glass-enclosed Veranda Lounge, or on an out-

---

Chart Symbols. Ships at a Glance. ●: *Fully equipped;* ◑: *Partially equipped;* ○: *Not equipped.* Cabins and Rates. **D:** *Double bed;* **K:** *King-size bed;* **Q:** *Queen-size bed;* **T:** *Twin bed;* **U/L:** *Upper and lower berths;* ●: *All cabins have this facility;* ○: *No cabins have this facility;* ◑: *Some cabins have this facility*

side deck, weather permitting. Other food service includes early morning coffee and croissants, plus afternoon tea. Limited room service is available 24 hours a day for Continental breakfast or canapés and beverages.

Entertainment The little entertainment that is planned is strictly low-key. Every evening the ship's band or local musicians play in the lounge; there is also a piano bar and nightly dancing. The library has a selection of videotapes for use in the cabins. When the ship is in port, many passengers go ashore to sample the local nightlife.

Service and Tipping Service is comprehensive, competent, and designed to create an elite and privileged ambience. Tipping is not expected.

Destinations The *Wind Spirit* and *Wind Star* spend late autumn, winter, and spring in the Caribbean. A third sister, *Wind Song*, is based in Tahiti. (For detailed itineraries, *see* Chapter 3.)

For More Information Windstar Cruises (300 Elliott Ave. W, Seattle, WA 98119, tel. 800/258–7245).

Wind Spirit and Wind Star

Specifications *Type of ship:* Motor-sail   *Passengers:* 148
Cruise experience: Casual   *Crew:* 91 (British)
Size: 5,350   *Officers:* Norwegian
Number of cabins: 74   *Passenger/crew ratio:* 1.6 to 1
Outside cabins: 100%   *Year built:* 1988/1986

Ship's Log Inspired by the great sailing ships of a bygone era, *Wind Spirit* and *Wind Star* are white, long, and lean, with bow masts and brass-rimmed portholes. To satisfy international safety regulations, the hulls are steel, not wood; the interiors, however, glow with wood paneling and teak trim—a look rare among modern cruise ships. Instead of the chrome-and-glass banisters so popular on other ships, Windstar vessels feature white-painted iron ones with teak handrails. Although the ships are narrow—a necessity for sail-powered vessels—the interiors are unusually spacious, mainly because there are so few passengers. The sense of space is heightened by huge glass windows that allow plenty of light into the public rooms.

Cabins and Rates

	Beds	Phone	TV	Sitting Area	Fridge	Tub	Average Per Diem*
Suite	T/Q	●	●	●	●	○	$456

*Rates are for Caribbean. Airfare and port taxes are extra.

Windstar cabins represent the height of sailing luxury. Every cabin is an outside suite, appointed in burled maple veneer and outfitted with plentiful closet space and mirrors. Portholes are trimmed in brass, the white laminated cabinetwork is accented with rich wood moldings, and bathroom floors are made of teak. All are outside suites with stocked refrigerators, sitting areas, safes, CD players, and VCRs. In-cabin TVs show CNN broadcasts. The larger Owner's Suite costs 30% more. Some cabins can accommodate a third passenger.

Outlet voltage: 110 AC.

Single supplement: 150% of double-occupancy rate; 200% for Owner's Suite.

Discounts: A third passenger in a cabin pays 50% of the double occupancy rate.

Sports and Fitness **Health club:** Exercise equipment, sauna, massage, hot tub.

Recreation: Exercise classes, sailing, scuba diving (for certified divers), snorkeling, waterskiing, windsurfing, swimming platform, pool, scheduled morning walks on unobstructed circuit.

Facilities **Public rooms:** Two bars, entertainment lounge, small casino (slots and blackjack), disco, library (books and videotapes).

Shops: Boutique, sports shop, hairstylist.

Health care: Doctor on call.

Child care: Bringing children on board is discouraged; no provisions are made for them.

Services: Laundry service.

Accessibility The lack of an elevator makes moving through the ship almost impossible for wheelchair users. Tenders are used to transport passengers from ship to shore in most ports.

World Explorer Cruises

The Fleet SS *Universe*

The *Universe*'s origin as a freighter is still evident in the cargo booms that dominate the bow. Later, the vessel sailed as a transatlantic liner; from those days it retains a glass-enclosed promenade and steam propulsion. As a cruise liner, the *Universe* carries a 12,000-volume library (the largest at sea), an onboard herbarium, and a constantly changing display of Pacific Northwest artwork.

Ship at a Glance

	Dining Rooms	Bars	Casino	Fitness Center	Pools	Average Per Diem
Universe	1	6	○	●	0	$200

Cruise Experience If you're intellectually inclined and willing to forgo some creature comforts of cruise-ship life, then an Alaskan cruise on the *Universe* might be for you. There is no casino or disco. Instead, World Explorer specializes in low-cost educational and cultural cruises of the Great Land, and they are superb. When you sail on the *Universe*, you can expect to learn more about Alaska and see more of the ports than on any other ocean liner. If, on the other hand, you sleep through music recitals or cringe at the idea of a lecture on native art and culture, take another ship.

A unique feature aboard the *Universe* is the 500-specimen herbarium. Passengers take botanical walks in selected ports with forest-service guides, collecting new samples every cruise. The ship also carries an artist-in-residence, who conducts informal workshops and painting demonstrations. The work is then displayed on the Promenade Deck.

Activities Days at sea and mornings en route to a port are packed with classes, slide presentations, videotape demonstrations, and educational films. Four or five experts give a series of lectures on subjects ranging from Alaskan anthropology to history, glaciers, whales, and oceanography. Much time is spent observing passing scenery and wildlife, but bridge, table tennis, board games, and jigsaw puzzles are popular pastimes, too. The ship also offers a selection of first-run movies, bingo, trivia contests, and competitions.

Dining World Explorer's food and dining-room service now get moderate to high marks from passengers, especially first-time cruisers; however, experienced cruisers complain that the food is often overcooked and fairly institutional when compared with other lines. The cuisine is mostly American, with Oriental, Italian, or Mexican dishes frequently on the menu. Low-salt and vegetarian selections are available every evening as well. Once during each two-week cruise, the

Chart Symbols. Ships at a Glance. ●: *Fully equipped;* ◐: *Partially equipped;* ○: *Not equipped.* Cabins and Rates. **D:** *Double bed;* **K:** *King-size bed;* **Q:** *Queen-size bed;* **T:** *Twin bed;* **U/L:** *Upper and lower berths;* ●: *All cabins have this facility;* ○: *No cabins have this facility;* ◐: *Some cabins have this facility*

crew prepares an Oriental theme dinner. It's generally the best meal of the voyage. Breakfast and lunch are served in a single, open seating. Dinner is served at two assigned seatings (6 and 7:45) and a classical guitarist or string quartet often plays during the meal. Two semiformal evenings are held each cruise. Make special diet requests in writing 30 days prior to sailing (no kosher available).

Continental breakfast, afternoon tea, and late-night snacks are served buffet-style on the enclosed Promenade Deck. The food selection tends to be skimpy, however. Self-serve coffee and tea are available at all times, but there is no room service.

Entertainment Lecturers become the entertainment on these cruises. Otherwise, you'll enjoy outstanding classical and folk performances by singers, string quartets, a pianist or violinist, a harp-and-dulcimer duo, or perhaps a flamenco guitarist. There's also a smattering of more traditional cruise fun: dancing, passenger talent competitions, and costume shows.

Service and Crew members are friendly, but service is not of the pampering kind
Tipping usually associated with cruise ships. Filipino stewards in the dining room receive consistently high marks from passengers. There is no room service, not even coffee in the morning. Tip the room steward and the waiter $2.50 each per passenger per diem.

Destinations Two-week summer cruises to Alaska are the only sailings aboard the *Universe* sold to the general public through World Explorer Cruises. From September to May, the ship operates as a floating university, taking students from the University of Pittsburgh, and a few leisure passengers, around the world. (For detailed itineraries, *see* Chapter 3.)

For More World Explorer Cruises (555 Montgomery St., San Francisco, CA
Information 94111, tel. 800/854–3835). For information on the floating university, contact Semester at Sea/I.S.E. (University of Pittsburgh, 811 William Pitt Union, Pittsburgh, PA 15260, tel. 412/648–7490 or 800/854–0195).

SS Universe

Specifications *Type of ship:* Cruise liner   *Passengers:* 550
Cruise experience: Casual   *Crew:* 220 (Chinese,
Size: 18,100 tons   Filipino, American, Cana-
Number of cabins: 314   dian)
Outside cabins: 47%   *Officers:* Chinese, Taiwanese
Year built: 1953   *Passenger/crew ratio:* 2.5 to 1

Ship's Log The *Universe*, with its emphasis on learning, is noteworthy mostly for its facilities that contribute to the Alaskan experience: the herbarium, library, artwork, and large picture windows along the enclosed promenade that provide wonderful views of the Alaskan landscape and wildlife.

Passengers who would rather not be distracted by the scenery can move inside to the cozy Mandarin Lounge, which is more like a living room. The stern lounge and bar on the Boat Deck is an excellent spot for socializing, reading, or having a nightcap. All the public rooms have been refurbished during the past several years and are comfortable, if less than luxurious.

Cabins and Rates	Beds	Phone	TV	Sitting Area	Fridge	Tub	Average Per Diem*
Outside	T or U/L	○	○	◐	○	◐	$260
Inside	T or U/L	○	○	○	○	○	$200

Rates are for Alaska. Airfare and port taxes are extra.

The tiny cabins have all been refurbished with new drapes, bed-spreads, and fresh paint during the course of the past several years, although steel lockers are still found in the place of closets and built-in steel bunks and desks (typical of a ship built in the 1950s) resist more comfortable furniture. In the postage-stamp bathrooms, you'll find a painted concrete floor and exposed pipes, another example of how these cabins were designed for function rather than form and appeal. Staterooms on the Boat Deck look onto a public promenade.

Outlet voltage: 110 AC.

Single supplement: A number of inside and outside single cabins are available.

Discounts: A third or fourth passenger in a cabin pays $57 per diem. Vancouver airport transfers are complimentary; Seattle airport transfers cost $30 one-way per passenger.

Sports and Fitness

Health club: Weights, stationary bikes, rowing machines, massage.

Recreation: Aerobics, table tennis, unobstructed indoor-outdoor circuit (12 laps = 1 mile) for jogging.

Facilities

Public rooms: Two bars, six lounges, cinema, library.

Shops: Gift shop, beauty salon/barber.

Health care: Doctor on call.

Child care: Playroom, children's program.

Services: Self-service laundry.

Accessibility

Some doorways have raised thresholds. The elevator doesn't reach the Main Deck cabins or the Coral Deck, where the cinema and beauty salon are located. Passengers with mobility problems must be accompanied by an able-bodied companion.

Western Hemisphere Cruise Fleet

Ship	Cruise Line	Cruising Regions	Size (in tons)	Type of Ship	Cruise Experience	Average Per Diem	Length of Cruise	Number of Passengers
American Queen	Delta Queen Steamboat	Mississippi River	4,700	Riverboat	Casual	$397	3–12-day	43(
Britanis	Fantasy	NA	26,000	Classic	Casual	$80–$180	NA	92(
Caribbean Prince	Amer. Canadian Caribbean	Central America/ N.E. U.S. & Canada	89.5	Coastal cruiser	Casual	$185	12-,15-day	7(
Celebration	Carnival Cruise	Caribbean	48,000	Cruise liner	Casual	$208	7-day	148(
Century/ Galaxy	Celebrity	Caribbean	70,000	Megaship	Semiformal	$285–$378	7-day	175(
Club Med 1	Club Med	Caribbean	14,000	Motor-sail	Casual	$300	7-day	38
Constitution	American Hawaii	Hawaii	30,090	Classic	Casual	$256	7-day	79
Costa Allegra	Costa	Caribbean	30,000	Cruise liner	Semiformal	$250	7-day	80
CostaClassica	Costa	Caribbean	53,000	Cruise liner	Semiformal	$285	7-day	130
CostaRomantica	Costa	Caribbean	54,000	Cruise liner	Semiformal	$285	7-day	130
Crown Odyssey	Royal	Hawaii/Panama Canal/ Mexican Riviera	34,250	Cruise liner	Semiformal	$278	8–16-day	105
Crown Princess	Princess	Caribbean/ Alaska/Panama Canal	70,000	Megaship	Semiformal	$300	7–11-day	159(
Cunard Countess	Cunard	Caribbean	17,593	Cruise liner	Casual	$160	7-day	79(
Cunard Crown Dynasty	Cunard	Caribbean/ Alaska/Panama Canal	20,000	Cruise liner	Semiformal	$338	7–14-day	80
Cunard Royal Viking Sun	Cunard	South America/ Caribbean/world cruise	38,000	Cruise liner	Formal	$615	14-114 day	75(
Crystal Harmony	Crystal	Panama Canal/ Caribbean/Amazon	49,400	Cruise liner	Formal	$455	10–13-day	96
Crystal Symphony	Crystal	Mexican Riviera/ world cruise	50,000	Cruise liner	Formal	$455	7–96-day	96
Delta Queen	Delta Queen Steamboat	Mississippi River	3,360	Riverboat	Casual	$397	3–12-day	17(
Dolphin IV	Dolphin	Bahamas	13,007	Cruise liner	Casual	$191	3–4-day	58
Dreamward	Norwegian	Caribbean/ Bermuda	30,440	Cruise liner	Casual	$270–$320	7-day	124

Passenger/Crew Ratio	Sanitation Rating*	Accessibility	Special Dietary Options	Gymnasium	Walking/Jogging Circuit	Swimming Pool	Whirlpool	Sauna/Massage	Deck Sports	Casino	Disco	Cinema/Theater	Library	Boutiques/Gift Shops	Video Arcade	Child Care
2.6:1	NA	◐	◐	●	●	1	○	○	○	○	○	●	●	●	○	○
.7:1	96	○	●	◐	●	1	○	◐	●	●	●	●	●	●	○	◐
4.6:1	86	○	●	○	●		○	○	○	○	○	○	○	○	○	○
2.2:1	89	●	◐	●	●	2	●	●	●	●	●	○	●	●	●	●
.1:1	NA	●	●	●	●	2	●	●	●	●	●	●	●	●	●	●
.1:1	89	○	◐	●	●	2	○	●	●	●	●	◐	●	●	○	○
.5:1	NA	○	◐	●	◐	2	○	●	●	○	●	●	○	●	●	◐
:1	92	●	●	●	●	1	●	●	●	●	●	○	●	●	○	●
:1	92	●	●	●	●	2	○	●	●	●	●	○	●	●	●	●
:1	93	●	●	●	●	2	●	●	●	●	●	○	●	●	●	●
.2:1	90	●	●	●	●	2	●	●	●	●	●	●	●	●	○	○
.2:1	97	●	●	●	●	2	●	●	●	●	●	●	●	●	○	◐
.3:1	92	◐	●	●	◐	1	●	●	●	●	●	●	●	●	●	◐
.5:1	96	●	◐	●	●	1	●	●	○	●	●	●	●	●	○	○
.6:1	95	●	●	●	●	2	●	●	●	●	●	●	●	●	○	◐
.7:1	96	●	●	●	●	2	●	●	●	●	●	●	●	●	●	◐
.8:1	NA	●	●	●	●	2	●	●	●	●	●	●	●	●	●	◐
.3:1	NA	○	◐	◐	●		○	○	○	○	○	○	○	◐	○	○
.1:1	93	◐	●	○	●	1	○	○	●	●	●	○	●	●	●	◐
.6:1	98	●	●	●	●	2	●	●	●	●	●	●	●	●	●	●

Ship	Cruise Line	Cruising Regions	Size (in tons)	Type of Ship	Cruise Experience	Average Per Diem	Length of Cruise	Number of Passengers
Ecstasy	Carnival	Bahamas/ Mexico	70,367	Megaship	Casual	$180	3-, 4-day	2040
Enchanted Isle	Commodore	Caribbean	23,395	Classic	Casual	$140–$155	7-day	731
Enchanted Seas	Commodore	Caribbean	23,500	Classic	Casual	$140–$155	7-day	726
Explorer	Abercrombie & Kent	South America/ Antarctica	2,398	Expedition	Casual	$460	14-19-day	96
Fantasy	Carnival	Bahamas	70,367	Megaship	Casual	$180	3-, 4-day	2044
Fascination	Carnival	Caribbean	70,367	Megaship	Casual	$208	7-day	2040
Festivale	Carnival	Caribbean	38,175	Classic	Casual	$208	7-day	1146
Golden Princess	Princess	Alaska	28,000	Cruise liner	Semiformal	$350	7-day	830
Hanseatic	Radisson Seven Seas	Antarctica/South America/ North America	9,000	Expedition	Casual	$750	8–15-day	188
Holiday	Carnival	Mexican Riviera	46,052	Cruise liner	Casual	$180–$197	3-, 4-day	1452
Horizon	Celebrity	Caribbean/Alaska	46,811	Cruise liner	Semiformal	$285–$349	7–day	1354
Imagination	Carnival	NA	70,367	Megaship	Casual	NA	NA	2040
Independence	American Hawaii	Hawaii	30,090	Classic	Casual	$256	7-day	828
Inspiration	Carnival	NA	70,367	Megaship	Casual	NA	NA	2040
Island Princess	Princess	Outside Western Hemisphere	20,000	Cruise liner	Semiformal	$350		640
Jubilee	Carnival	Mexico	47,262	Cruise liner	Casual	$208	7-day	1486
Leeward	Norwegian	Bahamas/Mexico	25,000	Cruise liner	Casual	$255–$277	3-, 4-day	950
Legend of the Seas	Royal Caribbean	Alaska/Hawaii/ Panama Canal	70,000	Megaship	Casual	$321	7–11-day	1804
Maasdam	Holland America	Caribbean/ Panama Canal	55,451	Cruise liner	Semiformal	$320	7-, 10-, 14-day	1266
Majesty of the Seas	Royal Caribbean	Caribbean	73,941	Megaship	Casual	$299–$314	7-day	2354

Passenger/Crew Ratio	Sanitation Rating*	Accessibility	Special Dietary Options	Gymnasium	Walking/Jogging Circuit	Swimming Pool	Whirlpool	Sauna/Massage	Deck Sports	Casino	Disco	Cinema/Theater	Library	Boutiques/Gift Shops	Video Arcade	Child Care
2.2:1	91	●	◐	●	●	2	●	●	●	●	●	○	●	●	●	●
2.2:1	87	◐	●	◐	○	1	○	◐	●	●	●	●	●	●	●	◐
2.1:1	91	◐	●	◐	○	1	○	◐	●	●	●	●	●	●	●	◐
1.4:1	NA	○	○	●	○	1	○	◐	○	○	○	○	○	○	○	○
2.2:1	94	●	◐	●	●	2	●	●	●	●	●	○	●	●	●	●
2.2:1	90	●	◐	●	●	2	●	●	●	●	●	○	●	●	●	●
2:1	96	○	◐	●	●	2	○	●	●	●	●	●	●	●	●	●
2:1	93	◐	●	●	●	2	●	●	●	●	●	○	●	●	○	●
1.5:1	NA	◐	●	●	○	1	●	●	○	○	◐	●	◐	●	○	○
2.2:1	90	●	◐	●	●	2	●	●	●	●	●	○	●	●	●	●
2.1:1	87	●	●	●	●	2	●	●	●	●	●	○	●	●	●	●
2.2:1	NA	●	◐	●	●	2	●	●	●	●	●	○	●	●	●	●
2.5:1	NA	○	◐	●	◐	2	○	●	●	○	●	○	●	●	●	◐
2.2:1	NA	●	◐	●	●	2	●	●	●	●	●		●	●	●	●
1.8:1	94	◐	●	●	●	2	○	●	●	●	●	●	●	●	●	◐
2.2:1	92	●	◐	●	●	2	●	●	●	●	●	○	●	●	●	●
2.4:1	NA	●	●	●	●	1	●	●	●	●	●	○	●	●	○	●
2.4:1	NA	●	◐	●	●	2	●	●	●	●	●	●	●	●	●	●
2.2:1	97	●	●	●	●	2	●	●	●	●	●	●	●	●	●	◐
2.8:1	96	●	◐	●	●	2	●	●	●	●	●	●	●	●	●	●

Ship	Cruise Line	Cruising Regions	Size (in tons)	Type of Ship	Cruise Experience	Average Per Diem	Length of Cruise	Number of Passengers
Mayan Prince	American Canadian Caribbean	Central America/ Panama Canal/ New England	92	Coastal cruiser	Casual	$182	6-,12-day	92
Meridian	Celebrity	Caribbean/Bermuda	30,440	Classic	Semiformal	$254–$331	7, 10, 11-day	1106
Mississippi Queen	Delta Queen Steamboat	Mississippi River	3,364	Riverboat	Casual	$397	3–12-day	420
Monarch of the Seas	Royal Caribbean	Caribbean	73,941	Megaship	Casual	$299–$314	7-day	2354
Nantucket/ Yorktown Clipper	Clipper	Alaska/Caribbean/ Panama Canal/N.E. U.S. & Canada	99.5	Coastal cruiser	Casual	$330	6–14-day	102/ 138
Niagara Prince	American Canadian Caribbean	Mid-America/ Caribbean	99	Coastal cruiser	Casual	$188	12-, 15-day	84
Nieuw Amsterdam	Holland America	Alaska/ Caribbean/ Panama Canal	33,930	Cruise liner	Semiformal	$285	7–22-day	1214
Noordam	Holland American	Alaska/ Caribbean/ Panama Canal	33,930	Cruise liner	Semiformal	$285	7–16-day	1214
Nordic Empress	Royal Caribbean	Bahamas	48,563	Cruise liner	Casual	$309	3,4-day	1600
Norway	Norwegian	Caribbean	76,049	Classic	Semiformal	$270	7-day	2032
OceanBreeze	Dolphin	Caribbean/ Panama Canal	21,486	Classic	Casual	$235	7-day	776
Pacific Princess	Princess	Caribbean/Amazon/ Panama Canal/ South America	20,000	Cruise liner	Semiformal	$350	11–17-day	640
Polaris	Special Expeditions	Amazon/Caribbean/ Panama Canal	2,214	Expedition	Casual	$550	8–55-day	80
Queen Odyssey	Royal	Caribbean/Amazon/ Panama Canal	10,000	Cruise yacht	Formal	$481	7–13-day	212
Queen Elizabeth 2	Cunard	N.E. U.S. & Canada/ Bermuda/Caribbean/ Transatlantic	67,139	Classic	Semiformal –formal	$437	5–95-day	1850
Radisson Diamond	Radisson Seven Seas	Caribbean/ Panama Canal	20,000	Cruise liner	Semiformal	$600	4–9-day	354
Regal Princess	Princess	Caribbean/ Alaska/Panama Canal	70,000	Megaship	Semiformal	$300	7–15-day	1590
Regent Isle	Regency	Caribbean/Alaska	25,000	Classic	Casual	$157	2–7-day	890
Regent Rainbow	Regency	Alaska/ Panama Canal	25,000	Classic	Casual	$242	7,14-day	960
Regent Sea	Regency	South America/ world cruise	22,000	Classic	Casual	$186	49–90-day	729

Passenger/Crew Ratio	Sanitation Rating*	Accessibility	Special Dietary Options	Gymnasium	Walking/Jogging Circuit	Swimming Pool	Whirlpool	Sauna/Massage	Deck Sports	Casino	Disco	Cinema/Theater	Library	Boutiques/Gift Shops	Video Arcade	Child Care
5:1	NA	○	●	○	●		○	○	○	○	○	○	○	○	○	○
1.9:1	95	◐	●	●	●	2	●	●	●	●	●	●	●	●	●	●
2.6:1	NA	◐	◐	●	●	1	●	●	●	○	○	◐	●	●	○	○
2.8:1	96	●	◐	●	●	2	●	●	●	●	●	●	●	●	●	●
3.2:1/3.5:1	93/93	○	◐	○	●		○	○	○	○	○	◐	○	○	○	○
5:1	NA	○	●	○	●		○	○	○	○	○	○	○	○	○	○
2.2:1	93	●	●	●	●	2	●	●	●	●	●	●	●	●	●	◐
2.2:1	93	●	●	●	●	2	●	●	●	●	●	●	●	●	●	◐
2.3:1	93	●	◐	●	●	1	●	●	●	●	●	○	○	●	●	●
2.3:1	90	●	●	●	●	3	●	●	●	●	●	●	●	●	●	●
2.5:1	NA	◐	●	●	●	1	●	●	◐	●	●	●	◐	◐	●	◐
1.8:1	94	◐	●	●	●	2	○	●	●	●	●	●	●	●	●	◐
1.8:1	NA	○	○	○	○		○	◐	○	○	○	○	●	●	○	○
1.6:1	95	●	●	●	●	1	●	●	●	●	○	○	●	●	○	○
1.8:1	90	◐	●	●	●	4	●	●	●	●	●	●	●	●	●	●
1.8:1	99	●	●	●	●	1	●	●	●	●	●	○	●	●	○	○
2.2:1	94	●	●	●	●	2	●	●	●	●	●	●	●	●	○	◐
2:1	95	◐	●	●	◐	3	●	●	●	●	●	●	●	●	○	◐
2.3:1	91	●	●	◐	●	1	●	●	◐	●	●	○	●	●	○	●
2:1	89	●	●	●	●	1	●	●	●	●	●	●	●	●	○	◐

Ship	Cruise Line	Cruising Regions	Size (in tons)	Type of Ship	Cruise Experience	Average Per Diem	Length of Cruise	Number of Passengers
Regent Spirit	Regency	Central America	12,500	Classic	Casual	$199	7-day	400
Regent Star	Regency	Panama Canal/Alaska	24,500	Classic	Casual	$295	7-day	950
Regent Sun	Regency	Caribbean/N.E. U.S. & Canada	25,500	Classic	Casual	$253	7-day	836
Renaissance IV	Renaissance	Caribbean	4,500	Cruise yacht	Semiformal	$225	7-day	104
Rotterdam	Holland America	Hawaii/Panama Canal/Alaska/world cruise	38,000	Classic	Semiformal	$353	7–99-day	1114
Royal Majesty	Majesty	Bahamas/Mexico/Bermuda	32,400	Cruise liner	Semiformal	$239	3-, 4-, 7-day	1056
Royal Odyssey	Royal	Alaska/ N.E. U.S. & Canada/Panama Canal/world cruise	28,000	Cruise liner	Semiformal	$300	7-102-day	749
Royal Princess	Princess	N.E. U.S. & Canada	45,000	Cruise liner	Semiformal	$350	10-, 11-day	1200
Ryndam	Holland America	Alaska/Caribbean/Panama Canal	55,451	Cruise liner	Semiformal	$320	7–18-day	1266
Sagafjord	Cunard	Caribbean/N.E. U.S. & Canada/Panama Canal/Alaska	24,474	Cruise liner	Formal	$545	10–20-day	589
Sea Bird	Special Expeditions	Alaska/Baja CA/Pacific N.W.	99.7	Coastal cruiser	Casual	$400	5–10-day	70
Sea Cloud	Special Expeditions	Caribbean	2,323	Motor-sail	Casual	$700	9-day	60
Sea Goddess I	Cunard	Caribbean/Amazon	4,250	Cruise yacht	Formal	$642	7-,10-, 11-day	116
Sea Lion	Special Expeditions	Alaska/Baja CA/Pacific N.W.	99.7	Coastal cruiser	Casual	$400	5–10-day	70
Seabourn Pride/Seabourn Spirit	Seabourn	Alaska/Mexico or N.E. U.S. & Canada Caribbean/Amazon	10,000	Cruise yacht	Formal	$875–$995	5–16-day	204
SeaBreeze	Dolphin	Caribbean	21,000	Classic	Casual	$192	7-day	840
Seaward	Norwegian	Caribbean	42,000	Cruise liner	Casual	$255	7-day	1504
Seawind Crown	Seawind	Caribbean	24,000	Classic	Semiformal	$275	7-day	624
Sensation	Carnival	Caribbean	70,367	Megaship	Casual	$208	7-day	2040
Silver Cloud/Silver Wind	Silversea	Caribbean N.E. U.S. & Canada/South America	16,500	Cruise yacht	Formal	$640	7–14-day	296

225

Passenger/Crew Ratio	Sanitation Rating*	Accessibility	Special Dietary Options	Gymnasium	Walking/Jogging Circuit	Swimming Pool	Whirlpool	Sauna/Massage	Deck Sports	Casino	Disco	Cinema/Theater	Library	Boutiques/Gift Shops	Video Arcade	Child Care
2:1	NA	●	●	●	●	1	○	●	●	●	●	●	●	●	○	●
2:1	93	◑	●	●	◑	1	●	●	●	●	●	●	●	●	○	◑
2:1	90	◑	●	●	○	2	○	●	●	●	●	●	●	●	●	◑
1.6:1	NA	○	●	○	●	1	●	●	◑	◑	○	○	●	●	○	○
1.9:1	78	●	●	●	●	2	○	◑	●	●	●	●	●	●	●	◑
2.1:1	95	●	●	●	●	1	●	○	○	●	●	○	●	●	○	◑
1.8:1	95	◑	●	●	●	1	●	●	●	●	●	●	●	●	○	○
2.4:1	96	●	●	●	●	3	●	●	●	●	●	●	●	●	●	◑
2.2:1	91	●	●	●	●	2	●	●	●	●	●	●	●	●	●	◑
1.7:1	88	●	●	●	●	2	●	●	●	●	●	●	●	●	○	◑
3.3:1	95	○	○	○	○		○	○	○	○	○	◑	○	◑	○	○
.92:1	97	○	○	○	●		○	○	○	○	○	○	●	○	○	○
1.3:1	96	○	●	●	●	1	○	●	●	●	○	○	●	●	○	◑
3.3:1	94	○	○	○	○		○	○	○	○	○	◑	○	◑	○	○
1.5:1	94/92	●	●	●	●	1	●	●	●	●	○	○	●	●	○	◑
2.1:1	92	◑	●	●	●	1	●	◑	●	●	●	●	○	●	●	◑
2.4:1	88	●	●	●	●	2	●	●	●	●	●	○	○	●	○	●
2.1:1	NA	●	●	●	●	2	○	●	●	●	●	●	●	●	○	●
2.2:1	94	●	◑	●	●	2	●	●	●	●	●	○	●	●	●	●
1.6:1	97/NA	●	◑	●	●	1	●	●	●	●	●	○	●	●	○	○

Ship	Cruise Line	Cruising Regions	Size (in tons)	Type of Ship	Cruise Experience	Average Per Diem	Length of Cruise	Number of Passengers
Sky Princess	Princess	Panama Canal/ Alaska	46,000	Cruise liner	Semiformal	$300	7-15-day	1200
Song of America	Royal Caribbean	Caribbean/ Bermuda	37,584	Cruise liner	Casual	$292	7-day	1402
Song of Norway	Royal Caribbean	Panama Canal	23,000	Cruise liner	Casual	$308	10,11-day	1004
Sovereign of the Seas	Royal Caribbean	Caribbean	73,192	Megaship	Casual	$299–$314	7-day	2278
Spirit of Alaska	Alaska Sightseeing	Alaska/San Francisco Bay	97	Coastal cruiser	Casual	$406	7-10-day	82
Spirit of Columbia	Alaska Sightseeing	Columbia and Snake rivers	98	Coastal cruiser	Casual	$351	7-day	70
Spirit of Discovery	Alaska Sightseeing	Alaska/ Pacific N.W.	94	Coastal cruiser	Casual	$412	7-day	84
Spirit of '98	Alaska Sightseeing	Alaska/Columbia and Snake rivers	96	Coastal cruiser	Casual	$420	7-10-day	101
Splendour of the Seas	Royal Caribbean	Caribbean	70,000	Megaship	Casual	$321	7-day	1804
Star Clipper	Star Clippers	Caribbean	3,025	Motor-sail	Casual	$185	7-day	180
Star Flyer	Star Clippers	Caribbean	3,025	Motor-sail	Casual	$185	7-day	180
Star Odyssey	Royal	Outside Western Hemisphere	28,000	Cruise liner	Semiformal	$300		750
Star Princess	Princess	Alaska/ Caribbean/ Panama Canal	63,500	Megaship	Semiformal	$300	7-15-day	1494
Star/Ship Atlantic	Premier	Bahamas	36,500	Cruise liner	Casual	$259	3,4-day	1550
Star/Ship Oceanic	Premier	Bahamas	40,000	Classic	Casual	$259	3,4-day	1609
Statendam	Holland America	Caribbean/ Panama Canal/ Alaska	55,451	Cruise liner	Semiformal	$320	7-19-day	1266
Stella Solaris	Sun Line	Caribbean/ Panama Canal/ Amazon	18,000	Cruise liner	Semiformal	$300	7-16-day	620
Sun Viking	Royal Caribbean	Caribbean	18,556	Cruise liner	Casual	$277	7,10, 11-day	714
Tropicale	Carnival	Caribbean/ Alaska	36,674	Cruise liner	Casual	$208	7-day	1022
Universe	World Explorer	Alaska	18,100	Cruise liner	Casual	$200	14-day	532

Passenger/Crew Ratio	Sanitation Rating*	Accessibility	Special Dietary Options	Gymnasium	Walking/Jogging Circuit	Swimming Pool	Whirlpool	Sauna/Massage	Deck Sports	Casino	Disco	Cinema/Theater	Library	Boutiques/Gift Shops	Video Arcade	Child Care
2.2:1	94	●	●	●	●	3	●	●	●	●	●	●	●	●	●	●
2.6:1	88	◐	◐	●	●	2	○	●	●	●	●	●	○	●	○	◐
2.4:1	90	◐	◐	●	●	1	○	●	●	●	●	○	○	●	○	◐
2.8:1	98	◐	◐	●	●	2	●	●	●	●	●	●	●	●	●	●
4:1	95	◐	●	◐	●		○	○	○	○	○	○	○	○	○	○
3.9:1	NA	◐	●	◐	●	1	○	○	○	○	○	○	○	○	○	○
4:1	96	○	●	◐	○		○	○	○	○	○	○	○	○	○	○
4.4:1	91	●	●	◐	●		○	○	○	○	○	○	○	○	○	○
2.4:1	NA	●	◐	●	●	2	●	●	●	●	●	●	●	●	●	●
2.6:1	80	○	○	○	○	2	○	○	○	○	○	○	●	●	○	○
2.6:1	88	○	○	○	○	2	○	○	○	○	○	○	●	●	○	○
1.8:1	91	◐	●	●	●	1	●	●	●	●	●	●	●	●	○	○
2.5:1	91	●	●	●	●	3	●	●	●	●	●	●	●	●	●	●
3.1:1	90	◐	●	●	●	3	●	◐	●	●	●	●	○	●	●	●
3:1	96	◐	●	●	●	2	●	◐	●	●	●	●	○	●	●	●
2.2:1	93	●	●	●	●	2	●	●	●	●	●	●	●	●	●	◐
2:1	92	◐	●	●	●	1	○	●	●	◐	●	●	●	●	○	◐
2:1	94	◐	◐	●	●	1	○	◐	●	◐	●	○	○	●	○	◐
1.9:1	88	●	◐	●	●	2	○	●	●	●	●	○	●	●	●	●
2.3:1	90	◐	◐	●	●		○	◐	●	○	○	●	●	●	○	◐

Ship	Cruise Line	Cruising Regions	Size (in tons)	Type of Ship	Cruise Experience	Average Per Diem	Length of Cruise	Number of Passengers
Viking Serenade	Royal Caribbean	West Coast U.S.	40,132	Cruise liner	Casual	$296	3,4-day	1512
Vistafjord	Cunard	Caribbean/ Panama Canal	24,492	Cruise liner	Formal	$442	14-, 15-day	736
Veendam	Holland America	Caribbean	55,451	Cruise liner	Semiformal	$320	7-day	1266
Westerdam	Holland America	N.E. U.S. & Canada/ Caribbean/ Alaska	53,872	Cruise liner	Semiformal	$285	7–10-day	1494
Wind Spirit/ Wind Star	Windstar	Caribbean	5,350	Motor-sail	Casual	$456	7-day	148
Windward	Norwegian	Caribbean/ Alaska	41,000	Cruise liner	Casual	$270–$320	7-day	1246
World Discoverer	Clipper	Alaska/South America/S. Pacific Antarctica	3,153	Expedition	Casual	$475	9–19-day	138
Zenith	Celebrity	Caribbean/ Bermuda	47,811	Cruise liner	Semiformal	$285–$349	7-day	1374

Passenger/Crew Ratio	Sanitation Rating*	Accessibility	Special Dietary Options	Gymnasium	Walking/Jogging Circuit	Swimming Pool	Whirlpool	Sauna/Massage	Deck Sports	Casino	Disco	Cinema/Theater	Library	Boutiques/Gift Shops	Video Arcade	Child Care
2.4:1	88	●	◐	●	●	1	●	●	●	●	●	○	●	●	●	●
1.9:1	87	●	●	●	●	2	●	●	●	●	○	●	●	●	○	◐
2.2:1	NA	●	●	●	●	2	●	●	●	●	●	●	●	●	●	○
2.4:1	95	●	●	●	●	2	●	●	●	●	●	●	●	●	●	◐
1.6:1	94/NA	○	●	●	●	1	○	●	●	◐	●	○	●	●	○	○
2.6:1	97	●	●	●	●	2	●	●	●	●	●	●	●	●	●	●
1.8:1	88	○	◐	◐	○	1	○	◐	●	○	○	●	●	●	○	○
2.1:1	91	●	●	●	●	2	●	●	●	●	●	○	●	●	●	●

*Sanitation ratings are provided by the Vessel Sanitation Program, Center for Environmental Health and Injury Control. Ships are rated on water, food preparation and holding, potential contamination of food, and general cleanliness, storage, and repair. A score of 86 or higher indicates an acceptable level of sanitation. According to the center, "a low score does not necessarily imply an imminent outbreak of gastrointestinal disease." Chart ratings come from the center's April 21, 1995, report. Not all ships are covered.

2 Ports of Call

Going Ashore

Traveling by cruise ship presents an opportunity to visit many different places in a short time. The flip side is that your stay will be limited in each port of call. For that reason, cruise lines invented shore excursions, which maximize passengers' time by organizing their touring for them. There are a number of advantages to shore excursions: In some destinations, transportation may be unreliable, and a ship-packaged tour is the best way to see distant sights. Also, you don't have to worry about being stranded or missing the ship. The disadvantage is that you will pay more for the convenience of having the ship do the legwork for you. Of course, you can always book a tour independently, hire a taxi, or use foot power to explore on your own.

Disembarking

When your ship arrives in a port, it either ties up alongside a dock or anchors out in a harbor. If the ship is docked, passengers just walk down the gangway to go ashore. Docking makes it easy to go back and forth between the shore and the ship.

Tendering If your ship anchors in the harbor, however, you will have to take a small boat—called a launch or tender—to get ashore. Tendering is a nuisance. When your ship first arrives in port, everyone wants to go ashore. Often, in order to avoid a stampede at the tenders, you must gather in a public room, get a boarding pass, and wait until your number is called. This continues until everybody has disembarked. Even then, it may take 15–20 minutes to get ashore if your ship is anchored far offshore. Because tenders can be difficult to board, passengers with mobility problems may not be able to visit certain ports. The larger the ship, the more likely it is to use tenders. It is usually possible to learn before booking a cruise whether the ship will dock or anchor at its ports of call. (For more information about where and whether ships dock, tender, or both, *see* Coming Ashore for each port, *below*.)

Before anyone is allowed to walk down the gangway or board a tender, the ship must first be cleared for landing. Immigration and customs officials board the vessel to examine passports and sort through red tape. It may be more than an hour before you're actually allowed ashore. You will be issued a boarding pass, which you must have with you to get back on board.

Port Stays

Most vessels spend the morning and afternoon in port. In ports that have a vibrant nightlife, like San Juan or Nassau, many ships stay until midnight or overnight. In Bermuda, vessels stay in port for one–five days, acting more as floating hotels than ships. In Hawaii, too, ships may overnight in Maui or at ports on the Big Island. Estimated times of arrival and departure in each port are provided in the cruise lines' brochures.

Currency Passengers can change money at the ship's purser's office or ashore, but don't exchange large amounts of dollars. At most cruise destinations, the dollar is welcome, and it can be difficult to change local money back into dollars. At the most, change a few dollars for public transportation, telephones, and museum passes.

Shore With the exception of a handful of cruise lines that include shore ex-
Excursions cursions in their basic ticket price, almost all ships sell these tours at extra cost. Shore excursions usually follow well-established formulas, although the quality of the tours varies enormously. Information about the shore excursions offered by a ship is sent to

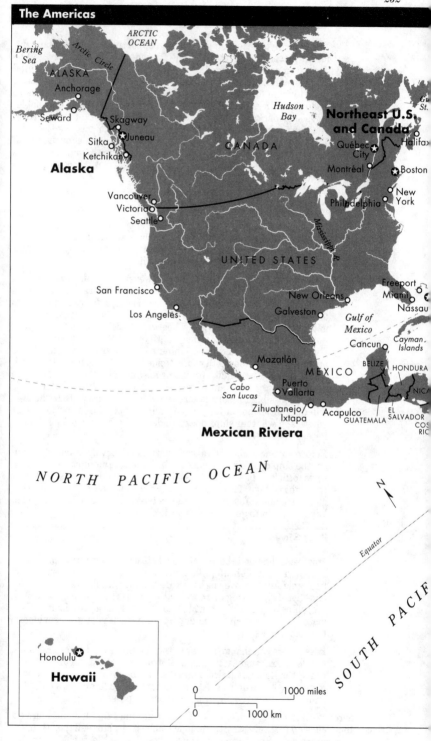

The Americas

ARCTIC OCEAN

Bering Sea

Arctic Circle

ALASKA
Anchorage

Seward

Skagway

Sitka

Juneau

Ketchikan

Alaska

Vancouver
Victoria
Seattle

San Francisco

Los Angeles

CANADA

Hudson Bay

Northeast U.S. and Canada

Québec City

Montréal

Halifax

Boston

New York

Philadelphia

UNITED STATES

Mississippi R.

New Orleans

Galveston

Gulf of Mexico

Cancun

Freeport

Miami

Nassau

Cayman Islands

Mazatlán

MEXICO

BELIZE

HONDURA

Cabo San Lucas

Puerto Vallarta

Zihuatanejo/ Ixtapa

Acapulco

GUATEMALA

EL SALVADOR

NICA

COS RIC

Mexican Riviera

NORTH PACIFIC OCEAN

N

Equator

SOUTH PACIF

Honolulu

Hawaii

0 — 1000 miles

0 — 1000 km

of
awrence

Tropic of Cancer

NORTH ATLANTIC OCEAN

Bermuda
o Hamilton

Bahamas

Virgin
Islands
Lesser
Antilles
Puerto
Rico

**FRENCH
GUIANA**

Devil's Island

Caribbean
Netherlands
Antilles
Aruba
Jamaica
Cartagena o
*Caribbean
Sea*
RAGUA
PANAMA
**Panama
Canal**
TA

Caracas
VENEZUELA

Cayenne

*Mouths of
the Amazon*

South America

Fortaleza

SURINAME

GUYANA

COLOMBIA

Manaus o

ECUADOR

PERU

BOLIVIA

B R A Z I L

Salvador o

Rio de
Janeiro

PARAGUAY

URUGUAY
Montevideo

Buenos
Aires
ARGENTINA

IC
OCEAN

Tropic of Capricorn

CHILE

Tierra del
Fuego

Cape Horn

**To
Antarctica**

passengers before the cruise. Often there is a shore excursion lecture given early in the sailing, when the cruise or shore-excursion director describes the tours and answers passengers' questions. With the exception of a few lines that require certain excursions to be reserved in advance in order to make the appropriate arrangements, most excursions can only be booked aboard ship. (For recommendations on which tours are good choices, *see* Shore Excursions for each port, *below.*)

If a shore excursion offered by the ship is fully booked, you might be able to purchase the same tour from a local vendor—and often at a better price. Tourist information offices, usually located on or near the pier (*see* Coming Ashore for each destination, *below*) can tell you about local attractions and all the tours, including some not offered by the ships. Free maps are often available. In some ports, you will find local walking-tour guides for hire.

Bus Tours The most common shore excursion is an **island or city tour**—usually the best, fastest, and most economical way to see the sights. A good bus tour gives a sampling of the most noteworthy historical and cultural attractions, as well as some of the local color. Passengers spend plenty of time in the bus, with a few stops for brief tours, photo opportunities, souvenir shopping, and sometimes lunch. Everything is strictly scheduled, with a limited amount of time spent at any one sight.

As a rule, few bus tours of the Mexican Riviera can be recommended. In the Caribbean, however, we do recommend a few bus tours for their scenic beauty or historical interest. The tour from Martinique's Fort-de-France to St. Pierre is a fascinating, though lengthy, trip to a part of the island that would otherwise be hard to reach, unless you rented a car and braved the local roads yourself.

If you're feeling adventurous, renting a car with a few friends will almost always save you money, and you can spend as long as you'd like wherever you'd like. However, this is a risky undertaking: If you get lost or for any other reason are late returning to the ship, you'll have to find a way to reach the next port on your own. Renting a car is best in ports where your ship overnights.

Boat Tours The typical **harbor boat tour** sails past small islands and waterfront sights where large cruise ships can't go; it may be combined with a bus tour or a stopover for lunch at a resort hotel. These tours usually don't provide music or entertainment. In some regions, especially Alaska, the boat tour brings passengers closer to nature, watching for whales, glaciers, or eagles. A variation of the harbor boat tour is a circumnavigation of the island or a cruise to a nearby island.

In stark contrast to sedate harbor tours are **party boats** or **booze cruises.** Party boats are noisy, boisterous, and fun. Most boats have an open bar or a free rum punch, and a local mariachi band or rock group. Depending on the boat, which can range from a barge to a trimaran, it may even have a dance floor. Many booze cruises combine a beach party with the boat excursion. A **sunset sail** on a catamaran or trimaran can be a romantic, relaxing excursion. However, don't confuse a sunset sail with a sunset booze cruise; they are entirely different.

Glass-bottom boats are small vessels with a panel of glass set into the bottom, through which passengers sitting on benches view the underwater life. Although the tours are worthwhile for those who do not snorkel or dive, the sea life seen from such boats is often sparse and colorless. Nighttime tours are usually better, because the underwater lights attract fish from the reef.

A more exciting option is a **submarine tour.** (The submarine does not usually dive deep, and a surface boat accompanies it at all times.) Large windows give an excellent view of coral and marine life. The pilot points out unusual fish; display charts help with identification. Some submarine tours have scuba divers outside feeding and frolicking with the fish.

Aerial Tours Helicopter or small-plane tours tend to be short and expensive, but the view they provide is spectacular. This is especially true in Alaska, where the aircraft flies over, or even lands on, glaciers. Before booking a helicopter ride, find out if the helicopter holds three or four passengers. In a four-passenger aircraft, one person has to sit in the middle seat and won't be able to see properly out the windows.

Beach Parties Beach parties come in two varieties. In the first, all the ship's passengers are brought to an isolated island or private beach much like a **port call.** Passengers pass the day with limbo contests, volleyball, swimming, and snorkeling. Although the barbecue and the games are free, passengers usually must pay for soft drinks and alcoholic beverages, as well as for rental of snorkels and other water-sports equipment.

The second kind of beach party is sold as a **paid excursion.** Before signing up for an extra-charge beach outing, make sure you know exactly what you're getting for your money. For instance, are lunch and drinks included? Are there changing rooms, lockers, and toilets? Are beach towels, chaises, and umbrellas provided, and is the use of sports equipment included in the price?

Nightclub Tours A variation on the daytime bus tours, with a drink or two and sometimes dinner thrown in, nightclub tours are offered in ports where ships stay late or overnight. Although some nightclub tours are quite good (San Juan's is notable), more often than not the entertainment is amateurish.

Participant Sports You can arrange to participate in a variety of sporting activities during your stopover. If the ship doesn't offer an excursion, the shore-excursion director can usually make arrangements. Time limits obviously put some restrictions on what sports passengers can pursue.

One of the best ways to experience Alaska is hiking through the wilderness or canoeing in the many bays and waterways. White-water rafting is available at some ports, and charter-boat fishing is offered everywhere.

In Mexico, the Caribbean, Bermuda, and the Bahamas, the emphasis is on water sports. Some beach excursions include waterskiing, windsurfing, parasailing, and snorkeling. These activities can also usually be found on any beach that borders a large resort hotel.

Almost every tropical port has several scuba-diving operators offering instruction and dives over coral reefs or wrecks. Though charter fishing boats can easily be hired, take the excursions offered by your ship, if possible, since Mexican and Caribbean charters can rarely be relied upon to get passengers back to the ship before it sails.

Golf and tennis are the most popular land sports in tropical regions. If the ship does not offer an excursion, the shore-excursion director may, for a fee, arrange guest passes at private golf and tennis clubs, including some very exclusive ones. It may also be possible for the pro at your home club to arrange a guest pass. Golf equipment can usually be rented, although many passengers bring their own clubs aboard. Some lines, especially NCL, Premier, Royal Caribbean, and Seabourn, have specific cruises that focus on tennis and/or golf, including onboard instruction, "19th-hole" parties, and celebrity pros. Ask a travel agent or the cruise lines about the dates for these sports-theme cruises.

Shopping Shopping is now a legendary sport among cruise passengers attracted by the heady perfume of duty-free merchandise. In reality, many of the typical consumer items, including electronics, jewelry, and liquor, carry price tags equivalent to those found at home. Add to this the hassle of hauling these goods around with you, and you may find that it is not worth the effort. Some bargains can be found, however. If you know what you want to buy, check its price at home first. Also consider the cost of any tax you may have to pay upon clearing customs. (*See* Arriving and Departing *in* Cruise Primer.)

In South America, Mexico, and certain areas of the Caribbean, shoppers are expected to haggle. The price first asked by most salespeople is about 50% more than what they'll accept.

Before arrival at a port, cruise directors give a shopping talk. Although passengers can learn a great deal about the merchandise offered in a port, they should be wary of endorsements for particular stores. Cruise directors often receive commissions from these stores to promote their wares.

Returning to the Ship

Cruise lines are strict about sailing times, which are posted at the gangway and elsewhere as well as announced in the daily schedule of activities. Be certain to be back on board at least a half hour before the announced sailing time or you may be stranded. If you are on a shore excursion that was sold by the cruise line, however, the captain will wait for your group before casting off. If the ship must leave without you, the cruise company will fly you, at its expense, to the next port. That is one reason many passengers prefer ship-packaged tours.

If you are not on one of the ship's tours and the ship does sail without you, immediately contact the cruise line's port representative, whose name and phone number are often listed on the daily schedule of activities. You may be able to hitch a ride on a pilot boat, though that is unlikely. Passengers who miss the boat must pay their own way to the next port of call.

Alaska

"Cruise everywhere else in the world before visiting Alaska," experienced passengers often advise, "because once you've seen Alaska, everything else pales by comparison."

Detached from the contiguous United States, Alaska has Canada and Russia as its nearest neighbors, and some localities are closer to Japan than to Juneau, the state capital. But more than scale and geography set Alaska apart from the rest of North America: Alaska is youth, energy, space, and wilderness. The sense of excitement and adventure is palpable from the moment you step ashore in a misty port, where dramatic mountains tower over narrow streets and humanity is dwarfed by the power of nature.

Just 13 miles from downtown Juneau, you can come face to face with a calving glacier. Outside Ketchikan, wander in hushed awe through a haunting totem-pole park, where sea breezes blow through a grove of Tlingit-carved poles and ancient spruce trees. Gliding through Glacier Bay National Park, watch from the ship rails as huge slabs of ice break away from a glacier, sounding like gunshots, and tumble into the bay, creating waves that rock the vessel. Harbor seals and their pups ride the ice floes like stowaways on a raft while passengers cool their cocktails with slivers of glacial ice created millions of years ago.

Alaskans are proud of their heritage and offer visitors ample opportunity to see and learn about totem poles, traditional dances, and artists' colonies. In the Southeastern Panhandle, where Tlingit Indians are the predominant Native American community, bookstores offer a great selection of literature on the land's native and Russian heritage.

About a dozen cruise lines deploy ships in Alaska. Sailings come chiefly in two varieties: round-trip southeastern sailings and one-way cruises that also visit the south-central part of the state. The first, weeklong loops from Vancouver, are cruise-only and sail entirely within the Inside Passage—the protected waterway between Vancouver and Skagway that winds through thousands of big and small islands. Three- or four-day segments are one-way and allow the option of exploring farther inland. The second, one-way, seven-day cruises to or from Vancouver, add the Gulf of Alaska to the Inside Passage, visiting the communities and glaciers of Prince William Sound. With an optional land tour, passengers can explore farther north and still spend a full week at sea. A few lines schedule longer one-way or round-trip sailings from Vancouver or San Francisco. (For detailed itineraries, *see* Chapter 3.)

When to Go The Alaska cruise season runs from spring through fall, but midsummer is the most popular time to sail. Cruise lines schedule first sailings in mid-May and final sailings in late September. May and June are the driest cruise months. At least two cruise lines price sailings by five "seasons," with spring and fall departures the least expensive and midsummer sailings the most costly. Virtually every line offers "early booking discounts" to passengers for deposits in advance. Some lines promote early-season cruises with special shoreside events and shopping discounts tied to a celebration known as "Mayfest." Holland America and Royal Cruise Line schedule theme cruises throughout the season. Topics include photography, country music, and nature and the environment.

Shore Excursions Shore excursions in Alaska give cruise passengers a chance to get closer to the state's natural beauty. For this reason, active or adventure-oriented tours are usually the best choices.

Aerial Tours Anyone unwilling to hike or boat in the backcountry should take at least one helicopter or small-plane tour to see the state in its full glo-

Alaskan Cruising Region

ALASKA RANGE

Mt. McKinley

ALASKA RR

Fairbanks

Porcupine R.

A L A S K A

Mt. Hayes

ALASKA RANGE

Yukon R.

Klondike R.

KENAI MTS

Anchorage

Whittier

GLENN HWY.

Dawson

Kenai Peninsula

Seward

Valdez

YUKON TERRITORY

Kodiak Island

College Fjord

Prince William Sound

Mt. St. Elias

Icy Bay

ALASKA HWY.

Whitehorse

Gulf of Alaska

Carcross

Haines

Skagway

Glacier Bay National Park and Preserve

Juneau

Sitka

Baranof Island

Inside Passage

Petersburg

Wrangell

BRITISH COLUMBIA

Revillagigedo Island

Ketchikan

Prince Rupert

Queen Charlotte Islands

Peace R.

P A C I F I C   O C E A N

N

Prince George

Fraser R.

Kamloops

Vancouver Island

Vancouver

Victoria

Seattle

Tacoma

Columbia R.

WASHINGTON

0   250 miles
0   375 km

KEY

Ports of Call

Rail Lines

ry. The aircraft fly over glaciers and waterways; the best helicopter tours actually land on a glacier and let passengers out for a walk.

Fishing The prospect of bringing a trophy king salmon or a rainbow trout to net is the reason many people choose an Alaskan cruise. Every ship offers optional fishing excursions on charter boats.

Hiking Trekking through woods and mountains and along the beaches is southeastern Alaska's unofficial pastime. Some trails are abandoned mining roads; others are natural routes or game trails that meander over ridges, through forests, and alongside streams and glaciers. Many ships offer hiking excursions, but every port is within easy access of at least some hiking. Trails go through real wilderness, so check with local park rangers or tourist offices for current conditions, and leave your intended itinerary with someone on the ship. Look under the hiking section for each port to find trails and paths convenient to cruise passengers.

Salmon Bake Alaska is famous for outdoor salmon barbecues, called salmon bakes. Fresh fish is grilled on an open fire and served with plenty of fixings. Quality varies, so ask locals for advice on which bake to attend. Juneau's Gold Creek salmon bake is a good choice.

Whale-Watching Whales are plentiful in these waters, and several small-boat excursions offer excellent opportunities to see them up close. The captains of these craft keep in contact and let one another know when a whale pod is near.

Shopping Alaskan Native American handicrafts range from Tlingit totem poles—a few inches high to several feet tall—to Athabascan beaded slippers. Tlingit, Inuit, and Aleut wall masks, dance rattles, baskets, and beaded items in traditional designs can be found at gift shops up and down the coast. To ensure authenticity, buy items tagged with the state-approved AUTHENTIC NATIVE HANDCRAFT FROM ALASKA "Silverhand" label. Or buy at Saxman Village outside Ketchikan or similar Native American–run shops. Better prices are found the farther you go to the north and away from the coast.

Salmon—smoked, canned, or fresh—is another popular item. Most towns have a local company that packs and ships local seafood.

Dining Not surprisingly, seafood dominates most menus. In summer, king salmon, halibut, king crab, cod, and prawns are usually fresh. Restaurants are uniformly informal; clean jeans and windbreakers are the norm.

Category	Cost*
$$$	over $40
$$	$20–$40
$	under $20

per person for a three-course meal, excluding drinks, service, and sales tax

Anchorage

A local newspaper columnist once dubbed Anchorage "a city too obviously on the make to ever be accepted in polite society." And for all its cosmopolitan trappings, this city of 225,000 does maintain something of an opportunistic, pioneer spirit. Its inhabitants, whose average age is just 28, hustle for their living in the banking, transportation, and communications fields.

Superficially, Anchorage looks like any other western American city, but sled-dog races are as popular here as surfing is in California, and moose occasionally roam along city bike trails. This is basically a modern, relatively unattractive city, but the Chugach Mountains form a striking backdrop, and spectacular Alaskan wilderness is found just outside the back door.

Anchorage took shape with the construction of the federally built Alaska Railroad (completed in 1923), and traces of the city's railroad heritage remain. With the tracks laid, the town's pioneer forefathers actively sought expansion by hook and—not infrequently—by crook. City fathers, many of whom are still alive, delight in telling how they tricked a visiting U.S. congressman into dedicating the site for a federal hospital that had not yet been approved.

Boom and bust periods followed major events: an influx of military bases during World War II; a massive buildup of Arctic missile-warning stations during the Cold War; and most recently, the discovery of oil at Prudhoe Bay and the construction of the trans-Alaska pipeline.

Anchorage today is the only true metropolis among Alaskan port cities. There's a performing-arts center, a diversity of museums, and a variety of ethnic eateries for cruise passengers to sample.

Shore Excursions Other than a typical city bus tour, few shore excursions are scheduled in Anchorage. Most cruise passengers are only passing through the city as they transfer between the airport and the ship or a land tour and their cruise. For passengers who arrive early or stay later, independently or on a pre- or post-cruise package, there is much to see and do (*see* Exploring Anchorage, *below*).

Coming Ashore Cruise ships visiting Anchorage most often dock at the port city of Seward, 125 miles away on the east coast of the Kenai Peninsula; from here passengers must travel by bus or train to Anchorage. Ships that do sail directly to the city dock just beyond downtown. A tourist information booth is located right on the pier. The major attractions are a 15- or 20-minute walk away; turn right when you disembark and head south on Ocean Dock Road.

Getting Around *By Bus* The municipal **People Mover** (tel. 907/343–6543) bus system covers the whole Anchorage bowl. It's not convenient for short downtown trips but can be used for visits to outlying areas. The central depot is at 6th Avenue and G Street. The fare is $1, plus an additional 10¢ for transfers.

By Taxi Prices for taxis start at $2 for pickup and $1.50 for each mile. Most people in Anchorage telephone for a cab, although it is not uncommon to hail one. Contact **Alaska Cab** (tel. 907/563–5353), **Checker Cab** (tel. 907/276–1234), or **Yellow Cab** (tel. 907/272–2422).

Exploring Anchorage *Numbers in the margin correspond to points of interest on the Downtown Anchorage map.*

The downtown is easily toured on foot in less than two hours. Start ❶ at the **Log Cabin Visitor Information Center** at the corner of 4th Avenue and F Street. A marker in front shows the mileage to various world cities. Fourth Avenue sustained heavy damage in the 1964 earthquake. The businesses on this block withstood the destruction, but those a block east, where the McDonald's now stands, fell into the ground as the earth under them slid toward Ship Creek. Most of these buildings have since been rebuilt.

❷ The **Old City Hall** is to the east, beside the visitor center. It was built in 1936. The marble sculpture out front is a monument to William Seward, the secretary of state who engineered the purchase of Alaska from Russia in 1867.

To the west on 4th Avenue, between F and G streets, is the Art Deco ❸ **Fourth Avenue Theater.** This restored movie palace has been put to new use as a museum and gift shop. Historic photos and the theater's original bronze murals tell the story of Alaska's past. Note the

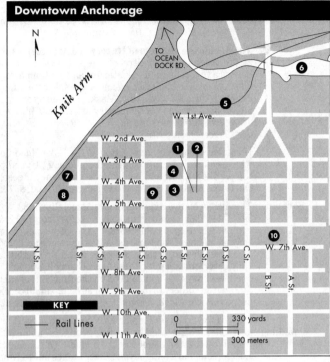

Downtown Anchorage

N

TO OCEAN DOCK RD.

Knik Arm

W. 1st Ave.

W. 2nd Ave.

W. 3rd Ave.

W. 4th Ave.

W. 5th Ave.

W. 6th Ave.

W. 7th Ave.

N St.   L St.   K St.   I St.   H St.   G St.   F St.   E St.   D St.   C St.   B St.   A St.

W. 8th Ave.

W. 9th Ave.

KEY

W. 10th Ave.

—— Rail Lines

0   330 yards

0   300 meters

W. 11th Ave.

lighted stars in the ceiling that form the big dipper against a field of blue—it's the Alaska state flag. Catercorner from the visitor center at 4th Avenue and F Street is the **Alaska Public Lands Information Center.** The center has displays about Alaska's national parks, forests, and wildlife refuges and shows films highlighting different parts of the state.

Walk north (downhill) on F Street to 2nd Avenue. The houses in this neighborhood are original 1915 town-site homes built by the Alaska Engineering Commission, which built the Alaska Railroad. A plaque by each house tells its history.

Turn east (right) on 2nd Avenue and head 1½ blocks to the stairway leading downhill to the **Alaska Railroad depot.** Outside are totem poles and a 1907 locomotive. A monument here relates the history of the railroad.

Just north of the depot, **Ship Creek** tumbles into Cook Inlet. Salmon run up this creek all summer; they are visible from the nearby viewing platform.

The paved walking and cycling **coastal trail,** which runs along the water for about 12 miles, can be reached by returning to 2nd Avenue and heading west three blocks to the marked entrance. Mt. Susitna (known as the Sleeping Lady) is the prominent low mountain to the northwest. To her north, Mt. McKinley is often visible. On the left is Resolution Park, a cantilevered viewing platform above the trail, dominated by the Captain Cook monument.

The **Oscar Anderson House** is next to the trail at the north end of **Elderberry Park,** near 5th Avenue between L and N streets. It was Anchorage's first permanent frame house, built in 1915. Tours are free. The park is also a good place to watch for whales off the coast.

Walk uphill on 5th Avenue from the park and continue east to H Street. The **Imaginarium,** an interactive science museum with a great shop, is a fun stop for kids and adults. *725 W. 5th Ave., tel. 907/276–3179. Admission: $4 adults, $3 senior citizens, $3 children 2–12. Open Mon.–Sat. 10–6, Sun. noon–5.*

⑩ The **Anchorage Museum of History and Art** occupies the whole block at 6th Avenue and A Street. The entrance is on 7th Avenue. It houses a fine collection of historical and contemporary Alaskan art, displays on Alaskan history, and a special section for children. One gallery is devoted to views of Alaska, as seen by early explorers, resident painters, and contemporary artists. *121 W. 7th Ave., tel. 907/ 343–4326. Admission: $4 adults, $3.50 senior citizens, children under 19 free. Open daily 9–6.*

If you have the time, take a taxi to the Lake Hood floatplane base, where colorful aircraft come and go hourly. A good place to watch the planes take off and land is from the Fancy Moose lounge inside the Regal Alaskan Hotel. *4800 Spenard Rd., tel. 907/243–2300.*

Shopping The **Alaska Native Arts and Crafts Association** (333 W. 4th Ave., tel. 907/274–2932; closed Sun.) sells items from all native Alaskan groups and carries the work of the best-known carvers, silversmiths, and bead workers, as well as unknown artists. The best buys on native Alaskan artists' work are found at the **Alaska Native Medical Center** gift shop (3rd Ave. and Gambell St., tel. 907/257–1150; open weekdays 10–2, also 11–2 on the first Sat. of each month). The **Stonington Gallery** (415 F St., tel. 907/272–1489) carries the work of better-known Alaskan artists, both native and nonnative.

Jogging/ The coastal trail (*see* Exploring Anchorage, *above*) and other trails
Walking in Anchorage are used by cyclists, runners, and walkers. The trail from Westchester Lagoon at the end of 15th Avenue runs 2 miles to Earthquake Park and, beyond that, 7 miles out to Kincaid Park. For bike rentals, contact **Adventures and Delights** (K St. between 4th and 5th Aves., tel. 907/276–8282).

Dining **Aladdin's.** In a strip-mall setting on the south side of Anchorage, the former director of catering for the Anchorage Hilton has created one of the city's most interesting dining experiences. The menu features dishes from virtually every country that rings the Mediterranean. The wine selection is equally diverse. *4240 Old Seward Hwy., tel. 907/561–2373. AE, D, DC, MC, V. Closed Sun. No lunch Sat. $$*
Club Paris. It's dark and smoky up front in the bar, where for decades old-time Anchorage folks have met to drink and chat. Halibut and fried prawns are available, but the star attractions are the big, tender, flavorful steaks. If you forget to make a reservation, have a drink at the bar and order the hors d'oeuvres tray—a sampler of steak, cheese, and prawns that could be a meal for two people. *417 W. 5th Ave., tel. 907/277–6332. Reserve early that day. AE, D, DC, MC, V. $$*
Lucky Wishbone. At this old Anchorage eatery, where old-timers sit around the brightly lit Formica tables and waitresses never seem to have a bad day, great fried chicken is the fare. Order all white meat, with just the wishbone and no ribs, or try the livers or gizzards. *1033 E. 5th Ave., tel. 907/272–3454. No credit cards. Closed Sun. $*

Glacier Bay National Park and Preserve

Cruising Glacier Bay is like revisiting the Little Ice Age, when glaciers covered much of the northern hemisphere. It is one of the few places in the world where you can get within a quarter mile of tidewater glaciers, which have their base at the water's edge. Sixteen of them line the 60 miles of narrow fjords at the northern end of the Inside Passage, rising up to 7,000 feet above the bay. Huge chunks of ice break off the glaciers and crash into the water, producing a dazzling show known as calving.

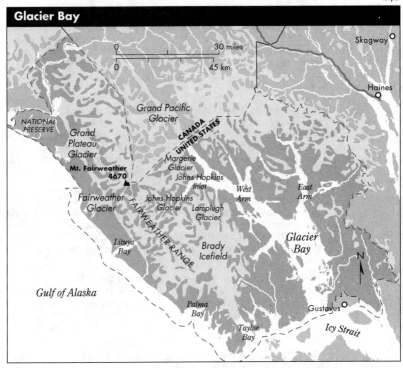

Glacier Bay

Although the Tlingit Indians have lived in the area for 10,000 years, the bay was first popularized by naturalist John Muir, who visited in 1879. Just 100 years before, the bay was completely choked with ice. By 1916, though, the ice had retreated 62 miles—the most rapid glacial retreat ever recorded. To preserve its clues to the world's geological history, the bay was declared a national monument in 1925. It became a national park in 1980. Today, a few of the glaciers are advancing again, but very slowly.

Competition is fierce among cruise ships for entry permits into Glacier Bay. The park service limits the number of ships that can call to protect the humpback whale, which feeds here in summer. Check your cruise brochure to make sure that Glacier Bay is included in your sailing. Most ships that do visit spend at least one full day exploring the park. There are no shore excursions or landings in the bay, but a park-service naturalist boards every cruise ship to provide narration on its history and scientific importance. It is often misty or rainy, so rain gear is essential. The average summer temperature is 50°. As always in Alaska, be prepared for the cold. Also, make sure to bring binoculars, extra film, and a telephoto lens.

The glaciers that most cruise passengers see are located in the west arm of Glacier Bay. Ships linger in front of four glaciers so passengers may view their stunning appearance. **Lamplugh,** one of the bluest in the park, is at the mouth of Johns Hopkins Inlet and is often the first stop on the glacier tour. Next is **Johns Hopkins Glacier** at the end of the inlet, where cruise passengers are likely to see a continuous shower of calving ice. Sometimes there are so many icebergs in the inlet that ships must avoid the area. Moving farther north, to the end of the western arm, **Margerie Glacier** is also quite active. Adjacent is **Grand Pacific Glacier,** the largest glacier in the park.

Your experience in Glacier Bay will depend partly on the size of your ship. Ocean liners tend to stay mid-channel, while small yachtlike ships spend more time closer to shore. Passengers on smaller ships may get a better view of the calving ice and wildlife—such as brown and black bear, mountain goats, moose, and seals with their pups—but big-ship passengers, on vessels with much higher decks, get a loftier perspective.

Juneau

Juneau owes its origins to a trio of colorful characters: two pioneers, Joe Juneau and Dick Harris, and a Tlingit chief named Kowee, who discovered rich reserves of gold in the stream that now runs through the middle of town. That was in 1880, and shortly after the discovery a modest stampede led first to the formation of a camp, then a town, then the Alaska district (now state) capital.

For nearly 60 years after Juneau's founding, gold remained the mainstay of the economy. In its heyday, the Alaska Juneau gold mine was the biggest low-grade-ore mine in the world. Then, during World War II, the government decided it needed Juneau's manpower for the war effort, and the mines ceased operations. After the war, mining failed to start up again, and government became the city's principal employer.

Juneau is a charming, cosmopolitan frontier town. It's easy to navigate, has one of the best museums in Alaska, is surrounded by beautiful wilderness, and has a glacier in its backyard. To capture the true frontier ambience, stop by the Red Dog Saloon and the Alaskan Hotel. Both are on the main shopping drag, just a quick walk from the cruise-ship pier.

Shore Excursions The following are good choices in Juneau. They may not be offered by all cruise lines. All times and prices are approximate. Unless otherwise noted, children's prices are for those under 13.

Adventure **Mendenhall Glacier Helicopter Ride.** One of the best helicopter glacier tours, including a landing on an ice field for a walk on the glacier. Boots and rain gear provided. *2 hrs. Cost: $140–$154.*

Mendenhall River Float Trip. A rafting trip down the Mendenhall River passes through some stretches of gentle rapids. Experienced oarsmen row the rafts; rubber boots, ponchos, and life jackets are provided. The minimum age is six. An excellent first rafting experience for those in good health. Great fun. *3½ hrs. Cost: $83–$95 adults, $54–$60 children.*

Salmon Bakes **Gold Creek Salmon Bake.** This all-you-can-eat outdoor meal features Alaskan king salmon barbecued over an open alderwood fire. After dinner, walk in the woods, explore an abandoned mine, or pan for gold. *1½–2 hrs. Cost: $22–$25 adults, $15 children.*

Taku Glacier Lodge Wilderness Salmon Bake. Fly over the Juneau Ice Field to Taku Glacier Lodge. Dine on barbecued salmon, then explore the virgin rain forest or enjoy the lodge. It's expensive, but this trip consistently gets rave reviews. *2½–3 hrs. Cost: $152–$173.*

Coming Ashore Cruise ships dock or tender passengers ashore at **Marine Park,** or at the old **Ferry Terminal,** nearby. A small visitor kiosk on the pier at Marine Park is filled with tour brochures, bus schedules, and maps (staffed according to cruise-ship arrivals). There is a tourist information center at the old ferry terminal as well. The downtown shops along South Franklin Street are just minutes away. The **Davis Log Cabin** (3rd and Seward Sts., tel. 907/586–2201) also dispenses information.

Getting Around *By Taxi* Taxis wait for cruise-ship passengers at Marine Park. There are no standard rates; they must be negotiated. Elsewhere in town, call **Taku Glacier Cab Co.** (tel. 907/586–2121); rates begin at $1.85 for pickup, and $1.80 per mile.

Exploring *Numbers in the margin correspond to points of interest on the Ju-*
Juneau *neau map.*

❶ Begin at the visitor information kiosk at **Marine Park,** then head
east a block to South Franklin Street. Buildings here and on Front
Street, which intersects South Franklin several blocks north, are
among the oldest and most interesting in the city. Many reflect the
architecture of the '20s and '30s; some are even older.

At No. 278 is the **Red Dog Saloon.** With a sawdust-covered floor, a
stuffed bear, and big-game heads mounted on the walls, this is
Alaska's most famous saloon. Just down the street is the small **Alaskan Hotel** (167 S. Franklin St.); it was called "a pocket edition of the
best hotels on the Pacific Coast" when it opened in 1913. Owners
Mike and Betty Adams have restored the building with period trappings. The barroom's massive, mirrored oak bar, accented by Tiffany lamps and panels, is a particular delight.

Also on South Franklin Street is the **Alaska Steam Laundry Building,** a 1901 structure with a windowed turret. It now houses a coffee-
house, a film processing service, and other stores. Across the street,
the equally venerable **Senate Building Mall** contains one of the two
Juneau Christmas Stores, a children's shop, and a place to buy Russian icons.

Head uphill on Franklin and turn left onto 4th Street; at the corner
❷ of Seward Street is the **Alaska State Capitol,** constructed in 1930,
with pillars of southeastern Alaska marble. The structure now
houses the governor's offices and other state agencies, and the state
legislature meets here for four months each year. *Tel. 907/465–2479.
Tours daily 8:30–5.*

❸ Uphill again and to the east on 5th Street is little **St. Nicholas Russian Orthodox Church,** built in 1894 and the oldest original Russian
church in Alaska. *Donation requested. Open daily in summer, but
hrs vary. Check at the visitors' kiosk.*

Back at the top of Seward Street, between 5th and 6th streets,
❹ stands a **totem pole** that is one of Juneau's finest; it tells a symbolic
story of Alaska. Walk up the hill to the totem pole and continue up
❺ the stairs to 7th Street, where you'll find the **House of Wickersham,**
the 1899 residence of James Wickersham, a pioneer judge and dele-
gate to Congress. Memorabilia from the judge's travels ranges from
rare Native American basketry and ivory carvings to historic photos, 47 diaries, and a Chickering grand piano that came "round the
horn" to Alaska while the Russians still ruled the region. *Tel. 907/
586–9001. Admission: $2. Tours Sun.–Fri. noon–5.*

❻ Back down the hill and to the west on 4th Street, you'll pass the **State
Office Building.** On Friday at noon in the four-story atrium you can
listen to organ music played on a grand old theater pipe organ, a veteran of the silent-movie era.

❼ Across the street is the **City Museum** and another totem pole. Head-
❽ ing along Calhoun Avenue, you'll come to the **Governor's House,** a
three-level colonial-style home completed in 1912.

Continuing on Calhoun Avenue, past the Gold Creek Bridge, you'll
❾ reach **Evergreen Cemetery,** where many Juneau pioneers (including
Joe Juneau and Dick Harris) are buried. At the end of the gravel
❿ lane is the **monument to Chief Kowee,** who was cremated on this
⓫ spot. Turn left here onto Glacier Avenue. Walk past the **Federal
Building and Post Office,** at 9th Street and Glacier Avenue, and the
⓬ **Juneau-Harris Monument** near Gold Creek (Glacier Ave. is now Willoughby Ave.), then on to Whittier Street, where a right turn takes
⓭ you to the **Alaska State Museum.** This is one of the best museums in
Alaska, with exhibits on the state's history, native cultures, wild-

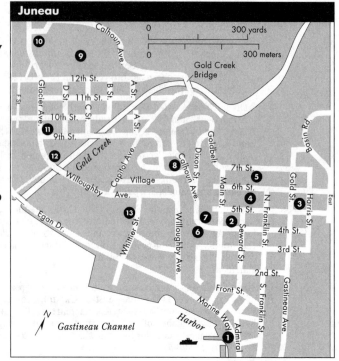

life, and industry. *395 Whittier St., tel. 907/465–2901. Admission: $2. Open weekdays 9–6, weekends 10–6.*

Mendenhall Glacier is only 13 miles from downtown, and you can walk right up to it. The bus ($1.25) that stops at South Franklin Street can take you within 1¼ miles of the Mendenhall visitor center. Plan on spending a total of three or four hours if you take the bus, including sightseeing. (*See* Hiking, *below.*)

Shopping South Franklin Street is the place in Juneau to shop. The variety of merchandise is good (especially the hand-knit sweaters); prices are moderate to expensive.

In the Senate Building Mall on South Franklin Street is the **Russian Shop** (tel. 907/586–2778), a repository of icons, samovars, lacquered boxes, nesting dolls, and other items that reflect Alaska's 18th- and 19th-century Russian heritage. For a souvenir from one of Alaska's most famous saloons, stop by the gift shop at the **Red Dog Saloon** (*see* Exploring Juneau, *above*).

Knowledgeable locals frequent the **Rie Munoz Gallery** (2101 N. Jordon Ave., tel. 907/789–7411) for fine art. Munoz is one of Alaska's favorite artists, and her stylized, colorful design technique is much copied. Other artists' works are also on sale, including wood-block prints by nationally known artist Dale DeArmond.

Sports Contact **Beartrack Charters** (tel. 907/586–6945) or **Juneau Sportfish-**
Fishing ing (tel. 907/586–1887).

Hiking Surrounded by the **Tongass National Forest,** Juneau is a hiker's paradise. For trail maps, information, and advice, stop by Centennial Hall on Willoughby at Egan Drive. The Davis Log Cabin (3rd and Seward Sts., tel. 907/586–2201) sells two useful booklets, "90 Short Walks Around Juneau" ($5) and "Juneau Trails" ($4). Good trails for cruise passengers begin just behind the **Mendenhall Glacier** Visitor Center (*see* Exploring Juneau, *above*).

For guided walks, **Parks and Recreation/Juneau** (tel. 907/586–5226 or 907/586–2635) sponsors open Wednesday- and Saturday-morning group hikes. On Saturday, there's free car-pool pickup at the docks. **Alaska Rainforest Treks** (tel. 907/463–3466) offers guided day hikes through Tongass National Forest. Day packs and rain gear are provided. Tours are limited in size, so call before leaving home. Departure times can be customized according to your ship's schedule. The price of $95 includes lunch.

Kayaking **Alaska Discovery** (tel. 907/780–6226) offers escorted day tours for $95 per person plus $10 round-trip transportation. Lunch and rain gear are included. Trips leave around mid-morning and return about dinner time, so participation is practical only for passengers whose ships make daylong calls.

Dining **Silver Bow Inn.** The ground floor of this little hotel houses one of Juneau's best restaurants. The dining room is furnished with mismatched antiques from the city's early days, and there's limited seating outdoors. Local fish is a specialty. Try the halibut in berries and port sauce or the mixed seafood grill in lemon garlic sauce. The rich dessert menu features homemade ice cream. The wine list is extensive. *120 2nd St., tel. 907/586–4146. AE, D, DC, MC, V. $$*

Fiddlehead. This is probably the favorite restaurant of Juneau locals, a delightful place of light wood, softly patterned wallpaper, stained glass, and historic photos. Food is healthy, generously served, and *different.* How about a light dinner of black beans and rice? Or pasta Greta Garbo (locally smoked salmon tossed with fettuccine in cream sauce). The homemade bread is laudable. *429 W. Willoughby Ave., tel. 907/586–3150. Reservations advised. AE, D, DC, MC, V. $–$$*

Ketchikan

Ketchikan sits at the base of 3,000-foot Deer Mountain. Until miners and fishermen settled here in the 1880s, the mouth of Ketchikan Creek was a summer fishing camp for Tlingit Indians. Today, commercial and recreational fishing are still important to the area.

Ketchikan is Alaska's totem-pole port: At the nearby Tlingit village of Saxman, 2½ miles south of downtown, there is a major totem park and residents still practice traditional carving techniques. The Ketchikan Visitors Bureau on the dock can supply information on getting to Saxman on your own, or you can take a ship-organized tour. Another outdoor totem display is at Totem Bight State Historical Park, a coastal rain forest 10 miles north of town. The Totem Heritage Center preserves historic poles, some nearly 200 years old.

Ketchikan is easy to explore, with walking-tour signs to lead you around the city. It is not advisable to walk to outlying areas, such as Saxman, because there are no sidewalks en route. Expect rain at some time during the day, even if the sun is shining when you dock: average annual precipitation is more than 150 inches.

Shore Excursions The following are good choices in Ketchikan. They may not be offered by all cruise lines. All times and prices are approximate. Unless otherwise noted, children's prices are for those under 13.

Adventure **Misty Fjords Flightseeing.** Aerial views of granite cliffs rising 4,000 feet from the sea, waterfalls, rain forests, and wildlife. A landing on a high wilderness lake is the highlight. *1½–2 hrs. Cost: $140–$159.*

Sportfishing. You're almost sure to get a bite in the "Salmon Capital of the World." Charter boats hold from four to six passengers; fish can be butchered and shipped home for an additional charge. *4–5 hrs, including 3–4 hrs of fishing. Cost: $135–$150.*

Native Culture **Saxman Village.** See 27 totem poles and totem-carvers at work at this native community. The gift shop is among the best for Alaska native crafts. *2–2½ hrs. Cost: $39–$42 adults, $21 children.*

Totem Bight Tour. This look at Ketchikan's native culture focuses on Tlingit totem poles in Totem Bight State Historical Park. Guides interpret the myths and symbols in the traditional carvings. *2½ hrs. Cost: $29–$31 adults, $14.50–$15.50 children.*

Coming Ashore Ships dock or tender passengers ashore directly across from the Ketchikan Visitors Bureau on Front and Mission streets, in the center of downtown. Here you can pick up brochures and maps. Most of the town's sights are within easy walking distance.

Getting Around By Taxi To reach the sights outside downtown on your own, you'll want to hire a cab. Metered taxis meet the ships right on the docks and also wait across the street. Rates are $2.10 for pickup, 23¢ each ⅒ mile.

Exploring Ketchikan *Numbers in the margin correspond to points of interest on the Ketchikan map.*

❶ From the **Ketchikan Visitors Bureau** on the dock, head up Mission Street, past the Trading Post and post office, and make a left on **❷** Bawden Street. On your left is **St. John's Church and Seamen's Center.** The 1903 church structure is the oldest house of worship in Ketchikan; its interior was formed from red cedar cut in the sawmill in Saxman. The Seamen's Center, next to the church, was built as a **❸** hospital in 1904. Catercorner from the church is **Whale Park,** site of the **Chief Johnson Totem Pole,** a 1989 replica of the 1901 original that stood on the same site.

❹ Turn right on Dock Street to reach the **Tongass Historical Museum and Totem Pole,** where you can learn about the early days of fishing and mining. *Dock and Bawden Sts., tel. 907/225–5600. Admission: $2; free on Sun. after 1. Open daily 8–5 during cruise season.*

Continue north on Bawden, bear right onto Park Avenue, and look **❺** up and to the left to see **Grant Street Trestle,** constructed in 1908. Virtually all of Ketchikan's walkways and streets were once wood trestles, but only this one remains. As you turn the corner and walk **❻** right, get out your camera and set it for fast speed at the **Salmon Falls** and **Fish Ladder** just off Park Avenue on Married Man's Trail. When the salmon start running in midsummer, thousands of fish leap the falls (or take the easier ladder) to spawn in Ketchikan Creek upstream.

As you continue up Park Avenue, notice that some of the intersecting streets are actually wooden staircases. Soon after passing the Fish Ladder, look for Venetia Avenue on your right, and follow the **❼** curving road up to the **Westmark Cape Fox Lodge.** Aside from providing stunning views of the harbor and fine dining, the lodge also runs tramway rides ($1) down the mountainside to popular Creek Street *(see below).*

Retrace your steps back down Venetia and turn right along Park until you reach **Deer Mountain Hatchery,** where tens of thousands of **❽** salmon are released annually into local waters. Farther down Woodland Avenue, at the corner of Deermont Street, is the **Totem Heri-** **❾** **tage Center and Nature Park.** *Tel. 907/225–5900. Admission: $2; free on Sun after 1. Open daily 8–5 during cruise season.*

❿ Trails from either the hatchery or the heritage center lead to **City Park,** where you can see small ponds that were once holding areas for the area's first hatchery, which ran from 1923 to 1928.

To return to the downtown area, follow Deermont to Stedman Street **⓫** and turn right. You will pass a colorful wall mural called *Return of the Eagle.* It was created by 25 Native American artists on the walls of the Robertson Building on the Ketchikan campus of the Universi-

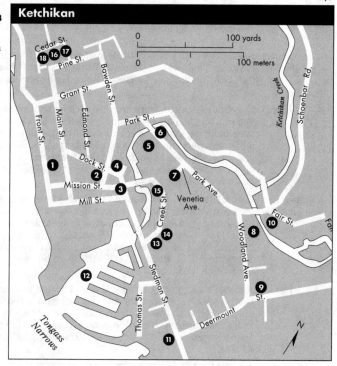

Ketchikan

⑫ ty of Alaska–Southeast. Next comes Thomas Street, built in 1913 as part of the New England Fish Company cannery, and **Thomas Basin,** one of four harbors in Ketchikan.

⑬ Return to Stedman Street and head north to **Creek Street,** formerly Ketchikan's infamous red-light district. Its small houses, built on stilts over the creek, have been restored as trendy shops. The ⑭ street's most famous brothel, **Dolly's House** (admission: $2.50), has been preserved as a museum, complete with furnishings and a short history of the life and times of Ketchikan's best-known madam. ⑮ There's more good salmon viewing in season at the **Creek Street Footbridge.** You can catch the tram here for a ride up to the Cape Fox Lodge, if you missed it before (*see above*).

If you're into steep street climbing, head left on Mission Street, then ⑯ right up Main Street past the fire department to the **Kyan Totem Pole,** a replica of an 1880s original that once stood near St. John's ⑰ Church. Adjacent is **Monrean House,** a 1904 structure on the Nation- ⑱ al Register of Historic Places. Nearby on Cedar Street is a **scenic lookout** onto City Float boat basin and the waters of Tongass Narrows.

Shopping The **Saxman Village** gift shop has some superb handcrafted Tlingit merchandise, along with cheaper mass-produced souvenirs. Because artists are local, prices for Native American crafts are better here than at most other ports.

Creek Street has several attractive boutiques. At **Parnassus Bookstore** (28 Creek St., tel. 907/225–7690), coffee and pastries are served amid an eclectic collection of books. Try **Soho Coho** (5 Creek St., tel. 907/225–5954) for novelty gifts.

Scanlon Gallery (318 Mission St., tel. 907/225–4730) handles not only major Alaskan artists and local talent but also traditional and contemporary native art, soapstone, bronze, and walrus ivory.

Salmon, Etc. (322 Mission St., tel. 907/225–6008) sells every variety of Alaskan salmon, which can be sent, frozen and processed, to your home.

Sports Fishing Salmon are so plentiful in these waters that the town has earned the nickname "Salmon Capital of the World." Contact **Chinook Charters** (tel. 907/225–9225) or **Tchaika Fishing Guide Service** (tel. 907/247–8526).

Hiking Check at the visitors bureau on the dock for trail maps and advice. If you're a tough hiker with sturdy shoes, the 3-mile trail from downtown (starting at the end of Fair Street) to the top of **Deer Mountain** will repay your effort with a spectacular panorama of the city below and the wilderness behind. **Ward Cove** recreation area, about 6 miles north of town, offers easier hiking along lakes and streams and beneath towering spruce and hemlock trees.

Kayaking and Canoeing Contact Juneau-based **Alaska Travel Adventures** (tel. 907/789–0052) for a Native American canoe excursion on Harriet Hunt Lake north of town; smoked fish and other native delights are part of the experience. This 3½-hour trip costs $69 per person for adults, $45 for children, and is often sold aboard ships as a shore excursion. **Southeast Exposure** (507 Stedman St.,tel. 907/225–8829) offers kayak rentals, instruction, and tours.

Dining **Annabelle's Keg and Chowder House.** Located in Gillmore's Hotel, this popular seafood restaurant takes you back to the '20s. The walls are covered with photos and paintings depicting the Ketchikan of years past. Specials include steamers, oysters on the half shell, and clam chowder. *326 Front St., tel. 907/225–6009. AE, D, DC, MC, V. $$–$$$*

Seward

On the southeastern coast of the Kenai Peninsula, Seward is surrounded by four major federal land holdings—**Chugach National Forest, Kenai Wildlife Refuge, Kenai Fjords National Park,** and the **Alaska Maritime National Refuge.** The entire area is breathtaking, and you should not miss it in your haste to get to Anchorage.

Seward was founded in 1903, at the time that planning for the railroad to Alaska's interior began. The tidal wave that followed the 1964 earthquake devastated the town but, fortunately, most residents saw the harbor drain almost entirely, knew the wave would follow, and ran to high ground. Since then the town has relied heavily on commercial fishing, and its harbor is important for shipping coal to the Orient.

If you're in Seward on the Fourth of July, stick around for the insane Mt. Marathon foot race, 3,000 feet straight uphill from downtown. (*See* Hiking, *below.*)

Shore Excursions Like Anchorage, Seward is mainly a transfer point for embarking and disembarking cruise passengers. If your ship is one that calls here for the day, though, the following excursion is a good choice.

Adventure **Mt. McKinley Flightseeing.** From Anchorage, fly to Denali National Park (filled with bears, wolves, caribou, and moose) to see North America's highest peak. The trip is often canceled due to cloudiness. *3 hrs, 2 hrs flying time. Cost: $288.*

Coming Ashore Cruise ships dock within a half mile of downtown. The Kenai Fjords National Park visitor center is within walking distance: Turn left as you leave the pier, then left again onto 4th Avenue; the center is two blocks ahead. The Chugach National Forest Ranger District Information Center is at 334 4th Avenue.

Getting Around Public bus routes include stops timed to meet ships. For a taxi call 907/224–5000 or 907/224–5555 from the pay phones at the dock. Rates are $2 for pickup, $1.50 per mile.

Exploring Seward Seward offers little to compare with the splendor of its surroundings: Most passengers head into Anchorage or explore the federal parks of the Kenai Peninsula. Don't miss the fjords in **Resurrection Bay**, with their bird rookeries and sea-lion colonies.

Shopping The **Alaska Shop** (210 4th Ave., tel. 907/224–5420) has a variety of souvenirs from T-shirts to jewelry to Alaska books. The **Treasure Chest** (Small Boat Harbor, tel. 907/224–8087) also has T-shirts and sweatshirts, plus a wide selection of Alaskan gifts. **Ranting Raven Bakery** (228 4th Ave., tel. 907/224–2228) has a gift shop stocked with Russian and Ukrainian imports. Don't forget to try the home-baked breads, pastries, and cakes. **Bardarson Studio** (Small Boat Harbor, tel. 907/224–5448) has local Alaskan art—originals and reproductions—as well as imported goods.

Sports
Fishing The Seward Jackpot Halibut Tournament runs through July, and the Seward Silver Salmon Derby is in August. For fishing, sightseeing, and drop-off/pickup tours, contact **Fish House** (tel. 800/257–7760 or 907/224–3674 in AK), Seward's oldest operator; **Kenai Fjords Tours** (tel. 907/224–8068), which has four charter boats for sightseeing; or Anchorage-based **Mariah Charters** (tel. 907/224–8623 or 907/243–1238).

Hiking The **Mt. Marathon** trail starts at the west end of Lowell Street and runs practically straight uphill. An easier and more convenient hike for cruise passengers is the **Two Lakes Trail**, a loop of footpaths and bridges on the edge of town. A map is available from the Seward Chamber of Commerce (Box 749, Seward 99664, tel. 907/224–8051).

Few areas in the world are as rich in hiking possibilities as the **Kenai Peninsula**. The hard part is getting there from the ship. One way is to go with a tour group specializing in hiking. **Alaska Treks-n-Voyages** (Small Boat Harbor, tel. 907/224–3960) can arrange hiking and glacier treks, as well as kayak tours and rentals.

Dining **Harbor Dinner Club & Lounge.** The lounge is decorated with hand-painted murals depicting Alaskan wildlife and the halibut is great at this house downtown. Try a halibut burger with homemade french fries. *5th Ave., tel. 907/224–3012. AE, D, DC, MC, V. $–$$*

Sitka

For centuries before the 18th-century arrival of the Russians, Sitka was the home of the Tlingit nation. But Sitka's beauty, mild climate, and economic potential caught the attention of outsiders. Russian Territorial Governor Alexander Baranof saw in the island's massive timbered forests raw materials for shipbuilding, and its location suited trading routes to California, Hawaii, and the Orient. In 1799 Baranof established an outpost that he called Redoubt St. Michael, 6 miles north of the present town, and moved a large number of his Russian and Aleut fur hunters there from Kodiak Island.

The Tlingits attacked Baranof's people and burned his buildings in 1802, but Baranof returned in 1804 with a formidable force, including shipboard cannons. He attacked the Tlingits at their fort near Indian River (site of the present-day, 105-acre Sitka National Historical Park) and drove them to the other side of the island. The Tlingits and Russians made peace in 1821, and, eventually, the capital of Russian America was shifted to Sitka from Kodiak.

Sitka today is known primarily for its onion-domed Russian Orthodox church, one of Southeast Alaska's most famous landmarks, and the Raptor Rehabilitation Center, a hospital for injured bald eagles and other birds of prey. Don't miss the 15 totem poles scattered throughout the grounds of the historical park.

Shore Excursions The following are good choices in Sitka. They may not be offered by all cruise lines. All times and prices are approximate. Unless otherwise noted, children's prices are for those under 13.

Adventure **Kayak Adventure.** Get down at sea level to search for marine and land wildlife in two-person sea kayaks. Sightings of eagles, seals, bears, and deer are likely. If your ship doesn't offer this excursion, contact Baidarka Boats (*see* Kayaking, *below*). *3 hrs, includes 1½ hrs of kayaking. Cost: $65–$75 adults, $44–$50 children.*

Wildlife Up Close **Eagle Hospital.** Visit the Alaska Raptor Rehabilitation Center, where injured birds of prey are nursed back to health. *3–3¾ hrs. Cost: $36–$39 adults, $18–$19 children. Minimum age is 6.*

Coming Ashore Only the smallest excursion vessels can dock at Sitka. Ocean liners must drop anchor in the harbor and tender passengers ashore near the Centennial Building, with its big Tlingit war canoe. Inside is the Sitka Visitors Bureau, which provides maps and brochures. A taxi ride downtown costs about $3, though the distance can easily be walked.

Getting Around *By Taxi* Taxis meet the cruise ships, but if none is around, call 907/747–8888 or 907/747–5001. A 30-minute taxi tour costs $20 per carload, an hour tour costs $40. Pay phones are in the Centennial Building and across the way in the Bayview Trading Company.

Exploring Sitka *Numbers in the margin correspond to points of interest on the Sitka map.*

❶ Begin at the Sitka Visitors Bureau, in the **Centennial Building.** To get one of the best views in town, turn left on Harbor Drive and head
❷ for **Castle Hill,** where Alaska was handed over to the United States on October 18, 1867, and where the first 49-star U.S. flag was flown on January 3, 1959, signifying the spirit of Alaska's statehood. Take the first right off Harbor Drive, then look for the entrance to Baranof Castle Hill State Historic Site. Make a left on the gravel path that takes you to the top of the hill overlooking Crescent Harbor.

With your back to the water, look down to your right. The large, four-story, red-roof structure with the imposing 14-foot statue in
❸ front is the **Sitka State Pioneers' Home,** built in 1934 as the first of several state-run retirement homes and medical-care facilities. The statue, symbolizing the spirit of Alaska's frontier sourdough (as the locals are nicknamed), was modeled after an authentic pioneer, William "Skagway Bill" Fonda. It portrays a determined prospector with pack, pick, rifle, and supplies, headed for gold country.

Go down the steps that lead to the Pioneer Home to face **Totem Square,** where there are three old anchors found in local waters and believed to be from 19th-century British ships. Notice the double-headed eagle of czarist Russia on the park's totem pole.

Walk past the Pioneer Home on Lincoln Street and make a left on Barracks Street, which becomes Marine Street after one block. On
❹ your left is an old **Russian Blockhouse,** and on your right are the
❺ **Russian and Lutheran cemeteries.** Make a right from Marine Street onto Seward Street and the cemetery entrance will be to your left. The most distinctive grave marks the final resting place of Princess Maksutoff, one of the most famous members of the Russian royal family buried on Alaskan soil.

❻ Back on Lincoln Street, **St. Michael's Cathedral** had its origins in a frame-covered log structure built in the 1840s. In 1966 the church burned in a fire that swept through the business district. Using original blueprints, an almost-exact replica of St. Michael's was built

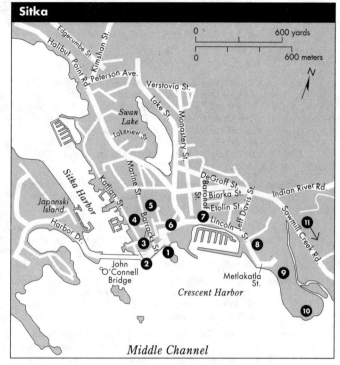

and dedicated in 1976. *Tel. 907/747–8120. $1 donation requested. Open daily 9–3.*

Several blocks east, past the cathedral on Lincoln Street and facing the harbor, is the **Russian Bishop's House.** Constructed in 1842, this is one of the few remaining Russian log homes in Alaska. Inside are exhibits on the history of Russian America and the Room Revealed, where a portion of the house's structure is peeled away to expose Russian building techniques. *Admission free. Open daily 8–5.*

Keeping the cathedral to your back and the water to your right, a 10- to 15-minute walk farther on Lincoln Street will lead you to the octagonal **Sheldon Jackson Museum,** built in 1895. It contains priceless Native American items collected by Dr. Sheldon Jackson from the remote regions of Alaska. Carved masks, Chilkat Indian blankets, dogsleds, kayaks—even the helmet worn by Chief Katlean during the 1804 battle between the Sitka Tlingits and the Russians—are displayed here. *Tel. 907/747–8981. Admission: $2 adults. Open daily 8–5.*

Sitka National Historical Park Visitor Center is a short walk farther along Lincoln Street. Audiovisual programs and exhibits including Native American and Russian artifacts give an overview of southeast Alaskan cultures, both old and new. Native American artists and craftspeople are on hand to demonstrate and interpret traditional crafts of the Tlingit people, such as silversmithing, weaving, and basketry. A self-guided trail (maps available at the visitor center) to the site of the **Tlingit Fort** passes by some of the most skillfully carved totem poles in the state; some of the 15 poles date back more than eight decades. *Tel. 907/747–6281. Admission free. Open daily 8–6.*

For die-hard walkers, a journey to the **Alaska Raptor Rehabilitation Center** is next. Visitors can see Buddy, a bald eagle that thinks he's human. To reach the rehabilitation center, exit the historical park at

Sawmill Creek Road and make a left. The center is 15 minutes down the road, across the street. *Tel. 907/747–8662. Admission: $10 adults, $5 children under 5. Open daily 7–6.*

Shopping　Shopping in Sitka is limited, though the town has its share of souvenir shops. Other ports offer a better selection.

At the **Sitka National Historical Park Visitor Center,** you can purchase interesting booklets on interpreting totem poles and other Tlingit art. A few stores, such as the **Russian-American Company** (407 Lincoln St., tel. 907/747–6228) and the **New Archangel Trading Co.** (335 Harbor Dr., across from the Centennial Building, tel. 907/ 747–8181), sell Russian items, including the popular *matruchka* nesting dolls. For books on Alaska, stop by **Old Harbor Books** (201 Lincoln St., tel. 907/747–8808).

Sports　Fishing is excellent here. Contact **Steller Charters** (tel. 907/747–
Fishing　6711), or see the information desk in the Centennial Building for a list of other charter operators.

Hiking　Sitka's best hiking can be done along the 2 miles of trails in **Sitka National Historical Park.** Here you can find some of the most dramatic totem poles in Alaska, relax in the picnic areas, and see spawning salmon during the seasonal runs on the Indian River.

Kayaking　**Baidarka Boats** (tel. 907/747–8996) rents sea kayaks ($25–$45) and offers guided trips in the island-strewn waters around Sitka ($75 minimum plus rental fee). Be sure to make arrangements in advance so that your guide and/or kayak is waiting for you at the harbor.

Dining　**Channel Club.** This is Sitka's best gourmet restaurant—a five-time winner of the Silver Spoon award from the Gourmet Club of America. Halibut cheeks are a favorite, and the recipe for the steak's delicious seasoning is a closely held secret. Decor is nautical, with glass fishing balls, whale baleen, and Alaska pictures on the walls. *Mile 3.5 on Halibut Point Rd., tel. 907/747–9916. AE, DC, MC, V. $$–$$$*

Skagway

The early gold-rush days of Alaska, when dreamers and hooligans descended on the Yukon via the murderous White Pass, are preserved in Skagway. Now a part of the Klondike Gold Rush National Historical Park, downtown Skagway was once the picturesque but sometimes lawless gateway for the frenzied stampede to the interior goldfields.

Local park rangers and residents now interpret and re-create that remarkable era for visitors. Old false-front stores, saloons, brothels, and wood sidewalks have been completely restored. You'll be regaled with tall tales of con artists, golden-hearted "ladies," stampeders, and newsmen. Such colorful characters as outlaw Jefferson "Soapy" Smith and his gang earned the town a reputation so bad that, by the spring of 1898, the superintendent of the Northwest Royal Mounted Police had labeled Skagway "little better than a hell on earth." But Soapy was killed in a duel with surveyor Frank Reid, and soon a civilizing influence, in the form of churches and family life, prevailed. When the gold played out just a few years later, the town of 20,000 dwindled to its current population of 700.

Shore　The following are good choices in Skagway. They may not be offered
Excursions　by all cruise lines. All times and prices are approximate. Unless otherwise noted, children's prices are for those under 13.

Adventure　**Glacier Bay Flightseeing.** If your ship doesn't sail through Glacier Bay—or even if it does—here's your chance to see it from above. *1¼–1¾ hrs, includes 70–75-min flight. Cost: $112–$124.*

Gold Rush Helicopter Tour. Fly over the Chilkoot Gold Rush Trail into a remote mountain valley for a landing on a glacier. Special boots are provided for walking on the glacier. *1½ hrs. Cost: $135–$159.*

Gold-Rush **White Pass and Yukon Railroad:** The 20-mile trip in vintage railroad
History cars, on narrow-gauge tracks built to serve the Yukon goldfields, runs past the infamous White Pass, skims along the edge of granite cliffs, crosses a 215-foot-high steel cantilever bridge over Dead Horse Gulch, climbs to a 2,865-foot elevation at White Pass Summit, and zigzags through dramatic scenery—including the actual Trail of '98, worn into the mountainside a century ago. A must for railroad buffs; great for children. *3 hrs. Cost: $72–$78 adults, $36–$39 children.*

Coming Cruise ships dock just a short stroll from downtown Skagway. From
Ashore the pier you can see the large yellow-and-red White Pass & Yukon Railroad Depot, now the National Park Service Visitor Center. Inside is an excellent photographic exhibit and superb documentary film. Ask the rangers about where to find the nearby hiking trails and a brochure on exploring the gold-rush cemetery.

Getting Virtually all the shops and gold-rush sights are along Broadway, the
Around main strip that leads from the visitor center through the middle of town, so you really don't need a taxi. Horse-drawn surreys, antique limousines, and modern vans pick up passengers at the pier and along Broadway for tours. The tracks of the White Pass and Yukon Railway run right along the pier; train departures are coordinated with cruise-ship arrivals.

Exploring *Numbers in the margin correspond to points of interest on the Skag-*
Skagway *way map.*

Skagway is perhaps the easiest port in Alaska to explore on foot. Just walk up and down Broadway, detouring here and there into the side streets.

① From the cruise-ship dock, follow the road into town to the **Red Onion Saloon** (Broadway and 2nd Ave.), where a lady-of-the-evening mannequin peers down from the former second-floor brothel and drinks are still served on the original mahogany bar. A couple of
② doors up is the **Arctic Brotherhood Hall,** with its curious driftwood-mosaic facade. Around the corner on 2nd Avenue is a tiny, almost
③ inconsequential shack that was **Soapy's Parlor,** but it is rarely open to tourists.

You'll find down-home sourdough cooking at the **Golden North Hotel** (Broadway and 3rd Ave.) and a rip-roaring revue, "Skagway in the
④ Days of '98," at the **Eagles Hall** (Broadway and 6th Ave.). Keep an eye out for the humorous architectural details and advertising irreverence that mark the Skagway spirit.

Turn right off Broadway onto 7th Avenue and walk about two blocks
⑤ to City Hall, where the **Trail of '98 Museum** is located. Here you will find interesting facts about the real lives of the people who settled here at the turn of the century.

Shopping Broadway is filled with somewhat overpriced curio shops, although some merchandise is unusual. **David Present's Gallery** (tel. 907/983-2873) has outstanding but pricey art by Alaskan artists. **Dedman's Photo Shop** (tel. 907/983-2353) has been a Skagway institution since the early days; here you'll find unusual historical photos, guidebooks, and old-fashioned newspapers. **Kirmse's** (tel. 907/983-2822) has a large selection of expensive, inexpensive, and downright tacky souvenirs. On display is the world's largest, heaviest, and most valuable gold-nugget watch chain.

Sports Real wilderness is within a stone's throw of the docks, which makes
Hiking this an excellent hiking port. Try the short jaunt to beautiful **Upper**

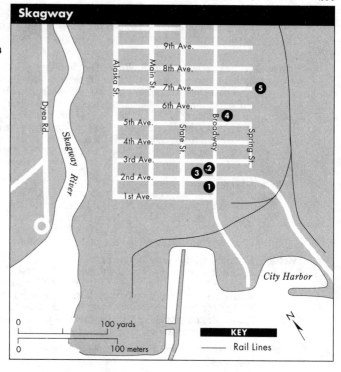

Skagway

9th Ave.

8th Ave.

7th Ave.

6th Ave.

5th Ave.

4th Ave.

3rd Ave.

2nd Ave.

1st Ave.

Alaska St.

Main St.

State St.

Broadway

Spring St.

Dyea Rd.

Skagway River

City Harbor

| 0 | 100 yards |
| 0 | 100 meters |

KEY

— Rail Lines

Dewey Lake. Start at the corner of 4th Avenue and Spring Street, go toward the mountain, cross the footbridge over Pullen Creek, and follow the trail.

A less strenuous hike is the trip through **Gold Rush Cemetery,** where the epitaphs offer strange but lively bits of social commentary. To get there, keep walking up Broadway, turn left onto 8th Avenue, then right onto State Street. Go through the railroad yards and follow the signs to the cemetery, which is 1½ miles, or a 30- to 45-minute walk, from town. To reach 300-foot-high **Reid Falls,** continue through the cemetery for a quarter mile. The National Park Service Visitor Center offers trail maps, advice, and the helpful brochure, *Skagway Gold Rush Cemetery Guide.*

Dining **Golden North Restaurant.** To eat in the Golden North Hotel's dining room is to return to the days of gold-rush con man Soapy Smith, heroic Frank Reid, and scores of pioneers, stampeders, and dance-hall girls. The decor is authentic and has been tastefully restored. Popular choices include sourdough pancakes for breakfast; soup, salad bar, and sandwiches for lunch; and salmon or other seafood for dinner. *3rd Ave. and Broadway, tel. 907/983–2294. AE, DC, MC, V. $–$$*

Prospector's Sourdough Restaurant. "Sourdough" is the nickname for locals, who often outnumber the tourists here. Breakfast specialties are hotcakes and snow-crab omelets. *4th Ave. and Broadway, tel. 907/983–2865. AE, DC, MC, V. $*

Victoria, British Columbia

Though Victoria is not in Alaska, it is a port of call for several Alaskan cruises. The city had its own gold-rush stampede in the 1800s, when 25,000 miners flocked to British Columbia's Cariboo country. Today the city is a mix of stately buildings and English traditions. Flower baskets hang from lampposts, shops sell Harris tweed and

Irish linen, locals play cricket and croquet, and visitors sightsee aboard red double-decker buses or horse-drawn carriages. Afternoon tea is still held daily at the city's elegant Empress Hotel. No visit to Victoria is complete without a stroll through Butchart Gardens, a short drive outside the city.

Shore Excursions The following are good choices in Victoria. They may not be offered by all cruise lines. All times and prices are approximate. Unless otherwise noted, children's prices are for those under 13.

Grand City Drive and Afternoon High Tea. This drive through downtown, past Craigdarrock Castle and residential areas, finishes with a British-style high tea at a hotel. A variation of this excursion takes visitors on a tour of the castle in lieu of high tea. *2½ hrs. Cost: $18–$30 adults, $10–$20 children.*

Short City Tour and Butchart Gardens. Drive through key places of interest, like the city center and residential areas, on the way to Butchart Gardens—a must for garden aficionados. *3½ hrs. Cost: $30–$38 adults, $15–$19 children.*

Coming Ashore Only the smallest excursion vessels can dock downtown in the Inner Harbour. Ocean liners must tie up at the Ogden Point Cruise Ship Terminal, a C$4–C$5 cab ride from downtown. Metered taxis meet the ship. The tourist information office (812 Wharf St., tel. 604/382-2127) is in front of the Empress Hotel, midway along the Inner Harbour.

Getting Around Most points of interest are within walking distance of the Empress Hotel. For those that aren't, public and private transportation is readily available from the Inner Harbor.

By Bus The public bus system is excellent. Pick up route maps and schedules at the tourist information office.

By Taxi Rates are C$2.15 for pickup, C$1.30 per kilometer. Contact **Bluebird** (tel. 604/382-3611) or **Victoria Taxi** (604/383-7111).

Exploring Victoria *Numbers in the margin correspond to points of interest on the Inner Harbour, Victoria, map. Prices listed below are in Canadian dollars.*

Victoria's heart is the **Inner Harbour,** always bustling with ferries, seaplanes, and yachts from all over the world. The ivy-covered
❶ **Empress Hotel** (721 Government St., tel. 604/384-8111), with its well-groomed gardens, is the dowager of Victoria. High tea in this little patch of England is a local ritual: Recline in deep armchairs and nibble on scones or crumpets with honey, butter, jam, and clotted cream while sipping blended tea.

❷ The **Crystal Gardens,** on Douglas Street behind the hotel, were built in 1925 under a glass roof as a public saltwater swimming pool. They have been renovated into a tropical conservatory and aviary, with flamingos, parrots, fountains, and waterfalls. Tea is served from 2 to 5 o'clock under garden umbrellas on the Upper Terrace, overlooking the lush, indoor jungle.

❸ Catercorner on Belleville Street, **Thunderbird Park** displays a ceremonial longhouse (a communal dwelling) and the finest collection of totem poles outside Alaska.

❹ Next to the park is **Helmcken House,** the province's oldest residence, which has a display of antique medical instruments. *10 Elliot St. Sq., tel. 604/361-0021. Admission: $3.75 adults, $2.75 senior citizens, $1.75 children 6–12. Open daily 11–5.*

❺ Next door is the superb **Royal British Columbia Museum.** Plan to spend at least an hour there. *675 Belleville St., tel. 604/387-3014. Admission: $5 adults, $3 senior citizens and children 13–18, $2 children 6–12. Open daily 10–5:30.*

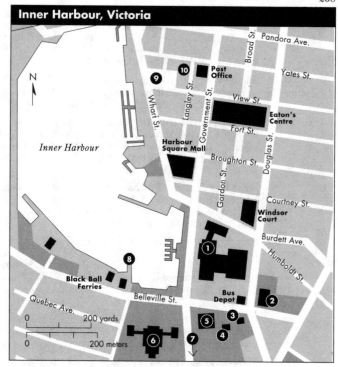

Bastion Square, **9**

British Columbia Parliament Buildings, **6**

Crystal Gardens, **2**

Emily Carr House, **7**

Empress Hotel, **1**

Helmcken House, **4**

Maritime Museum of B.C., **10**

Pacific Underseas Gardens, **8**

Royal British Columbia Museum, **5**

Thunderbird Park, **3**

Inner Harbour, Victoria

⑥ Across from the museum on Government Street are the stately, neo-Gothic **British Columbia Parliament Buildings,** constructed of local stone and wood and opened in 1898. At night the harbor is brilliantly lit with thousands of electric lights, like a fairy-tale castle.

⑦ Down Government Street a short way is the **Emily Carr House,** the beautifully restored residence of the famous early 20th-century painter. Prints by Carr, who was a member of the "Canadian Group of Seven," adorn the walls. *207 Government St., tel. 604/387–4697. Admission: $3.75 adults, $2.75 senior citizens, $1.75 children 6–12. Open Thurs.–Mon. 11–5.*

⑧ Return up Government Street and turn left at Belleville. One block on your right, opposite the Parliament Buildings, is the **Pacific Underseas Gardens,** a natural aquarium with more than 5,000 species from the area. You actually descend beneath the water for a live scuba show with Armstrong, the Pacific octopus. *490 Belleville St., tel. 604/382–5717. Admission: $6.50 adults, $6 senior citizens, $5 children 12–17, $3.25 children under 12. Open 9–9.*

⑨ Just a short walk from the Inner Harbour is **Bastion Square.** Follow Government Street to Humboldt Street. With the water to your left, bear left onto Wharf Street, and look for the square on your right. Established in 1843 as the original site of Ft. Victoria, it now boasts several restored buildings open for viewing. On the far side of the ⑩ square, the old courthouse is now the **Maritime Museum of British Columbia.** It has a collection of artifacts—including a 38-foot Indian dugout canoe and the 20-foot ketch *Trekka*, which has sailed around the world. In the Captain Cook gallery, nautical maps and other tools of 17th-century exploration are on display. *28 Bastion Sq., tel. 604/385–4222. Admission: $5 adults, $4 senior citizens, $3 children 12–17, $2 children 6–11. Open daily 9–4:30.*

Take a taxi (or a shore excursion) to **Butchart Gardens.** In a city of gardens, these 35 acres rank among the most beautiful in the world.

14 mi north of Victoria on Hwy. 17, tel. 604/652–5256. Admission: $11 adults, $5.75 children 13–17, $1.50 children 5–12. Open daily at 9, call for closing hrs.

Shopping   Save your receipts to receive a 7% GST tax refund from the Canadian government when you leave Canada; ask for a form at customs. Victoria stores specializing in English imports are plentiful, though Canadian-made goods are usually a better buy for foreigners. Look for Hudson's Bay Co. blankets and other woolens. From the Empress Hotel walk along Government Street to reach **George Straith Ltd., Piccadilly Shoppe British Woolens,** and **Sasquach Trading Company,** all of which sell high-quality woolen clothing.

Turn right onto Fort Street and walk four blocks to **Antique Row,** between Blanchard and Cook streets. The **Connoisseurs Shop** and **David Robinson, Ltd.** offer a wide variety of 18th-century pieces.

Dining   **Bengal Lounge.** Buffet lunches in the elegant Empress Hotel include curries with extensive condiment trays of coconuts, nuts, cool *raita* (yogurt with mint or cucumber), and chutney. Popular with cabinet ministers and bureaucrats, the Bengal Lounge offers splendid garden views. *721 Government St., tel. 604/384–8111. AE, D, DC, MC, V. $$*

La Ville d'Is. This cozy and friendly seafood house, run by Brittany native Michel Duteau, is one of the best bargains in Victoria. Although seafood, like *perche de la Nouvelle Aelande* (orange roughie in Muscadet with herbs), is the chef's strong suit, rabbit, lamb, and beef tenderloin are also available. The wine list is limited but imaginative. On warm days there's seating outside. *26 Bastion Sq., tel. 604/388–9414. Reservations advised. AE, DC, MC, V. Closed Sun. $$*

Antarctica

Antarctica is bigger than the continental United States, drier than the Sahara, colder than Siberia, and less populated than the Arabian Empty Quarter. Of all the fresh water in the world, 60% is locked in Antarctica's ice, which in places is more than 10 times thicker than the Empire State Building is tall.

First visited by only a handful of hearty whalers and intrepid explorers, Antarctica has been almost exclusively the domain of research scientists. Its purity and distance from civilization make it an ideal laboratory in which to study many problems that plague the rest of the planet.

In the late 1950s, a small company that specialized in adventure vacations began offering cruises to Antarctica. Although only a few ships followed over the next quarter century, a sudden, recent surge of interest in travel to the "White Continent" has produced a flood of inquiries and bookings. This year an estimated 9,000 visitors will make landfall on Antarctica. Among the major cruise ships with voyages scheduled are Abercrombie & Kent's *Explorer*, Radisson Seven Seas Cruises' *Hanseatic*, and Society Expeditions' *World Discoverer*. (For detailed itineraries, *see* Chapter 3.)

Now is a particularly good time to visit Antarctica, because there are still no limitations on tourists or cruise ships. Sentiment is building, however, to restrict visitors. Some environmentalists want to ban them entirely. Still, many scientists and ecologists are delighted that cruise passengers want to see Antarctica, because passengers return home among the most ardent supporters and lobbyists for protecting and preserving this as yet unspoiled continent.

Cruising to Antarctica requires a certain temperament and a moderate level of physical fitness. It involves a small degree of inconvenience, discomfort, and even risk. Ships leaving from South America must navigate the Drake Passage, one of the roughest stretches of ocean in the world. Because there are no landing wharfs or tour buses on the continent, getting from the ship to land means bundling up in bulky jackets and life preservers, climbing into small rubberized craft called Zodiacs, maneuvering in as close to the shore as possible, and, quite often, wading through the shallow surf. Then the only way to get inland to the research stations or penguin rookeries is by walking up rocky beaches or uneven ice surfaces. While all ships carry doctors and nurses, the nearest hospital is several thousand miles away.

Since the weather conditions in Antarctica are so unpredictable, itineraries are extremely flexible and are more commonly subject to last-minute changes. Heavy seas may prevent your ship from landing at a particular research station, and floating ice may cut a half-day tour down to an hour-long stop.

Catching your ship entails flying great distances to ports in either South America, New Zealand, or Australia. Flights are expensive and often arduous; it can take more than 24 hours to get to your initial departure point. For a cruise to the Antarctic Peninsula, you must fly first to either Santiago, Chile, or Buenos Aires, Argentina, and you'll usually be put up in a hotel overnight. The next day, you'll fly to Ushuaia on Tierra del Fuego or, less often, Port Stanley in the Falkland Islands, to meet your ship. If your cruise leaves from Christchurch, New Zealand, or Hobart in Tasmania, Australia, your route to the ship will be more direct, if no less time consuming.

When to Go   Cruise ships visit Antarctica only from early December to February—the austral summer. The best time is between mid-December and mid-January, when the weather is mildest and the wildlife most active.

What to Bring Packing for Antarctica is quite different from preparing for any other cruise. Forget about elegance and formality, although you may wish to take a sports jacket and tie or a simple all-purpose dress for the captain's informal get-together.

The most common mistake in packing for an Antarctic cruise is bringing gear designed for subzero temperatures. While it gets as cold as $-100°$F in the dead of winter (July and August), the median coastal temperatures in December and January average 35°F–55°F. The cruise lines supply recommended packing lists, as well as the bulky red parka that will provide your primary protection. Waterproof pullover pants and waterproof boots at least 12 inches high are necessities (check if your line provides these or if you must supply their own). You'll also want a good pair of binoculars, a 35mm camera with telephoto and wide-angle lenses, and lots of color film—remember, it's illegal to take a single stone, bone, feather, or artifact as a souvenir.

It's a nice idea to bring small gifts for the scientists and other workers in the research stations: recent magazines, books, candy, and fresh fruit.

Currency Since there are practically no stores or shops in Antarctica, you won't need much money here. Some of the research stations sell sweatshirts and T-shirts with Antarctica logos, decorative patches that can be sewn or ironed onto your parka, and postcards with Antarctic postmarks that you can mail to friends or relatives (the mail goes out with your ship and can take days, weeks, or months to be delivered). You can pay for these in U.S. dollars. In some places the merchandise is available only to station personnel, who will sometimes barter with you for books, magazines, and patches.

Passports and Visas No one visiting or living in Antarctica needs any kind of documents, but to get there, you will have to fly through Argentina, Chile, Australia, or New Zealand, all of which require passports and visas from U.S., Canadian, and British citizens.

Shore Excursions The only stops in Antarctica are at the research stations of various nations, historic huts built by explorers from the heroic era early in the century, and the penguin and seal rookeries and other places of interest to naturalists. Weather conditions as well as the needs and wishes of the research station personnel will dictate your itinerary.

Research Stations If you do visit a research station, you may or may not be invited into the common room, may or may not be able to buy a souvenir postcard or patch, and may or may not meet with scientists who speak English. Also, because of the dramatic increase in tourists, many stations have cut back, not only on the number of cruise ships permitted to visit, but on the areas open to visitors.

If you come from South America, you'll explore the area known as the Antarctic Peninsula, home to **Palmer Station,** a U.S. base with a PX; **Gonzalez Videla Station,** or **Esperanza;** and the nine bases on King George Island, including the Polish **Arctowski.** Your ship may also stop at **Deception Island, Nelson Island,** the **South Georgia Islands,** or the **South Orkney Islands.** Some adventure ships stop at the **Falkland Islands,** one of the most remote and forbidding inhabited places on earth. Argentina calls these islands the Malvenas and went to war with Britain in 1982 in an unsuccessful attempt to seize sovereignty; who owns them is still a hot issue in this part of the world. You may visit **Port Stanley,** the Falklands' picturesque capital, which seems like a transplanted northern Scotland village; or **New Island,** a 5-square-mile rock that is home to several species of penguin and albatross.

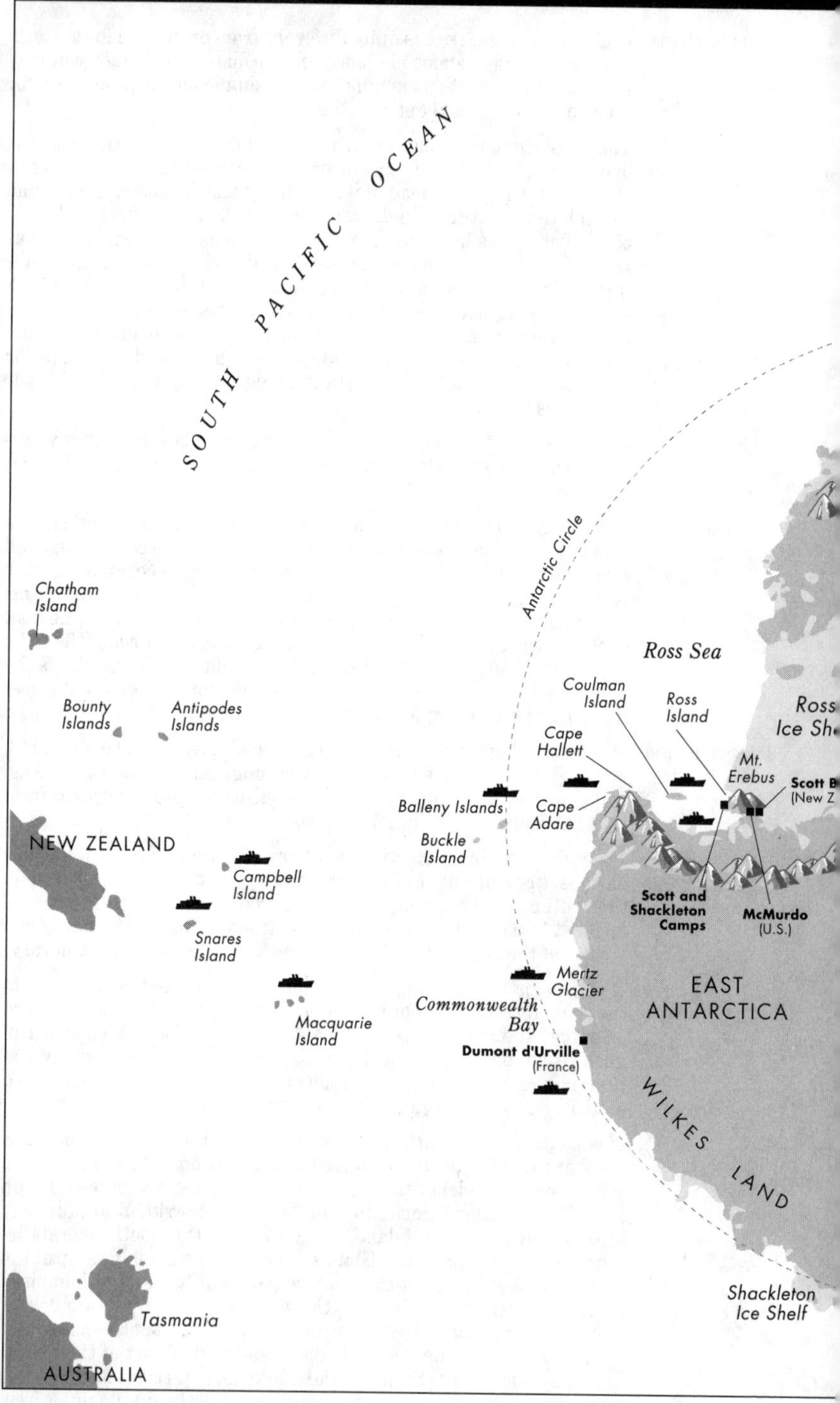

SOUTH PACIFIC OCEAN

Antarctic Circle

Ross Sea

Chatham Island

Bounty Islands

Antipodes Islands

Coulman Island

Ross Island

Ross Ice Sh

Cape Hallett

Mt. Erebus

Scott B (New Z

Balleny Islands

Cape Adare

NEW ZEALAND

Buckle Island

Campbell Island

Scott and Shackleton Camps

McMurdo (U.S.)

Snares Island

Mertz Glacier

EAST ANTARCTICA

Commonwealth Bay

Macquarie Island

Dumont d'Urville (France)

WILKES LAND

Tasmania

AUSTRALIA

Shackleton Ice Shelf

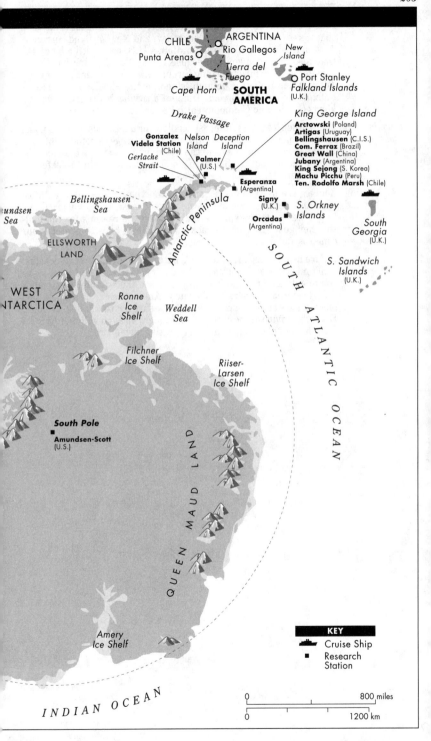

CHILE
Punta Arenas
ARGENTINA
Rio Gallegos
New Island
Tierra del Fuego
SOUTH AMERICA
Cape Horn
O Port Stanley
Falkland Islands (U.K.)

Drake Passage

King George Island
Arctowski (Poland)
Artigas (Uruguay)
Bellingshausen (C.I.S.)
Com. Ferraz (Brazil)
Great Wall (China)
Jubany (Argentina)
King Sejong (S. Korea)
Machu Picchu (Peru)
Ten. Rodolfo Marsh (Chile)

Gonzalez Videla Station (Chile)
Nelson Island *Deception Island*
Gerlache Strait
Palmer (U.S.)

Esperanza (Argentina)

Signy (U.K.)
Orcadas (Argentina)
S. Orkney Islands

South Georgia (U.K.)

Bellingshausen Sea

Antarctic Peninsula

ELLSWORTH LAND

...undsen Sea

WEST ANTARCTICA

Ronne Ice Shelf

Weddell Sea

Filchner Ice Shelf

Riiser-Larsen Ice Shelf

SOUTH ATLANTIC OCEAN

S. Sandwich Islands (U.K.)

South Pole
Amundsen-Scott (U.S.)

QUEEN MAUD LAND

Amery Ice Shelf

KEY
🚢 Cruise Ship
■ Research Station

INDIAN OCEAN

0   800 miles
0   1200 km

Those traveling from Australia or New Zealand cruise to the Ross Sea. Here is New Zealand's **Scott Base,** which has a souvenir shop that takes credit cards, U.S. currency, and New Zealand currency. Also in this area is **McMurdo Station,** a U.S. base with a Navy PX that also sells souvenirs (because it's a PX, the merchandise is cheaper here). Ships traveling through these waters may visit **Cape Adare, Cape Hallett, Coulman Island,** or the **Shackelton and Scott huts,** as well as **Mt. Erebus. Dumont d'Urville,** a French base, and **Mertz Glacier** and **Commonwealth Bay** are less-visited stops.

Penguins and Other Wildlife You will see lots of wildlife, especially penguins, seals, sea lions, and birds. Whales are less plentiful, but there are occasional sightings. Unlike in most other parts of the world, wild creatures here have no fear of people, but it's illegal to get closer than within 15–30 feet of the animals.

Getting Around Zodiacs are used to get ashore and to explore bays filled with ice floes and icebergs. Sitting on the edge of these craft, you are likely to get wet from the spray—that's one of the reasons for the foul-weather gear. Be sure to pack plastic Ziploc bags to protect your cameras and film.

Before heading ashore, the ship's naturalists give orientation talks. Don't miss these: You'll learn where it is safe to walk and what areas you should avoid, as well as where to see the wildlife. Remember that, despite its unparalleled beauty, Antarctica can be a dangerous place. There are no marked trails, so be sure not to wander off alone. Heed the advice of the naturalists, though, and you will find Antarctic to be a safe, exciting, and invigorating adventure.

The Bahamas

The Bahamas is an archipelago of more than 700 islands that begins in the Atlantic Ocean off the coast of Florida and stretches in a great southeasterly arc for more than 750 miles to the Caribbean Sea. Each island is bordered by soft, white-sand beaches lined with whispering casuarinas and swaying palms. Offshore, the islands are fringed by coral reefs and surrounded by a palette of blue and green waters of unbelievable clarity.

Fewer than 250,000 people live in the Bahamas, most of them in the two major urban resort centers of Nassau and Freeport. The Bahamas are one of cruising's most popular destinations. Three- and four-day cruises from Florida to Nassau and Freeport are a big hit among young and budget-conscious travelers. Many cruise lines also include a port call in the Bahamas as part of a longer sailing, sometimes for a beach party or barbecue at one of several isolated Bahamian islands. For some passengers, these excursions are the highlight of a cruise. One of the best such destinations is Blue Lagoon Island (also called Sale Cay). It is used by Dolphin Cruise and Premier Cruise Lines. (For detailed itineraries, *see* Chapter 3.)

A cruise to the Bahamas is ideal for first-time cruisers, shopping fanatics, beach bums, and party goers. You can sail and scuba dive all day, and if your ship ties up overnight, gamble and dance well into the evening. But don't expect an unspoiled paradise: Nassau and Freeport/Lucaya are crowded and far less scenic than most Caribbean islands.

When to Go Winter, from mid-December through April, is the traditional high season. However, Bahamas cruises are offered all year, and the weather remains consistently mild, in the 70s and 80s. The Goombay Summer, from June through August, is filled with social, cultural, and sporting events. June through October is the rainy season, and humidity is high.

Currency The Bahamian dollar is held at a par with the U.S. dollar, and the two currencies are used interchangeably. Be sure to request U.S. dollars and coins when you receive change, however. Traveler's checks and major credit cards are accepted by most fine restaurants and stores.

Passports and Visas U.S., Canadian, and British citizens do not need passports or visas if they have proof of citizenship; however, a passport is preferable.

Telephones and Mail Long-distance credit-card and collect calls can be made from most public phones. Airmail rates to the United States and Canada are 55¢ for first-class letters and 40¢ for postcards.

Shore Excursions Many ships offer excursions to a casino for round-the-clock gaming action, plus bars, restaurants, and entertainment, including elaborate floor shows and topless revues. Some ships stay overnight in Freeport or Nassau.

In addition, many ships offer shopping excursions. Both Freeport and Nassau have a host of malls and stores (*see below*). Water sports are a major draw, and most ships offer snorkeling or boat trips to outlying islands, as well as fishing.

Shopping Duty-free bargains in the Bahamas include imported china, crystal, leather, electronics, sweaters, liquor, watches, and perfume. Figure a 25% savings on most goods, and a 35%–60% savings on liquor. Though no store will deliver to your ship, most shopping is within a 10-minute walk of the pier. Most stores are open Monday–Saturday 9–5; some close at noon on Thursday.

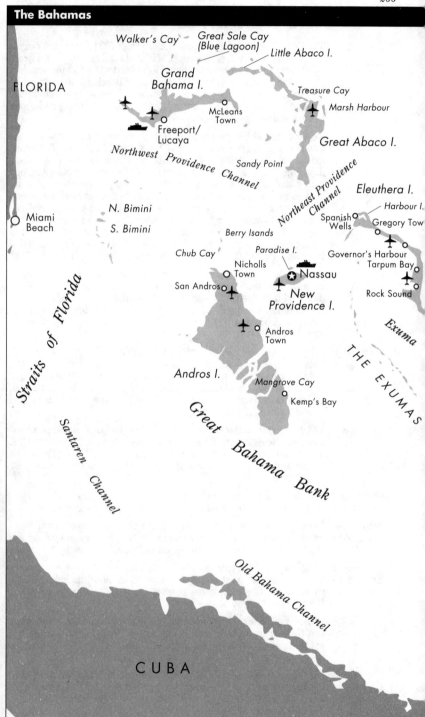

The Bahamas

Walker's Cay

Great Sale Cay
(Blue Lagoon)

Little Abaco I.

FLORIDA

Grand
Bahama I.

Treasure Cay

Marsh Harbour

McLeans
Town

Freeport/
Lucaya

Great Abaco I.

Northwest Providence Channel

Sandy Point

Northeast Providence Channel

Eleuthera I.

Harbour I.

Spanish
Wells

Gregory Tow

Miami
Beach

N. Bimini

S. Bimini

Berry Isands

Paradise I.

Governor's Harbour

Chub Cay

Nicholls
Town

Nassau

Tarpum Bay

San Andros

New
Providence I.

Rock Sound

Straits of Florida

Andros
Town

Exuma

THE EXUMAS

Andros I.

Mangrove Cay

Kemp's Bay

Great Bahama Bank

Santaren Channel

Old Bahama Channel

CUBA

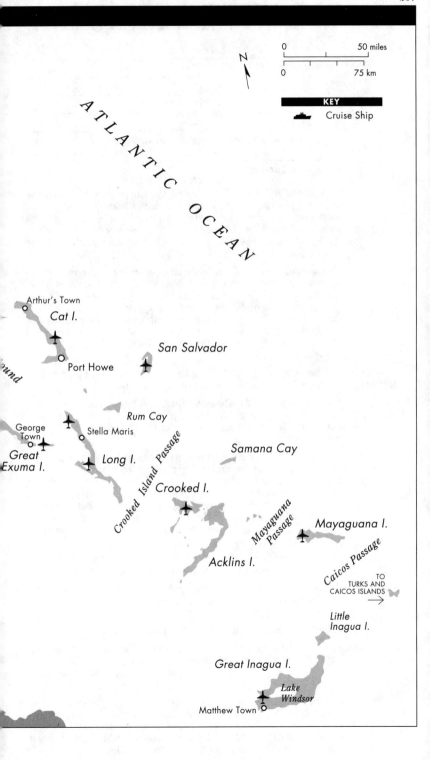

Dining Most Bahamian restaurants have adopted the European custom of adding a service charge to your bill—usually 15%, sometimes as little as 10%.

Category	Cost*
$$$	over $30
$$	$20–$30
$	under $20

per person for a three-course meal, excluding drinks and service

Freeport/Lucaya

Freeport is on Grand Bahama Island, the fourth largest island in the archipelago. Its 530-square-mile interior is heavily forested with palmetto, casuarina, and Caribbean pines. The 96-mile southern coastline is made up of sheltered harbors bordered by miles of unspoiled white-sand beaches and fringed with a nearly unbroken line of spectacular reefs.

Virtually unknown and unpopulated a generation ago, Grand Bahama was developed in the early 1950s. Modern, well-planned Freeport is the centerpiece of Grand Bahama. Its boulevards and shops are linked by a palm-lined road to Lucaya, a suburb set among thousands of acres of tropical greenery that sprawls along canals and ocean beach. Scattered here and there are hotels, the International Bazaar, four golf courses, two casinos, and Port Lucaya, the new shopping mall/tourist area.

Shore Excursion The following is a good choice in Freeport. It may not be offered by all cruise lines. Time and price are approximate.

Freeport Shopping & Sightseeing Tour. This bus trip covers about 26 miles round-trip, stopping along the way for a half hour at the Garden of the Groves and for shopping at the International Bazaar. *3 hrs. Cost: $12.*

Coming Ashore The cruise-ship harbor is an industrial center in the middle of nowhere. A cab from the cruise-ship piers to downtown costs $10 for two passengers. A Bahamas Ministry of Tourism office is at the port, but depending on where your ship is berthed, it may be a short walk across the parking lot or a long hike. You'll also find a Ministry of Tourism Information Center at the International Bazaar on West Sunrise Highway. Pick up maps, brochures, and information from either office.

Getting Around Everything in Freeport/Lucaya is far apart, so you need to sign up for a shore excursion, take a cab, or rent a car or moped.

By Bus Buses serve downtown Freeport and Lucaya; the fare is about 75¢. Service between Freeport and Lucaya costs $1.

By Car Car rentals average $48–$85 daily, and a significant deposit is required. In Lucaya, contact **Avis** (tel. 809/373–1102).

By Bicycle, Moped, or Scooter Rental mopeds and bicycles are available dockside in Freeport. Rates for bicycles start at about $10 per day, with a $50 deposit; scooters cost $40 per day with a $50–$100 deposit. Helmets are mandatory.

By Taxi Metered taxis meet all the incoming cruise ships. Rates are $2 for the first ¼ mile and 30¢ for each additional ¼ mile. A taxi tour costs $12–$18 an hour, but rates for longer trips are negotiable. Always settle the fare in advance. Taxis are also available in most major tourist areas. Try **Freeport Taxi** (tel. 809/352–6666).

Exploring Freeport/ Lucaya

Numbers in the margin correspond to points of interest on the Freeport/Lucaya map.

You will enjoy driving or riding around Freeport/Lucaya as long as you remember to drive on the left. Broad, landscaped "dual carriageways"—British for highways—and tree-lined streets wind through parks, past lovely homes, and along lush green fairways.

1 **Churchill Square** and the Freeport town center is where residents shop and tend to business. If you're hungry, **Mum's Coffee Shop and Bakery,** at 7 Yellow Pine Street, has delicious homemade breads, soups, and sandwiches. Head north on the Mall to Settler's Way **2** East, then turn right and follow the tree-lined highway to the **Rand Memorial Nature Center.** The 100-acre park, composed of natural woodland, preserves more than 400 indigenous varieties of subtropical plants, trees, and flowers. It is also a sanctuary for thousands of native and migratory birds. A mile of well-marked nature trails leads to a 30-foot waterfall. Guided walks are conducted by the resident naturalists.

Leaving the nature center, continue east on Settler's Way, then turn **3** south (right) onto West Beach Road to the **Garden of the Groves** (admission free; closed Wed.). The 11-acre park features some 5,000 varieties of rare and familiar subtropical and tropical trees, shrubs, plants, and flowers. Well-marked paths lead past clearly identified plants, a fern gully and grotto, and a tiny, stone interdenominational chapel.

From here, head for the sea, then turn right onto Royal Palm Way **4** and drive until you come to the **Underwater Explorers Society** (UNEXSO), the famous scuba-diving school of the Bahamas, which trains more than 2,500 divers annually. *Tel. 809/373–1244. Dive lesson and 1 dive $79; snorkeling trip including all equipment $15. Open daily 8–6.*

5 Within walking distance is **Lucayan Harbour,** with a 50-slip marina at which *El Galleon* is moored. This replica of a 16th-century Spanish galleon offers day and dinner cruises.

6 The **Dolphin Experience** at Sanctuary Bay is the world's largest dolphin sanctuary. A $25 ferry ride from the UNEXSO dive shop takes you there to see the dolphins and take pictures. For $59, you can wade into the waist-deep water and cavort with the dolphins for about 20 minutes.

Shopping

The **International Bazaar and Strawmarket** is on West Sunrise Highway, next to the Princess Casino. You enter through the 35-foot, red-lacquer Torii Gate, traditional symbol of welcome in Japan. Within the bazaar are a straw market and exotic shops with merchandise from around the world. Most items are priced at 20%–40% below U.S. *retail* prices, which means that you may or may not be getting a bargain when compared with prices in discount stores at home. Two dozen countries are represented in the 10-acre bazaar, with nearly a hundred shops. The vendors in the straw market expect you to haggle over the price, but don't bargain in the stores. For a less touristy experience, go to **Churchill Square** and the Freeport town center. An open-air produce market offers mangoes, papayas, and other fruit for snacking as you walk. To the east of Freeport is **Port Lucaya,** an attractive waterfront marketplace with 85 shops, boutiques, restaurants, and lounges. You'll need to drive or take a taxi to get here from downtown Freeport.

Sports
Diving

One of the most famous scuba schools and NAUI centers in the world is the **Underwater Explorers Society** (UNEXSO), adjacent to Port Lucaya (*see* Exploring Freeport/Lucaya, *above*). Beginners can learn to dive for $89, which includes three hours of professional instruction in the club's training pools, and a shallow reef dive. For experienced divers, there are three trips daily (tel. 809/373–1244 or

Freeport/Lucaya

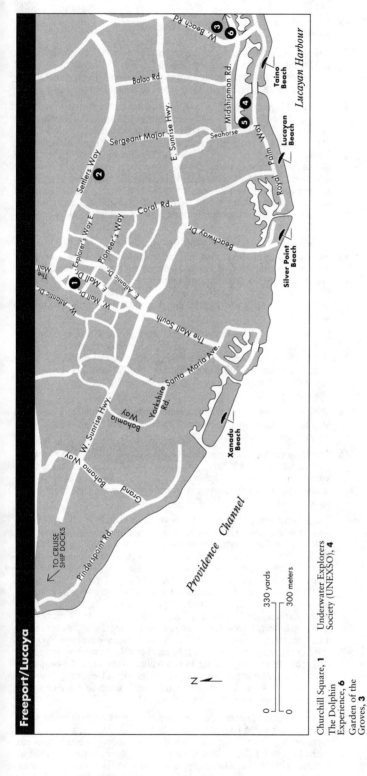

0 ——— 330 yards

0 ——— 300 meters

N

Providence Channel

Lucayan Harbour

TO CRUISE SHIP DOCKS

Pinderspoint Rd.

Grand Bahama Way

W. Sunrise Hwy.

Bahamia Way

Yorkshire Rd.

Santa Maria Ave.

The Mall South

W. Atlantic Dr.

E. Atlantic Dr.

The Mall

Explorer's Way E.

Pioneer's Way

W. Mall Dr.

E. Mall Dr.

Coral Rd.

Settlers Way

Sergeant Major

E. Sunrise Hwy.

Balao Rd.

W. Beach Rd.

Midshipman Rd.

Seahorse

Beachway Dr.

Royal

Palm

Way

Xanadu Beach

Silver Point Beach

Lucayan Beach

Taino Beach

Churchill Square, **1**

The Dolphin Experience, **6**

Garden of the Groves, **3**

Lucayan Harbor, **5**

Rand Memorial Nature Center, **2**

Underwater Explorers Society (UNEXSO), **4**

800/992–3483, or write to UNEXSO, Box F-2433, Freeport, Grand Bahama).

Fishing   Contact **Reef Tours** (tel. 809/373–5880). Boat charters cost $300 for a half day, $600 for a full day.

Golf   Grand Bahama's four championship 18-hole courses are among the best in the Caribbean: **Bahamas Princess Hotel & Golf Club** (2 courses, tel. 809/352–6721), **Fortune Hills Golf & Country Club** (tel. 809/373–4500), and **Lucayan Golf & Country Club** (tel. 809/373–1066). Fees are about $35 for nine holes.

Parasailing   Contact the **Clarion Atlantik Beach** (Royal Palm Way, tel. 809/373–
and   1444) or **Bahamas Sea Adventures** (at the Radisson Hotel, tel. 809/
Windsurfing   373–3923). Parasail rides cost $20–$25 for seven minutes. Windsurfing boards cost $10–$15 an hour; private lessons cost $25–$30.

Tennis   Cruise passengers are welcome at several hotels. Try **Xanadu Beach Resort** (3 clay courts, tel. 809/352–6782) and the **Lucayan Beach Resort & Casino** (4 courts, tel. 809/373–7777). Court time costs $5 an hour.

Beaches   The closest beach to the cruise-ship dock is **Xanadu Beach,** which has a mile of white-sand beach. South of Port Lucaya stretch three delightful beaches: **Fortune Beach, Smith's Point,** and **Taino Beach,** where sunbathers will also find the Stone Crab (tel. 809/373–1442)—a popular seafood restaurant.

Dining   **Pub on the Mall.** Opposite the International Bazaar, this splendid English pub has authentic atmosphere and decor. The Prince of Wales Lounge serves good fish-and-chips, and steak-and-kidney pie. Bass ale is on tap. Baron's Hall serves superb dinners at night—try the coquilles St. Jacques, Cornish game hen, or roast beef with Yorkshire pudding. *At Ranfurly Circus, tel. 809/352–5110. AE, MC, V. $$*
Pusser's Co. Store and Pub. Fashioned after an old Welsh pub, this amiable establishment overlooking Port Lucaya is part bar, part restaurant, and part maritime museum. It has a nautical decor with antique copper measuring cups and Tiffany lamps suspended from the wood-beam ceiling. Locals swap tall tales and island gossip with tourists over rum-based Pusser's Painkillers. Solid English fare is favored: shepherd's pie, fisherman's pie, steak-and-ale pie. *Port Lucaya Marketplace, tel. 809/373–8450. AE, MC, V. $*

Nassau

The 17th-century town of Nassau, the capital of the Bahamas, has witnessed Spanish invasions and hosted pirates, who made it their headquarters for raids along the Spanish Main. The new American navy seized Ft. Montagu here in 1776, when they won a victory without firing a shot.

The cultural and ethnic heritage of old Nassau includes the southern charm of British loyalists from the Carolinas, the African tribal traditions of freed slaves, and a bawdy history of blockade-running during the Civil War and rum-running in the Roaring Twenties. Over it all is a subtle layer of civility and sophistication, derived from three centuries of British rule.

Reminders of the island's British heritage are everywhere in Nassau. Court justices sport wigs and scarlet robes. The police wear colonial garb: starched white jackets, red-striped navy trousers, tropical pith helmets. Traffic keeps to the left, and the language has a British-colonial lilt, softened by a slight drawl.

New Providence Island's charm, however, is often lost in its commercialism. Downtown Nassau's colonial facade is barely visible, painted over with duty-free shop signs. Away from town, high-rise resorts and glittering casinos line the beaches. Lovely Old Nassau sold its soul to keep the tourists coming, and come they do in ever-increasing numbers.

Shore Excursions
The following are good choices in Nassau. They may not be offered by all cruise lines. Times and prices are approximate. Unless otherwise noted, children's prices are for those under 13.

Undersea Creatures
Coral World. A 100-foot observation tower soars above the landscape, but the real views are of turtles, stingrays, and starfish. Budget about three hours, but you can stay as long as you want—the ferry back to the cruise-ship docks leaves every half hour. *Cost: $21 adults, $15 children ($24 and $18 with ferry transfers).*

Snorkeling Adventure. The Bahamas is an underwater wonderland. On this tour you can learn to snorkel, then join an escorted tour or set off on your own. *2½–3 hrs. Cost: $20–$25.*

Coming Ashore
Cruise ships dock at one of three piers on Prince George's Wharf. Taxi drivers who meet the ships may offer you a $2 ride into town, but the historic government buildings and duty-free shops lie just outside the dock area. The one- or two-block walk takes five to 10 minutes. As you leave the pier, look for a tall pink tower: Diagonally across from here is the tourist information office. Stop in for maps of the island and downtown Nassau. You can join a free one-hour walking tour conducted by well-trained guides on most days. Outside the office, an ATM dispenses U.S. dollars.

Getting Around
By Bus
Jitney service runs to most points on the island. Walk from the pier to Frederick Street between Bay Street and Woodes Rogers Walk to catch a bus. The fare is 75¢ and buses run until 8:30 PM.

By Carriage
Across from the docks, along Rawson Square, are surreys drawn by straw-hatted horses that will take you through the old city and past some of the nearby historic sites. The cost is $10 for two for 25 minutes, but verify prices before getting on.

By Car
Car-rental rates begin at $50 a day; a substantial deposit is required. **Hertz** (tel. 809/327–6866) has an office in downtown Nassau.

By Ferry
A ferry commutes between the dock area and Paradise Island ($2 round-trip). Another goes to Coral World ($3 round-trip).

By Scooter
Scooters may be rented as you exit Prince George's Wharf. Rates average $25 per half day, $40 per full day. Helmets are mandatory.

By Touring Car or Taxi
As you disembark from your ship you will find a row of taxis and luxurious air-conditioned limousines. The latter are Nassau's fleet of tour cars, useful and comfortable for a guided tour of the island. Taxi fares are fixed at $2 for the first ¼ mile, 30¢ each additional ¼ mile. Sightseeing tours cost about $20–$25 per hour.

Exploring Nassau
Numbers in the margin correspond to points of interest on the Nassau map.

❶❷ As you leave the cruise wharf, you enter **Rawson Square.** Directly across Bay Street is **Parliament Square.** Dating from the early 1800s and patterned after southern U.S. colonial architecture, this cluster of yellow colonnaded buildings with green shutters is striking. In the center of the square is a statue of the young Queen Victoria, and the **Bahamas House of Parliament.**

❸ At the head of Elizabeth Avenue is the **Queen's Staircase,** a famous Nassau landmark. Its 66 steps, hewn from the coral limestone cliff by slaves in the late 18th century, were designed to provide a direct route between town and **Ft. Fincastle** at the top of the hill. The staircase was named more than a hundred years later, in honor of the 66 years of Queen Victoria's reign.

❹ Climb the staircase to reach **Ft. Fincastle.** The fort, shaped like the bow of a ship, was built in 1793. It never fired a shot in anger but

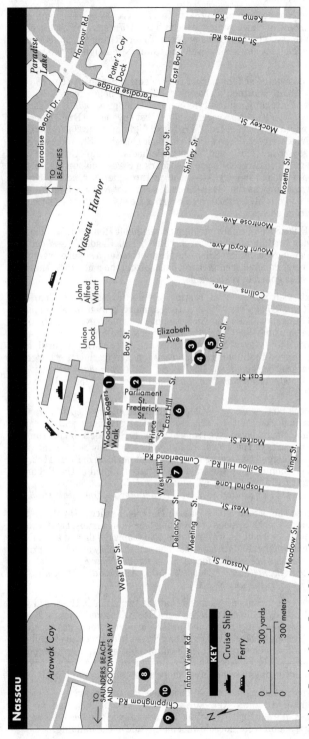

Nassau

273

Ardastra Gardens, **9**
Ft. Charlotte, **8**
Ft. Fincastle, **4**
Graycliff, **7**
Gregory Arch, **6**
Nassau Botanic Gardens, **10**
Parliament Square, **2**
Queen's Staircase, **3**
Rawson Square, **1**
Water Tower, **5**

served as a lookout and signal tower. For a really spectacular view of the island of New Providence, climb the 225 steps (or ride the elevator) to the top of the nearby **Water Tower.** Rising to 126 feet, more than 200 feet above sea level, the tower is the highest point on the island.

Head back toward the harbor to Parliament Street. At No. 48 you'll find **Green Shutters,** a charming Bahamian house from 1865, converted into an English-style pub (*see* Dining, *below*). On East Hill Street, you'll see historic mansions. Just beyond the **Bank House,** on the north side of the street, is a broad flight of stairs that leads down to Prince Street. Here are two historic churches, **St. Andrew's Kirk, Presbyterian** (1810) and **Trinity Methodist** (1866). Continue west along Prince Street. As you pass Market Street look up the hill for a good view of **Gregory Arch,** the picturesque entrance to **Grant's Town.** Known as the "over-the-hill" section of Nassau, Grant's Town was laid out in the 1820s by Governor Lewis Grant as a settlement for freed slaves.

On Duke Street, follow the high Government House wall around the corner to Baillou (pronounced "blue") Hill Road. Take West Hill Street; across Baillou Hill is the **Graycliff** hotel, a superb example of Georgian colonial architecture, dating from the mid-1700s, that now houses a gourmet restaurant.

Next, visit the most interesting fort on the island, **Ft. Charlotte,** built in 1787 replete with a waterless moat, drawbridge, ramparts, and dungeons. Like Ft. Fincastle, no shots were ever fired in anger from this fort. Ft. Charlotte is located at the top of a hill and commands a fine view of Nassau Harbor and Arawak Cay, a small, manmade island that holds huge storage tanks of fresh water barged in from Andros Island. *Off W. Bay St. at Chippingham Rd., tel. 809/ 322-7500. Admission free. Local guides conduct tours Mon.–Sat. 8:30–4.*

A block farther west, on Chippingham Road, are the **Ardastra Gardens and Zoo,** with 5 acres of tropical greenery and flowering shrubs, an aviary of rare tropical birds, and exotic animals from different parts of the world. The gardens are renowned for the pink, spindly legged, marching flamingos that perform daily at 11, 2, and 4. The flamingo, by the way, is the national bird of the Bahamas. *Near Ft. Charlotte, off Chippingham Rd., tel. 809/323–5806. Admission: $7.50 adults, $3.75 children under 10. Open daily 9–5.*

Across the street is the **Nassau Botanic Gardens.** On its 18-acre grounds are 600 species of flowering trees and shrubs; two freshwater ponds with lilies, water plants, and tropical fish; and a small cactus garden that ends in a grotto. The many trails wandering through the gardens are perfect for leisurely strolls. *Near Ft. Charlotte, off Chippingham Rd., tel. 809/323–5975. Admission: $1 adults, 50¢ children. Open daily 8–4:30.*

Shopping *Forbes* magazine once claimed that the two cities in the world with the best buys on wristwatches were Hong Kong and Nassau. Most of the stores selling these and other duty-free items are clustered along an eight-block stretch of Bay Street in old Nassau or spill over onto a few side streets downtown. Most stores are open Monday–Saturday 9–5; some close at noon on Thursday. The straw market is open seven days a week. Most shops accept major credit cards.

If you're interested in old-fashioned maps and prints, seek out **Balmain Antiques** (tel. 809/323–7421). Though located on Bay Street, it's a little hard to find: The doorway to the second-floor gallery is set off from the sidewalk on the side of the building.

Sports Contact **Chubasco Charters** (tel. 809/322–8148) or **Brown's Charters**
Fishing (tel. 809/324–1215). Boat charters cost $300 for a half day, $600 for a full day.

Golf Three excellent 18-hole championship courses are open to the public: **Crystal Palace Golf Course** (opposite the Wyndham Ambassador Hotel, tel. 809/327–6000, 800/222–7466 in the United States), **Paradise Island Golf Club** (eastern end of Paradise Island, tel. 809/363–3925, 800/321–3000 in the United States), and **South Ocean Beach & Golf Resort** (adjacent to Divi Bahamas Beach Resort, tel. 809/362–4391). Fees are $45–$70 for 18 holes, $22–$27 for nine holes.

Parasailing and Windsurfing Windsurfing is available at **Le Meridien Royal Bahamian Hotel** (tel. 809/327–6400). Board rental costs $12 an hour, lessons cost $30. Parasailing is available from **Sea Sports Ltd.** (in front of the Nassau Beach Hotel, tel. 809/327–6058). A six-minute ride costs $30.

Beaches **Paradise Beach,** the Bahamas' most famous beach, stretches for more than a mile on the western end of Paradise Island. The $3 admission includes a welcome drink, towels, and use of changing rooms and locker. The **Western Esplanade** sweeps westward from the British Colonial Hotel on Bay Street (a 10-minute walk from the cruise-ship pier). It's just across the street from shops and restaurants, and has rest rooms, a snack bar, and changing facilities. A little farther west, just past the bridge that leads to Coral World, is **Saunders Beach. Goodman's Bay,** a bit farther west of Saunders, is popular with Bahamians for picnics and cookouts on weekends and holidays.

Dining **Graycliff.** Situated in a magnificent, 200-year-old colonial mansion, Graycliff is filled with antiques and English country-house charm. The outstanding Continental and Bahamian menu includes beluga caviar, grouper *au poivre vert*, and chateaubriand, with elegant pastries and flaming coffees for dessert. The wine cellar is excellent. *West Hill St., across from Government House, tel. 809/322–2796 or 800/633–7411. Reservations required. Jacket required. AE, DC, MC, V. $$$*

Green Shutters. Shades of Fleet Street! This very British pub is a cozy place awash with wood paneling. Steak-and-kidney pie, bangers and mash, and shepherd's pie are featured alongside such island favorites as cracked conch and Bahamian crawfish tail. *48 Parliament St., tel. 809/325–5702. Reservations advised. AE, MC, V. $$*

Poop Deck. Coiled rope wraps around beams, life preservers hang on the walls, and port and starboard lights adorn the newel posts of this favorite haunt of Nassau residents. Tables overlook the harbor and Paradise Island. Cuisine is exceptional Bahamian-style seafood, served in a festive, friendly atmosphere. The food is spicy, the wine list extensive. Save room for guava duff, a warm guava-layered local dessert, and a Calypso coffee, spiked with secret ingredients. *E. Bay St. (an 8-min cab ride from the pier), tel. 809/393–8175. Reservations are advised for outside tables. AE, DC, MC, V. $$*

Shoal Restaurant and Lounge. Saturday mornings at 9 you'll find hordes of jolly Bahamians digging into boiled fish and johnnycake, the marvelous specialty of the house. A bowl of this peppery dish, filled with chunks of boiled potatoes, onions, and grouper, keep the locals coming back to this dimly lit, basic, and off-the-tourist-beat "ma's kitchen," where standard Nassau dishes, including peas 'n' rice and cracked conch, are served. If it suits you, you'll find native mutton here, too, which is sometimes hard to find. *Nassau St., tel. 809/323–4400. No reservations. AE. $*

Nightlife Some ships stay late into the night or until the next day so that passengers can enjoy Nassau's nightlife. You'll find nonstop entertainment nightly along Cable Beach and on Paradise Island. All the larger hotels offer lounges with island combos for listening or dancing, and restaurants with soft guitar or piano background music.

Casinos The three casinos on New Providence Island—**Crystal Palace Casino, Paradise Island Resort and Casino,** and **Ramada Inn Casino**—open early in the day, remain active into the wee hours of the morning, and offer Continental gambling and a variety of other entertainment. Visitors must be 18 or older to enter a casino, 21 or older to gamble.

Discos **Club Waterloo** (tel. 809/393–7324), on East Bay Street, is one of Nassau's most swinging nightspots. Disco and rock can be heard nightly at **Club Pastiche** (tel. 809/363–3000), at the Paradise Island Resort and Casino.

Local The **Drum Beat Club** (tel. 809/322–4233) on West Bay Street, just up
Entertainment from the Best Western British Colonial Hotel, features the legendary Peanuts Taylor, still alive and well and beating away at those tom-toms; his band and gyrating dancers put on two shows nightly at 8:30 and 10:30.

Bermuda

Blessed with fabulous beaches and surrounded by a turquoise sea, Britain's oldest colony and most famous resort island lies isolated in the Atlantic Ocean, more than 500 miles from Cape Hatteras, North Carolina, the nearest point on the U.S. mainland. Although it looks like one island, Bermuda actually consists of about 150 islands—the six largest connected by bridges and causeways—all arranged in the shape of a giant fishhook. Bermuda, which is 21 square miles, is never more than a mile wide. The islands are surrounded by coral reefs that offer not only protection from Atlantic storms but wonderful scuba diving as well.

Bermuda's residents are known as "onions"—after the sweet, succulent Bermuda onion that was their livelihood a century ago. Their homes are studies in color—pink and yellow, lime and turquoise—all topped with stepped white roofs that funnel rainwater into cisterns. (The islands have no freshwater supply of their own.)

Bermuda was stumbled upon accidentally by Spaniard Juan de Bermudez in 1503. In 1609 the British ship *Sea Venture*, commanded by Sir George Somers and on its way to Jamestown, Virginia, struck one of the reefs that surround the islands. Some of the shipwrecked colonists stayed to build a settlement. Bermuda has thrived ever since and is now home to nearly 60,000 residents.

In spite of its proximity to the American mainland, Bermuda has maintained a distinctly British visage. Cricket and pubs, for instance, are very much a part of Bermudian life. Today, Bermudians are protective of their country, and change is not undertaken lightly. To avoid road congestion and air pollution, the number of cars is limited to one per residential household. There are no rental cars, so most visitors buzz around the island on mopeds or scooters. You can also take public transportation or hire a taxi.

Proper dress is stressed on Bermuda. Tourists in short shorts are frowned upon, and bathing suits are unacceptable away from the beach. Bare feet are not acceptable in public, nor is appearing without a shirt or in just a bathing-suit top.

Bermuda has long been a favorite destination of cruise passengers, and it is usually a cruise's only port of call. Most ships make seven-day loops from New York, with three days spent at sea and four days tied up in port. Three Bermuda harbors serve cruise ships: Hamilton (the capital), St. George's, and the Royal Naval Dockyard. Concerned about overcrowding, the Bermudian government limits the number of regular cruise-ship visits. Cruise lines with weekly sailings are Celebrity, Majesty, Norwegian Cruise Line, and Royal Caribbean. Lines that call occasionally include Crystal, Cunard, Holland America, and Silversea. (For detailed itineraries, *see* Chapter 3.)

When to Go The Bermuda cruise season runs from April through October, when temperatures are in the 70s and 80s. One or two ships sail here in November.

Currency The Bermuda dollar (BD$) is pegged on a par with the U.S. dollar, so there is no need to exchange currency. Most shops take credit cards, but a few hotels and restaurants do not. U.S. traveler's checks, however, are widely accepted. Ask for change in U.S. dollars and coins; all shopkeepers have them. All other currencies must be exchanged at banks for local tender.

Passports and Visas U.S. citizens need proof of citizenship. A passport is preferable, but a stamped birth certificate or voter registration card with photo ID are also acceptable. Canadian and British citizens need a valid passport.

Bermuda

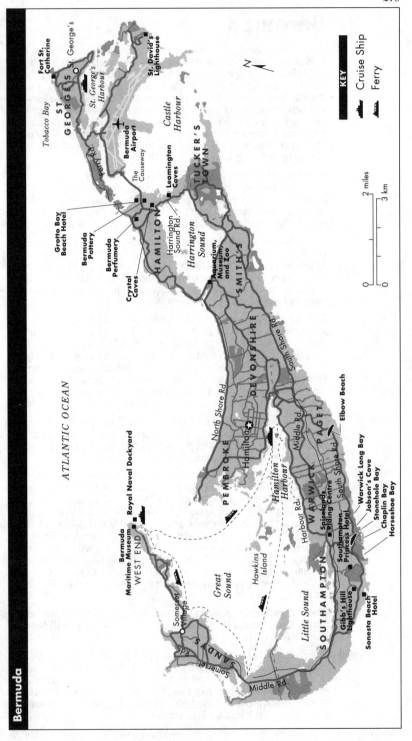

KEY
- Cruise Ship
- Ferry

ATLANTIC OCEAN

Royal Naval Dockyard

Bermuda Maritime Museum

WEST END

Great Sound

Hawkins Island

Little Sound

Somerset village

SANDYS

Somerset Rd.

Middle Rd.

Gibb's Hill Lighthouse

Sonesta Beach Hotel

SOUTHAMPTON

Southampton Princess Hotel

Spicelands Riding Centre

WARWICK

Warwick Long Bay

Jobson's Cove

Stonehole Bay

Chaplin Bay

Horseshoe Bay

South Shore Rd.

Harbour Rd.

PAGET

Elbow Beach

Middle Rd.

PEMBROKE

Hamilton

Hamilton Harbour

North Shore Rd.

South Shore Rd.

DEVONSHIRE

SMITH'S

Aquarium, Museum, and Zoo

Harrington Sound

HAMILTON

Harrington Sound Rd.

Crystal Caves

Bermuda Perfumery

Bermuda Pottery

Grotto Bay Beach Hotel

Leamington Caves

The Causeway

Bermuda Airport

TUCKER'S TOWN

Castle Harbour

ST. GEORGE'S

St. George's Harbour

Ferry Rd.

Tobacco Bay

Fort St. Catherine

St. George's

St. David's Lighthouse

2 miles

3 km

Reality check. Call home.

—— *AT&T USADirect® and World Connect.® The fast, easy way to call most anywhere.* ——

Take out AT&T Calling Card or your local calling card.** Lift phone. Dial AT&T Access Number for country you're calling from. Connect to English-speaking operator or voice prompt. Reach the States or over 200 countries. Talk. Say goodbye. Hang up. Resume vacation.

Anguilla.............................1-800-872-2881	French Antilles 19011
Antigua (Public Card Phones)....................#1	Grenada†. 1-800-872-2881
Bahamas.....................1-800-872-2881	**Haiti†■....................001-800-972-2883**
Barbados•••■...............1-800-872-2881	Jamaica††.......................0-800-872-2881
Bermuda†■.................1-800-872-2881	**Netherland Antilles...001-800-872-2881**
Bonaire 001-800-872-2881	St. Kitts/Nevis 1-800-872-2881
British V.I. 1-800-872-2881	St. Lucia ....Special USADirect Dedicated Locations
Cayman Islands 1-800-872-2881	St. Vincent •••..................1-800-872-2881
Dom. Rep.††■ 1-800-872-2881	**Trinidad&Tobago ..**Special USADirect Dedicated Locations
Dominica 1-800-872-2881	Turks & Caicos•••.............1-800-872-2881

AT&T
Your True Choice

**You can also call collect or use most U.S. local calling cards. Countries in bold face permit country-to-country calling in addition to calls to the U.S. World Connect® prices consist of USADirect® rates plus an additional charge based on the country you are calling. Collect calling available to the U.S. only. *Public phones require deposit of coin or phone card. † May not be available from every phone. †† Collect calling only. •••Only available from public phones. ■World Connect calls can only be placed *to* this country. ©1995 AT&T

For a free wallet sized card of all AT&T Access Numbers, call: 1-800-241-5555.

All the best trips start with **Fodor's**.

EXPLORING GUIDES

At last, the color of an art book combined with the usefulness of a complete guide.

"As stylish and attractive as any guide published." —*The New York Times*

"Worth reading before, during, and after a trip." —*The Philadelphia Inquirer*

More than 30 destinations available worldwide. $19.95 each.

BERKELEY GUIDES

The budget traveler's handbook

"Berkeley's scribes put the funk back in travel."
—*Time*

"Fresh, funny, and funky as well as useful."
—*The Boston Globe*

"Well-organized, clear and very easy to read."
—*America Online*

14 destinations worldwide. Priced between $13.00 - $19.50. ($17.95 - $27.00 Canada)

AFFORDABLES

"All the maps and itinerary ideas of Fodor's established gold guides with a bonus—shortcuts to savings." —*USA Today*

"Travelers with champagne tastes and beer budgets will welcome this series from Fodor's." —*Hartfort Courant*

"It's obvious these Fodor's folk have secrets we civilians don't." —*New York Daily News*

Also available: Florida, Europe, France, London, Paris. Priced between $11.00 - $18.00 ($14.50 - $24.00 Canada)

At bookstores, or call **1-800-533-6478**

Fodor's
The name that means smart travel.™

Telephones and Mail Calling home from Bermuda is as easy as from any city in the United States, and public phones can be found everywhere, including the docks. Federal Express can provide overnight package service to the United States. First-class airmail postage stamps are 60¢ for letters and postcards.

Shore Excursions The following are good choices in Bermuda. They may not be offered by all cruise lines. Times and prices are approximate.

Island Sights **St. George's Highlight Tour.** A quick overview of the area around St. George's includes Ft. St. Catherine, Ft. William, Gates Fort, the Unfinished Church, Somers Garden, Tobacco Bay, and the government housing complex. The guide is informative and will point out the popular shopping areas. *2 hrs. Cost: $60 (depending on where you are docked).*

West End Highlight Tour. Visit Island Pottery, the Bermuda Art Centre, the Crafts Market, Maritime Museum, Heydon Trust Chapel, and Gibb's Hill Lighthouse during a drive through Somerset. This tour is a must if you are docked in Hamilton or St. George's and won't go to the West End on your own. *4 hrs. Cost: $35 (depending on where you are docked).*

Undersea Creatures **Bermuda Glass-Bottom Boat Cruise.** A tame but pleasant cruise through the harbor and over reefs. You can feed the fish from the boat. *2 hrs. Cost: $30.*

Helmet Diving. Walk on the bottom of the sea, play with fish, and learn about coral, all without getting your hair wet. Helmets cover your head and feed you air from the surface. *3½ hrs. Cost: $44.*

Snorkeling Tour. Equipment, lessons, and an underwater guided tour are included. Underwater cameras are available for an extra charge. *3¾ hrs. Cost: $44.*

Coming Ashore Ships dock in Hamilton on Front Street, at the doorstep to the capital's prestigious shops. Passengers whose ships tie up at St. George's have an easy walk from either Ordnance Island or Penno's Wharf to Bermuda's equivalent of Colonial Williamsburg. The pier at the Royal Naval Dockyard, on the West End of the island, is within walking distance of the restored fortifications that now house the Maritime Museum, but you'll have to rent a moped or take public transportation to other sites of interest. Free ferry service is provided to and from Hamilton.

The Bermuda Department of Tourism maintains an information booth in the Hamilton cruise-ship terminal; on King's Square in St. George's; in Hamilton at 8 Front Street; and at the Royal Naval Dockyard in the West End.

Getting Around Buses are a good way to get around, although some stop running in the evening. A fare of $4 (exact change) will get you just about anywhere on the island. A three-day pass, which is ideal for cruise passengers, costs $15 and entitles you to unlimited use in all zones and ferry passage between Hamilton and the West End. This can be purchased at the central bus terminal next to City Hall on Washington Street in Hamilton. Bus stops are marked by green-and-white or pink-and-blue striped posts, and the pink-and-blue buses are easy to spot. Most operate about every 15–25 minutes, except on weekends.

By Carriage Horse-drawn carriages line up along Front Street in Hamilton, near the cruise-ship dock. A ride costs $20 per half hour.

By Ferry Ferry service between the West End and Hamilton costs $3.50 one way, and an extra $3.50 for a moped; the ride takes about 30 minutes. If your ship is tied up at the Royal Navy Dockyard, this crossing is free. Other ferries connect various points in Paget and Warwick for $2. Bicycles can be taken aboard for no charge, but mopeds and scooters are not allowed.

By Moped and Scooter Most visitors to Bermuda drive around on mopeds or scooters. However, be careful: The number of accidents is considerable. Mopeds can be rented all over the island at a daily rate of about $30. Riders are required to wear a strapped helmet. Most gas stations are open Monday–Saturday 7 AM–7 PM. A few remain open until 11 PM; some are also open on Sunday. Stop by a tourist information office to pick up a map for the Railway Trail, which is an especially fun ride.

By Taxi Taxis are plentiful and meet every ship. The blue flag signifies that the driver has passed a written examination to qualify as a guide. The drivers of these blue-flag taxis do not charge more than other taxi drivers. Meter rates are $2.60 for pickup plus 20¢ for each additional minute. A 25% surcharge is added between 10 PM and 6 AM. You can also hire a taxi by the hour. Rates are $30 per hour with a three-hour minimum for up to six passengers.

Exploring Hamilton *Numbers in the margin correspond to points of interest on the Hamilton map.*

❶ Begin your tour of Bermuda's capital at the **Birdcage,** where a policeman sometimes directs traffic. Turn right onto Queen Street. On

❷ your left is **Par-la-Ville Park,** once the private garden of William B. Perot, Bermuda's first postmaster and the creator of the famous 1848 Perot Stamp. His post office is still in operation here. The huge rubber tree was planted by Perot in 1847. In front of the park are the

❸ **Bermuda Public Library and Museum of the Bermuda Historical Society,** housed in what used to be Perot's home. *Admission to public library free. Open weekdays 9:30–6, Sat. 9:30–5. Museum admission free, donation suggested. Open Mon.–Sat. 9:30–12:30 and 1:30–4:30.*

Continue up Queen Street and turn right onto Church Street. The

❹ large building to the left is **City Hall,** a handsome modern structure with a traditional Bermudian feeling and a weather vane in the shape of the *Sea Venture.* The second-floor of the East Wing houses the **Bermuda National Gallery's** permanent displays. Works by the Old Masters as well as painters who visited Bermuda from the 19th to 20th centuries can be seen here. The second-floor of the West Wing is home to the **Bermuda Society of Arts Gallery,** with its changing exhibits of work by local artists in a range of media. City Hall is also home to a theater which hosts many Bermuda Festival events. *Admission to Bermuda National Gallery: $3 adults, children under 16 free. Open Mon.–Sat. 10–4, Sun. 12:30–4. Admission to Bermuda Society of Arts Gallery free, donation suggested. Open weekdays 10–4, Sat. 9–noon.*

❺ On the next block of Church Street is Bermuda's **Cathedral of the Most Holy Trinity,** the seat of the Anglican Church of Bermuda, which was consecrated in 1911. Commonly called the Bermuda Cathedral, it was built mainly from native limestone; decorative touches are of marble, granite, and English oak. *Open daily 8–4:45.*

❻ Turning right down Parliament Street you will see **Sessions House** on the left, its Italianate towers and colonnade decorated with red terra-cotta. In this building, the House of Assembly meets upstairs under the portraits of King George III and Queen Charlotte. The Speaker of the House, as well as the Supreme Court chief justice and barristers, all wear the traditional English wig and black robes. Climb up to the visitor galleries in the upper floors. *Admission free. Open weekdays 9–4:30.*

Walk back to Church Street and turn right onto it, then turn left onto King Street. Here you can walk or ride up (if you've rented a moped or scooter) the steep incline to Happy Valley Road, then con-

❼ tinue into **Ft. Hamilton** for a spectacular panoramic view of the city and harbor. Visitors approach the main gate over a moat—now dry and filled with exotic plants—which can be reached from the fort's

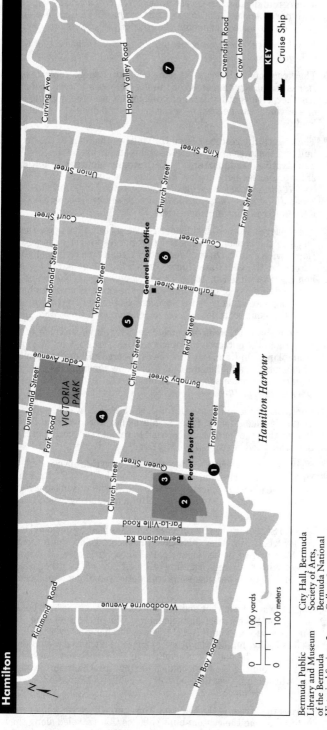

Hamilton

KEY

⚓ Cruise Ship

Richmond Road

Pitts Bay Road

Woodbourne Avenue

Bermudiana Rd.

Par-la-Ville Road

Church Street

Queen Street

VICTORIA PARK

Park Road

Dundonald Street

Cedar Avenue

Victoria Street

Church Street

Dundonald Street

Court Street

Union Street

Curving Ave.

Happy Valley Road

General Post Office

Parliament Street

Court Street

Church Street

King Street

Reid Street

Burnaby Street

Front Street

Front Street

Perot's Post Office

Cavendish Road

Crow Lane

Hamilton Harbour

N

0   100 yards

0   100 meters

Bermuda Public
Library and Museum
of the Bermuda
Historical Society, **3**

Birdcage, **1**

Cathedral of the
Most Holy Trinity, **5**

City Hall, Bermuda
Society of Arts,
Bermuda National
Gallery **4**

Ft. Hamilton, **7**

Par-la-Ville Park, **2**

Sessions House, **6**

underground galleries. On the upper level, now a grassy slope filled with park benches, the Royal Arms of Queen Victoria are emblazoned on the main armaments. *Admission free. Open daily 9–5.*

Exploring St. *Numbers in the margin correspond to points of interest on the St.*
George's *George's map.*

❶ The heart of St. George's is **King's Square,** where replicas of the **stocks and pillory** that stood on the site 300 years ago are on display. Another 17th-century form of punishment was the **ducking stool,** one of which can be seen near the cruise ship dock at Ordnance Island.

❷ The beautifully restored **Town Hall** follows the lines of the original building that was erected in 1782 and is still in use as the town's administrative headquarters. "The Bermuda Journey" multimedia show presented here depicts Bermuda's past and present. *Tel. 441/297–1642. Admission to Town Hall free. Open Mon.–Sat. 9–4. "Bermuda Journey" admission: $3 adults, $2 senior citizens, $1.75 children under 12. Call for show times.*

❸ Northeast of Town Hall is **Bridge House,** a circa 1700 home that belongs to the National Trust and now houses an art gallery. From there, walk east on Duke of York Street, then turn right on Princess
❹ Street for the **Old State House,** Bermuda's oldest surviving stone house, constructed in 1620. The first building on the island constructed entirely of native limestone, the State House was built in the Italianate style because Governor Butler believed Bermuda to be on the same latitude as Italy. *Admission free. Open Wed. 10–4.*

Heading back up Princess Street, you'll return to Duke of York
❺ Street and the entrance to **Somers Gardens,** created out of a former
❻ swampland. On Kent Street is the **St. George's Historical Society,** a museum set in a 1725 home that shows how Bermudians lived more than two centuries ago. *Admission: $1 adults, 50¢ children 6–16. Open weekdays 10–4.*

❼ Continue up the hill to the **Unfinished Church.** It was begun in 1874 as a replacement for St. Peter's Church, but work was abandoned in 1899 so that the funds could be used to rebuild the church in Hamilton, which had been destroyed by fire.

Walk west on Governor's Alley, turn left onto Clarence Street, then
❽ right onto Church Lane. Here is the churchyard of **St. Peter's,** the site of the oldest Anglican church in the Western Hemisphere, constructed in 1620. The tombstones offer a fascinating lesson in social history.

West of St. Peter's are two interesting lanes leading down to Duke of York Street. Silk Alley, also called Petticoat Lane, got its name in 1834 when two newly emancipated slave girls walked down the street with their new, rustling silk petticoats. The other is called Old Maid's Lane because some spinsters lived along here a century ago.

Head toward the harbor and you will come to Water Street, boasting
❾ one of the town's most historic homes. When the **President Henry Tucker House** was built in 1711, it was not hanging over the street, as it is today, but faced a broad expanse of lawn that went down to the harbor. The house was acquired in 1775 by Henry Tucker, who was president of the town council during the American Revolution and whose family was divided over the conflict. *Admission: $4. Open Mon.–Sat. 9:30–4:30.*

❿ Across the street is the **Carriage Museum,** where you can spend an hour admiring the custom-built vehicles that traveled along the island's roads before the automobile arrived in 1946. *Admission free, donation suggested. Open weekdays 10–5.*

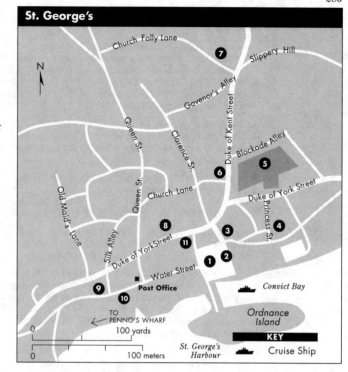

St. George's

Bridge House, **3**

Carriage Museum, **10**

Confederate Museum, **11**

King's Square, **1**

Old State House, **4**

President Henry Tucker House, **9**

St. George's Historical Society, **6**

St. Peter's, **8**

Somers Gardens, **5**

Town Hall, **2**

Unfinished Church, **7**

Church Folly Lane

Slippery Hill

Governor's Alley

Duke of Kent Street

Queen St.

Clarence St.

Blockade Alley

Old Maid's Lane

Queen St.

Church Lane

Duke of York Street

Silk Alley

Duke of York Street

Princess St.

Water Street

Post Office

Convict Bay

Ordnance Island

TO PENNO'S WHARF

100 yards

100 meters

St. George's Harbour

KEY

Cruise Ship

⓫ Back toward King's Square along Water Street is the post office. The pink structure on the corner of the block is the **Confederate Museum** and site of the old Globe Hotel. During the U.S. Civil War, this part of the island sided with the southern Confederates for economic reasons. The town of St. George became the focus of gunrunning between the southern United States and Europe. *Admission: $4. Open Mon.–Sat. 9:30–4:30.*

Exploring the West End Until the mid-1950s the West End was a working dockyard of the British Royal Navy. The area is now a shopping/sightseeing mini-village for tourists.

The **Maritime Museum,** in the inner fortifications of the Royal Naval Dockyard, is the most spectacular of the restored buildings. On the grounds are exhibits of Bermuda's seagoing history. A self-guided tour starts in the **Queen's Exhibition Hall,** originally built in 1850 to store gunpowder, and continues to the gun emplacements that surround the dockyard. Displays in the museum's several buildings include relics from Bermuda's famous shipwrecks. *Admission: $7.50 adults, $6 senior citizens, $3 children 4–12. Open daily 10–5.*

Across the street from the Maritime Museum, the old Cooperage now houses the **Neptune Cinema,** which shows first-run films from the United States and Europe, and the Frog & Onion pub (*see* Dining, *below*). *Admission: $7.*

The **Craft Market,** in the adjacent Bermuda Arts Centre, displays the work of local artisans. The Dockyard also has two nightclubs, branches of Hamilton-based stores, and stalls selling ice cream and pizza. In the nearby village of Somerset are more restaurants and branch shops of the main department stores in Hamilton.

Shopping There is no sales tax in Bermuda—the price you see is what you pay. This is a place to shop for luxury items, and topping the list of good buys are cashmere sweaters, bone china, Irish linens, Scottish tweeds, perfumes, and liquor. Local handicrafts include pottery and cedar ware.

Hamilton The majority of stores are located on Front Street and in the arcades of Reid Street. Bermuda's top department stores, all located on Front Street, Hamilton, are **H.A.&E. Smith's, A.S. Cooper, St. Michael's,** and **Trimingham's.** Each is a full-service department store, with good buys in cashmere and woolens. Smith's is arguably the best men's clothier in Bermuda.

Archie Brown & Son, on Front Street, carries affordably priced lambs-wool sweaters, while several outlets of the **English Sports Shop** stock some of Britain's finest woolens, particularly men's sports coats.

Fine jewelry and gems can be found at several locations of **Crisson's** and of **Astwood Dickinson.** The best for fine china is **Bluck's,** found on Front and Reid streets, Clocktower Mall at the Dockyard, and on Somers Wharf and Water Street in St. George's.

St. George's **Frangipani** is one of St. George's best shops, selling resort-style clothes. Just west on Water Street, opposite the post office, is **Taylor's,** which carries an array of British woolens.

Sports Fishing is excellent in Bermuda, with numerous boats going out
Fishing from just about every marina on the island. Do some comparison shopping at the tourist information booths. Or contact the **Bermuda Charter Fishing Boat Association** (tel. 441/292–6246), the **Bermuda Sport Fishing Association** (tel. 441/295–2370), or **St. George's Game Fishing & Cruising Association** (tel. 441/297–8093).

Golf Bermuda has seven golf courses open to cruise passengers. Among the best are the courses at the **Belmont Hotel** (Warwick, tel. 441/236–1301) and **Marriott's Castle Harbour Resort** (Tucker's Town, tel. 441/293–0795). Challenging links can also be found at the **Port Royal Golf Course** (Southampton, tel. 441/234–0972) and **St. George's Golf Course** (St. George's, tel. 441/297–8353). All are 18 holes. Greens fees range from $30 to $90.

Horseback The "breakfast rides" at the **Spicelands Riding Centre** (tel. 441/238–
Riding 8212), on Middle Road in Warwick, are an invigorating way to start a Bermuda day. Reservations are a must. Riders should wear sneakers or boots; hats are provided.

Tennis Visitors have access to more than 60 courts island-wide. Hourly rates for nonguests are about $10–$20 per hour; tennis balls are quite expensive. The best courts are found at the **Southampton Princess Hotel** (Southampton, tel. 441/238–1005), the **Belmont Hotel** (Warwick, tel. 441/236–1301), the **Elbow Beach Hotel** (Paget, tel. 441/236–3535), and the **Sonesta Beach Hotel** (Southampton, tel. 441/238–8122).

Water Sports Bermuda's clear waters are perfect for scuba diving, helmet diving, and snorkeling. Check at the tourist information booths about which operators are offering dives and snorkel tours. Excellent programs are offered by **Nautilus Diving** (at the Southampton Princess, tel. 441/238–2332), **Blue Waters Divers** (at Robinson's Marina in Sandys, tel. 441/234–1034), and **South Side Scuba** (at the Grotto Bay Hotel, tel. 441/293–2915).

Waterskiing is allowed only in certain protected waters, and by law can be offered only by licensed skippers. **Island Waterskiing** (Grotto Bay Beach Hotel, tel. 441/293–2915) and **Bermuda Waterski Centre** (Robinson's Marina, Somerset, tel. 441/234–3354) both offer lessons and outings.

Windsurfers should contact **Mangrove Marina Ltd.** (Mangrove Bay, Somerset, tel. 441/234–0914), **Pompano Beach Club Watersports Centre** (tel. 441/234–0222), and **South Side Scuba Water Sports**

(Grotto Bay Beach Hotel and Marriott's Castle Harbour Resort, tel. 441/293–2915). Board rental is $20 per hour; one-hour lessons are $25–$35.

Beaches Bermuda has some of the most beautiful beaches in the world. The cream of the crop are along the south shore from Southampton to Tucker's Town: **Horseshoe Bay, Chaplin Bay, Stonehole Bay, Jobson's Cove, Warwick Long Bay,** and **Elbow Beach.** Some are long sweeps of unbroken pink sand; others are divided by low coral cliffs into protected little coves. All are easily accessible by bicycle, moped, or taxi.

Dining Many restaurants require gentlemen to wear a jacket and tie, and women to be appropriately dressed. When the gratuity is not included in the bill, an overall tip of 10%–15% is the accepted amount. Reservations are recommended for most restaurants.

Category	Cost*
$$$$	over $50
$$$	$35–$50
$$	$20–$35
$	under $20

per person for a three-course meal, excluding drinks, service, and sales tax

Fourways Inn. At the very top of fine dining in Bermuda is this gourmet restaurant in an 18th-century Georgian home. The menu is impressive; specialties include fresh mussels simmered in white wine and cream, fresh veal sautéed in lemon butter, Caesar salad, and strawberry soufflé. The wine list is excellent. A gourmet brunch is offered on Sunday in cruise season. *Paget, tel. 441/236–6517. Reservations required. AE, MC, V. $$$$*

Once Upon a Table. Many locals consider this the finest restaurant on Bermuda. Guests dine in an 18th-century home, surrounded by Victorian furnishings. Dishes include rack of lamb and roast duckling, served on elegant china. *Serpentine Rd., Hamilton, tel. 441/ 295–8585. Reservations recommended. Jacket and tie. No lunch. AE, DC, MC, V. $$$*

Frog & Onion. An instant hit with locals when it opened in 1992, this pub-style eatery is housed in one of Dockyard's restored 19th-century buildings. Despite its cavernous size and soaring ceilings, the restaurant manages a cozy ambience, thanks in part to subdued lighting. Seafood and pub grub are recommended over the steak offerings. *Cooperage Bldg., Dockyard, tel. 441/234–2900. Reservations suggested. MC, V. $$*

Pub on the Square. Smack on King's Square in St. George's, this British-style pub is nothing fancy but offers cool draft beer, juicy hamburgers, and fish-and-chips. *King's Sq., St. George's, tel. 441/ 297–1522. AE, MC, V. $$*

Caribbean

Nowhere in the world are conditions better suited for cruising than in the ever-warm, treasure-filled Caribbean Sea. Tiny island nations, within easy sailing distance of one another, form a chain of tropical enchantment that curves from Cuba in the north all the way down to the coast of Venezuela. There is far more to life here than sand and coconuts, however. The islands are vastly different, with their own cultures, topographies, and languages. Colonialism has left its mark, and the presence of the Spanish, French, Dutch, Danish, and British is still felt. Slavery, too, has left its cultural legacy, blending African overtones into the colonial/Indian amalgam. The one constant, however, is the weather. Despite the islands' southerly position, the climate is surprisingly gentle, due in large part to the cooling influence of the trade winds.

The Caribbean is made up of the Greater Antilles and the Lesser Antilles. The former consists of those islands closest to the United States: Cuba, Jamaica, Hispaniola (Haiti and the Dominican Republic), and Puerto Rico. (The Cayman Islands lie south of Cuba.) The Lesser Antilles, including the Virgin, Windward, and Leeward islands and others, are greater in number but smaller in size, and constitute the southern half of the Caribbean chain. Cruise lines often include Caracas, Venezuela, and Mexico's Yucatan Peninsula in their Caribbean itineraries as well.

More cruise ships ply these waters than any others in the world. There are big ships and small ships, fancy ships and party ships. In peak season, it is not uncommon for several ships to disembark thousands of passengers into a small town on the same day—a phenomenon not always enjoyed by locals. Despite some overcrowding, however, the abundance of cruise ships in the area allows you to choose the itinerary that suits you best. Whether it's shopping or scuba diving, fishing or sunbathing, you're sure to find the Caribbean cruise of your dreams. (For detailed itineraries, *see* Chapter 3.)

When to Go Average year-round temperatures throughout the Caribbean are 78°F–85°F, with a low of 65° and a high of 95°; downtown shopping areas always seem to be unbearably hot. High season runs from December 15 to April 14; during this most fashionable, most expensive, and most crowded time to go, reservations up to a year in advance are necessary for many ships. A low season (summer) visit offers certain advantages: Temperatures are virtually the same as in winter (even cooler on average than in parts of the U.S. mainland), island flora is at its height, and the water is smoother and clearer. Some tourist facilities close down in summer, however, and many ships move to Europe, Alaska, or the northeastern United States.

Hurricane season runs from August through October. Although cruise ships stay well out of the way of these storms, they can affect the weather throughout the Caribbean for days, and damage to ports can force last-minute itinerary changes.

Currency Currencies vary throughout the islands, but U.S. dollars are widely accepted. Don't bother changing more than a few dollars into local currency for phone calls, tips, and taxis.

Passports and Visas In general, American citizens need only proof of identity and nationality (two pieces of I.D., or a passport) to travel through the Caribbean; British travelers need a passport. For island specifics, *see* individual port sections, *below*.

Shore Excursions Typically, these include a bus tour of the island or town, a visit to a local beach or liquor factory, boat trips, snorkeling or diving, and charter fishing. As far as island tours go, it's always safest to take a ship-arranged excursion, but it's almost never cheapest. You also sacrifice the freedom to explore at your own pace and the joys of venturing off the beaten path.

If you seek adventure, find a knowledgeable taxi driver or tour operator—they're usually within a stone's throw of the pier—and wander around on your own. A group of four–six people will find this option more economical and practical than will a single person or a couple.

Renting a car is also a good option on many islands—again, the more people, the better the deal. But get a good island map before you set off, and be sure to find out how long it will take you to get around. The boat will leave without you unless you're on a ship-arranged tour.

Conditions are ideal for water sports of all kinds: scuba diving, snorkeling, windsurfing, sailing, waterskiing, and fishing excursions abound. Your shore-excursion director can usually arrange these activities for you individually if the ship offers no formal excursion.

Many ships throw beach parties on a private island or an isolated beach in the Bahamas, the Grenadines, or (depending on the current political climate) Haiti. These parties are either included in your fare, with snorkeling gear and other water-sports equipment extra, or offered as an optional tour for which you pay.

Golf and tennis are popular among cruise passengers, and several lines—particularly NCL, Royal Caribbean, and Seabourn—offer special packages ashore. Most golf courses rent clubs, although many passengers bring their own.

Dining Cuisine on the Caribbean's islands is hard to classify. The region's history as a colonial battleground and ethnic melting pot creates plenty of variety. The gourmet French delicacies of Martinique, for example, are far removed from the hearty Spanish casseroles of Puerto Rico and even further from the pungent curries of St. Lucia.

The one quality that defines most Caribbean cooking is its essential spiciness. Seafood is naturally quite popular. Some of it is even unique to the region, such as Caribbean lobster: Clawless and tougher than other types, it is more like crawfish than Maine lobster. And no island menu is complete without at least a half dozen dishes featuring conch, a mollusk similar to escargots that is served in the form of chowder, fritters, salad, and cocktail. Dress is generally casual—though in Caracas men should not wear shorts.

Category	Cost*
$$$	over $30
$$	$15–$30
$	under $15

per person for a three-course meal, excluding drinks, service, and sales tax

Antigua

Some say Antigua has so many beaches that you could visit a different one every day for a year. Most have snow-white sand, and many are backed by lavish resorts offering sailing, diving, windsurfing, and snorkeling.

The larger of the British Leeward Islands, Antigua was the headquarters from which Lord Horatio Nelson made his forays against the French and pirates in the late 18th century. A decidedly British atmosphere still prevails, underscored by a collection of pubs that will raise the spirits of every Anglophile. Cruise passengers with a

The Caribbean

U.S.A. Miami

Nassau

Key West

THE BAHAMAS

Havana

Turks
and
Caicos
Islands

Cuba

CUBA

Little
Cayman

Cayman
Brac

Puerto Plata

George Town

Grand
Cayman

Montego
Bay

G R E A T E R

HAITI Hispaniola

Port-au-Prince

Ocho
Rios

Jamaica

T E R

Caribbean

Cartagena

Maracaibo

Panama
Canal

Colon **PANAMA**

Panama City

COLOMBIA

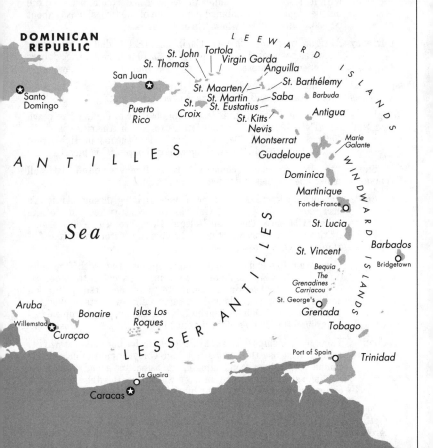

ATLANTIC OCEAN

DOMINICAN
REPUBLIC

LEEWARD ISLANDS

St. John   Tortola
St. Thomas   Virgin Gorda
                          Anguilla
San Juan   St. Barthélemy
⭐   St. Maarten/   Saba   Barbuda
Santo   St. Martin
Domingo   St. Eustatius   Antigua
        St.   St. Kitts
Puerto Croix   Nevis
Rico   Montserrat   Marie
                                    Galante
A N T I L L E S   Guadeloupe

                              Dominica

                              Martinique
                          Fort-de-France

Sea   St. Lucia
                                          Barbados
                          St. Vincent
                                       Bridgetown
                          Bequia
                          The
                          Grenadines
                          Carriacou
                  St. George's
Aruba   Bonaire   Islas Los   Grenada
Willemstad   Roques   Tobago
Curaçao

              L E S S E R   A N T I L L E S

                              Port of Spain   Trinidad
                  La Guaira
        Caracas
        ⭐

VENEZUELA

0   200 miles
0   300 km

N

taste for history will want to explore English Harbour and its carefully restored Nelson's Dockyard, as well as tour an 18th-century Royal Naval base, old forts, historic churches, and tiny villages. Hikers can wander through a tropical rain forest lush with pineapples, bananas, and mangoes. Those of an archaeological bent will head for the megaliths of Greencastle to seek out some of the 30 excavations of ancient Indian sites.

About 4,000 years ago Antigua was home to a people called the Siboney. They disappeared mysteriously, and the island remained uninhabited for about 1,000 years. When Columbus sighted the 108-square-mile island in 1493, the Arawaks had already set up housekeeping. The English moved in 130 years later, in 1623. Then a sequence of bloody battles involving the Caribs, the Dutch, the French, and the English began. Africans had been captured as slaves to work the sugar plantations by the time the French ceded the island to the English in 1667. On November 1, 1981, Antigua, with its sister island 30 miles to the north, Barbuda, achieved full independence. The combined population of the two islands is about 90,000—only 1,200 of whom live on Barbuda.

Currency Antigua uses the Eastern Caribbean (E.C.) dollar, commonly known as beewees. Figure about E.C. $2.70 to U.S. $1. U.S. dollars are generally accepted, but you may get your change in beewees.

Passports and Visas U.S. and Canadian citizens need only proof of identity, but a passport is preferred. British citizens need a passport.

Telephones and Mail Calling the United States is a simple matter of dialing 1 to reach AT&T's USADirect. Airmail letters to North America cost E.C. 60¢; postcards, E.C. 40¢. The post office is at the foot of High Street in St. John's, beside the Heritage Quay Shopping Complex.

Shore Excursions The following is a good choice in Antigua. It may not be offered by all cruise lines. Times and prices are approximate.

Island Sights **Nelson's Dockyard and Clarence House.** Driving through Antigua's lush countryside, you will visit the 18th-century residence of the duke of Clarence. Then visit Nelson's Dockyard, a gem of Georgian British maritime architecture and a must for history buffs and Anglophiles. *3 hrs. Cost: $25–$40.*

If you want to feel like Indiana Jones, opt for a tour with **Tropikelly** (tel. 809/461–0383). You'll be given an insider's look at the whole island by four-wheel-drive, complete with deserted plantation houses, rain-forest trails, ruined sugar mills and forts, and even a picnic lunch with drinks. The highlight is the luxuriant tropical forest around the island's highest point, Boggy Peak. *5 hrs. Cost: $55.*

Coming Ashore Though some ships dock at the deep-water harbor in downtown St. John's, most use the town's Heritage Quay, a multimillion-dollar complex with shops, condominiums, a casino, and a food court. Most St. John's attractions are an easy walk from Heritage Quay; the older part of the city is eight blocks away. A tourist information booth is in the main docking building.

Getting Around Avoid public buses. They're unreliable and hard to find. If you don't want to explore St. John's on foot, hire a taxi. If you intend to tour beyond this port city consider renting a car or hiring a taxi driver/guide.

By Car To rent a car, you'll need a valid driver's license and a temporary permit, which is available through the rental agent for $12. Rentals average about $50 per day, with unlimited mileage. Driving is on the left, and Antiguan roads are generally unmarked and full of potholes. Rental agencies are on High Street in St. John's, or they can be called from the terminal. Contact **Budget** (tel. 809/462–3009 or 800/648–4985), **Carib Car Rentals** (tel. 809/462–2062), or **National** (tel. 809/462–2113 or 800/468–0008), all in St. John's.

By Taxi Taxis meet every cruise ship. They are unmetered; fares are fixed, and drivers are required to carry a rate card. Tip drivers 10%. All taxi drivers double as guides, and you can arrange an island tour for about $15–$20 per person, for up to four passengers. A tour of the Royal Dockyard takes about three hours and costs up to $60 for four. The most reliable and informed driver-guides are at **Capital Car Rental** (High St., St. John's, tel. 809/462–0863).

Exploring *Numbers in the margin correspond to points of interest on the Anti-*
Antigua *gua map.*

❶ **St. John's** is home to about 40,000 people (nearly half the island's population). The city has seen better days, but there are some notable sights.

At the far south end of town, where Market Street forks into Valley and All Saints roads, locals jam the marketplace every Friday and Saturday to buy and sell fruits, vegetables, fish, and spices. Be sure to ask before you aim a camera, and expect the subject of your shot to ask for a tip.

If you have a serious interest in archaeology, see the historical displays at the **Museum of Antigua and Barbuda.** The colonial building that houses the museum is the former courthouse, which dates from 1750. *Church and Market Sts., tel. 809/462–1469. Admission free. Open weekdays 8:30–4, Sat. 10–1.*

Walk two blocks east on Church Street to **St. John's Cathedral.** The Anglican church sits on a hilltop, surrounded by its churchyard. At the south gate are figures said to have been taken from one of Napoleon's ships. A previous structure on this site was destroyed by an earthquake in 1843, so the interior of the current church is completely encased in pitch pine to forestall heavy damage from future quakes. *Between Long and Newcastle Sts. Admission free.*

A favorite car excursion is to follow Fort Road northwest out of
❷ town. After 2 miles you'll come to the ruins of **Ft. James,** named for King James II. If you continue on this road, you'll arrive at **Dickenson Bay,** with its string of smart, expensive resorts on one of the many beautiful beaches you will pass.

In the opposite direction from St. John's, 8 miles south on All Saints
❸ Road is **Liberta,** one of the first settlements founded by freed slaves.
❹ East of the village, on Monk's Hill, are the ruins of **Ft. George,** built in 1669.

❺ **Falmouth,** 1½ miles farther south, sits on a lovely bay, backed by former sugar plantations and sugar mills. **St. Paul's Church,** dating from the late 18th and early 19th centuries, held services for the military in Nelson's time; it has been restored and is now used for Sunday worship.

❻ **English Harbour,** the most famous of Antigua's attractions, lies on the coast just south of Falmouth. The Royal Navy abandoned the
❼ station in 1889, but it has been restored as **Nelson's Dockyard,** which epitomizes the colonial Caribbean. Within the compound are crafts shops, hotels, a marina, and restaurants. The **Admiral's House Museum** has several rooms displaying ship models, a model of English Harbour, and various artifacts from Nelson's days. *Tel. 809/463–1053. Admission: $2. Open daily 8–6.*

On a ridge overlooking the dockyard is **Clarence House,** built in 1787 and once the home of the duke of Clarence. As you leave the dockyard, turn right at the crossroads in English Harbour and drive up
❽ to **Shirley Heights** for a spectacular harbor view.

❾ Nearby, the **Dows Hill Interpretation Center** chronicles the island's history and culture from Amerindian times to the present. A highlight of the center is its multimedia presentation in which illumi-

Antigua

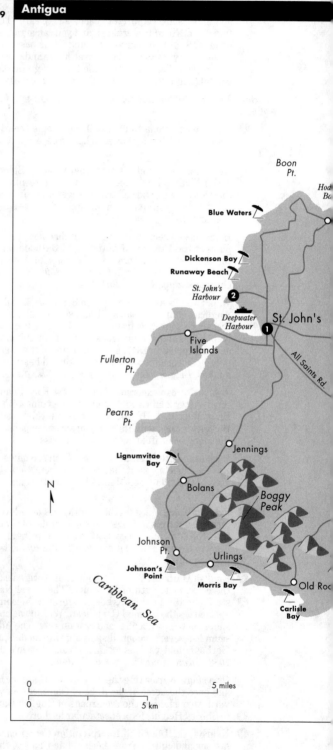

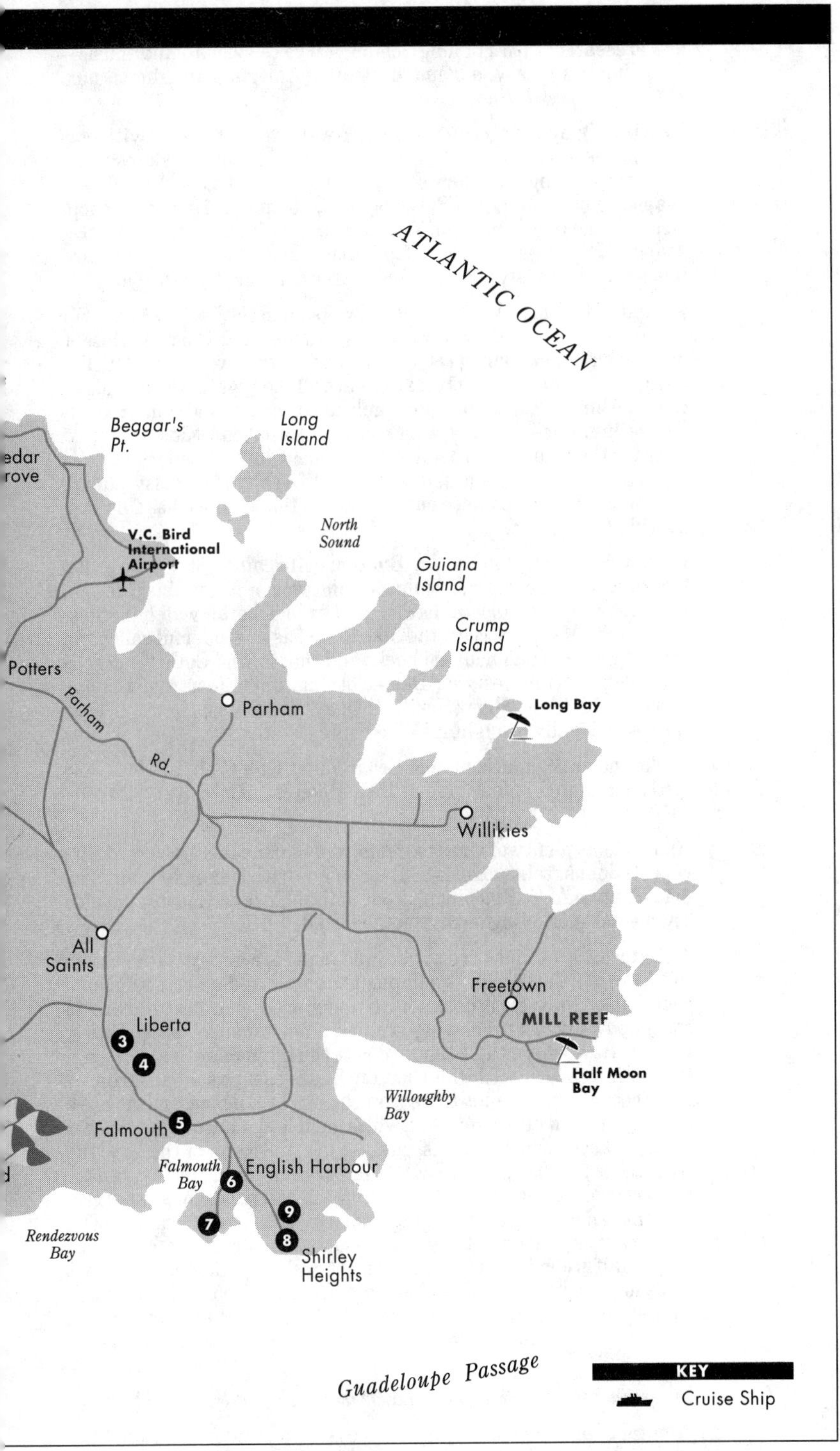

ATLANTIC OCEAN

Beggar's Pt.

Long Island

edar rove

V.C. Bird International Airport

North Sound

Guiana Island

Crump Island

Potters

Parham

Parham

Long Bay

Rd.

Willikies

All Saints

Freetown

Liberta

MILL REEF

❸
❹

Half Moon Bay

❺ Falmouth

Willoughby Bay

Falmouth Bay English Harbour

❻

❼ ❾

❽ *Shirley Heights*

Rendezvous Bay

Guadeloupe Passage

nated displays, incorporating lifelike figures and colorful tableaux, are presented with running commentary, television, and music—resulting in a cheery, if bland, portrait of Antiguan life. *Admission: E.C. $15. Open daily 9–5.*

Shopping   **Redcliffe Quay** and **Heritage Quay** are waterfront markets with boutiques, restaurants, and snack bars. The main tourist shops in St. John's are along **St. Mary's, High,** and **Long streets.** In general, shops are open Monday–Saturday 8:30–noon and 1–4; some shops close for the day at noon on Thursday and Saturday. The duty-free shops of Heritage Quay cater to tourists and often have more flexible hours; however, you may find better deals at Redcliffe Quay.

At Redcliffe Quay, Antiguan pottery is sold in the **Pottery Shop.** For batiks, sarongs, and swimwear, try **A Thousand Flowers. Base** is where you'll find striped cotton-and-Lycra beachwear from English designer Steven Giles; his creations are all the rage on the island. At the **Goldsmitty,** Hans Smit turns gold and precious and semiprecious stones into one-of-a-kind works of art. **Karibbean Kids** has great gifts for the younger set, and **Windjammer Clothing** sells nautically inspired attire for men and women. Off the little grassy square where African slaves were once penned is **Bona,** which has fine Italian china.

In downtown St. John's, **La Boutique Africaine** (St. Mary's St.) stocks Kenyan soapstone sculpture and woven bags, Masai flasks, Ibo ebony combs, colorful batiks, and even Tibetan wall hangings. Also on St. Mary's Street, the **Map Shop** has a wonderful collection of antique maps and nautical books and charts, and **CoCo Shop** sells Sea Island cotton designs, Daks clothing, and Liberty of London fabrics. The **Cigar Shop** (Heritage Quay) has Cuban cigars. (These cannot be legally brought into the United States.)

Sports   You'll find an 18-hole course at **Cedar Valley Golf Club** (tel. 809/462–
Golf   0161) and a nine-hole course at **Half Moon Bay Hotel** (tel. 809/460–4300).

Scuba Diving   Antigua has plenty of wrecks, reefs, and marine life. **Dockyard Divers** (St. Johns, tel. 809/464–8591), run by British ex–merchant seaman Captain A. G. Finchman, is one of the oldest and most reputable diving and snorkeling outfits on the island.

Beaches   Antigua's 366 beaches are public, and many are dotted with resorts that provide water-sports equipment rentals and a place to grab a cool drink. Since most hotels have taxi stands, you can get back to the ship easily. The following are just a few excellent possibilities: **Carlisle Bay,** where the Atlantic meets the Caribbean Sea, is a long, snow-white beach with the Curtain Bluff resort as a backdrop. A large coconut grove adds to its tropical beauty. **Dickenson Bay** has a lengthy stretch of powder-soft white sand and a host of hotels that cater to water-sports enthusiasts. At the south end of the bay, the **Buccaneer Club** is open only when ships are in port and is geared toward cruise passengers. It has a stretch of sandy beach, a small restaurant and lounge, changing rooms, and beach chairs. The Buccaneer is convenient, but the resorts farther up the beach are nicer. **Half Moon Bay,** a ¾-mile crescent of shell-pink sand, is a great place for snorkeling and windsurfing. The Half Moon Bay hotel will let you borrow gear with a refundable deposit. **Johnsons Point** is a deliciously deserted beach of bleached white sand on the southwest coast.

Dining   *In restaurants a 10% service charge is usually added to the bill.*

Admiral's Inn. Known simply as "The Ad" to yachtsmen around the world, this historic inn in the heart of English Harbour is a must for Anglophiles and mariners. Dine on curried conch, fresh snapper with lime, or lobster thermidor while taking in the splendid harbor views. *Nelson's Dockyard, tel. 809/460–1027. Reservations required. AE, MC, V. $$*

Redcliffe Tavern. Set amid the courtyards of Redcliffe Quay, on the second floor of a colonial warehouse, this appealing restaurant has an inventive menu that is part Northern Italian, part Continental, part Creole, and all fresh. Antique water-pumping equipment, salvaged from all over the island, adds to the unusual dining experience. *Redcliffe Quay, St. John's, tel. 809/461–4557. AE, MC, V. $$*

Aruba

Though the "A" in the ABC (Aruba, Bonaire, Curaçao) Islands is small—only 19.6 miles long and 6 miles at its widest—the island's national anthem proclaims "the greatness of our people is their great cordiality," and this is no exaggeration. Once a member of the Netherlands Antilles, Aruba became independent within the Netherlands in 1986, with its own royally appointed governor, a democratic government, and a 21-member elected parliament. Long secure in a solid economy, with good education, housing, and health care, the island's population of about 70,000 regards tourists as welcome guests and treats them accordingly. Waiters serve you with smiles and solid eye contact. English is spoken everywhere. In addition to the ships that call at Aruba on southern Caribbean itineraries, the island is the home port for Seawind's Seawind Crown and Dolphin's OceanBreeze.

The island's distinctive beauty lies in the stark contrast between the sea and the countryside: rocky deserts, cactus jungles, secluded coves, and aquamarine panoramas with crashing waves. It's famous mostly, however, for its casinos.

Currency Arubans accept U.S. dollars, so you've no need to exchange money, except for pocket change for bus fare or pay phones. Local currency is the Aruban florin (AFl). At press time, U.S. $1 will get you AFl 1.77 cash, or AFl 1.79 in traveler's checks. Note that the Netherlands Antilles florin used in Bonaire and Curaçao is not accepted on Aruba.

Passports and U.S. and Canadian residents need only proof of identity—a valid
Visas passport, original birth certificate, naturalization certificate, green card, valid nonquota immigration visa, or valid voter registration card. Other foreigners must have a valid passport.

Telephones International calls are placed at the phone center in the cruise ter-
and Mail minal. To reach the United States, dial 001, area code, and the local number. An airmail letter from Aruba to anywhere in the world costs AFl 1, a postcard AFl .70. The post office is catercorner to the St. Francis Roman Catholic Church in Oranjestad.

Shore The following are good choices on Aruba. They may not be offered
Excursions by all cruise lines. Times and prices are approximate. Unless otherwise noted, children's prices are for those under 13.

Island Sights **Aruba Town and Countryside Drive.** A comprehensive town-and-country bus tour. Passengers may then choose to stay in town, on the beach, or at the casino. *3 hrs. Cost: $25.*

Undersea **Atlantis Submarine.** Aboard a 65-foot submarine, passengers dive
Creatures 50–90 feet below the surface along Aruba's Barcadera Reef. *1½ hrs. Cost: $68 adults, $34 children.*

Glass-Bottom Boat Tour. A 60-passenger vessel (some with cash bar) allows you to view Aruba's extensive underwater life. *1½ hrs. Cost: $25.*

Coming Ships tie up at the Aruba Port Authority cruise terminal; inside is a
Ashore tourist information booth and duty-free shops. From here, you're a

five-minute walk from various shopping districts and downtown Oranjestad. Just turn right out of the cruise terminal entrance.

Getting Around By Bus Buses run hourly between the beach hotels and Oranjestad. They also stop across the street from the cruise terminal on L.G. Smith Boulevard. Round-trip fare is $1.50, exact change.

By Car It's easy to rent a car, Jeep, or motorbike in Aruba, and most roads are in excellent condition. Contact **Avis** (tel. 297/8–28787), **Budget** (tel. 297/8–28600), or **Hertz** (tel. 297/8–24545). Rates begin at about $45 a day.

By Taxi A dispatch office is located at Alhambra Bazaar and Casino (tel. 297/8–21604). Taxis can also be flagged down on the street. Because taxis have no meters, rates are fixed but should be confirmed before you get in. All drivers have participated in the government's Tourism Awareness Programs and have received a Tourism Guide Certificate. An hour tour of the island by taxi will cost about $35 for up to four people.

Exploring Aruba *Numbers in the margin correspond to points of interest on the Aruba map.*

❶ Aruba's charming capital, **Oranjestad,** is best explored on foot. If you're interested in Dutch architecture, begin at the corner of Oude School Straat and go three blocks toward the harbor to Wilhelminastraat, where some of the buildings date back to Oranjestad's 1790 founding. Walk west and you'll pass old homes, a government building, and the Protestant church. When you reach Shuttestraat again, turn left and go one block to Zoutmanstraat. The small **Archaeology Museum** here has two rooms of Indian artifacts, farm and domestic utensils, and skeletons. *Zoutmanstraat 1, tel. 297/8–28979. Admission free. Open weekdays 8–noon and 1:30–4:30.*

A block east lies **Ft. Zoutman,** the island's oldest building, built in 1796 and used as a major fortress in skirmishes between British and Curaçao troops. The Willem III tower was added in 1868. The fort's Historical Museum displays island relics and artifacts in an 18th-century Aruban house. *Tel. 297/8–26099. Admission: $1. Open weekdays 9–noon and 1–4.*

One block south is **Wilhelmina Park,** a small grove of palm trees and flowers overlooking the sea. Head back to Caya G.F. Betico Croes and turn north to the corner of Hendrikstraat to see the **St. Francis Roman Catholic Church.** Just behind the church is the **Numismatic Museum,** displaying coins and paper money from more than 400 countries. *Iraussquilnplein 2–A, tel. 297/8–28831. Admission free. Open weekdays 8:30–noon and 1–4:30.*

The "real" Aruba—or what's left of its wild, untamed beauty—can be experienced only by taking a car or taxi into the countryside. (Be aware that there are no public bathrooms anywhere, except in a few restaurants.)

❷ For a shimmering panorama of blue-green sea, drive east on L.G. Smith Boulevard toward San Nicolas. Past the airport, you'll soon see the 541-foot peak of **Hooiberg** (Haystack Hill). Climb 562 steps to the top for an impressive view of the city.

❸ Turn left where you see the drive-in theater. At the first intersection, turn right, then follow the curve to the right to **Frenchman's Pass,** a dark, luscious stretch of highway arbored by overhanging trees. Legend claims the French and native Indians warred here during the 17th century for control of the island. Nearby are the cement ruins of the **Balashi Gold Mine** (take the dirt road veering to the right), a lovely place to picnic, listen to the parakeets, and contemplate the towering cacti. A gnarled divi-divi tree stands guard at the entrance.

⑤ Backtrack all the way to the main road (back past the drive-in) and drive through the area called **Spanish Lagoon,** where pirates once hid to repair their ships.

⑥ Back on the main road, visit **San Nicolas,** Aruba's oldest village. During the heyday of the Exxon refineries, the town was a bustling port; now it's dedicated to tourism, with the Main Street promenade full of interesting kiosks. **Charlie's Bar** on the main street is a popular tourist lunch spot, good for both gawking at the thousands of license plates, old credit cards, baseball pennants, and hard hats covering every inch of the walls and ceiling, and for gorging on "jumbo and dumbo" shrimp.

Shopping Caya G.F. Betico Croes in Oranjestad is Aruba's chief shopping street. The stores are full of Dutch porcelains and figurines, as befits the island's Netherlands heritage. Also consider the Dutch cheeses (you are allowed to bring up to one pound of hard cheese through U.S. Customs), hand-embroidered linens, and any product made from the native plant aloe vera, such as sunburn cream, face masks, and skin fresheners. There is no sales tax, and Arubans consider it rude to haggle.

Artesania Arubiano (L.G. Smith Blvd. 47, next to the Aruba Tourism Authority) has charming home-crafted pottery and folk objets d'art. **Aruba Trading Company** (Caya G.F. Betico Croes 14) discounts brand-name perfumes and cosmetics (first floor), jewelry (second floor), men's and women's clothes, and liqueurs up to 30%. **Gandleman's Jewelers** (Caya G.F. Betico Croes 5–A) sells jewelry, including a full line of watches. **Wulfsen & Wulfsen** (Caya G.F. Betico Croes 52, tel. 297/8–23823) is one of Holland's best stores for fine-quality clothes and shoes.

Sports Contact **De Palm Tours** in Oranjestad (tel. 297/8–24400) for informa-
Fishing tion on fishing charters.

Golf There's a new, 18-hole course designed by Robert Trent Jones (at the Hyatt Regency Hotel; tel. 297/8–31234). The **Aruba Golf Club** near San Nicolas (tel. 297/8–42006) has a nine-hole course with 25 sand traps, roaming goats, and lots of cacti. Greens fees are $7.50 for nine holes, $10 for 18. Golf carts and clubs can be rented.

Hiking **De Palm Tours** (tel. 297/8–24400) offers a guided three-hour trip to remote sites of unusual natural beauty accessible only on foot. The fee is $25 per person, including refreshments and transportation; a minimum of four people is required.

Horseback At **Rancho El Paso** (tel. 297/8–23310), one-hour jaunts ($15) take
Riding you through countryside flanked by cacti, divi-divi trees, and aloe-vera plants; two-hour trips ($30) go to the beach as well. Wear lots of sunblock.

Water Sports **De Palm Tours** (tel. 297/8–24400) has a near monopoly on all water sports, including equipment and instruction for scuba, snorkeling, and windsurfing. **Pelican Watersports,** also in Oranjestad (tel. 297/8–31228), offers water-sports packages, including snorkeling, sailing, windsurfing, fishing, and scuba.

Beaches Beaches in Aruba are not only beautiful but clean. On the north side the water is too choppy for swimming, but the views are great. **Palm Beach**—which stretches behind the Americana, Aruba, Concorde, Aruba Palm Beach, and Holiday Inn hotels—is the center of Aruban tourism, offering the best in swimming, sailing, and fishing. In high season, however, it's packed. **Manchebo Beach,** by the Manchebo Beach Resort, is an impressively wide stretch of white powder and Aruba's unofficial topless beach. On the island's eastern tip, tiny **Baby Beach** is as placid as a wading pool and only 4 or 5 feet deep—perfect for tots and bad swimmers. Thatched shaded areas provide relief from the sun.

Aruba

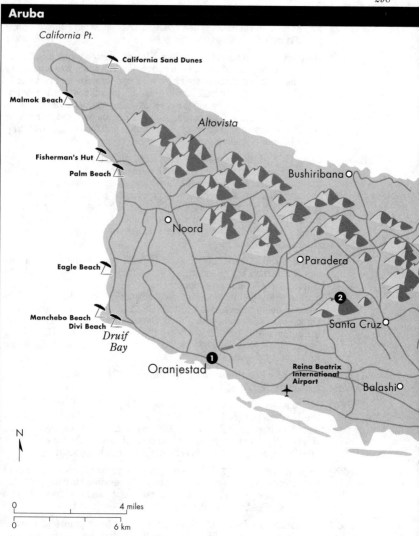

California Pt.

California Sand Dunes

Malmok Beach

Altovista

Fisherman's Hut

Bushiribana○

Palm Beach

○ Noord

Eagle Beach

○Paradera

❷

Manchebo Beach

Divi Beach

Santa Cruz○

Druif Bay

❶

Oranjestad

Reina Beatrix
International
Airport

Balashi○

N

| 0 | | 4 miles |
| 0 | | 6 km |

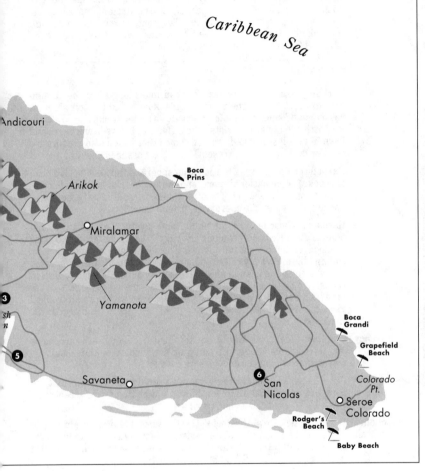

Caribbean Sea

Andicouri

Arikok

Boca Prins

Miralamar

Yamanota

Boca Grandi

Grapefield Beach

Colorado Pt.

Savaneta

San Nicolas

Seroe Colorado

Rodger's Beach

Baby Beach

Dining *Restaurants usually add a 15% service charge.*

Bali Floating Restaurant. Floating in an Oriental houseboat in Oranjestad's harbor, the Bali has some of the best Indonesian food on the island. Service is terminally slow but well-meaning. *L.G. Smith Blvd., tel. 297/8–22131. AE, MC, V. $$*

La Paloma. The low-key, lovely "Dove" serves up fresh seafood with no gimmicks, and it's usually packed. The restaurant ensures freshness with its own fishing boat. Try conch stew with *pan bati* (pancakelike bread), and fried plantains. *Noord 39, tel. 297/8–62770. AE, MC, V. Closed Tues. $*

Barbados

Barbados has a life of its own that continues long after the passengers have packed up their suntan oil and returned to their ships. A resort island since the 1700s, Barbados has slowly cultivated a civilized attitude toward tourists. The difference between the haves and have-nots is less marked than on some other islands, so visitors are neither fawned upon nor resented for their assumed wealth.

Barbados retains a very British atmosphere. Afternoon tea is a ritual, cricket is the national sport, and the tradition of dressing for dinner is firmly entrenched. The atmosphere is hardly stuffy, however, and even here, people operate on "island time."

Barbadian beaches are all public and lovely. The Atlantic surf pounds gigantic boulders along the rugged east coast, where Bajans themselves have vacation homes. The northeast is dominated by rolling hills and valleys covered by acres of impenetrable sugarcane. Elsewhere on the island, which is linked by almost 900 miles of good roads, are historic plantations, stalactite-studded caves, a wildlife preserve, and the Andromeda Gardens, an attractive, small tropical garden. Bridgetown, the capital, is a busy city with more traffic than charm.

Currency One Barbados dollar (BDS$) equals about U.S. 50¢. Both currencies and the Canadian dollar are accepted everywhere on the island. Always ask in which currency prices are quoted.

Passports and Visas American and Canadian citizens need proof of citizenship. A U.S. passport or original birth certificate and photo ID are acceptable. British citizens need a valid passport.

Telephones and Mail Public phones are at the docks. Use the same dialing procedure as in the United States, or dial for assistance for collect and credit-card calls. Airmail letters to the United States or Canada cost BDS 90¢ per half ounce; airmail postcards cost BDS 65¢.

Shore Excursions The following are good choices on Barbados. They may not be offered by all cruise lines. Times and prices are approximate. Unless otherwise noted, children's prices are for those under 13.

Island Sights **Harrison's Cave.** After a bus tour to the center of the island, passengers board an electric tram into an underground cave. At the lowest point, a 40-foot waterfall plunges into a deep pool. *3 hrs. Cost: $33 adults, $21 children.*

Undersea Creatures **Atlantis Submarine.** An excursion on a real submarine for an exciting view of Barbados's profuse marine life. For non–scuba divers, this trip to the depths is a thrilling experience. *1½ hrs. Cost: $70 adults, $40 children.*

Coming Ashore Up to eight ships at a time can dock at the Deepwater Harbour in Bridgetown, on the northwest side of Carlisle Bay. The cruise-ship terminal has duty-free shops, a post office, telephone station, tourist information desk, and taxi stand. To get downtown, follow the Careenage. By foot, it will take you about half an hour, or you can take a taxi for $3–$4.

Getting Around By Bus The bus system is good, connecting Bridgetown with all parts of the island, but the buses can be crowded and late. Fare is BDS$1.50 wherever you go.

By Car Barbados is a pleasure by car, provided you take the time to study a good map and don't mind asking directions. Unfortunately for North Americans, driving is on the left; this is not a pleasure. You'll need an international driver's license to rent a car; get one at the rental agency for $5 with your valid home license. Contact **National** (tel. 809/426–0603) or **P&S Car Rentals** (tel. 809/424–2052). Cars with automatic transmission cost $60–$65 per day. Gas costs about $3 a gallon.

By Taxi Taxis await ships at the pier. The fare to Paradise, Brandon, or Brighton beaches runs $3–$5, to Holetown it's $7. Drivers accept U.S. dollars and expect a 10% tip. Taxi tours cost $20 per hour for up to four passengers.

Exploring Barbados *Numbers in the margin correspond to points of interest on the Barbados map.*

Bridgetown Area The narrow strip of sea known as the **Careenage** made early **Bridgetown** a natural harbor. Here, working schooners were careened ❶ (turned on their sides) to be scraped of barnacles and repainted. Today, the Careenage serves mainly as a berth for pleasure yachts.

At the center of the bustling city is **Trafalgar Square,** with its monument to Lord Nelson that predates its London counterpart by about two decades. Also here are a war memorial and a three-dolphin fountain commemorating the advent of running water in Barbados in 1865.

The principal shopping area is **Broad Street,** which leads west from Trafalgar Square past the **House of Assembly** and **Parliament Buildings.** These Victorian Gothic structures, like so many others in Bridgetown, stand beside a growing number of modern office buildings.

East of the square is **St. Michael's Cathedral,** where George Washington is said to have worshiped on his only trip outside the United States. The structure was nearly a century old when he visited in 1751; destroyed twice by hurricanes, it was rebuilt in 1780 and again in 1831. Farther east, in **Queen's Park,** is an immense baobab tree more than 10 centuries old. The historic **Queen's Park House,** former home of the commander of the British troops, has been converted into a theater and a restaurant. The park is a long walk from Trafalgar Square; consider taking a taxi. *Open daily 9–5.*

About a mile south of Bridgetown on Highway 7, housed in what used to be a military prison, the **Barbados Museum** has artifacts and mementos of military history and everyday life in the 19th century; wildlife and natural history exhibits; a well-stocked gift shop; and a good café. *Garrison Savannah, tel. 809/427–0201. Admission: BDS$10 adults, BDS$5 children. Open Mon.–Sat. 9–5, Sun. 2–6.*

Central Barbados **Folkstone Marine Park,** north of Holetown on Highway 1, features a snorkeling trail around Dottin's Reef; nonswimmers can ride in a ❷ glass-bottom boat. A barge sunk in shallow water is home to myriad fish. The barge and the reef are popular dive sites.

A drive along Highway 2 passes several interesting sights, including ❸ touristy **Harrison's Cave.** The pale-gold limestone caverns, complete with subterranean streams and waterfalls, can be toured by tram. *Tel. 809/438–6640. Admission: BDS$15 adults, BDS$7.50 children. Open daily 9–6.*

❹ Nearby **Welchman Hall Gully** offers a similar opportunity to commune with nature, with acres of labeled flowers, the occasional

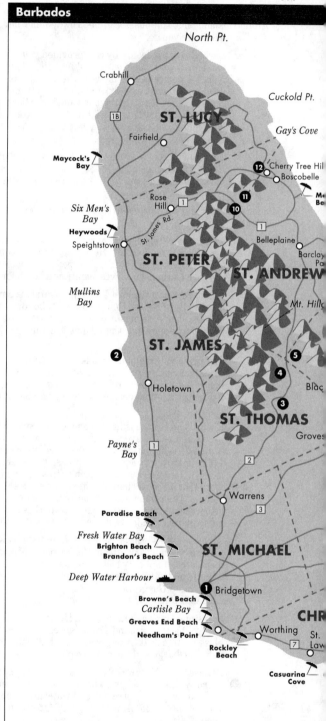

Barbados

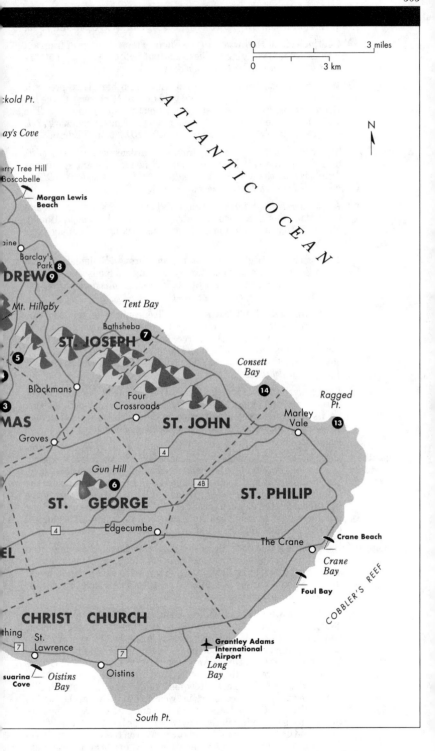

0   3 miles

0   3 km

A T L A N T I C   O C E A N

N

:kold Pt.

ay's Cove

rry Tree Hill
Boscobelle

**Morgan Lewis
Beach**

aine

Barclay's
Park **8**

DREW 9

Mt. Hillaby

Tent Bay

ST. JOSEPH

Bathsheba **7**

*Consett
Bay*

5

Blackmans

Four
Crossroads

14

*Ragged
Pt.*

Marley
Vale

13

3

MAS

Groves

ST. JOHN

4

Gun Hill

4B

ST. PHILIP

ST. GEORGE

6

Edgecumbe

4

EL

The Crane

Crane Beach

*Crane
Bay*

Foul Bay

COBBLER'S REEF

CHRIST CHURCH

thing

St.
Lawrence

7

7

**Grantley Adams
International
Airport**

suarina
Cove

*Oistins
Bay*

Oistins

*Long
Bay*

South Pt.

green monkey, and great peace and quiet. *Hwy. 2, tel. 809/438–6671. Admission: BDS$10 adults, BDS$5 children. Open daily 9–5.*

⑤ Continue along Highway 2 to the **Flower Forest,** 8 acres of fragrant bushes, canna and ginger lilies, and puffball trees. *Tel. 809/433–8152. Admission: BDS$10. Open daily 9–5.*

⑥ Highway 4 leads to **Gun Hill.** The view from here is so pretty it seems unreal. Fields of green and gold extend all the way to the horizon, and brilliant flowers surround a picturesque gun tower. The white limestone lion behind the garrison is a famous landmark. *Tel. 809/429–1358. Admission: BDS$5 adults, BDS$2.50 children.*

Eastern Shore/ The small but fascinating **Andromeda Gardens,** set into the cliffs
Northern overlooking the sea, holds unusual and beautiful plant specimens
Barbados from around the world. *Tel. 809/433–9384. Admission: BDS$10*
⑦ *adults, BDS$5 children. Open daily 9–5.*

⑧ A little north of the gardens, **Barclay's Park** offers a similar view and
⑨ picnic facilities in a wooded seafront area. At the nearby **Chalky Mount Potteries** you'll find craftspersons making and selling their wares.

Taking a left on Highway 1 after passing through Belleplaine, you'll
⑩ reach **Farley Hill,** a national park whose rugged landscape explains why this has been dubbed the Scotland area. *Admission: BDS$2 per car; walkers free. Open daily 8:30–6.*

⑪ At the **Barbados Wildlife Reserve,** you'll encounter herons, land turtles, screeching peacocks, innumerable green monkeys, geese, brilliantly colored parrots, a kangaroo, and a friendly otter. The fauna roam freely, so step carefully and keep your hands to yourself. *Tel. 809/422–8826. Admission: BDS$15 adults, BDS$10 children under 12. Open daily 10–5.*

⑫ Back toward the coast, near Cherry Tree Hill, is **St. Nicholas Abbey** (circa 1650), the oldest house on the island and well worth visiting for its stone and wood architecture in the Jacobean style. *Tel. 809/422–8725. Admission: $2.50. Open weekdays 10–3:30.*

Eastern Shore/ Driving east on highways 4 and 4B, note the many **chattel houses**
Southern along the route; the property of tenant farmers, these ever-expand-
Barbados able houses were built to be dismantled and moved when necessary.
⑬ On the coast, the aptly named **Ragged Point Lighthouse** is where the sun first shines on Barbados. About 4 miles to the northwest of the lighthouse, in the eastern corner of St. John Parish, the coral-stone
⑭ buildings and serenely beautiful grounds of **Codrington Theological College,** founded in 1748, stand on a cliff overlooking Consett Bay.

Shopping Barbados is a free port. In most stores, you can purchase imported items duty-free by showing your passport. Shopping is found mostly along Broad Street in Bridgetown. Stores are usually open weekdays 9–5 and Saturday 8–1. Many downtown shops have branches at the cruise-ship terminal.

At Bridgetown's **Pelican Village Handicrafts Center** (tel. 809/426–4391), on the Princess Alice Highway near the Cheapside Market, you can watch goods and crafts being made before you purchase them; rugs and mats are good buys. For antiques and fine memorabilia, try **Greenwich House Antiques** (tel. 809/432–1169), in Greenwich Village, Trents Hill, St. James Parish; and **Antiquaria** (tel. 809/426–0635), on St. Michael's Row next to the Anglican cathedral in Bridgetown. Exclusive designs in "wearable art" by Carol Cadogan are available at **Cotton Days Designs** in Ramsgate Cottage, opposite St. Patrick's Cathedral in Bridgetown (Lower Bay St., tel. 809/427–7191), and on the wharf in Bridgetown. Also on the wharf, **Origins—Colours of the Caribbean** (tel. 809/436-8532) has original—and expensive—handmade clothing and accessories.

Sports
Fishing Contact **Blue Jay Charters** (tel. 809/422–2098) for information on fishing charters.

Golf Several courses are open to the public. Try **Almond Beach Village** (9 holes, tel. 809/422–4900), **Club Rockley Barbados** (9 holes, tel. 809/435–7873), and **Sandy Lane Club** (18 holes, tel. 809/432–1145).

Horseback Riding The **Caribbean International Riding Center** (tel. 809/433–1246) offers one- or two-hour scenic trail rides for cruise-ship passengers. Prices begin at BDS$55.

Water Sports Waterskiing, snorkeling, and parasailing are available on most beaches of St. James and Christ Church parishes. Windsurfing is best learned on the south coast at **Benston Windsurfing Club Hotel** (Maxwell, Christ Church Parish, tel. 809/428–9095). For scuba divers, Barbados is a rich and varied underwater destination. Two good dive operators are the **Dive Shop Ltd.** (Grand Barbados Beach Resort, tel. 809/426–9947) and **Dive Boat Safari** (Barbados Hilton, tel. 809/427–4350).

Beaches The west coast has the stunning coves and white-sand beaches dear to the hearts of postcard publishers, plus calm, clear water for snorkeling, scuba diving, and swimming. Beaches here are seldom crowded. Good spots for swimming include **Paradise Beach,** just off the Paradise Village & Beach Hotel; **Brandon's Beach,** a 10-minute walk south; and **Greave's End Beach,** south of Bridgetown at Aquatic Gap. Just north of Paradise Beach, **Holetown** has several fine resorts; the Sandy Lane Hotel welcomes cruise passengers. If you don't mind a short drive along Highway 7, the **Crane Beach Hotel,** where the Atlantic meets the Caribbean, is a great find. Waves pound in, but a reef makes it safe for good swimmers and the sands are golden. For refreshment, there's the hotel's dining room on the cliff above.

Dining *A 5% tax and 10% service charge are added to most restaurant bills. When no service charge is added, tip waiters 10%–15%.*

Waterfront Cafe. A sidewalk table overlooking the Careenage is the perfect place to enjoy a drink, snack, or Bajun meal. It's a popular gathering place for locals and tourists alike. *Bridge House, Bridgetown, tel. 809/427–0093. MC, V. $*

Caracas/La Guaira, Venezuela

The busy harbor of La Guaira is the port for nearby Caracas, the capital of Venezuela. Most passengers go directly from the dock into air-conditioned excursion buses for the 15-mile (45-minute) drive into the big city. Those who want to explore historical La Guaira will find the colonial zone most interesting.

Caracas is a bustling, multiethnic, cosmopolitan city of 6 million people. It isn't the safest spot in the world, so passengers should travel in groups if touring the capital city on their own. In La Guaira, too, it's best to explore in a group or with a local taxi driver/guide: the colonial district is filled with "banditos." And unless you want to stick out like a sore thumb, and a rather rude one at that, men should wear long slacks and women should wear slacks or a short-sleeve dress.

Due to its rapid growth, Caracas is a hodgepodge of styles. Many of the buildings, such as Centro Banaven, a black, glass-sided box, display innovative touches; but there is also a healthy share of neoclassical buildings, like the 19th-century Capitol and the 20th-century Fine Arts Museum, as well as heavier, neogothic structures. The colonial dwellings of La Guaira are fascinating symbols of affluence long gone: Few have been restored, and they stand in silent, weathered testimony to the passage of time.

Currency The monetary unit is the bolivar (Bs). At press time the dollar exchange stood at Bs 100 on the free market. Store owners prefer U.S. dollars, however, and may even give you a discount for paying in greenbacks.

Passports and You will need a passport and a tourist card, which should be issued
Visas by your cruise line. If you don't receive a card with your tickets, check with your travel agent or the cruise line.

Telephones International calls, which are quite expensive, are best made from a
and Mail CANTV office. Ask at the cruise terminal for the nearest one. For operator-assisted international calls, dial 122. AT&T now offers a collect-call service to the United States: Dialing 800/11120 connects you directly with an English-speaking operator. Airmail letters to North America cost Bs 80, postcards Bs 40. There is a post office at the edge of the colonial zone in La Guaira, just east of the cruise-ship terminal.

Shore The following are good choices in Caracas. They may not be offered
Excursions by all cruise lines. Times and prices are approximate. Unless otherwise noted, children's prices are for those under 13.

Angel Falls and Canaima Lagoon. A jet ride carries you into the lush jungle interior and over Angel Falls—at 3,212 feet, the world's highest waterfall. After landing, you travel by canoe to a resort jungle camp to see another waterfall and the rich vegetation up close. Lunch is followed by a swim in a lagoon, with enough time to hike and explore. Not all ships offer this unforgettable tour. If yours doesn't, ask your shore-excursion director if it can be arranged for you. *9 hrs. Cost: $200.*

Caracas. If you want to see the city, a shore excursion is a much better choice than hiring a car. The half-day tour will show you all you need to see, and still leave you time to explore the area around the ship. *4 hrs. Cost: $30 adults, $18 children.*

Coming Cruise ships dock at a modern terminal with souvenir stands and
Ashore shops inside. Taxi drivers will quote negotiable prices for the round-trip ride to Caracas. Pay no more than $60, and never pay in advance or you may be left stranded. If you plan to explore La Guaira, it's best to hire an English-speaking driver/guide. Although the colonial zone is just a short distance east of the cruise-ship terminal, the walk along the highway is neither particularly scenic nor safe. Pay no more than $15–$20 to see the sights and return to the ship.

Getting The modern and handsome Metro, with its elegant French cars, cov-
Around ers 13 miles between Propatria in the west and Palo Verde in the
By Subway east. A million passengers a day ride the quiet rubber-wheeled trains in air-conditioned comfort. It is such a pleasant experience that some city-tour shore excursions include a jaunt on the subway as a highlight. Individual fares are from Bs 13 to Bs 16.

By Taxi Taxis are the best means of independent exploration. Private tours can be arranged just inside the cruise-ship terminal.

Exploring La Begin a quick survey of the colonial district at **Plaza Vargas,** on the
Guaira main shore road. Locals gather here around the statue of José Maria Vargas, a Guaireño who was Venezuela's third president. Across the plaza is Calle Bolívar, running between the shore road and the mountains. Lined by the cool and cavernous warehouses of another century's trade and by one- and two-story houses with their colonial windows and red-tile roofs, the street funnels the sea breezes like voices from a more gracious age. Have your driver/guide wait for you at the plaza while you walk down this narrow street.

With your back to the water (you'll be facing the mountains), turn right out of Plaza Vargas to find one of the best-preserved colonial buildings: **Boulton Museum,** a pink house with an ample wood balcony. It will be on your left as you walk down Calle Bolívar. Inside is a treasury of paintings, maps, documents, pistols, and other miscellany collected by the family of John Boulton, occupants of the house for more than 140 years. Unfortunately, the museum is now closed.

At the foot of Calle Bolívar, turn right and pass the post office. Next door is one of the most important old buildings in La Guaira, **Casa Guipuzcoana.** Built in 1734, it was the colony's largest civic structure, housing first the Basque company that held a trading monopoly for 50 years, then the customs office. Restored as a cultural center, it is now the Vargas District Town Hall. Follow the main shore road back to Plaza Vargas, where your driver should be waiting for you.

Exploring Caracas   *Numbers in the margin correspond to points of interest on the Caracas map.*

❶ Caracas radiates from its historic center, **Plaza Bolívar.** The old Cathedral, City Hall, and Foreign Ministry (or Casa Amarilla) all face Plaza Bolívar, a pleasant shady square with benches, pigeons, and the fine equestrian statue of Simón Bolívar, who was born only a
❷ block away. Nearby also are the **Capitol,** the presidential offices in
❸ ❹ **Miraflores Palace,** and the 30-story twin towers of the **Simón Bolívar Center** in El Silencio.

Now replacing the twin towers as the symbol of modern Caracas is
❺ the concrete **Parque Central,** with its two 56-story skyscrapers. Built over 16 years, the office and apartment complex was finished in 1986. Designed for 10,000 people, with seven condominiums and two towers, Parque Central encompasses not only shops, supermarkets, and restaurants, but also schools, a swimming pool, a convention center, a hotel, and the **Museum of Contemporary Art.** A pedestrian
❻ bridge links Parque Central to the **Museum of Natural Sciences,** the
❼ ❽ **Museum of Fine Arts,** and **Los Caobos Park.** Beyond this bower of mahogany trees, once a coffee plantation, lies the circular fountain
❾ of **Plaza Venezuela.**

Across the *autopista* (highway) from Plaza Venezuela are the
❿ ⓫ **Botanical Gardens** and the **City University campus.** In its courtyards and buildings are a stained-glass wall by Fernand Léger; murals by Léger and Mateo Manaure; sculptures by Antoine Pevsner, Jean Arp, and Henry Laurens; and, in the **Aula Magna Auditorium,** acoustic "clouds" by Alexander Calder.

The great fountain with colored lights in Plaza Venezuela is part of the urban renewal undertaken by the **Caracas Metro.** The Metro is changing the face of Caracas. When entire avenues were torn up, architects and landscapers converted the commercial street of Sabana Grande into a pedestrian boulevard of shops, popular sidewalk cafés, potted plants, and chess tables. Cars are banned between the
⓬ **Radio City** theater and Chacaito, the pedestrian mall popularly
⓭ known as the **Bulevar de Sabana Grande.** People of all ages and nationalities come to savor the best cappuccino and conversation in town, from midday to midnight.

Shopping   Many of Caracas's sophisticated shops are in modern complexes known as *centros commerciales,* less stocked with imports than formerly, since devaluation has put foreign goods beyond most local shoppers' purses. Caracas is a buyer's market for fine clothing, tailored suits, elegant shoes, leather goods, and jewelry.

For wholesale jewelry go to **Edificio La Francia,** whose nine floors off Plaza Bolívar hold some 80 gold workshops and gem traders; profit margins are low, so buys are attractive. Since alluvial gold is found in Venezuela, nuggets of *cochanos* are made into pendants, rings, and bracelets. Expert gold designer **Panchita Labady,** who originated the popular gold orchid earrings and pins, works in a small shop at No. 98 Calle Real de Sabana Grande, opposite Avenida Los Jabillos (tel. 02/712016).

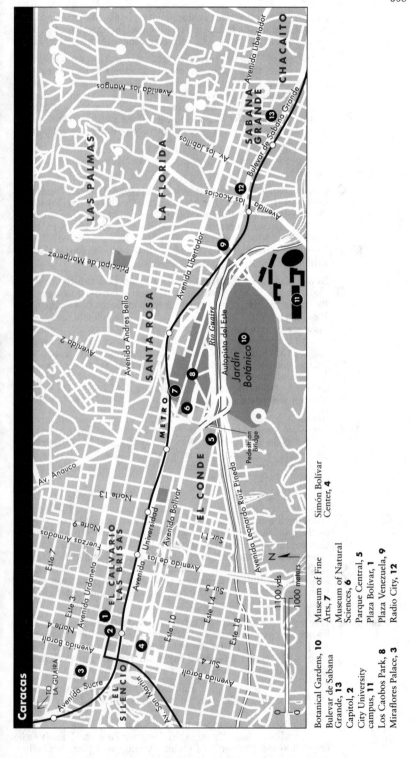

308

Caracas

Botanical Gardens, **10**
Bulevar de Sabana
Grande, **13**
Capitol, **2**
City University
campus, **11**
Los Caobos Park, **8**
Miraflores Palace, **3**

Museum of Fine
Arts, **7**
Museum of Natural
Sciences, **6**
Parque Central, **5**
Plaza Bolívar, **1**
Plaza Venezuela, **9**
Radio City, **12**

Simón Bolívar
Center, **4**

Devil's masks are much sought after for colorful souvenirs. Used in ritual dances marking the Corpus Christi festival (usually in early June), they are made of brightly painted papier-mâché. A good place to find these and other uniquely Venezuelan gifts is El Taller de La Esquina, Nivel Galeria, in the Paseo Las Mercedes shopping center. Explore other *artesanía* (folk art) shops in Paseo Las Mercedes.

Dining   *There is a 10% service charge in Venezuelan restaurants, and it is customary to tip the waiter another 10%.*

La Estancia. Black-and-white photos of famous bullfighters seem right at home in this traditional Spanish-style restaurant. But despite the obvious Spanish influence, criollo dishes are the house specialty. Start with the lobster bisque and move on to the *parillas* (criollo-style grill) or rabbit or chicken basted in orange sauce. *Av. Principal de la Castellana, Esquina Urdaneta, tel. 02/261–2363. Reservations advised. AE, MC, V. $$–$$$*

Le Coq d'Or. Probably the best French restaurant for the money in Caracas. The menu varies but it's always dependable. *Calle Los Mangos at Av. Las Delicias (between Bulevar de Sabana Grande and Av. Francisco Solano), tel. 02/761–0891. AE. Closed Mon. $*

Cozumel, Mexico

Sun-saturated Cozumel, its ivory beaches fringed with coral reefs, fulfills the tourist's vision of a tropical Caribbean island. More Mexican than Cancún and far less developed, Cozumel surpasses its better-known, fancier neighbor to the north in several ways. It has more—and lovelier—secluded beaches, superior diving and snorkeling, more authentically Mexican cuisine, and a greater diversity of handicrafts at better prices.

Life on this flat jungle island centers on the town of San Miguel. The duty-free shops stay open as long as a ship is in town, and most of the salespeople speak English. With the world-renowned Palancar Reef nearby, San Miguel is also a favorite among divers.

Cozumel is becoming an increasingly popular port of call for cruise ships on western Caribbean itineraries; one line, Regency, has even homeported the *Regent Spirit* here. As more and more cruise passengers arrive, the island has grown more commercial. Waterfront shops and restaurants have taken on a more glitzy appearance— gone are the hole-in-the-wall craft shops and little diners, replaced by high-dollar duty-free shops, gem traders, and slick eateries. There are also no less than half a dozen American fast-food chains and a Hard Rock Cafe.

Cruise ships visiting just for the day call at Cozumel; ships staying for two days usually call at Cozumel on one day and anchor off Playa del Carmen, across the channel on the Yucatan Peninsula, on the other. From here, excursions go to Cancún, or to the Mayan ruins at Tulum, Cobá, and Chichén Itzá.

Currency   In Mexico, the currency is the peso, but you may find items priced in as many as three different designations, P$ (the least common), NP$ (for *nuevo pesos*), or just N$ (the most common). If you see something you want to buy priced in P$, just knock off three zeros. (For instance, a pair of silver earrings marked P$5000 is equal to N$5). At press time, the exchange rate was about N$6 to $1, but the situation was highly changeable due to Mexico's financial crisis. Although U.S. dollars are widely accepted, you'll want some pesos in hand if you plan to take the ferry to Playa del Carmen or go exploring on your own.

Passports and   U.S. and Canadian citizens need only proof of citizenship (a passport
Visas   is best). All British subjects require a passport and a Mexican tourist card.

Telephones The best place to make long-distance calls is at the **Calling Station**
and Mail (Av. Rafael E. Melgar 27 and Calle 3 S., tel. 987/21417, open mid-
Dec.–April, daily 8 AM–11 PM; rest of the year, Mon.–Sat. 9 AM–10 PM
and Sun. 9–1 and 5–10), where you'll save 10%–50%. You can also exchange money here. Though postal rates are quite low in Mexico, service is notoriously slow. Postcards to the United States cost P$1.50; to
Britain, P$2. Letters (up to 10 grams) cost P$2 to the United States
and P$3 to Britain.

Shore The following are good choices in Cozumel. They may not be offered
Excursions by all cruise lines. Times and prices are approximate.

Archaeological **Chichén Itzá.** This incredible and awe-inspiring ruin of a great
Sites Mayan city is a 45-minute flight from Cozumel or a 12-hour round-
trip bus ride from Playa del Carmen. A box lunch is included. *Full
day. Cost: $130 (by plane), $85 (by bus).*

Tulum Ruins and Xel-ha Lagoon. An English-speaking guide leads a
tour to this superbly preserved ancient Mayan city, perched on the
cliffs above a beautiful beach. A box lunch is usually included. A stop
is made for a swim in the glass-clear waters of Xel-ha. The tour
leaves from Playa del Carmen. *7–8 hrs. Cost: $70.*

Undersea **Glass-Bottom Boat.** For those who don't dive, a tour boat with a see-
Creatures through floor takes passengers to the famed Paraiso and Chankanaab sites to view schools of tropical fish. *2 hrs. Cost: $27.*

Snorkeling. This region has been acknowledged by experts from
Jacques Cousteau to *Skin Diver Magazine* as one of the top diving
destinations in the world. If your ship offers a snorkeling tour, take
it. Equipment and lessons are included. *3 hrs. Cost: $30.*

Coming As many as six ships call at Cozumel on a busy day, tendering pas-
Ashore sengers to the downtown pier in the center of San Miguel or docking
at the international pier 4 miles away. From the downtown pier you
can walk into town or catch the ferry to Playa del Carmen. The international pier is close to many beaches, but you'll need a taxi to get
into town. There's a tourist information directory on the main
square, immediately across from the downtown pier, and an information office upstairs in the Plaza del Sol mall, at the east end of the
square (open weekdays 9 AM–2:30 PM).

Getting To get to Playa del Carmen from Cozumel, you can take a ferry or a
Around jetfoil from the downtown pier. It costs about $10 round-trip and
By Ferry takes 40–60 minutes each way. Travelers prone to seasickness
should take medications before embarking. Ferries depart every
hour; the last ferry back to Cozumel leaves around 8:30 PM, but be
sure to double-check because the schedule changes frequently.

By Car or Mopeds are great fun, and you can circumnavigate the island on one
Moped tank of gas. The only gas station is at the corner of Avenida Juárez
and Avenida 30 (open 7 AM–midnight). Wear a helmet and be careful:
Accidents are frequent on Cozumel. Four-wheel drive is recommended
if you're planning to explore the many dirt roads around the island. For
two- or four-wheel rentals, contact **Auto Rent** (tel. 987/20844, ext.
712), **Budget** (tel. 987/21732), **National Interrent** (tel. 987/23263), or
Rentadora Cozumel (tel. 987/21429). Rates start at about $50 per
day in summer, $75 in winter. Mopeds cost about half the price of a
car.

In Playa del Carmen you can rent a car from **PlayaCar Rental** (tel.
987/30241).

By Taxi Taxis are everywhere in Cozumel. Stands are on Avenida Melgar,
just north of the downtown pier, and in front of all the major hotels.
At Playa del Carmen, you can usually find a cab just off the ferry
pier. Taxis to surrounding towns and archaeological sites are not
cheap unless you're traveling in a group. Expect to pay about $45 to
Cancún and $25 to Tulum or Akumal. Agree on the fare in advance.

Exploring Cozumel San Miguel is tiny—you cannot get lost—and best explored on foot. The main attractions are the small eateries and shops that line the streets. Activity centers on the ferry and the main square, where the locals congregate in the evenings. The lovely **Museo de le Isla de Cozumel,** with exhibits devoted to the island environment and to the ecosystem of the surrounding reefs and water, is on the main coastal drag, near the ferry dock. On the second floor are displays on Mayan and colonial life and on modern-day Cozumel. *Av. Melgar and Calle 4 N. Admission: $3. Open daily 10–6.*

It's not necessary to go to the mainland to explore ancient Mayan and Toltec ruins because Cozumel has several sites of archaeological interest. Start with a visit to the **Cozumel Archaeological Park,** five minutes by cab from the downtown pier/plaza area. Three thousand years of pre-Columbian Mexican culture and art are showcased here. More than 65 full-size replicas of Toltec, Mexicas, and Mayan statues and stone carvings are surrounded by jungle foliage. A guided walking tour, included in the admission price, takes about an hour. *65th Av. S, tel. 987/20914. Admission $3. Open daily 8 AM–6 PM.*

To see the largest Mayan and Toltec site on Cozumel, head inland to the jungle. The ruins at **San Gervasio** once served as the island's capital and probably its ceremonial center, dedicated to the fertility goddess Ixchel. What remains today are numerous ruins scattered around a plaza and a main road leading to the sea (probably a major trade route). There's no interpretive signage, so you'll need to hire a guide in order to get much out of your visit. Guides charge $12 for groups of up to six, so try to get a group together aboard ship. *Admission: $1 to private road, $3.50 for ruins. Open daily 8–5.*

To sample Cozumel's natural beauty, head south out of town on Avenida Melgar; after 6½ miles your first stop will be the **Chankanaab Nature Park.** The natural aquarium has been designated an underwater preserve for more than 50 species of tropical fish, as well as crustaceans and coral. Snorkeling and scuba equipment can be rented, and instruction and professional guides are available, along with gift shops, snack bars, and a restaurant (open 10–5) serving fresh seafood. *Admission: $5. Open daily 6 AM–5:30 PM.*

Shopping San Miguel's biggest industry—even bigger than diving—is selling souvenirs and crafts to cruise-ship passengers. The primary items are ceramics, onyx, brass, wood carvings, colorful blankets and hammocks, reproductions of Mayan artifacts, shells, silver, gold, sportswear, T-shirts, perfume, and liquor. Almost all stores take U.S. dollars.

The shopping district centers on the Plaza del Sol and extends out along Avenida Melgar and Avenida 5 S and N. Good shops for Mexican crafts are **Los Cinco Soles** and **La Concha** (both on Av. Melgar) and **Unicornio** (Av. 5a S1, just off the Plaza del Sol). The most bizarre collection of shops on the island is the **Cozumel Flea Market,** on Avenida 5 N between Calles 2 and 4, which sells reproductions of erotic Mayan figurines, antique masks, rare coins, and Xtabentún, the local anise-and-honey liqueur. Down the street at Avenida 5 N #14, **Arte Na Balam** sells high-quality Mayan reproductions, jewelry, batik clothing, and a typical array of curios. For atmosphere, fresh fruit, and other foods, go to the **Municipal Market** at Avenida 25 S and Calle Salas.

Sports
Fishing In Cozumel contact **Yucab Reef Diving and Fishing Center** (tel. 987/24110) or **Club Naútico Cozumel** (tel. 987/20118 or 800/253–2701 in the U.S.)

Scuba Diving and Snorkeling Cozumel is famous for its reefs. In addition to **Chankanaab Nature Park,** another great dive site is **La Ceiba Reef,** in the waters off La

Ceiba and Sol Caribe hotels. Here lies the wreckage of a sunken airplane that was blown up for a Mexican disaster movie. Cozumel's dive shops include **Aqua Safari** (tel. 987/20101), **Blue Angel** (Hotel Villablanca, tel. 987/21631), **Dive Paradise** (tel. 987/21007), and **Fantasia Divers** (tel. 987/22840 or 800/336–3483 in the U.S.) and **Michelle's Dive Shop** (tel. 987/209470).

Dining *Although it is not common in Mexico, a 10%–15% service charge may be added to the bill. Otherwise, a 10%–20% tip is customary.*

Pancho's Backyard. A jungle of greenery, trickling fountains, ceiling fans, and leather chairs set the tone at this inviting restaurant, located on the cool patio of Los Cincos Soles shopping center. The menu highlights local standards such as black bean soup, *carmone al carbon* (grilled prawns), and fajitas. Round out your meal with coconut ice cream in Kahlua. *Av. Rafael Melgar N 27 at Calle 8 N, tel. 987/22141. AE, MC, V. Closed Sun. No lunch Sat. $$*

Rincón Maya. This is the top place on the island for Yucatecan cuisine and a popular spot with locals and divers. Lobster and fresh fish *a la plancha* (grilled) and *poc chuc* (marinated grilled pork) are among the excellent dishes. The decor is festive; a colorful mural, hats, masks, and fans adorn the walls. *Av. 5A S between Calles 3 and 5 S, tel. 987/20467. No lunch. No credit cards. $$*

Prima Pasta & Pizza Trattoria. Since Texan Albert Silmai opened this Northern Italian diner just south of the plaza, he's attracted a strong following of patrons who come for the hearty, inexpensive pizzas, calzones, sandwiches, and pastas. The breezy dining area, located on a second-floor terrace above the kitchen, smells heavenly and has a charming Mediterranean mural painted on two walls. *A. Rosado Salas 109, tel. 987/24242. MC, V. $*

Nightlife After 10 PM, **Carlos 'n' Charlie's** (Av. Melgar 11 between Calles 2 and 4 N, tel. 987/20191) and **Chilly's** (Av. Melgar near Av. Benito Juarez, tel. 987/21832) are the local equivalent of college fraternity parties. The new **Hard Rock Cafe** (Av. Rafael Melgar 2A near Av. Benito Juarez) is similarly raucous. A favorite with ships' crews is **Scaramouche** (Av. Melgar at Calle Rosada Salas, tel. 987/20791), a dark, cavernous disco with a crowded dance floor surrounded by tiered seating.

Curaçao

Try to be on deck as your ship sails into Curaçao. The tiny Queen Emma Floating Bridge swings aside to open the narrow channel. Pastel gingerbread buildings on shore look like dollhouses, especially from the perspective of a large cruise ship. Although the gabled roofs and red tiles show a Dutch influence, the riotous colors of the facades are peculiar to Curaçao. It is said that white gave the first governor of Curaçao migraines, so all the houses were painted in colors.

Thirty-five miles north of Venezuela and 42 miles east of Aruba, Curaçao is, at 180 square miles, the largest of the Netherlands Antilles. While always sunny, it is never stiflingly hot here, due to the cooling influence of the trade winds. Water sports attract enthusiasts from all over the world, and the reef diving is excellent.

History books still don't agree as to whether Alonzo de Ojeda or Amerigo Vespucci discovered Curaçao, only that it happened around 1499. In 1634 the Dutch came and promptly shipped off the Spanish settlers and the few remaining Indians to Venezuela. To defend itself against French and British invasions, the city built massive ramparts, many of which now house unusual restaurants and hotels.

Today, Curaçao's population, which comprises more than 50 nationalities, is one of the best educated in the Caribbean. The island is known for its religious tolerance, and tourists are warmly welcomed and almost never pestered by vendors and shopkeepers.

Currency U.S. dollars are fine, so don't worry about exchanging money, except for pay phones or soda machines. The local currency is the guilder or florin, indicated by "fl" or "NAf" on price tags. The official rate of exchange at press time was NAf 1.79 to U.S. $1.

Passports and Visas U.S. and Canadian citizens need only proof of citizenship and a photo ID. British citizens must have a passport.

Telephones and Mail The telephone system is reliable and there's an overseas phone center in the cruise-ship terminal. Dialing to the United States is exactly the same as dialing long distance within the United States. To airmail a letter to anywhere in the world costs NAf 1.25; a postcard costs NAf .70.

Shore Excursions The following are good choices in Curaçao. They may not be offered by all cruise lines. Times and prices are approximate.

Island Sights **Country Drive.** This is a good tour if you'd like to see Westpunt and Mt. Christoffel but don't want to risk driving an hour there yourself. Other stops are the Museum of Natural History, Boca Tabla, and Knip Beach. *3½ hrs. Cost: $25.*

Undersea Creatures **Sharks, Stingrays, and Shipwrecks.** Curaçao's seaquarium, a marine park, and two sunken ships reached by a 30-minute submarine trip highlight this tour of the island's marine environment. *3 hrs. Cost: $40.*

Coming Ashore Ships dock at the cruise-ship terminal just beyond the Queen Emma Bridge, which leads to the floating market and shopping district. The walk from the berth to downtown takes 5–10 minutes. Easy-to-read tourist information maps are posted dockside and in the shopping area. The terminal has a duty-free shop, a telephone office, and a taxi stand.

Getting Around Willemstad is small and navigable on foot; you needn't spend more than two or three hours wandering around here. English, Spanish, and Dutch are widely spoken. Narrow Santa Anna Bay divides the city into the Punda, where the main shopping district is, and the Otrabanda (literally, the "other side"), where the cruise ships dock. The Punda is crammed with shops, restaurants, monuments, and markets. The Otrabanda has narrow winding streets full of homes notable for their gables and Dutch-influenced designs.

You can cross from the Otrabanda to the Punda in one of three ways: Walk across the Queen Emma Pontoon Bridge; ride the free ferry, which runs when the bridge swings open (at least 30 times a day) to let seagoing vessels pass; or take a cab across the Julianna Bridge (about $7).

By Car To rent a car, call **Avis** (tel. 599/9–681163), **Budget** (tel. 599/9–683420), or **National** (tel. 599/9–683489). All you'll need is a valid U.S. or Canadian driver's license. Rates begin at $35 per day.

By Moped Rentals are available right at the pier. If you want to explore farther into the countryside, mopeds are an inexpensive alternative to renting a car or hiring a taxi.

By Taxi Taxis are metered, but confirm the price before getting in. Taxis meet every cruise ship, and they can be picked up at hotels. Otherwise, call **Central Dispatch** (tel. 599/9–616711). A taxi tour for up to four people will cost about $25 an hour.

Exploring Curaçao *Numbers in the margin correspond to points of interest on the Curaçao map.*

Willemstad A quick tour of downtown **Willemstad** covers a six-block radius. Be-
❶ gin at the **Queen Emma Bridge,** which the locals call the Lady. The toll to cross the original bridge, built in 1888, was 2¢ per person if

Curaçao

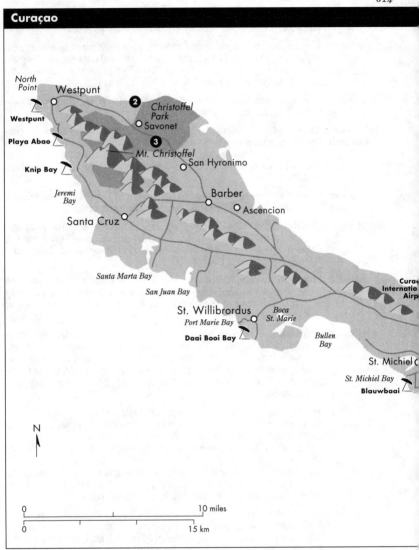

North
Point

Westpunt

Westpunt

Playa Abao

Knip Bay

Jeremi
Bay

Santa Cruz

2 Christoffel
Park
○ Savonet

3
Mt. Christoffel
○ San Hyronimo

Barber
○ Ascencion

Santa Marta Bay

San Juan Bay

St. Willibrordus
Port Marie Bay
Boca
St. Marie

Daai Booi Bay

Bullen
Bay

Cura
Internatio
Airp

St. Michiel

St. Michiel Bay

Blauwbaai

N

0   10 miles
0   15 km

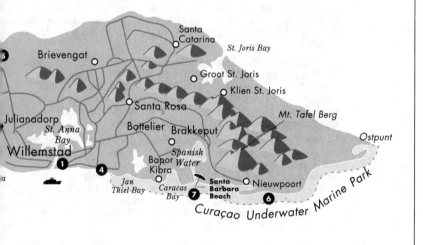

Caribbean Sea

Brievengat

Santa Catarina

St. Joris Bay

Groot St. Joris

Klien St. Joris

Julianadorp

Santa Rosa

St. Anna Bay

Bottelier

Brakkeput

Mt. Tafel Berg

Ostpunt

Willemstad

Spanish Water

Bapor Kibra

Jan Thiel Bay

Caracas Bay

Santa Barbara Beach

Nieuwpoort

Curaçao Underwater Marine Park

KEY

Cruise Ship

wearing shoes and free if barefoot. Today it's free, regardless of what is on your feet.

Once on the Punda side, turn left and walk up the waterfront along **Handelskade** to take a closer look at the charming buildings. The original red roof tiles came from Europe on trade ships as ballast. Walk down to the corner at the end of the street and turn right at the customs building onto Sha Caprileskade. At the bustling **floating market** that convenes here each morning, dozens of Venezuelan schooners arrive laden with tropical fruits and vegetables. Any produce bought at the market should be thoroughly washed before eating.

Keep walking down Sha Caprileskade toward the Wilhelmina Drawbridge, which connects the Punda with the once-flourishing district of **Scharloo.** The early Jewish merchants built stately homes in Scharloo; it is now a red-light district. At the bridge turn right and walk down Columbusstraat to the **Mikveh Israel-Emmanuel Synagogue,** founded in 1651 and the oldest temple still in use in the Western Hemisphere. It draws 20,000 visitors a year. Enter through the gates around the corner on Hanchi Snoa. A museum in the back displays Jewish antiques and fine Judaica. *Hanchi Di Snoa 29, tel. 599/ 9–611067. Small donation expected. Open weekdays 9–11:45, 2:30–5.*

Continue along Columbusstraat until you reach **Wilhelminaplein.** The statue keeping watch is of Queen Wilhelmina, a popular monarch of the Netherlands who gave up her throne to her daughter Juliana after her Golden Jubilee in 1948. At the far side of the square is the impressive Georgian facade of the McLaughlin Bank and, to its right, the courthouse with its stately balustrade.

Returning back across Wilhelminaplein, turn left at Breedestraat and go down toward the Pontoon Bridge, turning left at the waterfront. At the foot of the bridge are the mustard-color walls of **Ft. Amsterdam;** take a few steps through the archway and enter another century. In the 1700s the structure was actually the center of the city and the most important fort on the island. Now it houses the governor's residence, the Fort Church, the ministry, and several other government offices.

Western Curaçao The road that leads to the northwest tip of the island winds through landscape that Georgia O'Keeffe might have painted—towering cacti, flamboyant dried shrubbery, aluminum-roofed houses. In these parts you'll see fishermen hauling in their nets, women pounding cornmeal, and donkeys blocking traffic. Landhouses—large estate homes, most of which are closed to the public—can often be glimpsed from the road.

2 3 Past **Boca Tabla,** where the sea has carved a magnificent grotto, is **Christoffel Park.** It's a good hour from Willemstad (so watch your time), but worth a visit. This fantastic 4,450-acre garden and wildlife preserve with Mt. Christoffel at its center consists of three former plantations. As you drive through the park, watch for tiny deer, goats, and other small wildlife that might suddenly dart in front of your car. If you skip everything else on the island, it's possible to drive to the park and climb 1,239-foot Mt. Christoffel, which takes from two to three strenuous hours. The island panorama you get from the peak is amazing—on a clear day you can even see the mountain ranges of Venezuela, Bonaire, and Aruba. *Savonet, tel. 599/9– 640363. Admission: $5 adults, $3 children. Open Mon.–Sat. 8–5, Sun. 8–3.*

Eastern Curaçao At the **Curaçao Seaquarium,** more than 400 varieties of exotic fish and vegetation are displayed. Outside is a 495-yard-long artificial
4 beach of white sand, well-suited to novice swimmers and children.

Tel. 599/9–616666. Admission: $6 adults, $3 children. Open daily 9 AM–10 PM.

⑤ Near the airport is **Hato Caves,** where you can take an hour-long guided tour into various chambers containing water pools, a voodoo chamber, fruit bats' sleeping quarters, and Curaçao Falls—where a stream of silver joins a stream of gold. Hidden lights illuminate the limestone formations and gravel walkways. This is one of the better Caribbean caves open to the public. *Tel. 599/9–680378. Admission: $4.25 adults, $2.75 children. Open Tues.–Sun. 10–5.*

⑥ **Curaçao Underwater Marine Park** (*see* Sports, *below*) is the best spot for snorkeling—though the seabed is sadly litter-strewn in places. The park stretches along the southern shore from the Princess Beach Hotel in Willemstad to the eastern tip of the island.

Along the southern shore, you'll pass several private yacht clubs that attract sports anglers from all over the world for international tournaments. Stop at **Santa Barbara Beach,** especially on Sunday, when the atmosphere approaches party time. **Caracas Bay,** off
⑦ Bapor Kibra, is a popular dive site, with a sunken ship so close to the surface that even snorkelers can balance their flippers on the helm.

Shopping Curaçao has some of the best shops in the Caribbean, but in many cases the prices are no lower than in U.S. discount stores. Hours are usually Monday–Saturday 8–noon and 2–6. Most shops are within the six-block area of Willemstad described above. The main shopping streets are Heerenstraat, Breedestraat, and Madurostraat, where you'll find Bamali (tel. 599/9–612258) for Indonesian batik clothing and leather, and the African Queen (tel. 599/9–612682), an exotic bazaar of fine African jewelry, batik clothes, and Kenyan pocketbooks handmade of coconut husk and sisal. Fundason Obra di Man (Bargestraat 57, tel. 599/9–612413) sells native crafts and curios.

Arawak Craft Products (tel. 599/3–627249), conveniently located between the Queen Emma bridge and the cruise-ship terminal, is open whenever ships are in port. You can buy a variety of tiles, plates, pots, and tiny landhouse replicas here.

Along the Gomezplein, a pedestrian mall in the center of the shopping district, **Spritzer & Fuhrmann** (Gomezplein 1, tel. 599/9–612600), the top jeweler in the Netherlands Antilles, carries gold, watches, crystal, diamonds, emeralds, and china. Try **New Amsterdam** (Gomezplein 14, tel. 599/9–613823) for hand-embroidered tablecloths, napkins, and pillowcases.

Sports **Christoffel Park** (*see* Exploring Curaçao, *above*) has a number of
Hiking challenging trails.

Scuba Diving The **Curaçao Underwater Marine Park** (tel. 599/9–618131) is about
and Snorkeling 12½ miles of untouched coral reef that have been granted national park status. Mooring buoys mark the most interesting dive sites. If your cruise ship doesn't offer a diving or snorkeling excursion, contact **Curaçao Seascape** (tel. 599/9–625000, ext. 177), **Peter Hughes Divers** (tel. 599/9–614944, ext. 5047), or **Underwater Curaçao** (tel. 599/9–618131).

Beaches Curaçao doesn't have long, powdery stretches of sand. Instead you'll discover the joy of inlets: tiny bays marked by craggy cliffs, exotic trees, and scads of interesting pebbles. Westpunt, on the northwest tip of the island, is rocky with very little sand, but shady in the morning and with a bay view worth the one-hour trip. On Sunday watch the divers jump from the high cliff. Knip Bay has two parts: Groot (Big) Knip and Kleine (Little) Knip. Both have alluring white sand, and Kleine Knip is shaded by (highly poisonous) manchineel trees. Take the road to the Knip Landhouse, then turn right; signs will direct you. Blauwbaai (Blue Bay)—one of the largest, most spectacular beaches on Curaçao—offers plenty of white sand and shade, as well as showers and changing facilities. Admission is about $2.50 per car. Take the road that leads past the Holiday Beach Hotel north toward Julianadrop, and follow the sign to Blaauwbaai and San Michiel.

Dining *Restaurants usually add a 10%–15% service charge to the bill.*

Bistro Le Clochard. This romantic gem is built into the 18th-century Rif Fort and is suffused with the cool, dark atmosphere of ages past. The use of fresh ingredients in consistently well-prepared French and Swiss dishes makes dining a dream. Try the fresh fish platters or the tender veal in mushroom sauce. Save room for the chocolate mousse. *On the Otrabanda Rif Fort, tel. 599/9–625666. Reservations required. AE, DC, MC, V. Closed Sun. off-season. No lunch Sat. $$$*

Jaanchi's Restaurant. Tour buses stop regularly at this open-air restaurant for lunch and for weird-sounding but mouthwatering native dishes. The main-course specialty is a hefty platter of fresh fish, potatoes, and vegetables. *Westpunt 15, tel. 599/9–640126. AE, DC, MC, V. $*

Grand Cayman

The largest and most populous of the Cayman Islands, Grand Cayman is one of the hottest cruise destinations in the Caribbean, largely because it doesn't suffer from the ailments afflicting many larger ports: panhandlers, hasslers, and crime. Instead, the Cayman economy is a study in stability, and residents are renowned for their courteous behavior. Though cacti and scrub fill the dusty landscape, Grand Cayman is a diver's paradise, with translucent waters and a colorful variety of marine life protected by the government.

Compared with other Caribbean ports, there are fewer things to see on land; instead, the island's most impressive sights are under water. Snorkeling, diving, and glass-bottom-boat and submarine rides top every ship's shore-excursion list and also can be arranged at major aquatic shops. Grand Cayman is also famous for the 554 offshore banks in George Town; not surprisingly, the standard of living is high and nothing is cheap.

Currency The U.S. dollar is accepted everywhere. The Cayman Island dollar (C.I.$) is worth about U.S. $1.20. Prices are often quoted in Cayman dollars, so make sure you know which currency you're dealing with.

Passports and Visas Passports are not required for U.S. or Canadian citizens, but you must have proof of citizenship. British and Commonwealth subjects do not need a visa but must carry a passport.

Telephones and Mail Phone service is better here than on most islands. Calling the United States is the same as calling long distance in the States: Just dial 01 followed by the area code and telephone number. Sending a postcard to the United States or Canada costs C.I. 15¢; an airmail letter, C.I. 30¢ per half ounce. To Europe, rates are C.I. 20¢ for a postcard and C.I. 40¢ per half ounce for airmail letters. The main post office in downtown George Town is open Monday–Friday 8:30–3:30 and Saturday 8:30–11:30.

Shore Excursions The following are good choices in Grand Cayman. They may not be offered by all cruise lines. Times and prices are approximate. Unless otherwise noted, children's prices are for those under 13.

Undersea Creatures **Atlantis Submarine.** A real submarine offers an exciting view of Grand Cayman's profuse marine life. *1 hr. Cost: $75.*

Seaworld Explorer Cruise. A glass-bottom boat takes you on an air-conditioned, narrated voyage where you sit 5 feet below the water's

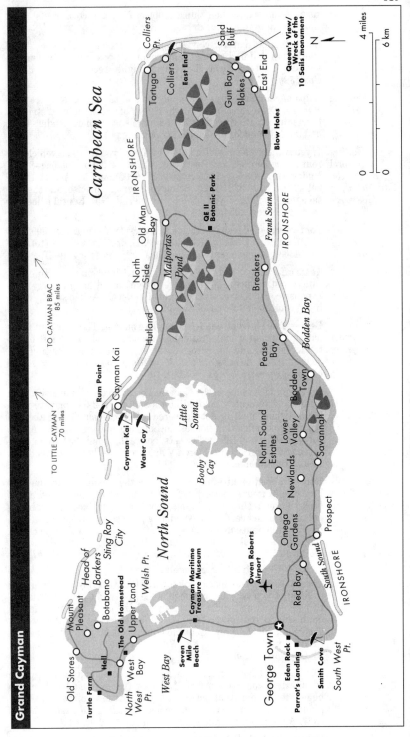

Grand Cayman

Caribbean Sea

TO CAYMAN BRAC 85 miles

TO LITTLE CAYMAN 70 miles

Colliers Pt.

Sand Bluff

Colliers

East End

Tortuga

Gun Bay

Blakes

East End

Queen's View/Wreck of the 10 Sails monument

IRONSHORE

Old Man Bay

QE II Botanic Park

Blow Holes

North Side

Malportas Pond

Hutland

Breakers

IRONSHORE

Frank Sound

Rum Point

Cayman Kai

Cayman Kai

Water Cay

Pease Bay

Bodden Bay

Little Sound

North Sound

Booby Cay

North Sound Estates

Lower Valley

Bodden Town

Savannah

Head of Barkers

Sting Ray City

Mount Pleasant

Botabano

The Old Homestead

Upper Land

Welsh Pt.

Cayman Maritime Treasure Museum

Omega Gardens

Newlands

Prospect

Old Stores

Hell

Turtle Farm

North West Pt.

West Bay

West Bay Pt.

Seven Mile Beach

Owen Roberts Airport

Red Bay

South Sound

IRONSHORE

George Town

Eden Rock

Parrot's Landing

Smith Cove

South West Pt.

N

0   4 miles

0   6 km

surface and see sunken ships, tropical fish, and coral reefs. *1 hr. Cost: $29 adults, $19 children.*

Snorkeling Adventure. Novices can take lessons and experienced snorkelers will find good adventure on this boat trip to one or two snorkeling sites—Sting Ray City is highly recommended. *2 hrs. Cost: $28.*

Coming Ashore

Ships anchor in George Town harbor and tender passengers onto Harbour Drive, placing you in the center of the shopping district. A tourist information booth is located on the pier where tenders land, and taxis line up for disembarking passengers.

Getting Around

By Bicycle, Car, Moped, or Motorcycle

If you want to see more than George Town, you'll need a vehicle. To rent a car, contact **Ace Hertz** (tel. 809/949–2280 or 800/654–3131), **Budget** (tel. 809/949–5605 or 800/527–0700), or **Cico Avis** (tel. 809/949–2468 or 800/228–0668). Bring your driver's license, and the rental agency will issue you a temporary permit ($5). Rental prices for cars range from $35 to $55 a day.

For two-wheeled transportation, try **Bicycles Cayman** (tel. 809/949–5572), **Cayman Cycle** (tel. 809/947–4021), or **Soto Scooters** (tel. 809/947–4363). Mopeds rent for $25–$30 a day, bikes for $10–$15.

By Taxi

Taxis offer island-wide service. Fares are determined by an elaborate rate structure set by the government, and although it may seem expensive, cabbies rarely try to rip off tourists. Ask to see the chart if you want to double-check the quoted fare.

Exploring Grand Cayman

George Town is small enough to explore on foot. The small but fascinating **Cayman Islands National Museum,** found to the left of the tender landing and just across the street, is well worth visiting. *Tel. 809/949–8368. Admission: C.I. $5 adults, $2.50 students and senior citizens. Open weekdays 9–5, Sat. 10–4.*

On Cardinal Avenue is the **General Post Office,** built in 1939, with strands of decorative colored lights and about 2,000 private mailboxes (island mail is not delivered). Behind that is **Elizabethan Square,** a complex that houses clothing and souvenir stores. At the corner of Fort and Edward streets, notice the small **clock tower** dedicated to Britain's King George V and the huge fig tree pruned into an umbrella shape.

Rent a moped or hire a taxi to get to the **Cayman Maritime and Treasure Museum,** located in front of the Hyatt Hotel, and a real find. Dioramas show how Caymanians became seafarers, boat builders, and turtle breeders. Owned by a professional treasure-salvaging firm, the museum displays a lot of artifacts from shipwrecks. A shop offers excellent buys on authentic ancient coins and jewelry. *West Bay Rd., tel. 809/947–5033. Admission: $5 adults, $3 children 6–12. Open Mon.–Sat. 9–5.*

The **Old Homestead,** formerly known as the West Bay Pink House, is probably the most photographed home in Grand Cayman. This picturesque pink-and-white cottage was built in 1912 of waddle and daub around an ironwood frame. Tours are led by Mac Bothwell, a cheery guide who grew up in the house. Not far away from here is the Hell post office. *West Bay Rd., tel. 809/949–7639. Admission: $5. Open Mon.–Sat. 8–5.*

The **Cayman Island Turtle Farm** is the most popular attraction on the island. Here you'll see turtles of all ages, from day-old hatchlings to huge 600-pounders that can live to be 100. In the adjoining café, sample turtle soup or turtle sandwiches. *West Bay Rd., tel. 809/949–3893. Admission: $5 adults, $2.50 children 6–12. Open daily 9–5.*

Queen Elizabeth II Botanic Park is a 60-acre wilderness preserve showcasing the variety of habitats and plants native to the Caymans. Interpretive signs identify the flora along the mile-long walking trail. Halfway along the trail is a walled compound housing the rare blue iguana—it's found only in remote sections of the islands. *Frank Sound Rd., tel. 809/947–9462. Admission $3. Open daily 7:30–5:30.*

On the way to the East End are the **Blow Holes,** a great photo opportunity as waves crash into the fossilized coral beach, forcing water into caverns and sending geysers shooting up through the ironshore. Next is the village of **East End,** the first recorded settlement on Grand Cayman. Farther on, as the highway curves north, you'll come to **Queen's View** lookout point. There's a monument commemorating the legendary **Wreck of the Ten Sails,** which took place just offshore.

Shopping Grand Cayman is known for its turtle and black-coral products, but these are banned in the United States. **Fort Street** and **Cardinal Avenue** are the main shopping streets in George Town. On Cardinal Avenue is **Kirk Freeport Plaza,** with lots of jewelry shops, and the **George Town Craft Market,** with more kitschy souvenirs than crafts. On South Church Street and in the Hyatt Hotel, **Pure Art** (tel. 809/949–4433) features the work of local artists. The **Tortuga Rum Company's** (tel. 809/949–7701) scrumptious rum cake makes a great souvenir; most shops on Grand Cayman carry it.

Sports For fishing enthusiasts, Cayman waters are abundant with blue and
Fishing white marlin, yellowfin tuna, sailfish, dolphin fish, bonefish, and wahoo. If your ship does not offer a fishing excursion, about 25 boats are available for charter. Ask at the tourist information booth on the pier.

Scuba Diving Contact **Bob Soto's Diving Ltd.** (tel. 809/947–4631 or 800/262–7686),
and Snorkeling **Don Foster's Dive Grand Cayman** (tel. 809/949–5679 or 800/833–4837), **Eden Rock** (tel. 809/949–7243), and **Parrot's Landing** (tel. 809/949–7884 or 800/448–0428). The best snorkeling is off the **ironshore reef** (within walking distance of George Town on the west coast) and in the reef-protected shallows of the north and south coasts, where coral and fish are much more varied and abundant.

Beaches The west coast, the island's most developed area, is where you'll find the famous **Seven Mile Beach.** The white powdery beach is free of both litter and peddlers, but it is also Grand Cayman's busiest vacation center, and most of the island's resorts, restaurants, and shopping centers are located along this strip. The Holiday Inn rents Aqua Trikes, Paddle Cats, and Banana Rides.

Dining *Many restaurants add a 10%–15% service charge.*

Lantana's. Try the American-Caribbean cuisine at this fine eatery, where the decor is as imaginative and authentic as the food, and both are top quality. Lobster quesadillas, blackened King salmon over cilantro linguine with banana fritters and cranberry relish, and incredible roasted garlic soup and apple pie are favorites from the diverse menu. *Caribbean Club, West Bay Rd., Seven Mile Beach, tel. 809/947–5595. Reservations suggested. AE, D, MC, V. No lunch weekends. $$–$$$*

Cracked Conch. Specialties here include conch fritters, conch chowder, spicy Cayman-style snapper, and turtle steak. The key lime pie is divine. Locals flock to the Cracked Conch on weekdays for the low-priced lunch buffet—hot entrée, soup, and salad for C.I.$6.50. The bar, also big with the local crowd, has karaoke, dive videos, and great happy-hour specials. *West Bay Rd. near the Hyatt, tel. 809/947–5217. MC, V. $–$$*

Grenada

The aroma of cinnamon and nutmeg, mace and cocoa, fill the air and all memories of Grenada (pronounced gruh-NAY-da). Only 21 miles long and 12 miles wide, Grenada is a tropical gem of lush rain forests, green hillsides, white-sand beaches, secluded coves, and the startling colors of exotic flowers.

Until 1983, when the U.S.–Eastern Caribbean invasion of Grenada catapulted this little nation into the headlines, it was a relatively obscure island providing a quiet hideaway for lovers of fishing, snorkeling, or simply lazing in the sun. Today Grenada is back to normal, a safe and secure vacation spot with enough good shopping, restaurants, and sights to make it a regular port of call. But expansion to accommodate the increased tourist trade is controlled: No building can stand taller than a coconut palm, and new construction on the beaches must be at least 165 feet back from the high-water mark. As a result, Grenada has retained a distinctly West Indian identity.

Currency Grenada uses the Eastern Caribbean (E.C.) dollar. Figure about E. C. $2.70 to U.S. $1. Always ask which currency is referred to when asking prices—unless otherwise noted, prices quoted here are in U.S. dollars, which are readily accepted.

Passports and Passports are not required of U.S., Canadian, or British citizens if
Visas they have two proofs of citizenship including one photo ID.

Telephones Phones and phone cards are available at the Welcome Center, where
and Mail passengers come ashore. U.S. and Canadian numbers can be dialed directly. Airmail rates for letters to the United States and Canada are E.C. 75¢ for a half-ounce letter and E.C. 35¢ for a postcard.

Shore The following are good choices in Grenada. They may not be offered
Excursions by all cruise lines. Times and prices are approximate. Unless otherwise noted, children's prices are for those under 13.

Island Sights **Grenada Tour.** Ride through the countryside to see a nutmeg processing station, small villages, the rain forest, and Grand Anse Beach. *3 hrs. Cost: $25–$30 adults, $15–$17 children.*

Undersea **Rhum Runner Cruise Tour.** Hop on a glass-bottom party boat and sip
Creatures unlimited rum punch or soda while you watch fish and coral pass beneath your feet. Stops on the beach for sunbathing and snorkeling are included. *3 hrs. Cost: $26 adults, $16 children.*

Coming Big ships anchor off St. George's and tender passengers to the east
Ashore end of the Carenage, a horseshoe-shaped thoroughfare that surrounds the harbor. Smaller ships can pull right alongside the Welcome Center on the pier, where water taxis, cabs, and walking tour guides ($5 per hour) can be hired. From here, you can easily walk to town or take a taxi ($3 one-way). The capital can be toured easily on foot, but be prepared to climb up and down steep hills.

Getting Minivans ply the winding road between St. George's and Grand
Around Anse Beach. Hail one anywhere along the way, pay E.C. $1, and
By Minivan hold onto your hat.

By Car If you want to venture outside St. George's, hiring a taxi or arranging a guided tour is more sensible than renting a car, unless you're at ease driving on the left side of these narrow, winding roads and willing to pay at least $50 for a day's rental, plus about $11 for a local license. In St. George's, contact **Avis** (tel. 809/440–3936) at Spice Island Rentals, **David's** (tel. 809/440–3038), or **McIntyre Brothers** (tel. 809/444–3944).

By Taxi Taxis are plentiful, and fixed rates to popular island destinations are posted at the pier on the Carenage. Hiring a cab on an hourly basis runs $15 per hour; island tours cost $16–$50.

By Water Taxi For $2, you can take a water taxi from one end of the Carenage to the other; water taxis are also the quickest and cheapest way to get to most beaches. The fare is $4 round-trip to Grand Anse; $10 to Morne Rouge.

Exploring Grenada *Numbers in the margin correspond to points of interest on the Grenada map.*

St. George's **St. George's** is one of the most picturesque and authentic West Indian towns in the Caribbean. Pastel warehouses cling to the curving shore along the Carenage; rainbow-colored houses rise above it and disappear into the steep green hills. You can walk the town in about two hours.

From the Welcome Center, follow the curve of the **Carenage** to the far end of the harbor. From here, you can walk up the hillside for a commanding view of the ocean and your ship at anchor. Make a right on Young Street. Halfway up on the left is the **Grenada National Museum,** housing a small but interesting collection of archaeological and colonial artifacts and recent political memorabilia. *Young and Monckton Sts., tel. 809/440-3725. Admission: $1 adults, 50¢ children under 18. Open weekdays 9–4:30, Sat. 10–1:30.*

If you'd prefer not to walk up the steep hill, the fastest way from the Carenage to the **Esplanade** is through the **Sendall Tunnel** just a little farther down the road from the museum entrance. The intrepid will want to continue climbing Young Street, turning left at the top onto Church Street. Continue past the Gothic-style Presbyterian Church to **Ft. George,** built by the French in 1708, which rises above the point that separates the harbor from the ocean. The inner courtyard is now the police headquarters; it was here that the prime minister was murdered in 1983, sparking the U.S. intervention. *Admission free. Open daily during daylight hrs.*

Past the fort, where the road overlooks the sea, a stone stairway on your right leads down to the Esplanade—the thoroughfare that runs along the ocean side of town and has a number of interesting shops. A right onto Granby Street leads to **Market Square,** which comes alive every Saturday from 8 AM to noon with vendors selling baskets and fresh produce, including spices and exotic tropical fruit.

The West Coast The coast road north from St. George's winds past mountains and valleys covered with banana and breadfruit trees, palms, bamboo, and tropical flowers. **Concord Falls,** about 8 miles out, is a great spot for hiking—about 2 miles to the main falls, another hour to the second spectacular waterfall. *Admission: $1.*

Continuing north to the town of **Gouyave,** the **Dougaldston Estate** has a spice factory where you can see cocoa, nutmeg, mace, cloves, cinnamon, and other spices in their natural state, laid out on giant trays to dry in the sun. Old women walk barefoot through the spices, shuffling them so they dry evenly. *No phone. Admission free. Open weekdays 9–4.*

The East Coast **Westerhall,** a residential area about 5 miles east of St. George's, is known for its beautiful villas, gardens, and panoramic views. From here, a dirt road leads north to **Grand Bacolet Bay,** a jagged peninsula on the Atlantic where the surf pounds against deserted beaches. Some miles north is **Grenville,** Grenada's second-largest city, where schooners set sail for the outer islands. As in St. George's, Saturday is market day, and the town fills with locals shopping for the week.

Take the interior route back to town to fully appreciate the lush, mountainous nature of Grenada. In the middle of the island is **Grand Etang Lake National Park,** a bird sanctuary and forest reserve where you can fish, hike, and swim. The lake, in the crater of an extinct volcano, is a 13-acre glasslike expanse of cobalt-blue water. *Main Interior Rd., between Grenville and St. George's, tel. 809/442-7425. Admission: $1. Open weekdays 8–4.*

Grand Anse/ South End Most of Grenada's hotels and nightlife are in Grand Anse or the adjacent community of L'Anse aux Epines. There's a small shopping

Grenada (and Carriacou)

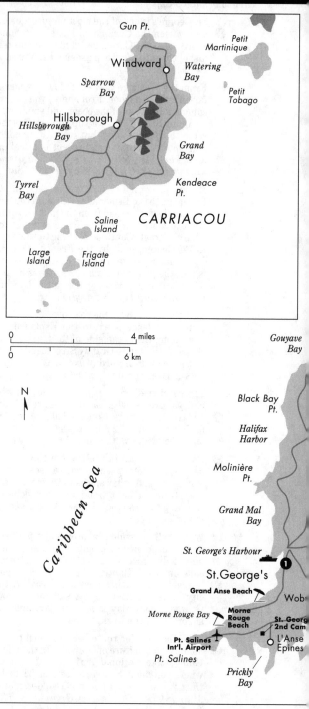

Gun Pt.

Petit
Martinique

Windward

Watering
Bay

Sparrow
Bay

Petit
Tobago

Hillsborough

*Hillsborough
Bay*

Grand
Bay

Tyrrel
Bay

Kendeace
Pt.

CARRIACOU

Saline
Island

Large
Island

Frigate
Island

0   4 miles

0   6 km

N

*Gouyave
Bay*

Black Bay
Pt.

*Halifax
Harbor*

Molinière
Pt.

*Grand Mal
Bay*

St. George's Harbour

Caribbean Sea

St.George's ❶

Grand Anse Beach

Wob

Morne Rouge Bay

**Morne
Rouge
Beach**

**St. Georg
2nd Cam**

**Pt. Salines
Int'l. Airport**

L'Anse
Épines

Pt. Salines

*Prickly
Bay*

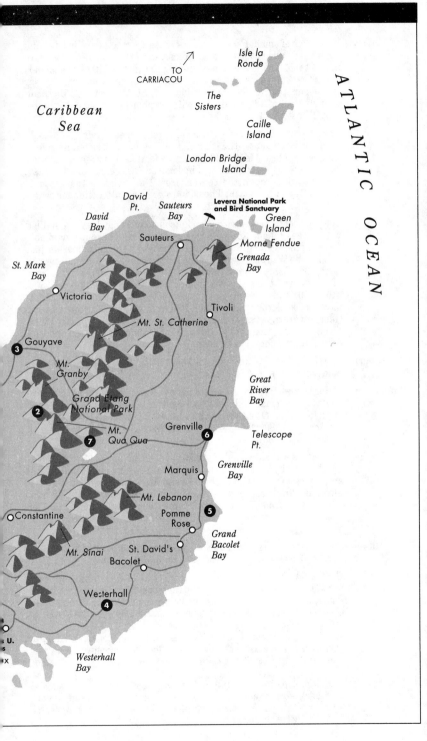

Isle la Ronde

TO CARRIACOU

The Sisters

Caille Island

Caribbean Sea

London Bridge Island

ATLANTIC OCEAN

David Pt.

Sauteurs Bay

Levera National Park and Bird Sanctuary

David Bay

Green Island

Sauteurs

Morne Fendue

Grenada Bay

St. Mark Bay

Victoria

Tivoli

Mt. St. Catherine

❸ Gouyave

Mt. Granby

Great River Bay

Grand Etang National Park

❷

Grenville ❻

❼ *Mt. Qua Qua*

Telescope Pt.

Marquis

Grenville Bay

Mt. Lebanon

○Constantine

Pomme Rose

❺

Grand Bacolet Bay

Mt. Sinai

St. David's

Bacolet

Westerhall

❹

U.

X

Westerhall Bay

center, too, but beautiful **Grand Anse Beach** is the main attraction here.

Carriacou   A number of smaller ships, such as those operated by Windstar and Club Med, call at Carriacou, 16 miles north of Grenada. At 13 square miles, the island is the largest among the chain of 100 small islands and cays known as the Grenadines. Other increasingly popular cruise ports in the chain are **Bequia** (near St. Vincent) and **Mayreau,** a tiny island of 182 residents, with no phones but some of the region's most beautiful beaches.

The colonial history of Carriacou (pronounced "Kair-ee-uh-koo") parallels Grenada's—the island's tiny size has restricted its role in the area's political history. Like Grenada, it is mountainous, but not as lush. In fact, it is quite arid in some areas. A chain of hills cuts a wide swath through the center, from Gun Point in the north to Tyrrel Bay in the south. The island's greatest attraction for cruise passengers is its water sports.

Shopping   Six-packs of tiny handwoven baskets lined with bay leaves and filled with spices (about $8) make good souvenirs. These are available from peddlers along the Carenage, including the spice market just outside the Welcome Center. For Caribbean art and antique engravings, visit **Yellow Poui Art Gallery** (tel. 809/444–3001), at the corner of Cross Street and the Esplanade in St. George's. **Tikal** (tel. 809/440–2310) and **Art Fabrik** (809/440–0568), both on Young Street, have batik clothing and other handcrafted items. Stores in St. George's are generally open weekdays 8–noon and 1–4, Saturday 8–noon; most are closed on Sunday, though many shops open and vendors appear if ships are in town.

Sports   The **Grenada Golf Club** (tel. 809/444–4128) in Grand Anse has a nine-
Golf   hole golf course. Fees are E.C. $7.

Water Sports   Major hotels on **Grand Anse Beach** have water-sports centers where you can rent small sailboats, Windsurfers, and Sunfish. For scuba diving, contact **Dive Grenada** at Grand Anse Beach's Grenada Renaissance (tel. 809/444–4372). On Carriacou try **Dive Silver Beach** (tel. 809/443–7337).

Beaches   Grenada has about 80 miles of coastline, 65 bays, and 45 white-sand beaches, many with secluded coves. Beaches are public and within an easy cab ride of the harbor. **Grand Anse,** the most popular, is a gleaming 2-mile curve of sand and clear, gentle surf about a 10-minute taxi ride from St. George's. **Morne Rouge Beach,** a little farther southwest, is less crowded and has a reef offshore that's terrific for snorkeling.

Dining   *Some restaurants add a 10% service charge to your bill. If not, a 10%–15% gratuity should be added for a job well done.*

Canboulay. You'll have to hop a ride to Grand Anse Beach and trade in your shorts for something a little more chic, but it's worth the trouble for the best cuisine on the island and a drop-dead view of St. George's Harbour. *Morne Rouge Beach, tel. 809/444–4401. AE, D, MC, V. Closed Sun. No lunch Sat. $$*
The Nutmeg. Fresh seafood like grilled turtle steaks, lobster, or shrimp is the specialty at this second-floor restaurant with a great view of the harbor. *The Carenage, St. George's, tel. 809/440–2539. AE, D, MC, V. $$*
Rudolf's. This informal pub offers fine West Indian fare—such as crab back, *lambi* (conch), and delectable nutmeg ice cream—along with the best gossip on the island. *The Carenage, St. George's, tel. 809/440–2241. No credit cards. Closed Sun. $$*

Guadeloupe

On a map, Guadeloupe looks like a giant butterfly resting on the sea between Antigua and Dominica. Its two wings—Basse-Terre and Grande-Terre—are the two largest islands in the 659-square-mile Guadeloupe archipelago. The Rivière Salée, a 4-mile seawater channel flowing between the Caribbean and the Atlantic, forms the "spine" of the butterfly. A drawbridge over the channel connects the two islands.

If you're seeking a resort atmosphere, casinos, and white sandy beaches, your target is Grande-Terre. Basse-Terre's Natural Park, laced with mountain trails and washed by waterfalls and rivers, is a 74,100-acre haven for hikers, nature lovers, and anyone yearning to peer into the steaming crater of an active volcano.

This port of call is one of the least touristy (and least keen on Americans). Guadeloupeans accept visitors, but their economy does not rely on tourism. Pointe-à-Pitre, the port city, is a kaleidoscope of smart boutiques, wholesalers, sidewalk cafés, a throbbing meat and vegetable market, barred and broken-down buildings, little parks, and bazaarlike stores. Though not to everyone's liking, the city has more character than many other island ports.

French is the official language, and few locals speak English. (It's sensible to carry a postcard of the ship with the name of where it is docked written in French. This will come in handy in an emergency.) Like other West Indians, many Guadeloupeans do not appreciate having their photographs taken. Always ask permission first, and don't take a refusal personally. Also, many locals take offense at short shorts or swimwear worn outside bathing areas.

Currency Legal tender is the French franc, composed of 100 centimes. At press time, the rate was 5.2F to $1.

Passports and Visas U.S. and Canadian citizens need only proof of citizenship, but a passport is best. British citizens need a valid passport.

Telephones and Mail To call the United States from Guadeloupe, dial 191, the area code, and the local number. For calls within Guadeloupe, dial the six-digit number. Postcards to the United States cost 3.80F; letters up to 20 grams, 4.60F. To Canada, the rate is 3.60F for postcards and letters.

Shore Excursions The following is a good choice in Guadeloupe. It may not be offered by all cruise lines. Time and price are approximate.

Pointe-à-Pitre/Island Drive. Grande-Terre's various districts and residential areas are surveyed in this half-day drive that includes a visit to Ft. Fleur d'Epée and a refreshment stop at a hotel. *3 hrs. Cost: $30.*

Coming Ashore Cruise ships dock at the Maritime Terminal of Centre St-John Perse in downtown Pointe-à-Pitre, about a block from the shopping district. To get to the tourist information office, walk along the quay for about five minutes to the Place de la Victoire. The office is across the road at the top of the section of the harbor called La Darse (*see* Exploring Guadeloupe, *below*), just a few blocks from your ship. There's also a small tourist information booth in the terminal, but its hours and the information available are limited.

Getting Around
By Car Guadeloupe has 1,225 miles of excellent roads (marked as in Europe), and driving around Grande-Terre is relatively easy. Cars can be rented at **Avis** (tel. 590/82–33–47), **Budget** (tel. 590/82–95–58), **Hertz** (tel. 590/84–57–94), or **Thrifty** (tel. 590/91–55–66). Rentals begin at about $60 a day.

By Taxi Taxi fares are regulated by the government and posted at taxi stands. Fares are more expensive here than on other islands. If your

French is good, you can call for a cab (tel. 590/82–00–00, 590/82–13–67, or 590/20–74–74). Tip drivers 10%. Before you agree to use a taxi driver as a guide, make sure you speak a common language.

By Moped   Vespas can be rented at **Vespa Sun** in Pointe-à-Pitre (tel. 590/82–17–80).

Exploring *Numbers in the margin correspond to points of interest on the*
Guadeloupe *Guadeloupe map.*

❶ **Pointe-à-Pitre,** a city of some 100,000 people, lies almost on the "backbone" of the butterfly, near the bridge that crosses the Salée River. Bustling and noisy, with its narrow streets, honking horns, and traffic jams, it is full of pulsing life. The most interesting area, with food and clothing stalls, markets, tempting pastry shops, and modern buildings, is compact and easy to see on foot.

The **Musée St-John Perse** is dedicated to the Guadeloupean poet who won the 1960 Nobel Prize in literature. Inside the restored colonial house is a complete collection of his poetry, as well as many of his personal effects. *Corner rue Noizières and Achille René-Boisneuf, tel. 590/90–01–92. Admission: 10F. Open daily except Wed. 9–5.*

You'll find the **Marketplace** by backtracking one block from the museum and turning right on rue Frébault. Located between rues St-John Perse, Frébault, Schoelcher, and Peynier, it's a cacophonous and colorful place where locals bargain for papayas, breadfruit, christophines, tomatoes, and a vivid assortment of other produce.

A left at the corner of rue Schoelcher onto rue Peynier leads to the **Musée Schoelcher,** which honors the memory of Victor Schoelcher, the 19th-century Alsatian abolitionist who fought slavery in the French West Indies. Exhibits trace his life and work. *24 rue Peynier, tel. 509/82–08–04. Admission: 10F. Open weekdays 8:30–11:30 and 2–5.*

Walk back three blocks along rue Peynier, past the market, to **Place de la Victoire.** Surrounded by wood buildings with balconies and shutters and lined by sidewalk cafés, the square was named in honor of Victor Hugues's 1794 victory over the British. The sandbox trees in the park are said to have been planted by Hugues the day after the victory. During the French Revolution a guillotine here lopped off the heads of many an aristocrat.

Rue Duplessis runs between the southern edge of the park and **La Darse,** where fishing boats dock and motorboats depart for the choppy ride to the neighboring islands of Marie-Galante and Les Saintes. Walk away from the harbor along rue Bebian, the western border of the square, and turn left onto rue Alexandre Isaac. There you'll see the imposing **Cathedral of St. Peter and St. Paul.** Earthquakes and hurricanes have wrought havoc on the 1847 church, now reinforced with iron ribs. Note the lovely stained-glass windows.

Basse-Terre   If you have a car, high adventure is to be had by driving across Basse-Terre, which swirls with mountain trails and lakes, waterfalls, and hot springs. Basse-Terre is the home of the Old Lady, as the Soufrière volcano is called, and of the capital, also called Basse-Terre.

Begin your tour by heading west from Pointe-à-Pitre on Route N1, crossing the Rivière Salée on the **pont de la Gabare** drawbridge. At the Destralen traffic circle turn left and drive 6 miles south through sweet-scented fields of sugarcane to the **Route de la Traversée** (D23), where you turn west.

Five miles from where you picked up D23, turn left at the junction and go a little over a mile south to **Vernou.** On a path that leads be-
❷ yond the village through lush forest is a pretty waterfall at **Saut de la Lézarde.**

❸ Back on La Traversée and 3 miles farther is **Cascade aux Ecrevisse,** where a marked trail leads to a splendid waterfall. Two miles farther **❹** is the **Parc Tropical de Bras-David,** where you can park and explore various nature trails. The **Maison de la Forêt** has displays on the park's flora, fauna, and topography, signposted in French. There are picnic tables. *Admission free. Open daily 9–5.*

❺ Two and a half miles away are the two mountains known as **Les Mamelles** ("The Breasts"). The pass that runs between Les Mamelles to the south and a lesser mountain to the north offers a spectacular view. Trails ranging from easy to arduous lace the surrounding mountains.

You don't have to be much of a hiker to climb the stone steps leading **❻** from La Traversée to the **Zoological Park and Botanical Gardens.** Titi the raccoon is the mascot of the park, which also features cockatoos, iguanas, and turtles. *Tel. 590/98–83–52. Admission: 30F adults, 20F children. Open daily 9–5.*

Shopping For serious shopping in Pointe-à-Pitre, browse the boutiques and stores along **rue Schoelcher, rue Frébault,** and **rue Nozières.** The market square and stalls of **La Darse** are filled with mostly vegetables, fruits, and housewares, but you will find some straw hats and dolls.

There are dozens of shops in and around the cruise terminal, **Centre St-John Perse.** Many stores here offer a 20% discount on luxury items purchased with traveler's checks or major credit cards. You can find good buys on anything French—perfume, crystal, wine, cosmetics, and scarves. As for local handcrafted items, you'll see a lot of junk, but you can also find island dolls dressed in madras, finely woven straw baskets and hats, salako hats made of split bamboo, madras table linens, and wood carvings.

The following shops are all in Point-à-Pitre: For Baccarat, Lalique, Porcelaine de Paris, Limoges, and other upscale tableware, check **Selection** (rue Schoelcher), **A la Pensée** (44 rue Frébault, tel. 590/82–10–47), and **Rosebleu** (5 rue Frébault, tel. 590/82–93–44). Guadeloupe's exclusive purveyor of Orlane, Stendhal, and Germaine Monteil is **Vendôme** (8–10 rue Frébault, tel. 590/83–42–44). **Tim Tim** (16 rue Henri IV, tel. 590/83–48–71) is an upscale nostalgia shop with elegant (and expensive) antiques; be sure to see the museum-quality displays. For native "doudou" dolls, straw hats, baskets, and madras table linens, try **Au Caraibe** (4 rue Frébault, no phone). The largest selection of perfumes is at **Phoenicia** (8 rue Frébault, tel. 590/83–50–36). You many also want to try **Au Bonheur des Dames** (49 rue Frébault, tel. 590/82–00–30). For discount liquor and French wines, try **Seven Sins** on rue Schoelcher.

Sports Contact **Caraibe Peche** (Marina Bas-du-Fort, tel. 590/90–97–51) or
Fishing **Le Rocer de Malendure** (Pigeon, Bouillante, tel. 590/98–28–84).

Golf **Golf Municipal Saint-François** (St-François, tel. 590/88–41–87) has an 18-hole Robert Trent Jones course, an English-speaking pro, and electric carts for rent.

Hiking Basse-Terre's **Parc Tropical de Bras-David** is abundant with trails, many of which should be attempted only with an experienced guide. Trips for up to 12 people are arranged by **Organisation des Guides de Montagne de la Caraibe** (Maison Forestière, Matouba, tel. 590/81–05–79).

Horseback Beach rides and picnics are available through **Le Criolo** (St-Felix,
Riding tel. 590/84–04–06).

Water Sports Windsurfing, waterskiing, and sailing are available at almost all beachfront hotels. The main windsurfing center is at **UCPA** hotel club (tel. 590/88–64–80) in St-François. You can also rent equipment at Holywind (Résidence Canella Beach, Pointe de la Verdure,

Guadeloupe

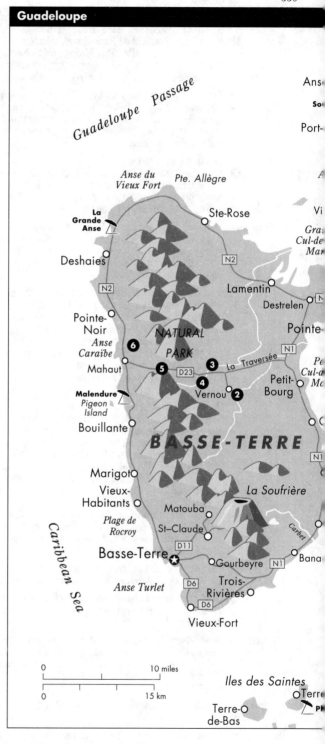

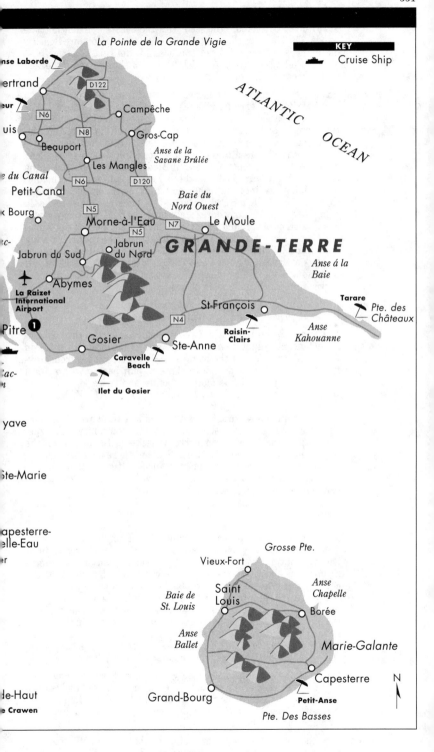

La Pointe de la Grande Vigie

ATLANTIC OCEAN

KEY
Cruise Ship

nse Laborde

ertrand

eur

uis N6

Beauport N8

Campêche

Gros-Cap

Anse de la
Savane Brûlée

Les Mangles

e du Canal N6 D120

Petit-Canal

Baie du
Nord Ouest

Bourg N5

Morne-à-l'Eau N5 N7

Le Moule

ec-

Jabrun du Sud

Jabrun
du Nord

GRANDE-TERRE

Anse á la
Baie

Abymes

La Raizet
International
Airport

N4

St-François

Tarare
Pte. des
Châteaux

Pitre ❶

Gosier

Ste-Anne

Raisin-
Clairs

Anse
Kahouanne

Caravelle
Beach

ac-
n

Ilet du Gosier

yave

Šte-Marie

apesterre-
elle-Eau
r

Grosse Pte.

Vieux-Fort

Anse
Chapelle

Baie de
St. Louis

Saint
Louis

Borée

Anse
Ballet

Marie-Galante

Capesterre

N

le-Haut

Grand-Bourg

Petit-Anse

e Crawen

Pte. Des Basses

Gosier, tel. 590/90–44–00) and at the Tropical Club Hotel (tel. 590/93–97–97) at Le Moule, blessed with the constant Atlantic trade winds. The Nautilus Club (tel. 590/98–89–08) at Malendure Beach is one of the island's top scuba operations and offers glass-bottom-boat and snorkeling trips to Pigeon Island, just offshore—one of the best diving spots in the world.

Beaches Some of the island's best beaches of soft white sand lie on the south coast of Grande-Terre from Ste-Anne to Pointe des Châteaux. For $5–$10 per passenger, hotels allow nonguests to use changing facilities, towels, and beach chairs. Caravelle Beach, just outside Ste-Anne, has one of the longest and prettiest stretches of sand. Protected by reefs, it's a fine place for snorkeling, and water-sports equipment can be rented from Club Med, located at one end of the beach. Raisin-Clairs, just outside St-François, offers windsurfing, waterskiing, sailing, and other activities, with rentals arranged through the Méridien Hotel. Tarare is a secluded cove close to the tip of Pointe des Châteaux where locals tan in the buff. There are several secluded coves around Pointe des Châteaux, where the Atlantic and Caribbean waters meet and crash against huge rocks, sculpting them into castlelike shapes. La Grande Anse, just outside Deshaies on the northwest coast of Basse-Terre, is a secluded beach of soft beige sand sheltered by palms. The waterfront Karacoli restaurant serves rum punch and Creole dishes.

Dining *Restaurants are legally required to include a 15% service charge in the menu price. No additional gratuity is necessary.*

La Canne à Sucre. Innovative Creole cuisine has earned this two-story restaurant a reputation for being the best (and most expensive) in Pointe-à-Pitre. Fare at the main-floor Brasserie ranges from crayfish salad with smoked ham to skate in puff pastry with saffron sauce. Dining upstairs is more elaborate and twice as expensive. *Quai No. 1, Port Autonome, tel. 590/82–10–19. AE, V. No lunch Sat. $$$*

Le Rocher de Malendure. The setting on a bluff above Malendure Bay overlooking Pigeon Island makes this restaurant worth a special trip for lunch. The tiered terrace is decked with flowers, and the best choices on the menu are fresh fish, but there are also meat selections, such as veal in raspberry vinaigrette and tournedos in three sauces. *Malendure Beach, Bouillante, tel. 590/98–70–84. Reservations advised. DC, MC, V. No dinner Sun. $$*

Jamaica

The third-largest island in the Caribbean, the English-speaking nation of Jamaica enjoys a considerable self-sufficiency based on tourism, agriculture, and mining. Its physical attractions include jungle mountains, clear waterfalls, and unforgettable beaches, yet the country's greatest resource may be its people. Although 95% of Jamaicans trace their bloodlines to Africa, their national origins also lie in Great Britain, the Middle East, India, China, Germany, Portugal, and South America, as well as many other islands in the Caribbean. Their cultural life is a wealthy one; the music, art, and cuisine of Jamaica are vibrant with a spirit easy to sense but as hard to describe as the rhythms of reggae or the streetwise patois.

Don't let Jamaica's beauty cause you to relax the good sense you would use in your own hometown. Resist the promise of adventure should any odd character offer to show you the "real" Jamaica. Jamaica on the beaten track is wonderful enough, so don't take chances by wandering too far off it.

Currency Currency exchange booths are set up on the docks at Montego Bay and Ocho Rios whenever a ship is in port. The U.S. dollar is accepted virtually everywhere, but change will be made in local currency.

Check the value of the J$ on arrival—it fluctuates greatly. At press time the exchange rate was J$30 to U.S.$1.

Passports and Visas
Passports are not required of U.S. or Canadian citizens, but every visitor must have proof of citizenship. British visitors need passports but not visas.

Telephones and Mail
Direct telephone, telegraph, telefax, and telex services are available in communication stations at the ports. Phones take phone cards, which are available from kiosks or variety shops. Airmail postage from Jamaica to the United States and Canada is J$1.50 for letters, J$1.20 for postcards.

Shore Excursions
The following are good choices in Jamaica. They may not be offered by all cruise lines. Times and prices are approximate. Unless otherwise noted, children's prices are for those under 13.

Natural Beauty
Prospect Plantation. The beautiful gardens of Prospect Plantation are the highlight of this tour, with a brief stop at Dunn's River Falls. *3½ hrs. Cost: $39 adults, $30 children.*

Rafting on the Martha Brae River. Glide down this pristine river in a 30-foot, two-seat bamboo raft, admiring the verdant plant life along the river's banks. *4 hrs. Cost: $45 adults, $40 children.*

Coming Ashore
In Montego Bay
A growing number of cruise ships are using the city of Montego Bay (nicknamed "Mo Bay"), 67 miles to the west of Ocho Rios, as their Jamaican port of call. The cruise port in Mo Bay is a $5 taxi ride from town. There is one shopping center within walking distance of the Montego Bay docks. The Jamaica Tourist Board office is about 3½ miles away on Gloucester Avenue.

In Ocho Rios
Most cruise ships dock at this port on Jamaica's north coast, near the famous Dunn's River Falls. Less than a mile from the Ocho Rios cruise-ship pier are the Taj Mahal Duty Free Shopping Center and the Ocean Village Shopping Center, where the Jamaica Tourist Board maintains an office. Getting anywhere else in Ocho Rios will require a taxi.

Getting Around
Neither Montego Bay nor Ocho Rios is a walking port, and driving is not recommended for cruise passengers. Renting a car tends to be a time-consuming hassle because you must reserve a car and send a deposit *before* you reach Jamaica.

By Moped
Mopeds are available for rent, but be especially careful: Jamaicans are not admired for their driving skills, and driving is on the left. Daily rates run from about $45. Deposits of $200 or more are usually required. Ask at the tourist office for rental shops near your port.

By Taxi
Some of Jamaica's taxis are metered; rates are per car, not per passenger. Cabs can be flagged down on the street. All licensed and properly insured taxis display red Public Passenger Vehicle (PPV) plates. Licensed minivans also bear the red PPV plates. If you hire a taxi driver as a tour guide, be sure to agree on a price *before* the vehicle is put into gear.

Exploring Jamaica
Montego Bay
Rose Hall Great House, perhaps the most impressive in the West Indies in the 1700s, enjoys its popularity less for its architecture than for the legend surrounding its second mistress. The story of Annie Palmer—credited with murdering three husbands and a plantation overseer who was her lover—is told in two novels sold everywhere in Jamaica: *The White Witch of Rose Hall* and *Jamaica Witch*. The great house is east of Montego Bay, across the highway from the Rose Hall resorts. *Tel. 809/953–2323. Admission: $10 adults, $6 children. Open daily 9–6.*

Greenwood Great House, 15 miles east of Montego Bay, has no spooky legend to titillate visitors, but it's much better than Rose Hall at evoking the atmosphere of life on a sugar plantation. Highlights of Greenwood include oil paintings of the family, china made

Jamaica

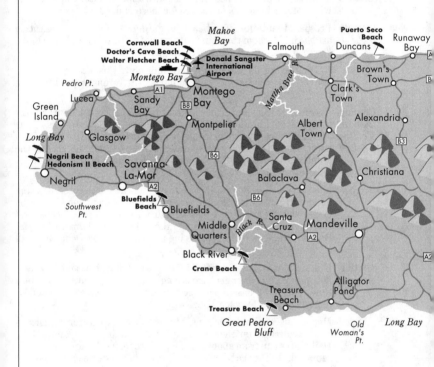

Mahoe Bay · Falmouth · **Puerto Seco Beach** · Duncans · Runaway Bay

Cornwall Beach · **Doctor's Cave Beach** · **Walter Fletcher Beach** · *Montego Bay* · **Donald Sangster International Airport** · Brown's Town

Pedro Pt. · Lucea · Sandy Bay · Montego Bay · Clark's Town

Green Island · Glasgow · Montpelier · *Martha Brae R.* · Albert Town · Alexandria

Long Bay · **Negril Beach** · **Hedonism II Beach** · Savanna-La-Mar · Balaclava · Christiana

Negril · **Bluefields Beach** · Bluefields · Black R. · Santa Cruz · Mandeville

Southwest Pt. · Middle Quarters · Black River · **Crane Beach**

Treasure Beach · Treasure Beach · Alligator Pond

Great Pedro Bluff · *Old Woman's Pt.* · *Long Bay*

N

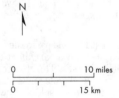

0 — 10 miles
0 — 15 km

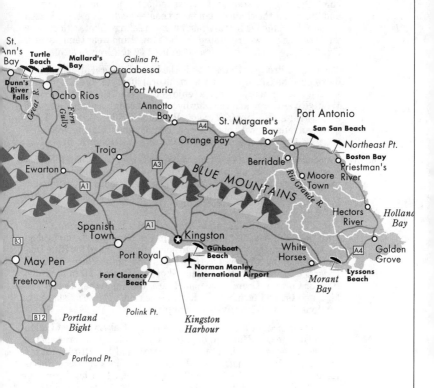

St. Ann's Bay
Turtle Beach
Mallard's Bay
Galina Pt.
Oracabessa
Dunn's River Falls
Great R.
Ocho Rios
Fern Gully
Port Maria
Annotto Bay
Troja
A4
Orange Bay
St. Margaret's Bay
Port Antonio
San San Beach
A3
Berridale
Northeast Pt.
Boston Bay
Priestman's River
BLUE MOUNTAINS
Ewarton
A1
Rio Grande R.
Moore Town
Hectors River
Holland Bay
Spanish Town
A1
Kingston
White Horses
A4
Golden Grove
B3
May Pen
Port Royal
Gunboat Beach
Freetown
Fort Clarence Beach
Norman Manley International Airport
Morant Bay
Lyssons Beach
B12
Portland Bight
Polink Pt.
Kingston Harbour
Portland Pt.

Caribbean Sea

KEY
Cruise Ship

especially for them by Wedgwood, a library filled with rare books, fine antique furniture, and a collection of exotic musical instruments. *Tel. 809/953–1077. Admission: $10 adults, $5 children. Open daily 9–6.*

One of the most popular excursions in Jamaica is rafting on the **Martha Brae River** (tel. 809/952–0889 for reservations), a gentle waterway filled with the romance of a tropical wilderness. Wear your swimsuit for a plunge at the halfway point and pick a raft that has a comfortable cushion. The ride costs less than $40 for two people.

Ocho Rios   **Dunn's River Falls** is 600 feet of cold, clear mountain water splashing over a series of stone steps to the warm Caribbean. Don a swimsuit, climb the slippery steps, take the hand of the person ahead of you, and trust that the chain of hands and bodies leads to an experienced guide. The climb leaders are personable, reeling off bits of local lore while telling you where to step. Bring a towel and wear tennis shoes. *Tel. 809/974–2857. Admission: $5 adults, $2 children 2–11.*

The tour of **Prospect Plantation** is the best of several offerings that delve into the island's former agricultural lifestyle. It's not just for specialists; virtually everyone enjoys the beautiful views over the White River Gorge and the tour by jitney through a plantation with exotic fruits and tropical trees. Horseback riding through 1,000 acres is available, with one hour's notice, for about $20 per hour. *Tel. 809/974–2058. Admission: $12 adults, children under 13 free.*

Shopping   Jamaican artisans express themselves in resort wear, hand-loomed fabrics, silk-screening, wood carvings, and paintings. Jamaican rum makes a great gift, as do Tia Maria (Jamaica's famous coffee liqueur) and Blue Mountain coffee. Cheap sandals are good buys (about $20 a pair).

Avoid the "craft" stalls in Mo Bay and Ocho Rios, which are filled with peddlers desperate to sell touristy straw hats, T-shirts, and cheap jewelry. If you're looking to spend money, head for **Blue Diamond Shopping Center, Overton Plaza, Westgate Plaza, Miranda Ridge Plaza,** or **St. James's Place Shopping Center,** all in Montego Bay, or **Coconut Grove, Pineapple Place,** the **Taj Mahal, Ocean Village,** and **Island Plaza** in Ocho Rios. Some cruise lines run shore excursions devoted exclusively to shopping.

For Jamaican and Haitian paintings, go to the **Gallery of West Indian Art** (1 Orange La., Montego Bay, tel. 809/952–4547). A corner of the gallery is devoted to hand-turned pottery and beautifully carved birds and jungle animals. Six miles east of the docks in Ocho Rios is **Harmony Hall** (tel. 809/975–4222), a huge house that has been converted into an art gallery, restaurant, and bar. Wares here include arts and crafts, carved items, ceramics, antiques, books, jewelry, fudge, spices, and Blue Mountain coffee.

Sports   The best courses are at the **Half Moon Club** (tel. 809/953–2560) in
Golf   Montego Bay or **Runaway Bay** (tel. 809/973–2561) and **Sandal's Golf and Country Club** (tel. 809/974–2528) in Ocho Rios. Rates range from $25 to $50 for 18 holes at the Ocho Rios courses to $110 (with cart) at the Half Moon Club.

Horseback   **Chukka Cove** (St. Ann, tel. 809/972–2506), near Ocho Rios, is the
Riding   best equestrian facility in the English-speaking Caribbean. Riding is also available at **Prospect Plantation** (between Negril and Green Island, tel. 809/974–2058) and **Rocky Point Stables** (Half Moon Club, Montego Bay, tel. 809/953–2286).

Beaches   **Doctor's Cave Beach** at Montego Bay is getting crowded, attracting Jamaicans and tourists alike. The 5-mile stretch of sugary sand has been spotlighted in so many travel articles and brochures that it's no secret to anyone anymore. Two other popular beaches near Montego Bay are **Cornwall Beach,** farther up the coast, which has food and drink options, and **Walter Fletcher Beach,** on the bay near the center of town. Fletcher offers protection from the surf on a windy day and has unusually calm waters for swimming. **Mallard's** is Ocho Rios's busiest beach; two large resort hotels are here, spilling out large convention groups at all hours of the day. **Turtle Beach** is the islanders' favorite place to swim in Ocho Rios.

Dining *Many restaurants add a 10% service charge to the bill. Otherwise, a tip of 10%–15% is customary.*

Sugar Mill. One of the finest restaurants in Jamaica, the Sugar Mill (formerly the Club House) serves seafood with flair on a terrace. Steak and lobster are usually garnished in a pungent sauce that blends Dijon mustard with Jamaica's own Pickapeppa. *At Half Moon Golf Course, Montego Bay, tel. 809/953–2228. Reservations recommended. AE, DC, MC, V. $$$*

Almond Tree. This very popular restaurant prepares Jamaican dishes enlivened by a European culinary tradition. The swinging rope chairs of the terrace bar and the tables perched above a lovely Caribbean cove are great fun. *83 Main St., Ocho Rios, tel. 809/974–2813. Reservations required. AE, DC, MC, V. $$–$$$*

Pork Pit. Enjoy Jamaica's fiery jerk pork at this open-air hangout. Plan to arrive around noon, when the first jerk is lifted from its bed of coals and pimiento wood. *Gloucester Av. across from Walter Fletcher Beach, Montego Bay, tel. 809/952–1046. No reservations. No credit cards. $*

Key West

The southernmost city in the continental United States was originally a Spanish possession. It, along with the rest of Florida, became an American territory in 1819. Through much of the 19th century, Key West was Florida's wealthiest city per capita. The locals made their fortunes from "wrecking"—rescuing people and salvaging cargo from ships that foundered on nearby reefs. Cigarmaking, fishing, shrimping, and sponge-gathering also became important industries.

Nicknamed "The Conch Republic," Key West today makes for a unique port call for the 10 or so ships that visit each week. A genuinely American town, it nevertheless exudes the relaxed atmosphere and pace of a typical Caribbean island. Major attractions for cruise passengers are the home of the Conch Republic's most famous citizen, Ernest Hemingway, the birthplace of now-departed Pan American World Airways, and, if your cruise ship stays in port late enough, the island's renowned sunset celebrations.

Shore Excursions The following are good choices in Key West. They may not be offered by all cruise lines. Times and prices are approximate. Unless otherwise noted, children's prices are for those under 13.

Island Sights **Historic Homes Walking Tour.** You'll see three notable 19th-century residences—the Harry S. Truman Little White House, the Donkey Milk House, and the Audubon House and Gardens—on a short guided stroll through the historic district. *2 hrs. Cost: $16 adults, $8 children.*

Undersea Creatures **Reef Snorkeling.** The last living coral reefs in continental America are the destination of this 65-foot catamaran. Changing facilities, snorkeling gear, and unlimited beverages are included. *3 hrs. Cost: $38.*

Coming Ashore Cruise ships dock at Mallory Square or near Truman Annex. Both are within walking distance of Duval and Whitehead streets, the two main tourist thoroughfares. For maps and other tourism information, the Chamber of Commerce (402 Wall St.) is found just off Mallory Square.

Getting Around Key West is easily explored on foot. There is little reason to rent a car or hire a cab; public transportation is virtually nonexistent. If you plan to venture beyond the main tourist district, a fun way to get around is by bicycle or scooter.

By Taxi The **Maxi-Taxi Sun Cab System** (tel. 305/294–2222) and **Five 66666** (tel. 305/296–6666) provide service in and around Key West. Taxis meet ships at the pier, but they are not recommended for sightseeing.

By Bicycle or Moped Key West is a cycling town. In fact, there are so many bikes around that cyclists must watch out for each other as well as cars. Try renting from **Keys Moped & Scooter** (tel. 305/294–0399) or **Moped Hospital** (tel. 305/296–3344); both can be found on Truman Avenue. Bikes rent for about $3–$5 per day, mopeds for $18.

By Tour Train or Trolley The **Conch Tour Train** (tel. 305/294–5161) is a 90-minute, narrated tour of Key West that covers 14 miles of island sights. Board at the Mallory Square Depot every half hour. The first train leaves at 9 AM and the last at 4:30 PM.

Old Town Trolley (tel. 305/296–6688) operates 12 trackless, trolley-style buses for 90-minute, narrated tours of Key West. You may get off at any of 14 stops and reboard later.

Exploring Key West *Numbers in the margin correspond to points of interest on the Key West map.*

1 Begin at **Mallory Square,** named for Stephen Mallory, secretary of the Confederate Navy, who later owned the Mallory Steamship Line. On nearby Mallory Dock, a nightly sunset celebration draws street performers, food vendors, and thousands of onlookers. Facing **2** the square is **Key West Aquarium,** which houses hundreds of brightly colored tropical fish and other fascinating sea creatures from local waters. *1 Whitehead St., tel. 305/296–2051. Admission: $6.50 adults, $5.50 senior citizens, $3.50 children. Open daily 10–6; guided tours and shark feeding at 11 AM, 1, 3, and 4:30 PM.*

3 Not far away, up Greene Street, the **Mel Fisher Maritime Heritage Society Museum** symbolizes Key West's "wrecking" past. On display are gold and silver bars, coins, jewelry, and other artifacts recovered in 1985 from two Spanish treasure ships that foundered in 1622. *200 Greene St., tel. 305/294–2633. Admission: $6 adults, $2 children. Open daily 9:30–5.*

4 At the end of Front Street, the **Truman Annex** is a 103-acre former military parade grounds and barracks. Also here is the **Harry S. Truman Little White House Museum,** the former president's vacation home. *111 Front St., tel. 305/294–9911. Admission: $6 adults, $3 children. Open daily 9–5.*

5 Head back to Whitehead Street to see the **Audubon House and Gardens.** The museum here commemorates ornithologist John James Audubon's 1832 visit to Key West. On display are a large collection of the artist's engravings. *205 Whitehead St., tel. 305/294–2116. Admission: $6 adults, $4 children 6–12, $2 children under 6. Open daily 9:30–5:30.*

6 At **301 Whitehead Street,** a sign proclaims the birthplace of Pan American World Airways, the first U.S. airline to operate scheduled international air service. The inaugural flight took off from Key West International Airport on October 28, 1927.

7 A little farther up Whitehead is **Hemingway House.** Built in 1851, this two-story, Spanish-colonial dwelling was the first house in Key West to have running water and a fireplace. Hemingway bought the place in 1931 and wrote 70% of his life's works here. Descendants of Hemingway's cats still inhabit the grounds. Half-hour tours begin

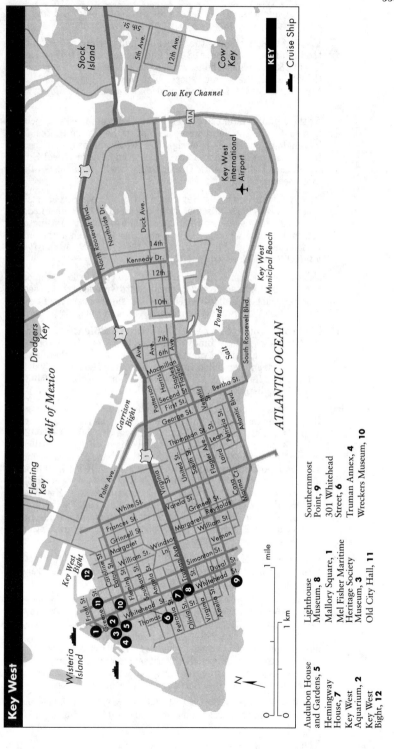

Key West

Audubon House
and Gardens, **5**

Hemingway
House, **7**

Key West
Aquarium, **2**

Key West
Bight, **12**

Lighthouse
Museum, **8**

Mallory Square, **1**

Mel Fisher Maritime
Heritage Society
Museum, **3**

Old City Hall, **11**

Southernmost
Point, **9**

301 Whitehead
Street, **6**

Truman Annex, **4**

Wreckers Museum, **10**

KEY

⚓ Cruise Ship

every 10 minutes. *907 Whitehead St., tel. 305/294–1575. Admission: $6.50 adults, $6 senior citizens, $2 children. Open daily 9–5.*

8 Up the block and across the street, behind a white picket fence, is the **Lighthouse Museum,** a 92-foot lighthouse built in 1847 and an adjacent 1887 clapboard house where the keeper lived. You can climb the 98 steps to the top for a spectacular view of the island. *938 Whitehead St., tel. 305/294–0012. Admission: $5 adults, $1 children 7–12. Open daily 9:30–5.*

9 At the foot of Whitehead Street, a huge concrete marker proclaims this spot to be the **Southernmost Point** in the United States. Turn left on South Street. To your right are two dwellings that both claim to be the **Southernmost House.** Take a right onto Duval Street, which ends at the Atlantic Ocean, and you will be at the **Southernmost Beach.**

10 Return toward downtown Key West by way of Duval Street until you reach the **Wrecker's Museum,** which is said to be the oldest house in Key West. It was built in 1829 as the home of Francis Watlington, a sea captain and wrecker. It now contains 18th- and 19th-century period furnishings. *322 Duval St., tel. 305/294–9502. Admission: $3 adults, 50¢ children. Open daily 10–4.*

11 Take Duval to Front Street, turn right, go two blocks to Simonton Street, turn right again and go one block to Greene Street to see the restored **Old City Hall** (510 Greene St.). Inside is a permanent exhibit of old Key West photographs, dating back to 1845.

12 Three blocks down Greene Street lies **Key West Bight** (also known as Harbor Walk), the last funky area of Old Key West. Numerous charter boats and classic old yachts call its slips home, and there's a popular waterfront bar called the Schooner Wharf (*see* Pub Crawling, *below*). The Reef Relief Environmental Center (tel. 305/394–3100) has videos, displays, and free information about the coral reef.

Shopping Passengers looking for T-shirts, trinkets, and other souvenirs will find them on the northern half of Duval Street and around the cruise ship piers. **Fast Buck Freddie's** (500 Duval St., tel. 305/294–2007) sells such novelties as battery-operated alligators that eat Muenster cheese, banana leaf–shaped furniture, fish-shaped flatware, and every flamingo item anyone has every dreamed up. **H.T. Chittum & Co.** (725 Duval St., tel. 305/292–9002) sells Key West–style apparel and accessories, from aviator hats to fish-cleaning knives. **Key West Island Bookstore** (513 Fleming St., tel. 305/294–2904) is the literary bookstore of the large Key West writer's community, while **Lucky Street Gallery** (919 Duval St., tel. 305/294–3993) carries the work of Key West artists and others.

Sports **Captain's Corner** (tel. 305/296–8918) leads excursions to reefs and
Diving wrecks for spear or lobster fishing and archaeological and treasure hunting.

Fishing and A variety of fishing vessels, glass-bottom boats, and sailing char-
Boating ters sail from Key West. The *Discovery* (tel. 305/293–0099) and *Fireball* (tel. 305/296–6293 or 305/294–8704) are two glass-bottom boats, and the *Wolf* (tel. 305/296–9653) is a schooner that sails on day and sunset cruises with live music. *Linda D III* (tel. 305/296–9798), captained by third-generation Key West seaman Bill Wickers, runs full- and half-day sportfishing outings. The Chamber of Commerce on Front Street, by the pier, has a full list of other operators.

Golf **Key West Resort Golf Course** (tel. 305/294–5232) is an 18-hole course on the bay side of Stock Island. Fees are $30 for 18 holes ($15 for a cart).

Snorkeling The last living coral reef in North America and clear, warm Gulf of Mexico waters make Key West a good choice for getting your flippers wet (*see* Shore Excursions, *above*, and Beaches, *below*).

Beaches Facing the Gulf of Mexico, **Simonton Street Beach,** at the north end of Simonton Street and near the cruise-ship piers, is a great place to watch the boats come and go in the harbor. On the Atlantic Ocean, **Fort Zachary Taylor State Historic Site** has several hundred yards of beach near the western end of Key West. The beach is relatively uncrowded; snorkeling is good here. **Smathers Beach** features almost 2 miles of sand beside South Roosevelt Boulevard. Trucks along the road will rent you rafts, Windsurfers, and other beach toys. **Southernmost Beach** is found at the foot of Duval Street (*see* Exploring, *above*).

Dining **Pier House Restaurant.** Steamships from Havana once docked at this pier jutting into the Gulf of Mexico. Now, it's an elegant place to dine, indoors or out, and to watch the boats glide by. The menu highlights American and Caribbean cuisine. Specialties include such dishes as grilled tuna with cracked peppercorns and lobster ravioli in a creamy pesto sauce. *1 Duval St., tel. 305/296–4600. Reservations advised. AE, DC, MC, V. $$$*

Half Shell Raw Bar. "Eat It Raw" is the motto, and even during the off-season this oyster bar keeps shucking. You eat at shellacked picnic tables in a shed, with model ships, life buoys, and old license plates hung overhead. If shellfish isn't to your taste, try the broiled dolphin sandwich or linguine seafood marinara. *Land's End Marina, tel. 305/294–7496. No reservations. MC, V. $–$$*

Pub Crawling Three spots stand out for first-timers among the many local saloons frequented by Key West denizens. **Capt. Tony's Saloon** (428 Greene St.) is where Ernest Hemingway used to hang out when it was called **Sloppy Joe's.** The current **Sloppy Joe's** is found nearby at 201 Duval Street and has become a landmark in its own right. **Schooner Wharf** (Key West Bight; *see* Exploring Key West, *above*) is the most authentically local saloon and doesn't sell T-shirts. All are within easy walking distance of the cruise-ship piers.

Martinique

One of the most beautiful islands in the Caribbean, Martinique is lush with wild orchids, frangipani, anthurium, jade vines, flamingo flowers, and hundreds of hibiscus varieties. Trees bend under the weight of tropical treats such as mangoes, papayas, bright red West Indian cherries, lemons, and limes. Acres of banana plantations, pineapple fields, and waving sugarcane fill the horizon.

The towering mountains and verdant rain forest in the north lure hikers, while underwater sights and sunken treasures attract snorkelers and scuba divers. Martinique is also wonderful if your idea of exercise is turning over every 10 or 15 minutes to get an even tan, or if your adventuresome spirit is satisfied by a duty-free shop.

The largest of the Windward Islands, Martinique is 4,261 miles from Paris, but its spirit and language are decidedly French, with more than a soupçon of West Indian spice. Tangible, edible evidence of that fact is the island's cuisine, a superb blend of classic French and Creole dishes.

Fort-de-France is the capital, but at the turn of the 20th century, St-Pierre, farther up the coast, was Martinique's premier city. Then, in 1902, volcanic Mont Pelée blanketed the city in ash, killing all its residents—save for a condemned man in prison. Today, the ruins are a popular excursion for cruise passengers.

Currency Legal tender is the French franc, which consists of 100 centimes. At press time, the rate was 5.2F to U.S. $1. Dollars are accepted, but if you're going to shop, dine, or visit museums on your own, it's better to convert a small amount of money into francs.

Passports and Visas U.S. and Canadian citizens must have a passport or proof of citizenship. British citizens are required to have a passport.

Telephones and Mail It is not possible to make collect or credit-card calls from Martinique to the United States. There are no coin telephone booths on the island. If you must call home and can't wait until the ship reaches the next port, go to the post office and purchase a Telecarte, which looks like a credit card and is used in special booths marked TELECOM. Long-distance calls made with Telecartes are less costly than operator-assisted calls. Airmail letters to the United States are 4.60F for up to 20 grams; postcards, 3.80F. The main post office is conveniently located on rue de la Liberté in central Fort-de-France.

Shore Excursions The following is a good choice on Martinique. It may not be offered by all cruise lines. Time and price are approximate. Unless otherwise noted, children's prices are for those under 13.

Island Sights **Martinique's Pompeii.** A bus or taxi drive through the lush green mountains, past picturesque villages, to St-Pierre, with a stop at the museum there. This is one of the best island tours in the Caribbean. *2½–4 hrs. Cost: $40–$50 adults, $30 children.*

Coming Ashore Cruise ships that dock call at the Maritime Terminal east of the city. The only practical way to get into town is by cab ($16 round-trip). To get to the Maritime Terminal tourist information office, turn right and walk along the waterfront. Ships that anchor in the Baie des Flamands (*see* Exploring Martinique, *below*) tender passengers directly to the downtown waterfront. A tourist office is just across the street from the landing pier in the Air France building. Guided walking tours ($15 for 1½ hrs.) can be arranged at the nearby open-air marketplace.

Getting Around Martinique has about 175 miles of well-paved roads marked with international road signs. Streets in Fort-de-France are narrow and clogged with traffic, country roads are mountainous with hairpin turns, and the Martiniquais drive with controlled abandon. If you drive in the country, be sure to pick up a map from one of the tourist offices; an even better one is the *Carte Routière et Touristique*, available at any local bookstore.

By Car

For rental cars, contact **Avis** (tel. 596/70–11–60), **Budget** (tel. 596/63–69–00), or **Hertz** (tel. 596/60–64–64). Count on paying $60 a day.

By Ferry Weather permitting, *vedettes* (ferries) operate daily between Fort-de-France and the marina Méridien, in Pointe du Bout, and between Fort-de-France and the beaches of Anse-Mitan and Anse-à-l'Ane. The Quai d'Esnambuc is the arrival and departure point for ferries in Fort-de-France. The one-way fare is 16F; round-trip, 27F.

By Taxi Taxi rates are regulated by the government; the minimum charge is 9.50F (about $1.90). Pick up cabs at taxi stands. Before you agree to use a taxi driver as a guide, check to make sure his English is good. For destinations beyond Fort-de-France, you will find taxis expensive and drivers keen to overcharge you.

Exploring Martinique *Numbers in the margin correspond to points of interest on the Martinique map.*

Fort-de-France On the island's west coast, on the beautiful Baie des Flamands, lies
❶ the capital city of **Fort-de-France.** Its narrow streets and pastel buildings with ornate wrought-iron balconies are reminiscent of the French Quarter in New Orleans—though whereas New Orleans is flat, Fort-de-France is hilly.

Bordering the waterfront is **La Savane,** a 12½-acre landscaped park filled with gardens, tropical trees, fountains, and benches. It's a popular gathering place and the scene of promenades, parades, and impromptu soccer matches. Near the harbor is a **marketplace** where beads, baskets, pottery, and straw hats are sold. The crafts here are among the nicest in the Caribbean.

On rue de la Liberté, which runs along the west side of La Savane, look for the **Musée Départmentale de Martinique.** Artifacts from the pre-Columbian Arawak and Carib periods include pottery, beads, and part of a skeleton that turned up during excavations in 1972. One exhibit examines the history of slavery; costumes, documents, furniture, and handicrafts from the island's colonial period are on display. *9 rue de la Liberté, tel. 596/71–57–05. Admission: 15F adults, 5F children 5–12. Open weekdays 8:30–1 and 2:30–5, Sat. 9–noon.*

Leave the museum and walk one block away from La Savane on rue Blénac to rue Victor Schoelcher. There you'll see the Romanesque **St-Louis Cathedral,** whose steeple rises high above the surrounding buildings. The cathedral has lovely stained-glass windows. A number of Martinique's former governors are interred beneath the choir loft.

Rue Schoelcher runs through the center of the capital's primary **shopping district**—a six-block area bounded by rue de la République, rue de la Liberté, rue Victor Sévère, and rue Victor Hugo (*see* Shopping, *below*).

Three blocks north of the cathedral, up rue Schoelcher, turn right onto rue Perrinon and go one block. At the corner of rue de la Liberté is the **Bibliothèque Schoelcher,** the wildly elaborate Byzantine-Egyptian-Romanesque public library named after Victor Schoelcher, who led the fight to free the slaves in the French West Indies in the 19th century. The eye-popping structure was built for the 1889 Paris Exposition, after which it was dismantled, shipped to Martinique, and reassembled piece by piece on its present site. Inside is a collection of ancient documents recounting Fort-de-France's development. *Admission free. Open daily 8:30–6.*

The North Martinique's "must do" is the drive north through the mountains from Fort-de-France to St-Pierre and back along the coast. The 40-mile round-trip can be done in an afternoon, although there is enough to see to fill your entire day in port. A nice way to see the lush island interior and St-Pierre is to take the N3, which snakes through dense rain forests, north to Le Morne Rouge; then take the N2 back to Fort-de-France via St-Pierre.

② Along the N3 (also called the Route de la Trace), stop at **Balata** to see the **Balata Church,** an exact replica of Sacré-Coeur Basilica in Paris, and the **Jardin de Balata** (Balata Gardens). Jean-Phillipe Thoze, a professional landscaper and devoted horticulturalist, spent 20 years creating this collection of thousands of varieties of tropical flowers and plants. There are shaded benches where you can relax and take in the panoramic views of the mountains. *Rte. de Balata, tel. 596/72–58–82. Admission: 30F adults, 10F children. Open daily 9–5.*

③ Continuing north on the N3, you'll reach **Le Morne Rouge,** on the southern slopes of Mont Pelée. This town was, like St-Pierre, destroyed by the volcano and is now a popular resort. Signs will direct you to the narrow road that takes you halfway up the mountain—you won't really have time to hike to the 4,600-foot peak, but this side trip gets you fairly close and offers spectacular views.

Northeast of here on the N3, a few miles south of **Basse-Pointe** on the **④** Atlantic coast, is the flower-filled village of **Ajoupa-Bouillon.** This 17th-century settlement in the midst of pineapple fields is a beautiful area, but skip it if you've never seen St-Pierre and are running out of time. From Le Morne Rouge, you'll need a good three hours to enjoy the coastal drive back to Fort-de-France.

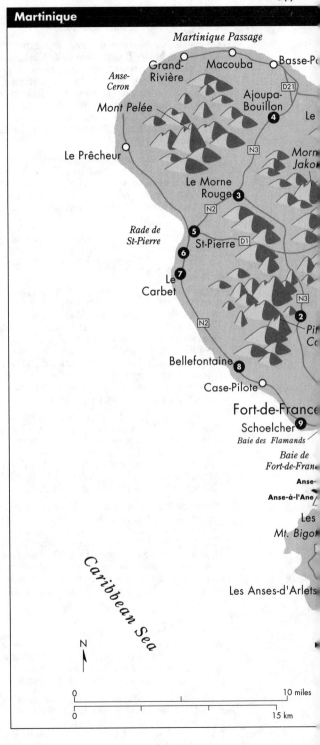

Martinique

Martinique Passage

Grand-Rivière

Macouba

Basse-Po

Anse-Ceron

Mont Pelée

Ajoupa-Bouillon **4**

D21

Le

Le Prêcheur

N3

Morn Jako

Le Morne Rouge **3**

N2

Rade de St-Pierre

5

St-Pierre

D1

6

Le Carbet **7**

N3

N2

2

Pit Co

Bellefontaine **8**

Case-Pilote

Fort-de-France

Schoelcher **9**

Baie des Flamands

Baie de Fort-de-Fran

Anse-

Anse-à-l'Ane

Les

Mt. Bigo

Les Anses-d'Arlets

Caribbean Sea

N

0   10 miles

0   15 km

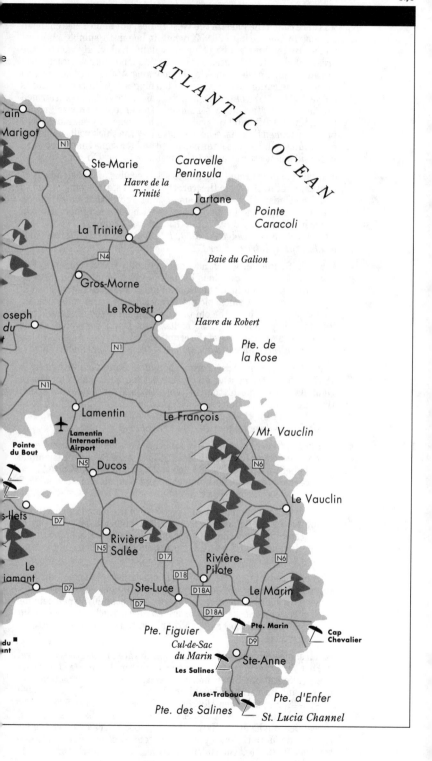

❺ Take the N2 west a few miles to **St-Pierre,** the island's oldest city. It was once called the Paris of the West Indies, but Mont Pelée changed all that in the spring of 1902, when it began to rumble and spit steam. By the first week in May, all wildlife had wisely vacated the area, but city officials ignored the warnings, needing voters in town for an upcoming election. On the morning of May 8, the volcano erupted, belching forth a cloud of burning ash with temperatures above 3,600°F. Within three minutes, Mont Pelée had transformed St-Pierre into Martinique's Pompeii. The entire town was annihilated, its 30,000 inhabitants calcified. There was only one survivor: a prisoner named Siparis, who was saved by the thick walls of his underground cell. He was later pardoned and for some time afterward was a sideshow attraction at the Barnum & Bailey Circus.

You can wander through the site to see the ruins of the island's first church, built in 1640; the theater; the toppled statues; and Siparis's cell. The Cyparis Express is a small tourist train that runs through the city, hitting the important sights with a running narrative (in French). *Departs from Pl. des Ruines du Figuier every 45 min weekdays 9:30–1 and 2:30–5:30, tel. 596/55–50–92. Tickets: 30F adults, 10F children under 12.*

While in St-Pierre, which now numbers only 6,000 residents, you might pick up some delicious French pastries to nibble on the way back after stopping in at the **Musée Vulcanologique.** Established in 1932 by American volcanologist Franck Perret, the collection includes photographs of the old town, documents, and excavated relics, including molten glass, melted iron, and contorted clocks stopped at 8 AM, the time of the eruption. *Tel. 596/78–15–16. Admission: 15F adults, 5F children under 12. Open daily 9–noon and 3–5.*

❻ A short way south is **Anse-Turin,** where Paul Gauguin lived briefly in 1887 with his friend and fellow artist Charles Laval. The **Musée Gauguin** traces the history of the artist's Martinique connection through documents, letters, and reproductions of paintings he completed while on the island. *Tel. 596/77–22–66. Admission: 15F adults, 5F children under 12. Open daily 10–5.*

❼ Continuing down the coast, **Le Carbet** is where Columbus is believed to have landed on June 15, 1502. In 1635, Pierre Belain d'Esnambuc arrived here with the first French settlers. The **Zoo de Carbet** here features rare birds, snakes, wildcats, and caimans. *Admission: 20F adults, 10F children. Open daily 9–6.*

❽ On your way back to port, you'll pass two of the island's more interesting towns. **Bellefontaine** is a small fishing village with pastel houses spilling down the hillsides and colorful boats bobbing in the **❾** water. Just north of Fort-de-France, **Schoelcher** is home of the University of the French West Indies and Guyana.

Shopping French products, such as perfume, wines, liquors, designer scarves, leather goods, and crystal, are all good buys in Fort-de-France. In addition, luxury goods are discounted 20% when paid for with traveler's checks or major credit cards. Look for Creole gold jewelry, white and dark rum, and handcrafted straw goods, pottery, and tapestries.

Small shops carrying luxury items proliferate around the cathedral in Fort-de-France, particularly on rue Victor Hugo, rue Moreau de Jones, rue Antoine Siger, and rue Lamartine. Look for Lalique, Limoges, and Baccarat at **Cadet Daniel** (72 rue Antoine Siger, tel. 596/71–41–48) and at **Roger Albert** (7 rue Victor Hugo, tel. 596/71–71–71), which also sells perfume. A wide variety of dolls, straw goods, tapestries, and pottery is available at the **Caribbean Art Center** (Centre de Métiers Art, opposite the tourist office, Blvd. Alfassa, tel. 596/70–32–16). The **Galerie d'Art** (89 rue Victor Hugo, tel. 596/

63–10–62) has some unusual and excellent Haitian art at reasonable prices.

Sports Fishing For charter excursions, contact **Bathy's Club** (Hôtel Méridien, Anse-Mitan, tel. 596/66–00–00).

Golf **Golf de l'Impératrice Joséphine** (tel. 96/68–32–81) has an 18-hole Robert Trent Jones course with an English-speaking pro, a pro shop, a bar, and a restaurant. Located at Trois-Ilets, a mile from the Pointe du Bout resort area and 18 miles from Fort-de-France, the club offers special greens fees for cruise-ship passengers.

Hiking **Parc Naturel Régional de la Martinique** (Caserne Bouille, Fort-de-France, tel. 596/73–19–30) organizes inexpensive guided hiking tours. Information is available at the island tourist offices.

Horseback Riding Excursions and lessons are available at the **Black Horse Ranch** (near La Pagerie in Trois-Ilets, tel. 596/68–37–80), **La Cavale** (near Diamant on the road to the Novotel hotel, tel. 596/76–22–94), and **Ranch Jack** (near Anse-d'Arlets, tel. 596/68–37–67).

Water Sports Hobie Cats, Sunfish, and Sailfish can be rented by the hour from hotel beach shacks. If you're a member of a yacht club, show your club membership card and enjoy the facilities of **Club de la Voile de Fort-de-France** (Pointe Simon, tel. 596/70–26–63) and **Yacht Club de la Martinique** (blvd. Chevalier, Ste-Marthe, tel. 596/63–26–76). To explore the old shipwrecks, coral gardens, and other undersea sites, you must have a medical certificate and insurance papers. Among the island's dive operators are **Bathy's Club** (Hotel Méridien, Anse-Mitan, tel. 596/66–00–00) and the **Sub Diamant Rock** (Diamant-Novotel, tel. 596/76–42–42).

Beaches Topless bathing is prevalent at the large resort hotels. Unless you're an expert swimmer, steer clear of the Atlantic waters, except in the area of Cap Chevalier and the Caravelle Peninsula. **Pointe du Bout** has small, white-sand beaches, most of which are commandeered by resort hotels. **Anse-Mitan**, south of Pointe du Bout, is a white-sand beach with superb snorkeling. **Anse-à-l'Ane** offers picnic tables and a nearby shell museum; bathers cool off in the bar of the Calalou Hotel. **Grande-Anse** is less crowded—the preferred beach among people who know the island well. **Les Salines** is the best of Martinique's beaches, whether you choose to be with other sun worshippers or to find your own quiet stretch of sand. However, it's an hour's drive from Fort-de-France and 5 miles beyond Ste-Anne.

Dining *All restaurants include a 15% service charge in their menu prices.*

Relais Caraibes. For a leisurely lunch, a magnificent view of Diamond Rock, and possibly a swim in the pool, head out to this tasteful restaurant and hotel. (A taxi will take you there for about 180F from Fort-de-France, less from Pointe du Bout.) Dishes include a half lobster in two sauces, fresh-caught fish in a basil sauce, and fricassee of country shrimp. *La Cherry (on the small road leading to the Diamant-Novotel), Le Diamant, tel. 596/76–44–65. AE, MC, V. Closed Mon. $$$*

Le Second Soufflé. The chef uses fresh vegetables and fruits—nutrition is a top priority here—to make soufflés ranging from aubergine (eggplant) to *filet de ti-nain* (small green bananas) with chocolate sauce and other tempting creations, like eggplant ragout and okra quiche. *27 rue Blénac, Fort-de-France, tel. 596/63–44–11. No credit cards. No lunch Sat. $*

St. Croix

St. Croix is the largest of the three U.S. Virgin Islands that form the northern hook of the Lesser Antilles. Its position, 40 miles south of its sisters, unfortunately put the island in the path of 1989's Hurricane Hugo, which stalled over St. Croix for several hours, ripping the island to shreds with 150-mile-an-hour winds. Hugo's wrath is now just a memory; St. Croix today remains quite beautiful and maintains a slow, quiet pace that is far more attractive than the hustle and bustle of St. Thomas.

Christopher Columbus landed here in 1493, skirmishing briefly with the native Arawak Indians. Since then, the three U.S. Virgin Islands have played a colorful, if painful, role as pawns in the game of European colonialism. Theirs is a history of pirates and privateers, sugar plantations, slave trading, and slave revolt and liberation. Through it all, Denmark had staying power; from the 17th to the 19th century, Danes oversaw a plantation slave economy that produced molasses, rum, cotton, and tobacco. Many of the stones you see in buildings or tread on in the streets were once used as ballast on sailing ships, and the yellow fort of Christiansted is a reminder of the value once placed on this island treasure.

Currency The U.S. dollar is the official currency of St. Croix.

Passports and Visas U.S. and Canadian citizens need proof of citizenship; a passport is best. British citizens need a passport.

Telephones and Mail Calling the mainland from St. Croix is as easy as calling within the United States. Local calls from a public phone cost 25¢ for every five minutes. Postal rates are the same as elsewhere in the United States: 32¢ for a letter and 20¢ for a postcard. Post offices are within walking distance of the piers in Frederiksted and Christiansted.

Shore Excursions The following are good choices on St. Croix. They may not be offered by all cruise lines. Times and prices are approximate.

Island Sights **Plantation Hike.** At the ruins of this plantation, discovered right outside Frederiksted in 1984, you can get a glimpse into St. Croix's past as you hike through the verdant rain forest. *3 hrs. Cost: $25–$30 adults, $15–20 children.*

Tee Time **Golf at Carambola.** Robert Trent Jones designed this 18-hole, par-72 course, considered one of the Caribbean's finest. Includes shared golf cart and greens fees. *Half day. Cost: $58.*

Coming Ashore Smaller ships (less than 200 passengers) dock in Christiansted, larger ones in Frederiksted. Information centers are found near both piers. In Christiansted, pick up a copy of the *Walking Tour Guide* at the visitor center. Both towns are easily explored on foot; beaches are nearby.

Getting Around
By Car Driving is on the left-hand side of the road, although steering wheels are on the left-hand side of the car. Rentals are available from **Avis** (tel. 809/778–9355), **Budget** (tel. 809/778–9636), and **Hertz** (tel. 809/778–1402), which are all near the airport; **Caribbean Jeep & Car** (tel. 809/773–4399) in Frederiksted; and **Olympic** (tel. 809/773–2208) in Christiansted. Rates begin at about $40 daily.

By Taxi Taxis of all shapes and sizes are available at the cruise piers and at various shopping and resort areas; they also respond quickly when telephoned. Taxis do not have meters, so you should check the list of standard rates available from the visitor centers and settle the fare with your driver before you start. Taxi drivers are required to carry a copy of the official rates and must show it to you when asked. Remember, too, that you can hail a taxi that is already occupied. Drivers take multiple fares and sometimes even trade passengers at midpoints. Try **St. Croix Taxi Association** (tel. 809/778–1088) or **Antilles Taxi Service** (tel. 809/773–5020).

Exploring St. Croix *Numbers in the margin correspond to points of interest on the St. Croix map.*

Most of this tour must be done by car, with the exceptions of Frederiksted and Christiansted. Next to the cruise-ship pier in ❶ **Frederiksted** is the restored **Ft. Frederik**, completed in the late 18th century. Here, in 1848, the slaves of the Danish West Indies were freed by Governor Peter van Scholten. Down Market Street is the **Market Place,** where you can buy fresh fruit and vegetables early in the morning.

Around the corner on Prince Street is the **Old Danish School,** designed in the 1830s and now part of the Ingeborg Nesbett Clinic. **St. Paul's Episcopal Church,** a mixture of classic and Gothic Revival architecture, is two blocks south on Prince Street; it has survived several hurricanes since its construction in 1812 and became Episcopal when the United States purchased the island in 1917. A few steps away, on King Cross Street, is **Apothecary Hall,** which survived the great fire of 1878. Walk south and turn right on Queen Cross Street to the **Old Public Library,** or **Bell House,** which now houses an arts-and-crafts center and the **Dorsch Cultural Center** for the performing arts. Back at the waterfront, walk up Strand Street to the **fish market.** By the cruise-ship pier is **Victoria House,** on your right. Once a private home and the town's best example of Victorian gingerbread architecture, it was heavily damaged by Hurricane Hugo but is currently undergoing renovation.

2 South of Frederiksted is the **West End Salt Pond,** rife with mangroves and little blue herons. In the spring, large leatherback sea turtles clamber up the white sand to lay their eggs. You will also see brown pelicans.

3 Head up Centerline Road to the **Estate Whim Plantation Museum.** The lovingly restored estate, with windmill, cookhouse, and other buildings, gives a real sense of what life was like for the owners of St. Croix's sugar plantations in the 1800s. The great house, with a singular oval shape and high ceilings, features antique furniture and utensils, as well as a major apothecary exhibit. Note the house's fresh and airy atmosphere—the waterless moat was used not for defense but for gathering cooling air.

4 A little farther along Centerline Road are the **St. George Village Botanical Gardens,** 17 lush and fragrant acres amid the ruins of a 19th-century sugarcane plantation village. Across Centerline Road off **5** Route 64 is the **Cruzan Distillery,** where rum is made with pure rainwater, making it (so it is said) superior to any other. Visitors are welcome for a tour and a free rum-laced drink (the concoction changes daily).

Turn left off Centerline Road onto Northside Road (Route 75), and **6** continue into **Christiansted.** Dominated by its yellow fort, the town is well worth an hour of your time.

7 Retrace your route along Northside Road to **Judith's Fancy,** on your right. Once home to the governor of the Knights of Malta, this old great house and tower are now in ruins. The "Judith" comes from the name of a woman buried on the property. From here you have a good view of **Salt River Bay,** where Columbus landed.

Continue west on Northside Road and then north on Route 80 toward the coast, pulling over at windy **Cane Bay.** This is one of St. Croix's best beaches for scuba diving; near the small stone jetty you may see a few wet-suited figures making their way to the "drop-off," which descends to 12,000 feet. Rising behind you is **Mt. Eagle,** at 1,165 feet St. Croix's highest peak.

8 Leaving Cane Bay and passing North Star Beach, follow the beautiful coast road to **Davis Bay,** both for the panoramic views of the sea along this winding corniche and for a glimpse of the striking setting of Carambola, a luxury resort. The road ends here, so backtrack to Route 69 and turn right. Turn right again onto Centerline Road and head for Frederiksted, then travel north on Route 63. The area north and east of town is **rain forest,** much of it private property but laced with roads open to the public. Just north of Frederiksted, turn

St. Croix

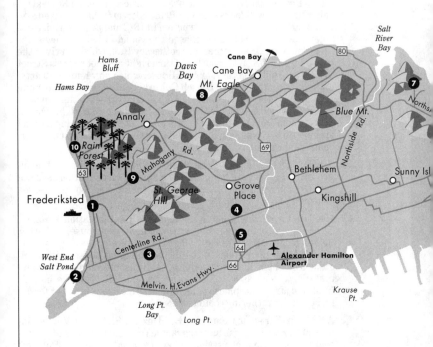

KEY

⚓ Cruise Ship

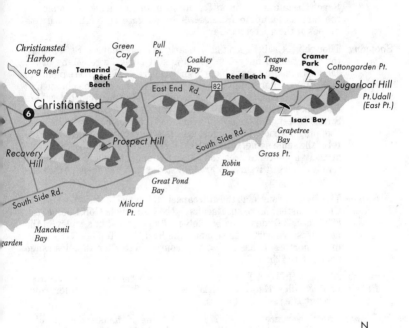

Buck Island

Buck Island Beach

Christiansted Harbor
Long Reef

⑥ *Christiansted*

Green Cay
Pull Pt.

Tamarind Reef Beach

East End Rd. 82

Coakley Bay

Reef Beach

Teague Bay

Cramer Park

Cottongarden Pt.

Sugarloaf Hill
Pt. Udall (East Pt.)

Isaac Bay

Prospect Hill

South Side Rd.

Grapetree Bay

Grass Pt.

Recovery Hill

Robin Bay

South Side Rd.

Great Pond Bay

Milord Pt.

Manchenil Bay

garden

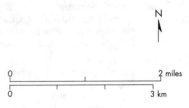

N

0   2 miles
0   3 km

⑨ right onto Route 76, or **Mahogany Road** (the best of the roads in this area), and watch for the sign on the right to **St. Croix Leap,** where you can purchase handsome articles of mahogany, saman, or thibet wood carved by local artisans. You'll find the rain-forest air surprisingly cool.

⑩ Return west to the coast road (Route 63) and head north to **Sprat Hall Plantation,** owned and run for generations by the Hurd Family and famed for its home-cooked food. The beautiful great house is the oldest in the Virgin Islands. Pull up a chair at the breezy **Sprat Hall Beach Restaurant** to sip on a cooling soda or rum drink and munch on the famous pumpkin fritters while you gaze through beach sea-grapes at the glistening Caribbean.

Shopping Though St. Croix doesn't have nearly as many shops as St. Thomas, the selection of duty-free goods is still fairly large. Many of St. Thomas's leading shops have branches here, and there are plenty of independent merchants who carry items you may not be able to find in Charlotte Amalie. The best shopping is in **Christiansted,** where most shops are in the historic district near the harbor. **King Street, Strand Street,** and the arcades that lead off them comprise the main shopping district. The longest arcade is **Caravelle Arcade,** in the hotel of the same name. **Gallows Bay,** just east of Christiansted, has an attractive boutique area that features unusual island-made silver jewelry and gift items. In **Frederiksted,** a handful of shops face the cruise-ship pier.

Sports The 18-hole course at the **Buccaneer** (tel. 809/773–2100) is close to
Golf Christiansted. More spectacular is the **Carambola Golf Course** (tel. 809/778–5638), designed by Robert Trent Jones, in a valley in the northwestern part of the island. The **Reef Club** (tel. 809/773–8844), in the northeast, has a nine-hole course. Rates for 18 holes range from $18 to $25.

Horseback At Sprat Hall (*see* Exploring St. Croix, *above*), near Frederiksted,
Riding **Paul & Jill's Equestrian Stables** (tel. 809/772–2627) offer rides through the rain forest.

Scuba Diving **Dive Experience** (tel. 809/773–3307) is one of the island's best dive
and Snorkeling specialists. **Mile-Mark Charters** (tel. 809/773–2628) offers a full range of water sports including sailing, snorkeling, and scuba diving. Both are in Christiansted.

Beaches **Buck Island** and its reef, which is under environmental protection, can be reached only by boat from Christiansted but is well worth a visit. The beach is beautiful, but its finest treasures are those you see when you plop off the boat and adjust your face mask, snorkel, and flippers. At **Cane Bay,** a breezy north-shore beach, the waters are not always gentle but the diving and snorkeling are wondrous, and there are never many people around. Less than 200 yards out is the drop-off, called Cane Bay Wall, or just swim straight out to see elkhorn and brain corals. Three miles north of Frederiksted you'll find **Rainbow Beach** where you can enjoy the sand, snorkel at a small nearby reef, and get a bite to eat at the bar. **Tamarind Reef Beach** is a small but attractive beach with good snorkeling east of Christiansted. Green Cay and Buck Island seem smack in front of you and make the view arresting.

Dining **Le St. Tropez.** A dark-wood bar and soft lighting add to the Mediterranean feel at this pleasant bistro, tucked into a courtyard off Frederiksted's main thoroughfare. Daily specials highlight local seafood, while light French cuisine, such as quiches, brochettes, and crepes, are the menu's mainstays. *67 King St., Frederiksted, tel. 809/772–3000. Reservations accepted. AE, MC, V. Closed Sun. $$*
Camille's. This tiny, lively spot is perfect for lunch or a light supper. Sandwiches and burgers are the big draw, but each day there's a

seafood special—often wahoo or mahimahi. *Queen Cross St.,
Christiansted, tel. 809/773-2985. No credit cards. Closed Sun. $*

St. Lucia

Oval, lush St. Lucia—a ruggedly beautiful island, with towering
mountains, green valleys, and acres of banana plantations—sits in
the middle of the Windward Islands. In addition to its beaches, it is
distinguished by two special topographical features: the twin peaks
of the Pitons (Petit and Gros), each soaring more than 2,400 feet, and
Soufrière's bubbling sulfur springs, part of a low-lying volcano that
erupted thousands of years ago, which attract visitors for their curative waters. Other attractions are the diving and, no less, the "lim-
ing"—the Caribbean term for hanging out.

St. Lucia changed hands between the French and English 14 times
before 1814, when England took final possession. Since 1979, the island has been an independent state within the British Commonwealth of Nations. The official language is English, and St. Lucians
are among the friendliest inhabitants of the Caribbean.

Currency St. Lucia uses the Eastern Caribbean (E.C.) dollar. Figure about
E.C. $2.70 to U.S. $1. U.S. dollars are widely accepted, but you'll
usually get change in E.C. dollars. Major credit cards are widely accepted, as are traveler's checks.

Passports and U.S., Canadian, and British citizens need proof of citizenship; a
Visas passport is best.

Telephones Long-distance connections from St. Lucia are excellent, and num-
and Mail bers can be dialed directly. International telephone and telex services are available at Pointe Seraphine, where most ships dock.
Postage for airmail letters to foreign countries is E.C. 95¢ for up to 1
ounce; postcards cost E.C. 75¢.

Shore The following is a good choice in St. Lucia. It may not be offered by
Excursions all cruise lines. Time and price are approximate.

Natural Beauty **La Soufrière and the Pitons.** Tour the countryside by bus, surveying
the mountains, sulfur springs, volcano, and Diamond Baths. A buf-
fet lunch accompanies this beautifully scenic overview of the island.
8 hrs. Cost: $43.

Coming Most cruise ships call at the capital city of Castries, except for a cou-
Ashore ple of tiny vessels that sail into Soufrière. Both are on the island's
west coast, Castries to the north and Soufrière to the south. In
Castries, most ships dock at Pointe Seraphine, a duty-free shopping
complex and cruise-ship terminal, or across the harbor at the noisy
downtown industrial dock. Ferry service connects the two dock areas. In Soufriere, most ships drop anchor and tender passengers
ashore. Tourist information offices are at Pointe Seraphine and
along the waterfront in Soufrière. Neither Castries nor Soufrière
offers much in the way of a walking tour.

Getting The best way to see the sights on St. Lucia is to take a ship-organ-
Around ized shore excursion. Passengers who want to tour on their own are
advised to rent a car or hire a taxi driver.

By Car To rent a car, you have to buy a temporary St. Lucian license, which
costs E.C. $16. Rates begin at $40 a day. Remember that driving is
on the *left* side of the road. Rental agencies include **Avis** (tel. 809/
452-2700), **Dollar** (tel. 809/452-0994), and **National** (tel. 809/450-
8721).

By Taxi Taxis are unmetered, and although the government has issued a list
of suggested fares, they're not regulated. Negotiate with the driver
before you depart, and be sure that you both understand whether
the price you've agreed upon is in E.C. or U.S. dollars. Taxi drivers
expect a 10% tip. Drivers know the island well and make excellent

guides; a taxi tour takes six hours and costs about $120 for up to four people, $20 per person thereafter.

Exploring St. Lucia *Numbers in the margin correspond to points of interest on the St. Lucia map.*

The John Compton Highway connects Pointe Seraphine to down-
① town **Castries.** When you reach Bridge Street (by car or taxi), head east past **Government House,** the official residence of the governor-general of St. Lucia, until you come to **Morne Fortune.** Driving up the "hill of good fortune," you'll see beautiful tropical plants—frangipani, lilies, bougainvillea, hibiscus, oleander.

② **Ft. Charlotte** on the Morne was begun in 1764 by the French as the Citadelle du Morne Fortune. Before it was completed 20 years later, several battles were waged, and it changed hands a number of times. The **Inniskilling Monument** is a tribute to a famous battle of 1796, when the 27th Foot Royal Inniskilling Fusiliers wrested the hill from the French.

The North End and Gros Islet The west coast north of Castries is the most developed part of the island and is easy and safe to navigate. Take the John Compton
③ Highway north for about 15 minutes to **Rodney Bay,** an 80-acre, man-made lagoon and resort complex named after 18th-century
④ British Admiral Rodney. Farther north of the lagoon is **Gros Islet,** a quiet little fishing village typical of the undeveloped side of the Windward Islands.

⑤ A couple of miles farther up the coast, **Pigeon Point** juts into the sea. According to island tales, pirate Jambe de Bois (Wooden Leg) used this island as his hideout (a causeway has been built since, connecting it with the mainland). This 40-acre hilltop is now a national park, with long sandy beaches, calm waters for swimming, and areas for picnicking. On the grounds you'll see ruins of barracks, batteries, and garrisons dating from the French and British battles for control of St. Lucia. *Pigeon Point, no phone. Admission: E.C. $3. Guided tours E.C. $10. Open Mon.–Sat. 9–4.*

Soufrière and the South It's a 90-minute drive from Castries to **Soufrière,** which dates from the mid-18th century and was named after the nearby volcano. At
⑥ ⑦ the **Diamond Falls** and **Mineral Baths,** see the waterfalls and gardens before slipping into your swimsuit for a dip in the steaming curative waters, fed by an underground flow from the volcano's sulfur springs. *Admission: E.C. $5. Open daily 10–5.*

⑧ St. Lucia's dense tropical **rain forest** is east of Soufrière on the road to Fond St. Jacques; the trek through the lush landscape takes three hours. You'll need a guide and plenty of stamina (contact the Forestry Division, tel. 809/452–3231). The road south out of Soufrière is awful and leads up a steep hill, but if you persevere, you'll be re-
⑨ warded by the best land view of the **Pitons.**

⑩ South of Soufrière, a left turn leads to **La Soufrière,** the drive-in volcano and its sulfur springs—more than 20 pools of black, belching, smelly sulfurous waters. Take the guided tour offered by the Tourist Board. *Admission: E.C. $3 (including tour). Open daily 9–5.*

Shopping St. Lucia's best-known products are the unique silk-screened and hand-printed designs of **Bagshaw Studios,** which are designed, printed, and sold only on St. Lucia. The island is also home to **Windjammer Clothing,** which is sold throughout the Caribbean. Other indigenous souvenirs include native-made wood carvings, pottery, and straw hats and baskets.

St. Lucia entered the duty-free market with the opening of **Pointe Seraphine,** a modern, Spanish-style complex by the harbor where 23 shops sell designer perfume, china and crystal, jewelry, watches, leather goods, liquor, and cigarettes; to get the duty-free reduction, you must show your boarding pass or cabin key. Native crafts are also sold here. Otherwise, Soufrière is not much of a shopping port.

Castries has a number of shops, mostly on **Bridge Street** and **William Peter Boulevard,** that sell locally made souvenirs. At **Caribelle Batik** (Old Victoria Rd., The Morne, tel. 809/452–3785), visitors are welcome to watch artisans creating batik clothing and wall hangings. At **Eudovic Art Studio** (Morne Fortune, 15 min south of Castries, tel. 809/452–2747), trays, masks, and figures are carved from mahogany, red cedar, and eucalyptus trees. Hammocks, straw mats, baskets and hats, and carvings, as well as books and maps of St. Lucia, are at **Noah's Arkade** (Jeremie St. and Pt. Seraphine, tel. 809/452–2523). **Artsibit** (corner Brazil and Mongiraud Sts., tel. 809/452–7865) features works by top St. Lucian artists.

Sports

Fishing Among the sea creatures in these waters are dolphin, Spanish mackerel, barracuda, and white marlin. Contact **Captain Mike's** (tel. 809/452–7044) or **Mako Watersports** (tel. 809/452–0412).

Golf There are nine-hole courses at **St. Lucia Sandals** (tel. 809/452–3081) and **Cap Estate Golf Club** (tel. 809/452–8523). A caddy is required at the former. Greens fees are $15–$20 at either for 18 holes; club rentals are $10. These courses are scenic and good fun, but they're not of a professional caliber.

Hiking St. Lucia is laced with trails, but you should not attempt the challenging peaks on your own. The Tourist Board or the **Forestry Division** (tel. 809/452–3231) can provide you with a guide. The **St. Lucia National Trust** (tel. 809/452–5005) runs tours of several sites, including Pigeon Point (*see* Exploring St. Lucia, *above*).

Horseback Riding For trail rides on the beach, contact **Trim's Riding School** (Gros Islet, tel. 809/452–8273), **North Point Riding Stables** (tel. 809/450–8853), or **Jalousie Plantation** (tel. 809/459–7666).

Scuba Diving **Scuba St. Lucia** (tel. 809/459–7355) is a PADI five-star training facility that offers daily beach and boat dives, resort courses, underwater photography, and day trips. Trips can also be arranged through **Buddies Scuba** (tel. 809/452–5288), **Dive Jalousie** (tel. 809/459–7666), **Moorings Scuba Centre** (tel. 809/451–4357), and **Windjammer Diving** (tel. 809/452–0913).

Tennis **St. Lucia Racquet Club** (adjacent to Club St. Lucia, tel. 809/450–0551) is one of the top tennis facilities in the Caribbean. **Jalousie Plantation** (tel. 809/459–7666) has four lighted courts open to nonguests.

Beaches All of St. Lucia's beaches are public. Many are flanked by hotels where you can rent water-sports equipment and have a rum punch, but the resorts are sometimes less than welcoming to cruise-ship passengers. About a 30-minute ride from Pointe Seraphine is **Pigeon Point** (admission E.C. $3), which has a long white-sand beach and a small restaurant; it's great for picnicking and swimming. **Reduit Beach,** 20 minutes from Castries, is a long stretch of beige sand facing Rodney Bay. Water-sports equipment can be rented at the two beachfront hotels.

Near Soufrière, **Anse Chastanet** is a gray-sand beach with a backdrop of green hills and the island's best reefs for snorkeling and diving. A dive shop and bar are located on the beach. The black-sand **Anse des Pitons** sits directly between the Pitons and is accessible by Jalousie Plantation or by boat from Soufrière. It, too, offers great snorkeling and diving.

Dining *Most restaurants add a 10% service charge to the bill.*

Castries **Jimmie's.** It's a 10–15-minute ride from the ship, but worth it for the great views. Popular with locals as well as visitors, Jimmie's specializes in seafood—from creole stuffed crab for an appetizer to the

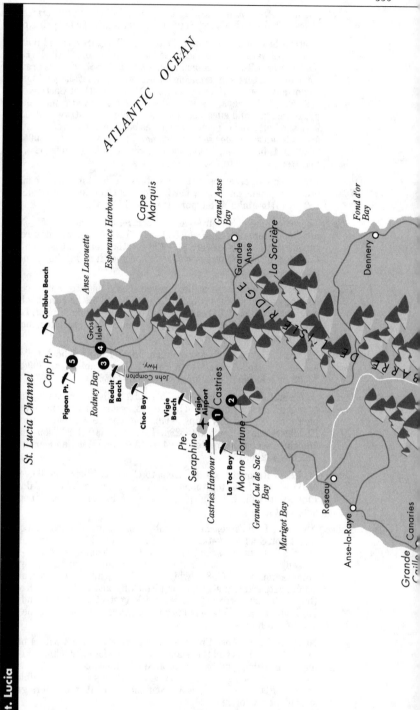

ATLANTIC OCEAN

St. Lucia Channel

Cap Pt.

Cariblue Beach

Pigeon Pt. **5**

Anse Lavonette

Esperance Harbour

Cape Marquis

Gros Islet **4**

Rodney Bay **3**

Reduit Beach

John Compton Hwy.

Grand Anse Bay

Grande Anse

La Sorcière

Choc Bay

Vigie Beach

Vigie Airport

Castries **1**

2

La CAPE DE L'ISLE RIDGE

Fond d'or Bay

Dennery

Pte. Seraphine

Castries Harbour

La Toc Bay

Morne Fortune

Grande Cul de Sac Bay

BARRE DE L'ISLE

Marigot Bay

Roseau

Anse-la-Raye

Grande Caille

Canaries

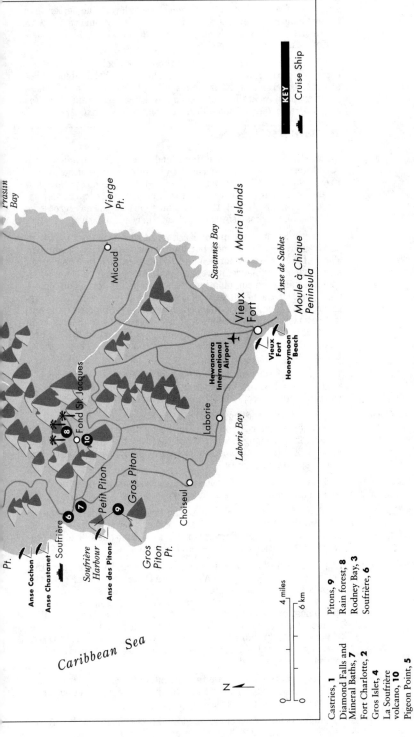

Praslin Bay

Vierge Pt.

Micoud

Maria Islands

Savannes Bay

Vieux Fort

Anse de Sables

Moule à Chique Peninsula

Hewanorra International Airport

Vieux Fort Honeymoon Beach

Laborie

Laborie Bay

Fond St. Jacques

8

10

6

7

Petit Piton

9

Gros Piton

Soufrière

Choiseul

Gros Piton Pt.

Soufrière Harbour

Anse des Pitons

Anse Cochon

Anse Chastanet

Pt.

Caribbean Sea

N

0

0

4 miles

6 km

KEY

Cruise Ship

Castries, **1**

Diamond Falls and Mineral Baths, **7**

Fort Charlotte, **2**

Gros Islet, **4**

La Soufrière volcano, **10**

Pigeon Point, **5**

Pitons, **9**

Rain forest; **8**

Rodney Bay, **3**

Soufrière, **6**

special seafood platter for an entrée. Dessert lovers had better be in a banana mood—everything from fritters to ice cream is made with St. Lucian "figs." *Vigie Cove, Castries, tel. 809/452–5142. No reservations. AE, MC, V. $$–$$$*

Soufrière **Camilla's.** Just a shore walk from the cruise docks, this friendly, second-floor restaurant serves local dishes such as the catch-of-the-day curried, creole-style, or grilled with lemon sauce. There's also a list of tropical cocktails bigger than the entire restaurant. *7 Bridge St., Soufrière, tel. 809/459–5379. Reservations advised. AE. $*

St. Martin/St. Maarten

St. Martin/St. Maarten: one tiny island, just 37 square miles, with two different accents, and ruled by two separate nations. Here French and Dutch have lived side by side for hundreds of years, and when you cross from one country to the next there are no border patrols, no customs. In fact, the only indication that you have crossed a border at all is a small sign and a change in road surface.

St. Martin/St. Maarten epitomizes tourist islands in the sun, where services are well developed but life remains distinctly Caribbean. The Dutch side is ideal for people who like plenty to do. The French side has more ambience, more fashionable shopping, and more Continental flair. The combination of the two halves makes an almost ideal port. On the negative side, the island has been thoroughly discovered and completely developed. There is gambling, but table limits are so low that high rollers will have a better time gamboling on the beach. It can be fun to shop, and you'll find an occasional bargain, but many goods (particularly electronics) are cheaper in the United States.

Though Dutch is the official language of St. Maarten, and French of St. Martin, almost everyone speaks English. If you hear a language you can't quite place, it's Papiamento, a Spanish-based Creole.

Currency Legal tender on the Dutch side is the Netherlands Antilles florin (guilder), written NAf; on the French side, the French franc (F). In general, the exchange rate is about NAf 1.80 to U.S. $1, and 5F to U.S. $1. There's little need to exchange money, though, as dollars are accepted everywhere.

Passports and Visas U.S. citizens need proof of citizenship; a passport is preferred. British and Canadian citizens need valid passports.

Telephones and Mail
Intra-island calls To phone from the Dutch side to the French side, dial 06 plus the local number. From the French side to the Dutch side, dial 011–5995 plus the local number. Remember that a call from one side to the other is an international call and not a local one.

Overseas Calls At the Landsradio in Philipsburg, St. Maarten, there are facilities for overseas calls and an AT&T USADirect telephone. On the French side, it's not possible to make collect calls to the United States, but you can make credit-card calls from a phone on the side of the tourist office in Marigot. The operator will assign you a PIN number, valid for as long as you specify. Calls to the U.S. are about $4 per minute. To call from other public phones, you'll need to go to the special desk at Marigot's post office and buy a Telecarte, which looks like a credit card.

Postal Rates Letters from the Dutch side to the United States and Canada cost NAf1.30, postcards NAf.60. From the French side, letters up to 20 grams cost 4.10F, postcards 3.50F.

Shore Excursions The following is a good choice in St. Martin/St. Maarten. It may not be offered by all cruise lines. Time and price are approximate.

Undersea **Snorkel Tour.** Take a boat to a beach where you will be taught how to
Creatures snorkel, then given the choice of joining a group or setting off on
your own. Refreshments may be served. *3 hrs. Cost: $27.*

Coming Except for a few vessels that stop on the French side, cruise ships
Ashore drop anchor off the Dutch capital of Philipsburg or dock in the marina at the southern tip of the Philipsburg harbor. If your ship anchors, tenders will ferry you to the town pier in the middle of town,
where taxis await passengers. Next to the pier, on Wathey Square,
is the Tourist Bureau, where you can pick up information and maps.
If your ship docks at the marina, downtown is a 15-minute taxi ride
away. The walk is not recommended.

Getting One of the island's best bargains, public buses cost from 80¢ to $2
Around and run frequently between 7 AM and 7 PM, from Philipsburg through
By Bus Cole Bay to Marigot.

By Car The island's roads are good, and it would be quite difficult to get lost.
Because everything is within an easy drive of Philipsburg, and taxis
are very expensive, this is a good port for renting a car. The cost is
about $35 a day. It's best to reserve a car before you leave home, es-
pecially at the height of the winter season. Contact **Avis** (tel. 800/
331–1212), **Budget** (tel. 800/527–0700), **Hertz** (tel. 800/654–3131), or
National (tel. 800/328–4567).

By Taxi Taxis are government-regulated and costly. Authorized taxis display stickers of the St. Maarten Taxi Association. Taxis are also
available at Marigot.

Exploring St. *Numbers in the margin correspond to points of interest on the St.*
Martin *Martin/St. Maarten map.*

❶ The Dutch capital of **Philipsburg,** which stretches about a mile along
an isthmus between Great Bay and Salt Pond, is easily explored on
foot. It has three parallel streets: Front Street, Back Street, and
Pond Fill. Little lanes called *steegjes* connect Front Street (which
has been recobbled and its pedestrian area widened) with Back
Street, considerably less congested because it has fewer shops. Al-
together, a walk from one end of downtown to the other takes a half
hour, even if you stop at a couple of stores.

Head first for **Wathey Square,** in the middle of the isthmus, which
bustles with vendors, souvenir shops, and tourists. The streets to
the right and left are lined with hotels, duty-free shops, restaurants, and cafés, most in West Indian cottages decorated in pastels
with gingerbread trim. Narrow alleyways lead to arcades and flower-filled courtyards with yet more boutiques and eateries.

If you have use of a car, start at the west end of Front Street. The
road (which becomes Sucker Garden Road) leads north along Salt
Pond and begins to climb and curve just outside town. Take the first
❷ right to **Guana Bay Point,** from which you get a splendid view of the
island's east coast, tiny deserted islands, and little St. Barts in the
distance.

Sucker Garden Road continues north through spectacular scenery.
❸ Follow the paved, roller-coaster road down to **Dawn Beach,** an excellent snorkeling beach, then continue to **Oyster Pond,** with an active
sailing community. The rough, potholed road winds around the
❹ shore to join the main road at **Orléans.** This settlement, also known
as the French Quarter, is the island's oldest.

A rough dirt road leads east to **Orient Beach,** the island's best-
❺ known nudist beach. North of Orléans is the **French Cul de Sac,**
where you'll see the French colonial mansion of St. Martin's mayor
nestled in the hills. From here the road swirls south through green
hills and pastures, past flower-entwined stone fences. Past
❻ L'Espérance Airport is the town of **Grand Case,** known as the "Restaurant Capital of the Caribbean." Scattered along its mile-long

St. Martin/St. Maarten

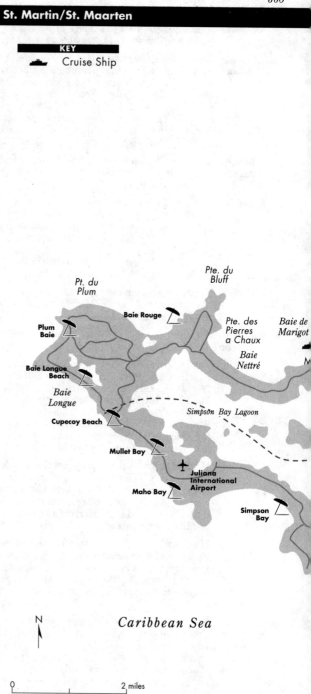

KEY

⛴ Cruise Ship

Pt. du Bluff

Pt. du Plum

Baie Rouge

Pte. des Pierres a Chaux

Baie de Marigot

Plum Baie

Baie Nettré

Baie Longue Beach

Baie Longue

Simpson Bay Lagoon

Cupecoy Beach

Mullet Bay

Juliana International Airport

Maho Bay

Simpson Bay

N

Caribbean Sea

0   2 miles

0   3 km

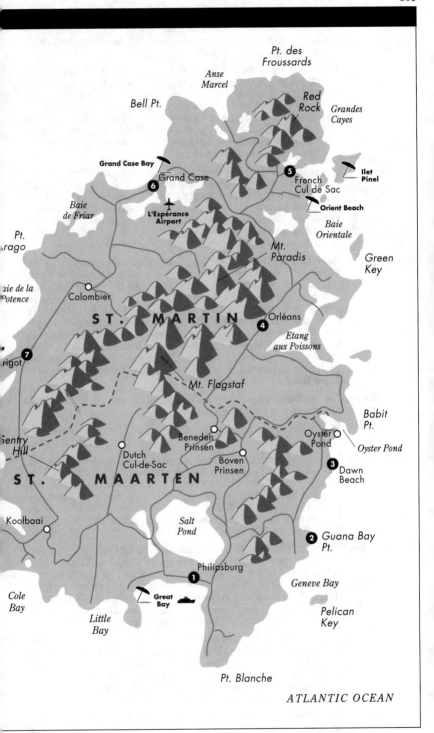

main street are more than 20 restaurants serving French, Italian, Indonesian, and Vietnamese fare, as well as fresh seafood. Along the shore, vendors known as "lolos" sell delicious barbecued chicken, beef on skewers, and other delicacies.

❼ Follow the signs south from Grand Case to rue de la République, which brings you to the French capital of **Marigot.** Marina Port La Royale is the shopping complex at the port; rue de la République and rue de la Liberté, which border the bay, are also filled with duty-free shops, boutiques, and bistros. The road south from Marigot leads to the official border, where a simple marker, placed here in 1948, commemorates 300 years of peaceful coexistence. This road will bring you back to Philipsburg.

Shopping Prices can be 25%–50% below those in the United States and Canada for French perfume, liquor, cognac and fine liqueurs, crystal, linens, leather, and other luxury items. However, it pays to know the prices back home; not all goods are a bargain. Caveat emptor: While most merchants are reputable, there are occasional reports of inferior or fake merchandise passed off as the real thing. When vendors bargain excessively, their wares are often suspect.

In Philipsburg, **Front Street** is one long strip of boutiques and shops; **Old Street,** near the end of Front Street, is packed with stores, boutiques, and open-air cafés. At Philipsburg's the **Shipwreck Shop,** look for Caribelle batiks, hammocks, handmade jewelry, the local guava-berry liqueur, and herbs and spices. You'll find almost 100 boutiques in **Mullet Bay** and **Maho** shopping plazas. In general, you will find smarter fashions in Marigot than in Philipsburg. In Marigot, wrought-iron balconies, colorful awnings, and gingerbread trim decorate the shops and tiny boutiques in the **Marina Port La Royale** and on the main streets, **rue de la Liberté** and **rue de la République.**

Sports Contact **Wampum** at Bobby's Marina, Philipsburg (tel. 599/5–22366)
Fishing for information on fishing charters.

Golf **Mullet Bay Resort** (tel. 599/5–52801) has an 18-hole championship course.

Water Sports Myriad boats can be rented at **Lagoon Cruises & Watersports** (tel. 599/5–52801) and **Caribbean Watersports** (tel. 599/5–42801). NAUI-, SSI-, and PADI-certified dive centers offer scuba instruction, rentals, and trips. On the Dutch side, try **Trade Winds Dive Center** (tel. 599/5–75176) and **St. Maarten Divers** (tel. 599/5–22446). On the French side, there's **Lou Scuba** (tel. 590/87–22–58) and **Blue Ocean** (tel. 590/87–89–73), both PADI-certified.

Beaches The island's 10 miles of beaches are all open to the public. Those occupied by resort properties charge a small fee (about $3) for changing facilities, and water-sports equipment can be rented at most hotels. Some of the 37 beaches are secluded; some are in the thick of things. Topless bathing is common on the French side. If you take a cab to a remote beach, be sure to arrange a specific time for the driver to return for you. Don't leave valuables unattended on the beach.

Baie Longue, the island's best beach, is a mile-long curve of white sand at the western tip offering excellent snorkeling and swimming but no facilities. **Cupecoy Beach** is a narrower, more secluded curve of white sand just south of Baie Longue near the border. There are no facilities, but a truck often pulls up with cold beer and sodas. Clothing becomes optional at the far end of the beach.

Dining *By law, restaurants on the French side figure a service charge into the menu prices, so no tips are expected. On the Dutch side, most restaurants add 10%–15% to the bill.*

Dutch Side **Chesterfield's.** Burgers and salads are served at lunch, but menus are more elaborate for dinner on this indoor/outdoor terrace overlooking the marina. Specialties include French onion soup, roast duckling with fresh pineapple and banana sauce, and chicken cordon bleu. The Mermaid Bar is popular with yachtsmen. *Great Bay Marina, Philipsburg, tel. 599/5–23484. AE, MC, V. $–$$*

Turtle Pier Bar & Restaurant. Chattering monkeys and squawking parrots greet you at the entrance to this classic Caribbean hangout, festooned with creeping vines and teetering over the lagoon. There are 200 animals in the zoo, but that's nothing compared to the menagerie at the bar during happy hour. Genial owners Sid and Lorraine Wathey have fashioned one of the funkiest, most endearing places in the Caribbean, with cheap beer on tap, huge American breakfasts, all-you-can-eat ribs for $9.95, and eclectic live music several nights a week. *Airport Rd., Philipsburg, tel. 599/5–52230. No credit cards. $*

French Side **Le Poisson d'Or.** At this posh and popular restaurant set in a stone house, the waters of the bay lap the 20-table terrace as you feast on hot foie gras salad in raspberry vinaigrette; smoked lobster boiled in tea with parsley cream sauce; or veal with Roquefort, hazelnut, and tarragon sauce. The young chef, François Julien, cooks with enthusiasm, but his cuisine must compete for attention with the striking setting. *Off rue d'Anguille, Marigot, tel. 590/87–72–45. Reservations recommended. AE, MC, V. No lunch Tues. in low season. $$$*

Cha Cha Cha Caribbean Cafe. Japanese gardens, gaudy colors, and a gaudier clientele have made this the island hot spot (the mouthwatering haute-Caribbean cuisine and reasonable prices don't hurt). Try the roasted pork tenderloin with ginger sauce or the grilled snapper with pesto, then wash it down with a "Grand Case Sunset." *Grand Case, tel. 590/87–53–63. MC, V. Closed Sun. No lunch. $$*

St. Thomas/St. John

St. Thomas is the busiest cruise port of call in the world. As many as a dozen ships may visit in a single day. Don't expect an exotic island experience: One of the three U.S. Virgin Islands (with St. Croix and St. John), St. Thomas is as American as any place on the mainland, complete with McDonald's franchises, HBO, and the U.S. dollar. The positive side of all this development is that there are more tours to choose from here than anywhere else in the Caribbean, and every year the excursions get better. Of course, shopping is the big draw in Charlotte Amalie, the main town, but experienced travelers remember the days of "real" bargains. Today, so many passengers fill the stores that it's a seller's market. One of St. Thomas's best tourist attractions is its neighboring island, St. John, with its beautiful national parks and empty beaches.

Passports and Visas U.S. and Canadian citizens need proof of citizenship; a passport is best. British citizens need a passport.

Telephones and Mail It's as easy to call home from St. Thomas as from any city in the United States. And public phones are all over the place, including right on the dock. Postal rates are the same as elsewhere in the United States: 32¢ for a letter, 20¢ for a postcard. The post office in downtown Charlotte Amalie is located one block up from the waterfront at the eastern end of the main shopping drag.

Shore Excursions The following are good choices in St. Thomas/St. John. They may not be offered by all cruise lines. Times and prices are approximate.

Adventure **Helicopter Tour.** An exciting aerial tour of St. Thomas and surrounding islands. *1–2 hrs, includes 1 hr flight time. Cost: $50–$100.*

Natural Beauty **St. John Island Tour.** Either your ship tenders you in to St. John in the morning before docking at St. Thomas, or you take a bus from the St. Thomas docks to the St. John ferry. On St. John, an open-air safari bus winds through the national park to a beach for snorkeling, swimming, and sunbathing. (If you have the option, go to Honeymoon Beach instead of Trunk Bay.) All tours end with a ferry ride back to St. Thomas. *4–4½ hrs. Cost: $22–$50.*

Undersea **Atlantis Submarine.** A surface boat ferries you out to a submarine *Creatures* with large picture windows; the *Atlantis* dives to explore the underwater world, with good accompanying narrative. *2 hrs. Cost: $68 adults, $34 children under 13.*

Coki Beach Snorkeling. A shallow reef just offshore next to Coral World, this busy locale has a large population of fish, coral, and snorkelers. Good for novices who want to learn snorkeling (instruction and equipment usually are included) and see a variety of wildlife. *3 hrs. Cost: $21–$22.*

Sailing and Snorkeling Tour. A romantic sail, a snorkeling lesson, and an attractive snorkeling site make this an excellent excursion for experiencing the true beauty of the Virgin Islands. The boat may be a modern catamaran, a single-hull sailing yacht, or a sailing vessel done up to look like a pirate ship. *3½–4 hrs. Cost: $32–$45.*

Scuba Diving. This excursion to one or two choice sites via boat or off a beach may be limited to certified divers, may be open to novices who have been taking lessons on the ship, or may include instruction for beginners. *3 hrs. Cost: $38–$75.*

Coming Depending on how many ships are in port, cruise ships drop anchor **Ashore** in the harbor at Charlotte Amalie and tender passengers directly to the waterfront duty-free shops, dock at the Havensight Mall at the eastern end of the crescent-shaped bay, or dock at Crown Point Marina a few miles west of town. The distance from Havensight to the duty-free shops is 1½ miles, which can be walked in less than half an hour, or a taxi can be hired for $4 per person, one-way ($3 if there is more than one passenger). Tourist information offices are located at the Havensight Mall (Bldg. No 1) for docking passengers and downtown at the eastern end of the waterfront shopping strip for those coming ashore by tender. Both distribute free island and downtown shopping maps. From Crown Point, it's also a half-hour walk or a $3 cab ride ($2 for more than one passenger).

Getting Driving is on the left side of the road, though steering wheels are on **Around** the left side of the car. Car rentals are available from numerous *By Car* agencies, including **ABC Rentals** (by Havensight Mall, tel. 809/776–1222), **Budget** (Marriott's Frenchman Reef Hotel, tel. 809/776–5774), and **Hertz** (near the airport, tel. 809/774–1879). Rates for one day range from $55 to $70.

By Ferry You can get to St. John on your own via ferry from Charlotte Amalie. The cost is $6 round-trip. Get ferry schedules and information from the tourist information offices at Havensight or in Charlotte Amalie.

By Taxi Taxis meet every ship. They don't have meters, but rates are set. Check with the shore-excursion director for correct fares and agree on the price before getting in the cab. Most taxis are minivans, which take multiple fares and charge per person. Many of them will give you a guided tour of the island for far less than you'd pay for a ship-sponsored excursion. The most popular destination, Magens Bay, costs $4 from town and $6.50 from the Havensight pier, per person, one way.

Exploring St. *Numbers in the margin correspond to points of interest on the St.* **Thomas** *Thomas map.*

Charlotte **Charlotte Amalie** is a hilly, overdeveloped shopping town. There are *Amalie* plenty of interesting historical sights here, and much of the town is ❶ quite pretty. So while you're shopping, take the time to see at least a few of the sights. For a great view of the town and the harbor, begin at the beautiful Spanish-style **Hotel 1829,** whose restaurant (*see* Dining, *below*) is one of the best on St. Thomas. A few yards farther up the road is the base of the **99 Steps,** a staircase "street" built by the Danes in the 1700s. Go up the steps (there are more than 99) and continue to the right to **Blackbeard's Castle,** originally Ft. Skysborg. The massive five-story watchtower was built in 1679. It's now a dramatic perch from which to sip a drink and admire the harbor from the small hotel and restaurant.

With gravity now on your side, head back down the steps. To the left down Kongen's Gade is **Government House** (1867), the official residence of the governor of the U.S. Virgin Islands. Inside are murals and paintings by Pissarro. Continue down the steps in front of Government House to Norre Gade and turn right to reach the **Frederick Lutheran Church,** the second-oldest Lutheran church in the Western Hemisphere. Its walls date to 1793.

Walk down Tolbod Gade toward the water to **Emancipation Garden,** a park that honors the 1848 freeing of the slaves and features a smaller version of the Liberty Bell. As you stand in the park facing the water, you'll see a large red building to your left, close to the harbor; this is **Ft. Christian,** St. Thomas's oldest standing structure (1627–87) and a U.S. national landmark. The building was used at various times as a jail, governor's residence, town hall, courthouse, and church. The clock tower was added in the 19th century.

If you continue toward the water and cross Veterans Drive, you'll be at **Kings Wharf.** To the left is the lime-green **Legislature Building** (1874), the seat of the 15-member U.S.V.I. Senate since 1957.

The South Shore and East End
Leaving Charlotte Amalie, head east along the waterfront on Veterans Drive (Route 30), which becomes Route 32, called Red Hook Road as it passes **Benner Bay, East End Lagoon,** and **Compass Point.**
2 Staying on Route 32 brings you into **Red Hook,** which has grown from a sleepy little town, connected to the rest of the island only by dirt roads, into an increasingly self-sustaining village. There's luxury shopping at American Yacht Harbor, or you can stroll along the docks and visit with sailors and fishermen, stopping for a beer at Piccola Marina Cafe or Larry's Warehouse. Above Red Hook, the main road swings toward the north shore and becomes Route 38, or
3 Smith Bay Road, taking you past Sapphire Beach and on to **Coral World,** with its three-level underwater observatory, the world's largest reef tank, and an aquarium with more than 20 TV-size tanks providing capsulized views of sea life. *Tel. 809/775–1555. Admission: $14 adults, $9 children. Open daily 9–6.*

4 Farther west on Route 38 is **Tillet's Gardens** (*see* Shopping, *below*), where local artisans craft stained glass, pottery, and ceramics. Artist Jim Tillet's paintings and fabrics are also on display.

North Shore/ Center Islands
In the heights above Charlotte Amalie is **Drake's Seat,** the mountain lookout from which Sir Francis Drake was supposed to have kept
5 watch over his fleet and looked for enemy ships of the Spanish fleet. Magens Bay and Mahogany Run are to the north, with the British Virgin Islands and Drake's Passage to the east. Off to the left, or west, are Fairchild Park, Mountain Top, Hull Bay, and smaller islands, such as the Inner and Outer Brass islands.

6 West of Drake's Seat is **Mountain Top,** not only a tacky mecca for souvenir shopping, but also the place where the banana daiquiri was supposedly invented. There's a restaurant here and, at 1,500 feet above sea level, some spectacular views.

If you head west from Mountain Top on Crown Mountain Road
7 (Route 33), you'll come to **Four Corners.** Take the extreme right turn and drive along the northwestern ridge of the mountain through **Estate Pearl, Sorgenfri,** and **Caret Bay.** There's not much here except peace and quiet, junglelike foliage, and breathtaking vistas.

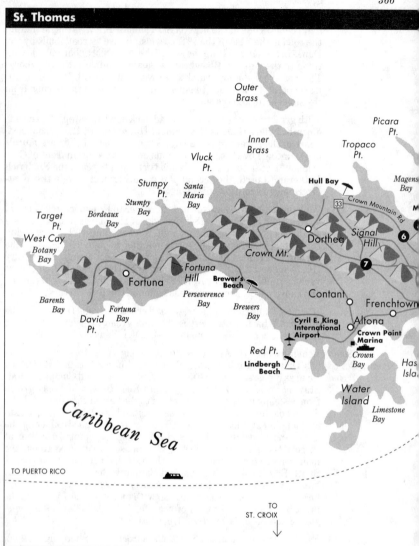

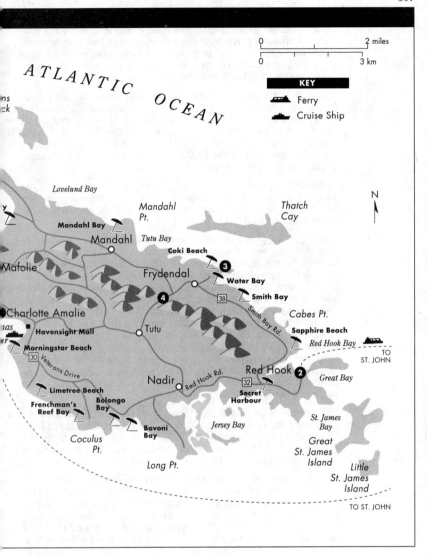

KEY

Ferry

Cruise Ship

ATLANTIC OCEAN

N

Lovelund Bay

Mandahl Pt.

Thatch Cay

Mandahl Bay

Mandahl

Tutu Bay

Coki Beach

3

Mafolie

Frydendal

Water Bay

38

Smith Bay

4

Cabes Pt.

Charlotte Amalie

Tutu

Sapphire Beach

Havensight Mall

Red Hook Bay

TO ST. JOHN

Morningstar Beach

30

Veterans Drive

Nadir

Red Hook Rd.

Red Hook

2

Great Bay

Limetree Beach

32

Frenchman's Reef Bay

Bolongo Bay

Secret Harbour

St. James Bay

Bovoni Bay

Jersey Bay

Great St. James Island

Coculus Pt.

Little St. James Island

Long Pt.

TO ST. JOHN

Shopping There are well over 400 shops in Charlotte Amalie alone, and near the Havensight docks there are at least 50 more, clustered in converted warehouses. Even die-hard shoppers won't want to cover all the boutiques, since a large percentage peddle the same T-shirts and togs. Many visitors devote their shopping time on St. Thomas to the stores that sell handicrafts and luxury items.

Although those famous "give-away" prices no longer abound, shoppers on St. Thomas can still save money. Today, a realistic appraisal puts prices on many items at about 20% off stateside prices, although liquor and perfume often are priced 50%–70% less. What's more, there is no sales tax in the U.S. Virgin Islands, and visitors can take advantage of the $1,200-per-person duty-free allowance. Remember to save receipts.

Prices on such goods as perfume do vary from shop to shop—if you find a good deal, take it. Prices on jewelry vary the most, and it's here that you'll still run across some real "finds." Major credit cards are widely accepted.

Shopping Districts The major shopping area is Charlotte Amalie, in centuries-old buildings that once served as merchants' warehouses and that, for the most part, have been converted to retail establishments. Both sides of **Main Street** are lined with shops, as are the side streets and walkways between Main Street and the waterfront. These narrow lanes and arcades have names like Drake's Passage, Royal Dane Mall, Palm Passage, Trompeter Gade, Hibiscus Alley, and Raadet's Gade. The **Bakery Square Shopping Mall** (1 block north of Main St. off Nye Gade) has about 15 boutiques. The streets adjacent to Bakery Square, notably Back Street, Nye Gade, Garden Street, Kongen's Gade, and Norre Gade, are also very good areas for browsing. At **Havensight Mall,** near the deep-water port where many cruise ships dock, you'll find branches of downtown stores, as well as specialty shops and boutiques.

Charlotte Amalie Unless otherwise noted, the following stores have branches both downtown and in Havensight Mall and are easy to find. If you have any trouble, shopping maps are available at the tourist offices and often from your ship's shore-excursion desk. U.S. citizens can carry back a gallon, or six "fifths," of liquor duty-free.

A.H. Riise Gift Shops: Waterford, Wedgwood, Royal Crown, Royal Doulton, jewelry, pearls, ceramics, perfumes, watches; liquors, cordials, and wines, including rare vintage cognacs, Armagnacs, ports, and Madeiras; tobacco and imported cigars; fruits in brandy; barware from England. **Al Cohen's Discount Liquor** (Havensight only): discount liquors. **Amsterdam Sauer** (downtown only): one-of-a-kind fine jewelry. **Blue Diamond** (downtown only): 14K and 18K jewelry crafted by European goldsmiths. **Boolchand's:** cameras, audio-video equipment.

The **Caribbean Marketplace** (Havensight Mall only): Caribbean handicrafts, including Caribelle batiks from St. Lucia; bikinis from the Cayman Islands; Sunny Caribee spices, soaps, teas, and coffees from Tortola. **Down Island Traders** (downtown only): hand-painted calabash bowls; jams, jellies, spices, and herbs; herbal teas made of rum, passion fruit, and mango; high-mountain coffee from Jamaica; Caribbean handicrafts. The **English Shop:** china and crystal from Spode, Limoges, Royal Doulton, Port Meirion, Noritaki, and Villeroy & Boch.

The **Gallery** (downtown only): Haitian and local oil paintings, metal sculpture, wood carvings, painted screens and boxes, figures carved from stone, oversize papier-mâché figures. **G'Day** (downtown only): umbrellas, artwork, sportswear. **Gucci:** wallets, bags, briefcases, totes, shoes. **H. Stern:** gems and jewelry. **Ilias Lalaounis** (downtown only): 18K and 22K gold jewelry by the Greek designer. **In the Bag** (in A.H. Riise, downtown): designer leather goods. **Janine's Boutique** (downtown only): women's and men's apparel and accessories from European designers and manufacturers, including Louis Feraud, Valentino, Christian Dior, Pierre Cardin. **Java Wraps** (downtown only): Indonesian batik, swimwear, leisure wear, sarongs, ceremonial Javanese puppets. **The Leather Shop:** Fendi, Bottega Veneta, other fine leather goods. **Little Switzerland:** Lalique, Baccarat, Waterford, Swarovski, Riedel, Orrefors, and other crystal; Villeroy & Boch, Aynsley, Wedgwood, Royal Doulton, and other china; Rolex watches. **Luisa** (downtown only): leather shoes and bags from Italy. **MAPes MONDe Ltd.** (in A.H. Riise, downtown): old-fashioned maps and engravings of Caribbean scenes. **Opals of Australia** (downtown only): the name says it all.

Pampered Pirate (downtown only): Caribbean handicrafts, spices, sauces, jams, and Jamaican coffee; gold chain by the inch. **Royal Caribbean** (Havensight Mall only): cameras, cassette players, audio-video equipment. **Sea Wench** (Havensight Mall only): swimwear, lingerie. **Traveler's Haven** (Havensight Mall only): leather bags, backpacks, vests, money belts. **Tropicana Perfume Shoppes** (downtown only): fragrances for men and women.

Tillet's Gardens **Tillet's Gardens and Craft Complex** (Estate Tutu, tel. 809/775–1405; *see* Exploring St. Thomas, *above*) is more than worth the cab fare to reach it. Jim Tillet's artwork is on display, and you can watch craftsmen and artisans produce watercolors, silk-screened fabrics, pottery, enamel work, candles, and other handicrafts.

St. John Opportunities for duty-free shopping are more limited and the prices a bit higher on St. John. One popular spot is **Wharfside Village,** an attractive, compact mall of some 30 shops overlooking Cruz Bay Harbor. **Mongoose Junction,** just north of Cruz Bay across from the Park Service Visitor Center, is one of the most pleasant places to shop in the Caribbean. Built from native stone, the graceful staircases and balconies wind among the shops, a number of which sell handicrafts designed and fashioned by resident artisans.

Sports Call **American Yacht Harbor** at Red Hook (tel. 809/775–6454) if
Fishing you're interested in some serious angling.

Golf Scenic **Mahogany Run** (tel. 809/775–5000), north of Charlotte Amalie, has a par-70, 18-hole course and a view of the British Virgin Islands. The rate for 18 holes is $85, cart included.

Water Sports **Underwater Safaris** (tel. 809/774–1350) is at the Ramada Yacht Haven Motel and Marina, near Havensight. Other reliable scuba and snorkeling operators are **Chris Sawyer Diving Center** (tel. 809/775–7320) and **Aqua Action** (tel. 809/775–6285).

Beaches All beaches in the U.S. Virgin Islands are public, but occasionally
St. Thomas you'll need to stroll through a resort to reach the sand. Government-run **Magens Bay** is lively and popular because of its spectacular loop of white-sand beach, more than a half mile long, and its calm waters. Food, changing facilities, and rest rooms are available. **Secret Harbour** is a pretty cove for superb snorkeling; go out to the left, near the rocks. **Morningstar Beach,** close to Charlotte Amalie, has a mostly sandy sea bottom with some rocks; snorkeling is good here when the current doesn't affect visibility. **Sapphire Beach** has a fine view of St. John and other islands. Snorkeling is excellent at the reef to the east, near Pettyklip Point, and all kinds of water-sports gear can be rented. Be careful when you enter the water; there are many rocks and shells in the sand.

St. John **Trunk Bay** is the main beach on St. John, mostly because of its underwater snorkeling trail. However, experienced snorkelers may find it tame and picked over, with too little coral or fish. Lifeguards are on duty.

Dining *Some restaurants add a 10%–15% service charge to the bill.*

Hotel 1829. Candlelight flickers over old stone walls and across the pink table linens at this restaurant on the gallery of a lovely old hotel. The award-winning menu and wine list are extensive, from Caribbean rock lobster to rack of lamb; many items, including a warm spinach salad, are prepared tableside. The restaurant is justly famous for its dessert soufflés: chocolate, Grand Marnier, raspberry, and coconut. *Government Hill, a few steps up from Main St., Charlotte Amalie, tel. 809/776–1829. Reservations required. AE, D, MC, V. $$$*

Gladys' Cafe. Even if the food was less tasty and the prices higher, it would be worth visiting just to see Gladys smile. Antiguan by birth, she won a local following as a waitress at Palm Passage before opening her own restaurant for breakfast and lunch in a courtyard off Main Street in Charlotte Amalie. Try the Caribbean lobster roll, the barbecue ribs, Gladys's hot chicken salad, or one of the filling salad platters. *17 Main St., tel. 809/774–6604. AE. $*

San Juan, Puerto Rico

Although Puerto Rico is part of the United States, no other city in the Caribbean is as steeped in Spanish tradition as San Juan. Old San Juan has restored 16th-century buildings, museums, art galleries, bookstores, 200-year-old houses with balustrade balconies overlooking narrow, cobblestoned streets—all within a seven-block neighborhood. In contrast, San Juan's sophisticated Condado and Isla Verde areas have glittering hotels, flashy Las Vegas–style shows, casinos, and discos.

Out in the countryside is the 28,000-acre El Yunque rain forest, with more than 240 species of trees growing at least 100 feet high. You can also visit dramatic mountain ranges, numerous trails, vast caves, coffee plantations, old sugar mills, and hundreds of beaches. No wonder San Juan is one of the busiest ports of call in the Caribbean. Like any other big city, San Juan has its share of crime, so guard your wallet or purse, and avoid walking in the area between Old San Juan and the Condado.

Passports and Visas U.S. citizens do not need passports. British citizens must have a passport. Canadians need proof of citizenship (preferably a passport).

Telephones and Mail You can use the long-distance telephone service office in the cruise-ship terminal, or call from any pay phone. A phone center by the Paseo de la Princesa charges 40¢ a minute for calls to the United States. Postal rates are the same as in the United States: 32¢ for a letter, 20¢ for a postcard.

Shore Excursions The following are good choices in San Juan. They may not be offered by all cruise lines. Times and prices are approximate.

Local Flavors **Bacardi Rum Distillery.** After seeing how it is made, you can sample and buy some Bacardi rum. *2 hrs. Cost: $15.*

San Juan Nightlife Tour. Several major hotels (like the Condado Plaza) have very exciting revues, especially those that feature flamenco or Latin dancers. Includes a drink or two. *3 hrs. Cost: $26–$34.*

Natural Beauty **El Yunque Rain Forest.** A 45-minute drive heads east to the Caribbean National Forest, where you may walk along various trails, see waterfalls, and climb the observation tower. The trip may include a stop at Luquillo Beach. *4 hrs. Cost: $20.*

Coming Ashore Cruise ships dock within a couple of blocks of Old San Juan. The Paseo de la Princesa, a tree-lined promenade beneath the city wall, is a nice place for a stroll to admire the local crafts and stop at the refreshment kiosks. A tourist information booth and long-distance telephone office are found in the cruise terminal area. From here a 10- or 15-minute taxi ride to New San Juan costs $8–$10. A five-minute ride to the Condado costs $3–$4.

Getting Around By Bus The **Metropolitan Bus Authority** operates buses that thread through San Juan. The fare is 25¢, and the buses run in exclusive lanes, against traffic, on all major thoroughfares, stopping at yellow posts marked *Parada* or *Parada de Guaguas*. The main terminal is Intermodal Terminal, at Marina and Harding streets in Old San Juan.

By Car U.S. driver's licenses are valid in Puerto Rico. All major U.S. car-rental agencies are represented on the island. Contact **Avis** (tel. 809/721–4499 or 800/331–1212), **Budget** (tel. 809/791–3685 or 800/527–0700), **Hertz** (tel. 809/791–0840 or 800/654–3131), or **L & M Car Rental** (tel. 809/725–8416). Prices start at $30 a day. If you plan to drive across the island, arm yourself with a good map and be aware that many roads up in the mountains are unmarked, and many service stations require cash. To keep you on your toes, speed limits are posted in miles, distances in kilometers, and gas prices are per liter.

By Taxi Taxis line up to meet ships. Metered cabs authorized by the Public Service Commission charge an initial $1; each additional ⅒ mile is 10¢. Waiting time is 10¢ for each 45 seconds. Demand that the meter be turned on, and pay only what is shown, plus a tip of 10%–15%.

By Trolley If your feet fail you in Old San Juan, climb aboard the free open-air trolleys that rumble through the narrow streets. Take one from the docks or board anywhere along the route.

Exploring Old San Juan *Numbers in the margin correspond to points of interest on the Old San Juan map.*

Old San Juan Old San Juan, the original city founded in 1521, contains authentic and carefully preserved examples of 16th- and 17th-century Spanish colonial architecture. Graceful wrought-iron balconies decorated with lush green hanging plants extend over narrow, cobblestoned streets. Seventeenth-century walls still partially enclose the old city. Designated a U.S. National Historic Zone in 1950, Old San Juan is packed with shops, open-air cafés, private homes, tree-shaded squares, monuments, plaques, pigeons, people, and traffic jams. It's faster to walk than to take a cab. Nightlife is quiet, even spooky during the low-season; you'll find more to do in New San Juan, especially the Condado area.

❶ **San Cristóbal,** the 18th-century fortress that guarded the city from land attacks, is known as the Gibraltar of the West Indies. San Cristóbal is larger than El Morro (*see below*), and offers spectacular views of both Old San Juan and the new city. *Tel. 809/729–6960. Admission free. Open daily 9–5.*

Return along Calle San Francisco; three or four blocks past **St. Francis Church** and the **Museum of the Puerto Rican Family/Museum of**
❷ **Colonial Architecture** is the **Plaza de Armas,** the original main square of Old San Juan. The plaza has a lovely fountain with statues
❸ representing the four seasons. West of the square stands **La Intendencia,** a handsome, three-story neoclassical building that was home to the Spanish Treasury from 1851 to 1898. *Calle San José at Calle San Francisco. Admission free. Open weekdays 8–noon and 1–4:30.*

❹ On the north side of the plaza is **City Hall,** called the *alcaldía.* Built between 1604 and 1789, it was fashioned after Madrid's city hall, with arcades, towers, balconies, and a lovely inner courtyard. An art gallery is on the first floor. *Tel. 809/724–7171, ext. 2391. Open weekdays 8–4.*

❺ Turn right onto Calle San José. Here, the **Casa de los Contrafuertes** —also known as the Buttress House because buttresses support the wall next to the plaza—is one of the oldest remaining private resi-

Casa de los
Contrafuertes, **5**

City Hall, **4**

Dominican
Convent, **8**

El Morro
(Fuerte San
Felipe del
Morro), **9**

La Fortaleza, **12**

La
Intendencia, **3**

Pablo Casals
Museum, **6**

Plaza de
Armas, **2**

Plazuela de la
Rogativa, **11**

San Cristóbal, **1**

San José
Church, **7**

San Juan
Cathedral, **10**

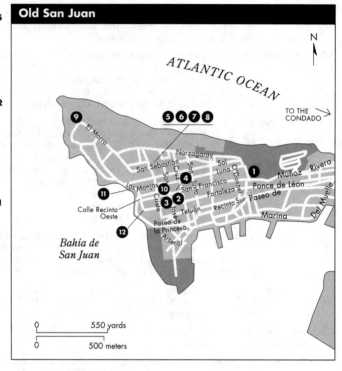

dences in Old San Juan. Inside is the Pharmacy Museum, a re-cre-ation of an 18th-century apothecary shop, and the Latin American Graphic Arts Museum and Gallery. *101 Calle San Sebastián, Plaza de San José, tel. 809/724–5949. Admission free. Open Wed.–Sun. 9–4:30.*

6 The **Pablo Casals Museum,** farther down the block, contains memo-rabilia of the famed Spanish cellist, who made his home in Puerto Rico for the last 20 years of his life. *101 Calle San Sebastián, Plaza de San José, tel. 809/723–9185. Admission free. Open Tues.–Sat. 9:30–5.*

7 In the center of Plaza San José is the **San José Church.** With its series of vaulted ceilings, it is a fine example of 16th-century Spanish Goth-ic architecture. *Calle San Sebastián, tel. 809/725–7501. Admission free. Open Mon.–Sat. 8:30–4; Sun. mass at 12:15.*

8 Next door is the **Dominican Convent.** Also built in the 16th century, the building now houses an ornate 18th-century altar, religious manuscripts, artifacts, and art. *98 Calle Norzagaray, tel. 809/724–0700. Admission free. Chapel museum open Wed.–Sun. 9–noon and 1–4:30.*

9 Follow Calle Norzagaray to **El Morro** (Fuerte San Felipe del Morro), set on a rocky promontory on the northwestern tip of the old city. Rising 140 feet above the sea, the massive, six-level Spanish fortress is a labyrinth of dungeons, ramps, turrets, and tunnels. Built to pro-tect the port, El Morro has a commanding view of the harbor and Old San Juan. Its small museum traces the history of the fortress. *Tel. 809/729–6960. Admission free. Open daily 9:15–6.*

10 Leaving El Morro, head for **San Juan Cathedral** on Calle Cristo. This great Catholic shrine of Puerto Rico had humble beginnings in the early 1520s as a thatch-top wood structure that was destroyed by a hurricane. It was reconstructed in 1540, when the graceful circular staircase and vaulted ceilings were added, but most of the work on the church was done in the 19th century. The remains of Ponce de León are in a marble tomb near the transept. *153 Calle Cristo. Open daily 8–4.*

⑪ Go west alongside the Gran Hotel El Convento on Caleta de las Monjas toward the city wall to the **Plazuela de la Rogativa.** In the little plaza, statues of a bishop and three women commemorate a legend in which the British, while laying siege to the city in 1797, mistook the flaming torches of a religious procession for Spanish reinforcements and beat a hasty retreat.

⑫ One block south on Calle Recinto Oeste is **La Fortaleza,** on a hill overlooking the harbor. The Western Hemisphere's oldest executive mansion in continuous use, La Fortaleza was built as a fortress. The original 16th-century structure has seen numerous changes, including the addition of marble and mahogany, medieval towers, and stained-glass galleries. Guided tours are conducted every hour on the hour in English, on the half hour in Spanish. *Tel. 809/721–7000. Admission free. Open weekdays 8:30–5.*

New San Juan In Puerta de Tierra, a half mile east of the pier, is Puerto Rico's white marble **Capitol,** dating from the 1920s. Another mile east, at the tip of Puerta de Tierra, tiny **Ft. San Jeronimo** perches over the Atlantic like an afterthought. Added to San Juan's fortifications in the late 18th century, the structure barely survived the British attack of 1797.

Santurce, the district between Miramar on the west and the Laguna San José on the east, is a busy mixture of shops, markets, and offices. The classically designed **Sacred Heart University** is home of the **Museum of Contemporary Puerto Rican Art** (tel. 809/268–0049).

San Juan From San Juan, follow Route 2 west toward Bayamón and you'll spot
Environs the **Caparra Ruins,** where, in 1508, Ponce de León established the island's first settlement. The ruins are those of an ancient fort. Its small **Museum of the Conquest and Colonization of Puerto Rico** contains historic documents, exhibits, and excavated artifacts. *Km 6.6 on Rte. 2, tel. 809/781–4795. Admission free. Open Wed.–Sun. 9–4.*

Continue on Route 2 to **Bayamón.** In the Central Park, across from the city hall, are some historic buildings and a 1934 sugarcane train that runs through the park. Along Route 5 from Bayamón to Catano, you'll see the **Barrilito Rum Plant.** On the grounds is a 200-year-old plantation home and a 150-year-old windmill, which is listed in the National Register of Historic Places.

The **Bacardi Rum Plant,** along the bay, conducts 45-minute tours of the bottling plant, museum, and distillery, which has the capacity to produce 100,000 gallons of rum a day. (Yes, you'll be offered a sample.) *Km 2.6 on Rte. 888, tel. 809/788–1500. Admission free. Tours Mon.–Sat. 9:30–3:30; closed Sun. and holidays.*

Shopping San Juan is not a free port, and you won't find bargains on electronics and perfumes. In fact, many Puerto Ricans go to Miami to do their shopping, and their savings usually pay for the trip. However, shopping for native crafts can be fun. Popular souvenirs and gifts include *santos* (small, hand-carved figures of saints or religious scenes), hand-rolled cigars, handmade lace, carnival masks, Puerto Rican rum, and fancy men's shirts called *guayaberas.*

Old San Juan is filled with shops, especially on **Calles Cristo, La Fortaleza,** and **San Francisco.** You can get discounts on Hathaway shirts and clothing by Christian Dior and Ralph Lauren at **Hathaway Factory Outlet** (203 Calle Cristo, tel. 809/723–8946) and on raincoats at the **London Fog Factory Outlet** (156 Calle Cristo, tel. 809/722–4334). For one-of-a-kind local crafts, head for **Puerto Rican Arts & Crafts**

(204 Calle La Fortaleza, Old San Juan, tel. 809/725–5596) or the **Haitian Gallery** (367 Calle Fortaleza, tel. 809/725–0986).

Sports There are four 18-hole courses shared by the **Hyatt Dorado Beach**
Golf **Hotel** and the **Hyatt Regency Cerromar Beach Hotel** (Dorado, tel. 809/796–1234). You'll also find 18-hole courses at **Palmas del Mar Resort** (Humacao, tel. 809/852–6000), **Club Ríomar** (Rio Grande, tel. 809/887–3964), **Punta Borinquén** (Aquadilla, tel. 809/890–2987), and **Bahia Beach Plantation** (Rio Grande, tel. 809/256–5600).

Hiking Dozens of trails lace **El Yunque**. Information is available at the Sierra Palm Visitor Center (Km 11.6, Rte. 191).

Water Sports Virtually all the resort hotels on San Juan's Condado and Isla Verde (*see* Beaches, *below*) strips rent paddleboats, Sunfish, and Windsurfers.

Beaches By law, all of Puerto Rico's beaches are open to the public (except for the Caribe Hilton's artificial beach in San Juan). The government runs 13 public beaches (*balnearios*), which have lockers, showers, and picnic tables; some have playgrounds and overnight facilities. *Admission free; parking $1. Open Tues.–Sun. 8–5 in summer, 9–6 in winter.*

Isla Verde is a white sandy beach close to metropolitan San Juan. Backed by several resort hotels, the beach offers picnic tables and good snorkeling, with equipment rentals nearby.

Dining *A 10%–15% tip is expected in restaurants.*

La Chaumière. Reminiscent of a French inn, this intimate yet bright white restaurant serves a respected onion soup, oysters Rockefeller, rack of lamb, and veal Oscar, in addition to daily specials. *327 Calle Tetuán, tel. 809/722–3330. Reservations advised. AE, DC, MC, V. Closed Sun. No lunch. $$$*
Amadeus. The atmosphere of this restaurant is gentrified Old San Juan, with an ever-changing menu of 20 appetizers, including *tostones* with sour cream and caviar, plantain mousse with shrimp, and Buffalo wings. Entrées on the nouvelle Caribbean menu range from Cajun-grilled mahimahito creamy pasta dishes and chicken and steak sandwiches. *106 Calle San Sebastián, tel. 809/722–8635. Reservations recommended. AE, MC, V. Closed Mon. $–$$*

Nightlife Almost every ship stays in San Juan late or even overnight to give passengers an opportunity to enjoy the nightlife—the most sophisticated in the Caribbean.

Casinos By law, all casinos are in hotels. Alcoholic drinks are not permitted at the gaming tables, although free soft drinks, coffee, and sandwiches are available. The atmosphere is quite refined, and many patrons dress to the nines, but informal attire is usually fine. Casinos set their own hours, which change seasonally, but generally operate from noon to 4 AM. Casinos are located in the following hotels: **Condado Plaza Hotel, Caribe Hilton, Carib Inn, Clarion Hotel, Dutch Inn, El San Juan, Ramada,** and **Sands.**

Discos In Old San Juan, young people flock to **Neon's** (203 Tanca St., tel. 809/725–7581) and to **Lazers** (251 Cruz St., tel. 809/721–4479). In Puerta de Tierra, Condado, and Isla Verde, the thirty-something crowd heads for **Amadeus** (El San Juan Hotel, tel. 809/791–1000), **Juliana's** (Caribe Hilton Hotel, tel. 809/721–0303), **Isadora's** (Condado Plaza Hotel, tel. 809/721–1000), and **Mykonos** (La Concha Hotel, tel. 809/721–6090).

Nightclubs The Sands Hotel's **Calypso Room** has a flamenco show nightly except Monday. El San Juan's **Tropicoro** presents international revues and, occasionally, top-name entertainers. The Condado Plaza Hotel has the **Copa Room,** and its **La Fiesta** sizzles with steamy Latin shows. Young professionals gather at **Peggy Sue** (tel. 809/722–4750), where the design is 1950s and the music mixes oldies and current dance hits.

The Hawaiian Islands

It's hard to believe such a gentle paradise sprang from such a violent beginning—mighty volcanic explosions. Over the centuries, crashing surf, strong sea winds, and powerful rivers carved and chiseled the great mountains and lush valleys that are Hawaii's pride.

Polynesian explorers stumbled upon these islands in the fourth century AD while navigating the South Pacific in their huge voyaging canoes. A succession of native rulers began in 1795 with King Kamehameha I and ended with the deposition of Queen Liliuokalani in 1893, when a provisional government was installed. In 1900 Hawaii was established as a U.S. territory, and in 1959 it became the 50th state. Today the islands retain a mystique that makes Hawaii America's most exotic state, with 132 islands and atolls stretching across 1,600 miles of ocean.

At one time many a ship brought travelers to the Hawaiian Islands, but when Pan Am's amphibious *Hawaii Clipper* touched down on Pearl Harbor's waters in 1936, it marked the beginning of the end of regular passenger-ship travel here. Since then, visitors have been flown in, and only a few cruise lines now pass through the islands. Among them are Cunard, Holland America, Princess, Regency, and Royal. One line, American Hawaii, sails exclusively in Hawaii. Its 800-passenger sister ships, the SS *Constitution* and the SS *Independence*, leave Honolulu on seven-day cruises that visit the Big Island, Maui, and Kauai. (For detailed itineraries, *see* Chapter 3.)

When to Go Hawaii is always temperate, sunny, and a pleasure. Although rainfall is slightly greater from December through February, the sun is rarely hidden behind the clouds for a solid 24-hour period. Summer is big with families, as are holidays. February and March are also busy cruising months because whales are most abundant during this period.

Passports and Visas Canadians need only prove their place of birth, with a passport, birth certificate, or similar document. Other foreign citizens require a passport and visa.

Shopping Distinctively Hawaiian gifts include Aloha shirts and muumuus, rich roasted Kona coffee, macadamia nuts, pineapples, and hand-carved wood. In general, major stores and shopping centers are open from 9 or 10 AM to 4:30 or 5 PM; some have evening hours.

Retail outlets abound in the Aloha State, from major tourist centers to small villages. Shopping malls are prevalent; many run free shuttles from the pier for cruise passengers. One of the largest on Oahu is the **Ala Moana Center**, which is just west of Waikiki—home of the **Royal Hawaiian Shopping Center**. Outside Waikiki are **Ward Warehouse,** the **Kahala Mall,** and **Pearlridge Center.**

On the Neighbor Islands smaller strips of shops are the rule, but larger stores exist in Kauai's **Kukui Grove Center** in Lihue, Maui's **Kahului Shopping Center,** and the Big Island's **Prince Kuhio Plaza** in Hilo. Kauai is known for its mom-and-pop shops and family-run boutiques. Exclusive shops are abundant in the luxury hotels.

Dining Hawaii's melting-pot population accounts for its great variety of epicurean delights. You can dine on Japanese sashimi, Thai curry, Hawaiian *laulau*, Chinese roast duck, and a mouthwatering array of French, German, Korean, American, Mexican, Indian, Italian, and Greek dishes.

There are, of course, a few uniquely tropical tastes, especially when it comes to fruit. Bananas, papayas, and pineapples grow throughout the year, while the prized mangos, watermelons, and litchis appear in summer. Seafood is equally exotic, with such delicacies as mahimahi (dolphin fish), *opakapaka* (pink snapper), *ulua* (crevelle), and *ahi* (yellowfin tuna).

Many tourists rate a trip to a luau among the highlights of their stay. At these feasts, you're likely to find the traditional *kalua* pig, often roasted underground in an *imu* (oven); *poi*, the starchy, bland paste made from the taro root; and *laulau*—fish, meat, and other ingredients wrapped and steamed in ti leaves.

Category	Cost*
$$$$	over $40
$$$	$30–$40
$$	$20–$30
$	under $20

per person for a three-course meal, excluding drinks, service, and 4% sales tax

The Big Island of Hawaii

Nearly twice the size of the other Hawaiian Islands combined, the Big Island is also the most diverse. With 266 miles of coastline of black-lava, white-coral, and green-olivine beaches, and with cliffs of lava and emerald gorges slashing into jutting mountains, the Big Island is so large and so varied that ships call at two ports, Hilo and Kona.

Shore Excursions The following are good choices on the Big Island. They may not be offered by all cruise lines. Times and prices are approximate. Unless otherwise noted, children's prices are for those under 13.

In Hilo **Volcanoes and Nuts.** Discover the sights, sounds, and tastes of the Big Island on this attraction-filled half-day tour. Travel from sea level to 4,000 feet, from desert to rain forest, and see steam vents and lava flows and explore an ancient lava tunnel. Includes a stop at a macadamia-nut farm, where you can buy freshly roasted nuts, chocolate-covered nuts, and nut-flavored coffee. *Half day. Cost: $30 adults, $21 children.*

Volcanoes by Helicopter. Hover over the still-active craters of Kilauea, which have been erupting steadily for a decade. If you're lucky, they'll be oozing lava. *45-min flight. Cost: $119.*

In Kona **Deep-Sea Fishing.** Fish the waters around Kona, renowned for their abundance of billfish. Blue marlin and yellowfin tuna are other prizes here. Bait, tackle, and ice are provided. *3 hrs. Cost: $75–$95.*

Spectacular Snorkeling. At least once during your cruise, put on your flippers and mask to explore below Hawaii's crystal-clear waters. A variety of snorkeling excursions are offered. *3–4½ hrs. Cost: $34–$59 adults, $19–$33 children.*

Coming Ashore
In Hilo Ships dock in an industrial area of tank farms and freight depots; the only thing within walking distance for cruise passengers is the Big Island Candies factory gift shop. It's about half a mile away from the pier. Make a right as you exit the dock area—it's a little ways down on the left. Across Hilo Bay, you can see the Big Island's small collection of resorts on Banyon Drive. There's also a Japanese garden, landscaped with bonsai trees and reflecting pools, and a small beach. It's about 2 miles away. The island's major attraction, **Volcanoes National Park,** is 30 miles from the ship. There's a State of Hawaii visitor information booth inside the cruise terminal.

In Kona Ships drop anchor off Kailua-Kona and tender passengers to shore. Walk off the tender and you're across the street from the toney shop-

The Hawaiian Islands

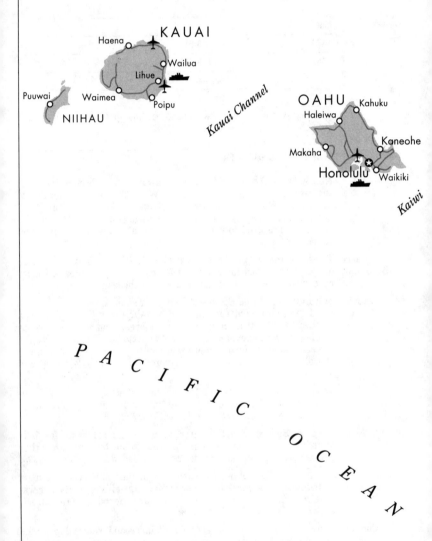

KAUAI

Haena

Wailua

Lihue

Puuwai

Waimea

Poipu

NIIHAU

Kauai Channel

OAHU

Kahuku

Haleiwa

Kaneohe

Makaha

Honolulu

Waikiki

Kaiwi

PACIFIC OCEAN

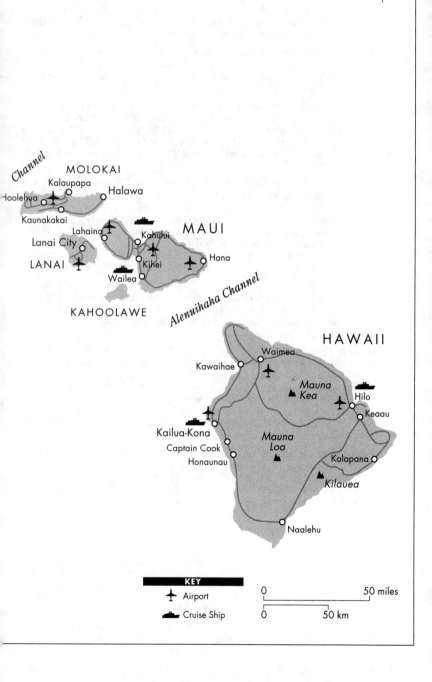

N

Channel
MOLOKAI
Kalaupapa   Halawa
Hoolehua
Kaunakakai
Lahaina   MAUI
Lanai City   Kahului
LANAI   Kihei   Hana
        Wailea

KAHOOLAWE   Alenuihaha Channel

                                HAWAII
                    Waimea
        Kawaihae   Mauna
                               Kea   Hilo
                                          Keaau
        Kailua-Kona
        Captain Cook   Mauna
        Honaunau   Loa   Kalapana
                                Kilauea

                        Naalehu

KEY
✈ Airport
🚢 Cruise Ship

0   50 miles
0   50 km

ping complex of the King Kamehameha Hotel. Just a short stroll away is historic Hulihee Palace; from here, the village of Kailua extends about a mile down the coast.

Getting Around By Car If you choose to tour the Big Island on your own, you'll need a car. **Avis** (tel. 800/331–1212), **Hertz** (tel. 800/654–3131), and **Budget** (tel. 800/527–0700) are among the national agencies with locations in both Hilo and Kona. In Hilo, also try **Harper's** (tel. 808/969–1478). American Hawaii ships can arrange car rentals through their shore excursions offices. Prices start at around $40 a day for a compact.

By Historic Auto An antique Sampan—an open-air, station wagon–like vehicle— runs on a continuous circuit in Hilo between the pier and Banyan Drive, the Nani Mau Gardens and shopping centers. For $7 you can ride all day (Hilo Sampan Co., tel. 808/935–6955).

By Taxi Several companies advertise guided tours by taxi, but it is an expensive way to travel: The trip around the island costs more than $300. Meter rates are $2 for pickup and $1.60 per mile. In Hilo, call **Ace Taxi** (tel. 808/935–8303) or **Hilo Harry's** (tel. 808/935–7091). In Kona, try **Paradise Taxi** (tel. 808/329–1234) or **Marina Taxi** (tel. 808/329–2481).

Beaches Don't believe anyone who tells you the Big Island lacks beaches; it actually has 80 or more. Small but beautiful, swimmable white-sand beaches dot the Kohala coastline. The surf is rough in summer, and few public beaches have lifeguards. In Hawaii beaches change constantly; a new black-sand beach, **Kamoamoa**, was formed in 1989 by molten lava encountering cold ocean waters. It was just as suddenly closed in 1992 by lava flow from Kilauea, which has been erupting since 1983. Lava also covered the Harry K. Brown and Kaimu beaches in 1990.

Near Kona The closest beach to ships that call at Kona is White Sands, a 10-minute drive from the tender landing. Another five minutes down the coast is Kahalu'u, a coarse-sand beach good for swimming, sunning, and snorkeling.

Near Hilo Three small beaches can be found 10–15 minutes from the pier. **James Keahola,** is a white-sand beach with rest rooms and picnic tables. **Onekahakaha** also has facilities and picnic tables. **Leleiwi Beach Park** is a lava-rock beach with small, protected coves for swimming. **Punaluu Beach Park** is 27 miles from Volcanoes National Park on the south side of the island. Turtles swim in the bay and lay their eggs in the black sand. Fishponds are just inland. There are rest rooms across the road.

Dining **Harrington's.** At this popular and reliable steak-and-seafood restaurant located right near the docks, two outstanding dishes are fresh ono or mahimahi *meunière*, served with brown butter, lemon, and parsley; and Slavic steak, thinly sliced and slathered with garlic butter. *135 Kalanianaole St., Hilo, tel. 808/961–4966. MC, V. $–$$*

Kauai

Nicknamed "the Garden Isle," Kauai is Eden epitomized. In the mountains of Kokee, lush swamps ring with the songs of rare birds, while the heady aroma of ginger blossoms sweetens the cool rain forests of Haena. Time and nature have carved elegant spires along the remote northern shore, called the Pali Coast, while seven powerful rivers give life to the valleys where ancient Hawaiians once dwelled.

Shore Excursions The following are good choices on Kauai. They may not be offered by all cruise lines. Times and prices are approximate. Unless otherwise noted, children's prices are for those under 13.

Natural Beauty **Helicopter Tour.** A bird's-eye view of Kauai visits canyons, waterfalls, and rain forests. *25–50 min. Cost: $76–$122.*

Waimea Canyon. A quick and convenient way to see Waimea Canyon, known as the "Grand Canyon of the Pacific," without renting a car. *Half day. Cost: $25 adults, $17 children.*

Coming Ashore
Ships calling along the "Coconut Coast" dock at Nawiliwili, a picturesque if somewhat industrial harbor in the shadows of the Hoary Head mountain range. A five-minute walk from the dock is the Anchor Cove shopping center. Make a right turn out of the dock area, and follow the road around to Kalapaki Bay, where there's a small white-sand beach lined with palm trees. A State of Hawaii visitor information booth is located inside the cruise terminal. To reach the island's natural attractions, such as **Waimea Canyon** or the **Wailua Falls,** you'll need to rent a car or take a shore excursion.

Getting Around
By Car
Kauai is easy to get around, since one major road almost encircles the island. **Avis** (tel. 800/331–1212), **Hertz** (tel. 800/654–3131), and **Budget** (tel. 800/527–0700) are among the national agencies with locations at Lihue airport. Also try local renter **Westside U-Drive** (tel. 808/332–8644). American Hawaii ships can arrange car rentals through their shore excursions offices. Prices start at around $40 a day for a compact.

By Taxi
A cab will take you island-wide, but you'll pay dearly, at $2 a mile, plus $2 for pickup. A trip from Lihue to Poipu costs $30, plus tip. The major cab company is **Kauai Cab** (tel. 808/246–9554).

Beaches
The Garden Isle is embraced by stretches of magnificent ivory sand, many with breathtaking mountains as a backdrop. Water is clean, clear, and inviting. Although some of the most scenic beaches are on the north shore, the surf there can be treacherous in winter. Beaches are free.

Kalapaki Beach (*see* Coming Ashore, *above*) is closest to the cruise-ship dock. There are rest rooms and showers. **Brennecke's Beach,** 25 minutes from the ship on the south shore near Poipu, is a bodysurfer's paradise. Showers, rest rooms, and lifeguards are on hand. **Lumahai Beach,** near Hanalei on the north coast, is one of the most scenic beaches. Its majestic cliffs, black lava rocks, and hala trees were the setting for the film *South Pacific.* There are no lifeguards, showers, or rest rooms, and swimming is not recommended. It's a 45-minute drive from the pier.

Dining
Gaylord's. A gracious 19th-century plantation is the charming setting in which to enjoy venison in blueberry-juniper sauce, or pan-blackened and highly spiced fresh salmon. The alfresco dining area opens to extensive gardens. *Kilohana Plantation, 3-2087 Kaumualii Hwy., 1 mi south of Lihue, tel. 808/245–9593. Reservations recommended. AE, D, DC, MC, V. $$*

Maui

Maui, say the locals, is *no ka oi*—the best, the most, the top of the heap. To those who know Maui well, there's good reason for superlatives. The second-largest island in the Hawaiian chain, the Valley Isle has made an international name for itself with its tropical allure, heady nightlife, and miles of perfect-tan beaches.

Shore Excursions
The following are good choices on Maui. They may not be offered by all cruise lines. Times and prices are approximate. Unless otherwise noted, children's prices are for those under 13.

Adventure
Bike Trip. Whiz more than 38 miles downhill from the summit of Mt. Haleakala. Bikes, helmets, windbreakers, and gloves are supplied; riders must bring their own eye protection and wear closed shoes. For a truly unforgettable experience, choose the sunrise departure. This trip can be dangerous; must be 12 or older. *7½ hrs. Cost: $99–$109.*

Natural Beauty **Haleakala Crater.** A motor coach takes you through Maui's beautiful interior to the Haleakala crater, the world's largest dormant volcano. The summit lies at 10,000 feet. *Half day. Cost: $30 adults, $21 children.*

Hana Drive. This drive along the rugged Hana Coast is beautiful but long and winding. It's more exciting to drive it yourself, but take this excursion if you don't rent a car. *Full day. Cost: $72 adults, $53 children.*

Coming Ships calling at Kahului dock in an industrial harbor. To reach the
Ashore island's natural attractions, such as **Iao Valley State Park, Haleakala**
In Kahului **Crater,** or the **Hana Highway,** you'll need to rent a car or take a shore excursion.

In Lahaina Ships that call at Lahaina drop anchor just offshore and tender passengers directly into the heart of this historic old whaling town. Along Front Street, the main drag, there are restaurants, shops, and a few small museums. A free shuttle bus runs from the Cinema Center (just across from the harbor) to the Kaanapoli beach resort area. To reach the island's major natural attractions, you'll need to rent a car or take a shore excursion.

Getting Those wishing to venture outside Lahaina, which is small enough to
Around explore on foot, should rent a car. **Avis** (tel. 800/331–1212), **Hertz**
By Car (tel. 800/654–3131), and **Budget** (tel. 800/527–0700) are among the many national agencies with locations at Kahului Airport. American Hawaii ships can arrange car rentals through their shore excursions offices. Prices start at around $40 a day for a compact.

By Taxi For short hops this can be a convenient way to go, but you'll have to call for pickup—even busy West Maui lacks curbside taxi service. Rates are $1.75 for pickup and $1.75 per mile. In Kahului and Central Maui, call **Kihei Taxi** (tel. 808/879–3000). In Lahaina, contact **West Maui Taxi** (tel. 808/667–2605).

Beaches Maui has more than 100 miles of coastline. Not all of this is beach, but striking white crescents do seem to be around every bend. Closest to ships that anchor off Lahaina are the beaches of **Kihei,** which stretch along the south coast of Maui. Another 10 minutes away are the white-sand beaches of **Wailea.** For passengers docking in Kahului, the beaches of Kanaha are close by. **Kaihalulu Beach** is a gorgeous cove with good swimming and snorkeling on the Hana Coast. Though a bit hard to reach, this red-sand beach is worth the hike. No facilities are available.

Dining **David Paul's Lahaina Grill.** Cap off a day of sightseeing and shopping with dinner at this amiable grill. Chef David Paul revises the menu regularly, marrying imaginative sauces and side dishes to poultry, meat, and seafood. Vanilla-bean rice, for example, is an innovative complement for grilled opakapaka. *127 Lahainaluna Rd., Lahaina, tel. 808/667–5117. AE, D, DC, MC, V. $$$*
Mama's Fish House. Looking for the best seafood on Maui? Head to this Old Hawaii restaurant a mile from Paia in a lovely oceanfront setting. Try the stuffed fish Lani, a fresh fillet baked with shrimp stuffing. *Hana Hwy. (Hwy. 36), Paia, tel. 808/579–8488. AE, MC, V. $$$*
Avalon Restaurant and Bar. The decor at this most trendy spot is 1940s Hawaii. The "Hawaiian Regional" cuisine features dishes made from local Hawaiian ingredients. *Mariner's Alley, 844 Front St., Lahaina, tel. 808/667–5559. AE, D, DC, MC, V. $$*

Oahu

The person who dreamed up Oahu's nickname, "The Gathering Place," was prophetic. Hawaii's most populated island boasts an eclectic blend of people, places, customs, and cuisines. Its geography ranges from peaks and plains to rain forests and beaches. The sands of Waikiki brim with honeymooners, couples celebrating anniversaries, Marines on holiday, and every other type of tourist imaginable. Beaches to the west and north are surprisingly unspoiled and uncrowded.

On cruises that begin and end in Honolulu, you can visit Oahu as part of your pre- or post-cruise vacation. American Hawaii Cruises offers hotel packages and shore excursions for those with late flights home.

Shore Excursions The following is a good choice in Oahu. It may not be offered by all cruise lines. Time and price are approximate. Unless otherwise noted, children's prices are for those under 13.

Pearl Harbor and the *Arizona* Memorial. A Navy launch takes you to the submerged hull of the U.S.S. *Arizona*, where 1,178 men lost their lives when the ship was sunk during the attack on Pearl Harbor. *Half day. Cost: $15 adults, $10 children.*

Coming Ashore Ships dock downtown at Aloha Tower, where there's a new waterfront complex of shops and restaurants. At the far side of the marketplace is the Hawaii Maritime Museum. Look for the tall ship, the *Falls of Clyde*, moored out front. There's a State of Hawaii visitor information desk inside the cruise terminal. A $1 trolley runs to the beaches and resorts of Waikiki, a 20-minute drive from Aloha Tower. American Hawaii passengers on fly/cruise packages will be shuttled from the airport to the pier. For those arriving independently, taxis wait outside the airport exit; the fare to the pier is about $12.

Getting Around By Car Don't bother renting a car unless you're planning to travel outside Waikiki, in which case a number of highly competitive car-rental companies offer deals and discounts. When making hotel or plane reservations, ask if there's a car tie-in. At peak times—summer, Christmas vacation, and February—reservations are a must. **Avis** (tel. 800/331–1212), **Hertz** (tel. 800/654–3131), and **Budget** (tel. 800/527–0700) are among the many national agencies with locations in Honolulu.

By Bus The fare to anywhere on the island is 85¢, including one free transfer; ask for one when boarding.

By Taxi Meter rates are $1.50 at the drop of the flag, plus $1.95 for each additional mile. The two biggest cab companies are **Charley's** (tel. 808/531–1333) and **SIDA of Hawaii** (tel. 808/836–0011).

Beaches Waikiki (*see* Coming Ashore, *above*) is a 2½-mile chain of beaches extending from the Hilton Hawaiian Village to the base of Diamond Head. The sand is harder and coarser, and the beaches more crowded, than at some of the less-frequented spots out of town, but food stands and equipment rentals are more abundant here. Other than Waikiki, **Ala Moana Beach Park**, a 10-minute drive from the cruise-ship pier, is the most popular beach in Honolulu. A protective reef keeps its waters calm. Amenities include playing fields, changing houses, indoor and outdoor showers, lifeguards, grills, concession stands, and tennis courts.

Dining **Orchids.** You can't beat this eatery's seaside setting: Diamond Head looms in the distance, and fresh orchids are everywhere. The popovers are huge, the salads light and unusual. The Sunday brunch buffet is a big hit. *Halekulani Hotel, 2199 Kalia Rd., Waikiki, tel. 808/923–2311. AE, DC, MC, V. $$$$*
Golden Dragon. Local Chinese consider this the best Chinese food in town. Set right by the water, it has stunning red-and-black decor. Best bets are stir-fried lobster with *haupia* (coconut) and Szechuan

beef. *Hilton Hawaiian Village, 2005 Kalia Rd., Waikiki, tel. 808/949–4321. AE, DC, MC, V. $$$*

Sloppy Joe's. Conveniently located right next to the docks at Aloha Tower, this outpost of the famous Key West saloon is fun for burgers and a beer. Eat inside or overlooking the water. *Aloha Tower, Honolulu, tel. 808/528–0007. AE, D, MC, V. $*

Mexican Riviera

Along the Mexican Riviera's 2,000-mile coast, cruise passengers find the exotic and the familiar. Among the McDonald's and Pizza Huts and the Fords and Chevys are adobe cantinas, breathtaking parasailing, and high-cliff divers. While Spanish and various Indian dialects predominate, most Mexicans involved in tourism speak some English.

The transformation of once sleepy fishing villages—most notably, Acapulco, Puerto Vallarta, and Mazatlán—into booming cities has been a direct result of the swarms of tourists who come by land, by air, and by sea. And the growth has not been gentle. Although the area's recorded history stretches back more than 400 years, cruise passengers will find few significant landmarks or archaeological sites. (These are more common along Mexico's Caribbean coast; *see* Cozumel, *above*.) If it's authentic history and genuine culture you want, go elsewhere. But for sun, sea, and sports, the colorful Mexican west coast is a fine choice. Indeed, Mexico's beaches compare favorably with the best in the world. Their talcum-powder sands are white, wide, and beckoning; the water is warm and clear.

Loop cruises of three, four, seven, and sometimes 10 days usually depart from Los Angeles for the Mexican Riviera. Among the lines sailing here are Carnival, NCL, Princess, and Royal Caribbean. (For detailed itineraries, *see* Chapter 3.)

When to Go November through March is the Mexican Riviera's cruising season—most ships reposition to Alaska for the summer. Still, it is possible to cruise here year-round, and prices are lowest from April through October. June has the best weather, though it is remarkably good almost all year, with daytime temperatures averaging from 82°F to 90°F. During the June–October rainy season, very brief showers can be expected.

Currency In Mexico, the currency is the peso, but you may find items priced in as many as three different designations, P$ (the least common), NP$ (for *nuevo pesos*), or just N$ (the most common). If you see something you want to buy priced in P$, just knock off three zeros. (For instance, a pair of silver earrings marked P$5000 is equal to N$5.) At press time, the exchange rate was about N$6 to $1, but the situation was highly changeable due to Mexico's financial crisis.

U.S. dollars and credit cards are accepted at most restaurants and large shops. Most taxi drivers take dollars as well. There is no advantage to paying in dollars, but there may be an advantage to paying in cash. To avoid having to change unused pesos back to dollars, change just enough to cover what you'll need for public transportation, refreshments, phones, and tips. Use up your Mexican coins; they can't be changed back to dollars.

Passports and Visas Although U.S. and Canadian citizens do not need a passport or visa to enter or leave Mexico, they must fill out a tourist card, issued by the cruise line, a Mexican embassy or consulate, or any airline flying to Mexico. This is free, but you must show proof of citizenship (passport or birth certificate) to have it validated. British travelers need a passport and a tourist card.

Telephones and Mail Until recently, phoning home from the Mexican Riviera could be frustrating because phone lines were few and the sound quality was poor. Since the introduction of AT&T USADirect service, calling has become much easier with better connections. You must use "Ladatel" phones, located on the dock in Acapulco, Mazatlán, Puerto Vallarta, and Zihuatanejo. Dial 95–800–462–4240 to be connected with an English-speaking operator, who will take your AT&T credit card number or place a collect call for you.

The Mexican Riviera

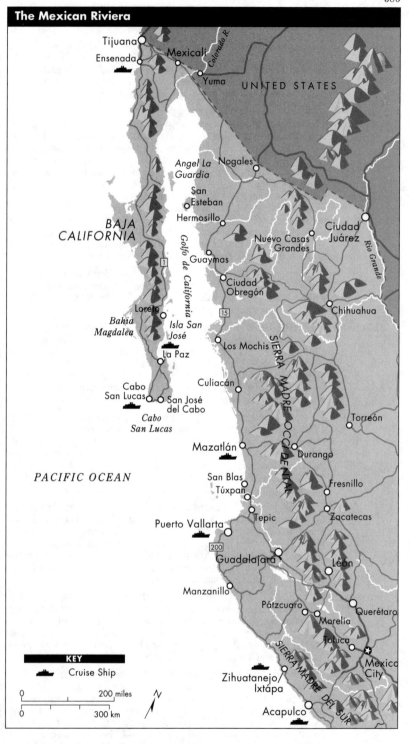

UNITED STATES

Tijuana
Ensenada
Mexicali
Yuma
Colorado R.

BAJA CALIFORNIA

Nogales

Angel La Guardia
San Esteban
Hermosillo

Ciudad Juárez
Rio Grande

Nuevo Casas Grandes

Guaymas
Ciudad Obregón

Chihuahua

Loreto
Bahia Magdalea
Isla San José
La Paz

Golfo de California

Los Mochis

SIERRA MADRE OCCIDENTAL

Cabo San Lucas
San José del Cabo
Cabo San Lucas

Culiacán

Torreón

PACIFIC OCEAN

Mazatlán

Durango

San Blas
Túxpan
Tepic

Fresnillo

Zacatecas

Puerto Vallarta

Guadalajara

León

Manzanillo

Pátzcuaro
Morelia
Querétaro

SIERRA MADRE DEL SUR

Toluca
Mexico City

KEY
Cruise Ship

0   200 miles
0   300 km

N

Zihuatanejo/ Ixtápa

Acapulco

The Mexican postal system is notoriously slow and unreliable; *never* send packages, as they may simply vanish without a trace. There are numerous post offices (*oficinas de correos*) in the larger cities. Always use airmail for overseas correspondence; it will take anywhere from 10 days to two weeks or more. Rates are quite low: N$2 for a letter (up to 20 grams) and N$1.5 for a postcard to the United States.

Tipping Everyone wants a dollar; not everyone expects one. It's wise to carry some pesos for those times when a dollar tip is too much. Don't tip less than N$3.

For taxi rides, tips are usually included in the negotiated rate. Good taxi tours, however, merit a small tip; about N$5 for a three-hour tour is average. If you stop for a cold soda, you are expected to buy your driver a bottle. Bus-tour guides expect a tip of about $1 per person per half-day tour. In restaurants a service charge of 15% is occasionally included; otherwise tip 10%–15%.

Shore Excursions Not surprisingly, some of the best excursions are those that take advantage of the area's wonderful beaches, where passengers indulge in parasailing, waterskiing, snorkeling, and windsurfing. Sunset sails and booze cruises are also popular.

Deep-sea fishing has long drawn sportfishing fans hoping to land trophy-size marlin and sailfish, as well as tuna, wahoo, and bonito. Most ships sailing the Mexican Riviera offer half-day or full-day fishing at rates comparable to what it would cost to charter a boat on your own. It's therefore prudent to take the ship-organized excursions: The locals' relaxed sense of time is not shared by cruise-ship captains, who will—and do—leave without late passengers.

And be wary of land tours. A substantial percentage of the bus tours range from mediocre to indifferent. Too often, guides speak poor English, the vehicles are in poor repair, and the tour itself is of limited interest. Typically, a bus tour of the *ciudad* (city) will drive past the *malecón* (sea wall), stop briefly at the central cathedral on the *zócalo* (main town square)—and then, bypassing the few historic sites or authentic native markets, pull up at various hotels and timeshare properties, where passengers are subjected to a sales pitch. Finally, passengers will be taken for an extended stop at a shopping area or crafts shop. While a few superb folkloric shows exist, most dance companies seen on bus tours are either young amateurs or jaded semiprofessionals who merely go through the motions.

Taxis are a worthwhile alternative to the bus tour, especially in Acapulco and Zihuatanejo/Ixtapa. Cabs are numerous and relatively cheap, and every driver accepts dollars. Taxis are not metered, however, nor are there fixed rates to specific destinations. Don't get in until you've negotiated an exact fare (including tip), and never pay the driver in advance. The cruise director usually knows the appropriate fare to various destinations, or how much it costs to hire a taxi by the hour. Not all taxi drivers are qualified to act as tour guides, however, and cabs almost never have air-conditioning.

Shopping It's possible to get great bargains and souvenirs, even in those ports where cruise ships call. Haggling is the rule of thumb in markets and with street vendors, but most boutiques have fixed prices. Start by offering no more than half the asking price, then raise your price very slowly but pay no more than 70%. For silver, first offer about one-quarter the asking price, and beware of disreputable shops that hawk faux silver—always check for the stamp ".925," which must by law appear on all sterling.

Most resort-area shops open at 9 or 10 AM, break between 2 and 4 for siesta, then reopen until 7 or 8 PM. Street vendors generally start packing up at 6 PM or when dusk falls, whichever comes first.

Dining Mexican restaurants run the gamut from humble, hole-in-the-wall shacks, street stands, and chairs and tables in the markets, to *taquerías* (taco stands), American-style fast-food joints, and acclaimed gourmet restaurants.

Ceviche—raw fish and shellfish (*mariscos*) marinated in lime juice and topped with cilantro, onion, tomato, and chili—is almost a national dish, though it originated in Acapulco. Shrimp, lobster, and oysters can be huge and succulent; the safest time to eat oysters is October–March. Avoid all foods sold by street vendors—especially meat and fruit—no matter how tempting. *Tacos al pastor*—thin pork slices grilled on a revolving spit and garnished with cilantro, onions, and chili—are delicious but dangerous for most non-Mexican stomachs. If you're not keen on spiciness, ask that your food be prepared *no muy picante*. Stick to bottled beverages, and ask for your drinks *sin hielo* (without ice).

Category	Cost*
$$$$	over $35
$$$	$25–$35
$$	$15–$25
$	under $15

*per person for a three-course meal, excluding drinks, service, and 10% sales tax

Acapulco

As the ship enters the harbor, passengers should be on deck for a panoramic view of Acapulco's gently curving, high-rise-studded waterfront backed by a series of dramatic hills. Distant mountains are shrouded in haze. As the ship passes Roqueta Island, a rock jutting almost straight up in the air, you see hundreds of boats and a sprawling fort. Acapulco, the largest city on the Mexican Riviera, bustles with crowded markets, trendy discos, fashionable restaurants, and spectacular gardens and scenery.

Shore Excursions The following is a good choice in Acapulco. It may not be offered by all cruise lines. Time and price are approximate.

Adventure **Helicopter Flightseeing:** A spectacular view of Acapulco's bay is the reward for those brave enough to step aboard one of these choppers. The copter then flies over the cliff divers at La Quebrada and the Acapulco Princess hotel and beach. *Flight time 15–30 min. Cost: $50–$95.*

Coming Ashore The municipal pier, where cruise ships dock, is alive with food hawkers, souvenir vendors, taxi drivers, and small boys ready to dive for coins. From the pier, it's a short stroll to Costera Miguel Alemán, the main boulevard that wraps around the harbor and includes the city's famous hotel zone. A taxi stand is located at the cruise terminal; a ride to the hotel zone shouldn't cost more than $5, to the main flea market about $3.

Getting Around For those who choose not to walk, a variety of wheeled vehicles may be employed to explore the city:

By Bus Public buses are cheap and can be a fun way to see the town. The bus marked HORNOS follows the Costera from the pier to the hotel zone; the fare is N$1 (N$2 for air-conditioned models).

By Carriage Buggy rides are available up and down the hotel zone on weekends. Bargain before you get in—fares are about $20 for a half hour.

By Taxi Taxis are cheap and plentiful. Fares are negotiable; Volkswagen Beetles are cheapest. Flagging a cab in the street costs less than at a hotel or at the cruise terminal, where hourly rates for tours run about $20 for a four–eight passenger vehicle.

Exploring *Numbers in the margin correspond to points of interest on the Aca-*
Acapulco *pulco map.*

Though it is within walking distance of the docks, in Old Acapulco you'll find more Mexicans than tourists. Colors are earthier, odors more pungent, and air-conditioning almost nonexistent. Near the ❶ municipal pier is the **zócalo,** a pleasant plaza crisscrossed with shaded promenades and alive with shoe-shine stands, vendors, children, and old men ogling a new generation of lovers. Sunday means music in the grandstand. The church of **Nuestra Señora de la Soledad** is a modern oddity, with a stark white facade and blue and yellow spires.

❷ Opposite the pier and towering over it is **El Fuerte de San Diego,** built in the 18th century as protection from pirates. An earlier fort, finished in 1616, was destroyed by an earthquake. Today the fort's air-conditioned rooms offer archaeological, historical, and anthropological exhibits, covering early Mexican exploration and Spanish trade. *Admission: about $4. Open Tues.–Sun. 10:30–5.*

❸ **La Quebrada,** where world-famous cliff divers perform daily, is a 15–20 minute walk west, up a rather steep hill, so consider a taxi (the fare is about $7). A $2-per-person entrance fee gives you access to a platform beside the **Plaza las Glorias El Mirador Hotel,** an excellent vantage point, or you can see the cliff-diving show while having drinks and dinner at the hotel's **La Perla** nightclub. Cliff-diving exhibitions are scheduled daily at 1 PM and every hour from 7:30 to 10:30 PM.

Shopping The best bargains are found in the public markets. In places like **El Mercado de Artesanías** in the hotel zone, **Noa Noa** near Papagayo Park, and any of the several open-air markets set up around town, you can haggle for woven blankets, puppets, colorful wood toys, leather, baskets, hammocks, and handmade wood furniture, but beware of pickpockets.

Along the Costera east of the cruise pier, between the Continental Plaza and Papagayo Park, is where you'll find many upscale boutiques. The **Galería Rudic** (across from the Continental Plaza, tel. 74/84–48–44) has great prices on authentic Mexican fine art. For silver jewelry and flatware, go to **Taxco Exporta** (La Quebrada 315, tel. 74/83–25–51). The expensive and formal **Esteban's,** the most glamorous shop in Acapulco, is on the Costera across the street from the Club de Golf.

Sports Try the **Pesca Deportiva,** the dock across from the zócalo. Boats ac-
Fishing commodating four to eight people cost $200 to $400 a day. Excursions leave about 7 AM and return at 2 PM. Most fishing operations get a license for you; otherwise, go to the **Secretaría de Pesca,** above the central post office at Costera Miguel Alemán 215.

Golf Two great 18-hole golf courses are shared by the **Princess and Pierre Marqués hotels.** Greens fees are $89 for cruise passengers. At the public nine-hole course on the Costera Miguel Alemán, next to the Centro Internacional Acapulco, the fee is about $21 for nine holes, about $35 for 18 holes.

Water Sports Water sports of all kinds can be arranged at any of the big beachfront hotels. Rates for the most popular activities are: Broncos (one-person motorboats; $30 per half hour), parasailing (about $25 for 10 minutes), sailing ($20–$30 an hour), snorkeling (equipment rental $10 per day), waterskiing (about $30–$40 per half hour), windsurfing ($15 per hour).

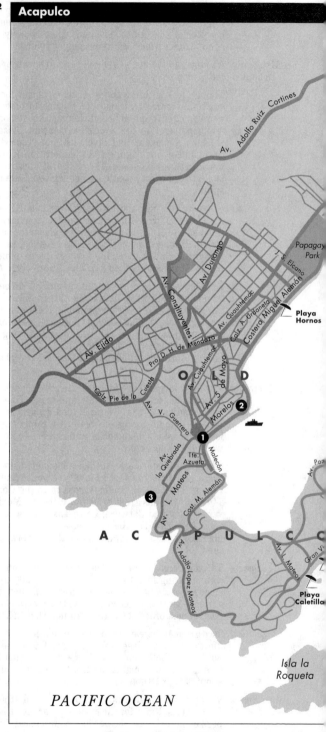

Acapulco

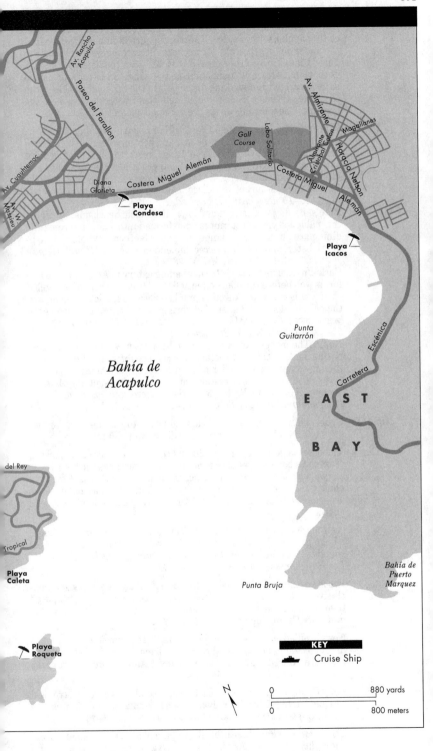

Av. Rancho Acapulco

Paseo del Farallon

Av. Cuauhtemoc

Av. W. Massieu

Diana Glorieta

Playa Condesa

Costera Miguel Alemán

Golf Course

Lobo Solitario

Av. Almirante

Costera Miguel Alemán

Almirante Cristobal Colón

Horacio Nelson

Magallanes

Playa Icacos

Costera Miguel Alemán

Bahía de Acapulco

Punta Guitarrón

Escénica

Carretera

E A S T

B A Y

del Rey

Tropical

Playa Caleta

Playa Roqueta

Punta Bruja

Bahía de Puerto Marquez

KEY

⛴ Cruise Ship

N

| 0 | 880 yards |
| 0 | 800 meters |

Beaches Acapulco's beaches are legendary. Smack in the middle of Acapulco Bay, **Playa Condesa** is a tourist-riddled stretch of sand that's especially popular with singles. The atmosphere is fun and festive, but the undertow is especially strong here. Stretching west of Papagayo Park, **Playa Hornos** is crammed with Mexican tourists who know a good thing: Graceful palms shade the sand, and scads of casual eateries are within walking distance. On the far eastern side of the bay, **Playa Icacos** is less populated than other beaches on the Costera. The morning waves are especially calm.

Dining **Blackbeard's.** The pirate-ship motif here sports walls decked with fishing nets and wood figureheads, and booths with maps on the tables. Photos of movie stars, from Bing Crosby to Liz Taylor, who've eaten here hang in the much-used lounge. A luscious salad bar and jumbo shrimp, lobster, and steak portions keep 'em coming back. Part of the restaurant is a disco. *Costera Miguel Alemán 101, tel. 74/84–25–49. Reservations advised. AE, MC, V. $$$$*

Beto's. By day you can eat and enjoy live music beachside; by night, this palapa-style restaurant is transformed into a dim and romantic dining area lighted by candles and paper lanterns. Whole red snapper, lobster, and ceviche are recommended. *Costera Miguel Alemán 99, tel. 74/84–04–73. AE, MC, V. $$*

Carlos 'n Charlie's. This is *the* happening eatery in Acapulco; the line forms well before the doors open at 6 PM. An atmosphere of controlled craziness is cultivated through prankster waiters, a jokey menu, and the eclectic decor. Ribs, stuffed shrimp, and oysters are among the best choices. *Costera Miguel Alemán 112, tel. 74/84–12–85 or 74/84–00–39. AE, DC, MC, V. No lunch. $$*

Pipi's. The owners are a mother-and-son team who have been preparing some of the best seafood in Acapulco for years. Seating is in the air-conditioned interior or on a terrace overlooking life on the Costera. This no-frills restaurant is a favorite spot for *Acapulquenos. Almirante Bretón 3 off the Costera and near the Centro Internacional Acapulco, tel. 74/82–22–37. AE, MC, V. $$*

Nightlife Cruise ships often dock in Acapulco late into the night or for two days to take advantage of the city's discos and nightclubs.

Discos The discos open late, around 10:30 PM, and stay open until sunrise. Most clubs have a cover charge of $10–$20. Sometimes you get a drink or two with that, perhaps even access to an open bar; sometimes you don't. Lines are common but usually move quickly. Since many discos are bunched together in the hotel zone, you can easily hop from one to another.

As if the spectacle of a crowded, pulsating dance floor weren't enough, a huge glass wall at **Extravaganzza** provides a breathtaking wraparound view of the harbor. *Carretera Escénica to Las Brisas, next to Los Rancheros restaurant, tel. 74/84–71–54.*

For stargazing, Hollywood-style, go to **Fantasy**; it's expensive, exclusive, and one of the few places in Acapulco where you're supposed to dress to the nines. *On Carretera Escénica, just below Las Brisas and near Extravaganzza, tel. 74/84–67–27.*

News is billed as a "disco and concert hall." It's enormous, with seating for 1,200 in booths and love seats. Theme parties and competitions are offered nightly. *Costera Miguel Alemán, across from the Hyatt Regency, tel. 74/84–59–02.*

Baby O, one of the best singles discos, resembles a cave in a tropical setting. A big 18-to-30 crowd of mostly tourists dominates the scene. *Costera Miguel Alemán near News, tel. 74/84–74–74.*

The decor of **D'Paradisse** is black, and the place has a fabulous after-midnight light show. As many as 500 vivacious night crawlers compete for the tables and chairs arranged on three levels overlooking the dance floor. *Across the Costera from Baby O, tel. 74/84–88–15.*

Entertainment One of Acapulco's best folkloric shows is performed Monday, Wednesday, and Friday at 7:30 at the **Acapulco International Center** (tel. 74/84–62–28), also called the convention center, located on the right side of the Costera, near Icacos beach. For about $22 per person you get an all-you-can-eat buffet, open bar, and a rousing show with dancers, singers, and a mariachi band. If you've eaten dinner on the ship, the charge for the show only is $14.

Tourists love watching the cliff divers at **La Quebrada** plunge into floodlighted waters. Where better to watch than from a boat below, sipping champagne and listening to strumming guitars? Several companies sell sunset cruises that end up at La Quebrada; one of the best is **Acapulco Divers** (tel. 74/83–11–09).

Cabo San Lucas

Cabo San Lucas sits at the southern tip of Baja California, where the Gulf of California and the Pacific Ocean meet. Here, the surf has shaped the dun-colored cliffs into bizarre jutting fingers and arches of rock. The desert ends in white-sand coves, with cacti standing at their entrances like sentries under the soaring palm trees. Big-game-fishing fans are lured from all over the world for marlin and sailfish. Although Cabo San Lucas and its neighboring town of San José del Cabo have little to offer in the way of sophistication, their isolation and beauty make them superb cruise destinations.

Shore Excursions The following are good choices in Cabo San Lucas. They may not be offered by all cruise lines. Times and prices are approximate.

Undersea Creatures **Los Arcos Glass-Bottom Boat Ride:** See the marine life below and pelicans and sea lions above and on the water as you sail Lovers Beach. *1–2 hrs. Cost: $16.*

Sail and Snorkel Fiesta: Boarding a catamaran, you stop for an hour to snorkel then sail out past Los Arcos. *2½ hrs. Cost: $30.*

Coming Ashore The shallow harbor makes it necessary for ships to anchor in the bay and tender passengers to shore. A flea market is on the wharf, and tour boats leave for Los Arcos and the beach at Playa del Amor from the pier. Downtown is a few blocks away and small enough so you can get anywhere on foot. San José del Cabo is 23 miles away. A cab ride from the pier into Cabo San Lucas costs about $1 per person with a $3 minimum; to San José del Cabo expect to pay about $25 per carload.

Getting Around Municipal buses run up and down the main drag. They are old and not air-conditioned, but they are cheap—about 30¢.

By Taxi Cab fares vary according to time, distance, and the mood of the driver, so establish the price before getting in the car. Rates for a tour should run about $20 an hour.

Exploring Cabo San Lucas *Numbers in the margin correspond to points of interest on the Cabo San Lucas map.*

① The main downtown street of Cabo San Lucas, Avenida Lázaro Cárdenas, passes a small **zócalo**. Most shops, services, and restaurants are between the avenida and the waterfront, two blocks east. From the inner harbor you can see the spectacular natural rock arches **②** called **Los Arcos**, but they are more impressive from the water.

About 15 minutes from town is a dramatic desert, populated by wild horses and incredible cacti.

Shopping Along the waterfront and on its side streets, Cabo San Lucas is a shopper's mecca; the selection of handicrafts and sportswear is especially good. As you step off the tender at the pier is the **Mercado de Artesanías**, a maze of thatched booths selling mediocre silver jewelry, mass-produced wood sculptures, T-shirts, and other souvenirs.

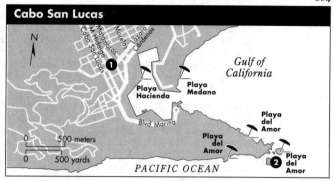

Sportswear shops—**Ferrioni, Bye-Bye, Fila,** and **Benetton**—are clustered around the **Plaza Cabo San Lucas,** on Avenida Madero near the waterfront, and at **Plaza Bonita,** at the marina in the inner harbor. **Temptations** (Lázaro Cárdenas and Matamoros, on the same block as the Giggling Marlin restaurant; *see* Dining, *below*) has some chic and original designs for women, including the Maria de Guadalajara line. **La Paloma** in town is another good spot for souvenirs, and the boutiques in the **Mexican Village** at the Hacienda Hotel are popular with tourists. **El Dorado Gallery,** across from the marina, is a must. Its two rooms are filled with sculptures in ceramic, papier-mâché, brass, and copper; the creations of Mario González; and contemporary Mexican paintings and handicrafts.

Sports The best fishing on the Baja is to be had here. You can charter a 28-
Fishing foot cruiser for about $300 a day from the Cabo San Lucas marina. Contact **Picis Fleet** (tel. 114/3–0588) or **Pesca Deportiva Solmar** (Hotel Solmar, tel. 114/3–0022).

Scuba Diving Los Arcos is the prime diving and snorkeling area, but several good rocky points are off the coast. Contact **Amigos del Mar** (near the sportfishing docks, tel. 114/3–0505), **Cabo Acuadeportes** (at the Cabo San Lucas, Hacienda, Plaza Las Glorias, and Pueblo Bonito hotels, tel. 114/3–0117), and **Cabo Divers** (Blvd. Marina and Av. Madero, tel. 114/3–0747).

Beaches **Playa del Amor** sits at the end of the peninsula, with the Gulf of California on one side and the Pacific on the other. The beach and nearby arches are some of the most romantic spots along the Mexican Riviera. The surf on the Pacific side is too rough for swimming. A water taxi ferries passengers from the tender landing to the beach for $6 per person round-trip.

The crowded 2-mile **Playa Medano,** just north of town, is the most popular stretch of beach for sunbathing and people-watching. **Playa Hacienda,** in the inner harbor by the Hacienda Hotel, has calm waters and good snorkeling around the rocky point. A water taxi from the marina in the inner harbor to the hotel costs about $2.50 per person.

Dining **El Galeón.** The choice seats at this posh eatery across from the marina are on terraces facing the water. The interior is an assemblage of heavy wood furniture. Seafood and traditional Italian fare are prepared expertly. Drop in for the piano music, which starts at 6 PM. *By the road to the Finesterra Hotel, tel. 114/3–0443. AE, MC, V. $$$*
Giggling Marlin. Five large color TVs broadcast major sporting events and other U.S. programs at this bar-restaurant, raking in a huge crowd during the Super Bowl, World Series, and other important spectacles. Though the menu is extensive—burgers, sandwiches, tostadas, burritos, steaks— regulars advise sticking with

tacos, appetizers, and drinks. *Av. Matamoros and Blvd. Marina, tel. 114/3-0606. MC, V. $$*
Las Palmas. Playa Medano's most popular hangout is headquarters to beach-volleyball competitors, dune-buggy enthusiasts, and beach bums of all types. The barbecued ribs are great; even better is the quail, lobster, and steak combo.*Tel. 114/3-0447. MC, V. $$*

Mazatlán

Mazatlán (an Aztec word meaning "place of the deer") is the only major city on the Mexican Riviera that has a raison d'être other than welcoming droves of tourists. With 350,000 inhabitants, it's a thriving seaport, home to a large shrimp fleet and other commercial-fishing boats. Long before the first cruise ships called and the tourist hotels were built, Mazatlán was a year-round mecca for sportfishermen and hunters in search of sailfish and marlin, duck and quail. Hunting is on the wane now as time-share condos and high-rises pop up, but the Mazatlán waterfront still has the feel of a working fishing town rather than a tourist resort.

Shore Excursions The following is a good choice in Mazatlán. It may not be offered by all cruise lines. Time and price are approximate.

Sierra Madre Tour: Go inland and up into the mountains, to visit the ancient towns of Copala and Concordia, with their baroque houses, wonderfully unspoiled plazas, a deserted silver mine, and shopping stopovers. Lunch is served in a local cantina that frequently features amateur musicians. *4–6½ hrs. Cost: $40.*

Coming Ashore Cruise ships tie up along a narrow channel leading from the Pacific Ocean, but passengers must take a short shuttle ride to the nearby cruise terminal. The downtown zócalo, where you'll find the cathedral and the *mercado municipal* (flea market), is about 12 blocks away.

Getting Around Mazatlán is spread far and wide, and walking from one section of town to another can take hours.

By Bus Air-conditioned minibuses, marked SABALO-CENTRO, run along the coastal road to the town plaza. The fare is N$1.10, the driver will accept a U.S. dollar if you don't have any pesos.

By Taxi Taxis are cheap and readily available. Fares are set, with the city divided into four zones. One-way fares for a private car range from $5 to $10 per carload, depending on your destination. If you don't mind sharing, so-called "ecotaxis" cost only $1.75 to $2.50, also depending upon your destination. You can flag one down anywhere, but you may have to make stops for other passengers.

Exploring Mazatlán *Numbers in the margin correspond to points of interest on the Mazatlán map.*

Mazatlán has two faces: the glitzy resort area known as the Zona Dorado and the authentically Mexican part of town. Downtown is filled with buses and locals rushing to and from work and the market.

❶ Head for the gold spires of the **Mazatlán Catedral.** Built in 1890 and made a basilica in 1935, it has an ornate triple altar, with murals of angels overhead and many small altars along the sides. Dress appropriately (no shorts or tank tops) to enter. Steps away, at the Plazuela Machado, peek in at the restored **Angela Peralta Theater,** Mazatlán's former opera house.

❷ Across the street is the **zócalo, Plaza Revolución,** with a fascinating gazebo: It looks like a '50s diner inside the lower level, with a wrought-iron bandstand on top. The green and orange tile on the walls, the ancient jukebox, and the soda fountain serving shakes, burgers, and hot dogs couldn't make a more surprising sight. Facing

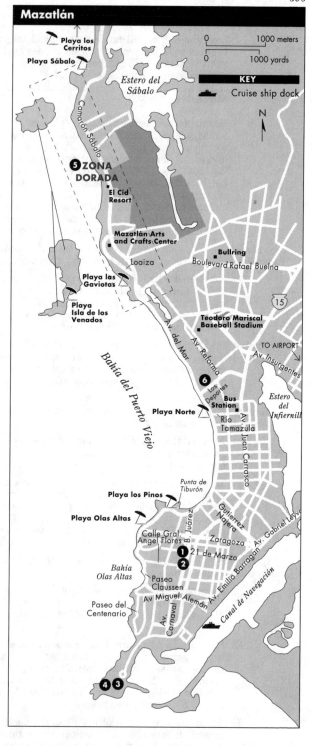

the zócalo are the City Hall, banks, the post office, and a telegraph office.

For a great view, take a taxi to the end of the peninsula, where you climb **Cerro del Crestón** (Summit Hill). At the top is **El Faro,** the second-tallest lighthouse in the world.

If you've headed instead to the **Zona Dorada,** north of the downtown center, on the way back stop by the **Acuario Mazatlán,** an aquarium with tanks of sharks, sea horses, eels, lobsters, and multicolor saltwater and freshwater fish. *Av. de los Deportes 111, tel. 69/81–7815. Admission: $5.30 adults, children $2.35. Open daily 9:30–6:30.*

Shopping Most tourists head for the **Mazatlán Arts and Crafts Center** (tel. 69/13–5022) in the Zona Dorada, a market where you can watch artists at work. You'll find some of the best prices on the Mexican Riviera here, although the handicrafts are only average. On the next block is **Sea Shell City** (tel. 69/13–1301), and there are dozens of other shops on the surrounding streets. **La Carreta,** at the El Cid and Playa Mazatlán hotels, is another worthwhile handicrafts center. The enormous **Mercado Central,** between Calles Juárez and Serdan, sells produce, meat, fish, and handicrafts at competitive prices as well.

Sports Mazatlán has the largest charter fishing fleet on the Mexican Rivi-
Fishing era. Charters cost $200–$350 for two to five people; a chair on a shared boat runs about $70. Contact **Bill Heimpel's Star Fleet** (tel. 69/82–2665), **De Oro** (tel. 69/82–3130), **Estrella** (tel. 69/82–3878), **Flota Bibi** (tel. 69/81–3640), or **Flota American Fleet** (tel. 69/81–5992).

Water Sports Rent Jet Skis, Hobie Cats, and Windsurfers from most hotels, and look for parasailing along the Zona Dorado. Mazatlán has no good diving spots.

Beaches **Playa los Cerritos,** the northernmost beach on the outskirts of town, runs from Camino Real Resort to Punta Cerritos, and is cleanest and least populated. It's too rough for swimming but great for surfing. The two most popular beaches are along the Zona Dorado— **Playa Sábalo** and **Playa las Gaviotas.** Here you'll find as many vendors selling blankets, pottery, lace tablecloths, and silver jewelry as you will sunbathers. Boats, Windsurfers, and parasailers line the shores. Boats make frequent departures from the Zona Dorado hotels for **Playa Isla de los Venados** on Deer Island. You can buy tickets at the El Cid Hotel ($8 round-trip). The amphibious vehicle leaves 10 AM, noon, and 2 PM, returning every two hours until 4 PM. It's only a 20-minute ride, but the difference is striking: The beach is pretty, uncluttered, and clean, and you can hike around the southern point of the island to small, secluded coves covered with shells.

Dining **Sr. Peppers.** This is an elegant yet unpretentious place, with ceiling fans, lush foliage, candlelit tables, and choice steaks and lobsters cooked over a mesquite grill. You can bop around the dance floor to live music. *Av. Camarón Sábalo, across from the Camino Real Hotel, tel. 69/84–0120. AE, DC, MC, V. $$$*

Costa Marinera. At the best seafood house on the Mexican Riviera, try the generous seafood platter, grilled on a hibachi at your table and piled high with frogs' legs, shrimp, oysters, octopus, and more, covered with melted cheese, and fresh fish. Also good is the shrimp *machaca*, sautéed in olive oil with tomatoes, chives, and chilis. *Privada del Camarón and Privada de la Florida, tel. 69/14–1928. AE, MC, V. $$*

Señor Frog. Almost every gringo eventually ends up here. Bandido waiters carry tequila bottles and shot glasses in their bandoliers, and patrons stand on tables to sign their names on the ceiling. Barbecued ribs and chicken, served with corn on the cob, and heaping portions of standard Mexican dishes are the specialties. The tortilla soup is excellent. *Av. del Mar 225, tel. 69/82–1925. DC, MC, V. $$*

Puerto Vallarta

Puerto Vallarta was an unknown fishing village until John Huston filmed *Night of the Iguana* here in 1964 with Richard Burton, who brought along his girlfriend Liz Taylor. The torrid romance made international headlines and launched Puerto Vallarta as one of the most popular resorts on the Riviera.

The area between the airport and Old Town, including the new Marina Vallarta complex, is overdeveloped; luxury high-rise hotels block sea views and mar the landscape. Downtown and the area south of the Río Cuale, however, have avoided the raw boomtown look that afflicts so many Mexican towns. Here, efforts are made to retain the image of the charming fishing village that once was: You'll still find the traditional whitewashed houses with red-tile roofs and lush bougainvillea, cobblestone streets, and fleets of colorful fishing boats hauling in their afternoon catches.

Shore Excursions The following are good choices in Puerto Vallarta. They may not be offered by all cruise lines. Times and prices are approximate.

City History **Puerto Vallarta City Tour:** An overview of the city includes a visit to Gringo Gulch, where Taylor and Burton built a bridge over the street to join their houses; Mismaloya Beach, where *Night of the Iguana* was filmed; and a stop in the downtown shopping district. *3 hrs. Cost: $25.*

Natural Beauty **Vallarta Horseback Riding:** Ride through the lush hillside or along the shore to a beach for a swim. *2½–4 hrs. Cost: $30–$55.*

Coming Ashore Cruise ships dock nearly 3 miles from downtown. Taking a bus tour or hiring a taxi is recommended if you want to see all of the large, sprawling town, but you can easily cover the downtown area on foot once you get there; a cab ride into town costs $2 per person; it will cost $5 per carload to return (*see* By Taxi, *below*). A cab ride to a beach costs $5 per person, about twice that back to the pier.

Getting Around **By Bus** Buses are cheap and crisscross the city, but figuring out which goes where is too much effort for most passengers with only a few hours ashore.

By Car Rental cars and motorbikes are expensive, but they may be the only practical way to visit the beaches at Boca de Tomatlán if you can't catch a convenient van or taxi. Contact **Avis** (Carretera Aeropuerto Km 2.5, tel. 322/1–1158), **Budget** (Carretera Aeropuerto Km 5, tel. 322/1–1888), **Dollar** (Paseo de las Palmas 1728, tel. 322/3–1354), **Hertz** (Paseo de las Palmas 1602, tel. 322/2–0024), **National** (Carretera Aeropuerto Km 1.5, tel. 322/2–0515), and **Quick** (Carretera Aeropuerto Km 1.5, tel. 322/2–4010).

By Taxi Cabs are the best way to travel between the pier and town or to the beaches. There are two types: Volkswagen combis or vans pick up passengers only at the pier. Yellow union cabs cruise the downtown and beach areas and return passengers to the pier. Combis/vans and union cabs charge different rates; either way, negotiate the fare before getting in. Combi tours should cost $20–$30 per hour, depending on the size of the car and if it's air-conditioned. There is a three-hour minimum, and a good guide should be able to show you the town and the outskirts in that time.

Exploring Puerto Vallarta *Numbers in the margin correspond to points of interest on the Puerto Vallarta map.*

There are three major regions: the northern hotels and resorts, the downtown, and the Río Cuale and Playa de los Muertos. Exploring downtown is best done on foot. Holes in the old cobblestone streets have recently been filled with cement, but you'll still want to wear comfortable walking shoes.

① Along the *malecón,* or sea wall, is the bronze sea horse that has become the town's trademark. A lovely promenade of palm trees and benches, the malecón and the beachfront are peppered with touristy sing-along bars, open-air restaurants, and boutiques.

Walk a few hundred yards, keeping the sea on your right, and you **②** will cross a bridge. Halfway across, descend a staircase to **Río Cuale Island,** where you'll find purveyors of paintings, folk art, stuffed **③** iguanas, and other interesting handmade wares. The **Museo Arqueológico** displays pre-Columbian artifacts that are hardly worth seeing. More appealing are the restaurants on the island and the view of the sea.

Head back over the bridge and to return to Old Town. The three streets that parallel the malecón are lined with shops, boutiques, **④** and car-rental agencies. Several blocks beyond is **La Iglesia de Nuestra Señora de Guadalupe** (Our Lady of Guadalupe Cathedral), with the distinctive crown on its clock tower and an impressive interior. The steps are often crowded with vendors and women weaving **⑤** colored shawls and bags. A cathedral dominates the **Plaza de Armas,** **⑥** the zócalo. On the north side is **City Hall,** where a colorful mural painted by the town's most famous artist, Manuel Lepe, depicts Puerto Vallarta before the tourist boom.

⑦ Hop in a cab to go the 8 miles to **Playa Mismaloya,** where *Night of the Iguana* was filmed. The drive south passes spectacular homes, some of the town's oldest and most refined resorts, and a slew of condo and time-share developments. Somewhat spoiled by the huge hotel complex La Jolla de Mismaloya, the pretty Mismaloya cove is backed by rugged, rocky hills and affords a good view of Los Arcos, a rock formation in the water.

Shopping The downtown is filled with shops, boutiques, and stalls charging inflated prices. Better prices can be found in the **Mercado Municipal** (open daily 9 AM–7:30 PM), a large public market at Avenida Miramar and Libertad, in front of the inland bridge (the one farthest from the sea). Among stalls of fish, meat, chicken, fruit, and vegetables, you will find serapes, cotton dresses, silver jewelry, and leather goods. One of the best places on the Mexican Riviera for handmade leather boots, belts, jackets, and wallets is **Rolling Stones** (on the Malecón at Galeana, tel. 322/2–5798; and Paseo Díaz Ordaz 802, tel. 322/3–1769). For silver jewelry, try **Mar de Plata** (Paseo Díaz Ordaz 824, tel. 322/2–6727) or **Sergio Bustamante** (Juárez 275, tel. 322/2–1129; Paseo Díaz Ordaz 700A, tel. 322/3–1407; and Paseo Díaz Ordaz 542, tel. 322/2–5480).

Sports Head over to the **Fishermen's Association** shack at the north end of
Fishing the malecón to find out about fishing trips. Large group boats cost about $60 per person; private charters start at $150 for up to six passengers.

Golf **Los Flamingos Country Club** (tel. 322/7–1515) has an 18-hole course; reservations should be made a day in advance and include transportation. **Club de Golf Marina** (tel. 322/1–0171) is also a good course.

Water Sports Snorkeling and diving are best at **Los Arcos,** a natural underwater preserve on the way to Mismaloya, but you'll have to take a motor launch from Boca de Tomatlán for about $15 per person, round-trip.

Beaches Beaches at Puerta Vallarta, many with a coarse sand, are not the best on the Mexican Riviera. **Playa Norte** stretches from the wharf to downtown and changes according to the character of the hotel it fronts. It's particularly pleasant by the Fiesta Americana and Krystal hotels. Within walking distance of town, **Playa de los Muertos** (Beach of the Dead) is said to have been the site of a battle between pirates and Indians. Budget travelers hang out here, along with myriad vendors selling kites, blankets, and jewelry.

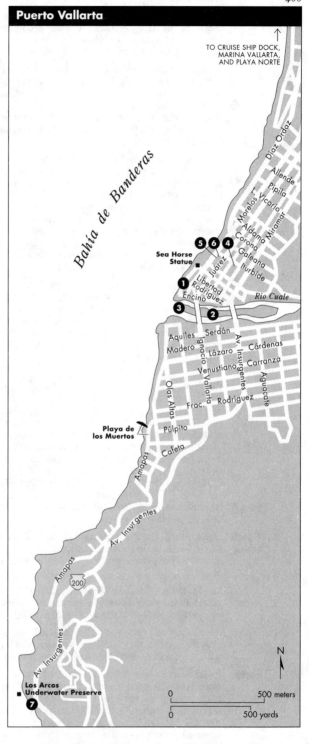

Puerto Vallarta

TO CRUISE SHIP DOCK, MARINA VALLARTA, AND PLAYA NORTE

Bahía de Banderas

Díaz Ordaz
Allende
Pipila
V. Vicario
Morelos
Aldama
Miramar
Corona
Galeana
Iturbide

Sea Horse Statue

Juárez
Libertad
Rodríguez
Encino
Río Cuale

Aquiles Serdán
Madero
Ignacio Vallarta
Lázaro
Venustiano
Av. Insurgentes
Cárdenas
Carranza
Aguacate
Olas Altas
Frac. Rodríguez
Púlpito
Cafeta

Playa de los Muertos

Amapas

Av. Insurgentes

Amapas

(200)

Av. Insurgentes

N

Los Arcos Underwater Preserve

0   500 meters
0   500 yards

Dining **El Dorado.** This is a popular hangout for American expatriates. The eclectic menu includes spaghetti, burgers, and crepes, but stick with Dorado-style fish, broiled with a thick layer of melted cheese. *Amapas and Pulpito, tel. 322/2–1511. AE, MC, V. $$*

Mr. Tequilla's Grill. Set on a second-floor perch above the malecón, this place's view alone is worth a visit. The menu includes tasty Mexican sandwiches, fresh seafood, and build-your-own tacos with oysters, peppers, and mushrooms among the fillings. *Galena 101–104, tel. 322/2–5725. AE, MC, V. $–$$*

Zihuatanejo/Ixtapa

Few Mexican resorts can claim the graceful balance between old and new reflected in the twin resort towns of Zihuatanejo ("zee-wha-tah-NAY-ho") and Ixtapa ("ees-TAH-pah"). Until the early 1970s Zihuatanejo was just another sleepy fishing village and neighboring Ixtapa was a swampy coconut plantation. But with some of the most beautiful beaches anywhere, the area could not go undiscovered by tourism. Developers would like to turn Ixtapa into another Cancún, but growth has been pleasantly slow. Ixtapa today is an isolated oasis of about a dozen hotels, and Zihuatanejo a charming village of small hotels and restaurants less glitzy than Ixtapa's. Hoping to boost tourism, investors have built a $500 million marina complex at the end of Ixtapa's hotel row, and a new 18-hole golf course. For now, at least, the area has something Cancún lacks: a quiet, easy pace and a way of life that more closely resembles that of a fishing village than a resort.

In this wild, rugged part of Mexico, Spanish colonization was never very successful. As a result, many natives still speak one of five Indian dialects, including the craftsmen who come here from Oaxaca to sell their wares. But the people are friendly, and despite the language barrier, it's somehow easier to make yourself understood here (even if communication is in sign language) than in other Mexican Riviera ports.

Shore Excursions The following is a good choice in Ixtapa. It may not be offered by all cruise lines. Time and price are approximate.

Undersea Creatures **Sail and Snorkel Tour:** A catamaran takes you to a less-populated beach, such as one in Manzanillo, for an hour of snorkeling. Drinks and snacks are served. *2½–3 hrs. Cost: $39.*

Coming Ashore Ships anchor in Zihuatanejo's harbor and tender passengers ashore to the town pier, in the center of the crescent-shape bay. To the right of the tender landing, the town covers about 2 square miles of cobblestone streets, and the main shopping area is concentrated in a few blocks near the town pier.

Getting Around While small Zihuatanejo is easily managed on foot, Ixtapa is 10 minutes away via the main highway.

By Bus Buses run between Zihuatanejo and the Ixtapa Hotel Zone approximately every hour for about N$1.

By Taxi The fare from Zihuatanejo to Ixtapa is about $6 per carload. Taxis are small, fitting three passengers comfortably. Minibuses also run between Zihuatanejo and Ixtapa; the fare is about $10 round-trip. Getting anywhere within the Ixtapa Hotel Zone is about $4.

Exploring Zihuatanejo/ Ixtapa Zihuatanejo's charm lies in its narrow sun-baked streets, its little shops and boutiques. A small museum and a folk-art store are beside the cathedral.

Ixtapa is strictly a resort town, with hotels strung for miles along the beach. Aside from the main boulevard, there is little to explore. However, with several malls clustered together, it's a shopping nirvana, and you'll find plenty of restaurants at the malls and in the resort hotels.

Shopping
Zihuatanejo
Budget at least an hour here. Unlike elsewhere on the Mexican Riviera, merchants leave you alone and let you browse. (But locals will often approach you on the street, wanting to sell you packs of gum for $1.) Locally produced goods include wood carvings, ceramics, weavings, and leather goods. Indians display handicrafts in a **street market** on Juan Alvarez. Casa Marina (tel. 753/4–2373), on the waterfront, has four distinctive shops: **El Embarcadero** has a large selection of indigenous embroidered clothing made of hand-loomed cotton, wool rugs, and wall hangings; **El Jumil** has native masks and hand-carved figurines; **La Zapoteca** has hand-woven wool Zapotec rugs and Yucatan hammocks; and **Manos** has toys, baskets, hats, and copper. **Coco Cabaña** (tel. 753/4–2518), the folk-art store on Vicente Guerrero, behind Coconuts restaurant, is fabulous.

Ixtapa
In Ixtapa browse at the **La Puerta** shopping mall along the Hotel Zone. It has more boutiques than Zihuatanejo, with pricey merchandise by such designers as Ralph Lauren, Christian Dior, and Calvin Klein, as well as a number of shops selling handicrafts and casual clothing and beachwear by local designers. There is also an open-air market for local crafts.

Sports
Fishing
You can charter a boat at the **Municipal Beach**'s Zihuatanejo Pier and at **Playa Quieta** in Ixtapa. Rates range from $150 to $350 per day.

Water Sports
Waterskiing, windsurfing, snorkeling, diving, and sailing can be arranged at the Hotel Zone beaches in Ixtapa. Waterskiing costs about $25 a half hour.

Beaches
Zihuatanejo has some very fine swimming spots, and there's really no reason to travel to Ixtapa to spend the day at a beach. A cab ride from the pier to the popular stretch of sand at Playa la Ropa costs about $3.

A few steps from downtown, **Municipal Beach** curves around Zihuatanejo Bay. It's lined with restaurants and hotels. **Playa la Ropa**, a calm, safe swimming beach, is across the bay—about a $3 taxi ride one-way. **Las Gatas** is reached by water taxi. Buy a ticket at the kiosk on the town pier (also $3) and hail one of the boats for the short ride across the harbor. There are several small restaurants and facilities here. Snorkeling equipment can be rented to explore the manmade reef that shelters the beach. One of the best swimming options is at the **Puerto Mío Hotel.** For the price of a drink and a snack you can spend the day at the stunning tile pool, cut into a cliff overlooking a small cove.

Dining
Zihuatanejo
Zi Wok. At this hilltop restaurant with a great panoramic view of the bay, stir-fried seafood with a Mexican accent is the fare. A touch of chili peppers spices up the specialty of the house: fresh tuna with broccoli. *Carr. Escénica a Playa La Ropa, tel. 753/4–3136. MC, V. $$*

La Bocana. This favorite with locals and visitors has been here for ages. Service is good, and so's the food. Musicians sometimes stroll through. *Juan Alvarez 13, tel. 753/4–3545. MC, V. $*

Puntarenas. Home-cooked, authentic Mexican food in a no-nonsense setting makes this a favorite with locals and visitors in the know. *Across the bridge at the end of Juan Alvarez, no phone. No credit cards. Closed Easter–mid-Dec. No dinner. $*

Ixtapa
Las Esferas. This is a complex of two restaurants and a bar in the Hotel Camino Real. **Portofino** specializes in Italian cuisine and is decorated with multicolor pastas and scenes of Italy. In **El Mexicano** you get Mexican food along with Mexican ambience—bright pink tablecloths, Puebla jugs, and a huge "tree of life." *Playa Vista Hermosa, tel. 753/3–2121, ext. 3444. AE, DC, MC, V. $$$*

Carlos 'n Charlie's. Hidden away at the end of the beach is an outpost of the famous Anderson's chain. Pork, seafood, and chicken are served in a Polynesian setting. *Next to Posada Real Hotel, tel. 753/ 3–0035. AE, DC, MC, V. $$*

Da Baffone. Italian dishes are the specialties of this restaurant, one of three eateries in La Puerta mall. *Tel. 753/3–11–22. AE, MC, V. $$*

Northeastern United States and Canada

Less crowded and less expensive than Alaska, New England and Canada's Maritimes offer beautiful scenery, historical sights, and wildlife (including whales). Prime attractions of a cruise in this area are tiny Maine fishing villages, the historic St. Lawrence Seaway, and hillsides ablaze with autumn colors. Major ports are New York, Boston, Nova Scotia, and Québec. Among the lines that sail here seasonally are American Canadian, Holland America, Princess, Regency, Royal, Seabourn, and Silversea. (For detailed itineraries, *see* Chapter 3.)

When to Go Cruises leave during the summer and through early autumn. The best cruising time is fall, when the leaves are turning color, or summer if you enjoy jazz and arts festivals. Some ships offer only a couple of cruises between their summer season in Europe and their Caribbean season, so the number of berths is limited. For that reason, few bargains are offered.

Boston

Boston is a popular terminus and port of call. Over the past decade, however, it has become increasingly difficult to find the "real" Boston. What was once thought of as the most staid and settled of American cities now defies such easy stereotyping. The historic shrines along the Freedom Trail (which remains an excellent walking tour) are surrounded today by forests of skyscrapers that many critics say represent the "Manhattanization" of Boston. The old Italian North End is slowly "going condo." The Back Bay is now better known for its shopping and chic restaurants than for its quiet residential blocks with their superlative architecture.

Coming Ashore Cruise ships dock at the Black Falcon Cruise Terminal, about a mile from downtown. Taxis generally meet incoming ships. The ride into town costs about $4. Buses run from the dock to downtown every 20 minutes, Monday–Friday 7 AM–6 PM. The fare is $1. Maps and brochures are available inside the terminal; the nearest manned information booth is at South Station.

Exploring Boston For traditionalists, a walk through Boston should start on **Beacon Hill**, taking in all the little side streets; then wind past **Government Center**, heading for the back corners of the North End, where landmarks like **Paul Revere's House** and the **Old North Church** reveal themselves at every turn. Continue through the downtown streets, through the Common and the Public Garden and along a Beacon Street that still belongs to the ghost of Oliver Wendell Holmes. As afternoon shadows lengthen, walk along the Charles River toward **Harvard Square**, as Archibald MacLeish did on the night he decided to become a poet rather than a lawyer. Cross the river into **Cambridge** and consider what possessed men to build a college in what in 1636 was the wilderness.

Newport

In contrast to Boston, the genteel community of Newport, Rhode Island, offers a very manageable day of exploring. Newport is best known for its Colonial beginnings and turn-of-the-century high-society splendor: Along Bellevue Avenue and Ocean Drive you can see the summer mansions (several sumptuous ones are open as museums). Newport is also famous as a navy town, and a visit to the Naval War College Museum will illustrate Rhode Island's role in America's naval history. Newport's colonial waterfront boasts more restored

Northeast United States and Canada

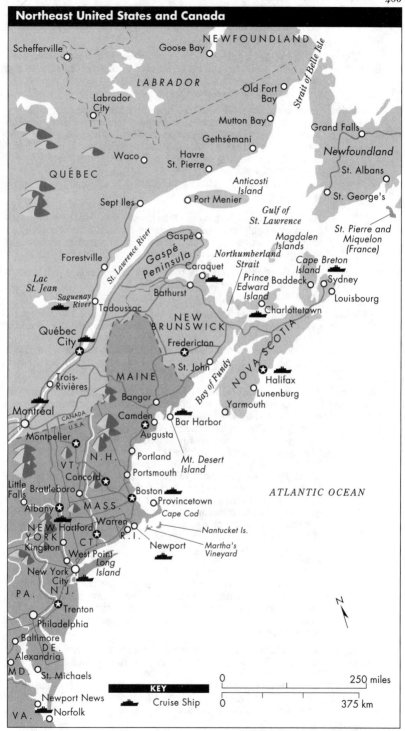

NEWFOUNDLAND

Schefferville

Goose Bay

LABRADOR

Strait of Belle Isle

Old Fort Bay

Labrador City

Mutton Bay

Grand Falls

Gethsémani

Newfoundland

Havre St. Pierre

Waco

St. Albans

Anticosti Island

QUÉBEC

St. George's

Port Menier

Sept Iles

Gulf of St. Lawrence

Magdalen Islands

St. Pierre and Miquelon (France)

Gaspé

Forestville

Gaspé Peninsula

Northumberland Strait

Cape Breton Island

Caraquet

Baddeck

Sydney

St. Lawrence River

Bathurst

Prince Edward Island

Louisbourg

Lac St. Jean

Saguenay River

Tadoussac

NEW BRUNSWICK

Charlottetown

Québec City

Fredericton

NOVA SCOTIA

Trois-Rivières

MAINE

St. John

Bay of Fundy

Halifax

Lunenburg

Montréal

Bangor

Yarmouth

CANADA

Camden

U.S.A.

Bar Harbor

Montpelier

Augusta

Mt. Desert Island

ATLANTIC OCEAN

VT.

N.H.

Portland

Little Falls

Concord

Portsmouth

Brattleboro

Boston

Albany

MASS.

Provincetown

Cape Cod

NEW

Warren

Hartford

Nantucket Is.

Kingston

C T.

R.I.

Newport

Martha's Vineyard

West Point

YORK

Long Island

New York City

N.J.

P A.

Trenton

Philadelphia

Baltimore

DE.

Alexandria

M D.

St. Michaels

KEY
⚓ Cruise Ship

0   250 miles

Newport News

0   375 km

V A.

Norfolk

18th-century homes than Williamsburg or Boston, first-rate restaurants, jazz and folk festivals, a lively nightlife, and special events throughout the year.

Shore Excursions If you'd rather a guided tour of Newport's sights, a good choices are the guided walking tour of the waterfront district (2 hrs, $18) and excursions that combine a ride along Ocean Drive with tours of the historic mansions (2–4 hrs, $20–$35).

Coming Ashore Ships anchor in the East Passage and tender passengers to nearby Goat Island. Shuttle buses transfer passengers from here to downtown, or they can walk the quarter-mile distance. Just across the causeway from Goat Island is the Gateway Visitors Center, stocked with maps and brochures, as well as friendly local staffers who will answer any questions.

Halifax

Halifax, Nova Scotia, has one of the finest harbors in the world, with a history of shipping and understated hospitality that makes it a wonderful port of call. If you are on one of the very few cruises that actually start or stop here, a pre- or post-cruise stay is a must.

Shore Excursions To see the sights beyond the town itself, a good choice in Halifax is the scenic drive along the rugged south shore and Peggy's Cove (3½ hrs, $50.)

Coming Ashore Ships dock at Pier 20/21 near the railway station, a 15-minute walk to downtown. A shuttle bus is usually arranged by the ship, but taxis also are on hand. The ride to downtown costs $5 (Canadian). The historic district is a pleasant half-mile walk along the waterfront; there you'll find the Nova Scotia Visitor Center. The closest branch of the Halifax Tourist Office is at Old City Hall.

Exploring Halifax The combination of old and new in Halifax is nowhere more apparent than in and around the area known as **Historic Properties,** on the waterfront. In the 1800s, the area was the center of business for the young city. The stone **Privateer's Warehouse** housed the cargoes captured by Nova Scotia privateers until the captured ships and cargoes could be auctioned off by the Admiralty. The area's historic buildings now hold boutiques, restaurants, nightclubs, and souvenir shops. Between June and October, you can hear the town crier, take helicopter and stern-wheeler tours, and sail on the *Bluenose II.* Other sites worth visiting are the **Citadel,** the **Nova Scotia Museum,** the excellent **Marine Museum of the Atlantic,** and the **Public Gardens.** For shopping, visit Spring Garden Road, and take a break at one of the many sidewalk cafés frequented by university students.

Montréal

In contrast to Québec (*see below*), Montréal is a thoroughly modern city, though also with a French accent and its own charming historic district. Montréal is so clean and organized that most visitors feel safe and comfortable as they wander its many vibrant neighborhoods, or *quartiers.*

Coming Ashore Ships dock within a few blocks of Place Jacques-Cartier, the main square in Old Montréal. Taxis are plentiful in the port area, and there are three Métro stations in Old Montréal to carry you to the Underground City and elsewhere. (Montréal's Métro is clean, quiet, and efficient.) The closest information booth is at 174 Notré Dame East, near Place Jacques-Cartier.

Exploring Montréal Downtown are boutiques, department stores, and 21 museums. Among these are such gems as the **Canadian History Museum,** the **Art Deco Museum,** the **International Humor Museum,** and the **Montreal Museum of Fine Arts.** Buildings linked by the **Underground City**

include several posh hotels and 11 shopping malls. Close to the docks, the **Latin Quarter** has a Métro station at Berride Montigny on St-Denis. Lower St-Denis has a typical student-quarter atmosphere, with bookstores, art galleries, and bistros. In summer, musicians in town for the Jazz Festival gather here for jam sessions. Off St-Denis, 19th-century homes on **St-Louis Square** surround a fountain and flower market. The square's west side leads to the **Prince Arthur pedestrian mall,** lined with restaurants (many of them inexpensive) and outdoor cafés. A healthy walk will lead you to **Place Jacques-Cartier** in Old Montréal, where you will see many historic sites.

Québec City

The birthplace of French-colonial North America, Québec City is a jewel. Perched high on a cliff overlooking the St. Lawrence River, it is rich in charm and history. Extremely proud of their heritage, Québecois have preserved dozens of buildings (many dating back to the 17th century), battle sites, and monuments. The result is a charming blend of winding cobblestone streets and old houses reminiscent of Europe. In fact, Québec is so full of architectural treasures that in 1985 UNESCO declared it a World Heritage Treasure site, ranking it with Egypt's pyramids and India's Taj Mahal.

Shore Excursions Good choices in Québec City are a tour that combines sights in the old and new cities (2½ hrs, $20), an escorted walking tour of the old city (2½ hrs, $18), and, in season, a fall foliage drive through the countryside (3½ hrs, $40).

Coming Ashore Ships dock downtown, below the cliffs and a few steps from the old walled city. Taxis are always near the dock, which is next to the ferry terminal. Typically, a tourist guide meets the ship to answer questions and provide maps, but in summer you can look for friendly youths on scooters handing out maps on street corners in the old town.

Exploring Québec City Most of the Old World charm is found in **Vieux Québec,** the historic walled city. The **Lower City** is the place to browse through art galleries and superb boutiques. Then take the funicular, or elevator tram, into the upper city (for about $1 [Canadian]) to stand on **Dufferin Terrace,** with its boardwalk and panoramic view of the waterway below. To your right is the **Château Frontenac,** probably the most photographed building in Canada. Street musicians and jugglers turn the **Place d'Armes** into an open-air theater in summer. Nearby is **Trésor Street,** the artists' alley, where you can buy paintings priced from $5 to $5,000.

Other Ports

As a cruise destination, the northeastern United States and Canada remain relatively unspoiled, full of charm, history, and a fresh perspective on very beautiful lands. Besides the major ports outlined above, places of interest include the historic French fortress city of Louisbourg, Nova Scotia; the quaint but upscale island of Nantucket, Massachusetts; Maine fishing villages; the scenic St. Lawrence Seaway; and Campobello Island on the Bay of Fundy, site of President Franklin D. Roosevelt's summer home. Small ships, such as those in the fleets of American Canadian Caribbean Line and Clipper Cruise Line, also sail through upstate New York's canal and lock system—a stunning trip in the autumn.

Panama Canal

Transit of the Panama Canal takes only one day. The rest of your cruise will be spent on islands in the Caribbean or at ports along the Mexican Riviera. Most Panama Canal cruises are one-way trips, part of a 10- to 14-day cruise between the Atlantic and Pacific oceans. Shorter loop cruises enter the canal from the Caribbean, sail around Gatún Lake for a few hours, and return to the Caribbean.

The Panama Canal is best described as a water bridge that "raises" ships up and over Central America, then down again, using a series of locks or water steps. Artificially created Gatún Lake, 85 feet above sea level, is the canal's highest point. The route is approximately 50 miles long, and the crossing takes from eight to 10 hours. Ships pay an average of $30,000 in cash for each transit, which is less than half of what it would cost them to sail around Cape Horn, at the southern tip of South America.

Just before dawn, your ship will line up with dozens of other vessels to await its turn to enter the canal. Before it can proceed, two pilots and a narrator will come on board. The sight of a massive cruise ship being raised dozens of feet into the air by water is so fascinating that passengers will crowd all the forward decks at the first lock. If you can't see, go to the rear decks, where there is usually more room and the view is just as intriguing. Later in the day you won't find as many passengers up front.

On and off throughout the day, commentary is broadcast over ship's loudspeakers, imparting facts and figures as well as anecdotes about the history of the canal. The canal stands where it does today not because it's the best route but because the railroad was built there first, making access to the area relatively easy. The railway had followed an old Spanish mule trail that had been there for more than 300 years.

Frenchman Ferdinand de Lesseps, builder of the Suez Canal, was determined to construct a sea-level canal here, as he had done at Suez, instead of an easier lock canal. Disease, scandal, corruption, rain, mud, and jungle took their toll, including 20,000 lives, and the French company went bankrupt. (One worker during 1886–87 was an unknown French painter named Paul Gauguin.)

By 1900 it was apparent that only the United States had the resources to complete the huge project. After the Panamanian revolution, the United States was able to negotiate a favorable treaty with the Panamanians rather than trying to deal with Colombia, which held the isthmus at that time. The main obstacle to building the canal was disease, which was rampant in the Panamanian jungle. In 1904 Colonel William Gorgas undertook one of the great sanitation campaigns in history, clearing brush, draining swamps, and eliminating areas where mosquitoes bred and swarmed. Within two years yellow fever had been wiped out and bubonic plague and malaria were on the decline.

The canal was completed in 1914, and, with constant dredging, it still functions smoothly. If you would like to learn more about its history, pick up a copy of David McCullough's *The Path Between the Seas.*

When to Go In spring and autumn a number of cruise ships use the Panama Canal to reposition between the Caribbean and Alaska. However, several ships offer regular transcanal and loop cruises throughout the winter season. (For detailed itineraries, *see* Chapter 3.)

Currency Passengers won't need to change money to transit the canal, but some ships stop in Costa Rica; in the San Blas Islands, off Panama; and at Cartagena, Colombia. In Costa Rica, the currency is the co-

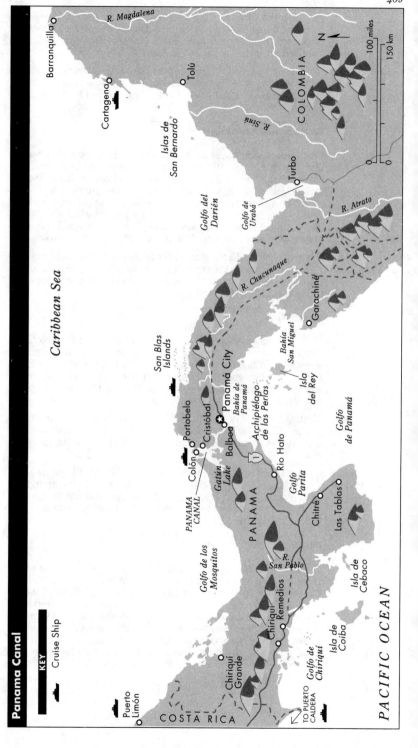

Panama Canal

KEY

⬛ Cruise Ship

Caribbean Sea

R. Magdalena

Barranquilla

Tolú

Cartagena

Islas de San Bernardo

COLOMBIA

N

100 miles

150 km

0

0

R. Sinú

Turbo

Golfo del Darién

Golfo de Urabá

R. Atrato

R. Chucunaque

San Blas Islands

Garachiné

Portobelo

Cristóbal

Panamá City

Bahía San Miguel

Colón

Balboa

Bahía de Panamá

Isla del Rey

PANAMA CANAL

Gatún Lake

Archipiélago de las Perlas

Rio Hato

Golfo de Panamá

Golfo de los Mosquitos

PANAMA

Golfo Parita

Chitré

Las Tablas

R. San Pablo

Isla de Cebaco

Remedios

Chiriquí

Isla de Coiba

Chiriquí Grande

Puerto Limón

Golfo de Chiriquí

TO PUERTO CALDERA

COSTA RICA

PACIFIC OCEAN

lón. At press time, one U.S. dollar was worth about 163 colón. In Panama, the balboa and the U.S. dollar are regular currency and both have the same value. In Colombia, the monetary unit is the peso, with one U.S. dollar worth about 580 pesos.

Passports and Visas No passport or visa is necessary to transit the Panama Canal because passengers do not disembark. A passport is needed for passengers on cruises that call in Costa Rica, the San Blas Islands, or Cartagena.

Cartagena, Colombia

Cartagena, Colombia, is one of the Western Hemisphere's most fascinating cities. Seventeenth-century walls divide Cartagena into the "old" and "new" city. In the old city, houses are in the Iberian style: thick walls, high ceilings, central patios, gardens, and balconies. The streets are narrow and crooked, designed for protection during assault. The cityscape is filled with historical sites, forts, and museums. Among Cartagena's major exports are coffee and emeralds—Colombia supplies 70% of the world's supply of these gems.

Shore Excursions The best choice in Cartagena for the first-time visitor is the city tour (3½ hrs, $26), which takes you through the city, stopping at a hilltop monastery for a sweeping view, and in the old town for a survey of the historic attractions and shopping.

Costa Rica

Costa Rica is emerging as a popular port of call on Panama Canal itineraries, due to its growing reputation as a land of unspoiled rain forests and other natural beauty. Twelve percent of Costa Rica's territory is protected wilderness—home to 560 species of mammals, amphibians, and reptiles; 850 species of birds; 130 species of freshwater fish, and 9,000 species of plants.

Coming Ashore Most ships dock in Puerto Caldera on the west coast or Puerto Limon on the Caribbean coast. From either landing spot, half-day and full-day excursions take passengers deeper into the lush interior.

Shore Excursions Good choices in Costa Rica include river rafting on the Rio Reventazon (8 hrs, $78), riding the historic Green Train through banana plantations (2½ hrs, $68), and exploring the countryside and visiting the rain forest to see toucans, scarlet macaws, monkeys, and brilliant flora (5 hrs, $45).

The San Blas Islands

The beautiful islands of the **San Blas** archipelago are home to the Cuna Indians, whose women are famous for hand-worked stitching. These women are a charming sight with their embroidered *molas*, strings of necklaces, gold jewelry in their noses, and arm and ankle bracelets. Some cruise lines organize shore excursions to Cuna villages on outlying islands. Travel is by motorized dugout canoe. A native dance performance may be scheduled, and native crafts are usually for sale. If you are wavering between two Panama Canal cruises, take the one that stops at the San Blas Islands.

South America

Cruising to South America to escape the cold Northern winter is one of cruising's more exotic adventures. The most common itineraries, sometimes known as Caribazon cruises, combine Caribbean ports of call with a navigation of the Amazon River. Other itineraries sail down to Rio de Janeiro to coincide with Carnival; a few head even farther south, rounding the tip of the continent at Tierra del Fuego. The grandest of all is a circumnavigation of South America, which takes in all the major ports in about 50 days.

The Amazon region has figured so prominently in novels and films that most people arrive with several preconceived notions. Often they expect an impenetrable jungle, herds of animals, flocks of swooping birds, and unfriendly Indians. In reality, ground cover is sparse, trees range from 50 to 150 feet in height, little animal life can be spotted, and the birds nest in the tops of the high trees. However, the natural romance of the Amazon River, the free-flowing water, and the hint of mystery remain.

Most of the Amazon basin has been explored and charted. The river itself is 3,900 miles long—the second-longest in the world—and has 17 tributaries, each over 1,000 miles long. About one-third of the world's oxygen is produced by the vegetation, and one-fifth of all the fresh water in the world is carried by the Amazon. Although more than 18,000 plant species thrive here, the extremely heavy rainfall leaches the soil of its nutrients and makes organized cultivation impractical. Poor in agricultural possibilities, the Amazon is rich in other products, including gold, diamonds, lumber, rubber, oil, and jute.

Listed below are brief overviews of South America's major cruise ports; your shore excursion director will have detailed information on getting around these ports, choosing excursions, and exchanging currency. The major cruise lines sailing to South America at press time were Clipper, Crystal Cunard, Princess, Regency, Royal, Seabourn, Silversea, Special Expeditions, and Sun Line. (For detailed itineraries, *see* Chapter 3.) Alternative sailings to South America can be found aboard some European cruise lines, such as Epirotiki, and passenger-freighter lines, such as Ivaran (*see* Special-Interest Cruises *in* Cruise Primer).

When to Go South America's cruising season is short—from the end of December or early January to the end of February or early March. The few ships going there tend to be booked quickly, so make your reservations early.

Health Travelers to the Amazon, and other South American rural areas and small cities, are advised to get vaccinated against yellow fever and to take medication against malaria. There are no formal vaccination requirements for entry, but the **Centers for Disease Control** (tel. 404/639–2572) in Atlanta offers up-to-the-minute advice on health precautions. Call their **International Travellers Hotline** for information on your destination. In addition to malaria and yellow fever, you'll be warned about hepatitis A (for which immune serum globulin is recommended), hepatitis B, typhoid fever, and cholera. Contact your health department for immunization information. Local offices of the **U.S. Public Health Service** (a division of CDC) handle inquiries. There are branches in Chicago, Hawaii, Los Angeles, Miami, New York, San Francisco, and Seattle.

Passports and Visas Brazil requires valid passports and tourist visas of visitors whose countries demand visas of Brazilians. This includes the United States and Canada, but not the United Kingdom. A tourist visa, valid for 90 days, is easily obtainable from a Brazilian consulate and free if you apply in person and bring your passport, a 2″-by-3″ pass-

South America

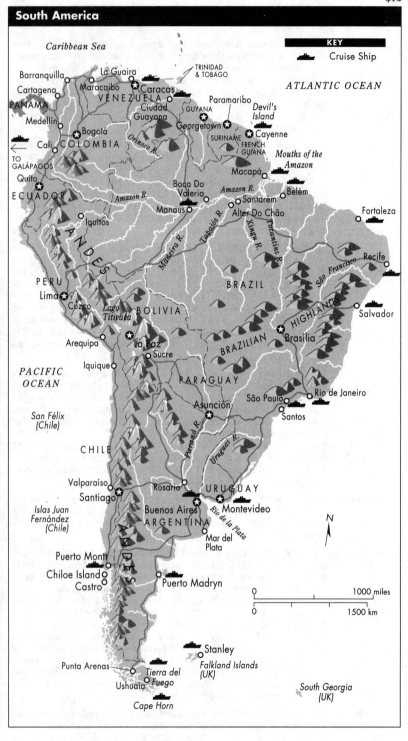

Caribbean Sea

ATLANTIC OCEAN

Barranquilla
La Guaira
Maracaibo
Caracas
TRINIDAD & TOBAGO
VENEZUELA
Ciudad Guayana
Paramaribo
Devil's Island
PANAMA
GUYANA
Medellín
Georgetown
SURINAME
Cayenne
Bogotá
COLOMBIA
Cali
FRENCH GUIANA
TO GALÁPAGOS
Orinoco R.
Macapá
Mouths of the Amazon
Quito
ECUADOR
Boca Do Valeria
Amazon R.
Belém
Iquitos
Amazon R.
Santarém
Manaus
Alter Do Chão
Fortaleza
Tapajós R.
Xingu R.
Tocantins R.
Madeira R.
São Francisco
Recife
PERU
BRAZIL
Lima
Cuzco
HIGHLANDS
Lago Titicaca
BOLIVIA
Salvador
Arequipa
La Paz
Sucre
Brasília
PACIFIC OCEAN
Iquique
BRAZILIAN
San Félix (Chile)
PARAGUAY
Rio de Janeiro
São Paulo
CHILE
Asunción
Santos
Paraná R.
Valparaíso
Rosario
URUGUAY
Islas Juan Fernández (Chile)
Santiago
Uruguay R.
Buenos Aires
Montevideo
Río de la Plata
ARGENTINA
Mar del Plata

N

Puerto Montt
Chiloe Island
Castro
Puerto Madryn

0 ——— 1000 miles
0 ——— 1500 km

Stanley
Falkland Islands (UK)
Punta Arenas
Tierra del Fuego
Ushuaia
South Georgia (UK)
Cape Horn

ANDES

port photo, and a round-trip ticket. Check requirements with your cruise line if your itinerary includes other countries.

Alter do Chão/Santarém, Brazil

Cruise ships that call at Alter do Chão generally spend half the day here and half at nearby Santarém—they're both on the Amazon about midway between Belém and Manaus. Shopping for such local handicrafts as masks, blowguns, earrings, necklaces, and straw baskets is a major pastime. You'll find the same wares sold by literally the same merchants in both towns.

Coming Ashore Ships drop anchor off Alter do Chão and tender passengers directly to the main square downtown. Most worthwhile sights are within walking distance. At Santarém, ships dock just a few minutes' walk from the downtown shopping district. Ships run shuttle buses to the **Mercado Modelo** (handicrafts market) for about $10 per person, but taxis are readily available and cheaper at $3–$5 per carload.

Exploring Alter do Chão/ Santarém There are no formal shore excursions in Alter do Chão, a small village on the Tapajós River with lush vegetation and fine river swimming. After tendering ashore, passengers can shop; visit the **Museum of Indigenous Art,** with exhibits and artifacts representing 58 Amazonian Indian tribes; or watch folk dances performed by local children. For a small fee ($2–$4), local fishermen will row you across the little harbor to a small but very clean beach.

Santarém, founded in 1661, is a city of 250,000 people. It's notable for its riches of timber, bauxite, and gold, and the colorful **waterfront** makes for an engaging stroll. There are no formal excursions here, either. Browsing and shopping are the major pursuits for cruise passengers.

Belém, Brazil

The Brazilian city of Belém is the gateway to the Amazon, 90 miles from the open sea. It has ridden the ups and downs of Amazon booms and busts since 1616, alternately bursting with energy and money and slumping into relative obscurity. This is evident in the city's architecture: Ultramodern high-rises mingle with older red-tile-roof buildings, Colonial structures survive alongside rubber-era mansions and ostentatious monuments.

Shore Excursions The following are good choices in Belém. They may not be offered by all cruise lines. Times and prices are approximate.

Belém City and the Goeldi Museum. Includes visits to the Ver-o-Peso market; the Goeldi Museum; the marble, turn-of-the-century Basilica of Our Lady of Nazareth; and a stop at the enormous, neoclassical Teatro de la Paz. *Half day. Cost: $35.*

Brazilian Jungle River Cruise. Cruise in riverboats into creeks and channels of the Guama River. Stop at Santa Maria Island for a walk into the Amazon rain forest, which can be muddy and is always hot and humid. *Half day. Cost: $50.*

Coming Ashore Ships must anchor pretty far offshore. With the strong local current, the tender ride can take 15–20 minutes one-way. Passengers land at a floating dock about a half-hour ride outside town. Taxis are available, but few drivers speak English.

Exploring Belém In the "old city" you will find the **Our Lady of Nazare** church, with its ornate interior; the former **city palace;** and the **Bolonha Palace.** Walk to the **Praca da Republica,** facing the Municipal Theatre, to see the Victorian marble statues. Nearby is the **handicrafts center** run by the state tourism office; at this daily fair you will find wood, leather, and straw objects, plus handmade Indian goods and examples of the region's colorful and distinctive pottery, called *marajoara*. In addition to the **Goeldi Museum**'s extensive collection of Indian artifacts and excellent photographs, there is a **zoo** with many local animals in their natural surroundings. The **Ver-o-Peso** market is short on cleanliness but long on local color, with vendors offering medicinal herbs, regional fruits, miracle roots from the jungle, alligator teeth, river fish, and good-luck charms for body and soul.

Boca de Valeria, Brazil

Calling tiny, undeveloped Boca de Valeria a port is a bit generous. Passengers are often met by a group of 50 or so Native Americans, who canoe into port when a ship arrives. The big draw here is a chance to capture on film little boys holding their pet monkeys, sloths, and alligators and little girls selling beaded necklaces. If you're one of the first ashore you'll get a fascinating, though somewhat contrived, picture of an Amazon village.

Coming Ashore Boca de Valeria is so small that cruise ships set up inflatable docks for disembarkation by tender at this village east of Manaus. There are no facilities, restaurants, or tourist offices. Crew members sometimes bring ashore coolers of refreshments. Exploring is done solely on foot along dirt paths.

Buenos Aires, Argentina

Buenos Aires has been called the most sophisticated city in South America. Most cruise lines recognize its late-night appeal by calling here overnight. Spending the evening in this city that never sleeps gives you the chance to see an Argentine folk dance or even venture out to a tango parlor on your own! Pre- or post-cruise packages in Buenos Aires or to Iguazú Falls are extremely popular.

Shore Excursions The following are good choices in Buenos Aires. They may not be offered by all cruise lines. Times and prices are approximate.

A Day in the Pampas. Drive out of the city into the nearby pampas to visit an *estancia* (ranch). Watch a performance of traditional gaucho guitar music and a show of horsemanship. A barbecue lunch is served. *7 hrs. Cost: $60–$80.*

Buenos Aires City Tour. The drive through Buenos Aires gives you a feel for this sprawling city, with its broad boulevards, narrow colonial streets, and famous landmarks, such as the Casa Rosada (the pink "White House"), the tomb of Evita Perón, the Obelisk, and the Teatro Colón. *Half day. Cost: $25.*

Steak Dinner and Tango Show. Combines an Argentine steak dinner at one of the city's barbecue and *parilla* (grill) restaurants with a stage show of tango Argentino and gaucho (cowboy) folk dancing. *5 hrs. Cost: $70–$89.*

Coming Ashore Ships dock in the deep-water harbor. The most interesting shopping areas are a long walk or short taxi ride away. Taxis are available, at the passenger terminal, and most drivers speak at least a smattering of English. The 10–15 minute ride into town costs $3–$5.

Caracas/La Guaira, Venezuela

Cruises that call along the Venezuelan coast are most often sailing on a southern Caribbean itinerary (*see* Caribbean, *above*).

Cartagena, Colombia

Cruises that call at Colombia's capital city are most often sailing on a Panama Canal itinerary (*see* Panama Canal, *above*).

Devil's Island, French Guiana

Many cruises that advertise a stop at Devil's Island may actually put ashore at another of French Guiana's three Iles du Salut, of which Devil's Island (Ile Royale) is one. All three were prisons, and today tourism is unwilling—and unable—to push back the rampant jungle. The area is picturesque, lush, and haunting, so don't forget your camera.

Coming Ashore Passengers tender ashore to explore the remains of the penal colony and follow the footpath that encircles the island.

Fortaleza, Brazil

Several hundred miles southeast of Belém, Fortaleza is Brazil's fifth-largest city. A long drought devastated this agrarian region during the 1980s, and only in recent years has Fortaleza begun to recover. On the Atlantic, you'll find wonderful (usually crowded) beaches and some of the best lobster in South America. Its famed lace industry is fast turning Fortaleza into one of Brazil's top fashion centers.

Shore Excursions The following is a good choice in Fortaleza. It may not be offered by all cruise lines. Time and price are approximate.

City Tour. Includes the gothic-style cathedral; the monument to former president of Brazil Castello Branco; the fortress; and a visit to an artisan's center—in the old city jail—to shop for such local handicrafts as lacework, leather, wooden figures, and sand paintings in bottles. *Half day. Cost: $35.*

Coming Ashore Ships dock within walking distance of the beaches. You can stroll along the waterfront and watch vendors parade by, dangling live crabs from sticks. An artisan's center, marketplace, and other attractions are minutes away by bus or taxi.

Galápagos Islands, Ecuador

Ecuador's "Enchanted Isles," the Galápagos archipelago includes 13 major islands and dozens of islets. This 3-million-year-old cluster of volcanic islands is home to giant tortoises (after which the Galápagos Islands are named); marine iguanas; sea lions; and such rare birds as the blue-footed boobies, cormorants, and albatross.

In 1994, the Ecuadorian government banned foreign cruise ships from calling at the Galápagos for a period of at least three years. For local cruise operators that visit the Galápagos, *see* Fodor's South America.

Manaus, Brazil

A sprawling city of nearly 1.5 million people, Manaus is built in the densest part of the jungle some 1,000 miles up the Amazon. After years of dormancy, it has reestablished its role as the key city of the Amazon. A number of cruise lines use it as the embarkation or disembarkation port for Caribazon sailings, making Manaus an ideal jumping-off point for a pre- or post-cruise overnight jungle experience.

Of the excursions listed below, the two river tours are most worthwhile. Because it's possible to tour the opera house by day, you may wish to skip the fabricated evening performance. You can hire a taxi to show you the sights described in the city shore excursion. Some jewelry companies, such as **H. Stern** and **Amsterdam Sauer,** give free taxi tours (stopping only upon request), provided you agree to end with a showroom visit.

Shore
Excursions
The following are good choices in Manaus. They may not be offered by all cruise lines. Times and prices are approximate.

Alligator Spotting. On this nighttime version of the Amazon River tour (*see below*), motorized canoes venture into alligator-populated creeks. Guides search for gators with a strong flashlight, spotting the creatures' gleaming red eyes in the darkness. Once hypnotized by the bright light, the alligator can be lifted by the guide for photographs and then released unharmed. *3 hrs. Cost: $55.*

Amazon River Tour. A local riverboat plies the black-tinted Rio Negro, until it meets the caramel-colored Solimoes River; they eventually blend to form the Amazon. At Lake Janauaca, motorized canoes whisk you along small *igarapés* (creeks) into the jungle. Water levels permitting, you'll cross a wooden bridge to view Victoria Regia water lilies. *4½ or 7 hrs. Cost: $48–$55.*

An Evening Performance at Teatro Amazonas (Manaus Opera House). Attend a 50-minute folklore performance, designed especially for cruise passengers, which provides an historic overview of Manaus's native population, rubber boom times, and the city today. *1½ hrs. Cost: $45.*

Manaus City Tour. Visit the art deco–style Municipal Market, housing meat, fruit, hat, and herb vendors; the turn-of-the-century Teatro Amazonas Opera House; the Indian Museum; and the Natural Science Museum, which showcases piranhas, electric eels, butterflies, beetles, and tarantulas. *3 hrs. Cost: $38.*

Coming
Ashore
Ships tie up at the floating dock, which comes alive with a festive atmosphere as peddlers, vendors, and other locals gather to greet the ships. Within walking distance is the *Mercado Municipal* (Municipal Market).

Exploring
Manaus
The **custom house** and **lighthouse** were imported piece by piece from England and reassembled alongside the floating dock, which was built to accommodate the annual 40-foot rise and fall of the river. Vestiges of Manaus's opulent rubber-boom days remain, including the famous **Teatro Amazonas Opera House,** where Jenny Lind once sang and the Ballets Russes once danced. Completed in 1910 and restored to its former splendor in 1990, the building is adorned with French ironwork and works of art and chinaware. Take a taxi to the suburbs to the **Salesian Mission Museum** to see a documentary on the now vanished "Floating City"; also visit the **Indian Museum** operated by the same religious order. For insight into the rubber-boom period, visit a **rubber plantation.** For shopping, try the **Credilar Teatro,** an imposing edifice of native red stone and glass.

Montevideo, Uruguay

An increasing number of cruise ships have begun calling at this sprawling capital city of nearly 2 million. Although Montevideo has no regal colonial past, this well-laid-out metropolis is a pleasant place to relax.

The best way to see the sights is on a ship-arranged city tour. From the harbor, a tour can take you past the downtown area's art deco– and nouveau-style buildings, the Prado district, and monuments, and then down the Rambla (the riverfront drive).

You can combine the city tour with a visit to an *estancia* (ranch) for a traditional barbecue of beef, chicken, and sausages, then watch a *gaucho* (cowboy) show of folkloric music and horsemanship. Another popular option is spending the day at the South American resort of Punta Del Este, on the Atlantic Ocean.

Coming
Ashore
Ships dock a long walk or short taxi ride from the city. Taxis are fairly inexpensive, and it's fairly easy to find drivers who speak English.

Many cabs are vintage 1920s–1950s autos. The restaurants immediately around the port area are a good choice for lunch.

Port Stanley, Falkland Islands (United Kingdom)

Although there are no formal shore excursions, some cruise ships—mostly expedition vessels—call here for a day. The islands (of which there are several hundred) are located 350 miles east of Cape Horn. The war in 1982 between Great Britain and Argentina put the Falkland Islands on the map.

Puerto Madryn/Ushuaia, Argentina

These two ports, several hundred miles apart on Argentina's east coast, are becoming increasingly popular with cruise ships.

A day in Puerto Madryn might be spent driving around **Peninsula Valdes** to observe the some 13,000 sea elephants reclining on the pebbled beaches. Another option is a drive to Punta Tombo through the Patagonian countryside to watch the thousands of migrating birds, including tuxedo-clad Magellan penguins, that gather here annually.

From Ushuaia, the southernmost town in the world (population 20,000), visit **Tierra del Fuego National Park,** take a catamaran ride to see the wildlife of the **Beagle Channel,** or spend a full day on **Fagnano Lake,** where you'll see beaver dams, peat bogs, and have lunch in a country inn.

Rio de Janeiro, Brazil

The approach to Rio de Janeiro by ship is one of cruising's most breathtaking sights, as the famous peak of Sugar Loaf grows ever bigger on the horizon. Rio is blessed with deep green, mountainous jungles; a profusion of birds, butterflies, and flowers; and long stretches of soft, sandy beaches lined with tall palm trees. To these natural blessings people have added colorful parades, colonial buildings vying for space with dramatic skyscrapers, and music everywhere—from honking automobile horns to soft singing voices to the thump of recorded drums accompanying street dancers. Several ships offer cruises that coincide with Carnival (four days before Ash Wednesday) and reserve grandstand seats for their passengers; if you enjoy crowds and pageantry, nowhere is more exciting.

At any time of year, though, the city offers many museums and historical sites, distinctive coffeehouses, and remarkable districts where shopping is good and affordable: You can buy a fine leather coat for less than a cloth one would cost back home. At the beaches you can watch barely clothed youths sunbathing and playing volleyball. Or head up to **Pão de Açúcar** (Sugar Loaf) for a rousing samba show. Be aware, however, that Rio is home to a great many poor settlers living in a country rife with economic problems. Watch your valuables, and don't walk down empty streets.

Shore Excursions The following is a good choice in Rio de Janeiro. It may not be offered by all cruise lines. Time and price are approximate.

Rio's Beaches and Sugar Loaf. Drive through the Reboucas Tunnel (the longest in Brazil) and along the famous beaches of Leblon, Ipanema, and Copacabana. Ride the cable car to the peak of Pão de Açúcar (Sugar Loaf). A stop is made for shopping. Half day. Cost: $35.

Coming Ashore Ships dock in the oldest part of the city. Restaurants and shops are found just outside the pier area, where an impromptu flea market springs up whenever a ship pulls in. The beaches and hotel district are a half-hour taxi ride away; cabs are readily available at the dock.

Free car tours (stopping only upon request) are supplied by jewelers such as H. Stern, but only if you agree to end your sightseeing at their showroom.

Salvador, Brazil

With a rich colonial past evident in its churches, forts, and other historical buildings, Salvador is known to Brazilians as the most Brazilian of their cities. For this it draws not only upon its history (Salvador was the country's first capital), but also upon its colors, tastes, sounds, and aromas—a blend of African, Native American, and European cultures. Salvador moves to its own rhythm, slow and sensual, more at ease than Rio and blessed with miles of practically untouched beaches. Plunge into the **Upper City,** home to Brazil's best-preserved colonial architecture. Walking around, you may happen upon a street exhibition of *capoeira,* a fight dance that originated in Bahia. Don't miss the chance to sample the special Bahian cuisine.

Shore Excursions The following is a good choice in Salvador. It may not be offered by all cruise lines. Time and price are approximate.

City tour. Includes visits to the *Mercado Modelo* (public market), the Upper City and colonial section, the Church of São Francisco and Carmo church (Salvador has nearly 200 churches), and Largo do Pelourinho—a plaza of Latin America's finest colonial buildings. Shops near the Plaza sell Bahian costumes and jewelry. *Half day. Cost: $35.*

Coming Ashore Ships dock within sight of the Upper City. There is a funicular to the colonial district, but it is more prudent to take a taxi. Cabs are readily available outside the pier; drivers speak at least a smattering of English.

Santos/São Paulo

Santos is São Paulo's port. São Paulo, overflowing with more than 14 million residents, is one of the largest cities in the world. It's the richest area in South America, the fastest growing, and the pride of all Brazilians. Sprawling over 589 square miles, São Paulo is covered by a semipermanent blanket of smog. Skyscrapers dominate the horizon in jagged concrete clusters. Coffee plantations made São Paulo what it is today; now a variety of industries thrive.

Santos is a lovely tropical retreat of sun-worshipping and swimming. Apart from the historic Basilica of Santo Andre, the city offers little in the way of culture.

Shore Excursions The following are good choices in Santos/São Paulo. They may not be offered by all cruise lines. Times and prices are approximate.

Santos Beach Party. A trip to the resort island of Ilha Porchat. Swimmers can choose among two swimming pools or the beach. *Half day. Cost: $45.*

São Paulo city tour. From Santos a two-hour bus ride passes banana plantations and oil refineries before glimpsing the skyscrapers of downtown São Paulo. A stop is made at Butanta Institute, where snakes are raised for antivenom. Lunch is included. *6–7 hrs. Cost: $100.*

Coming Ashore Santos has the largest dock area in South America. Ships tie up next to a small outdoor mall, where there is shopping for coffee and handicrafts. São Paulo is about 40 miles away.

Less Visited Ports

Brazil   A few cruise ships call at **Recife** on the east coast of Brazil or, as part of an Amazon River itinerary, Macapá, Parintins, or the Anavilhanas archipelago.

Chile   Ships visiting **Santiago,** the capital, call at **Valparaíso,** two to three hours away. Farther south, from **Puerto Montt,** passengers can explore the lake country of southern Chile. Down around Chile's tip, **Punta Arenas** provides an opportunity for adventurous travelers to board a flightseeing plane to view the White Continent, **Antarctica;** to take a drive up to Observation Point for a panoramic view of the city or of the **Strait of Magellan;** or to drive alongside Otway Bay to the **Penguin Caves.**

Peru   Calls may include **Callao,** the port city for **Lima,** the capital, which is half an hour away. From Lima, passengers can visit **Machu Picchu,** the ancient fortress of the Incas, high in the Andes Mountains. Calls are contingent upon Peru's unstable political conditions. Check with your travel agent or cruise line.

3 Itineraries

Sailing Schedules

The port-by-port itineraries listed below are for sailings in the Western Hemisphere only. When a ship is positioned outside the Western Hemisphere for all or part of the year, only the sailing region is given. Schedules begin with fall 1995 and run through summer 1996. Ship deployments and ports of call are subject to change; check with your cruise line or travel agent.

Abercrombie & Kent

Explorer **Early Fall:** Europe. **Fall:** Fourteen-day **Antarctica** cruises depart Ushuaia, Argentina, sailing the Drake Channel and calling at a research station. **Winter:** Fourteen-day **Antarctica** cruises same as fall. Fifteen-day **Antarctica** cruises include the Falkland Islands. Nineteen-day **Antarctica** sailings depart Port Stanley, Falkland Islands, and include the South Georgia Islands. **Spring: Amazon** cruises with port calls to be announced.

Alaska Sightseeing/Cruise West

Spirit of Alaska **Fall–early Spring:** Seven-night **San Francisco Bay/Sacramento River** delta loops depart Sausalito calling at Stockton, Sacramento, Napa, San Francisco. **Spring:** Ten-night **Alaska** cruises between Seattle and Juneau call at Ketchikan, Wrangell, Sitka, Skagway, Haines, and Glacier Bay. Seven-night **Alaska** cruises between Juneau and Ketchikan call at Wrangell, Skagway, Haines, and Glacier Bay. **Late Spring–Summer:** Seven-night **Alaska** cruises between Seattle and Juneau call at Ketchikan, Petersburg, Sitka, and Glacier Bay.

Spirit of Columbia **Fall:** Seven-night **Columbia and Snake river** loops depart Portland, Oregon, to Bonneville Dam and Maryhill Museum, Washington; Hell's Canyon, Idaho; Walla Walla, Washington; Hood River and Astoria, Oregon; and a side trip to Cannon Beach, Oregon. **Winter:** No cruises scheduled. **Spring–Summer:** Same as fall.

Spirit of Discovery **Fall:** Seven-night **British Columbia** loops from Seattle call at Campbell River, Chemainus, Victoria, Vancouver, Friday Harbor, Rosario Resort (Orcas Island), La Conner, and Port Townsend. **Winter:** No cruises scheduled. **Early Spring:** Same as fall. **Mid-Spring–Summer:** Seven-night **Alaska** cruises between Seattle and Juneau call at Ketchikan, Petersburg, Sitka, and Glacier Bay.

Spirit of '98 **Fall:** Same as *Spirit of Columbia* **Columbia River and Snake River** loops. **Winter:** No cruises scheduled. **Spring:** Ten-night **Alaska** cruises between Seattle and Juneau call at Ketchikan, Wrangel, Sitka, Skagway, Haines, and Glacier Bay. **Late Spring–Summer:** Seven-night **Alaska** cruises between Seattle and Juneau call at Ketchikan, Sitka, Skagway, and Haines.

American Canadian Caribbean Line

Caribbean Prince **Fall:** Twelve-day **Northeastern United States and Canada** cruises sail between Warren, Rhode Island, and Québec City, visiting Narragansett Bay; New York Harbor; the Hudson River Valley, including West Point, Kingston, Troy, Little Falls, Erie Canal Village, Sylvan Beach, Oswego, the Thousand Islands, Clayton, and Upper Canada Village, Ontario; and Montréal. A 15-day **eastern seaboard** cruise from Warren, Rhode Island, to Palm Beach Garden calls at Baltimore and Crisfield, Maryland; Norfolk, Virginia; Beaufort and Wrightsville Beach, North Carolina; Georgetown, Charleston, and Beaufort, South Carolina; Savannah and St. Simons Island, Georgia; and in Florida, St. Augustine and Titusville. **Winter:** Twelve-day **Central America** loops depart Belize City, calling at isolated islands and coves along the coasts of Guatemala and Belize, a barrier reef, and along the Rio Dulce. Twelve-day **Central America** cruises from Roatan (off Honduras) to Belize City call at Mayan sites. **Spring–Summer:** Same as fall.

Mayan Prince **Fall:** Same as *Caribbean Prince*. **Winter:** A 12-day **Panama Canal** transit calls at Panama City, Colón, El Porvenir, the San Blas Islands, Coronado de Jesus, Isla Tigre, Portobelo, Taboga, Contadora, La Esmeralda, Pt. Alegre, the Darien Jungle, and Balboa. Twelve-day positioning cruise sails from Balboa, Panama, to Belize City, visiting Costa Rica, Nicaragua, and Honduras. **Spring–Summer:** Same as fall. Six-day **New England Islands** cruises in July sail round-trip from Warren, Rhode Island, or between New York and Hyannis, Massachusetts, calling at Sag Harbor, Long Island; Block Island and Newport, Rhode Island; Martha's Vineyard and Nantucket, Massachusetts.

Niagara Prince **Fall:** 15-day **mid-America** cruises sail between Chicago and New Orleans, calling at Joliet and Peoria, Illinois; St. Louis and St. Genevieve, Missouri; Paducah, Kentucky; New Johnsonville and Shiloh, Tennessee; Columbus, Missouri; Demopolis and Mobile, Alabama; and Biloxi, Mississippi. **Winter:** Twelve-day **Virgin Islands** loops depart St. Thomas calling at St. John, Tortola, Virgin Gorda, Prickly Pear, Anegada, Beef Island, Jost Van Dyke, Sandy Cay, and Norman Island. Twelve-day **Venezuela** cruises between Trinidad and Tobago call at Ciudad Guayana/Angel Falls and sail the Macareo and Orinoco rivers. Twelve-day **southern Caribbean** cruises call at Aruba, Bonaire, and Curaçao. **Spring–Summer:** Fifteen-day **mid-America** cruises (same as fall). A 16-day **inland waterways** cruise between Chicago and Warren, Rhode Island, calls at Manistee, Mackinac Island, and Wyandotte, Michigan; Cleveland, Ohio; Erie, Pennsylvania; Buffalo and Rochester, New York; the Erie Canal and Hudson River. A 12-day **inland waterways** cruise between Warren, Rhode Island, and Buffalo, New York, sails the Erie Canal, Hudson River, Champlain Canal, Lake Champlain and visits Waterford, Little Falls, Rome, Lyons, Palmyra, Pittsford, Rochester, Brockport, Medina, Lockport, and Buffalo.

American Hawaii Cruises

Constitution **Year-round:** Seven-day **Hawaii** loops depart Honolulu Saturday, calling at Nawiliwili, Kaui; Kahului, Maui; Hilo and Kona, Big Island.

Independence **Year-round:** Seven-day **Hawaii** loops reversing the *Constitution*'s route depart Honolulu Saturday.

Carnival Cruise Lines

Celebration **Year-round:** Seven-day **Caribbean** loops depart Miami Saturday, calling at San Juan, St. Thomas/St. John, and St. Maarten/St. Martin.

Ecstasy **Year-round:** Three-day **Bahamas** loops depart Miami Friday, calling at Nassau. Four-day **Mexican Yucatan** loops depart Miami Monday, calling at Key West and Cozumel/Playa del Carmen.

Fantasy **Year-round:** Three-day **Bahamas** loops depart Port Canaveral Thursday, calling at Nassau. Four-day **Bahamas** loops depart Port Canaveral Sunday, calling at Nassau and Freeport/Lucaya.

Fascination **Year-round:** Seven-day **Caribbean** loops depart San Juan Saturday, calling at St. Thomas, Guadeloupe, Grenada, La Guaira/Caracas, and Aruba.

Festivale **Year-round:** Seven-day **Caribbean** loops depart San Juan Sunday, calling at St. Thomas/St. John; St. Maarten/St. Martin; Dominica; Barbados; and Martinique.

Holiday **Year-round:** Three-day **Mexican Riviera** loops depart Los Angeles Friday, calling at Ensenada, Mexico. Four-day **Mexican Riviera** loops depart Los Angeles Monday, calling at Ensenada, Mexico, and Catalina Island.

Jubilee **Year-round:** Seven-day **Mexican Riviera** loops depart Los Angeles Sunday, calling at Puerto Vallarta, Cabo San Lucas, and Mazatlán.

Sensation **Year-round:** From Miami, seven-day **eastern Caribbean** loops depart alternate Sundays calling at San Juan, St. Croix, and St. Thomas. Seven-day **western Caribbean** loops depart alternate Sundays, calling at Cozumel/Playa del Carmen, Mexico; Grand Cayman; and Ocho Rios, Jamaica.

Tropicale **Fall–mid-Spring:** From Tampa, seven-day **western Caribbean** loops depart Sunday, calling at Grand Cayman; Cozumel/Playa del Carmen, Mexico; and New Orleans. From New Orleans, seven-day **western Caribbean** loops depart Friday, calling at Tampa, Grand Cayman, and Cozumel/Playa del Carmen, Mexico. **Late Spring–Summer:** Seven-day **Inside Passage/Gulf of Alaska** cruises between Vancouver and Seward call at Juneau, Ketchikan, and Skagway. Northbound cruises also call at Sitka. Southbound cruises also call at Valdez.

Celebrity Cruises

Century **Year–round:** Seven-night **eastern Caribbean** loops depart Fort Lauderdale alternate Saturdays, calling at San Juan, St. Thomas, St. Maarten, and Nassau. Seven-night **western Caribbean** loops depart Fort Lauderdale alternate Saturdays, calling at Ocho Rios, Jamaica; Grand Cayman; Cozumel/Playa del Carmen, Mexico; and Key West.

Horizon **Fall–Spring:** Seven-day **Caribbean** loops depart San Juan Saturday, calling at Martinique, Barbados, St. Lucia, Antigua, and St. Thomas. A 15-night **Panama Canal** transit from San Juan to Los Angeles to San Juan calls at Aruba; Cartagena, Colombia; Puerto Caldera, Costa Rica; Acapulco and Cabo San Lucas, Mexico; and San Diego. An 11-night **Pacific Coast** cruise from Los Angeles to Vancouver calls at San Francisco, Victoria, Sitka, Juneau, Ketchikan, and Glacier Bay. **Summer:** Seven-night **Inside Passage** loops depart Vancouver, calling at Ketchikan, Juneau, Skagway, and Haines. Seven-night **Inside Passage/Gulf of Alaska** cruises between Vancouver and Seward call Sitka, Juneau, Skagway, Ketchikan, and Valdez.

Meridian **Fall–Winter:** Ten- and 11-night **Caribbean/Panama Canal** loops depart San Juan Friday and Monday and may call at Aruba, Caracas/La Guaira, Grenada, Barbados, St. Lucia, Martinique, St. Maarten, St. Thomas, Cartagena, or the San Blas Islands. An 11-night **Caribbean** cruise from Fort Lauderdale to San Juan calls at Nassau, Tortola, St. Maarten, Antigua, Martinique, Barbados, Grenada, and St. Thomas. **Spring–Summer:** Seven-night **Bermuda** loops depart New York or Fort Lauderdale, calling at King's Wharf (West End). Ten- and 11-night **Caribbean** loops (same as fall). A 12-night **Caribbean** cruise from San Juan to Fort Lauderdale calls at Grenada, Barbados, St. Lucia, Martinique, Antigua, St. Barts, St. Maarten, St. Thomas, and Nassau.

Zenith **Fall–Spring:** Seven-night **Caribbean** loops depart San Juan Saturday calling at St. Thomas, Guadeloupe, Grenada, Caracas/La Guaira, and Aruba. A seven-night **Caribbean** cruise between San Juan and New York calls at St. Thomas, St. Maarten, and Bermuda. **Spring–Summer:** Seven-night **Bermuda** loops depart New York Saturday, calling at Hamilton and St. George.

Clipper Cruise Line

Nantucket Clipper **Fall:** Seven- to 14-day **Northeastern United States and Canada** cruises may call at Camden and Campobello Island, Maine; Martha's Vineyard and Nantucket Island, Massachusetts; Newport, Rhode Island; Albany, Kingston, New York City, Rochester, and West Point, New York; Annapolis, Baltimore, and St. Michaels, Maryland; Washington, DC; Philadelphia; Alexandria, Norfolk, Richmond, and Yorktown, Virginia; Beaufort, New Bern, and Wilmington, North Carolina; Beaufort and Charleston, South Carolina; Savannah, St. Marys (Okefenokee Swamp), and St. Simons Island, Georgia; and Jacksonville, Florida. **Northeastern Canada** cruises call at the Gaspé Peninsula and Percé, Québec; Caraquet and St. Andrews, New Brunswick; Baddeck, Digby, Halifax, Louisbourg, and Lunenberg, Nova Scotia; Kingston and Prescott, Ontario; Charlottetown, Prince Edward Island; Montréal; and Québec City. **Winter:** Eight-day **Caribbean** loops depart St. Thomas calling at St. John, Jost Van Dyke, Tortola, Virgin Gorda, Salt Island, and Norman Island. **Spring:** Seven- to 14-day **Northeastern United States and Canada** cruises (same as fall). **Summer:** Eleven- and 12-day **Great Lakes** cruises between Québec City and Toledo, Ohio, or between Toledo and Sault Ste. Marie, Michigan, may call at Montréal; Kingston, Toronto, Windsor, Goderich and Midland, Ontario; or Presque Isle, Leland, and Mackinac Island, Michigan. Seven- to 14-day **Northeastern United States and Canada** cruises (same as fall).

Yorktown Clipper **Fall:** Eleven-day **Inside Passage** cruises between Juneau and Seattle call at Haines, Skagway, Glacier Bay, Wrangell, Ketchikan, and Victoria, British Columbia. Eleven-day **Pacific Northwest** cruises call in British Columbia and along the Columbia River. Six-day **Northern California** cruises call at Redwood City, Sausalito, Stockton, Sacramento, and Napa Valley. An eight-day **Sea of Cortez** cruise from La Paz to Cabo San Lucas calls along the Baja California coast. Eleven-day **Panama Canal** transits between Puerto Caldera, Costa Rica, and Colón, Costa Rica, call at Punta Leona, Quepos, Las Perlas Archipelago, the Darien Jungle, the San Blas Islands, and Portobelo. **Winter:** Eleven-day **Costa Rica/Panama Canal** transits (same as fall). Eleven-day **Lesser Antilles and Orinoco River, Venezuela,** cruises between Curaçao and Trinidad call at Ciudad Guayana/Angel Falls, Venezuela; Tobago; Islas Caracas/Mochimas National Park; and Bonaire. Eleven-day **Caribbean** cruises between Grenada and St. Martin call at Anguilla; Saba; St. Kitts; Iles des Saintes, Guadeloupe; Dominica; St. Lucia; Bequia and Union Island, Grenadines. **Spring:** **Panama Canal** transits, **Sea of Cortez** and **Northern California** cruises (same as fall). **Summer:** Eleven-day **Inside Passage** cruise (same as fall). Eight-day **Inside Passage** loops depart Juneau, calling at Baranof Island, Sitka, Haines, Skagway, and Glacier Bay.

Club Med

Club Med 1 **Mid-Fall:** Mediterranean. **Late Fall–Spring:** Seven-day alternating **Caribbean** loops depart Martinique Saturday, calling at such islands as Barbados; St. Kitts; Nevis; Grenada; St. Lucia; St. Barts; St. Thomas, Virgin Gorda, and Jost Van Dyke in the Virgin Islands; or Bequia, Mayreau, and Tobago Cays in the Grenadines. **Late Spring–Summer:** Transatlantic and Mediterranean cruises.

Commodore Cruise Line

Enchanted Isle **Year-round:** Seven-day western **Caribbean** loops depart New Orleans Saturday, calling at Montego Bay, Jamaica; Grand Cayman; and Cozumel/Playa del Carmen, Mexico. An alternate loop calls at Key West and Cozumel/Playa del Carmen.

Costa Cruise Lines

CostaAllegra **Early Fall:** Mediterranean. **Mid-Fall–mid-Spring:** Seven-day **southern Caribbean** loops depart San Juan Saturday, calling at St. Thomas/St. John; St. Maarten/St. Martin; Guadeloupe; St. Lucia; Tortola/Virgin Gorda; Serena Cay (Costa's private island); and Casa de Campo, Dominican Republic. **Late Spring–Summer:** Same as early fall.

CostaClassica **Early Fall:** Mediterranean. **Mid-Fall–mid-Spring:** Caribbean cruises with port calls to be announced.

CostaRomantica **Early Fall:** Mediterranean. **Late Fall–mid-Spring:** Seven-day alternating **eastern and western Caribbean** loops depart Miami Sunday, calling at San Juan; St. Thomas/St. John; Serena Cay (Costa's private island); Casa de Campo, Dominican Republic; and Nassau. The second route calls at Key West, Florida; Cozumel/Playa del Carmen, Mexico; Montego Bay, Jamaica; and Grand Cayman. **Summer:** Same as early fall.

Crystal Cruises

Crystal Harmony **Winter:** An 11-day **Panama Canal** transit between Fort Lauderdale and Acapulco calls at Nevis/Montserrat; Playa del Carmen/Cozumel and Huatulco, Mexico; Grand Cayman; and Puerto Limón, Costa Rica. Ten- and 11-day **Panama Canal** transits between Acapulco and San Juan may call at Puerto Caldera, Costa Rica; Aruba; St. Thomas; Curaçao; San Blas Islands; Huatulco, Mexico; and St. Maarten. Eleven-day **Caribbean/Amazon** cruises between San Juan and Manaus, Brazil, may call at Barbados; Grenada; Devil's Island, French Guiana; Belem, Alter de Chao, Macapa, or Santerem, Brazil. A 12-day **Panama Canal** transit between Acapulco and New Orleans calls at Puerto Quetzal, Guatemala; Puerto Caldera, Costa Rica; San Blas Islands; and Playa del Carmen/Cozumel, Mexico. **Spring:** Ten- and 12-day **Panama Canal** transits (same as winter). A 13-day **Panama Canal** transit between San Juan and Los Angeles calls at Curaçao, Aruba, and Huatulco and Acapulco, Mexico.

Crystal Symphony **Fall:** South Pacific and Asia. **Winter:** A seven-day **Mexican Riviera** loop departs Los Angeles calling at Puerto Vallarta, Mazatlán, and Cabo San Lucas. A 96-day **world cruise** departs Los Angeles calling at 38 ports including Honolulu and Lahania, Hawaii.

Cunard Line Limited

Cunard Countess **Fall–Spring:** Alternating seven-day **Caribbean** loops depart San Juan Saturday, calling at St. Maarten/St. Martin; Guadeloupe; Grenada; St. Lucia; St. Kitts; and St. Thomas/St. John. The alternate itinerary calls at Tortola; Antigua; Martinique; Barbados; and St. Thomas.

Cunard Crown Dynasty **Fall–Spring:** A 14-day **Panama Canal** transit from Los Angeles to Fort Lauderdale calls at Acapulco; Puerto Caldera, Costa Rica; Cartagena, Colombia; and Ocho Rios, Jamaica. Ten- and 11-day **Panama Canal** transits between Fort Lauderdale and Acapulco may call at Cozumel/Playa del Carmen, Mexico; Grand Cayman; Puerto Caldera, Costa Rica; Ocho Rios, Jamaica; and Key West, Florida.

Queen Elizabeth 2 **Fall:** A six-day **Northeastern United States and Canada** loop departs New York, calling at Halifax, St. John, Boston, and Newport. An eight-day **Bermuda** loop departs New York, calling Port Canaveral and Charleston. An 11-day **Caribbean** loop departs New York, calling at Fort Lauderdale; St. Maarten/St. Martin; Barbados; Martinique; and St. Thomas. A seven-day **Caribbean** loop departs Fort Lauderdale, calling at St. Maarten/St. Martin, Barbados, Martinique, and St. Thomas. **Winter–early Spring:** Eleven- and 15-day **Ca-**

ribbean loops depart New York and Fort Lauderdale, calling at St. Maarten/St. Martin, Aruba, La Guaira/Caracas, Grenada, Barbados, Martinique, and St. Thomas. A 95-day **world cruise** departs New York calling at Fort Lauderdale; Cozumel/Playa del Carmen, Acapulco, and Ensenada, Mexico; Cartagena, Colombia; Los Angeles; Lahaina and Honolulu, Hawaii; Rio de Janeiro and Salvador; Brazil; Barbados; and St. Thomas in the Western Hemisphere. **Late Spring:** A series of five-day **transatlantic crossings** depart New York or Southampton.

Royal Viking Sun **Late Fall–early Winter:** A 53-day **Circle South America** loop departs New York and calls at the San Blas Islands; Puerto Montt, Chile; Port Stanley, Falkland Islands; Buenos Aires; Bahia, Salvador; and Antigua. A 14-day **Caribbean** loop departs Fort Lauderdale calling at Tortola, St. Maarten/St. Martin, Dominica, Barbados, Aruba, St. Kitts, and St. Croix. **Mid-Winter–Spring:** A 114-day **world cruise** departs Fort Lauderdale calling at Aruba, Panama, Costa Rica, Mexico, San Francisco, Los Angeles, Honolulu, and Bermuda in the Western Hemisphere.

Sagafjord **Fall:** Fourteen-day **Northeastern United States and Canada** cruises between Fort Lauderdale and Montréal call at New York; Bar Harbor; St. John, New Brunswick; Halifax and Sydney, Nova Scotia; Cornerbrook, Newfoundland; and Québec City. An alternate voyage calls at Québec City; Gaspe; Charlottetown; Sydney; St. Pierre; Portland, Maine; Newport, Rhode Island; and New York. **Late Fall–early Winter:** Twelve-, 13-, or 16-day loops depart Fort Lauderdale and call at **eastern, western, and southern Caribbean** ports including Cozumel/Playa del Carmen, Mexico; Grand Cayman; Puerto Plata; Key West; St. Kitts; Fort-de-France; Tortola; and St. Thomas.

Sea Goddess I **Late Fall–Winter:** Seven-, 10-, or 11-day **Caribbean** loops depart St. Thomas Saturday, calling at St. John, St. Maarten/St. Martin, St. Barts, Antigua, Virgin Gorga, and Jost Van Dyke. Fourteen-day **Panama Canal** transits between Barbados and Acapulco call at Grenadines; Isla Margarita; Aruba; Cartagena, Colombia; San Blas Island; Puerto Caldera, Costa Rica; and Puerto Escondido. **Spring:** same as winter. **Summer:** Europe.

Vistafjord **Early Winter:** A 14-day **Panama Canal** transit from Fort Lauderdale to Los Angeles calls at Grand Cayman; Cartagena, Colombia; Puerto Caldera, Costa Rica; and Acapulco and Cabo San Lucas, Mexico. A 14-day **Caribbean** loop departs Fort Lauderdale calling at St. Thomas/St. John, St. Maarten/St. Martin, Montserrat, Martinique, Barbados, Aruba, and Grand Cayman. **Mid-Winter: Hawaii/Tahiti** sailings from Los Angeles. **Late Winter:** A 15-day **Panama Canal** transit from Los Angeles to Fort Lauderdale calls at Cabo San Lucas; Acapulco; Puerto Caldera, Costa Rica; Aruba; and Grand Cayman. **Spring–Summer:** Fourteen-day **Caribbean/Amazon** cruises between Fort Lauderdale and Manaus, Brazil, call at St. Thomas; St. Kitts; Martinique; Barbados; Devil's Island; and Santana, Santarem, and Alter do Chao, Brazil.

Delta Queen Steamboat Co.

American Queen **Year-round:** Three- to 16-night river cruises on the **Mississippi River System** departing New Orleans, Memphis, St. Louis, St. Paul, Cincinnati, Pittsburgh, Louisville, Nashville, and Chattanooga. Ports of call may include Burnside, White Castle, Oak Alley, Baton Rouge and St. Francisville, Louisiana; Natchez, Vicksburg, Greenville, and Helena, Arkansas; New Madrid, Cape Girardeau, Hannibal, and Ste. Genevieve, Missouri; Burlington and Dubuque, Iowa; Prairie du Chien, Winona, and Wabasha, Wisconsin; Cairo and Cave-in-Rock, Illinois; Evansville and Madison, Indiana; Maysville, Henderson, and Paducah, Kentucky; Marietta, Ohio; Blennerhasset

Island and Wellsburg, West Virginia; Dover, Camden, and Shiloh, Tennessee; and Florence and Decatur, Alabama.

Delta Queen   **Year-round:** Three- to 14-night river cruises on the **Mississippi and its tributaries** calling at such ports as Galveston and Port Arthur, Texas; New Orleans, Morgan City, Port of Iberia, Krotz Springs, Oak Alley, Homas House, Baton Rouge, and St. Francisville, Louisiana; Natchez, Vicksburg, Greenville, Helena, Pine Bluff, Petit Jean State Park, Fort Smith, and Van Buren, Arkansas; Muskogee and Tulsa, Oklahoma; Memphis, Shiloh, Camden, Dover, Chattanooga, and Nashville, Tennessee; Florence and Decatur, Alabama; New Madrid, Cape Girardeau, Ste. Genevieve, St. Louis, and Hannibal, Missouri; Burlington and Dubuque, Iowa; Wabasha, Winona, and St. Paul, Minnesota; Prairie du Chien, Wisconsin; Cairo and Cave-In-Rock, Illinois; Evansville and Madison, Indiana; Paducah, Henderson, and Maysville, Kentucky; Pittsburgh, Wellsburg, and Wheeling, West Virginia; Cincinnati and Marietta, Ohio.

Mississippi   **Year-round:** Three- and 12-night river cruises on the **Mississippi Riv-**
Queen   **er System** depart New Orleans, Memphis, St. Louis, St. Paul, Louisville, Little Rock, Tulsa, Galveston, Cincinnati, Nashville, Pittsburgh, and Chattanooga. Ports of call may include Burnside, White Castle, Oak Valley, Baton Rouge, and St. Francisville, Louisiana; Fort Smith, Pine Bluff, Jean State Park, Natchez, Vicksburg, and Greenville, Arkansas; New Madrid, Cape Girardeau, Hannibal, and Ste. Genevieve, Missouri; Cairo and Cave-In-Rock, Illinois; Burlington and Dubuque, Iowa; Prairie du Chien, Winona, and Wabasha, Wisconsin; Evansville and Madison, Indiana; Maysville, Henderson, and Paducah, Kentucky; Marietta, Ohio; Blennerhasset Island and Wellsburg, West Virginia; Dover, Camden, and Shiloh, Tennessee; Florence and Decatur, Alabama; Galveston, Texas; and Port of Iberia, Port Arthur, Krotz Springs, and Morgan City, Louisiana.

Dolphin Cruise Line

Dolphin IV   **Year-round:** Three-night **Bahamas** loops depart Miami Friday, calling at Nassau and Blue Lagoon Island. Four-night **Bahamas** loops depart Miami Monday, calling at Nassau, Blue Lagoon Island, and Key West.

OceanBreeze   **Year-round:** Alternating seven-night **southern Caribbean** or **Panama Canal** loops depart Aruba Sunday, calling at Dominica, Barbados, Martinique, and Curaçao; or Cartagena, Colombia; the San Blas Islands, Curaçao, and Gatun Lake (Panama Canal).

SeaBreeze   **Year-round:** Alternating seven-night **eastern and western Caribbean** loops depart Miami Sunday, calling at Nassau, San Juan, and St. Thomas/St. John; or Grand Cayman, Montego Bay in Jamaica, and Cozumel/Playa del Carmen in Mexico.

Fantasy Cruises

Britanis   Under long-term charter to the U.S. military.

Holland America Line

Maasdam   **Late Fall–early Winter:** Ten-day **Panama Canal** transits between Fort Lauderdale and Acapulco call at Georgetown, Grand Cayman; Puerto Caldera, Costa Rica; and Puerto Quetzal/Tikal, Guatemala. A 10-day **Panama Canal** transit between Acapulco and New Orleans calls at Puerto Quetzal/Tikal, Guatemala; Georgetown, Grand Cayman; and Cozumel, Mexico. **Winter–early Spring:** A 14-day **Panama Canal** loop departs New Orleans, calling at Cozumel, Mexico; Montego Bay, Jamaica; Bonaire; Curaçao; Aruba; and Castries in St. Lucia. Ten-day **Panama Canal** transits same as fall. A seven-day

western Caribbean loop departs Fort Lauderdale, calling at Key West; Playa del Carmen/Cozumel, Mexico; Ocho Rios, Jamaica; and Grand Cayman. **Mid-Spring–Summer:** Europe.

Nieuw Amsterdam **Early Fall:** A 22-day **Panama Canal** transit from Vancouver to New Orleans calls along the West Coast, Mexico, Costa Rica, and in the Caribbean. **Mid-Fall–mid-Spring:** Seven-day **western Caribbean** loops depart New Orleans Sunday, calling at Montego Bay, Jamaica; Grand Cayman; and Playa del Carmen/Cozumel, Mexico. **Late Spring–Summer:** Seven-day **Inside Passage** loops from Vancouver call at Ketchikan, Juneau, Sitka, and Glacier Bay.

Noordam **Early Fall:** A 16-day **Panama Canal** transit from Vancouver to Tampa calls at Los Angeles; Cabo San Lucas; Acapulco; Cartagena, Colombia; and Grand Cayman. **Mid-Fall–mid Spring:** Seven-day **western Caribbean loops** depart Tampa Saturday, calling at Cozumel/Playa del Carmen, Mexico; Ocho Rios, Jamaica; and Grand Cayman. Some departures add Key West. **Late Spring–Summer:** Seven-day **Inside Passage/Gulf of Alaska** cruises between Vancouver and Seward call at Ketchikan, Juneau, Sitka, and Valdez.

Rotterdam **Fall:** Sixteen-day **Hawaii** loops depart Los Angeles, calling at Ensenada, Mexico; Kona and Hilo, the Big Island; Port Allen, Kauai; Honolulu, Oahu; Lahaina, Maui. **Early Winter:** A 14-day **Panama Canal** transit from Los Angeles to Fort Lauderdale calls at Ensenada, Cabo San Lucas, and Acapulco, Mexico; Puerto Caldera, Costa Rica; and Curaçao. **Winter:** A 15-day **Caribbean** loop departs Fort Lauderdale, calling at St. Thomas/St. John, Martinique, St. Lucia, Trinidad, Barbados, Curaçao, and Ocho Rios. A 99-day **world cruise** from Los Angeles to Fort Lauderdale calls at 30 ports including Salvador and Recife, Brazil; Devil's Island, French Guiana; Barbados, and New York in the Western Hemisphere. **Late Spring–Summer:** Seven-day **Inside Passage/Gulf of Alaska** cruises between Vancouver and Seward call at Ketchikan, Juneau, Sitka, and Valdez.

Ryndam **Early Fall:** An 18-day **Panama Canal** transit from Vancouver to Fort Lauderdale calls at San Francisco; Cabo San Lucas and Acapulco, Mexico; Puerto Caldera, Costa Rica; Curaçao; and Ocho Rios, Jamaica. **Mid-Fall–mid-Spring:** Ten-day **southern Caribbean** loops from Fort Lauderdale call at St. Maarten/St. Martin; Castries and Soufriere, St. Lucia; Barbados; Dominica; St. John/St. Thomas; and Nassau. **Late Spring–Summer:** Seven-day **Inside Passage/Gulf of Alaska** cruises between Vancouver and Seward call at Ketchikan, Juneau, Sitka, and Valdez.

Statendam **Early Fall:** A 19-day **Panama Canal** transit between Vancouver and Fort Lauderdale calls at Los Angeles; Puerto Vallarta, Ixtápa, and Acapulco, Mexico; Puerto Quetzal/Tikal, Guatemala; San Blas Islands; Cartagena, Colombia; and Grand Cayman. **Late Fall:** Ten-day **southern Caribbean** loops depart Fort Lauderdale, calling at Curaçao, Caracas/La Guaira, Grenada, Martinique, St. Thomas/St. John, and Nassau. **Winter–mid-Spring:** Ten-day **southern Caribbean** loops depart Fort Lauderdale, calling at St. Thomas/St. John; Cabrits and Roseau, Dominica; Grenada, Caracas/La Guaira; and Curaçao. **Late Spring–Summer:** Seven-day **Inside Passage** loops from Vancouver call at Ketchikan, Juneau, Sitka, and Glacier Bay.

Veendam **Spring–Summer:** Alternating seven-day **eastern or western Caribbean** loops depart Fort Lauderdale Saturday or Sunday, calling at Key West, Cozumel/Playa del Carmen, Mexico; Ocho Rios, Jamaica; and Grand Cayman or Nassau, San Juan, and St. Thomas/St. John.

Westerdam **Early Fall:** Ten-day **Northeastern United States and Canada** loops depart New York, calling at Halifax, Ingonish, and Sydney, Nova Scotia; Québec City and Gaspe, Québec; and Newport, Rhode Island. An eight-day **Northeastern United States and Canada** loop departs New York, calling at Bar Harbor and Portland, Maine; Halifax,

Nova Scotia; St. John, New Brunswick; Boston; and Newport, Rhode Island. **Mid-Fall–Spring:** Seven-day **eastern Caribbean** loops depart Fort Lauderdale Saturday, calling at St. Maarten/St. Martin, St. Thomas/St. John, and Nassau. **Summer:** Seven-day **Inside Passage** loops from Vancouver call at Ketchikan, Juneau, Sitka, and Glacier Bay.

Majesty Cruise Line

Royal Majesty **Fall–mid-Spring:** Three-night **Bahamas** loops depart Miami, calling at Nassau, Key West, and Royal Isle (Majesty's private island). Four-night Mexican Yucatan loops depart Miami, calling at Key West and Cozumel/Playa del Carmen, Mexico. **Late Spring–Summer:** Seven-night **Bermuda** loops depart Boston every Sunday, calling at St. George's.

Norwegian Cruise Line

Dreamward **Fall–Spring:** Seven-day **western Caribbean** loops depart Fort Lauderdale Sunday, calling at Grand Cayman; Cozumel/Playa del Carmen, Mexico; Cancun; and Great Stirrup Cay, Bahamas. **Summer:** Seven-day **Bermuda** loops depart New York, calling at St. George's and Hamilton.

Leeward **Year-round:** Alternating three-day **Bahamas** loops call at Great Stirrup Cay and Nassau or Key West. Four-day **Mexican Yucatan** loops depart Monday calling at Key West; Cancun and Cozumel/Carmen del Playa, Mexico.

Norway **Year-round:** Seven-day **eastern Caribbean** loops depart Miami Saturday, calling at St. Maarten/St. Martin, St. Thomas/St. John, and Great Stirrup Cay, Bahamas.

Seaward **Year-round:** Alternating seven-day **Caribbean** loops depart San Juan Sunday calling at Barbados, Martinique, St. Maarten, Antigua, and St. John/St. Thomas. The alternate route calls at Aruba, Curaçao, Tortola/Virgin Gorda, and St. John/St. Thomas.

Windward **Fall–mid-Spring:** Same as *Seaward*. **Late Spring–Summer:** Inside **Passage** loops depart Vancouver Monday, calling at Skagway, Haines, Juneau, and Ketchikan. Some departures call at Glacier Bay.

Premier Cruise Lines

Star/Ship **Year-round:** Three- and four-day **Bahamas** loops depart Port Canaveral Thursday and Sunday, calling at Nassau and Freeport/Lucaya.
Atlantic

Star/Ship Same as *Star/Ship Atlantic*, above, departing Friday and Monday.
Oceanic

Princess Cruises

Crown Princess **Early Fall:** An 11-day **Panama Canal** transit from Acapulco to Fort Lauderdale calls at Puerto Caldera, Costa Rica; Grand Cayman; and Cozumel/Playa del Carmen, Mexico. **Mid-Fall–late Fall:** Seven-day **western Caribbean** loops depart Fort Lauderdale calling at Princess Cays, Bahamas; Montego Bay, Jamaica; Grand Cayman; and Cozumel/Playa del Carmen, Mexico. **Winter–mid-Spring:** Ten-day **eastern Caribbean** loops depart Fort Lauderdale calling at Nassau, St. Thomas, Guadeloupe, Barbados, Dominica, St. Maarten, and Princess Cays (Bahamas). **Late Spring–Summer:** Seven-day **Inside Passage/Gulf of Alaska** cruises between Vancouver and Seward call at Ketchikan, Juneau, Skagway, and Glacier Bay.

Golden **Fall–mid-Spring:** South Pacific and Asia. **Late Spring–Summer:**
Princess Twelve-day **Inside Passage** loops depart San Francisco, calling at Victoria, Vancouver, Juneau, Skagway, Sitka, and Ketchikan.

Island Princess   **Fall–Spring:** India/Asia/Africa. **Summer:** Europe.

Pacific Princess   **Late Fall–early Winter:** Fourteen-day **Strait of Magellan** cruise from Buenos Aires, Argentina, to Santiago, Chile, calls at Montevideo, Uruguay; Puerto Madryn and Ushuaia, Argentina; Pt. Stanley, Falkland Islands; Punta Arehas and Puerto Montt, Chile. A 17-day **Panama Canal/South America** cruise from Santiago, Chile, to San Juan, Puerto Rico, calls at Arica, Chile; Lima, Peru; Guayaquil, Ecuador; Cartagena, Colombia; Aruba; and La Guaira, Venezuela. **Winter:** A 16-day **Panama Canal** transit between Los Angeles and San Juan calls at St. Thomas; St. Barts; Curaçao; San Blas Islands, near Panama; Puerto Caldera, Costa Rica; and Acapulco. Fifteen-day **Panama Canal** transits between Fort Lauderdale and Los Angeles call at Princess Cays, Bahamas; Montego Bay, Jamaica; Cartagena, Colombia; Puerto Caldera, Costa Rica; and Acapulco and Cabo San Lucas, Mexico. **Spring:** Sixteen-day **Panama Canal** transits between San Diego to San Juan call at Acapulco, Mexico; Puerto Caldera, Costa Rica; San Blas Islands, near Panama; Virgin Gorda; St. Barts; and St. Thomas. An 11-day **Caribbean/Amazon** cruise from San Juan to Manaus, Brazil, calls at St. Thomas, Martinique, Barbados, Devil's Island, and along the Amazon River at Santana, Santarém, Alter do Cháo, and Boca do Valer. A 14-day **South America** cruise from Manaus, Brazil, to Buenos Aires, Argentina, calls at the Brazilian ports of Santana, Recife, Rio de Janeiro, Santos, and Montevideo.

Regal Princess   **Early Fall:** A 15-day **Panama Canal** transit from San Francisco to San Juan calls at Cabo San Lucas; Acapulco; Puerto Caldera, Costa Rica; Curaçao; and St. Thomas. **Fall–mid-Spring:** Seven-day **southern Caribbean** loops depart San Juan calling at Barbados; Mayreau, Grenadines; Martinique; St. Maarten; and St. Thomas. **Late Spring–Summer:** Seven-day **Gulf of Alaska** cruises between Vancouver and Seward, calling at Ketchikan, Juneau, Skagway, and Glacier Bay.

Royal Princess   **Early Fall:** Ten-day **Northeastern United States and Canada** cruises between New York and Montréal call at Newport, Boston, Bar Harbor, St. John, Halifax, and Québec. **Mid-Fall–Spring:** Ten-day **Panama Canal** transits between Acapulco and San Juan call at Puerto Caldera, Costa Rica; Cartagena, Colombia; St. Maarten/St. Martin; and St. Thomas. Eleven-day **Panama Canal** transits between San Juan and Acapulco call at St. Thomas, Martinique, Grenada, Caracas/La Guaira, and Curaçao.

Sky Princess   **Fall–mid-Spring:** Ten-day **Panama Canal** loops depart Fort Lauderdale, calling at Cozumel/Playa del Carmen, Mexico; Limón, Costa Rica; Cartagena, Colombia; Princess Cays, Bahamas; and Gatun Lake (Panama Canal). Fifteen-day **Panama Canal** transits between Los Angeles and Fort Lauderdale call at Cabo San Lucas and Acapulco, Mexico; Puerto Caldera, Costa Rica; Cartagena, Colombia; Montego Bay, Jamaica; and Princess Cays, Bahamas. **Late Spring–Summer:** Seven-day **Gulf of Alaska** cruises between Vancouver and Seward call at Ketchikan, Juneau, Skagway. Some departures also call at Glacier Bay.

Star Princess   **Early Fall:** A 16-day **Panama Canal** transit from San Diego to Fort Lauderdale calls at Cabo San Lucas, Puerto Vallarta, and Acapulco, Mexico; Puerto Caldera, Costa Rica; Cartagena, Colombia; St. Thomas; and Princess Cays, Bahamas. **Mid-Fall–mid-Spring:** Seven-day **eastern Caribbean** loops depart Fort Lauderdale, calling at Nassau; St. Thomas; St. Maarten; and Princess Cays, Bahamas. **Late Spring–Summer:** Seven-day **Gulf of Alaska** cruises between Vancouver and Seward call at Ketchikan, Juneau, Skagway, and Glacier Bay.

Sun Princess   **Winter–Spring:** Seven-day **western Caribbean** loops depart Fort Lauderdale calling at Princess Cays, Bahamas; Montego Bay, Jamaica; Grand Cayman; and Playa del Carmen/Cozumel. **Late**

Spring–Summer: Seven-day **Inside Passage** loops depart Vancouver, calling at Juneau, Skagway, and Sitka. Some departures also call at Glacier Bay.

Radisson Seven Seas Cruises

Hanseatic **Fall:** A nine-night **Northeastern United States and Canada** cruise from Boston to Montréal calls at Bar Harbor, Maine; St. John, New Brunswick; Halifax, Nova Scotia; Sydney, Cape Breton Island; Charlottetown, Prince Edward Island; and Québec, Canada. Eight-day **Caribbean** cruises between Philippsburg, St. Maarten, and San Juan, Puerto Rico, call at Roadtown, British Virgin Islands; Santo Domingo and Cayo Levantado, Dominican Republic; Port Antonio, Jamaica; and Great Inagua, Bahamas. The second route calls at Basseterre, St. Kitts; Roseau, Dominica; St. George's, Grenada; Port Elizabeth, Bequia; Bridgetown, Barbados; and Pointe-a-Pitre, Guadeloupe. A 13-day **Panama Canal** transit from Philippsburg, St. Maarten, to Esmeraldas calls at St. George's, Grenada; Cumana, Venezuela; Willemstad, Curaçao; the San Blas Islands; Cristobal/Colón; Isla del Rey; Coco Island, Costa Rica; and a flight from Esmeraldas to Baltra, Galapagos Islands. A 15-day **South America** cruise from Esmeraldas to Puerto Montt, Chile, calls at Salaverry; Callao, Lima; Peru; and Iquique, Antofagasta, Valparaiso, Isla Mocha, and Puerto Montt, Chile. A **Chile/Patagonia** loop departs Puerto Montt, calling at Castro, Chiloe Island; Laguna San Rafael and Puerto Natales, Chile, and sails the Messier Canal, Seno Ultima Esperanza, the Patagonian Icefields and Fjords, and the Chilean coast. A 19-night cruise departs from Puerto Montt, Chile, to Ushuaia, Argentina, visiting the Chilean Fjords, Falkland Islands, and Antarctica. **Winter–Spring:** Eleven- and 12-night **Antarctic/Falkland Islands** loops depart Ushuaia, Argentina, calling at various ports on the Falkland Islands; the South Shetland Islands; King George Island; Whaler's Bay on Deception Island; and Cape Horn, Chile. A 14-day **South America** cruise from Ushuaia to Rio de Janeiro calls at the Falkland Islands; Puerto Madryn and Mar del Plata, Argentina; Montevideo, Uruguay; and Ilha de St. Catarina and Paraty, Brazil.

Radisson Diamond **Fall:** Nine-night **Panama Canal** transits between Barbados or San Juan and Puerta Caldera, Costa Rica, call at Bequia or St. Thomas; Curaçao; Cartagena, Colombia; and the San Blas Islands. **Winter:** **Panama Canal** transits (same as fall). A seven-night **Caribbean** cruise between San Juan and Barbados calls at St. Thomas, St. Maarten, Montserrat, Bequia, and St. Lucia. Four- and five-night **Caribbean** loops depart San Juan calling at St. Thomas, St. Barts, St. Maarten, and Jost Van Dyke (five-night only). Alternating six-night **Caribbean** cruises between San Juan and Barbados call at Tortola, St. Kitts, Antigua, Martinique, and Carriacou. The alternative route calls at St. Lucia, Montserrat, St. Barts, St. Maarten, and St. Thomas. **Spring: Panama Canal** transits (same as fall). **Caribbean** loops (same as winter). Seven and eight-night **Panama Canal** transits between Puerta Caldera, Costa Rica, and Aruba call at the San Blas Islands; Cartagena, Colombia; and Curaçao.

Regency Cruises

Regent Isle **Fall:** Ten-day **Hawaii** cruises from Vancouver to Honolulu and from Honolulu to Mexico. **Winter–Spring:** Two-day weekend cruises to **Mexico** and five-day **western Caribbean** cruises from Tampa. **Summer:** Seven-day **Inside Passage/Gulf of Alaska** cruises between Vancouver and Seward call at Ketchikan, Juneau, Skagway, and Sitka. Some departures call at Glacier Bay.

Regent Rainbow **Winter–Spring:** Fourteen-day **Panama Canal** transits between Montego Bay and Los Angeles or San Diego may call at Cartagena, Colombia; Puerto Caldera, Costa Rica; Acapulco, Puerto Vallarta, and Zihuatanejo/Ixtápa, Mexico; Ocho Rios, Jamaica; or Grand Cayman. **Late Spring–Summer:** Seven-day **Inside Passage/Gulf of Alaska** cruises between Vancouver and Seward call at Ketchikan, Juneau, Skagway, and Sitka. Some departures call at Glacier Bay.

Regent Sea **Fall:** A 49-day circumnavigation of **South America** begins and ends in Fort Lauderdale. **Winter:** Three-month **world cruise** departs New York and ends in Fort Lauderdale. **Summer:** Mediterranean.

Regent Spirit **Fall–Winter:** Seven-day **Central America** loops depart Cozumel, calling at Caribbean coastal ports in Honduras, Guatemala, and Belize. **Spring–Summer:** Europe.

Regent Star **Fall–mid-Spring:** Seven-day **Panama Canal** loops depart Montego Bay, calling at Aruba; Cartagena, Colombia; Puerto Moin, Costa Rica; and Gatun Lake (Panama Canal). **Late Spring–Summer:** Seven-day **Inside Passage/Gulf of Alaska** cruises between Vancouver and Seward call at Ketchikan, Juneau, Skagway, and Sitka. Some departures call at Glacier Bay.

Regent Sun **Early Fall:** Seven-day **Northeastern United States and Canada** cruises between New York and Montréal may call at Newport, Rhode Island; Provincetown, Massachusetts; Portland or Bar Harbor, Maine; Halifax or Sydney, Nova Scotia; and Québec City. **Late Fall–Spring:** Seven-day alternating **southern Caribbean** loops depart San Juan, calling at St. Lucia, St. Kitts, Barbados, St. Croix, and St. Maarten/St. Martin. The alternate route calls at St. Barts, Antigua, Martinique, Grenada, and St. Thomas/St. John. **Summer:** Seven-day **Northeastern United States and Canada** (same as early fall).

Renaissance Cruises

Renaissance IV **Fall–Spring:** Seven-day alternating southern **Caribbean** cruises between Antigua and Barbados depart Sunday, calling at Montserrat, Martinique, Grenada, Tobago, Trinidad, and St. Lucia. **Summer:** Mediterranean.

Royal Caribbean Cruise Line

Legend of the Seas **Fall:** Ten-night **Hawaii** sailings between Vancouver to Honolulu or Honolulu and Ensenada call at Hilo, Kona, Kaunakakai, Kahului, and Port Allen. **Winter:** Ten-and 11-night **Panama Canal** transits between Acapulco and San Juan call at St. Thomas; Santo Domingo; Curaçao; and Puerto Caldera, Costa Rica. **Summer:** Seven-night **Inside Passage** loops depart Vancouver, calling at Skagway, Haines, Juneau, and Ketchikan.

Majesty of the Seas **Year-round:** Seven-night **western Caribbean** loops depart Miami Sunday, calling at Grand Cayman; Cozumel/Playa del Carmen, Mexico; Ocho Rios, Jamaica; and Labadee, Haiti.

Monarch of the Seas **Year-round:** Seven-night **southern Caribbean** loops depart San Juan Sunday, calling at Martinique; Barbados; Antigua; St. Maarten/St. Martin; and St. Thomas.

Nordic Empress **Year-round:** Four-night **Bahamas** loops depart Miami Monday, calling at Freeport/Lucaya; Nassau; and CocoCay, Bahamas. Three-night **Bahamas** loops depart Miami Friday, calling at Nassau and CocoCay, Bahamas.

Song of America **Fall:** Seven-night **Bermuda** loops depart New York Sunday, calling at St. George's and Hamilton. **Winter–Spring:** Seven-night **southern Caribbean** loops depart San Juan Saturday, calling at St. Croix, St. Kitts, Guadeloupe, St. Maarten/St. Martin, and St. Thomas. **Summer:** Same as fall.

Song of **Fall:** Europe. **Winter–Spring:** Ten- and 11-night **Panama Canal**
Norway transits between San Juan and Acapulco call at Puerto Caldera,
Costa Rica; Aruba; Curaçao; and St. Thomas.

Sovereign of the **Year-round:** Seven-night **eastern Caribbean** loops depart Miami Sat-
Seas urday, calling at Labadee, Haiti; San Juan; St. Thomas; and
CocoCay, Bahamas.

Sun Viking **Fall–Spring:** Seven-night **southern Caribbean** loops depart San
Juan, calling at St. Thomas, St. Maarten/St. Martin, Dominica, Gre-
nada, and Tobago. Ten- and 11-day **southern Caribbean** sailings be-
tween Miami and San Juan call at CocoCay, Bahamas; St. Barts;
Martinique; Grenada; Dominica; St. Martin/St. Maarten; and St.
Thomas. **Summer:** Far East.

Viking **Year-round:** Three- and four-night **West Coast** loops depart Los An-
Serenade geles, calling at Catalina Island and Ensenada.

Royal Cruise Line

Crown Odyssey **Winter:** A 14-day **Panama Canal** transit from San Juan to Los Ange-
les calls at Aruba; Puerto Caldera, Costa Rica; Acapulco,
Zihuatanejo/Ixtapa, and Puerto Vallarta, Mexico. A 12-day **Mexi-
can Riviera** loop departs Los Angeles, calling at Puerto Vallarta,
Zihuatanejo, Acapulco, Manzanillo, Mazatlán, and Cabo San Lucas.
A 12-day **Panama Canal** transit from Acapulco to San Juan calls at
Puerto Caldera, Costa Rica; Aruba; Curaçao; St. Croix; and St.
Thomas. A 16-day **Hawaii** loop departs San Diego, calling at
Nawiliwili, Kauai; Kahulu and Lahaina, Maui; Honolulu, Oahu; and
Hilo, the Big Island. An eight-day **Hawaii** cruise from Ensenada,
Mexico, to Honolulu calls at Nawiliwili, Kauai; and Kahulu and
Lahaina, Maui; a reverse sailing calls at Kona and Hilo, the Big Is-
land. A 12-day **Panama Canal** transit from San Diego to San Juan
calls at Acapulco and Aruba. **Spring–Summer:** Europe.

Queen Odyssey **Early Winter:** Seven-day **Caribbean** loops depart Barbados calling at
Grenada, Grenadines, Bequia, St. Vincent, and St. Lucia. Thirteen-
day **Amazon** cruises between Barbados and Manaus, Brazil, include
calls at Devil's Island; Trinidad; and Alter do Chão, Brazil. **Winter:**
Seven-day **Caribbean** cruises between Barbados and San Juan call at
Iles des Saintes, Montserrat, St. Kitts, St. Barts, and St. John/St.
Thomas. Ten-day **Panama Canal** transits between San Juan and
Puerto Caldera, Costa Rica, call at Bonaire; Antilles; Aruba; San
Blas Islands; Puerto Armuelles, Panama; and Puerto Quepos and
Santa Rosa, Costa Rica. **Spring–Summer:** Europe.

Royal Odyssey **Fall:** A 15-day **Panama Canal** transit between San Francisco and
Nassau calls at Cabo San Lucas; Puerto Vallarta; Acapulco; Puerto
Caldera, Costa Rica; and Ocho Rios, Jamaica. A nine-day **eastern
seaboard** cruise between Nassau and New York calls at Savannah;
Charleston; Williamsburg; Washington, DC/Baltimore; and Philadelphia. Seven-day **Northeastern United States and Canada** cruises
between New York and Montréal call at Bar Harbor; Halifax, Nova
Scotia; and Québec City. **Early Winter:** Nine-day **Panama Canal**
transits between Acapulco and Aruba call at Puerto Caldera, Costa
Rica; San Blas Islands; and Curaçao. Twelve-day **Panama Canal**
transits between Acapulco and Fort Lauderdale or Aruba may call
at Playa del Carmen/Cozumel and Zihuatanejo/Ixtapa/Mexico;
Grand Cayman; Ocho Rios, Jamaica; or Curaçao. **Winter–Spring:** A
102-day **world cruise** departs San Francisco calling at Honolulu and
Bermuda in the Western Hemisphere. **Summer:** Seven-night **Inside
Passage/Gulf of Alaska** cruises between Vancouver and Anchorage
call at Ketchikan, Juneau, and Skagway. A 10-day **Inside Passage**
cruise from Vancouver to San Francisco calls at Ketchikan, Juneau,
Skagway, Sitka, Victoria, and Glacier Bay. A 10-day **Inside Passage**

cruise between Vancouver and San Francisco calls at Victoria, Ketchikan, Juneau, Skagway, Sitka, and Glacier Bay.

Seabourn Cruise Line

Seabourn Pride **Fall:** Mediterranean. **Late Fall–Winter:** Africa/Seychelles. **Spring– Summer:** Ten-day **Alaska** cruises sail from Anchorage, Vancouver, or Seattle. A 14-day **Alaska** cruise sails from Vancouver to San Francisco. A 17-day **Alaska** loop departs San Francisco.

Seabourn Spirit **Fall:** A 14-day **Northeastern United States and Canada** loop departs New York, calling at North East Harbor, Maine; Halifax, Nova Scotia; Percé, Québec; Montréal; Québec City; Baddeck, Nova Scotia; and Lunenburg, Nova Scotia. A nine-day **Northeastern United States and Canada** loop departs New York, calling at Kennebunkport, Maine; North East Harbor, Maine; Charlottetown, Prince Edward Island; Baddeck, Halifax; and Lunenburg, Nova Scotia. **Late Fall–Winter:** Five- to 16-day **Caribbean and Caribbean– Amazon** cruises depart Fort Lauderdale; St. Thomas; or Manaus, Brazil. Caribbean sailings may call at Tortola, St. Croix, Virgin Gorda, Jost Van Dyke, St. Maarten/St. Martin, St. Barts, St. Kitts, the Grenadines, Antigua, San Juan, or Guadeloupe. Caribbean– Amazon cruises may also call at Parintins and Alter do Cháo, Brazil, and Devil's Island. **Spring–Summer:** Europe.

Seawind Cruise Line

Seawind Crown **Year-round:** Alternating seven-day **southern Caribbean** loops depart Aruba Sunday, calling at Curaçao, Grenada, Barbados, and St. Lucia. The alternate route calls at Antigua, Guadeloupe, Barbados, and Dominica.

Silversea Cruises

Silver Cloud Outside Western Hemisphere.

Silver Wind **Fall:** Ten-day **Northeastern United States and Canada** cruises between New York and Montréal may call at Halifax, Nova Scotia; Québec City, Québec; Baddeck and Lunenburg, Nova Scotia; Boston; or Newport. An eight-day **eastern seaboard** cruise from New York to Nassau calls at Yorktown; Baltimore; Charlestown; and Savannah. **Late Fall–Winter:** Seven- and 10-day **Caribbean** cruises between Fort Lauderdale and Barbados may call at St. Lucia, Martinique, Antigua, Aruba, Grand Cayman, St. Barts, Guadeloupe, Montserrat, Dominica, Virgin Gorda, St. Maarten/St. Martin. **Late Winter–Spring:** Fourteen-day **South America** cruises between Buenos Aires and Valparaiso call at Mar del Plata, Puerto Madryn, Ushuaia, Punta Arenas, and Puerto Montt. Seven-day cruises between Rio de Janeiro and Buenos Aires call at Montevideo, Mar del Plata, Punte del Este, San Francisco do Sul, and Parati. **Summer:** Mediterranean.

Society Expeditions

World Discoverer **Early Fall:** Nine-, 17-, and 18-day **South Pacific** cruises include calls in Hawaii, Easter Island, and in Ecuador, Peru, and Chile. **Mid-Fall–Winter:** Twelve- to 19-day **Antarctica** cruises sail from Puerto Montt, Chile; Port Stanley, Falkland Islands; or Ushuaia, Argentina, calling at a variety of small islands and research stations. Some itineraries visit the Chilean fjords. **Early Spring:** same as early fall. **Mid-Spring–Summer:** Eleven- or 12-night **Bering Strait** cruises between Alaska and the Russian Far East depart Nome or Homer, Alaska. Eleven-day **Inside Passage/Gulf of Alaska** cruises depart Seward or Prince Rupert, British Columbia, calling at Sitka and

Glacier Bay. A nine-day **South Pacific** cruise departs Seward for Honolulu.

Special Expeditions

Polaris **Fall:** Sixteen-day **Amazon** cruises between Belém, Brazil, and Iquitos, Peru, call at Manaus and explore the upper Amazon, lower Amazon, and Rio Negro. A 55-day **South America** circumnavigation. **Winter–early Spring:** An eight-day **Costa Rica and Panama** cruise between Colón and Puerto Caldera. Thirteen-day **Panama Canal** transits from Colón to Belize call at San Blas Islands, Nicaragua, and Honduras. A 15-day **Panama Canal–Caribbean** cruise from Colón to Antigua calls at the San Blas Islands, Panama; Los Hermanos; Trinidad; the Grenadines; St. Lucia; Isles des Saintes, Guadeloupe; and Dominica. **Summer:** Europe.

Sea Bird, Sea **Fall:** Seven-day **Pacific Northwest** cruises between Vancouver and
Lion Seattle call at the San Juan Islands and the Gulf Islands and Inlets of British Columbia. Seven-day **Columbia River and Snake River** loops depart Portland, Oregon, sailing the eastern Washington wine country; Clarkston and Hells Canyon; the Palouse River; Columbia River Gorge; and Hood River and the Bonneville Dam and also visiting Astoria. Five-day **San Francisco** loops call at Sausalito, Sacramento, the Sacramento–San Joaquin Delta, and the Sonoma Valley. **Winter–mid-Spring:** Eight- and 10-day **Baja California** cruises search for whales in the Sea of Cortez. Seven-day Columbia River and Snake River loops (same as in fall). **Late Spring–Summer:** Eight **Inside Passage** cruises between Juneau and Sitka call at the islands along British Columbia and southeast Alaska and sail Misty Fjords National Monument and Glacier Bay National Park.

Sea Cloud **Winter:** Nine-day **Caribbean** loops depart Antigua, calling at St. Lucia, Grenada, Tobago, Carriacou, Dominica, and Isles des Saintes. **Spring–Summer:** Europe.

Star Clippers

Star Clipper **Year-round:** Alternating seven-day **Caribbean** loops depart Barbados Saturday, calling at Tobago Cays, Grenadines; Grenada; Carriacou; St. Vincent; and St. Lucia. The alternate route calls at Bequia, Grenadines; Martinique; Dominica; St. Lucia; and Tobago Cays/Union Island.

Star Flyer **Fall–Spring:** Alternating seven-day **Caribbean** loops depart St. Maarten Sunday, calling at Anguilla, Tortola, Norman Island/Jost Van Dyke, Virgin Gorda, and St. Barts. The alternate route calls at Nevis/Montserrat, Isles des Saintes, Dominica, Antigua, St. Kitts, St. Barts, and St. Maarten/St. Martin. **Summer:** Europe.

Sun Line Cruises

Stella Solaris **Winter:** Eleven-day **Caribbean** loop departs Fort Lauderdale, calling at Nassau; St. Barts; St. Maarten/St. Martin; Isles des Saintes, Guadeloupe; Grenada; Barbados; and St. Croix. **Amazon/Caribbean** cruises sail from Fort Lauderdale or Manaus, Brazil. Fourteen-day cruises call at St. Thomas, St. Lucia, Barbados, Grenada and Tobago Cays/Grenadines in the Caribbean and Curua Una, Boca da Valeria, and Manaus on the Amazon. Thirteen or 16-day cruises call at Boca da Valeria and Santarém on the Amazon and Trinidad, St. Vincent, Antigua, and San Juan in the Caribbean. Twelve-day **Panama Canal** loops depart Galveston, Texas, calling at Grand Cayman; Cristóbal; San Blas Islands; Puerto Limon, Costa Rica; Cozumel/Playa del Carmen, Mexico; and Gatun Lake (Panama Canal). Seven-day **western Caribbean** loops depart Galveston, calling at Cozumel/

Playa del Carmen and Key West. One departure adds Grand Cayman.

Windstar Cruises

Wind Spirit **Late Fall:** Seven-day **Caribbean** loops depart St. Thomas Sunday, calling at St. Croix, St. John, St. Barts, Tortola, Virgin Gorda, and Jost Van Dyke. **Winter–Early Spring:** Seven-day **eastern Caribbean** loops depart St. Thomas Sunday, calling at St. Croix, Saba, Montserrat, St. Barts, Virgin Gorda, and St. John. A 10-day **Caribbean** loop departs St. Thomas calling at St. Maarten/St. Martin; St. Kitts; Isles des Saintes, Guadeloupe; Dominica; Martinique; St. Lucia; Bequia; and St. Barts. An 11-day **Caribbean** cruise departs Virgin Gorda calling at St. Barts, St. Maarten/St. Martin, Antigua, Guadeloupe, Saba, Jost Van Dyke, St. Croix, and St. John. **Spring–late Summer:** Europe.

Wind Star **Late Fall:** Alternating seven-day **eastern Caribbean** loops depart Barbados Saturday, calling at St. Lucia, Dominica, St. Maarten/St. Martin, St. Barts, and St. Kitts. The alternate route stops at Tobago Keys; Bequia; Martinique; Isles des Santes, Guadeloupe; St. Lucia; and Carriacou. **Winter:** Alternating seven-day **Caribbean** loops depart Barbados calling at Nevis, St. Maarten/St. Martin, St. Barts, Monserrat, and Martinique. The second route calls at Bequia, Carriacou, Grenada, Tobago Cays, and St. Lucia. **Spring–Summer:** Mediterranean.

World Explorer Cruises

Universe **Summer:** Fourteen-day **Inside Passage/Gulf of Alaska** loops depart Vancouver every other Sunday, calling at Ketchikan; Sitka; Seward; Valdez; Skagway; Juneau; Wrangell; Victoria, British Columbia, and Glacier Bay National Park.

Index

NOTES

What's hot, where it's hot!

Fodor's Travel Publications

Available at bookstores everywhere, or call 1–800–533–6478, 24 hours a day.

Gold Guides

U.S.

Alaska

Arizona

Boston

California

Cape Cod, Martha's
Vineyard, Nantucket

The Carolinas & the
Georgia Coast

Chicago

Colorado

Florida

Hawaii

Las Vegas, Reno,
Tahoe

Los Angeles

Maine, Vermont,
New Hampshire

Maui

Miami & the Keys

New England

New Orleans

New York City

Pacific North Coast

Philadelphia & the
Pennsylvania Dutch
Country

The Rockies

San Diego

San Francisco

Santa Fe, Taos,
Albuquerque

Seattle & Vancouver

The South

U.S. & British Virgin
Islands

USA

Virginia & Maryland

Waikiki

Washington, D.C.

Foreign

Australia &
New Zealand

Austria

The Bahamas

Barbados

Bermuda

Brazil

Budapest

Canada

Cancún, Cozumel,
Yucatán Peninsula

Caribbean

China

Costa Rica, Belize,
Guatemala

The Czech Republic
& Slovakia

Eastern Europe

Egypt

Europe

Florence, Tuscany
& Umbria

France

Germany

Great Britain

Greece

Hong Kong

India

Ireland

Israel

Italy

Japan

Kenya & Tanzania

Korea

London

Madrid & Barcelona

Mexico

Montréal &
Québec City

Morocco

Moscow, St.
Petersburg, Kiev

The Netherlands,
Belgium &
Luxembourg

New Zealand

Norway

Nova Scotia, New
Brunswick, Prince
Edward Island

Paris

Portugal

Provence &
the Riviera

Scandinavia

Scotland

Singapore

South America

South Pacific

Southeast Asia

Spain

Sweden

Switzerland

Thailand

Tokyo

Toronto

Turkey

Vienna & the Danube

Fodor's Special-Interest Guides

Branson

Caribbean Ports
of Call

The Complete Guide
to America's
National Parks

Condé Nast Traveler
Caribbean Resort and
Cruise Ship Finder

Cruises and Ports
of Call

Fodor's London
Companion

France by Train

Halliday's New
England Food
Explorer

Healthy Escapes

Italy by Train

Kodak Guide to
Shooting Great
Travel Pictures

Shadow Traffic's
New York Shortcuts
and Traffic Tips

Sunday in New York

Sunday in
San Francisco

Walt Disney World,
Universal Studios
and Orlando

Walt Disney World
for Adults

Where Should We
Take the Kids?
California

Where Should We
Take the Kids?
Northeast

Special Series

Affordables
Caribbean
Europe
Florida
France
Germany
Great Britain
Italy
London
Paris

Fodor's Bed & Breakfasts and Country Inns
America's Best B&Bs
California's Best B&Bs
Canada's Great Country Inns
Cottages, B&Bs and Country Inns of England and Wales
The Mid-Atlantic's Best B&Bs
New England's Best B&Bs
The Pacific Northwest's Best B&Bs
The South's Best B&Bs
The Southwest's Best B&Bs
The Upper Great Lakes' Best B&Bs

The Berkeley Guides
California
Central America
Eastern Europe
Europe
France
Germany & Austria
Great Britain & Ireland
Italy
London
Mexico

Pacific Northwest & Alaska
Paris
San Francisco

Compass American Guides
Arizona
Canada
Chicago
Colorado
Hawaii
Hollywood
Las Vegas
Maine
Manhattan
Montana
New Mexico
New Orleans
Oregon
San Francisco
South Carolina
South Dakota
Texas
Utah
Virginia
Washington
Wine Country
Wisconsin
Wyoming

Fodor's Español
California
Caribe Occidental
Caribe Oriental
Gran Bretaña
Londres
Mexico
Nueva York
Paris

Fodor's Exploring Guides
Australia
Boston & New England

Britain
California
Caribbean
China
Florence & Tuscany
Florida
France
Germany
Ireland
Italy
London
Mexico
Moscow & St. Petersburg
New York City
Paris
Prague
Provence
Rome
San Francisco
Scotland
Singapore & Malaysia
Spain
Thailand
Turkey
Venice

Fodor's Flashmaps
Boston
New York
San Francisco
Washington, D.C.

Fodor's Pocket Guides
Acapulco
Atlanta
Barbados
Jamaica
London
New York City
Paris
Prague
Puerto Rico

Rome
San Francisco
Washington, D.C.

Rivages Guides
Bed and Breakfasts of Character and Charm in France
Hotels and Country Inns of Character and Charm in France
Hotels and Country Inns of Character and Charm in Italy

Short Escapes
Country Getaways in Britain
Country Getaways in France
Country Getaways Near New York City

Fodor's Sports
Golf Digest's Best Places to Play
Skiing USA
USA Today The Complete Four Sport Stadium Guide

Fodor's Vacation Planners
Great American Learning Vacations
Great American Sports & Adventure Vacations
Great American Vacations
National Parks and Seashores of the East
National Parks of the West

Before Catching Your Flight, Catch Up With Your World.

Fueled by the global resources of CNN and available in major airports across America, CNN Airport Network provides a live source  of current domestic and international news,

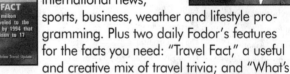

sports, business, weather and lifestyle programming. Plus two daily Fodor's features for the facts you need: "Travel Fact," a useful and creative mix of travel trivia; and "What's

Happening," a comprehensive round-up of upcoming events in major cities around the world.

With CNN Airport Network, you'll never be out of the loop.